AMERICAN CIVICS

Third Edition

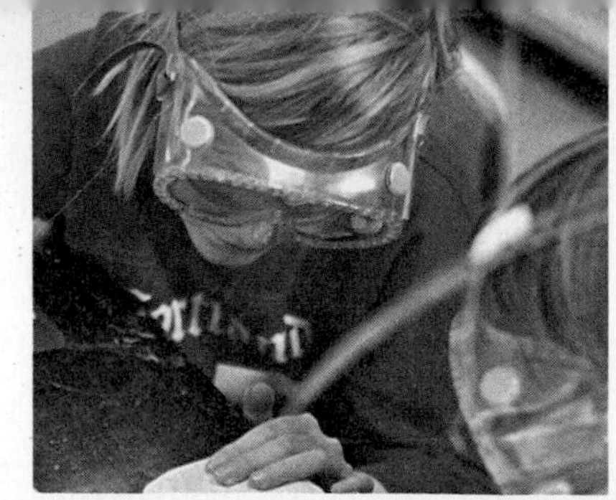

CLASS
OFFICERS

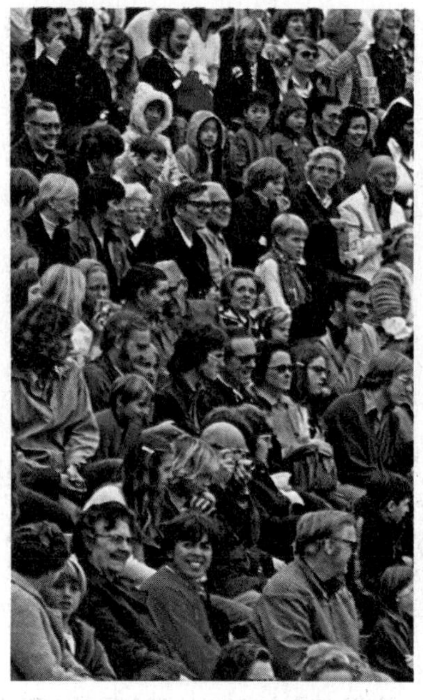

WILLIAM H. HARTLEY
WILLIAM S. VINCENT

AMERICAN CIVICS

Third Edition

Harcourt Brace Jovanovich
New York Chicago San Francisco
Atlanta Dallas *and* London

Authors

WILLIAM H. HARTLEY, a former classroom teacher, is Professor of Education, Emeritus, at the Towson State University, Baltimore, Maryland. He is well known to teachers of the social studies as a past president of the National Council for the Social Studies. His monthly article "Sight and Sound" was for many years a highlight of *Social Education.* Dr. Hartley has written several textbooks, a number of motion picture and filmstrip scripts, and many articles in the field of audio-visual education and techniques for learning.

WILLIAM S. VINCENT, a former teacher of junior high school social studies, is Professor of Education, Emeritus, at Teachers College, Columbia University, where he organized and directed the Citizenship Education Project. He now heads the school research firm of Vincent & Olson School Evaluation Services. Dr. Vincent has written several books on citizenship and has produced a number of educational films. His most recent work is *Indicators of Quality,* a method of training teachers to measure the educational quality of schools and school systems.

Special Features by Leonard C. Wood. Dr. Wood, formerly an editor of social studies textbooks for secondary schools, is now Professor of History and Director of Cooperative Education at Eastern Illinois University, Charleston, Illinois.

Reader Consultants

George G. Dawson
Dean, Empire State College
State University of New York
Old Westbury, New York

Richard H. Loftin
Social Studies Consultant
Aldine Independent School District
Houston, Texas

Erna Murphy
Head Teacher, Freshman Civics Team
Belleville Township High School West
Belleville, Illinois

Marcus Shannon
Coordinator, Social Studies
Metro Nashville Public Schools
Nashville, Tennessee

Charts by Cliff Line and Donald Crews

Map of the United States by Cliff Line on a base by Harold K. Faye

Printed in the United States of America

ISBN 0-15-371460-3

Contents

Charts

Special Features

Civics Skills

Physical and Political Map

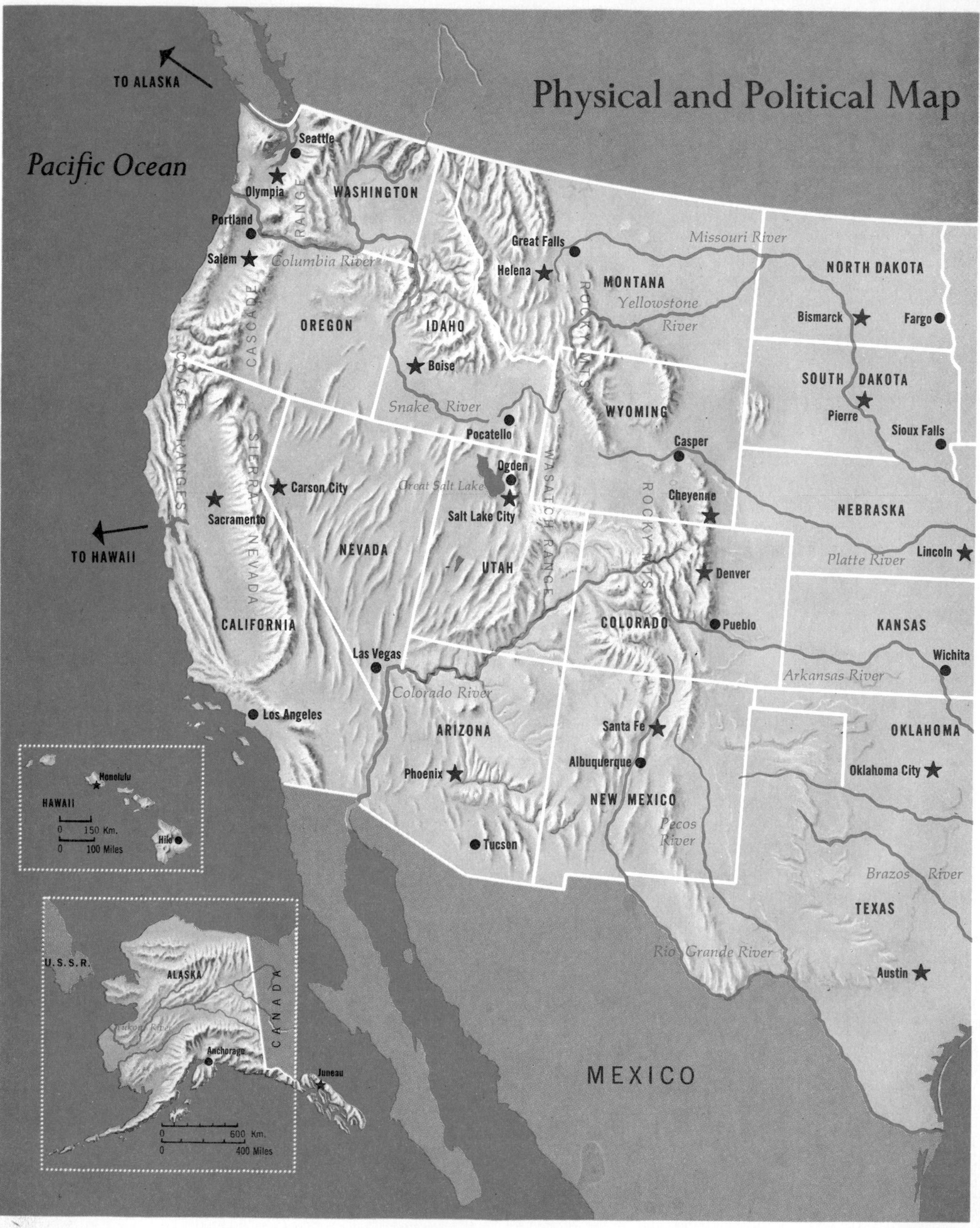

of the United States

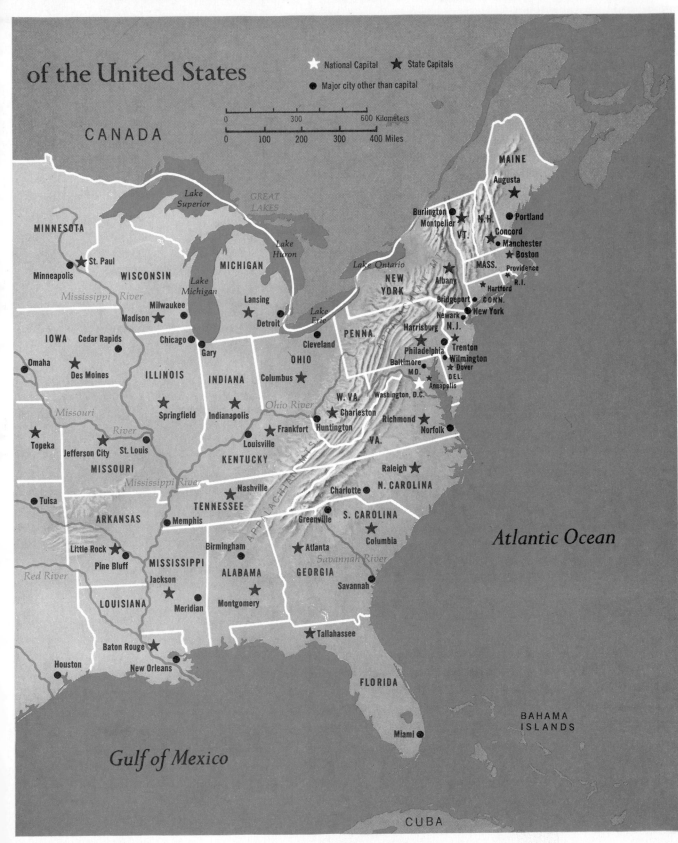

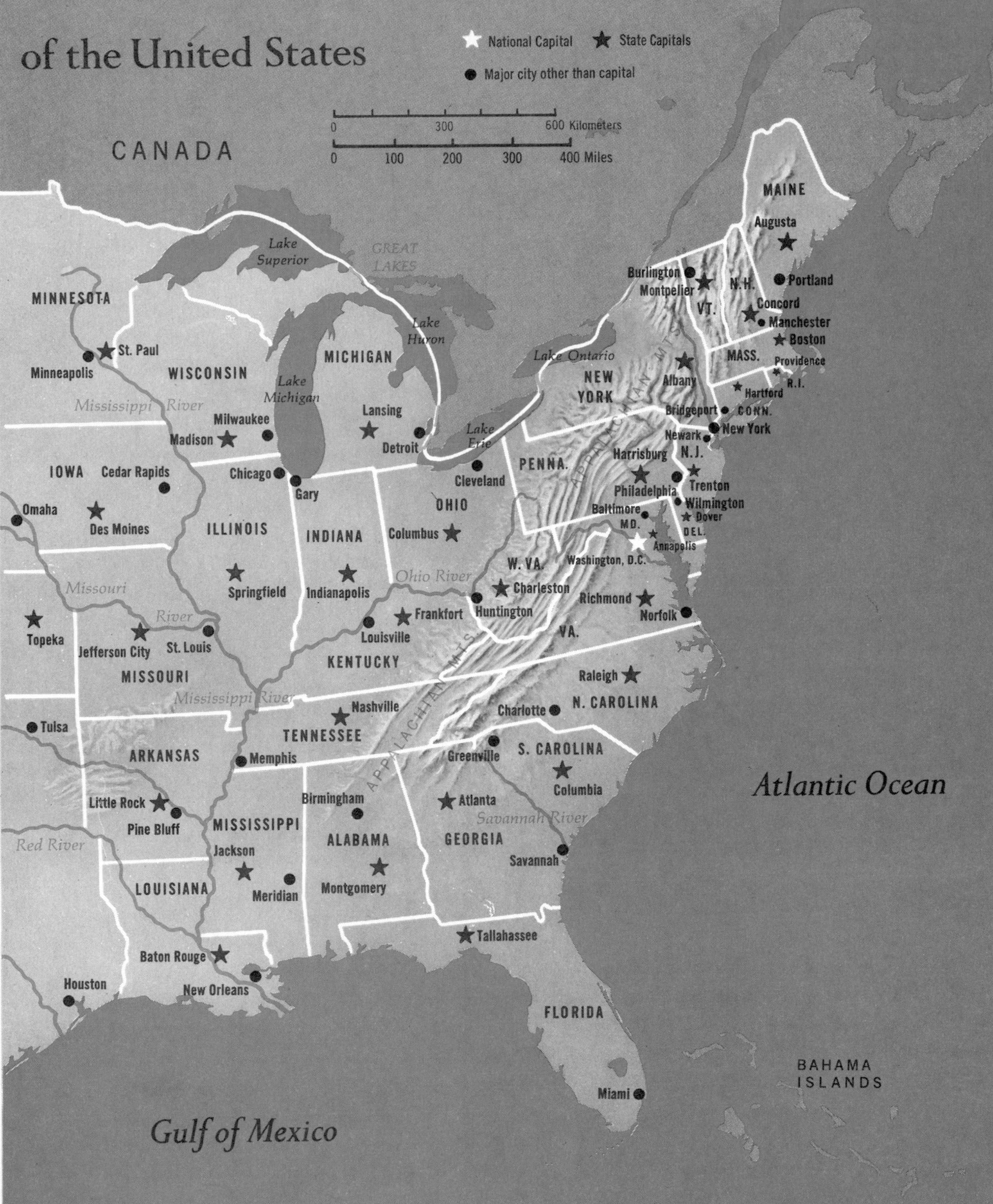

National Capital
State Capitals
Major city other than capital
0
300
600 Kilometers
0
100
200
300
400 Miles
CANADA
Lake Superior
GREAT LAKES
Lake Michigan
Lake Huron
Lake Ontario
Lake Erie
MAINE
Augusta
Portland
Burlington
Montpelier
N.H.
VT.
Concord
Manchester
Boston
MASS.
Providence
R.I.
Hartford
CONN.
Bridgeport
NEW YORK
Albany
New York
Newark
N.J.
Trenton
APPALACHIAN MTS.
Harrisburg
PENNA.
Philadelphia
Wilmington
Dover
DEL.
Baltimore
MD.
Annapolis
Washington, D.C.
MINNESOTA
St. Paul
Minneapolis
WISCONSIN
Mississippi River
Milwaukee
Madison
MICHIGAN
Lansing
Detroit
Cleveland
IOWA
Cedar Rapids
Chicago
Gary
Omaha
Des Moines
ILLINOIS
INDIANA
OHIO
Columbus
W. VA.
Charleston
Huntington
Richmond
Norfolk
VA.
Missouri River
Topeka
Springfield
Indianapolis
Ohio River
Frankfort
Louisville
Jefferson City
St. Louis
MISSOURI
KENTUCKY
Raleigh
N. CAROLINA
Charlotte
Mississippi River
Nashville
TENNESSEE
Tulsa
ARKANSAS
Memphis
Greenville
S. CAROLINA
Columbia
Little Rock
Pine Bluff
Birmingham
Atlanta
Savannah River
Atlantic Ocean
MISSISSIPPI
ALABAMA
GEORGIA
Red River
Jackson
Savannah
LOUISIANA
Meridian
Montgomery
Tallahassee
Baton Rouge
New Orleans
Houston
FLORIDA
BAHAMA ISLANDS
Miami
Gulf of Mexico
CUBA

UNIT
ONE

Citizenship in Our Democracy

CHAPTER

Introduction

The United States is built on a dream. It is a dream that has been shared by millions of people who believed that in this country all men and women could be truly free. The dream began in colonial times, and its power is still so great that it draws thousands of people to our shores each year.

What was the meaning of freedom to these people? There were those who came to find religious freedom. Others, living in poverty, believed that in a new land they could make a new start and find a better life for themselves. Still others fled from political persecution and wars. Throughout our past, America held the promise of excitement and adventure. It seemed a good place to invest one's energy, time, and money. Who could tell how far an ambitious, hard-working person could go in a growing land? These ideas and ideals were all part of the American Dream.

Today, the American Dream, with all its hopes, its promises, and its possibilities, is yet to be completely realized. Our nation has made great progress in many areas. Many Americans share in the wealth and freedom of the United States. But there are still a number of Americans who live in poverty, who do not have jobs, and who do not have equal opportunity. For some of these Americans the difference between the ideal and the real in the American Dream has led to bitterness and disillusionment.

Today, most Americans realize that their nation is far from perfect. "This is a great country," President John F. Kennedy once said, "but it must be greater." All of us as Americans must decide for ourselves how far America has to go to reach the ideals on which it was founded. But we must always remember that even if the ideal has not been reached, the goals are still there for us to strive for. Perhaps we can, by working together, make the American Dream of freedom and equality come true for all Americans. In order to do this we must understand our nation—its government, people, values, and problems. We shall begin by taking a closer look at the people who make up our country. In this chapter we will study the following topics:

1. One Nation from Many Nations
2. America's Immigration Policy
3. Who Are American Citizens?
4. The Meaning of American Citizenship

CHAPTER

1

We the People

1 One Nation from Many Nations

The motto of the United States of America is **E Pluribus Unum.** This is a Latin phrase meaning "out of many, one." It reminds us that the many people who make up our nation came from all over the world to share their hopes and dreams. It reminds us of our heritage. Today, there are about 220 million people living here. All of these individuals, with their different backgrounds and ideas, form one nation and one people.

Americans share an interesting and wonderful background. We are all **immigrants**—people who came here from other lands—or descendants of immigrants. This is as true of the Native Americans who first populated the continent thousands of years ago as it is of today's most recent arrivals. From their countries of origin, the settlers brought different languages, cultures, and customs. In America, they found a new language and way of life.

THE "MELTING POT" THEORY

All immigrants to America were members of **ethnic groups.** That is, they were part of a group of people of the same race or nationality who shared a common and distinctive culture and heritage. In America, all faced the problem of adapting their ethnic backgrounds to their new homeland.

For many years, the United States was looked upon as a **melting pot.** People thought that immigrants lost their old languages, customs, and beliefs and became "Americanized." But this idea was true only in part. Immigrants have become Americans. But the "melting process" has never really been completed. Instead, each immigrant group has kept part of its cultural heritage. Each group also has contributed some of its heritage to our nation. The customs and ideas brought by these groups mixed with the ideas developed in America. This wealth of difference has given a special energy and richness to our nation.

THE FIRST AMERICANS

The first people to settle in America were the Indians, or Native Americans. The name "Indian" was first used in 1492, when Christopher Columbus first landed in the Americas. Today, many Indians prefer to be called Native Americans, as a reminder that they were the first people to settle the Americas.

Many scientists believe that the ancestors of the Native Americans came here from Asia at least 20,000 years ago. Gradually, over thousands of years, they moved into many parts of North and South America. There, they developed cultures suited to the natural environments around them. Some groups lived mainly by hunting. Others learned how to farm — to grow crops for food. Still others built great cities and set up powerful empires in Mexico and in Central and South America.

No one knows exactly how many Native Americans lived here when the Europeans

The first settlers to come to America were the Native Americans who arrived over 20,000 years ago. Their knowledge helped the European settlers to survive in America.

first arrived. Experts think at least 1 to 3 million lived in what is now the United States. Without the help of the Native Americans, the European settlers would not have survived.

EARLY SPANISH SETTLERS

The Spanish were the first Europeans to build lasting settlements in the Americas. They defeated the great Indian empires in Mexico and South America and settled there. They also set up colonies in what is now the United States—in Florida, California, and the Southwest. Many of the early Spanish settlers married Native Americans. Their children were called **mestizos.** With the help of Native Americans, the Spanish built cattle ranches and farms. Spanish ideas and traditions—building styles, language, food, and customs—took root in the areas they colonized.

OUR COLONIAL HERITAGE

As you know from your study of American history, the original 13 colonies were settled mostly by people from England. But there were colonists from other countries as well. For example, German settlers came to Pennsylvania. The Dutch settled in New Netherland, their colony along the Hudson River. Swedes built settlements in New Jersey and Delaware.

The French were also among the early settlers in America. When the English defeated the French in America in the mid-1700's, some of the French settlers remained. Another group of colonists were the Scotch-Irish, who settled on the frontier along the foothills of the Appalachian Mountains from Maine to the Carolinas.

Americans owe much to these early settlers, especially the English. Our official language came from England. So, too, did many of our ideas about government and about our rights as free people. Yet our language and ideas, like our people and customs, are mixtures enriched by the contribution of people from many lands.

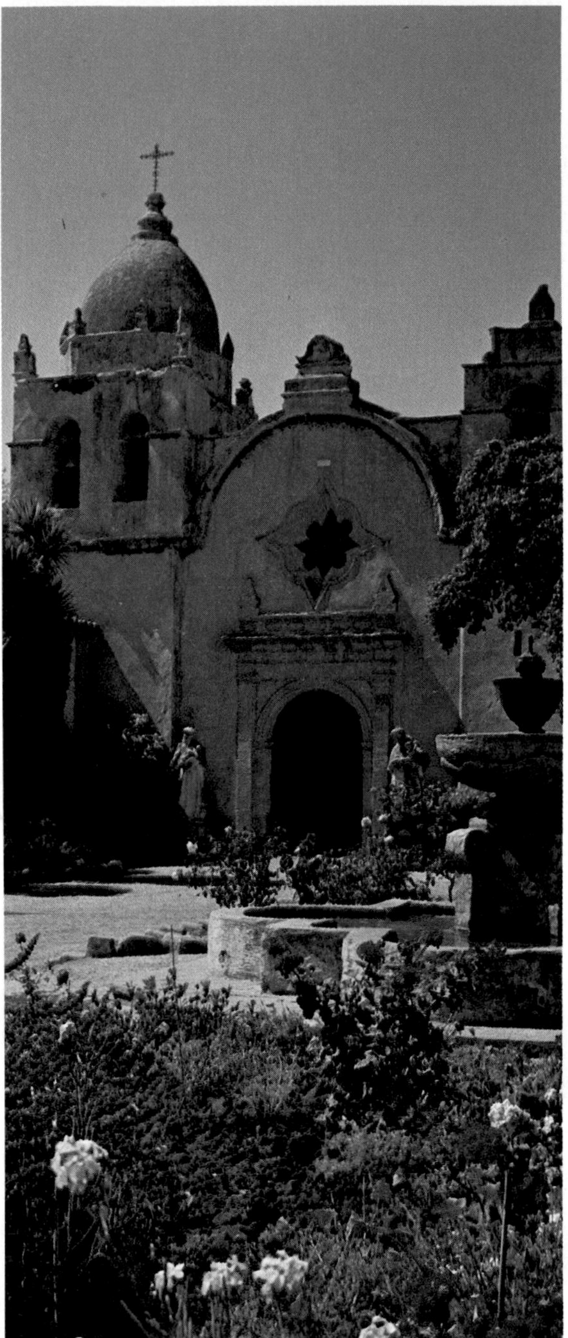

San Carlos Borromeo Mission in Carmel, California, was founded in 1770 by Father Junípero Serra, a Spanish missionary. The mission is still used as a church. Many churches and other buildings in different parts of our country show the influence of Spanish design.

PEOPLE FROM AFRICA

About 22 million Americans are descendants of people from Africa. A few of their ancestors came here as **indentured servants.** As indentured servants, they had to work a certain number of years for whoever bought them. But most of their ancestors were brought to America as slaves. They and their children were forced to live in bondage for many years.

Africans brought with them a rich and varied heritage of art, music, and skills. They took part in the building of our nation. As slaves, they helped to develop southern agriculture. They helped produce raw materials for northern factories. In spite of severe difficulties, the blacks entered many parts of American life.

THE GREAT IMMIGRATION OF THE 1800's

The first official count, or **census,** of the people in the United States was made in 1790. About 4 million people lived here at the time. Between 1790 and 1830, the population of the nation more than tripled, reaching nearly 13 million. Almost all of this growth was the result of births in the United States. During this period, fewer than 400,000 immigrants came. However, during the next 50 years, more than 10 million immigrants came to the United States. The majority of them came from the nations of northern and western Europe. Smaller numbers also came from Canada and Latin America. This immigration of people from the 1830's to the late 1880's is called the **Old Immigration.**

The Germans. One of the largest groups of immigrants to come to America during the 1800's were the Germans. About 1.5 million came between 1815 and 1860. They immigrated for a number of reasons. Some came because of crop failures in their homeland. Some came in search of political liberty. And some, like the German Jews, came in search of religious freedom. Many Germans settled in the Middle West, where they helped build farms and factories. They also helped to build cities such as Milwaukee, St. Louis, and Cincinnati.

Immigrants from northern Europe. In the 1800's, large numbers of Scandinavians also came to the United States. Almost 1 million Scandinavians arrived here between 1820 and the late 1880's. They came here to find better farmland and economic opportunity. The Swedes were the largest group of Scandinavian immigrants. Other settlers came from Norway, Finland, and Denmark. Many Scandinavian immigrants moved to the Middle West—especially to Wisconsin and Minnesota. There they became dairy and grain farmers, miners, and lumber workers.

The Irish. Over 2 million Irish arrived here between 1815 and 1860. Many came because a plant disease destroyed the potato crops in Ireland. This caused a famine, or a period of great hunger. The Irish settled in the large cities along the Atlantic coast. Many helped to build the canals and railroads that bound our nation together.

NEW IMMIGRANTS FROM EUROPE

The largest number of immigrants to America came between the late 1880's and 1920. More than 20 million newcomers settled here then. This period of immigration is often called the **New Immigration.** The people who came during this period were mainly from nations in southern and eastern Europe. Included in this group were Russians, Poles, Italians, Austrians, Hungarians, Greeks, Bulgarians, and Slavs. For the most part, the people of the New Immigration were poor and had few skills. They usually settled in large cities. Like earlier immigrants, they contributed to our nation's culture and economic life.

The Italians. One of the largest groups of people who came during the New Immigration period were the Italians. Some were craft workers. But most had been farmers. Many of these immigrants were poor and willing to take any kind of work. They settled in the large cities along the Atlantic coast.

These immigrants have just arrived in America. They were among the more than 20 million people who came here between the late 1880's and 1920.

Immigrants from eastern Europe. Many of the newcomers were Russians. They came in search of a better life. Some were Jews who came for religious and economic reasons. Many of these immigrants were skilled craft workers. For the most part they, too, settled in large cities.

At the same time, large numbers of people came from other parts of eastern Europe. Newcomers arrived from Poland, Czechoslovakia, Austria, Hungary, Rumania, Bulgaria, and Greece. They came to find better economic opportunities.

THE MEXICAN AMERICANS

Thousands of Mexicans lived in the Southwest when that area became part of the United States in the mid-1800's. Most of them stayed and became citizens of the United States. Some Mexican Americans went to work on ranches and farms. Others worked on the railroads or as laborers in the cities.

During the early 1900's, many thousands of Mexicans came to the United States looking for jobs. They went to work on farms and ranches, and in the cities. Some worked here for a while and then returned home to Mexico. But many Mexicans stayed. To set themselves apart from the Mexican immigrants, the descendants of the original Spanish settlers began to call themselves **Hispanos** or **Latinos.** More recently, many Mexican Americans throughout the United States have begun to call themselves **Chicanos,** a short version of the Spanish word for Mexican.

IMMIGRANTS FROM ASIA

Almost all of the early Asian immigrants were from China and Japan. Except for some Armenians, Turks, and Syrians, very few immigrants came from other Asian nations until the 1940's. Most of the early Chinese and Japanese immigrants settled on the West Coast, where they maintained their rich ethnic traditions and customs.

The Chinese. Asian immigrants began coming to America before the New Immigration. The first group of about 35,000 came from China in the 1850's and settled on the West Coast. They helped build the western railroads and did other kinds of physical labor. Other Chinese immigrants came in the later years of the 1800's. They farmed or started small businesses.

The Japanese. Japanese immigrants began to arrive in America in the late 1800's. About 40,000 Japanese came between 1900 and 1910. Most stayed in California, where they built productive farms and a flourishing fishing industry.

Recent immigrants from Asia. During the 1940's Asians also began to arrive from the Philippines, Hong Kong, Korea, and India. Recently, they have also come from Vietnam, Laos, Cambodia, and the Middle East. Most of the newcomers have been educated, skilled people in search of better economic opportunities. Some of these newcomers were escaping the unsettled conditions in their countries.

PEOPLE FROM THE CARIBBEAN LANDS

Today, immigrants arrive here from all over the world. They continue to come from Europe, Canada, and Mexico. But many also come from Central and South America, Africa, and the islands of the Caribbean. Since 1950, large numbers have come from the islands of the Caribbean, especially from Puerto Rico and Cuba.

The Puerto Ricans. Unlike other newcomers,

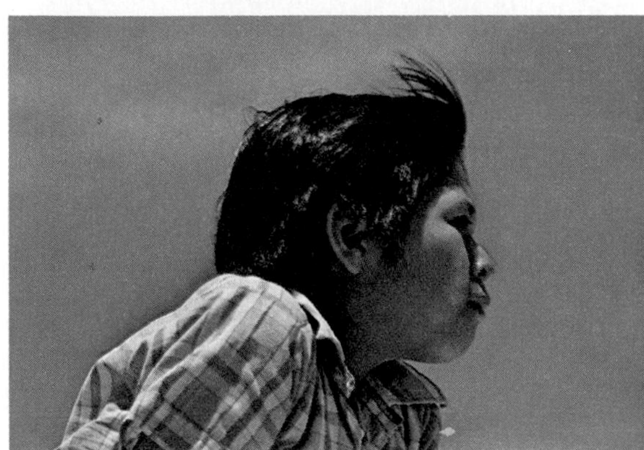

America's culture has been enriched by people from all over the world. How have people from other lands helped to enrich the area where you live?

the people of Puerto Rico have come here as citizens of the United States. They are citizens because Puerto Rico joined with the United States in 1898 after the Spanish-American War. In 1917, Puerto Ricans became American citizens. Today, Puerto Ricans can move freely between their island home and the mainland of the United States. During the late 1940's and the 1950's large numbers of Puerto Ricans came to the mainland to find jobs. Most of the newcomers settled in New York and other large cities. A few were craft workers and the owners of small businesses. But most were poor and had few skills. When conditions in Puerto Rico improved during the 1960's, many Puerto Ricans returned home.

The Cubans. In 1959, about 40,000 people from Cuba arrived in the United States. They came after a revolution led by Fidel Castro brought a new government to Cuba. In the years since then, hundreds of thousands of Cubans have found homes in various parts of the United States. A large majority have settled in Florida. Many have started flourishing businesses and entered almost every profession.

CONSIDER AND DISCUSS

Identify. E Pluribus Unum / immigrant / ethnic group / melting pot / mestizos / indentured servants / census / Old Immigration / New Immigration / Hispanos / Latinos / Chicanos

Review. 1. What was the "melting pot" theory? 2. Where in the United States did the Spanish settle and what influence did they have on those areas? 3. What contributions did the early English settlers make to the American way of life? 4. What group of settlers came unwillingly to America? 5. Give the reasons for German immigration in the 1800's.

Discuss. Should ethnic groups be encouraged to keep their traditional language, festivals, and other customs? Why or why not?

2 America's Immigration Policy

As you have read, the United States was settled and populated by people from all over the world. Europeans, Asians, and Africans helped to build our land. For many, America was a land of opportunity. Thousands came in search of a better life. Here they could plow farms out of the wilderness and build homes for their families. Here they could find work and a place to fulfill their dreams. For many people it meant the end of political or religious persecution.

But for some the promise of America was empty. The Africans came not to find a better life, but against their will. They arrived bound in chains, and they lived in slavery. For the Native Americans, the great movement of immigrants meant centuries of conflict.

EARLY IMMIGRATION POLICY

During our early history, the new American nation had to struggle hard to survive. Therefore, most immigrants were welcomed to the United States. Farm and factory workers were needed as our nation expanded from the Atlantic to the Pacific Ocean. During the first half of the 1800's, the federal government adopted an **"open shore" policy,** allowing unlimited immigration. The only persons who were not admitted were criminals and those with contagious diseases.

But as America began to fill up and land became less available, some Americans began to question our immigration policies. How many more immigrants could we take in, they wondered. During periods of hard times when jobs were scarce, bad feelings arose. Often the immigrants were blamed because there were not enough jobs for everyone.

RESTRICTIONS AGAINST IMMIGRATION

Slowly the United States began to limit the number of people who were allowed to immigrate here. The first group of people to be affected were the Chinese. By the late 1800's, thousands of Chinese had settled in California. When hard times hit the United States in 1873, many American workers lost their jobs. As unemployment rose, many California workers feared the Chinese would take their jobs because they were willing to work for lower wages. Bad feelings grew until violence broke out.

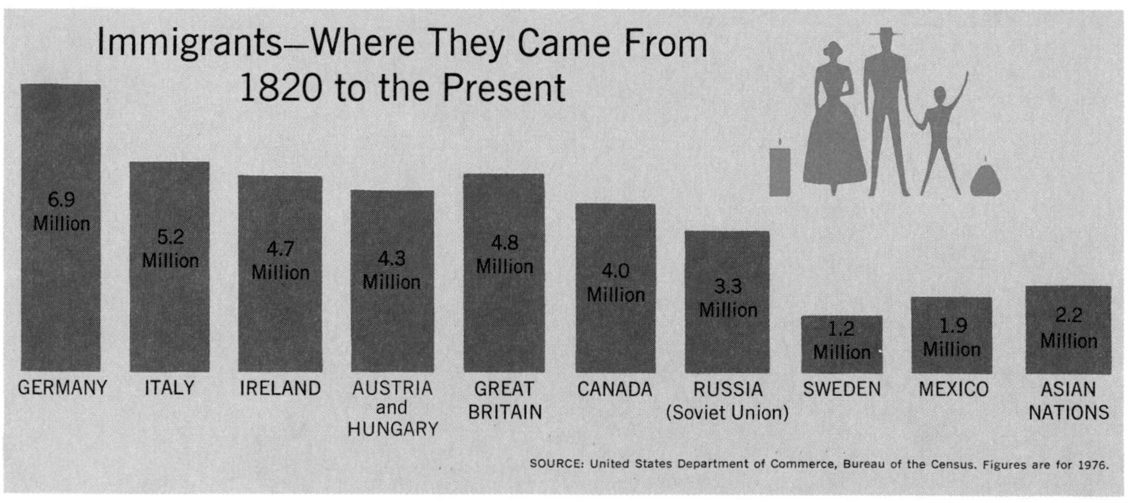

In 1882, Americans who opposed Chinese immigration convinced Congress to pass a law that prohibited further immigration from China. This law, the Chinese Exclusion Act, forbade the immigration of Chinese workers. Very few Chinese were admitted to the United States for the next 60 years.

The 1882 law was just the first in a series of restrictions on immigration. Within the next few years, laws were passed to keep out other foreign laborers and anyone who wanted to overthrow the government. In 1907 Japan and the United States signed an agreement that Japan would send no more unskilled laborers to the United States. A 1917 law forbade anyone who could not read or write, or who did not have employable skills, to enter our nation.

THE QUOTA SYSTEM

Despite these restrictions, huge numbers of immigrants continued to arrive in the early 1900's. Their customs, languages, and ways of life differed greatly from those of the earlier immigrants. Many Americans distrusted these differences. Some also feared that they would lose their jobs to the new immigrants. Therefore, some groups began to pressure Congress to limit immigration even further.

In 1921, Congress acted by setting up a **quota system.** This quota system placed a definite limit, or quota, on the number of immigrants who could be admitted from each country in any one year. Under the Emergency Quota Act of 1921, about 350,000 immigrants were to be admitted to the United States each year. The quota tended to favor the countries of the Old Immigration. Then in 1924, Congress passed another law that further restricted immigration. This law limited the yearly quota of immigrants to about 165,000 and excluded all Asians. In 1929, another law was passed that lowered the yearly quota to about 150,000. This law stayed in effect for many years.

CHANGES IN THE IMMIGRATION LAWS

In the 1950's and 1960's, many Americans began to feel that the immigration laws passed in the 1920's were unfair. They complained that the laws favored people from the nations of western Europe. The number of southern and eastern Europeans who were admitted was small.

As a result, in 1965 Congress passed a new immigration law. This law provided that, beginning in 1968, as many as 170,000 immigrants from nations outside the Western Hemisphere could be admitted to the United States each year. No specific quotas were set up for each nation. But no nation outside the Western Hemisphere could send more than 20,000 immigrants a year. The Western Hemisphere nations are permitted to send a total of up to 120,000 immigrants a year.

IMMIGRATION TODAY

Although immigration to our nation is limited, as it is in most nations, Congress has made certain exceptions. After World War II, many of Europe's homeless people, or **refugees,** were admitted to the United States even after their quotas were filled. Congress passed a law in 1948 that allowed about 600,000 refugees to come here. Since that time, the United States has allowed other groups of refugees from Hungary, Cuba, Vietnam, Laos, and Cambodia to enter our country.

In recent years, about 400,000 immigrants have been admitted to the United States each year. About 40 percent of these new arrivals come from Latin America, with large numbers from Mexico. Many immigrants still come from Europe, especially Italy. Other large groups of immigrants come from the Philippines and Korea. These immigrants enter our country under the immigration law of 1965.

MINORITY GROUPS

Immigrant groups from Cuba, Italy, the Philippines, and other places might all be referred

Throughout American history, minority groups have faced prejudice and discrimination. These are some of the thousands of Americans who attended the 1963 March on Washington to win equal rights for all Americans.

to as **minority groups.** The word "minority" in this case does not necessarily mean that the group is outnumbered. Rather, it means that it is not the group in power. It also means that the group is set apart from other people in the society because of race, nationality, language, customs, or religion.

Minority groups have often met with prejudice and discrimination. **Prejudice** is an unfair opinion of members of a particular group. **Discrimination** refers to unfair actions taken against people because they belong to a particular group. Black Americans, Native Americans, Mexican Americans, Asian Americans, and Puerto Ricans are other minority groups that have been discriminated against.

These two evils, prejudice and discrimination, have been present throughout human history. In the United States, too, some Americans have looked upon others who were "different" from them with fear, distrust, and hatred. These feelings were present in the early years of our nation. For example, some English settlers did not welcome the early Scotch-Irish and Germans. In later years, some Americans were unfriendly to newly arriving Catholics from Ireland and Germany. And still later, these people of the Old Immigration looked with distrust on the southern and eastern Europeans who arrived during the New Immigration. Many were alarmed by the huge numbers of these immigrants. They were also disturbed because their languages, ways of life, and customs were very different from those of northern and western Europe. Some Americans distrusted this difference. As a result, the new immigrant groups found much resentment and hostility.

In later times, the Mexican Americans suffered from prejudice and discrimination for the same reasons as earlier immigrant groups. Many lost their land, mining, and water rights.

They found it difficult to get good jobs. During the hard times that began in the late 1920's, many were pressured into leaving the United States.

RACIAL PREJUDICE AND DISCRIMINATION

The harshest prejudice and discrimination were experienced by those who were racially different from the white majority. From the earliest times, Native Americans were excluded from the benefits of American life. The European settlers took their land and pushed them farther and farther west. Fierce fighting broke out and continued throughout the 1800's. Finally, after a long, bitter struggle, the Native Americans were forced to move to reservations, where about half of them still live. Also, although Native Americans were the original inhabitants of America, they were not granted American citizenship until 1924.

Black Americans, too, suffered greatly as a result of prejudice and discrimination. Their ancestors were brought to this country as slaves. Most were denied their rights as free people even after an 1865 Constitutional amendment to end slavery. Blacks in the North won their freedom earlier than those in the South. But even then, they did not have the same opportunities as other Americans. Many were not allowed to vote or hold certain kinds of jobs. Only recently has there been a determined effort to gain equal rights for all.

You have already read how the Chinese and Japanese were forbidden by law from entering the United States. In addition, Asians who were here often faced prejudice and discrimination. One of the most tragic cases of unfair treatment occurred during World War II. After Japan bombed our naval base on Pearl Harbor, many Americans turned against the **Nisei**—those native-born Americans whose parents had come from Japan. Some 100,000 were forced to leave their homes and businesses. They were taken to camps where they stayed until the end of the war.

MINORITY GROUPS TODAY

Prejudice and discrimination are still serious problems in our nation today. Black Americans, Native Americans, Mexican Americans, Puerto Ricans, Asian Americans, and others are working hard to win equal rights as citizens. They have accomplished much. But much still needs to be done. All Americans must work to end the effects of prejudice and discrimination, if the American ideal of equal rights for all citizens is to be won.

CONSIDER AND DISCUSS

Identify. "open shore" policy / quota system / refugee / minority group / prejudice / discrimination / Nisei

Review. 1. What were some of the reasons why immigrants came to America? 2. Why was the Chinese Exclusion Act passed? 3. How did the quota system work? 4. What are the main provisions of the immigration law that is now in effect? 5. Why are some groups of people referred to as minority groups?

Discuss. Do you think the United States was justified in limiting immigration after 1920?

3 Who Are American Citizens?

Millions of immigrants have become American citizens. Some American citizens belong to families who have lived here for many generations. Other Americans were born in foreign countries. American citizens are of many different races and religions. All of us, regardless of our background, have the same legal rights and responsibilities of citizenship.

Most of you are citizens of the United States. **Citizenship** means membership in your nation. When you reach the voting age of 18, you

These people are attending a class in English as part of their preparation for American citizenship.

can take part in our system of self-government. You have a right to expect that the American government will protect your life, liberty, and property at home and abroad. In return, you are expected to be loyal to your country and to work to promote its welfare.

CITIZENSHIP BY BIRTH AND BLOOD

Americans gain their citizenship either by birth or by a legal process called naturalization. Since citizenship by birth is the way most of us became citizens of the United States, let us review it first.

If you were born in any one of the 50 states or any American territory, you automatically became a **native-born** citizen. If your parents were United States citizens, you were a citizen at birth even if they were living in a foreign land when you were born. Citizenship, then, can be acquired by the place of birth or through one's parents. These two ways of becoming a native-born American follow the principle of "birth and blood."

The "birth and blood" principle raises many questions. What about children born in this country whose parents are citizens of a foreign country? Are they citizens of the United States? In most cases they are if their parents were under the authority of the United States at the time the children were born. But what about children born in the United States of parents who are officials representing a foreign country? These children are not United States citizens, because their parents are under the authority of another country. All cases involving questions about whether a person can claim American citizenship are handled by the United States Department of Justice.

THE ALIEN IN AMERICA

More than six million people living in the United States are citizens of other countries. These people are called **aliens.** Some are here on a visit. Others live and work here, or attend school here, but expect someday to return to their homelands. However, most aliens in the United States expect to live here permanently. While in the United States all aliens must obey the laws of this country. They are also entitled to be protected by its laws. Aliens enjoy most of the benefits of American citizenship. But they cannot vote or hold most public offices. In January of each year, aliens are required to register with the United States Immigration and Naturalization Service.

HOW AN ALIEN BECOMES A CITIZEN

Under certain circumstances, citizens of other countries may become citizens of the United States through a legal process called **naturalization.** To be eligible to enter the country, foreigners must prove that they can support themselves and that they can read and write. They must prove that they do not have certain diseases, and are not mentally ill, drug addicts, or criminals. There are a number of other restrictions. One of them bars all persons who are in favor of violent revolution, that is, the overthrow of the government by force.

When foreigners enter the United States, they are immediately eligible to begin the process of naturalization. They may file a declaration of intention with the immigration authorities. This paper simply states that the person plans to become a citizen. Such a declaration is not required. But some employers ask for it as evidence that the worker plans to stay in this country.

After five years of living here, aliens may apply for citizenship. They must at this time be at least 18 years of age. When the immigration authorities receive the application, called a **petition for naturalization,** they set a date for the person to appear in a Naturalization Court. Two witnesses must come with the prospective citizen to testify to his or her good moral character. The person applying for citizenship must prove to the judge that he or she can read, write, and speak the English language in an acceptable fashion. The judge may also ask the person questions about the history and government of the United States.

After this preliminary hearing, there is a 30-day wait during which applicants may be investigated to make sure of their qualifications. If they prove to have the background of good citizens, they are called to the court for a final hearing. There they take an oath of allegiance to the United States and are granted a certificate of naturalization. Naturalized citizens now have all the rights, privileges, and duties of native-born Americans. There is only one exception. They are not eligible to become President or Vice-President of the United States.

How an Alien Becomes a Citizen

DECLARATION OF INTENTION (Optional)

An alien may file this declaration in any federal court. This written statement declares that the alien plans to seek American citizenship.

PETITION FOR NATURALIZATION

After an alien has lived in America at least 5 years (or 3 years if married to an American citizen), he or she files a petition. This petition requests American citizenship.

PETITION WITNESSED

Two American citizens appear as witnesses to declare that the petitioner has lived in America for 5 years, has good moral character, and believes in the principles of the Constitution.

EXAMINATION

An examiner, or judge, examines the alien to see that he or she can read and write English and knows American history and government.

CITIZENSHIP GRANTED

The alien becomes an American citizen. The alien swears an oath of allegiance and signs a certificate of naturalization.

CONSIDER AND DISCUSS

Identify. citizenship / native-born / aliens / naturalization / petition for naturalization

Review. 1. What are two ways of being a native-born American? 2. Give the main steps in the naturalization process. 3. What right does a native-born American have that naturalized citizens do not have? 4. What department of the United States government decides questions of citizenship?

Discuss. Would you change the required qualifications for becoming a naturalized citizen? Explain.

4 The Meaning of American Citizenship

We live in a **democracy.** The word "democracy" comes from a Greek term meaning "rule of the people." The leaders who wrote the Constitution of the United States and planned our system of government tried to set up a form of government in which the people would truly rule.

We as American citizens elect our own government officials. Through them we influence government policies and actions. Therefore, we the people are responsible for our government. It is up to us as citizens to see that American government lives up to the **ideals,** or beliefs, of its people.

THE IDEALS OF AMERICAN GOVERNMENT

What are these ideals? Perhaps the simplest and best statement may be found in the Declaration of Independence:

> We hold these truths to be self-evident: that all men are created equal, that they are endowed by their Creator with certain unalienable rights, that among these are life, liberty, and the pursuit of happiness.

There is no more famous phrase in American writing than "all men are created equal." In this phrase, the word "men" is used to include both men and women. The statement

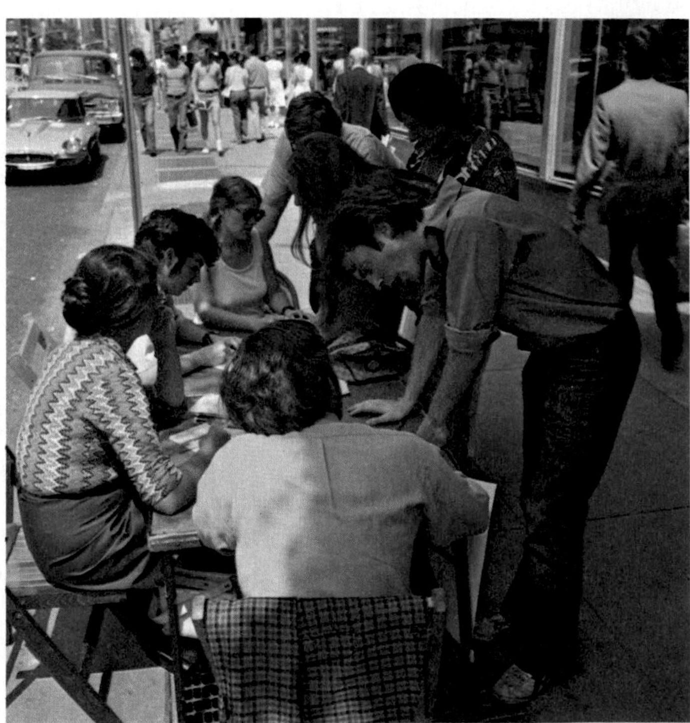

Voting is one of the most important responsibilities of American citizenship. In this picture, several young Americans are registering to vote.

does not mean that we are all born with the same mental and physical abilities. Instead, it means that we all have an equal claim to certain basic human rights. For example, all of us have the right to live our lives in liberty, or freedom. We also have the right to try to achieve happiness. The phrase also means that all of us are entitled to equal treatment by the law, regardless of our background or position. We must all obey the laws of the land. And we are all equally entitled to their protection. If American citizens are accused of a crime, they should receive a fair trial regardless of whether they are rich or poor, and regardless of their racial or religious background, education, or job.

The leaders who signed the Declaration of Independence realized that these ideals would be difficult to achieve. But they believed that these ideals were worth, in their own words, "our lives, our fortunes, and our sacred honor."

ACHIEVING AMERICAN IDEALS

Those who planned our system of government and wrote the Constitution of the United States took important steps toward achieving the ideals set forth in the Declaration of Independence. For example, Article I, Section 9, of the Constitution states, "No title of nobility shall be granted by the United States . . . or from any king, prince, or foreign state." Since all citizens were to be equal, there would be no class structure based on titles or heredity as there was in Europe. The United States was to be a land of equal opportunity where a person's position depended upon his or her ability.

The democratic ideal is also contained in the Constitution in what is not said. There are no religious, property, or class qualifications for holding public office. Every native-born citizen can aspire to become President. Rich or poor, a person who meets age and residence qualifications can be a Senator or Representative.

Since the early years of our nation, many other steps have been taken toward achieving equal rights for all Americans. But much still remains to be done. There are also many other ideals we have not yet achieved.

American citizenship involves certain duties and responsibilities that will be discussed in detail in the rest of this section. As you read, consider how, in fulfilling each duty and responsibility of citizenship, a citizen is given the opportunity to work toward national ideals.

THE DUTIES OF AMERICAN CITIZENS

Certain duties are required of all American citizens. These duties are the "musts" of citizenship. That is, all American citizens are required by law to perform these actions. The duties required of all citizens are described in the Constitution of the United States and in the laws of our nation and states.

Most Americans are familiar with these duties of citizenship, but sometimes we forget how important they really are. The success of our system of government depends upon all citizens fulfilling these duties:

1. American citizens must obey the laws.
2. American citizens must pay taxes to help pay the costs of government.
3. American citizens must serve as jury members if called upon to serve.
4. American citizens must testify in court if they have evidence to present.
5. American citizens may be called upon to help defend the nation by serving in the armed forces.
6. American citizens must attend school in order to obtain an education.

THE RESPONSIBILITIES OF AMERICAN CITIZENS

In addition to the required duties of citizenship, Americans have many responsibilities of citizenship. These responsibilities are the "shoulds" of citizenship. That is, American

Responsibilities of Citizenship

American citizens should vote in elections.

American citizens should be interested in their government and study its activities.

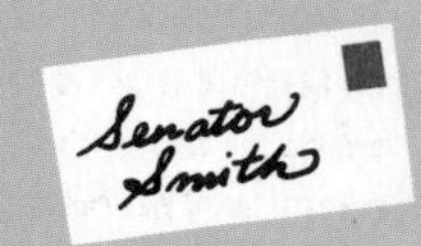

American citizens should tell their representatives what they think about the problems facing our government.

American citizens should be willing to serve as officials of government if elected or appointed to these jobs.

American citizens should be willing to support the work of their government.

American citizens should help their government to enforce the laws by cooperating with the police.

citizens are not required by law to carry out these actions. But most Americans accept these responsibilities because they are so important to the successful operation of our system of government. These are some of the most important responsibilities:

1. American citizens should vote in all elections for which they are eligible.

2. American citizens should be interested in their government and carefully study its activities.

3. American citizens have a responsibility to tell their representatives what they think about the problems facing their government.

4. American citizens should concern themselves with and support the work of their government either as members of a political party or as independent voters.

5. American citizens should be willing to serve as officials of government if they are elected or appointed to public office.

6. American citizens should help the government to enforce the laws. Citizens can also help by cooperating with their local police forces.

Voting is perhaps the most important responsibility of American citizens. By voting on election day, each citizen plays an important part in deciding who will be the leaders of our government. Each voter also helps to determine what actions our government will take, because the people who are elected will plan these actions when they are in office. In these ways, voting in free elections carries out our great Constitutional ideal of government by consent of the people governed.

In order for all citizens to cast their votes wisely, they must understand the problems that face the government. They must take an interest in the programs and the activities of the government. They must also learn what policies each candidate running for office favors. This means that if citizens are to vote responsibly, they first must fulfill the responsibilities of good citizenship.

The responsibilities of American citizenship are not easy ones. To fulfill them requires time and effort. But carrying them out gives all Americans a chance to take part in our representative democracy. And all Americans must take part if our nation is truly to have a "government of the people, by the people, for the people."

CONSIDER AND DISCUSS

Identify. democracy / ideals
Review. 1. What are some of the important ideals of American government? 2. What are the duties required of American citizens? 3. What are the responsibilities of American citizens?
Discuss. Which ideals of American government do you think we have achieved? Which ones do you think we have not yet achieved?

CHAPTER
Summary

Our nation, built upon the American Dream, has made great progress toward the fulfillment of its ideals. But there is still much work to be done to bring about the dream of equal opportunity for all. America is still growing, and such growth brings with it many problems.

Our nation has grown as our natural population has increased and as more and more immigrants have come to America to live. People have come from Asia, Europe, Africa, Latin America, and other areas of the world. Today, about 220 million people live in the 50 states of the United States.

Citizenship in our nation is gained by birth or by naturalization. An immigrant can become an American citizen by following certain legal steps in our courts. When immigrants become naturalized citizens, they enjoy the same rights as native-born citizens. The one exception is that they cannot become President or Vice-President.

Americans live in a representative democracy, a form of government in which the people rule through their elected representatives. As American citizens we must see that our government lives up to the ideals set forth in the Declaration of Independence and the Constitution. Citizenship in our nation requires certain very important duties and responsibilities. The good citizen supports our nation's democratic ideals and works to make certain that its freedoms are shared equally by all citizens.

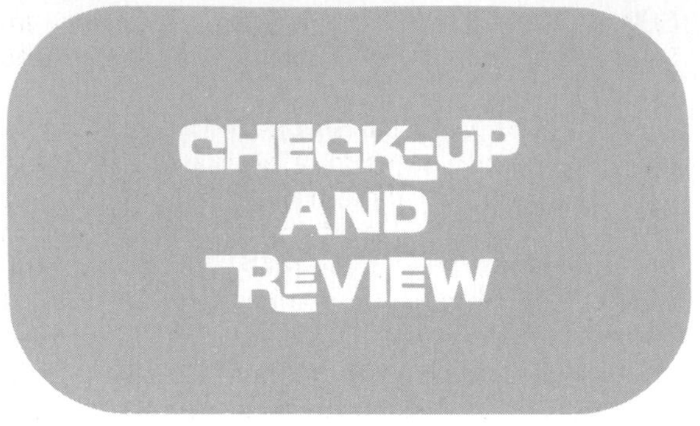

VOCABULARY

Each of the questions below may be answered by one of the words in the following vocabulary list. Set aside a portion of your civics notebook for vocabulary studies. There, list each word. After the word, write the number of the question it answers.

immigrant	refugee
citizenship	democracy
alien	prejudice
naturalization	quota system

1. What is the name used for a person who visits or lives in the United States but remains a citizen of another nation?
2. What word means to have full membership in a nation?
3. What do we call a person who comes to the United States to live here permanently?
4. By what means may a citizen of another country become an American citizen?
5. What term describes the limit that is placed on the number of immigrants admitted into a country in any one year?
6. What term applies to people who flee their homelands to find safety in a foreign land?
7. What do we call unfair opinions of people that are based on race, nationality, or creed?
8. What word is used to mean a government in which the people rule themselves?

CHECK-UP

The following questions will help you review this chapter:

1. What was the "melting pot" theory?
2. What were some of the contributions the English settlers made to the American way of life?
3. What was the major difference between the "Old Immigration" and the "New Immigration"?
4. From what nations have large numbers of immigrants come in recent years?
5. What are the main steps by which an alien becomes an American citizen?
6. Why did the United States adopt a quota system for immigrants?
7. What examples show that the United States is still a refuge for oppressed peoples?
8. What problems have minority groups had to face in the United States?
9. What are some of your duties and responsibilities as an American citizen? Which do you think are most important?
10. Why is it important that the people of the United States carefully guard the principle of "liberty and justice for all"?

CITIZENSHIP AND YOU

Many Americans think that the duties and responsibilities of citizenship include only such important matters as voting in national elections or paying their taxes. Good citizenship means much more. You and your classmates can engage daily in citizenship activities. Here are some suggestions.

1. Class Projects

Many communities set aside a special day to welcome newly naturalized citizens. Sometimes this is done on September 17, which was proclaimed by President Truman as "Citizenship Day." Civics classes may take part in the ceremonies that mark such occasions.

Your class may find it interesting to attend a naturalization court to watch the judge administer the oath of citizenship to new citizens.

Your class may decide to invite a naturalized citizen to come to class and tell how he or she became an American citizen.

2. Group or Committee Projects

A poster committee may prepare and display original posters on such challenging topics as "The American Dream," "Minority Rights," and "Good Citizenship."

A graph committee can prepare a large bar graph showing immigration to the United States from 1820 to the present. Use this graph as a basis for a discussion of America's immigration pattern.

A map committee, using an outline map of the world, can make a map showing the national origins of the class members or their ancestors.

3. Individual Projects

Write your own "American's Creed." List the things America means to you. This creed may be expressed in the form of an essay or a poem. Several creeds may be read and discussed in class.

CIVICS SKILLS

USING REFERENCE MATERIALS

Your textbook provides you with many of the basic facts concerning our nation, its opportunities, its problems, and its challenges. You will learn more from your textbook if you approach your study of civics with a questioning attitude. After you have read something, you may want to check the accuracy of what you read. Or you may want to get additional information. You may want to learn more about how these facts affect you and your community. In order to do this, you must know how and where to get information.

Social scientists such as sociologists develop useful methods and tools for finding out facts about individuals and groups within society. They ask questions, make surveys, and search for additional facts. They also test their facts and try to reach conclusions. Like other scientists, those who deal with the way people live in groups and interact with one another depend upon gathering reliable data. They learn to observe, define, interpret, and draw conclusions. They are interested in finding out.

Among the tools that students of civics should learn to use are standard reference books. These reference sources contain many facts that have been gathered by experts and put together in books. For example, if you are interested in finding facts concerning population trends, you might go to the library and obtain a copy of the most recent edition of the *World Almanac* or some other good almanac. These reference books contain tables on many subjects of national interest. Each year the United States government also issues a book called *Statistical Abstract of the United States*. Learn how to make good use of the tables of contents and indexes in such books.

Finding facts about local population is not so easy. In making your own local population survey, newspaper files may be helpful. Or local officials may be interviewed to find the facts you and your classmates need.

PRACTICING YOUR CIVICS SKILLS

Go to the school library or the public library and find the Reference section. What are the titles of the books in this section? Look through several of the books to see what kinds of information they contain. Then see if you can find the following information:

1. What is the present population of the United States?
2. How many children were born in the nation during the past year?
3. How many deaths occurred?
4. How many black Americans live in the United States?
5. How many people of Spanish origin live in the United States?
6. How many Asian Americans live in the United States?
7. How many Indians, or Native Americans, live in the United States?
8. How many immigrants came to the United States between 1841 and 1850?

If last year's figures are not listed in the reference books available, give figures for the most recent year you can find.

CHAPTER

Introduction

You are a citizen of the United States of America. You also are a citizen of your state and of your local city or town. As a good citizen you obey the laws of your nation, your state, and your community. Your family helps to support each of these governments by paying taxes. In return, you receive important services from each of these governments. These services include good schools, modern highways, police protection, mail delivery, and many others.

All of these services are intended to serve you, the citizen. If any of these government services do not satisfy you, you can write to your Congressman or Congresswoman, or your local representative. And when you are old enough to vote, you can help to elect leaders who will give you the kind of government you want.

What do we mean by the word "government"? You probably have a fairly good idea of what government means. But the chances are that you have never before tried to describe it in a few words. When you think of government perhaps you think of the Capitol building in Washington, D.C., or your state capital, or the city hall in your own community. Perhaps you think of the President of the United States, the Governor of your state, or the Mayor of your town. Perhaps you think of laws that you must obey or the rules of the student council in your school. If you do think of government in this way, you are on the right track.

But government is not only buildings and laws and leaders. It includes all of these. But it also includes much more. *Government* is the entire system of authority or power that acts on the behalf of a group of people.

Learning about your government will provide you with knowledge that will be useful the rest of your life. It will also help you to become a good citizen and to understand the aims and ideals of the United States. In the four parts of this chapter, you will study these important topics:

1. Why Americans Have Governments
2. How Our American Government Developed
3. Great Ideals in the Constitution
4. The Rights and Freedoms of Americans

CHAPTER

Government by the Consent of the Governed

1 Why Americans Have Governments

In times past, the governments of many nations were controlled by kings or queens. They often held all of the power in their nation's governments, and they were able to rule by force. For this reason, they were called **absolute monarchs.**

Today, there are few absolute monarchs left. Most nations that have monarchs greatly limit their power. And such rulers are called **limited monarchs.** There are still some nations, however, in which a single leader (or a group of leaders) rules by force. These absolute rulers are called **dictators.** Their nations are called **dictatorships.**

Americans are fortunate to live in a nation that is not ruled by force. We believe that the people should rule themselves. Indeed, the term **American government** refers to the authority, or power, that Americans have set up to help them rule their own affairs. We have developed a form of government in which the leaders are responsible to the people. And in our government the people have the power to change or abolish any part of our system that no longer works.

WHY DO WE NEED GOVERNMENT?

Wouldn't it be possible for all of us to live as we choose? Couldn't we manage our own affairs without a government? Do we really need to follow rules in order to get along

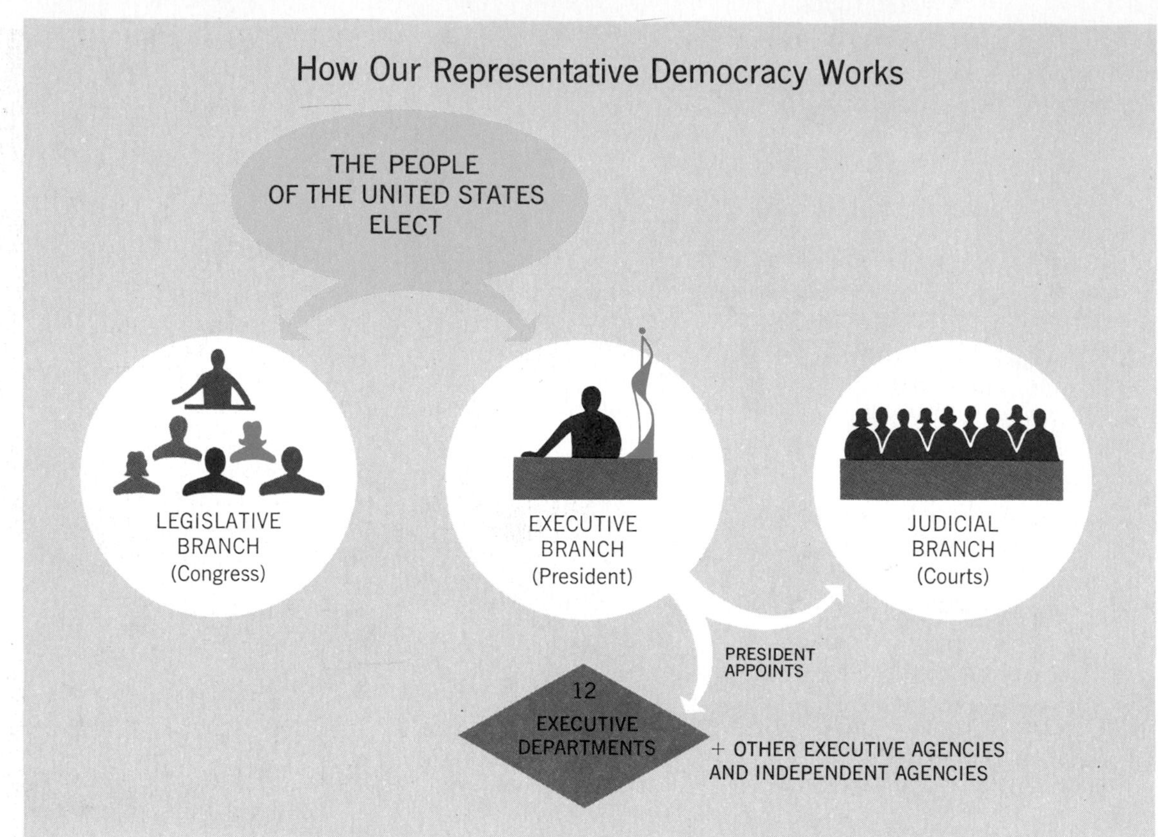

with one another? In order to answer these questions, we need to understand the purposes of government.

(1) GOVERNMENTS MAKE IT POSSIBLE FOR PEOPLE TO LIVE TOGETHER

Whenever large groups of people have lived together, they have found it necessary to have a government. **Anthropologists** are social scientists who study the physical, social, and cultural development of humans. They tell us that under early forms of government, the strongest person was sometimes made the leader of the people. This person could best help the people defend themselves against their enemies. At other times, the best hunter might be the leader because a hunter could help get a good food supply. In other matters, such as whether the entire group should move to better land, a group of the oldest and wisest leaders might make the decision.

One of the earliest lessons that people learned was that cooperation was useful. It was easier to hunt and kill a large animal for food if the group worked together. The tribe could be better protected against enemies if it was united. Even the simplest form of government helped to make life safer, easier, and more pleasant.

(2) GOVERNMENTS PERFORM MANY SERVICES FOR THE PEOPLE

Over the years, government has grown more and more complex. But its basic purposes have remained the same. It provides ways for people to live and work together. It also enables people to accomplish things that need to be done but cannot be done well by each person working alone.

For example, what would happen if each family in your community had to educate its own children? Even if the parents had time enough to teach, would they be able to teach well? How would they teach subjects that they had forgotten or perhaps had never studied when they went to school? How would they know how well their children were learning, compared with other children? Using government to set up schools avoids most of these problems. Government makes it possible for people to work together to provide a good education for all children.

Just as government has made schools possible, it performs other services that would be difficult or expensive for individual citizens to provide for themselves. Because of government, American citizens can travel over highways that stretch from sea to sea and from border to border. Their lives and property are protected by police. A system of money makes it easy for Americans to buy and sell things and to know their value. Trash is collected, and health laws are enforced. Homes are protected by fire departments. Libraries are built and operated. These and many more services are provided by government.

Government provides many services that we sometimes take for granted. But when a city's sanitation workers go on strike, the trash piles up quickly.

(3) GOVERNMENT PROVIDES RULES, OR LAWS, FOR THE PEOPLE

Large groups of people need rules to help them live together in peace. When there are rules, all people know what they may and may not do. Without good rules, any disagreement or dispute would probably end with the strongest members of the group settling things their way.

One of the most important reasons for establishing governments is to provide rules of conduct for the group. In American government, these rules are known as **laws** and are written down so that people can know them and obey them. Many of these laws are contained in **constitutions,** or written plans of government. Americans have used constitutions to establish their national and state governments. A constitution states the purposes of the government. It describes how the government is to be organized, or set up. And it contains some of the most important laws that the government is to uphold. In this way, American governments use laws and constitutions to set up rules for the people to follow.

(4) GOVERNMENT ENABLES A NATION TO PUT ITS IDEALS INTO PRACTICE

A nation's government helps put into practice the ideals of the people, or the things they believe in. Americans believe that the people should rule themselves. They also believe that each individual citizen is important, and that no citizen should be denied his or her rights.

What are these rights? In the Declaration of Independence, which we shall discuss in detail later in this chapter, they are described as "life, liberty, and the pursuit of happiness." This means that all Americans have the right to live their own lives in liberty, or freedom, and to try to achieve happiness for themselves. To safeguard a citizen's liberty, our governments guarantee certain freedoms, such as freedom of speech, freedom of the press, and freedom of religion. These freedoms can never be taken away from an American citizen. Nor can they be restricted in any way, except to keep people from using these freedoms to violate the rights of others.

Americans also believe that if any citizen is denied his or her rights, the liberty of all Americans is endangered. As you have read (Chapter 1), some minority groups in the United States have yet to achieve their equal rights as citizens. All Americans must work hard toward this goal if it is to be reached. But, with the willingness of American citizens, our government can put this ideal, and other ideals, into practice through its laws and institutions.

Government can help a nation put its ideals into practice through passing and enforcing new laws, and by setting a good example. Can you think of other ways? In regard to minority rights, for example, laws that forbid discrimination in education, housing, voting and many other fields have been passed and enforced. The governments on federal, state, and local levels have themselves used fair employment practices in hiring Americans to fill positions.

CONSIDER AND DISCUSS

Identify. government / absolute monarch / limited monarch / dictator / dictatorships / American government / anthropologist / laws / constitution

Review. 1. What are some of the services governments provide? 2. Give four reasons why we need government.

Discuss. Which of the reasons for establishing governments do you think is the most important one? Tell why.

2 How Our American Government Developed

As you may remember from your study of American history, our nation was once ruled by Great Britain. But Great Britain was far away, on the other side of the Atlantic Ocean. And so for many years, the colonists made most of their own rules and regulations. When the British government under King George III began to make laws that the colonists felt were unjust, Americans decided that they wanted to be free to govern themselves. They fought the Revolutionary War to gain their independence and to be free.

THE DECLARATION OF INDEPENDENCE

The reasons why the 13 colonies decided to separate from Great Britain and form a free nation are stated in the **Declaration of Independence.** (See the complete text of this important document on pages 512–13.) The Declaration also explained to the world, in clear and inspiring language, that the purpose of government was to protect the rights of the individual citizen.

The Declaration of Independence did *not* provide a government for the new American nation. As soon as the Declaration was signed, the people in each of the states adopted constitutions in which they assigned certain powers to their state governments. At the same time, while the Revolutionary War was still being fought, leaders from all the 13 states met in Philadelphia. This Second Continental Congress began to work out a plan for a national government that would reflect the ideals of the American people. This plan of national government was approved by the states and began to operate in 1781. The plan was called the **Articles of Confederation.**

THE ARTICLES OF CONFEDERATION

A **confederation** is a loose association rather than a firm union of states. The Articles of Confederation, the young nation's first plan of government, set up a "firm league of friendship" among the 13 states. Each state was to have equal powers, and in most ways was independent of the other states. The central government was given very limited powers. The people of the 13 states did not want a strong central government. They feared that such a government might use its power to limit the freedom of the separate states.

Under the Articles of Confederation, the national government consisted of a law-making body of one house, called **Congress.** The states sent Representatives to Congress, and each state had one vote in Congress regardless of the number of people living in the state. There was no provision for a President or any other strong leader to head the nation's government and to carry out the nation's laws. This was because the people were suspicious of strong leaders after their experience with King George III of Great Britain. There were also no national courts to judge the nation's laws and to punish lawbreakers. The states kept the power to enforce the laws passed by Congress.

During the Revolutionary War, the 13 states were willing to work together and make sacrifices to achieve victory. But things were different in the years following the Revolution. Many Americans suffered hard times after the war. Property had been destroyed. Trade with other countries had been cut off. And American business was badly hurt. Moreover, the war left the young nation deeply in debt. The new government tried its best to handle these difficult problems. But it was too weak to solve them.

THE WEAKNESSES OF THE CONFEDERATION

There were many causes for the weakness of our nation's government under the Articles of Confederation. Without a president to head the national government, the nation had no strong leadership. The Congress had trouble passing laws, because a vote of nine states was needed to pass a law. There were no officials to see that the laws were carried out. And there were no national courts to judge those who broke the laws. In addition, it was very difficult to change the Articles of Confederation in order to make the national government stronger. Any changes in the Articles required the unanimous vote of all the Representatives of the 13 states.

One of the main weaknesses of the new national government was that Congress lacked the power to collect taxes. Congress could ask the states to contribute money to help the national government meet its expenses. But Congress had no power to force states to make these contributions. Without money, Congress could not pay its debts or carry on any government programs that might be needed. Congress could not pay the soldiers who had fought in the Revolutionary War or repay its debts to foreign nations.

Under the Articles of Confederation, the national government also lacked other important powers. It could not regulate, or control, trade between the states or with foreign countries. Each state regulated its own trade.

WEAKNESSES OF GOVERNMENT ESTABLISHED BY THE ARTICLES OF CONFEDERATION

ONE-HOUSE CONGRESS

NO PRESIDENT

States kept most of the power, gave too little power to the national government.

No President or Chief Executive.

Congress had no power to collect taxes.

Laws were difficult to pass (9 out of 13 states' approval needed).

Congress was responsible to the state legislatures, not to the people.

There was no system of national courts.

Congress had no power to regulate trade.

Congress had no power to coin money.

Congress had no power to establish armed forces—each state kept its own troops.

STRENGTHS OF AMERICAN GOVERNMENT ESTABLISHED BY THE CONSTITUTION

TWO-HOUSE CONGRESS

A PRESIDENT

States kept many powers, gave important powers to the national government.

President, with enough powers, heads our nation's government.

Congress given power to collect taxes.

Laws easier to pass (majority vote required).

Congress responsible to the people directly (after 17th Amendment).

Supreme Court and system of national courts authorized.

Congress may regulate trade with other nations and trade between the states.

Congress may coin money.

Congress can establish an army and navy to defend our nation.

This caused many disputes among the states and with foreign nations. Most of the states issued their own money.

The states were acting more like small separate nations than as states in a confederation. The states often refused to obey the laws of Congress. As a result, relations between the states and Congress grew steadily worse.

WHY THE CONFEDERATION FAILED

The real trouble with the government set up by the Articles of Confederation was that the states refused to give the national government enough power to operate effectively. The states feared a strong central government and kept most of the real power in their own hands. The people of each state continued to think of themselves as belonging to their particular state rather than to the nation as a whole. This was natural because the states were separated by great distances, transportation was poor, and there was little contact between many of the states. It took years before the states began to think of themselves as parts of a single nation.

The weaknesses of the national government became clear as new problems faced the American nation. The states began to quarrel over the location of boundary lines, and they got into disputes over trade. But the national government was powerless to end these disagreements. It seemed as if the new nation were about to break up into several small nations. As a result, Congress called upon the states to send representatives to a meeting to consider what could be done to improve matters.

On May 25, 1787, a group of outstanding leaders met in Independence Hall in Philadelphia. They had been sent as **delegates,** or representatives, by their states to discuss ways of improving the national government. The 55 delegates included such leaders as George Washington, Benjamin Franklin, James Madison, Alexander Hamilton, James Wilson, William Paterson, and Edmund Randolph. The meeting is known as the **Constitutional Convention.** The wise and remarkable leaders who attended wrote a constitution that founded, or established, a government for the United States that has lasted for almost 200 years.

THE ENGLISH BACKGROUND

These leaders knew history well, and they had learned many important lessons from the past. They wanted the people of America to enjoy the rights that the English had fought for and won during the past centuries. This heritage from England included the rights mentioned in the Magna Carta (the Great Charter), which the English people had won from King John in 1215. This important document guaranteed that free people should not be arrested, put in prison, or forced to leave their country unless they were given a trial by other free people who were their equals. And they were to be judged by the laws of their country.

The members of the Constitutional Convention also wished the new American nation to have the rights contained in the English Bill of Rights of 1689. These rights included the right to **petition,** or request, the government to improve or to change laws, and the right to a fair punishment if a citizen were found guilty of a crime.

The Convention delegates at Philadelphia also studied carefully the example of the English Parliament. **Parliament** was the lawmaking body of the English government. It was a **bicameral,** or two-house, legislature. It was made up of the House of Lords, appointed by the King, and the House of Commons, elected by the people. It had the advantage of each house checking upon and improving the work of the other. The leaders at Philadelphia wanted no part of lords or kings. But they could see the advantage of the bicameral system.

THE CONSTITUTION OF THE UNITED STATES

The delegates to the Constitutional Convention decided that rather than **amending,** or changing, the Articles of Confederation, a new system of government was needed to solve the nation's problems. The delegates agreed that the national government had to be given greater power. At the same time, most of the members agreed that the states should keep the powers needed to govern their own affairs. In order to achieve this, the delegates established a system of government known as a **federal union** or a **federation.** In a federal union, the powers of government are divided between the national government, which governs the whole nation, and state governments, which govern the people of each state.

The delegates worked out the new plan of a federal union during their meetings at Philadelphia. The new plan of government that they drafted was the **Constitution of the United States.** The Constitution took only a few short months to write. But ever since it has continued to provide a system of free government for the United States.

During the hot summer months of 1787, the delegates discussed many ideas and proposals as they worked on the Constitution. There were many problems and disputes that needed to be solved. You may recall these disagreements from your study of American history.

The smaller states, for example, fearing the power of the large states, did not want a bicameral legislature. They favored a lawmaking body of one house, with each state having an equal number of representatives in it. The larger states favored a lawmaking body of two houses, with states represented in both houses according to the size of their population. Both sides argued strongly for their ideas.

Finally, both sides agreed to a compromise, that is, to an arrangement in which each side gives up part of its demands. This agreement provided for a lawmaking body of two houses called Congress. In one house, the Senate, the states were to have equal representation. In the other house, the House of Representatives, each state was to be represented according to the size of its population. This agreement is known as the **Great Compromise.**

A STRONG NEW NATION IS CREATED

Many other compromises and agreements were reached as the Convention delegates worked on the Constitution. The states agreed to give up some of their powers and to increase the powers of the new national government. The central government was given the power to tax, to regulate trade among the states and with foreign nations, to raise armed forces, and to coin and print money. Provision was made for a President to carry out the nation's laws. National courts would enforce these laws.

By September 1787, the delegates to the Constitutional Convention had completed their work. The Constitution of the United States was ready to be sent to the states and the people for their approval, or **ratification.** Most of the states ratified the Constitution in special conventions during the next year. The rest ratified it soon after. The new government of the United States began to operate in March 1789.

The Constitution of the United States is such a remarkable and important document that every American should read and study it with care. (The entire Constitution is found on pages 514–30.) You will learn more about the great beliefs and ideals in the Constitution in the next part of this chapter.

CONSIDER AND DISCUSS

Identify. Declaration of Independence / Articles of Confederation / confederation / Congress / delegates / Constitutional Convention / petition / Parliament / bicameral / amend / federal union / federation / Constitution of the United States / Great Compromise / ratification

Review. 1. What ideas of government did the delegates to the Constitutional Convention borrow from England? 2. Why were the states unwilling to give more power to the central government? 3. What were some of the weaknesses of the government under the Articles of Confederation?

Discuss. Do you think of yourself more as a citizen of your state or as a citizen of the nation? Why?

3 Great Ideals in the Constitution

A famous English leader, William Pitt, said many years ago that the Constitution of the United States "will be a pattern for all future constitutions and will receive the admiration of all future ages." Time has proved the truth of these words. The Constitution is now the world's oldest written plan of government still working successfully. The constitutions of many other nations have been patterned on it.

The Constitution of the United States has been successful because it is based upon many great ideals concerning government. And it provides a system of government that enables us to put these ideals into action. These ideals provide the key to understanding the American system of government.

GOVERNMENT BY CONSENT OF THE GOVERNED

The Declaration of Independence states that governments receive "their just [or well-deserved] powers from the consent [or approval] of the [people] governed." This is one of the basic ideals upon which our Nation's founders built the Constitution. They, too, believed that a government must receive all its powers from the people it governs, that it must not use any powers that the people do not grant it, and that the people must give their consent before the system of government goes into effect.

The idea of government by the **consent of the governed** is found in the opening sentence of the Constitution. It clearly states that this new plan of government is being established by the people themselves. "We the people of the United States . . . do ordain [order] and establish this Constitution. . . ." The Constitution of the United States was the work of representatives of the people. And, as you know, it was ratified in special conventions representing the people in each of the 13 states before it went into effect. To this day, not one word of it can be changed without the consent of the people or their representatives.

A REPRESENTATIVE DEMOCRACY OR REPUBLIC

But why was the Constitution drawn up and ratified by representatives of the people, rather than by the people themselves? And why didn't the Constitution set up a **direct democracy,** in which all voters would meet together at one place to make laws and to decide what actions the nation should take?

The answer is that the writers of the Constitution were practical. They knew that direct democracy might not work in a nation as large as ours. They decided instead to set up a form of government known as a **representative democracy,** or a **republic.** In a representative democracy, or a republic, the people elect representatives to carry on the work of government for them. Representative democracy is based upon the consent of the people who are governed. When the people are dissatisfied with the way their representatives are governing them, the people can let their representatives know what they think should be done. Also, the people can and often do elect new representatives at election time.

GOVERNMENT BASED ON A FEDERAL SYSTEM

Our system of government is based on a federal union, or a federal system. In this **federal system,** as you have read, the powers of government are divided between a national government, which governs the whole nation, and state governments, which govern the people of each state. The national government is often called our **federal government.** It is important to remember that the term "federal government" refers to the national government, which is centered at Washington, D.C. The term "federal system" refers to our entire system of government and includes both the federal government and the state governments.

In our American federal system, the federal government is given certain important powers. The state governments are given other important powers. The federal government's powers are meant to apply to matters concerning all the people. Among these powers are the control of trade among the states

The American Federal System

THE NATION

THE FEDERAL GOVERNMENT
has authority over the whole nation.

MAJOR POWERS

Foreign Relations — Foreign Trade
National Defense — Money System
Trade Among the States

EACH STATE

EACH STATE GOVERNMENT
has authority over most affairs within the state's borders.

MAJOR POWERS

Education — Public Building Programs
Police — Health and Safety
Highways

EACH COMMUNITY OR LOCAL AREA

EACH LOCAL GOVERNMENT
has authority over the affairs of a town or city or county or township.

MAJOR POWERS

Schools — Parks and Playgrounds
Police — Libraries
Fire Protection — Public Utilities
Sewage Systems — Streets and Traffic
Zoning and Building Codes

Each American is a citizen of the nation, of a state, and of a local community.

and with foreign nations, the printing and coining of money, the maintenance of an army and a navy, and the conduct of foreign relations.

The Constitution leaves to the states many important powers to manage their own affairs. Under our federal system, the states or the people keep all the powers not specifically given to the federal government. The state governments, for example, help build our highways, provide schools, conduct elections, and protect the health and welfare of the people.

The state and federal governments also share many powers. Both, for example, can raise funds through taxation. They also cooperate in building interstate highways, in looking after the welfare of the people, in enforcing health regulations, and in keeping the peace. When the federal government and the state governments both claim they have the power to do certain things, the federal government usually wins the dispute. The writers of the Constitution tried to prevent trouble of this kind by saying that the Constitution and the laws of the federal government shall be "the supreme law of the land." Whenever a state law disagrees with the Constitution or with a federal law, the state must give way to the federal government.

GOVERNMENT IN WHICH POWERS ARE LIMITED

By establishing the American federal system, the writers of the Constitution set up the stronger national government that our new nation needed. But they also were determined to keep this new federal government from becoming too powerful. Therefore, they spelled out very carefully the various powers of the federal government, in order that all Americans might know exactly what these powers are. The Constitution also provides that all powers not mentioned are therefore reserved, or set aside, for the states or the people. Furthermore, the Bill of Rights (see pages 524–25) specified certain powers that were forbidden to both the federal government and the states.

As you have read, the writers of the Constitution believed that all governments had to have the consent, or approval, of the people. Therefore, the government could have only as much power as the people wanted to give it. And the American people clearly wanted to limit, or to check, the power that their federal government would have. But why?

Nearly all Americans at the time of the Constitutional Convention were against strong governments. They feared that a strong national government might destroy their freedom, as the British king had attempted to do. They wanted to prevent any leader or small group of leaders from using the strong power of government to establish a dictatorship. They wanted to be sure that their new government would be responsible to the American people.

GOVERNMENT IN WHICH POWERS ARE SEPARATED

There are several provisions in the Constitution designed to prevent any person or group of people, or any part of the government, from taking too much power. One of the provisions sets up three separate branches, or divisions, in the federal government. This three-way division of power is known as the **separation of powers.** The Constitution provides for a **legislative branch,** called Congress, to make the laws. It also sets up an **executive branch,** headed by the President, to see that the laws are carried out. And it established a **judicial branch,** or system of courts, headed by the Supreme Court, to judge the laws and to punish lawbreakers.

GOVERNMENT WITH CHECKS AND BALANCES

To make doubly sure that no branch of the federal government can become too powerful, a system of **checks and balances** was included in the Constitution. Each branch of the government has powers that check, or limit, the powers of the two other branches. Each branch also has its own powers, which no other branch can assume. In this way, the powers of government are balanced, or equally divided, three ways.

The Separation of Powers

Makes the laws.

Carries out and enforces the laws.

Judges laws and punishes lawbreakers.

How does this system of checks and balances work? To take one example, how does the executive branch check the legislative branch? The President can check the lawmaking power of Congress because of the power to approve or disapprove **bills,** or proposed laws, passed by Congress. If the President favors a bill and signs it, the bill becomes a law. If the President does not favor a bill, the President has the power to veto, or turn down, the bill.

Does this mean that any bill that the President does not like cannot become a law? This would give too much power to the President. Therefore, the Constitution balances the President's power. It does so by giving Congress the power to pass bills over the President's veto. A two-thirds vote of both houses is required before Congress can pass any bill that the President has vetoed. But if Congress is determined to get the bill passed, it can do so by a two-thirds vote.

There are many other checks and balances in the working of our federal government. You will learn more about how the three branches check and balance each other as you study American government in the chapters that follow.

Checks and Balances in Making Laws in the Federal Government

POWERS		CHECKS ON POWERS
Passes laws. Can pass laws over the President's veto if two thirds of the Congress approve the law. Approves appointments of Supreme Court Justices.	 THE CONGRESS	President can veto laws. The Supreme Court can rule that a law is unconstitutional.
Can approve or veto laws. Carries out the laws. Appoints Supreme Court Justices.	 THE PRESIDENT	Congress can pass laws over the President's veto by a two-thirds vote. Congress may impeach or remove the President for high crimes or for misdemeanors. Congress approves the President's appointments to the Supreme Court.
Judges the meaning of laws. May rule that laws passed by Congress are unconstitutional.	 THE SUPREME COURT	Congress (or the states) may propose an amendment to the Constitution if the Supreme Court rules that a law is unconstitutional. Congress may refuse to approve the appointments to the Supreme Court.

Many of the delegates who helped write the Constitution also served as leaders in the new government. Here, President Washington meets with his first Cabinet.

GOVERNMENT THAT CAN CHANGE AND GROW

Our Constitution has the great advantage of being able to grow and change with the changing times. There are three ways in which the Constitution and the government can change. They are **amendment, interpretation,** and **custom.**

The process for amending, or changing, the Constitution is set forth in Article 5 of the Constitution of the United States. It is not easy to amend our Constitution. All amendments require the approval of a large majority of the American people. Also, they may take a long time to pass. This makes it more likely that long, careful thought will be given to any proposed amendment before it is passed. Since the Constitution went into effect in 1789, only 26 amendments have been added to it. (See Chapter 6 for a discussion of the amendments to the Constitution.)

Our government also changes by interpreting, or explaining, the meaning of some part of the law in a new way. For example, Congress may read a certain clause in the Constitution and decide that its wording gives Congress the right to take a certain action. Congress then passes a law based on its interpretation. If a citizen objects and challenges the law in the courts, then the Supreme Court may make a decision as to whether or not Congress has the right to interpret the Constitution in that way. The Supreme Court's ruling is final.

A number of changes in our government have also come about through custom and tradition. For example, the Constitution did not provide for regular meetings of the leaders in the executive branch of our federal government. But President George Washington brought these leaders together regularly to serve as his advisers, or **Cabinet.** Since the time of President Washington, regular meetings between a President and the Cabinet have become an accepted part of the American tradition of government. Many other important traditions have developed in our nation's government. These traditions are followed regularly. But they have seldom been written down or made into laws. For this reason, they are sometimes called our **unwritten Constitution.**

CONSIDER AND DISCUSS

Identify. consent of the governed / direct democracy / representative democracy / republic / federal system / federal government / separation of powers / legislative branch / executive branch / judicial branch / checks and balances / bill / amendment / interpretation / custom / Cabinet / unwritten Constitution

Review. 1. What is the difference between direct democracy and representative democracy? 2. Why does the Constitution limit powers granted to the federal government? 3. How does the system of checks and balances work in our federal government?

Discuss. Suppose a new system of television and telephones were set up. And suppose that each evening all Americans of voting age could watch debates over a proposed law and phone in their vote for or against it. Do you think such a system of direct democracy would work better or worse than our present system? Why?

4 The Rights and Freedoms of Americans

In drafting the Constitution, most of the convention delegates believed that the safeguards written into it would protect the rights of Americans. But when the Constitution was sent to the states in 1787 for ratification, many Americans were not happy with it. In Virginia, Patrick Henry protested strongly against the lack of a specific statement of rights. Other Americans from different states demanded that a Bill of Rights be added to the Constitution. A number of states ratified the Constitution only conditionally. That is, they would approve the Constitution only if it were changed to include a Bill of Rights.

Two years after the new American government went into effect, the **Bill of Rights** was added as the **first ten amendments** to the Constitution. Congress discussed nearly 200 proposals for amendments before it presented these ten to the states for approval. The states ratified these amendments, and they became part of the Constitution in 1791.

THE BILL OF RIGHTS

The first ten amendments to the Constitution, or the Bill of Rights, set forth the priceless rights or freedoms that all Americans may enjoy. A brief summary of these great freedoms is given here.

FREEDOM OF RELIGION

The first right, or freedom, guaranteed in the Bill of Rights is freedom of religion. This right is guaranteed in the First Amendment. **Freedom of religion** guarantees to all Americans the right to practice any religion they choose, or to practice no religion at all.

Congress is forbidden to establish any religion as our nation's official religion. Congress cannot favor any one religion over others or tax citizens in order to support any one religion.

FREEDOM OF SPEECH

The right to express your ideas and opinions when you speak is called **freedom of speech.** Freedom of speech also means the right to listen to the thoughts and opinions of others. This freedom guarantees that Americans are free to express their thoughts and ideas about anything. We may talk freely to our friends and neighbors or speak in public to a group of people. Of course, we should not use our freedom of speech to injure others. If someone knowingly says things that are false about others, that person may be sued in court by those who believe they have been harmed by what was said.

Americans are free to express opinions about their government or anything else. They are free to criticize the actions of the government and of government officials. In a dictatorship, where the nation's government has all the powers, the people have no right to speak like this. They do not dare to criticize the actions of the government. If they do, they may be imprisoned. But all Americans enjoy the freedom of speech, which is guaranteed in the First Amendment of the Constitution.

FREEDOM OF THE PRESS

The freedom to express your ideas and opinions in writing is known as **freedom of the press.** This freedom is closely related to freedom of speech and is also guaranteed by the First Amendment.

Freedom of the press gives all Americans the right to express their ideas and thoughts freely in writing. This writing may be in newspapers, books, magazines, or any other printed or written form. Americans are also free to read what others write. They may read any newspaper, book, or magazine they want. Because they are free to read a variety of facts and opinions, Americans can become better informed citizens.

FREEDOM OF ASSEMBLY

Another priceless freedom guaranteed by the First Amendment is **freedom of assembly,** or freedom to hold meetings. Americans are free to meet together to discuss problems and to plan their actions. Of course, such meetings must be carried on in a peaceful way.

FREEDOM OF PETITION

The **freedom of petition** is the right to ask your government to do something or to stop doing something. The First Amendment contains this guarantee, also. The freedom of petition gives you the right to write to your Representative and request him or her to work for the passage of laws you favor. You are free to ask your Representative to change laws that you do not like. The right of petition also helps government officials to know what Americans think and what actions they want the government to take.

continued on page 41

These women are exercising their right of free assembly—one of the basic freedoms guaranteed to all Americans.

A RIGHT TO BEAR ARMS?

WHAT DO YOU THINK?

Americans have owned guns and other firearms since colonial times. Until not too long ago guns were considered a necessary part of life in many areas of the United States. They were used for hunting, for self-defense, and for controlling wildlife. But more recently, as crime has increased throughout the nation, some people have demanded that guns be regulated. Each year, more than 18,000 people are murdered, about two thirds of them by guns. Moreover, several of our national leaders have been attacked with guns. In the 1960's, President John Kennedy, civil rights leader Martin Luther King, Jr., and Presidential candidate Robert Kennedy were shot and killed. In 1972, Governor George Wallace of Alabama was shot and crippled. In 1975, President Gerald Ford was the target of two unsuccessful assassination attempts.

In response to the demands of citizens, some gun control laws were passed. The Gun Control Act of 1968 outlawed the interstate shipment of long guns

(rifles and shotguns) to individuals. Interstate shipment of hand guns (pistols and revolvers) was already illegal. This means that you cannot order any kind of gun from a catalog and have it sent to you from another state. Some states, such as California and New York, also have laws requiring the registration of all guns and gun owners. But most states do not. Since there is no federal registration, most guns cannot be traced to their owners.

Much controversy surrounds the issue of gun control. One of the main reasons for the controversy is the Constitution of the United States. Read the following carefully:

Amendment 2: Right to Keep Arms

> A well regulated militia being necessary to the security of a free state, the right of the people to keep and bear arms shall not be infringed (disregarded or violated).

What do you think this Amendment means? Does it guarantee the right of every American to own guns? Or does it mean that the federal government cannot interfere with the right of states to organize militia (National Guards)?

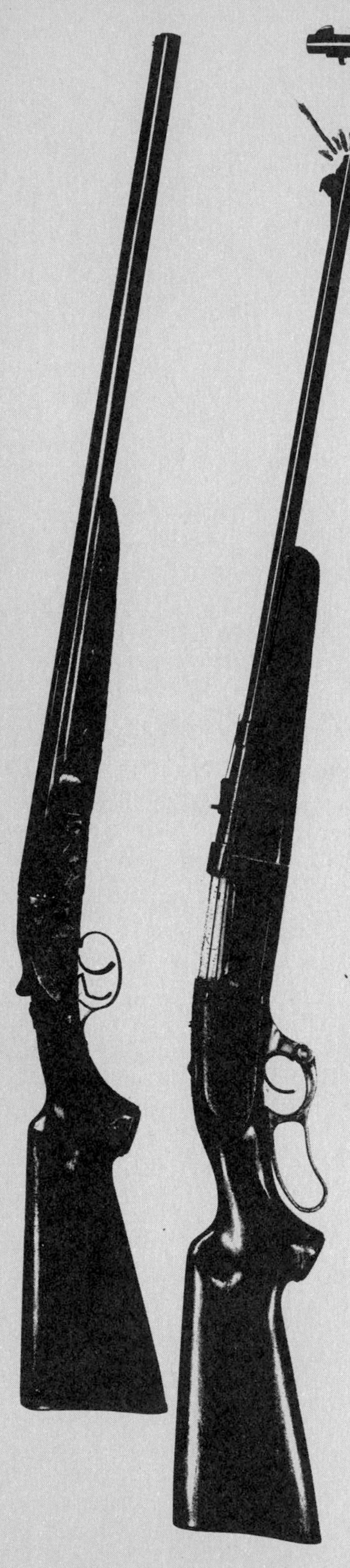

What other arguments can you think of for and against stricter gun control? Here are some of the arguments that have been used by those who think that people should have to get a license to own a gun:

1. Guns are used to commit many serious crimes in addition to murders. They are used in robberies, kidnappings, and terrorist activities, for example. Also, guns are involved in many suicides and are the cause of accidental deaths. The easier it is to get guns, the greater the danger of harm from them.

2. Nations with strict gun control laws, such as Great Britain, have much lower crime rates than the United States. In fact, ours is the only modern industrial nation that allows its citizens to keep arms for their private use.

3. Registration of guns and licensing of their owners would be only a small inconvenience for law-abiding hunters and sports enthusiasts. And it would make it harder for criminals to get guns, and much easier to trace a gun used to commit a crime.

4. The Supreme Court has upheld the idea of federal gun controls on individuals. Obviously, no one can claim a right to endanger other citizens.

Do these arguments seem reasonable to you? What arguments can you think of against gun control?

Here are some of the reasons given by those who oppose gun control laws:

1. "It isn't the gun that kills; it's the person who kills." Guns don't cause crimes. If people intend to kill or steal, they will do so with or without guns. If it's a question of dangerous items, other weapons besides guns are dangerous, and they're not outlawed.

2. "When guns are outlawed, only outlaws will have guns." A criminal who wants a gun won't pay attention to the law anyway. Only hunters and other ordinary citizens will be restricted.

3. Citizens should be able to defend themselves and their homes, with guns if necessary. The tradition of guns for self-defense goes back to frontier days and is part of the American way of life.

4. Any limitation on the constitutional right to bear arms would be a serious threat to our freedom. We must keep all of our rights, or we will end with very few of them left.

Can you think of any other reasons for or against gun control? Which arguments seem the most important to you? Do any of them seem unimportant or exaggerated? What other facts or figures would you want to know before you made up your mind on this question?

THE RIGHT TO BEAR ARMS

The Second Amendment to the Constitution guarantees Americans the **right to bear arms.** In the early years of our nation, Americans needed weapons in order to serve in the militia, or volunteer armies, that were established to defend our states. The militia provided protection during emergencies, too. Many Americans also believed that without weapons they would be powerless if the government tried to overstep its powers and rule by force.

"NO-QUARTERING" RIGHT

The Third Amendment states, "No soldier shall, in times of peace, be quartered [sheltered] in any house. . . ." Under British rule, the colonists sometimes had to feed and house British soldiers against their will. As a result, Americans wanted the **"no-quartering" right** entered into the Bill of Rights.

THE RIGHT TO EQUAL JUSTICE

The Bill of Rights contains many rights that are guaranteed to persons accused of a crime. Amendments Five, Six, Seven, and Eight are all concerned with these rights. Our nation places great importance on these rights in order to guarantee equal justice for all Americans.

1. A person must be **indicted,** or formally accused of a crime, by a group of citizens called a "grand jury" before being brought into court for trial.
2. A person accused of a crime is guaranteed the right to know what law he or she is accused of breaking.
3. A person accused of a crime has a right to a prompt public trial by a jury of citizens.
4. Accused persons cannot be put into prison and kept there for weeks or months while awaiting a trial. They have the right to leave jail, in most cases, if they can raise a certain sum of money, or bail, as a pledge that they will appear at the trial.
5. Accused persons have the right to a lawyer to represent them in court.
6. All the testimony and evidence against an accused person must be presented publicly in court.
7. Accused persons have the right to call any witnesses to appear if their testimony will help them.
8. Accused persons cannot be forced to testify or give evidence against themselves.
9. If the accused person is found guilty, that person cannot be given cruel or unusual punishment.
10. The accused person who is found not guilty of a serious crime, cannot be tried a second time for this same crime.

THE RIGHT TO OWN PRIVATE PROPERTY

The Fifth Amendment guarantees Americans the **right to own private property.** No person may take away anything that we own. Nor can the government seize our land, money, or other forms of property without cause, or without paying for it. The right to own private property is one of America's basic freedoms. Our free economic system is based upon this right.

THE RIGHT TO ENJOY MANY OTHER FREEDOMS

To make doubly sure that Americans should enjoy every right and freedom possible, Amendment Nine was added to the Constitution. This amendment states that the list of rights contained in the Bill of Rights is not complete. There are many other rights that all Americans have and will continue to have even though they are not mentioned in the Bill of Rights. Among them are the following:

1. Freedom to live or travel anywhere in our nation.

2. Freedom to work at any job for which we can qualify.

3. Freedom to marry and raise a family.

4. Freedom to receive a free education in good public schools.

5. Freedom to join a political party, a union, and other legal groups.

As a final guarantee of our rights, the Tenth Amendment set aside many powers of government for the states. This Amendment says that all powers not given to the federal government by the Constitution, nor forbidden to the states, are set aside for the states, or for the people. This provision leaves with the states the power to act in many ways to guarantee the rights of their citizens.

CONSIDER AND DISCUSS

Identify. Bill of Rights / first ten amendments / freedom of religion / freedom of speech / freedom of the press / freedom of assembly / freedom of petition / right to bear arms / "no-quartering" right / indicted / right to own private property

Review. 1. Why was the Bill of Rights added to the Constitution? 2. If you were accused of a crime, what rights would you have? 3. What freedoms do Americans enjoy in addition to those mentioned in the Bill of Rights?

Discuss. Which of the freedoms in the Bill of Rights do you think is the most important to Americans today? Why?

CHAPTER
Summary

Government is the authority or power that people establish to help them run their affairs.

Governments serve many important purposes. But the most important one is that government makes it possible for people to live and work together. Government provides us with rules of conduct we can follow. Government makes it possible for people to live by known laws, and helps provide many services that citizens acting alone could not perform themselves.

Our nation's government is based on the American Constitution. This Constitution, together with its Bill of Rights and other amendments, provides us with a workable plan of government. The Constitution also guarantees to all Americans many priceless rights and freedoms.

Our nation's government is based upon the approval, or consent, of the people who are governed. It is a federal system in which certain powers are given to the national government and other powers are left to the states and to the people. Certain powers are shared by both federal and state governments. In both federal and state governments, powers are separated and balanced among three branches of government.

VOCABULARY

A number of new civics words and terms have been explained in the chapter you have just studied. But reading about words is not the same as having to use words. To increase your communication skills, you need to use new words as tools that will make your ideas clear to others. The following exercise will give you valuable practice in the use of new civics words.

Write each of the words that appear below on a separate piece of paper. (This list can be added to your civics notebook after you begin to keep one.) Then read the numbered definitions that follow. Choose the one that best fits each word. Write the definition beside the word it fits.

Constitution	absolute monarch
bicameral	confederation
government	ratification
democracy	republic
amendment	anthropologist

1. The established authority that administers the affairs of a nation, state, or local community.
2. A form of government in which all power is in the hands of a king or queen who is able to rule by force.
3. A social scientist who studies the physical, social, and cultural development of humans.
4. The fundamental set of laws and principles set up to govern our nation and our states.
5. A league of states loosely bound together.
6. A two-house legislature, each with its own powers and authority.
7. The submission of a document or law to the people for approval.
8. A government of, by, and for the people.
9. A form of government in which the people elect representatives to carry on the work of government for them.
10. A change in a bill, a law, or a constitution.

CHECK-UP

One good way to see if you have really learned from studying a chapter is to answer questions about important ideas in it. Can you give good answers to the following questions? Try to answer fully without looking at your textbook. Then turn to the text and check your answers.

1. What are some of the important reasons we need governments?
2. How do governments help groups of people to run their own affairs?
3. What were some of the rights guaranteed to English subjects by the Magna Carta and the English Bill of Rights of 1689?
4. Why did Americans in 1781 fear a strong central government?
5. What were some of the principal weaknesses of the government under the Articles of Confederation?
6. How did the Great Compromise settle differences between the large states and the smaller states?
7. What are some of the powers granted to the federal government under the Constitution?
8. How does our system of checks and balances work?
9. What are some of the rights and freedoms you possess as an American citizen?
10. Why was the Bill of Rights added to the Constitution?

CITIZENSHIP AND YOU

You and your classmates will find civics more challenging and interesting if you begin to put your ideas about government into operation now. Projects are suggested here for the entire class, for small groups, and for the individual student.

1. Class Projects

Set up a student government for your civics class. The first step is to draw up a constitution setting forth the officers needed and their duties and powers. Give the constitution to the class for ratification. Then hold a class election to vote for these officers. Try to get permission to have the class president lead some of your civics lessons. The class secretary can take notes on the discussions.

Another class project that you may find useful in connection with this chapter is to put on a mock Constitutional Convention. Members of the class may role-play the parts of the major delegates. One student will be George Washington, Chairman of the Convention. Another will play the part of James Madison, expert on governmental organization. Several students can represent the small states. Others can represent the larger states. One class period can be used to reenact the Convention debate that led to the Great Compromise. Keep the mock convention informal and spontaneous. The actors should not deliver memorized speeches when they present the ideas of the delegates.

2. Group or Committee Projects

Groups may be set up to report on special topics. Some topics could be: "How Government Began," "The Democratic Ideas of Ancient Greece," "How George Washington Contributed to the Constitutional Convention," "Dictatorship Governments Today," and "Rights, Duties, and Privileges of the Teenage Citizen."

A bulletin-board committee may be appointed to prepare a display on "The Great Ideals of American Government." Posters, pictures, charts, and drawings may be prepared and arranged on the bulletin board to illustrate topics in this chapter.

3. Individual Projects

The bulletin-board committee described above will be responsible for the actual display. Each member of the class can contribute to its success by bringing in interesting materials.

Students talented in art may prepare drawings and posters on "American Ideals." These may be used to decorate the classroom or may be displayed on the bulletin board.

A large chart may be prepared to show the contrasts between government in a democracy, a limited monarchy, and a dictatorship.

CIVICS SKILLS

KEEPING A NOTEBOOK

Your notebook can become an important tool of learning. In it you can keep a record of essential information. If the material is well organized and classified, your notebook will be a good source of reference.

Organizing and classifying information in your notebook will help make the big ideas of civics more meaningful to you. Putting facts in your own words will help you to make sure you understand them. Writing down your tentative conclusions will help you weigh the evidence on each side of important questions.

Some students use their notebooks to outline information from their textbooks and other sources. They find such outlining to be a useful method of preparing for tests or reviewing the main points of each chapter. *American Civics* lends itself readily to outline form. Each chapter has several main headings (listed at the start of each chapter), and many subheadings. In addition, there are lists of important ideas worth remembering. The chapter headings will help you organize your own outline, especially if you get into the habit of writing down these headings in your own words. You will also find it helpful to write down the main points you want to remember under each heading.

PRACTICING YOUR CIVIC SKILLS

Prepare a "Table of Contents" for your civics notebook. Some suggested headings might be: Vocabulary, Outlines, Current Newspaper Clippings, Facts About the Constitution, Special Projects, Answers to Chapter Check-ups, Charts. What other headings can you think of to add? List them all in your Table of Contents.

In your notebook, make a list of Amendments 1–10 of the Constitution. Next to each amendment list the rights or freedoms it guarantees to each American. Then, write a short description of how each of these rights and freedoms affects you in your daily life. If you wish, illustrate your materials on the Bill of Rights with pictures from newspapers, magazines, pamphlets, or from other sources.

UNIT
TWO

The Federal Government

CHAPTER

Introduction

In January of each year, the 535 men and women who make our nation's laws set out on an important journey. They all leave their home states to travel to the capital of the United States, Washington, D.C. Some of them come from large states such as California, New York, Illinois, and Texas. Others come from small states such as Delaware and Vermont. Some of the Senators and Representatives come from such faraway places as Hawaii and Alaska. They all come to the nation's capital to prepare for a new session of Congress.

Together, these members of Congress make up the legislative, or law-making, branch of our national government. It is the branch of the government that is closest to the people because all of its members are chosen by the people to represent the people. For this reason, it is the central institution of our representative democracy. It is also the branch of the government to which the Constitution has given the greatest amount of power.

What is the job of these 535 members of Congress? Their main job is to make our nation's laws. Every day they must make important decisions that affect the lives and welfare of the American people. Members of Congress may have to decide such important questions as how large our armed forces should be, or how high federal taxes should be. Only Congress holds "the power of the purse." This means that only Congress has the right to tax, to regulate interstate and foreign commerce, and to coin and borrow money for the government. Members of Congress also may propose amendments to the Constitution. They may declare war. And, of course, they must find time to keep in touch with the people of their home states and take care of their problems.

In this chapter, you will learn more about Congress, its organization, and the way in which laws are passed, as you study these topics:

1. The Senate and the House of Representatives
2. How Congress Is Organized
3. Bills Take Shape in Committees
4. How a Bill Becomes a Law
5. The Powers of Congress

CHAPTER

3 Congress Makes Our Nation's Laws

1 The Senate and the House of Representatives

As you know, the work of our national government is divided among three separate branches, or divisions—the legislative branch, the executive branch, and the judicial branch. We shall begin with the legislative, or lawmaking, branch because it is the first branch of government mentioned in the American Constitution.

THE TWO HOUSES OF CONGRESS

The work of the legislative branch is carried out by the Congress of the United States. Congress is the lawmaking body of our national government. The Constitution provides that Congress shall be composed of two houses—the Senate and the House of Representatives.

The leaders who drew up our plan of government in 1787 had several good reasons for creating a lawmaking body of two houses, or a bicameral legislature. First, they believed that a lawmaking body of two houses would help to "check and balance" the work of this branch of the government. Having two houses to share the responsibility of making the nation's laws allows each house to check upon the actions of the other. As a result, there is less danger that Congress will pass laws in haste or pass laws not needed or wanted by the people.

Second, the writers of the Constitution established a two-house Congress in order to settle a dispute between the large and the small states. As you may recall, the smaller states feared that they would be dominated by the larger ones. They worried that their people would receive less consideration in the law-making process. The dispute was settled by the Great Compromise. It provided that the states should be represented equally in the Senate, and according to the size of their population in the House of Representatives.

THE HOUSE OF REPRESENTATIVES

The House of Representatives, or the House as it is sometimes called, has 435 members and is the larger of the two houses of Congress. The members of the House are known as **Representatives.** According to the Constitution, the number of Representatives that each state may elect to the House is based on the size of the state's population.

Originally, each state elected one Representative for every 30,000 persons living in the state. If the state's population was under 30,000 people, it was entitled to have one Representative. In the first Congress, which met in 1789, there were 59 Representatives in the House. Then, as new states joined the union and the nation's population increased, the House steadily grew in size. To prevent the membership from growing too large, Congress finally limited the size of the House of Representatives. In 1929 Congress set the limit at 435 members.

Every ten years, after the census is taken, Congress determines how the 435 seats in the House of Representatives are to be distributed. Congress itself divides these seats among the states according to population. If a state's population decreases from one census to the next, the number of its Representatives may be reduced. On the other hand, states whose population grows may be entitled to more Representatives. But the total size of the House of Representatives can never be more than 435 members. After the 1970 census, five states gained additional seats in the House while nine states lost seats. California, for instance, gained five seats, while New York and Pennsylvania each lost two seats.

CONGRESSIONAL ELECTIONS

Elections for members of the House of Representatives are held in November of each even-numbered year. All Representatives are elected for a two-year term, which begins on January 3 following the November election. Members of the House may be reelected to office, and there is no limit on the number of times they may serve. Because many Representatives are reelected, there are always a number of experienced lawmakers in the House. If a Representative dies or resigns before the end of his or her term, the governor of the state must call a special election to fill the vacancy.

CONGRESSIONAL DISTRICTS

The lawmaking body of each state government—the state legislature—is responsible for dividing the state into **Congressional districts.** Each state is divided into as many Congressional districts as it has members in the House. The voters in each Congressional district of the state elect one Representative. After each census, the state legislature must redivide the state's Congressional districts if the number of people has changed.

For many years, a number of the states did not adjust their districts according to changes in population. As cities gained in population, the state legislatures often failed to give them increased representation either in Congress or in the state legislatures. A rural district with few people might elect a Representative. And an urban district with a much larger population would have the same representation as the smaller district. As a result, state legislatures and the House

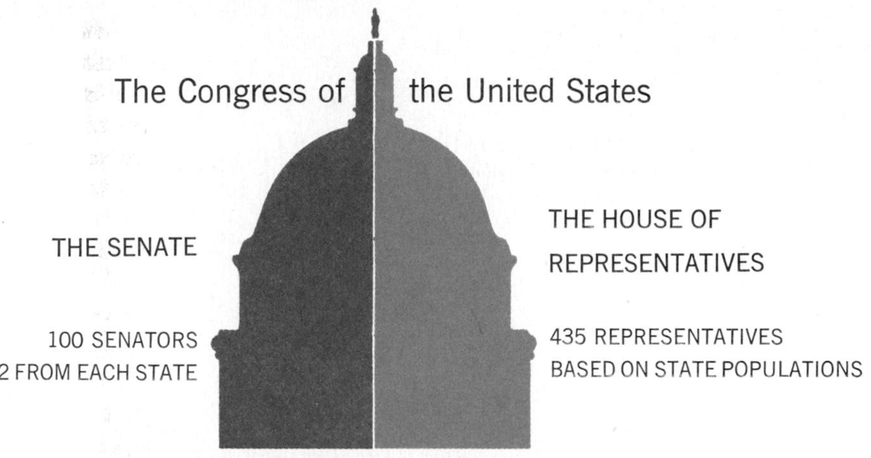

	LENGTH OF TERM	WHEN ELECTED	REQUIRED AGE	CITIZENSHIP	LEGAL RESIDENCE	SALARY
SENATORS	6 years	One third of Senate elected every 2 years	At least 30 years old	American citizen at least 9 years	Resident of state where elected	$57,500+ expenses
REPRESENTATIVES	2 years	Entire House elected every 2 years	At least 25 years old	American citizen at least 7 years	Resident of state where elected	$57,500+ expenses

of Representatives often represented rural interests and gave less attention to cities.

In 1964, in the case of *Reynolds v Sims*, the Supreme Court of the United States decided that Congressional districts within each state must be equal in population "as nearly as possible." This was known as the "one man, one vote" decision. It meant that every man, woman, and child is entitled to equal representation in Congress. As a result of this decision, the states must revise their Congressional districts after each census if the census figures show that the population of the districts is uneven.

THE SENATE

The Senate is the smaller of the two houses of Congress. The Constitution provides that each state, large or small, be represented equally in the Senate by two members. These members are known as **Senators.** The first Senate, which met in 1789, consisted of only 22 Senators because two of the 13 states had not yet accepted the Constitution. Today, the Senate has 100 members—two Senators elected from each of the 50 states.

Senators are elected by the voters of the state. The members of the Senate are elected for six-year terms and may be reelected any number of times. One third of the Senate's membership comes up for election every two years. Elections for Senators, like those for Representatives, are held in November of even-numbered years. Because only one third of the Senate seats are up for election at one time, a new Senate begins its work with at least two thirds of the members having had experience in the Senate.

The Senator from each state who has

served the longest period of time is called the state's **senior Senator.** If a Senator dies or resigns before the end of the term of office, the Governor of the state may appoint someone to fill the vacancy until the next regular election, or until a special state election is held.

THE QUALIFICATIONS OF MEMBERS OF CONGRESS

The Constitution sets forth the qualifications that members of Congress must meet. These are the qualifications for members of the House of Representatives:

1. A Representative must be at least 25 years old.
2. A Representative must be a citizen of the United States for at least seven years before being elected.
3. A Representative must be a legal resident of the state he or she represents. In addition, a Representative usually lives in the district from which he or she is elected. Although the Constitution does not make this a requirement for office, it has been established through custom.

The qualifications of members of the Senate differ slightly from those of Representatives. The Constitution sets forth these qualifications for Senators:

1. A Senator must be at least 30 years old.
2. A Senator must be a citizen of the United States for at least nine years before being elected.
3. A Senator must be a legal resident of the state he or she represents.

SALARY AND PRIVILEGES OF MEMBERS OF CONGRESS

Senators and Representatives each receive a yearly salary of $57,500. In addition, they are paid for certain traveling expenses while on official business. They are provided with office space in Washington. They receive an allowance to pay an office staff of assistants,

This aerial view shows Capitol Hill and the Senate and House office buildings where members of Congress pass our nation's laws.

clerks, and secretaries. Members of Congress may mail official letters free of charge. This right is sometimes referred to as the **franking privilege.**

Members of Congress are free from arrest when they are attending Congress or on their way to or from a meeting of Congress, unless they have committed a serious crime or are charged with treason. In this way, no one can interfere needlessly with federal lawmakers as they perform their duties.

Members of Congress cannot be sued for anything they may say while they are speaking in Congress. This provision is intended to protect their freedom of debate. On the other hand, members of Congress are not free to behave just as they wish. Both the Senate and the House of Representatives have rules of conduct that members must follow.

Both houses of Congress also have the right to decide who shall be seated as members. This means that if the Senate or House questions the methods by which any member was elected, the member may not be seated until an investigation is made. If either house finds that dishonest or questionable methods were used, it can refuse to seat this member. The Senate or the House can also require the state to hold a new election. Fortunately, Congress seldom has to refuse to seat a member. Most Congressional elections are conducted honestly.

Improper conduct by a member of the Senate or House may result in **expulsion** from office by a vote of two thirds of the Senators or Representatives. Expulsion of a member means that the member must give up his or her seat in Congress. Grounds for expulsion are limited to the most serious offenses, such as treason or the accepting of bribes. Lesser offenses may bring a vote of **censure,** or formal disapproval of a member's actions.

CONSIDER AND DISCUSS

Identify. Representative / Congressional district / Senator / senior Senator / franking privilege / expulsion / censure

Review. 1. How many members are there in Congress? in the House? in the Senate? 2. In what ways do the qualifications for Senators and Representatives differ? 3. What are some of the special privileges enjoyed by members of Congress?

Discuss. Do you think that members of Congress should vote on issues according to what they believe are the best interests of the country? Or should they vote according to the way the people of their state or district want them to vote? Explain.

2 How Congress Is Organized

The third day of January is always a busy and exciting day in the Capitol building in Washington, D.C. Doorkeepers take their places. Clerks prepare to keep careful records of all the proceedings. Guards and the Sergeant at Arms get ready for an orderly session. Attendants place materials on the desks of Senators and Representatives. A new session of Congress is about to begin.

TERMS AND SESSIONS OF CONGRESS

Beginning with the first Congress in 1789, each Congress has been given a number to identify it. Thus, the Congress that began its term in 1789 was known as the First Congress. The Congress that began its term in 1979 was the Ninety-sixth Congress. In each term of Congress, there are two **regular sessions,** or meetings. Each of these sessions begins in a different year. The first session begins on January 3 in the odd-numbered year following the Congressional election in November. The second session begins on January 3 of the next year. In the past, sessions usually lasted from January 3 until August or September. In recent years, however, the growing workload has made the sessions of Congress last longer. Each session may last as long as Congress wishes. And both houses must agree upon the date to **adjourn,** or to end the session.

Sometimes serious problems come up after Congress has adjourned its regular session. In such cases, the President of the United States may recall Congress to Washington for a **special session.** Usually the President calls both houses into special session. But the President may call only one of the two houses. The last special session of Congress was called by President Truman in 1948 to deal with various anti-inflation and welfare proposals.

THE ORGANIZATION OF CONGRESS

Congress must be well organized in order to carry out its job of making laws. The Consitution of the United States (Article 1, Section 2) states that "The House of Representatives shall choose their Speaker and other officers. . . ." Article 1, Section 3, states that the "Vice-President of the United States shall be President of the Senate. . . ." and that "The Senate shall choose their other officers. . . ." This is the only direction given to Congress by the Constitution about the organization of the two houses. Congress is free to choose what other officers it will have. It also can decide how they will be chosen.

Over the years, Congress has developed the following procedures to organize itself. Shortly after the opening day of each session of Congress, the Republican members and Democratic members in each house of Congress gather separately in private meetings to organize their members. These private meetings are called **party caucuses.** At these caucuses, the Republican members of each house choose their own leaders and the Democratic members choose theirs. The political party that has the most members in each house is called the **majority party.** The political party that has fewer members is called the **minority party.**

At their private caucus meetings, the members of the Democratic Party and the Republican Party each choose a **floor leader** for the Senate and another for the House. The floor leaders of the majority party are called the **majority leaders.** The floor leaders of the minority party are called **minority leaders.** The floor leaders of each party guide the party's bills through Congress. Each floor leader has an assistant called the **party whip** who helps persuade the members of the party to be present and to vote for party-sponsored bills.

At their private caucuses, the members of each party also appoint a **steering committee.** The steering committees in each house help the floor leaders to steer, or guide, bills through Congress. The steering committee also helps its party to decide which policies it favors and which bills it wants its members to support.

THE PRESIDENT OF THE SENATE

The Constitution provides that there shall be a presiding officer in each house of Congress. The Vice-President of the United States serves as the presiding officer of the Senate. The Vice-President is not a Senator, however, and cannot take part in Senate debate. The Vice-President may cast a vote only in the case of a tie. The chief duty of the presiding officer of the Senate is to see that the Senate works smoothly.

In recent years, the President of the United States has given the Vice-President many other duties to perform both at home and abroad. These duties cause the Vice-President to be absent from the Senate on many occasions. During the Vice-President's absence, the Senate is presided over by a **President pro tempore** – a President "for the time being." This presiding officer is elected by the members of the Senate, and is usually a member of the majority party.

THE SPEAKER OF THE HOUSE

The House of Representatives elects its own presiding officer who is called the **Speaker of the House.** The candidates for this office are chosen at party caucuses. Since the majority party has more votes, its candidate usually wins. Because this office is such an important one, the Speaker is usually a longtime member of the House who has had much experience in Congress.

The Speaker receives a yearly salary of $75,000 and $10,000 for expenses. The power of the Speaker is great. No Representative may speak until called upon, or "recognized," by the Speaker. The Speaker also has much in-

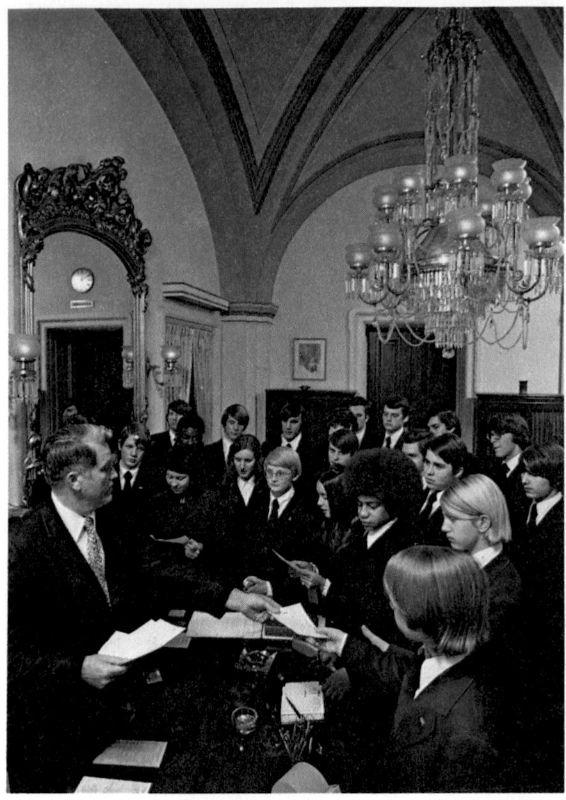

These teenagers are Congressional pages. They run errands and carry messages for members of Congress.

fluence in deciding the order of business in the House. The Speaker of the House becomes President of the United States if both the President and the Vice-President should die or become disabled.

CONGRESS WORKS THROUGH COMMITTEES

Every year, Congress has to consider thousand of **bills,** or proposed laws. Sometimes it considers as many as 20,000 a session. It would be impossible for all the members of each house to consider every bill that is proposed at each session. Therefore, the members divide their work among many smaller groups, or **committees.**

Each house of Congress has a number of permanent **standing committees.** These committees deal with bills in special areas of government such as foreign affairs, the armed services, and many others. For example, in the Senate the Committee on Aeronautical and Space Sciences handles all matters concerning space exploration. In the House, bills related to outer space go to the Committee on Science and Technology.

The Senate has 18 standing committees, and the House has 22. Before any bill is brought before Congress, it is carefully studied by a standing committee. After eliminating any bills not worth considering, the committee will hold hearings to gain information on the good and bad points of a bill, and revise it. The committee then sends the bill to the entire membership for its consideration, with their recommendation for or against it. This recommendation usually determines whether the membership will or will not consider the bill.

From time to time, each house of Congress appoints special committees called **ad hoc committees.** These ad hoc committees are set up to do special jobs and are disbanded when they finish their work. Sometimes, the two houses of Congress decide they can take care of certain matters better by working together in a committee. When this happens, they set up **joint committees.** Joint committees, composed of members of both houses, consider legislation or try to work out differences in bills passed by the two houses.

MEMBERSHIP ON COMMITTEES OF CONGRESS

Each member of the Senate and House of Representatives serves on at least one standing committee. Members of Congress eagerly seek assignment to the most important committees, such as the Senate Committee on Foreign Relations or the House Ways and Means Committee.

Each party in each house has its own **committee on committees.** This group nominates, or names, members of the party to serve on the various standing committees. Then a party caucus reviews the nominations of the committee on committees. Loyal party members are rewarded with the best committee assignments.

The chairperson of a standing committee of the House or Senate is very powerful. How does someone get this position? For many years, the post went automatically to the member of the majority party who had the most years of service on the committee. This person was said to have **seniority.**

In recent years, some people have questioned the use of the seniority system in choosing committee chairpersons. Should the position go to the person with the longest period of service or to the one who is best qualified to lead the committee? Critics believe that younger members with fewer years of service might provide more vigorous committee leadership. As a result of such criticism, the House changed its method of selecting chairpersons. The majority party now chooses the heads of the committees by secret vote in a party caucus. However, the person with the longest service is almost always chosen. The Senate still uses the seniority system.

PARTY REPRESENTATION ON COMMITTEES

The majority party in each house has a great advantage when committee members are chosen. Since the majority party elects the majority of members on each standing committee, it is able to control much of the work of the committee. The membership of the standing committees is divided in proportion to the number of members each party has in each house. For example, if the Senate contains 60 Democrats and 40 Republicans, a ten-member committee would include six Democrats and four Republicans.

When the committees have been formed and the leaders elected, the Congress is ready for the important business of lawmaking. As you can see, the committee system of Congress plays a vital part in the work of our nation's lawmakers.

CONSIDER AND DISCUSS

Identify. regular sessions / adjourn / special session / party caucus / majority party / minority party / floor leader / majority leader / minority leader / party whip / steering committee / President *pro tempore* / Speaker of the House / bill / committees / standing committee / ad hoc committee / joint committee / committee on committees / seniority

Review. 1. How are Congresses numbered? 2. Why is the Speaker of the House an important official? 3. What services do legislative committees perform? 4. What advantages does the majority party enjoy in Congress?

Discuss. Do you think the seniority system in Congress needs to be changed further?

3 Bills Take Shape in Committees

Each day that Congress is in session, an interesting scene takes place. As the members of the House enter their legislative hall, some of them approach the front of the chamber. Then they drop papers into a box on the clerk's desk. The box is called "the hopper." And the papers dropped in it are written proposals for laws, or bills.

HOW THE IDEA FOR A BILL BEGINS

Each year the Senate and the House of Representatives consider thousands of bills. These bills may be introduced in either

How Ideas for Bills Begin

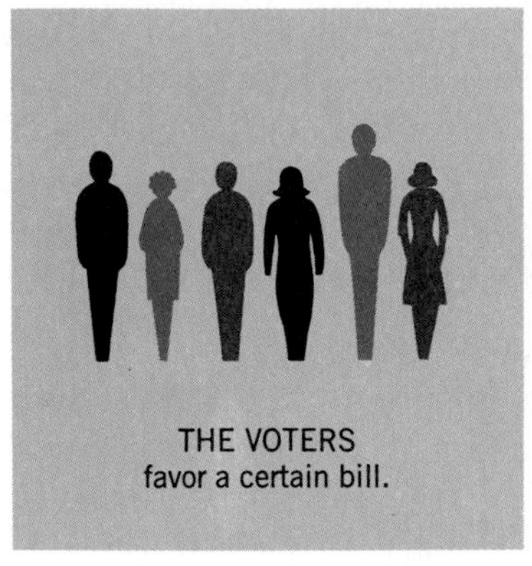

THE VOTERS
favor a certain bill.

INDIVIDUAL
MEMBERS OF CONGRESS
may introduce a bill they favor.

LARGE GROUPS OF AMERICANS
ask for a certain bill.

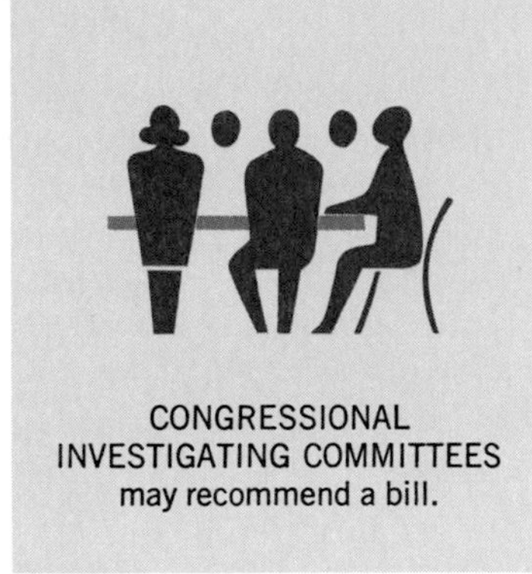

CONGRESSIONAL
INVESTIGATING COMMITTEES
may recommend a bill.

THE PRESIDENT
urges certain laws in
speeches to Congress.

house. The only exception to this rule is **appropriation bills,** or bills approving the spending of money. They must originate in the House of Representatives. Every bill must be passed by both houses of Congress before it may be signed by the President and become a law.

Where do these bills come from? Where do the ideas for all these bills begin?

1. Ideas for bills may come from any American citizen. The people are a powerful force. When enough Americans write to their Representatives asking for action, they usually get it. The staffs of the Representatives keep a careful check on the letters they receive. When a large number of **constituents**—the voters who live in the Representative's state or district—request a law, the Representative usually introduces a bill containing their ideas. This, of course, does not mean that the law will be passed. Our power is limited because the process of getting a law passed is long and difficult. This sometimes makes us think that government is not responsive enough. But in the long run this process helps to insure that our laws will be good laws.

2. Ideas for bills may come from organized groups. Members of Congress sometimes introduce bills because they are requested to do so by certain groups. Veterans' organizations may ask for a bill to provide better care for disabled American soldiers. Business people may want to prevent competition from industries in other countries. Labor groups often call for laws establishing improved working conditions. Parents' organizations

and church groups may present Congress with arguments for or against increased federal aid to education. Each of these groups deserves a hearing and usually gets it. As a result of pressure from such groups, bills are often introduced into Congress.

3. **Ideas for bills may come from committees of Congress.** Many bills begin in Congress itself. Suppose that a Congressional investigating committee conducts a study of certain kinds of crime. Suppose that its findings convince the committee that the federal government needs a new law for crime control. The committee can then draw up a bill and introduce it in Congress.

4. **Ideas for bills may come from members of Congress.** Members of Congress often become experts in certain fields. Senators who have had long experience with farm problems, for example, may introduce a bill to aid agriculture. Or Representatives from mining districts may get an idea for a bill that they believe will help their constituents and all miners with similar problems. They may then put the bill in written form and present it to the clerk of the House.

5. **Ideas for bills may come from the President of the United States.** The President has great influence on bills introduced into Congress. Early in each session of Congress, the President appears before a joint session of the two houses to deliver a "State of the Union" Message. In this speech, the President recommends the laws that are needed to improve our nation's well-being. Many of these ideas are soon introduced as bills by members of Congress.

HOW AN IDEA BECOMES A BILL

Although anyone can suggest an idea for a bill, only members of Congress can introduce the bill itself. Suppose, for example, that a group of citizens favors raising the federal tax on gasoline to help pay for a program to clean up the air. They write to their Senators or Representatives and explain their idea. The leader of the group arranges for a personal meeting with the Senator or Representative. At this meeting, he or she provides the Senator or Representative with facts and figures on the subject and urges that a bill be introduced. If the Senator or Representative is convinced that the group's idea is a good one, he or she may agree to introduce the bill.

To see how a bill becomes a law, let us study the progress of this bill to raise the tax on gasoline as it is considered first by the House and then by the Senate.

THE BILL IS INTRODUCED IN THE HOUSE

How does the Representative introduce this bill in the House? First, the proposed bill is carefully written out. The bill is not always written by the Representative. In fact, many bills are written by a committee, or by the group who suggested the bill, or by an assistant to the Representative. The bill is typed on specially lined paper. Each line is numbered so that it can be referred to easily.

After the bill is dropped into the hopper, it is given letters and a number. Let us suppose that the bill to raise the gasoline tax is marked HR 1215. The letters HR show that the bill is being considered by the House of Representatives. The number 1215 shows its place among all the bills presented in this particular session.

What happens to the bill after it is introduced? First, it is printed so that copies may be available to all who are interested. Then, it is sent to one of the standing committees for study. The Speaker of the House of Representatives decides which committee will consider the bill. Usually the subject of the bill determines which committee will study it. But in some cases, two committees may be interested in studying the bill. The Speaker then decides which committee to send it to.

How a Bill Becomes a Law

THE HOUSE OF REPRESENTATIVES

1. A BILL IS INTRODUCED IN THE HOUSE OF REPRESENTATIVES.

A Representative introduces the bill.

The Clerk of the House reads the title of the bill, gives the bill a number, and has it printed.

The Speaker of the House sends the bill to the proper House committee.

2. THE BILL IS STUDIED BY THE COMMITTEE.

The House committee or one of its subcommittees holds hearings on the bill, and may amend, rewrite, pigeonhole, or approve the bill.

If the bill is approved, the committee sends it back to the House with a favorable report. The bill is then placed on the House calendar.

When a bill comes up for consideration, it is given its second reading.

3. THE BILL IS DEBATED BY THE HOUSE OF REPRESENTATIVES.

The bill may be amended, or returned to the committee for revision, or approved by the House.

Before the final vote is taken, the bill is given its third reading.

If a majority of the Representatives approves it, the bill is passed.

HOUSE-SENATE CONFERENCE COMMITTEE

THE SENATE

4. THE BILL IS SENT TO THE SENATE.

In the Senate, the bill is given a number, its title is read, and it is printed.

The presiding officer of the Senate sends the bill to the proper committee.

The Senate committee studies the bill, and its actions are similar to the House committee (see 2).

5. THE BILL IS STUDIED BY THE COMMITTEE, THEN IS DEBATED BY THE SENATE.

Senate action is similar to that of the House (see 3).

If the Senate and the House bills are different, the bill is sent to a conference committee of Representatives and Senators.

The conference committee irons out differences and returns the revised bill to both houses for approval.

The House and the Senate pass the bill.

6. THE APPROVED BILL IS SENT TO THE PRESIDENT.

When the bill is approved by both House and Senate, the bill is sent to the President.

The President signs or vetoes the bill, or allows it to become law without signing it.

Congress can again pass the bill over the President's veto by a two-thirds vote of both houses.

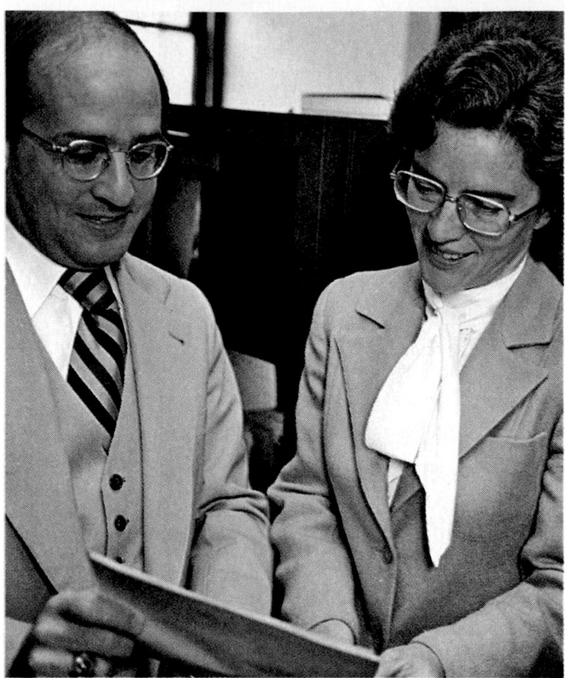

Members of Congress consider many points of view to reach a decision. Here, Representative Elizabeth Holtzman of New York considers a committee report.

THE BILL IS SENT TO A HOUSE COMMITTEE

In the case of HR 1215, the Speaker sends the bill to the House Ways and Means Committee. This is the committee that deals with all bills to raise or distribute money.

Each bill is given careful attention in committee. Many of the bills are found to be unnecessary. The committee by a majority vote **pigeonholes** these—that is, the committee puts them aside and spends no more time on them. Bills that are pigeonholed are said to "die in committee" because they are never sent back to the House for further action. In this way the committees cut down on the amount of legislation Congress must consider. If the bill is not pigeonholed, it is sent back to the House, with or without changes, together with the committee's report and recommendations.

THE COMMITTEE HOLDS HEARINGS

Because HR 1215 is an important bill, it is not pigeonholed. Instead, the House Ways and Means Committee holds special meetings called **hearings** to consider the bill. Most of these committee hearings are **public sessions,** or hearings open to the public. If you go to Washington, you can walk into a committee room and listen to the discussion. Some important public hearings are shown on television. Other meetings are held in private and are called **executive sessions.**

The Ways and Means Committee may hold several weeks of hearings on HR 1215. During this period, the committee calls witnesses to testify for and against the bill. These witnesses help to give the committee members the information they need in order to recommend that the bill be accepted, rejected, or perhaps changed.

Some of the witnesses who testify may be **lobbyists.** Lobbyists are persons who are paid to represent a certain group's point of view, or interests, at committee hearings. Lobbyists and expert witnesses, letters and telegrams from citizens, and evidence that committee members gather from many sources—all of these help the committee to reach a decision on the bill.

In the case of HR 1215, the representatives of the gasoline industry pointed out what the increased tax would do to their business, to the public, and to the nation's economy. On the other hand, supporters of the bill pointed to the need for funds to pay for a clean-air campaign and to the importance of the campaign itself. Other witnesses spoke in favor of entirely different bills to achieve the same effects.

THE COMMITTEE STUDIES THE BILL

You can see that the work of the committees is not easy. Committees are often flooded with bills. The hearing process is long and difficult, but necessary. Also, it is not always easy for committees to agree on what action to take on a bill. At the end of each session of Congress, the standing committees of both houses often leave unfinished bills under consideration. These bills will die in committee and never become laws unless their supporters succeed in having them reintroduced at the next session of Congress.

In the case of HR 1215, the Ways and Means Committee went into executive session after the public hearings were closed. Here the members decided to change the bill in certain ways. They reworded lines and added new sections to parts of the bill. When they were finished, the bill was very different from the one they had originally received. Some felt that it had been improved. Others were opposed to it and threatened to vote against it. But the majority of committee members decided to recommend that the House pass the bill as amended, or changed, by the committee.

In the next section, we shall follow the progress of HR 1215 after it leaves the committee and is brought before the House.

CONSIDER AND DISCUSS

Identify. appropriation bills / constituents / pigeonhole / hearings / public sessions / executive sessions / lobbyist

Review. 1. Where do ideas for bills introduced into Congress come from? 2. Who may introduce a bill into Congress? 3. Name at least three things that may happen to a bill in committee.

Discuss. The law requires lobbyists to register with Congress and tell who is paying them. Do you think this law is a good one? Why or why not?

Each committee in Congress must hold hearings on the bills it is considering. Here, witnesses are appearing before the Senate Committee on Foreign Relations.

LOBBIES:

The Third House of Congress

Imagine that you are a member of Congress. Next week you have to vote on an important bill. For the past three days you have received thousands of letters and telegrams from people in your home state. Each day you have received hundreds of phone calls. Fifty people from your home state came to see you today. And five representatives of organized groups dropped in to discuss the pros and cons of the bill. All of these people were interested in the bill and wanted to influence your vote.

Members of Congress face such pressure every day. Much of it comes from groups with special interests. People with shared, or special, interests are not formally represented in Congress. To make their voices heard, they send specialists, called "lobbyists," to represent them in the nation's capital. Lobbyists are so influential that they are sometimes called the "Third House of Congress." But unlike members of Congress, lobbyists are not answerable to the people. Who are these lobbyists? And what exactly do they do?

Each year, over 400 lobbyists attend sessions of Congress. They spend over $10 million a year trying to influence Senators and Representatives. Almost all of the important organized interests in our country have lobbyists in Washington, D.C. They include such groups as farmers, labor unions, consumers, teachers, manufacturers, doctors, veterans, churches, and minority groups. Can you think of any other groups that might have lobbyists in the nation's capital?

Lobbyists are paid to represent a certain group's point of view or interests. They work to block the passage of bills that are harmful to their group's interests, and to get bills passed that will aid them. Lobbyists are often highly skilled people with a staff of research assistants. Some lobbyists were once members of Congress. Others are lawyers, public relations experts, journalists, or specialists in different fields.

How have lobbyists become so powerful? For one thing, they often supply the raw material of legislation. Lobbyists may ask a member of Congress to sponsor a bill they are interested in. They supply facts for the bill. Sometimes they even help draw it up. When the bill comes up in committee, lobbyists representing different viewpoints appear before the committee. They come prepared with well-developed arguments and statistics.

Lobbyists will help committee members obtain any information they need. Committee members welcome this aid. Legislators are faced with over 20,000 bills a year. These bills cover many different topics and often are very technical. No legislator can be informed about all of these areas. And legislative staffs are small.

If the bill is approved by the committee, lobbyists are prepared to bring pressure on members of the House and the Senate, and even on the President, if necessary. Lobbyists often try to influence public opinion. They prepare pamphlets. They place advertisements and appeals in the news media. Lobbyists promise to help members of Congress in their next election campaign with workers and contributions. Sometimes, lobbyists urge local groups, individuals, and well-known people to send letters and telegrams to their Representatives and Senators. Pressure groups will use any legitimate means to influence votes.

What about illegal means? What happens when a lobbyist offers bribes or makes business deals with members of Congress, for example? A person who bribes a member of Congress can be fined up to $20,000 and go to jail for as long as 15 years. Any Representative or Senator accused of an illegal action and found guilty may be removed from office by Congress.

All Congressional lobbyists must register with Congress. They must also tell for whom they are working and how much they spend in lobbying. But not all lobbyists report everything they spend. And not all representatives of special interests register. They say that the law does not require them to do so. The lobbying law was passed in 1946. And there has been no new law since then. In many places, the wording of the 1946 law is vague. It has loopholes, or ways of evading the enforcement of a law.

Lobbyists were once viewed with suspicion because many of them worked behind closed doors. But today, most work in the open and are welcomed as sources of information and help by an overworked Congress.

Yet many people are critical of lobbyists. They feel that lobbying plays too great a role in the lawmaking process. They say that important interests —such as those of the poor, the sick, the general public, and many minorities—do not always get an equal hearing. The advantage often goes to the group that is best organized and has the most money and the best publicity.

Should lobbyists be restricted further? Would it be better to give Congress more research help so that it will not have to rely on lobbyists? On the other hand, don't interest groups have the right to make their opinions known? Don't they have the right to petition the government? What do you think?

4 How a Bill Becomes a Law

When HR 1215 is reported out of committee and is sent back to the House of Representatives, it is placed on the House's **calendar.** The calendar is the schedule that lists the order in which the bills are to be considered. Of course, in a real emergency a bill can be moved up on the calendar, and early action may be taken.

THE HOUSE CONSIDERS THE BILL

HR 1215 must be given three readings in the House of Representatives. By the time its turn comes on the calendar, however, the **first reading** really has already occurred. It took place when the Speaker first read the title of the bill to the House before sending it to the appropriate committee, in this case the Ways and Means Committee. The second reading will occur after the bill has been debated.

THE HOUSE DEBATES THE BILL

The Rules Committee decides how much time will be given to debate on this bill. The time to be spent in debate, or discussion, is divided evenly between those members in favor of the bill and those against the bill. In the case of HR 1215, the debate is limited to four hours equally divided between the two sides. After the formal debate, the House usually acts as a **Committee of the Whole.** As one big committee, the House can act less formally and really turn the meeting into a work session. The bill now is given its **second reading.** A clerk reads a paragraph, and then amendments may be offered. Debate on amendments to the bill is usually limited to five minutes for each member who wishes to speak. A vote is then taken on the amendment. It is usually a voice vote with all in favor shouting "aye" and those opposed, "no." Sometimes a **standing vote** is used with a clerk counting those for and against.

Each paragraph of the bill is read and amended in similar fashion until the entire bill has been considered. When the House once again meets in formal session, a member may demand a "quorum call." Since a **quorum,** or majority, of the members must be present in order to do business, the Speaker may ask the clerk to call the roll.

THE HOUSE VOTES ON THE BILL

When a quorum is present, the House is ready for the **third reading.** This reading is usually by title only. But any member may demand that the bill be read in its entirety. The vote is then taken. A majority of the members present is required to pass a bill.

On important bills, as few as 20 members may demand a **teller vote.** According to this procedure, the House members write their names on small green (yes) or red (no) cards and drop them in a ballot box. The teller vote provides a public record of the way in which each member voted on a bill.

Our bill to raise the federal gasoline tax, as amended, passes the House. But it is not yet a law. Like all bills, it must now be considered by the other house of Congress, the Senate.

THE SENATE RECEIVES THE BILL

After HR 1215 has been passed by the House of Representatives, it is sent to the Senate. In the Senate the bill is given a new letter and number. It is called S 2019. S stands for a Senate bill, and the number represents the bill's place among those being considered in the Senate.

The way a bill is handled in the Senate is very similar to the process we followed in the House of Representatives. After a bill is introduced in the Senate, its title is read by the presiding officer. This is the first reading of the bill in the Senate. It is then assigned to the appropriate Senate standing committee.

THE BILL IN THE SENATE COMMITTEE

In our example, bill S 2019 is read by title. It is then sent to the Senate Finance Committee. Since S 2019 is a bill to raise money, it originated in the House. Other kinds of bills may begin in the Senate and are then sent to the House.

Senate committees, like House committees, may pigeonhole a bill. They may revise it. Or they may recommend that it be accepted or rejected. Senate committees, too, hold hearings, gather evidence, and finally vote to send the bill back to the floor of the Senate.

S 2019, to raise the gasoline tax, is amended slightly in the Senate Finance Committee. The committee then reports on the bill to the entire Senate and recommends that the bill be passed.

THE SENATE DEBATES THE BILL

After a second reading in which a clerk reads the bill line for line, debate begins. The Senators are usually not limited in their debate as are members of the House of Representatives. In the Senate, speeches may go on and on. Some Senators have talked for many hours in order to prevent the Senate from taking a vote on a bill. This method of delay by making speeches is called **filibustering.** Filibustering is possible in the Senate because debate in that body can be limited only if three fifths of the full Senate votes to limit it. Limit on debate in the Senate is called **cloture.** It is seldom voted and it doesn't always work.

In this picture, the Senate is having a debate over the advantages and disadvantages of a bill they must vote on. Do you think the Senate's rule on unlimited debate is a good idea?

THE SENATE VOTES ON THE BILL

After the Senate finishes its debate on S 2019, the bill to raise the gasoline tax is given its third reading. This is almost always by title only. A voice vote is then taken. Let us suppose that S 2019 passes. What happens next?

THE HOUSE AND THE SENATE MUST AGREE ON THE FINAL BILL

When a bill passes the House and Senate in identical form, it is ready to be sent to the President. The chances are, however, that the original bill was changed, at least in some small way, by the Senate. If it was changed in any way, the bill must be sent back to the house in which it originated. In our example, the House of Representatives did not agree to the Senate changes. When this happens, a conference committee must be called.

A **conference committee** is made up of an equal number of Senators and Representatives. It meets to try to reach an agreement on the bill. The committee members from each house may have to give up something in order to reach a compromise. Finally, a compromise bill is sent back to both houses. Usually both houses approve the work of their conference committee. But sometimes they do not. In that case, the bill must be sent back to another conference committee. In due time, however, agreement is reached and the bill is passed.

THE PRESIDENT APPROVES THE BILL

The bill as passed by both houses is signed first by the Speaker of the House, and then by the President of the Senate. After this,

Bills must be approved by the President before they become law. In 1971, President Nixon, surrounded by teenagers, signed the bill that gave the vote to 18-year-olds in federal elections.

it is sent to the President of the United States. What happens when the bill to raise the gasoline tax is sent to the President?

The President may take one of three possible actions on a bill:

1. The President may sign the bill and declare it to be a law.

2. The President may refuse to sign the bill and send it back to Congress with a message giving the reasons for rejecting it. This action is called a **Presidential veto.**

3. The President may keep the bill for ten days without signing it. If Congress is in session during this ten-day period and the President does not sign it, the bill becomes a law without the President's signature. But if Congress is not in session and the President does not sign the bill within ten days, then the bill does not become a law. When this happens we say the bill has been killed by a **pocket veto.**

Actually, most bills passed by the Senate and the House of Representatives are signed into law by the President. The President does not use the veto often. When the President does, there are usually important issues at stake. Even then, Congress can pass a bill over the President's veto by a two-thirds vote of both houses. In the case of our gasoline tax bill, it becomes a law and goes into effect after the President signs it.

This long and involved process of making laws may be slow. However, it prevents hasty legislation while providing a way for the national government to pass needed laws.

CONSIDER AND DISCUSS

Identify. calendar / first reading / Committee of the Whole / second reading / standing vote / quorum / third reading / teller vote / filibuster / cloture / conference committee / Presidential veto / pocket veto

Review. 1. Trace the steps by which a bill becomes a law. 2. What may happen to a bill in committee? 3. What three courses of action are open to the President on a bill that has been passed by Congress?

Discuss. Some Americans think our process of lawmaking is too slow. What do you think?

5 The Powers of Congress

The Congress of the United States is a powerful lawmaking body. Its powers are given to it by the Constitution. This same document places clear-cut limitations upon Congressional powers. Now is a good time to examine the powers and limitations of Congress.

THE POWERS GIVEN TO CONGRESS

In Article 1, Section 8, of the Constitution of the United States, certain powers are granted to Congress. These specific powers are sometimes known as **delegated powers,** because they are granted, or delegated, to Congress by the Constitution. They give Congress the right to make laws in five important areas:

1. Financing our government. Congress can raise and collect taxes, borrow money, print and coin money, and pay the debts of the United States.

2. Regulating and encouraging trade and industry. Congress can regulate trade with foreign countries. It can also help American businesses by setting standards of weights and measures and by passing laws that protect the rights of investors and customers. Congress also establishes post offices and national roads that help business and industry in our nation. And Congress can set punishment for piracy and other crimes committed against American ships on the seas.

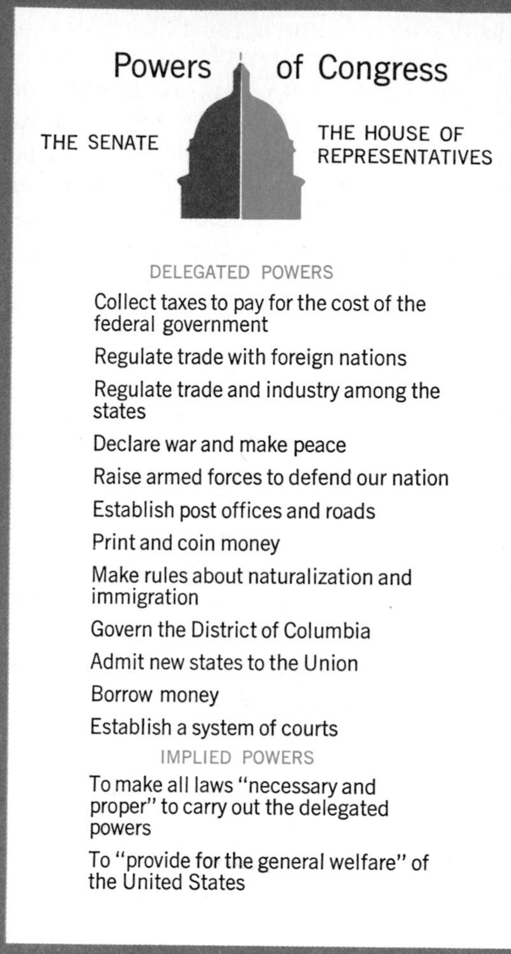

Powers of Congress
THE SENATE
THE HOUSE OF REPRESENTATIVES
DELEGATED POWERS
Collect taxes to pay for the cost of the federal government
Regulate trade with foreign nations
Regulate trade and industry among the states
Declare war and make peace
Raise armed forces to defend our nation
Establish post offices and roads
Print and coin money
Make rules about naturalization and immigration
Govern the District of Columbia
Admit new states to the Union
Borrow money
Establish a system of courts
IMPLIED POWERS
To make all laws "necessary and proper" to carry out the delegated powers
To "provide for the general welfare" of the United States

3. Defending the nation against its enemies. Congress has the power to declare war, and to maintain an army and a navy. It also can provide for a citizen army that can be called to duty during wartime or national emergencies.

4. Enforcing the nation's law. Congress can pass laws concerning such crimes as counterfeiting and treason. To see that these and other federal laws are upheld, Congress can establish a system of national courts.

5. Providing for the nation's growth. Congress has the power to pass naturalization laws. Naturalization laws make it possible for people born in foreign lands to become American citizens. In addition, the Costitution gives Congress the power to govern the nation's territories and to provide for the admission of new states.

THE "ELASTIC CLAUSE"

Article 1, Section 8, Clause 18, of the Constitution says that Congress shall have the power "To make all laws which shall be necessary and proper for carrying into execution [carrying out] the foregoing powers, and all other powers vested by this Constitution in the government of the United States, or in any department or officer thereof."

This is the famous **elastic clause.** It is called the elastic clause because it has allowed Congress to stretch the powers listed in the Constitution in order to cover many other subjects. The clause has permitted Congress to pass laws covering situations that developed long after the Constitution was written.

Congress, for example, has set up national military academies to train Army, Navy, and Air Force officers. The Constitution does not specifically give Congress this power. But Congress has claimed the power to establish military academies. It says that the academies are "necessary and proper" in order for it to carry out its Constitutional right to establish an army and a navy. Congress claims that this part of the Constitution implies, or suggests, that Congress has the right to establish military academies. For this reason, the powers that Congress claims under the elastic clause are sometimes called **implied powers.**

LIMITS ON THE POWERS OF CONGRESS

The powers of Congress are limited in several important ways. The Supreme Court has the power to decide when Congress has gone beyond the powers granted to it by the

Constitution (see Chapter 5). When the Court rules that Congress has passed a law that exceeds Congress' constitutional powers, this law has no force. It is declared unconstitutional, that is, in violation of the Constitution.

The second limit on Congress' powers is the provision in the Constitution declaring that the states shall keep all the powers not actually granted to the national government. The powers set aside, or reserved, for the state governments are known as **reserved powers.** They include the states' authority over elections, education, and marriage. The Constitution left these reserved powers to the states to prevent the national government from becoming too powerful and to allow the people of each state to keep control of many of their own affairs.

The powers of Congress are also limited by some provisions in the Constitution that deny certain powers to Congress. The Constitution specifically forbids the following powers to Congress:

1. Congress cannot pass *ex post facto* laws. An **ex post facto law** is a law that applies to some action that took place before the law was passed. For example, it is not against the law today to buy and sell foreign automobiles. If tomorrow Congress forbids the buying and selling of foreign cars, a person cannot be arrested for having bought one of these cars in the past.
2. Congress cannot pass bills of attainder. A **bill of attainder** is a law that sentences a person to jail without granting the person the right to a trial. The Constitution provides that anyone accused of a crime must be given a trial in a court of law. Congress cannot take this right away from anyone.
3. Congress cannot set aside, or suspend, the writ of *habeas corpus*. A **writ of habeas corpus** is a court order requiring that a person accused of a crime be brought to court to determine whether or not there is enough evidence to hold the person for a trial. If Congress had the right to set aside the writ of *habeas corpus*, a person might be kept in jail for weeks or even months with no formal charges being brought.
4. Congress cannot tax exports. **Exports** are goods and products that are sent to other countries. A tax on exports would harm our foreign and domestic trade. Congress can, however, tax products that are **imports**—those brought into the country from abroad.
5. Congress cannot pass any law that violates the Bill of Rights. The first ten amendments to the Constitution—the Bill of Rights—spell out the rights and freedoms of all American citizens. As a result, the Bill of Rights limits the powers of Congress, since Congress is forbidden to pass any law that violates these rights.
6. Congress cannot favor the trade or commerce of any one state over that of other states. Congress cannot pass a law giving any state or group of states an unfair advantage. Of course, Congress can pass laws regulating trade. But these laws must apply equally to all states.
7. Congress cannot grant titles of nobility to any American citizen. Americans believe that all people are created equal. Therefore, they are opposed to establishing a noble class, or small group of persons with rights superior to those of other citizens.
8. Congress cannot withdraw money from the United States Treasury unless a law permits the withdrawal. Congress must pass a law telling what money shall be spent and the exact amount to be spent before the public funds are made available. This means that Congress must pass appropriation laws, or money laws, to provide the money for carrying out the other laws it passes.

SPECIAL POWERS OF EACH HOUSE

The Constitution gives each house of Congress certain special powers. The House of Representatives has three special powers:

1. The House alone can start impeachment proceedings to dismiss the President

and certain other high officials from office.

2. All bills for raising money must start in the House of Representatives.

3. If no candidate for President receives a majority vote in a Presidential election, the members of the House of Representatives choose the President.

The Senate has these special powers:

1. The impeachment trial of the President and certain other high officials must be held in the Senate.

2. If no candidate for Vice-President receives a majority vote in a Presidential election, the members of the Senate choose the Vice-President.

3. All **treaties,** or written agreements, with foreign nations must be approved by the Senate by a two-thirds vote.

4. Certain high officials appointed by the President must be approved by the Senate by a majority vote.

CONGRESS' POWER TO IMPEACH

Congress has the power to impeach, or to accuse high federal officials of serious crimes against the nation and to bring them to trial. The highest officials in our government—the President, Vice-President, Cabinet members, and federal judges—may be removed from office if they are found guilty of treason or some other serious crime.

The charges against the accused officials must be drawn up in the House of Representatives. The charges are written down in a resolution that is read before the entire House. If the members vote in favor of the resolution, the accused official will be put on trial. The procedure of drawing up the charges and passing the resolution in the House is called **impeachment.**

The trial on the impeachment charges is held in the Senate. The members of the Senate act as the jury. The Chief Justice of the Supreme Court usually presides at impeachment trials. During this trial, the Senate becomes a court. The Senators hear the evidence and examine all witnesses. Then they vote on whether the official is innocent or guilty. Two thirds of the Senate must find the official guilty before he or she can be dismissed from office.

Only one President, Andrew Johnson, has ever been impeached, or had formal charges brought against him by the House. In the impeachment trial in the Senate, President Johnson was found not guilty by one vote. Altogether, 12 federal officials have been impeached. Only four of them, all judges, were found guilty and dismissed from office.

In 1974, the threat of impeachment caused President Richard M. Nixon to resign. The House Judiciary Committee had been holding impeachment hearings. It had been trying to find out whether the President had known about a break-in of the Democratic Party headquarters in Washington, D.C. The Committee found that the President had tried to obstruct the investigation of the break-in. It recommended that he be impeached.

CONGRESS HAS THE POWER TO INVESTIGATE

Either house of Congress, or a joint committee of both houses, may investigate conditions in the nation. The purpose of such investigations is to determine whether new laws are necessary to correct some condition in our nation. Congressional investigating committees can call witnesses and require their attendance before the committee. If a new law seems to be needed, the investigating committee may recommend that Congress pass new legislation.

CONGRESS AND THE DISTRICT OF COLUMBIA

The Constitution of the United States gives Congress the power to govern the nation's capital. Washington, D.C., is not part of any state. It is a **federal district**—the District of Columbia.

Until recently, the people of Washington,

D.C., were governed by appointed officials. The people of the District were not able to elect local officials nor to vote in national elections.

The Twenty-third Amendment, passed in 1961, gave the people of the District the right to vote for President and Vice-President. In 1971, Congress passed a law that allowed Washingtonians to elect a Representative to serve in the House. The Representative may debate and make the wishes of the people known, but cannot vote in Congress. The right to elect local officials was given to the people of the District of Columbia in 1973. Washington, D.C., is now governed by a mayor and a 13-member City Council.

CONSIDER AND DISCUSS

Identify. delegated powers / elastic clause / implied powers / reserved powers / *ex post facto* law / bill of attainder / writ of *habeas corpus* / exports / imports / treaty / impeachment / federal district

Review. 1. What are some of the delegated powers of Congress? 2. What are some things Congress cannot do? 3. What can the House do that the Senate cannot do? 4. What special powers does the Senate have?

Discuss. Do you think the Representative of the people of Washington, D.C., should be permitted to vote in Congress? Why or why not?

CHAPTER Summary

The lawmaking body of our federal government is called Congress. It consists of two houses, the House of Representatives and the Senate. Congress has the important job of making the laws that govern our nation.

The members of Congress are elected by the people of the United States. Each Senator and Representative represents the people of a state or of a Congressional district. Each must meet certain qualifications to hold office.

Congress meets for a two-year term. The two houses organize their work and operate in similar ways. Much of the actual work of Congress is carried out by committees. Each bill, or proposed law, in Congress must go through a long and involved process, be passed by both houses, and then signed by the President into law.

Congress has been given many important powers by the Constitution. The delegated powers set forth specific functions of Congress, and a few special powers are given to each of its two houses. The "elastic clause," too, has permitted Congress to exercise powers not specifically granted to it. To limit the jurisdiction of Congress, however certain powers have been reserved for the states, and others have been specifically forbidden to Congress.

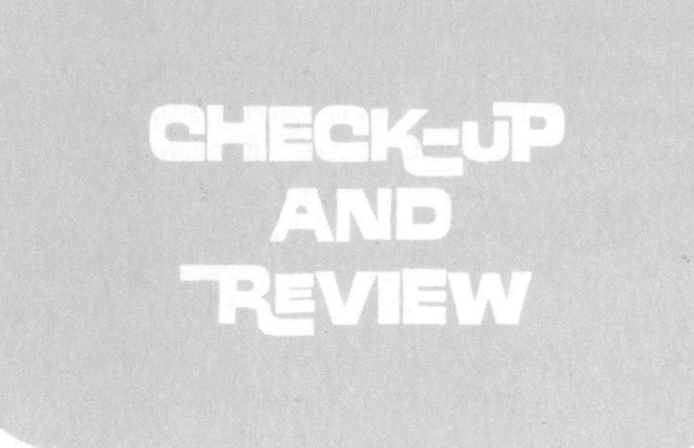

VOCABULARY

On a separate piece of paper or in the vocabulary section of your notebook, copy the following paragraph. Then, choosing from the list of words below, fill in the blanks in the paragraph.

A civics class, visiting Washington, D.C., learned that Congress consisted of (1) ________ houses, the (2) ________ and the (3) ________. The class members knew that a two-house legislature is also called a (4) ________ legislature. At the House Office Building they found a committee in closed, or (5) ________, session. In a Representative's office they saw people called (6) ________ trying to persuade the Representative to vote a certain way. Then, in the Senate, they saw the presiding officer, who was also the (7) ________ of the United States. In the House of Representatives, the presiding officer was the (8) ________. The members of Congress were discussing (9) ________ that might become laws if they passed both houses and were signed by the (10) ________.

lobbyists	bicameral
Senate	Vice-President
two	President
executive	bills
House of Representatives	Speaker of the House

CHECK-UP

Here are ten questions that will help you to review the main ideas in this chapter. Write down the answers and bring them to class with you.

1. Why is our national legislature divided into two houses?

2. During the 1970's, California was one of the fastest-growing states. What effect did this growth have on this state's representation in Congress?

3. What is the importance of Congressional districts in determining the membership of the House of Representatives? Do these divisions affect the election of Senators?

4. What is the difference between a conference committee and a joint committee?

5. Who calls special sessions of Congress? Why might such a session be called?

6. Who are some of the main officers of each political party in Congress and what do these officials do?

7. Name some of the important standing committees of each house. Why are they important?

8. What are the main steps by which a bill becomes a law?

9. What are some of the powers shared by both houses of Congress?

10. What are some of the things Congress cannot do?

CITIZENSHIP AND YOU

Here are some projects that you may find interesting and rewarding.

1. Class Projects

Classes that can visit Washington, D.C., will enjoy the interesting experience of a field trip to our nation's capital.

When a visit to the capital is not possible, the class may profit by viewing one of the many excellent motion pictures or filmstrips describing Washington, D.C., and the work of government that is done there.

Your class may wish to invite a current or former member of Congress to speak before the class and to answer your questions about the work of Congress.

2. Group or Committee Projects

A group or committee may want to learn about the members of Congress from your state. Who represents your Congressional district? What are the names of the Senators from your state? Who is the senior Senator? How many Representatives has your state? How did the last census affect your state's representation in Congress?

Another group may wish to study the current activities of Congress to see what major bills are being considered. How would these bills affect you if they became laws?

3. Individual Projects

Prepare a chart, tracing the steps by which a bill becomes a law. This may be a small chart for your notebook or a large chart for display on the bulletin board.

Find a map of your state showing Congressional districts. Make a large copy for display in class.

CIVICS SKILLS

UNDERSTANDING ORIGINAL DOCUMENTS

You will need to be familiar with certain basic laws, court decisions, treaties, and other official statements upon which governmental action may be based. Such official papers are called *documents.* You have already been introduced to two of the most famous and important documents in our nation's history—the Declaration of Independence and the Constitution of the United States.

Throughout your textbook you will find a number of documents. The complete Constitution and Declaration of Independence are reproduced at the end of the textbook. In the various chapters, the documents are brief passages taken from complete, original documents. Such passages are called *excerpts.* They tell you the main ideas contained in the complete documents.

These excerpts of documents serve three important purposes. First, they give you a definite idea of how laws and other documents are written. You will become familiar with the kind of language used by lawmakers and other government officials when they are handling public affairs. Second, the documents illustrate ideas in the text. The United States Bill of Rights, for example, shows how the first Congress provided extra protection for the fundamental rights of all Americans. Third, the documents provide information upon which students can base their own opinions. By studying original documents, you may discover facts for yourself.

PRACTICING YOUR CIVICS SKILLS

Turn to the Declaration of Independence on text page 512 and read the first paragraph. What does this paragraph say is the purpose of this document? Then, turn to the Constitution of the United States (page 514) and read the Preamble. What is the purpose of this document? How do the purposes of the two documents differ?

Look through the Constitution and read Article 1 and Amendment 20. See if you can find the following information:

1. What are the two penalties for conviction in impeachment cases?
2. On what date is the opening session of Congress held?
3. In which house of Congress do bills for raising money start?

CHAPTER

Introduction

"The terms of the President and Vice-President shall end at noon on the 20th day of January . . . and the terms of their successors shall then begin."
—Amendment 20 of the Constitution of the United States.

The day on which the new President takes office is called Inauguration Day. It is an exciting day in Washington, D.C., and indeed, throughout the nation. Visitors pour into the nation's capital from our 50 states and from foreign lands. The city is crowded with officials, newspaper and television reporters, and sightseers.

The Inaugural ceremony is held on a large, flag-draped platform set up in front of the Capitol building. The newly elected President arrives there after being driven from the White House down Pennsylvania Avenue. This broad avenue is lined on both sides with spectators waiting to catch a glimpse of the new President.

Now the Inaugural ceremony begins. The President walks down the steps of the Capitol to the platform as a band plays "Hail to the Chief." The highlight of the ceremony is the swearing in of the President. The President places one hand on the Bible and repeats the oath of office. The Chief Justice administers the oath, reading the following words from the Constitution:

"I do solemnly swear (or affirm) that I will faithfully execute [carry out] the office of the President of the United States, and will, to the best of my ability, preserve, protect, and defend the Constitution of the United States."

After the oath of office, the President delivers an *Inaugural Address.* Americans throughout the nation, as well as people in other lands, listen carefully to the President's words. They do so because they know they are listening to the person who will lead the American nation for the next four years.

In this chapter, you will study these important topics:

1. The President of the United States
2. The Cabinet and the Executive Departments
3. The President and the Executive Agencies
4. The Many Roles of the President

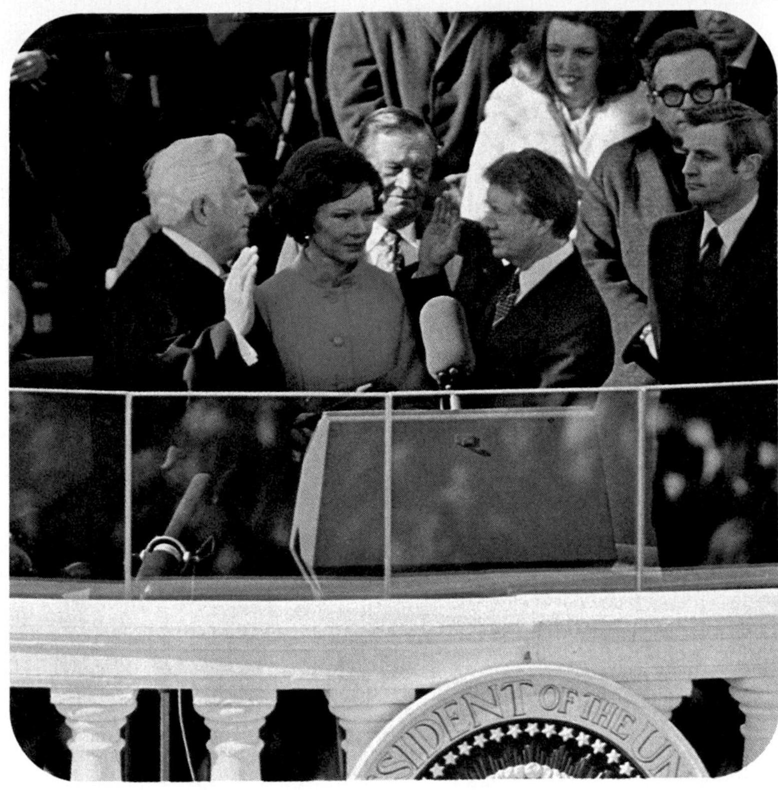

CHAPTER

4 The President Carries Out Our Nation's Laws

1 The President of the United States

In 1789, George Washington became the first President of the United States. Since then, 38 men, including George Washington, have served as President. Up to now, all American Presidents have been men. For this reason, in this book we refer to the President as he. This does not mean, however, that a woman could not become President. Although the Constitution sets forth certain qualifications for President, it does not specify whether the President shall be a man or a woman. In the future, American voters may be able to choose whether to elect a man or a woman candidate as their President.

QUALIFICATIONS OF THE PRESIDENT

The Constitution sets forth certain qualifications that the President of the United States must meet:

1. The President must be a native-born American citizen.
2. The President must be at least 35 years of age.
3. The President must be a resident of the United States for at least 14 years.

TERM OF OFFICE

The President serves a four-year term and receives a salary of $200,000 a year. In addition, the President receives a tax-free travel allowance of not more than $40,000, plus a taxable official expense allowance of $50,000.

The Vice-President must fulfill the same qualifications as the President. The Vice-President also serves a four-year term and receives a salary of $75,000 a year and $10,000 for expenses. The Vice-President becomes President of the United States if the President dies. The Vice-President may also act as President if the President becomes unable to carry out the duties of office.

A President may be reelected for a second term of office. The original Constitution did not state how many terms a President might serve. President George Washington set the tradition of a limit of two terms by refusing to run for the Presidency a third time when he was urged to do so. President Franklin D. Roosevelt ended this two-term custom when he was elected to a third term in 1940. And in 1944, he won a fourth term in office.

In 1951, the **Twenty-second Amendment** was added to the Constitution. This amendment set a two-term limit to the Presidency:

> No person shall be elected to the office of the President more than twice, and no person who has held the office of President, or acted as President, for more than two years of a term to which some other person was elected President shall be elected to the office of President more than once.

THE POWERS OF THE PRESIDENT

Article 2, Section 1, of the Constitution provides that "The executive power shall be vested in [given to] a President of the United States of America." This means that the President is responsible for executing, or carrying out, the laws passed by Congress. Because the President has the job of executing the nation's laws, the President is often called the country's **Chief Executive.** As Chief Executive the President must take an active role in all phases of government.

The President plays a large role in shaping the nation's laws by recommending, or suggesting, needed laws to Congress. In fact, the Constitution requires that the President "shall from time to time give to the Congress information of [about] the state of the Union, and recommend to their [Congress'] consideration such measures as he shall judge necessary . . . ." To carry out this constitutional provision, the President each year delivers several messages to Congress. Chief among these messages are the "State of the Union" Message, a Budget Message, and an Economic Message. These messages may be delivered as speeches before Congress or in writing.

The **"State of the Union" Message,** which the President usually delivers in person to a meeting of both houses of Congress, sets forth the programs and policies which he favors and which he recommends that Congress put into effect as laws. The **Budget Message** lists the sums of money the President believes should be spent by the national government. In his **Economic Message,** the President reviews the nation's economy and recommends laws that he thinks are needed.

THE VETO POWER

The President also influences legislation by the power to **veto,** or reject laws. Sometimes, just the threat of a Presidential veto is enough to discourage Congress from passing a bill. Congress knows how difficult it is to pass a bill after it has been vetoed by the President. To do so requires a two-thirds majority in both houses of Congress. For this reason, Congress considers carefully before passing a bill it knows the President does not approve.

SPECIAL SESSIONS

The President can influence lawmaking in still another way. He has the power to call special sessions of Congress. If Congress does not pass laws that the President feels are necessary, or if a national emergency arises, the President may call Congress back into special session to request that it take action to meet the emergency or to reconsider laws he favors. The last special session of Congress was called in 1948.

THE PRESIDENT AS COMMANDER-IN-CHIEF

As head of the armed forces of the United States, the President has great power in time of war or when war threatens. The President does not actually lead American forces into battle. However, the President

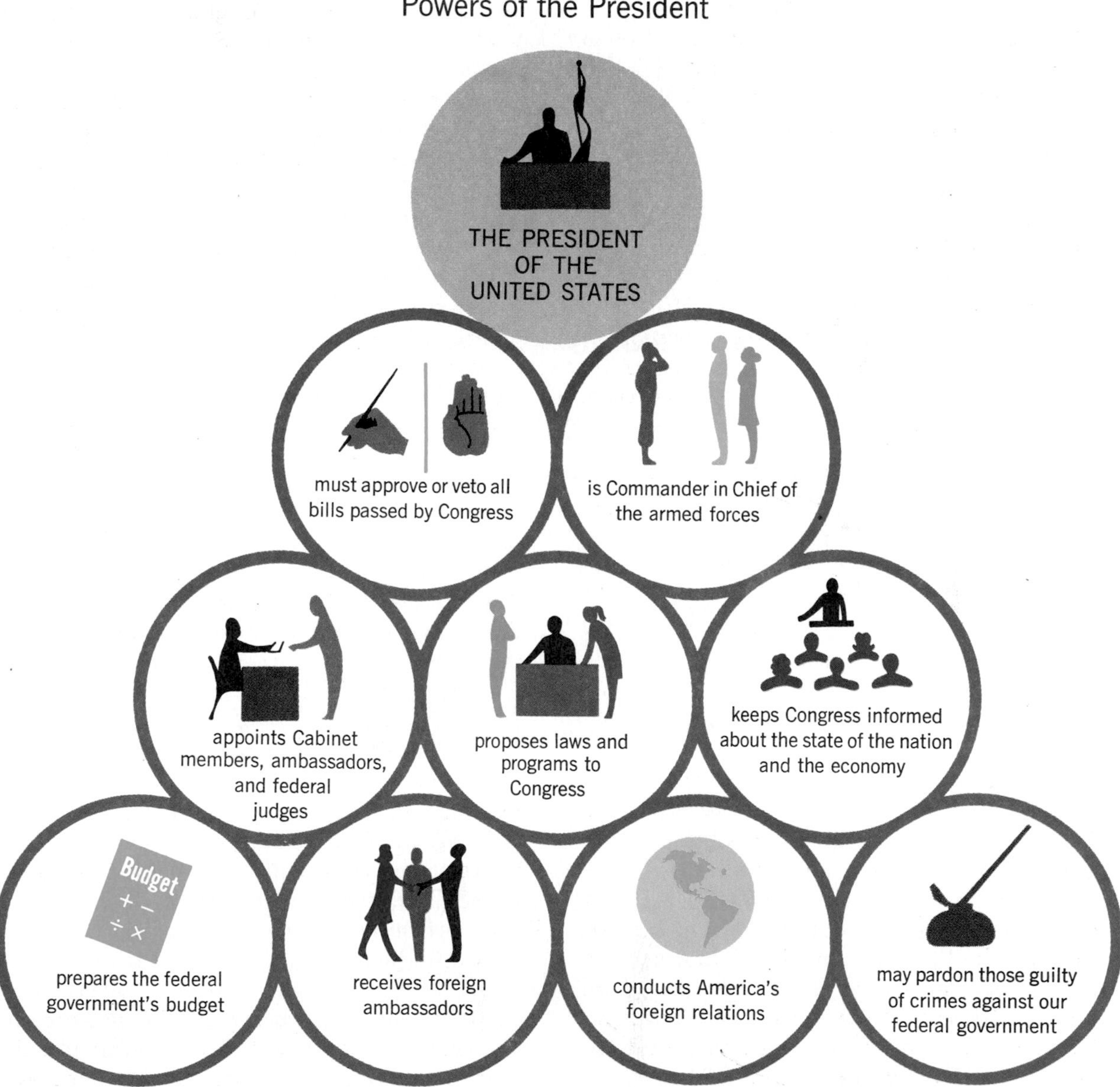
Powers of the President
THE PRESIDENT OF THE UNITED STATES
must approve or veto all bills passed by Congress
is Commander in Chief of the armed forces
appoints Cabinet members, ambassadors, and federal judges
proposes laws and programs to Congress
keeps Congress informed about the state of the nation and the economy
Budget
+ −
÷ ×
prepares the federal government's budget
receives foreign ambassadors
conducts America's foreign relations
may pardon those guilty of crimes against our federal government

Three men who were Presidents — Harry S. Truman, Dwight D. Eisenhower, and John F. Kennedy — are shown together in this picture. They were attending the funeral of Speaker of the House Sam Rayburn in Texas in 1962.

is in constant touch with our nation's military leaders. He also has the final word in planning how a war is to be fought.

The hydrogen bomb and other terrible weapons of modern war have placed a heavy burden on the President. Recent Presidents have had to make fateful decisions regarding the use of these terrible weapons. President Truman in 1945 had to decide whether to use the first atomic bomb. President Kennedy risked nuclear war when in October 1962 he forced the Soviet Union to stop building missile bases in Cuba.

As **Commander-in-Chief** of the armed forces, the President may send American forces into any part of the world where danger threatens. But sending American troops into certain situations sometimes involves the risk of war. To limit the President's power, Congress passed the War Powers Act in 1973. This law requires that troops sent abroad be recalled within 60 days unless Congress approves the President's action.

THE PRESIDENT CONDUCTS FOREIGN POLICY

The President carries out our **foreign policies.** He is responsible for the way our nation conducts its relations with other nations of the world. He seeks to secure friendly relations with foreign governments while preserving the security of our country.

To conduct our relations with other nations, the President appoints ambassadors to represent the United States in foreign countries. He also receives the official representatives that other nations send to the

United States. The President, however, has the power to refuse to **recognize** a new nation or a new government, though he seldom uses this power. That is, he may refuse to receive an ambassador from that nation or to send an American representative to that nation.

The government of the United States makes written agreements, called **treaties,** with other nations. Treaties with foreign nations are drawn up by the President or his representatives. However, all treaties must be made with the advice and consent of the Senate. The Senate must approve a treaty by a two-thirds vote before it becomes effective.

THE PRESIDENT'S OTHER POWERS

The President appoints many of the officials in our national government. The Constitution gives him the power to appoint Supreme Court justices, federal judges, and many other high government officials as vacancies occur. Most of these appointments must be approved by the Senate by a majority vote, or at least 51 votes.

The President also has the power to grant reprieves and pardons to those who have committed certain federal crimes. A **reprieve** postpones the carrying out of a sentence. It gives the convicted person the opportunity to gather more evidence to support his or her case or to appeal for a new trial. A **pardon** forgives the person convicted of a crime and frees him or her from serving out the sentence. The President also has the power of **commutation,** or making a convicted person's sentence less severe. The President's power of pardon, reprieve, and commutation may be applied only to persons who are guilty of breaking federal laws.

Because the President's duties and powers are so great, they require a person of outstanding ability to perform them efficiently. The President of the United States must serve as the Chief of State, the Chief Executive, the Chief of his Party, and the chief official in our nation's government.

CONSIDER AND DISCUSS

Identify. Inaugural Address / Twenty-second Amendment / Chief Executive / "State of the Union" Message / Budget Message / Economic Message / veto / Commander-in-Chief / foreign policy / recognize / treaties / reprieve / pardon / commutation

The Unwritten Constitution

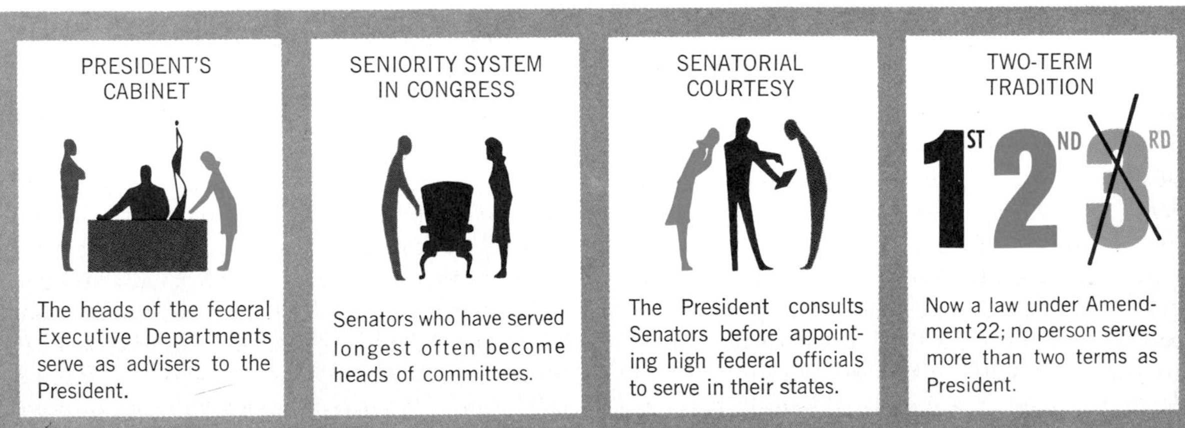

PRESIDENT'S CABINET
The heads of the federal Executive Departments serve as advisers to the President.
SENIORITY SYSTEM IN CONGRESS
Senators who have served longest often become heads of committees.
SENATORIAL COURTESY
The President consults Senators before appointing high federal officials to serve in their states.
TWO-TERM TRADITION
1ST 2ND 3RD
Now a law under Amendment 22; no person serves more than two terms as President.

Review. 1. What are the qualifications required of a President of the United States? 2. How can the President influence the lawmaking process? 3. What actions of the President must be approved by the Senate?
Discuss. Do you think the President of the United States has too much power? Why or why not?

2 The Cabinet and the Executive Departments

The people who wrote the Constitution drew up a plan of government with plenty of room for growth. They did not try to work out every detail of government. For example, they did not try to plan for each person who would help the President carry out the laws. The Constitution made no mention of the President's helpers except to state that "he may require the opinion, in writing, of the principal officer in each of the executive departments. . . ." This provision made it possible to establish each **executive department** as it was needed.

There are presently 12 departments in the executive branch of the federal government. Each department is headed by an official appointed by the President, with the advice and consent of the Senate. Congress has the power to establish departments, combine several under one head, or even drop a department. The President must then direct these departments, working within the structure that Congress sets up.

THE CABINET

George Washington had only three executive departments: the Department of State, Treasury, and War. Since President Washington's time, ten other departments have been added. One department—the Post Office Department—was dropped in 1970 and made an independent, self-supporting and self-governing agency.

President Washington began the tradition of calling together the heads of the executive departments to discuss policies with him and to advise him on important matters. Other Presidents followed this custom of meeting with the heads of the departments. This group of advisers became known as the President's **Cabinet.**

The President often consults the heads of the executive departments when planning policies. Here, President Carter meets with his Cabinet.

The present Cabinet consists of the heads of the 12 executive departments, plus the United States Representative to the United Nations. The heads of the 12 executive departments are the Secretary of State, Secretary of the Treasury, Secretary of the Interior, Secretary of Agriculture, Secretary of Commerce, Secretary of Labor, Secretary of Defense, Secretary of Health, Education, and Welfare, Secretary of Housing and Urban Development, Secretary of Transportation, Secretary of Energy, and the Attorney General, who is head of the Department of Justice. The President may also invite the Vice-President and other key government officials to attend Cabinet meetings.

THE EXECUTIVE DEPARTMENTS

In addition to serving as a member of the President's Cabinet, each department head directs the work of a department. Department heads may remain in office as long as their work is acceptable to the President.

What kind of work is done by the 12 executive departments represented in the Cabinet?

THE DEPARTMENT OF STATE

The conduct of our nation's relations with other countries is the special responsibility of the Department of State. The Secretary of State is the head of this department. The Department of State has a large staff of officials in Washington, D.C., who direct the worldwide work of the department. In addition, the officials who are sent to other countries by the President to represent our nation report to the Department of State.

The officials who represent the United States in dealings with the governments of foreign countries are called **ambassadors.** In a few of the smaller countries, these officials have the title of **ministers.** There is also another kind of representative called a **consul.** An American consul's office, or **consulate,** can be found in most large foreign cities. The consuls and the members of their staffs work hard to build up our foreign trade and commerce. They also help to protect citizens of the United States who do business and who own property in foreign lands. Citizens of the United States traveling in foreign lands may go to the consulate for help if they need it.

At home, the Department of State is the keeper of the Seal of the United States, which is affixed to all laws and treaties. It is the duty of the department to publish all laws and treaties of the United States. In addition, the Department of State issues documents known as **passports.** They allow our citizens to travel abroad.

THE DEPARTMENT OF THE TREASURY

The Secretary of the Treasury heads the Department of the Treasury. This is the department that collects taxes from our citizens. It pays out the money owed by our national government and, when necessary, borrows money for our government. It also supervises the coining and printing of money, and keeps the President informed about the financial condition of our country.

There are several important units within the Department of the Teasury. The Internal Revenue Service collects personal and corporate income taxes. The Customs Service collects taxes on all imported goods. The Treasurer of the United States sees that all money is spent as Congress directs. The Secret Service protects the President and helps prevent counterfeiting.

THE DEPARTMENT OF DEFENSE

Until 1947, the nation's armed forces were administered, or directed, by two separate departments, the Department of War and the Department of the Navy. Then, in 1947, Congress placed all the armed forces—the Army, Navy, and Air Force—under one de-

Principal Duties of the Executive Departments

EXECUTIVE DEPARTMENT (YEAR ESTABLISHED)		PRINCIPAL DUTIES
DEPARTMENT OF STATE (1789)		Conducts our foreign relations Protects our citizens abroad Issues passports
DEPARTMENT OF THE TREASURY (1789)		Prints, coins, and issues money Collects taxes and pays bills Manages government funds
DEPARTMENT OF JUSTICE (1789)		Investigates violations of laws Prosecutes cases before courts Administers naturalization laws Enforces immigration laws
DEPARTMENT OF THE INTERIOR (1849)		Controls our public lands Maintains our public parks Supervises Indian reservations Controls our water resources
DEPARTMENT OF AGRICULTURE (1862)		Conducts studies to help farmers Provides extension services to farmers Controls farm production and prices Directs soil conservation programs
DEPARTMENT OF COMMERCE (1903)		Fixes standards of weights and measures Encourages and regulates foreign trade Publishes reports on business and trade
DEPARTMENT OF LABOR (1913)		Determines standards of labor Publishes employment information Directs public employment services
DEPARTMENT OF DEFENSE (1949)		Maintains our armed forces Carries on military studies Operates military bases
DEPARTMENT OF HEALTH, EDUCATION, AND WELFARE (1953)		Directs our public health services Conducts studies for our schools Operates our Social Security program
DEPARTMENT OF HOUSING AND URBAN DEVELOPMENT (1965)		Aids urban housing programs Helps cities plan traffic control Helps cities plan mass transportation Cooperates with metropolitan area planners
DEPARTMENT OF TRANSPORTATION (1966)		Helps develop our nation's transportation policy Supervises federal-aid highway program Promotes air, highway, and railroad safety
DEPARTMENT OF ENERGY (1977)		Helps develop our nation's energy policy Promotes conservation of energy Controls use of nuclear energy Regulates hydroelectric power

partment, the Department of Defense. This department is headed by the Secretary of Defense, who is always a civilian. However, the Secretary has many military officers as assistants. These officers help the Secretary to plan the military defense of our nation and provide for the training and equipping of the armed forces. The Secretary is also aided by the Director of Defense Research and Engineering, who is a civilian. The Director is in charge of all the space and scientific research of the armed forces.

Within the Department of Defense, there are three major divisions: the Department of the Army, which commands our land forces; the Department of the Navy, which has charge of our seagoing forces and includes the Marine Corps; and the Department of the Air Force, which is responsible for our air defenses. Each of these divisions of the Defense Department is headed by a civilian Secretary.

In each of the three branches of our armed forces, the highest ranking military officer is called the **Chief of Staff.** Headed by a Chairman, they and the Commandant of the Marine Corps meet together to form the **Joint Chiefs of Staff.** The Joint Chiefs have the duty of advising the President on military matters.

The Corps of Engineers is also part of the Department of Defense. The Corps assists in such projects as flood control, river and harbor improvements, and the maintenance of the Panama Canal. The Department of Defense is also responsible for our four officer-training schools: the Military Academy at West Point, New York; the Naval Academy at Annapolis, Maryland; the Air Force Academy at Colorado Springs, Colorado; and the Coast Guard Academy at New London, Connecticut.

THE DEPARTMENT OF JUSTICE

The Attorney General of the United States is the head of the Department of Justice. The officials of the department see that federal laws are obeyed. They defend the United States in court when a lawsuit is brought against the federal government.

The Federal Bureau of Investigation (FBI) is an important agency of the Justice Department. The FBI investigates violations of federal laws and arrests those accused of crimes against the United States. The Immigration and Naturalization Service and the Bureau of Prisons are also within the Justice Department.

THE DEPARTMENT OF THE INTERIOR

The Department of the Interior, headed by the Secretary of the Interior, manages our nation's natural resources. Its duties are to encourage the wise use of America's land, minerals, water, fish, and wildlife. The Department also manages our national parks and federal dams.

Among the many **bureaus,** or divisions, of the Department of the Interior, the following are the most important: the Bureau of Indian Affairs, which deals with matters involving Native Americans; the Bureau of Reclamation, which sponsors water irrigation projects; and the Office of Territories, which supervises American overseas territories. Other bureaus within the Department of the Interior are the National Park Service, the Bureau of Mines, and the Fish and Wildlife Service.

THE DEPARTMENT OF AGRICULTURE

The Department of Agriculture, headed by the Secretary of Agriculture, aids American farmers in the important task of raising and marketing crops. Special agencies in the Department, such as the Agricultural Research Service and the Soil Conservation Service, try to encourage better methods of farming. The Department also prepares reports on market conditions for crops and livestock to aid farmers in their planning and planting. Other bureaus within this department include the Farmers Home Administration, the Rural Electrification Administration, and the Forest Service, which helps to protect our nation's woodlands. The Food and Nutrition Service manages the food stamp and food lunch programs.

THE DEPARTMENT OF COMMERCE

American trade and business are encouraged by the Secretary of Commerce and the staff. There are many important agencies within the Department of Commerce. The Office of Business Economics studies business conditions in the United States. The Domestic and International Business Administration promotes America's foreign trade. The Patent and Trademark Office protects the rights of inventors. The National Bureau of Standards establishes official weights and measures. Also under this department are the Bureau of the Census and the Maritime Administration, which aids American ocean shipping and commerce. The Weather Bureau is part of the department's National Oceanic and Atmospheric Administration.

THE DEPARTMENT OF LABOR

The American worker receives important services from the Department of Labor. This department is headed by the Secretary of Labor. It gathers information on working conditions in various businesses and industries. The Wage and Hour Division is responsible for carrying out federal laws that regulate the wages and hours of workers in businesses that are engaged in interstate commerce.

Various bureaus of the Labor Department study such matters as Apprenticeship and Training, Unemployment Insurance, Employment Standards, Veterans' Reemployment Rights, Labor Statistics, and International Labor Affairs. The Office of Comprehensive Economic Development creates jobs in places that have a high rate of unemployment.

The Department of Housing and Urban Development aids cities and states to help solve urban problems.

THE DEPARTMENT OF HEALTH, EDUCATION, AND WELFARE (HEW)

This department is directed by the Secretary of Health, Education, and Welfare. It gathers information, does research, and conducts programs to promote the health, education, and well-being of all citizens.

The important work of assisting the aged, the unemployed, and other persons in need is carried on by a division of this department —the Social Security Administration. Other divisions within this department include the Food and Drug Administration, the Public Health Service, the Office of Education, the Social and Rehabilitation Service, and the Community Services Administration. These divisions furnish advice and information to school systems. They train the physically handicapped and disabled for jobs. They also see that the food we eat is safe and pure, and they work to promote health.

THE DEPARTMENT OF HOUSING AND URBAN DEVELOPMENT

This department is sometimes referred to by the initials HUD. It offers aid to city and state governments in working out programs for such local problems as housing, mass transportation, traffic, and better parks and playgrounds. The Department assists metropolitan areas in solving regional problems such as those concerning water conservation and air pollution.

THE DEPARTMENT OF TRANSPORTATION

Established in 1966 and headed by the Secretary of Transportation, this department helps to coordinate and develop our nation's rail, highway, and air transportation.

Among the important agencies of the Department of Transportation are the Federal Aviation Administration, the Federal Railroad Administration, the Urban Mass Transportation Administration, and the Federal Highway Administration. The Coast Guard is part of the Transportation Department in peacetime. In wartime it becomes part of the Navy.

THE DEPARTMENT OF ENERGY

At the request of the President, Congress created the Department of Energy in 1977. It is headed by the Secretary of Energy. One of the main goals of the department is to lessen the amount of energy that is wasted in our nation. It also is responsible for stretching our oil and gas supplies until new sources of energy can be found.

The Department of Energy took over the work of three independent agencies. They were the Federal Energy Administration, the Energy Research and Development Administration, and the Federal Power Commisssion. Parts of other departments and agencies that dealt with energy also became part of the new department. The Department of Energy is responsible for carrying out our energy laws. It regulates the development and use of our hydroelectric power, gas and oil pipelines, nuclear power, and energy deposits.

CONSIDER AND DISCUSS

Identify. executive departments / Cabinet / ambassadors / ministers / consuls / consulate/ passport / Chief of Staff / Joint Chiefs of Staff / bureaus

Review. 1. What is the Cabinet? 2. Describe the work of each executive department.

Discuss. Which of the executive departments affects your life most? Why?

3 The President and the Executive Agencies

In addition to the 12 executive departments, Congress has set up a number of **independent agencies.** These agencies help the President carry out the duties of office. The independent agencies are separate from the executive departments because they perform specialized duties that often do not fit into any regular department. In addition, some of these agencies serve all of the departments. Therefore, they function best as separate and independent organizations.

THE INDEPENDENT AGENCIES

There are about 50 of these independent agencies. Congress has given some of them considerable power. Some independent agencies can make rules and bring violators into court. Their decisions often have the force of law.

The **Interstate Commerce Commission,** for example, has the power to regulate railroad, bus, and truck transportation that crosses state lines. The Commission can even regulate rates, routes, and stops to be made.

The **Securities and Exchange Commission** make rules for the buying and selling of stocks and bonds.

The **Environmental Protection Agency** works to end water and air pollution. It also regulates the disposal of solid wastes.

The **Civil Aeronautics Board** is responsible for regulating all airlines flying in the United States. Such law-enforcing agencies are called **regulatory agencies.**

A number of independent agencies have been established to offer assistance to the people:

The **Veterans Administration** is one of the largest of these. It provides needed services to persons who have served in the armed forces and to their families. Among these services are veterans' hospitals, life insurance, education loans, and other benefits.

The **Farm Credit Administration** helps farmers obtain needed loans.

The **National Labor Relations Board** helps settle disputes between workers and their employers.

The work of the entire government is assisted by many other independent agencies:

The **United States Civil Service Commission** gives examinations to persons who apply for jobs with the federal government. It helps to place most of the 2.8 million workers who are on the payroll of the United States government.

The **Equal Employment Opportunity Commission** works to end discrimination in hiring and in all employment practices.

The **General Services Administration** buys supplies for the federal government. It also builds and maintains public buildings belonging to the federal government, and keeps public documents and records.

A number of independent agencies provide the President with the accurate information necessary to strengthen our national security:

When an international crisis arises, the President may call in the members of the **National Security Council.** The council is the top-ranking group of advisers on all matters concerning the nation's defense and security. The Council is made up of the President of the United States, the Vice-President, the Secretary of State, and the Secretary of Defense. The head of the Joint Chiefs of Staff and the Director of the Central Intelligence Agency attend all of the Council meetings.

The **Central Intelligence Agency** provides secret information that may aid the President to make decisions and to act wisely in any troubled spot in the world.

INDEPENDENT AGENCIES AND BUREAUCRACY

The independent agencies were given independence so that they could have the freedom they needed to do their jobs. The members are appointed by the President. But they have long terms, often as long as 14 years.

This independence has often been criticized on the grounds that it makes the agencies too powerful. When a government is made up of many powerful agencies with appointed officials who enforce rules and regulations, it may be called a **bureaucracy.** Under such a system, mix-ups, conflicts, and delays may occur. Some experts feel that our government should be completely reorganized. Others point out that we need many agencies in our government. They say that without them, the government could not do all of the things that it does for the people of the United States.

THE EXECUTIVE AGENCIES

The executive departments and independent agencies established by Congress help the President of the United States to carry out the laws passed by Congress. You have already studied how the 12 executive departments (each with many bureaus and divisions) and the many independent agencies play a vital part in helping the President carry out his complex duties. Now you will read about some other executive agencies that are equally important in assisting the President in his work.

THE EXECUTIVE OFFICE OF THE PRESIDENT

Congress established the **Executive Office of the President** in 1939. It has been reorganized in every Presidential administration since then. The agencies and offices that make up the Executive Office are staffed by the President's closest advisers. They advise the President on economic and domestic matters, energy resources, foreign trade, the quality of the environment, and national science and technology matters. The **Council of Economic Advisers,** for example, furnishes the President with facts and figures about the nation's economy. It helps him to decide what laws or recommendations he should propose to Congress in his yearly Economic Message. The **Office of Management and Budget** similarly helps the President to prepare his yearly federal Budget Message.

In order for the President to manage the many departments and agencies that are under his supervision, he needs plenty of help. Members of the **White House Office** perform this function. They include senior advisers, special assistants, researchers, clerical staff, social secretaries, and the White House doctor. Aides help the President with speeches

The President often must travel to foreign nations. In this picture, President Jimmy Carter meets with the leaders of Saudi Arabia.

and assist him in his relations with the public, representatives of foreign governments, the news media, Congress, and the other departments and agencies of government.

CONSIDER AND DISCUSS

Identify. independent agencies / regulatory agencies / National Security Council / bureaucracy / Executive Office of the President / White House Office / Council of Economic Advisers / Office of Management and Budget

Review. 1. Why are the independent agencies separate from the executive departments? 2. Name three independent agencies and describe what they do.

Discuss. What are the dangers of a federal bureaucracy? What do you think could be done to avoid these dangers?

4 The Many Roles of the President

In addition to the many important decisions the President makes, he must find time to carry on a hundred and one activities from day to day. President Truman worked a 70-hour week. President Eisenhower usually got up at 6 a.m. and worked until early evening. Presidents Kennedy and Johnson put in long and busy working days. Subsequent Presidents have continued this tradition.

Even the weekends are busy times for the President. Try as he may, the Chief Executive has found it difficult to cut down on Saturday appointments. If he goes away for a weekend in the country, he is surrounded by members of his staff, secret service agents, and often newspaper reporters. At all times he and his assistants must be in touch with other high officials of the nation's government. The President can never be far away from the telephone.

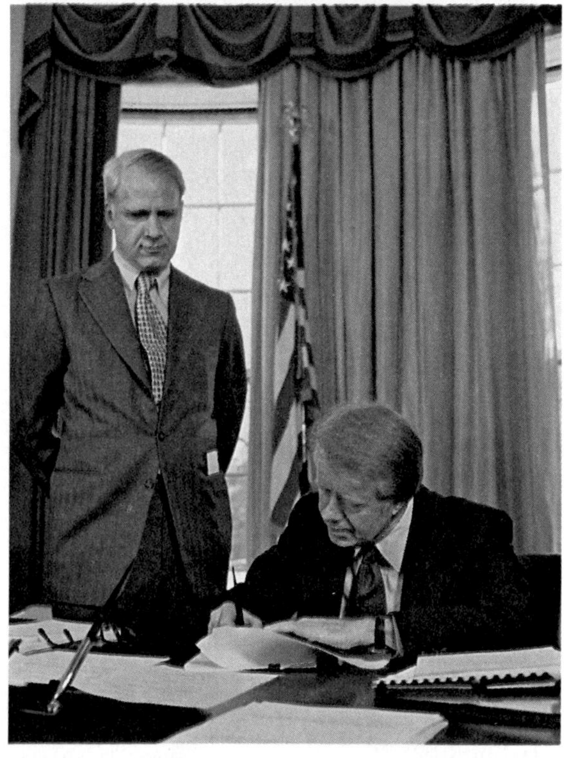

As President of the United States, Jimmy Carter is one of the busiest people in the world. Here, he meets with members of Congress and signs papers given to him by the Secretary of Energy.

THE PRESIDENT'S DAY

The activities that occupy the President's time are varied. When Congress is in session, he often has breakfast or luncheon meetings with Congressional leaders. He also meets during the day with members of his party and talks over the bills before Congress, appointments to be made, or political plans of importance to the party.

The National Security Council, which plans the nation's defense, meets regularly with the President. The President also meets with the Cabinet on a regular basis. The Council of Economic Advisers and the Director of the Office of Management and Budget are frequent visitors.

Every day of the week a steady stream of visitors calls on the President. He receives Cabinet members, foreign visitors, ambassadors, and representatives of farm, labor, and business organizations. The President's staff must carefully arrange his schedule so that he can also give time to his many important tasks.

SPEECHES! SPEECHES! WORK! WORK!

The President delivers speeches by the dozens. President Franklin D. Roosevelt established the custom of reporting directly to the American people. He did so by radio talks, which he called "fireside chats." More recently, the President has appeared on television to speak directly to the people, to inform them of his programs, and to ask for their support.

The President's most important speech is the annual "State of the Union" Message. Each January, as directed by the Constitution, he appears before both houses of Congress to outline the programs he intends to recommend. As you have read, he also delivers an Economic Message and a Budget Message to Congress once each year. Hundreds of church, labor, business, education, and charitable organizations are eager to have the President speak before their groups. And each year, he does address many of them. There are also interviews with newspaper and television reporters.

All of these speeches and public appearances take a lot of time. But the President also must find time to attend to his many other important duties. He must sign (or veto) bills, write messages, appoint officials, examine budget figures, deal with foreign nations, and reach decisions on national defense problems. The President also must find time to read several newspapers and magazines a day, study many reports received from government officials at home and abroad, and discuss problems with his advisers.

CHIEF DIPLOMAT

The President, as Chief Executive of one of the leading nations of the world, must give constant attention to our foreign relations. He is required to show great skill and tact in dealing with friendly and unfriendly nations. The art of dealing with foreign governments is called **diplomacy,** and the President is our chief diplomat.

The President depends heavily upon the Secretary of State in matters concerning our nation's foreign relations. The Secretary of State often represents the President at conferences and in dealings with the leaders of foreign governments. When problems of great importance are considered, the President sometimes attends conferences with the leaders of other nations. Such meetings are called **summit conferences.**

The President meets with ambassadors sent here to represent other nations of the world. From these foreign representatives, the President gains information that helps to conduct American foreign relations. It has also become the custom in recent years for the President of the United States to make visits to foreign nations to build up international friendship and security.

THE PRESIDENT MAKES TREATIES

The President uses treaties to help carry out our nation's foreign policy. The President is responsible for making these treaties with foreign governments. Some of these written agreements deal with trade and are intended to promote business between nations. Other treaties establish friendly alliances for the purpose of increasing our nation's security in case of war or threat of war.

American ambassadors and the Secretary of State usually do most of the actual work in reaching agreements with other nations. The President of the United States, however, assumes the final responsibility for the treaty. Therefore, it is the President's treaty. He must send it to the Senate and try to get the Senate's approval by the necessary two-thirds vote. If the treaty is approved, it is the President's job to see that its provisions are carried out.

DIPLOMATIC NOTES

The President also influences our foreign relations in other ways. For example, he often corresponds with the heads of foreign governments. These written communications are called **diplomatic notes.** Such an exchange of views between world leaders is helpful, since it often prevents governments from taking actions that might have dangerous results.

In addition, in these days of rapid communication, the President is able to contact any of our diplomatic representatives in a matter of minutes. He can also telephone other world leaders. On his desk there is a special phone that enables him to make direct connection with the government of the Soviet Union in an emergency.

THE PRESIDENTIAL SUCCESSION

The Constitution provides that if the President of the United States dies, resigns, is removed from office, or is unable to carry out his duties, the Vice-President becomes President. Eight Presidents of the United States have died while in office. Upon the death of each of the Presidents, the Vice-President took the oath of office and became President as provided by the Constitution.

But what would happen if both the President and the Vice-President should die while in office? The Constitution gave Congress the right to decide who should then fill the office of President.

In 1947, Congress passed the law establishing the present order in which the office of President is to be filled. This is known as the order of **Presidential succession.** This law provides that the Speaker of the House of Representatives shall become President if both the regularly elected President and Vice-President die while in office. If the Speaker should die or be removed from office, then the President *pro tempore* of the Senate succeeds to the Presidency. Following them in order of succession to the Presidency are the members of the Cabinet, in the order in which their departments were created.

THE TWENTY-FIFTH AMENDMENT

If the President dies while in office and the Vice-President succeeds him, who then is the Vice-President? Until 1967 the answer to this question was, no one. The office of the Vice-President remained empty when the Vice-President moved up to the Presidency. Under the **Twenty-fifth Amendment** to the Constitution, the new President shall nominate a person for the office of Vice-President. The nomination must then be approved by a majority vote of both houses of Congress.

The Twenty-fifth Amendment also provides that if the President is too ill to serve, then the Vice-President will serve as Acting President until the President is again able to serve. Suppose, however, that the President wants to return to his duties, but the Cabinet and the Vice-President do not think that he is fit to do so. Then Congress must decide by a two-thirds vote whether the President will return to office or whether the Vice-President will continue as Acting President.

The first test of the Twenty-fifth Amendment came in 1973. Vice-President Spiro Agnew resigned after he was charged with income tax evasion. President Nixon nominated Gerald R. Ford as the new Vice-President. The Congress confirmed him. When President Nixon resigned because of the Watergate scandal in 1974, Vice-President Ford became President. He then nominated Nelson Rockefeller as Vice-President and the Congress approved the nomination. Thus, for the first time in our history, the nation had a President and a Vice-President who had not been elected by the vote of the people.

CONSIDER AND DISCUSS

Identify. diplomacy / summit conference / diplomatic notes / Presidential succession / Twenty-fifth Amendment

Review. 1. What are some of the official responsibilities and powers of the President? 2. How does the President influence our foreign policy? 3. What is the order of Presidential succession?

Discuss. In your opinion, what is the President's most important responsibility? Why?

CHAPTER
Summary

The President is the leader of our nation's government and is elected by all the people. The President is responsible for seeing that our nation's laws are carried out and enforced.

The President has a difficult and demanding job. The President must provide leadership in a great many vital areas, such as foreign relations, conservation, budget making, planning our nation's defense needs, promoting our nation's prosperity, and helping to secure equal rights for all citizens.

For aid in these tasks, the President turns to the members of the Cabinet —the various heads of the federal executive departments. These departments carry on a great deal of the work of the executive branch of the federal government.

The President also may turn to other executive agencies for advice and aid on such matters as atomic energy, communications, interstate commerce, the stock market, veterans' affairs, and many other important activities of government.

The President is the Chief Executive of one of the most powerful nations in the world. As such, the President's actions and words play a large part in shaping the history of our nation and the world.

CHECK-UP AND REVIEW

VOCABULARY

Tell how each of the following words or phrases is related to the powers and duties of the President.

Inaugural Address
Chief Executive
Budget Message
Economic Message
veto
special session
executive departments
ambassadors
passport
independent agencies
summit conference
State of the Union Message
Commander-in-Chief
foreign policies
treaties
reprieve
pardon
commutation
Cabinet
consul
Secret Service
Chief Diplomat
Central Intelligence Agency

CHECK-UP

Answer the following questions to review what you have learned from this chapter.

1. What are the President's powers as Commander-in-Chief?
2. What are the qualifications for the President of the United States?
3. What purpose did the Twenty-second Amendment serve?
4. In what three ways can the President influence the lawmaking powers of Congress?
5. How can Congress check the powers of the President?
6. What department of the federal government aids the school system?
7. To which department would the President turn for advice on foreign affairs? Why?
8. Name the executive departments whose heads are in the President's Cabinet.
9. What are some of the reasons for calling the President of the United States "the busiest person in the world"?
10. In case the President becomes unable to serve, what official takes his place? Who is third in succession?

CITIZENSHIP AND YOU

Here are some activities that will help you to understand the executive branch of the government of the United States. Newspapers, magazines, and television programs are good sources of project materials.

1. Class Projects

Practice your discussion skills by taking part in an open-forum debate on one of the following topics:

Will a woman ever become President of the United States?
Should a President be limited to two terms in office?
How can we better protect the lives of our Presidents?
Do you think that the President of the United States has too much, too little, or just the right amount of power?

Another kind of group discussion may be based upon a televised press conference with the President. Watch the program in school or at home. Listen carefully to what the President says. Take notes on the main points. Then, come to class prepared to discuss the President's ideas.

2. Group or Committee Projects

A group may prepare a chart showing the executive branch of the federal government.

Prepare a panel report on the activities of the President of the United States. Each member of the panel should come to class prepared to report on specific Presidential activities.

3. Individual Projects

List in order the five Presidents of the United States who, in your opinion, did the most for our country. Come to class prepared to explain your choices.

Draw a cartoon showing some of the activities of the President. A display of these cartoons will add to the interest of the class.

Keep a record of news reports of the President's daily activities. Relate each of these reported activities to the President's responsibilities. To which responsibility has the President been giving the most attention during this period of time? Report your findings to the class.

Keep a scrapbook of the activities of each of the executive departments.

CIVICS SKILLS

USING CHARTS AND GRAPHS

In order to show amounts and figures in easy-to-read form, social scientists often use graphs. They also use charts to point out important facts and information and to make them easier to learn and remember. Sometimes the term *chart* is used to mean either a graph or a chart. However, graphs and charts are usually used for different purposes.

The main purpose of graphs is to show amounts – how many, how much, how far, how long. Graphs use symbols to show these amounts. Amounts may be shown with bars, parts of a circle, lines, or with pictorial symbols to represent houses, workers, automobiles, and so on. Many graphs compare two or more accounts. They are used to show comparisons or relationships. Bar graphs, picture graphs, and most other graphs permit you to see the comparison at a glance. But some graphs, especially line graphs, usually require more careful study.

Charts illustrate an important idea and often contrast or compare information. Flow charts are often used in civics. For example, the chart on page 57 shows how a bill becomes a law. It traces the various steps, or the "flow" in the lawmaking process. Often, symbol figures and arrows are used in such charts to make clearer what happens at each step.

Organization charts are also useful in studying civics. These charts show, for example, how the various branches of government are organized, how business corporations are established, and how courts are set up.

The first step in learning to read and understand a graph or a chart is to read its title. The title tells you what information the chart or graph contains. Then try to sum up the chart or graph's main points by putting them in your own words. Ask yourself, what are the main ideas being stressed? How does the chart or graph use color to help make these ideas clearer? Graphs and charts will be easier to read and to understand if you practice making them. A good way to summarize important ideas or to illustrate facts in this book is to put them in chart form in your notebook. You will find that they will help you to learn more and learn it faster.

PRACTICING YOUR CIVICS SKILLS

Turn to the chart on page 80 and find the following information:

1. What is the title of the chart? What information does the chart present?
2. What do the symbols on the chart represent?
3. Which executive departments were the first ones to be established? Which is the newest one?

Draw a bar graph that compares the location of our population in 1900 and 1970. (For an example of a bar graph turn to page 10.) Use the following information in drawing your bar graph:

1. The total population of the United States in 1900 was 75,994,000. Of this number 30,159,000 people lived in cities, and 45,834,000 lived in areas outside of cities.
2. In 1970 America's total population was 203,212,000, with 149,325,000 living in city areas and 53,887,000 living outside of cities.

What other kind of graph might be drawn to show this information?

CHAPTER
Introduction

One of the most impressive sights in our nation's capital is the majestic Supreme Court building. Its rows of Corinthian columns remind one of a temple in ancient Greece. In a sense it is a temple. The Supreme Court building is a temple dedicated to the American ideal of justice for all. Carved in bold letters over the entrance is the motto "Equal Justice Under Law."

The Supreme Court stands at the head of a court system that affects the life of every citizen. The national, district, state, and local courts make decisions that directly influence our lives. The courts are designed to help "insure domestic tranquility." At their best they protect the weak from injury by the strong. They also protect the individual citizen from the tyranny of bad government. In accordance with the American ideal of justice, our courts should protect, defend, and uphold the rights guaranteed by the Constitution.

No function of government is more important to study than the way in which the enforcement of good laws helps to improve the lives of free people. The idea of justice for all is one of democracy's great achievements. Without equal justice for all our republican form of government cannot exist. In this chapter you will learn how our legal system works as you study these topics:

1. Equal Justice Under Law
2. Our Federal Courts
3. Our Federal Courts at Work

CHAPTER

5

The Federal Courts Judge Our Nation's Laws

1 Equal Justice Under Law

We enjoy freedom in the United States because we have laws to protect our rights. Of course, some laws limit our freedom. For example, a law against robbery denies the robber's freedom to steal. But it gives the rest of us freedom to use and enjoy our own property. Laws usually represent the feelings of the majority as to what is right and what is wrong. When most of the American people feel strongly that something should or should not be done, then a law is passed on the subject. In this way, our laws constantly grow and change with the times.

THE IDEA OF LAW

There are certain rules which have been accepted by Americans as the proper ways in which to act. Some of these rules are based on common sense and common practice. For example, parents who treated their children very badly might be punished even if there were no law dealing with the matter. The judge would apply the rule of common sense and common practice in reaching a decision in such a case.

This same decision might be remembered by another judge hearing a similar case. Eventually, most judges might follow the same **precedent,** or earlier decision in such cases. In time, those guilty of cruel treatment of their children would be punished according to this customary rule. This rule would become a part of our customary law, known as **common law.** Common law, therefore, is law that comes from judges' decisions. In time, most common law is passed by the nation's lawmaking body. In this way, it is written down so that all of the nation's citizens may know it.

Laws that are passed by lawmaking bodies are known as **statutory laws.** America has a great many statutory laws. They are passed by city, state, and national governments. All these statutory laws must follow the principles set forth in the Constitution of the United States, which is the supreme law of the land.

Every American citizen is responsible for knowing and obeying the laws. It is our responsibility to get to know the laws that concern any activity we expect to undertake. The man or woman who drives an automobile, for example, must know about speed laws, road signs, signaling, and traffic regulations. "Ignorance of the law excuses no one," is an old saying that holds true today. The law-abiding citizen realizes that laws are passed for the good of all. By learning and obeying the nation's laws, the citizen is practicing good citizenship.

THE IDEA OF COURTS

To be just, a law must be enforced fairly. Suppose, for example, that the Congress of the United States passed a law forbidding workers in an atomic energy plant to give or sell secrets about their work to a foreign government. This might be a very good law, intended to protect the American people.

What would happen if an FBI agent found an engineer who worked in an atomic energy plant talking to a foreign spy? Could the federal government arrest the engineer on suspicion of treason, and put him or her in jail for 20 years? The answer is no! Under our American system of justice, the engineer must be given a fair public trial.

To guarantee justice in the United States, we have accepted the important idea that a person is innocent until proven guilty. The proper way to determine whether a person is guilty or not is to hold a trial in a court of law. Our courts are made up of persons who have been given the authority to administer justice. We believe that only a system of courts can assure equal justice to all people. Equal justice for all is the ideal we try to achieve, even though our court system sometimes falls short of the ideal.

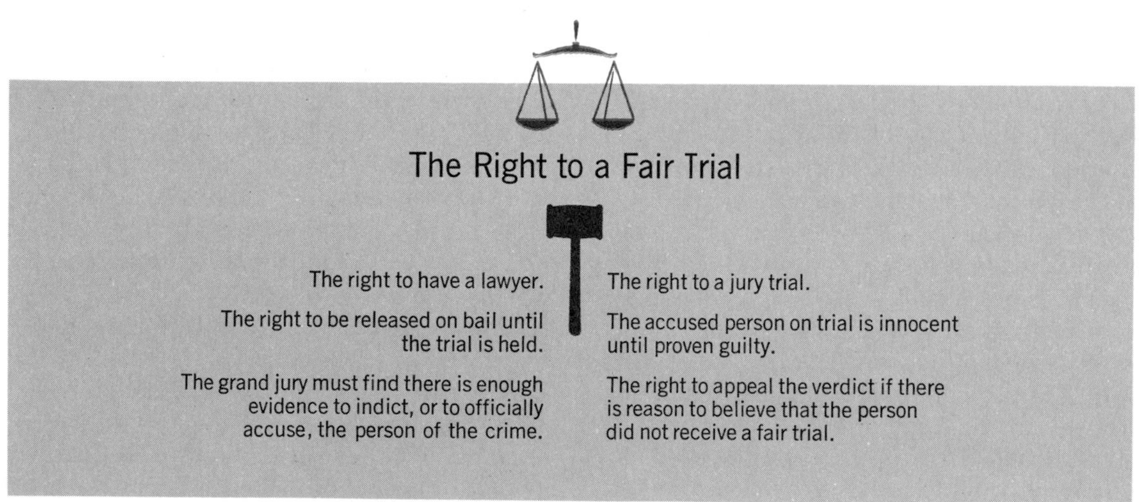

The Right to a Fair Trial
The right to have a lawyer.
The right to be released on bail until the trial is held.
The grand jury must find there is enough evidence to indict, or to officially accuse, the person of the crime.
The right to a jury trial.
The accused person on trial is innocent until proven guilty.
The right to appeal the verdict if there is reason to believe that the person did not receive a fair trial.

A person accused of crime has a right to a trial by jury, such as that pictured here.

THE RIGHT TO A FAIR TRIAL

The Constitution guarantees every American the right to a fair public trial. It is important that you understand this guarantee as you study our federal court system and learn how equal justice under the law works in the United States. What does the right to a fair trial mean? Consider our example of the atomic engineer who is accused of giving secret information to a foreign government.

1. The right to have a lawyer. All persons accused of a crime are entitled to the services of a lawyer who will represent them in court and help to protect their rights. The atomic engineer can claim this right to be represented by a lawyer. If the engineer cannot afford one, the court will appoint a lawyer and pay the lawyer's fees out of public funds.

2. The right to be released on bail. A person accused of a crime does not, ordinarily, have to spend months in prison waiting for the case to come to trial. Usually, the accused may be released if he or she can put up bail. **Bail** is a sum of money that is deposited with the court as a pledge that the accused will appear in court at the time of trial. The amount of bail is set by a judge. The Constitution (Amendment 8) states that "Excessive bail shall not be required . . . ." But a person accused of a serious crime, such as murder or treason, may be denied bail and have to remain in jail until the trial is held. Who decides whether there is enough evidence against a person to justify holding him or her for trial?

3. A person must be indicted (accused) by a grand jury. Just because a person is arrested on suspicion of a crime does not mean that this person must come to trial. There must be enough evidence against someone to justify bringing that person into court for trial. The group of persons that decides whether there is enough evidence to bring the accused to trial is called the **grand jury.**

In federal courts, the grand jury is made up of 16 to 23 citizens who live in the district in which the trial is to be held. The grand jury is chosen by the clerk of the court, who draws names at random from a box containing the names of all residents who are eligible to serve. The grand jury examines the evidence against the person accused. It calls witnesses to testify and investigates all the facts in the case. If a majority of the grand jury decides that the evidence against the accused is strong enough, then the person is indicted and held for trial. In the case of the atomic engineer, the grand jury found the evidence strong enough. As a result, the engineer was indicted.

4. The right to a jury trial. Individuals who go on trial must be judged on the basis of the evidence for and against them. But who shall judge the evidence? In the United States, a person on trial is entitled to be judged by a **trial jury,** or petit jury, as it is also called. The Constitution (Amendment 6) provides this right:

> In all criminal prosecutions, the accused shall enjoy the right to a speedy and public trial, by an impartial jury of the state and district wherein the crime shall have been committed . . . and to be informed of the nature and cause of the accusation; to be confronted with the witnesses against him; to have compulsory process for obtaining witnesses in his favor, and to have the assistance of counsel for his defense.

The trial jury is made up of from 6 to 12 persons who live in the community. The men and women of the trial jury who judge the evidence are called trial jurors. Jurors are selected from among the list of qualified voters in the community. The court clerk chooses names at random from this list and notifies them to appear in court on a certain date. From this group, or panel of jurors, the required number of jurors are chosen for the trial.

The trial jury must determine the true answer, or **verdict,** in the case. Usually the jury's verdict must be a **unanimous** vote. This means that all of the members must agree on whether the accused person is guilty or innocent.

5. Innocent until proven guilty. The burden of proof in a jury trial rests with those who bring charges against the person on trial. They must prove their case "beyond a reasonable doubt." Accused persons cannot be forced to testify against themselves. Their lawyers have the right to question all witnesses to make sure their testimony is accurate and honest. Accused persons have the right to present their own witnesses to help them defend themselves.

The atomic engineer accused by the federal government of selling secrets to a foreign power was found not guilty by the trial jury. The jury of **peers,** or equals, found the engineer innocent because the government lawyers could not prove guilt. As you see, the American system of justice is carefully designed to protect the innocent and to punish the guilty.

6. The right of appeal. Since courts are made up of human beings, it is only natural that courts sometimes make mistakes. To make sure that justice is done, our nation's court system provides the right to **appeal,** or to ask for a review of a case. If there is reason to doubt that justice was done in the court trial, the convicted person can appeal to a higher court. The person may carry the appeal to the Supreme Court of the United States.

CONSIDER AND DISCUSS

Identify. precedent / common law / statutory law / bail / grand jury / trial jury / verdict / unanimous / peers / appeal

Review. 1. How may law be established by the decisions of judges? 2. What is meant by the saying, "Ignorance of the law excuses no one"? 3. Why do we have courts? 4. What rights to a fair trial are guaranteed by the Constitution? 5. Why is it important that citizens have the right of appeal?

Discuss. Some people think that it would be better to have criminal cases decided by several trained judges rather than by a jury. What do you think?

2 Our Federal Courts

Article 3 of the Constitution of the United States provides that "The judicial power of the United States shall be vested in one Supreme Court, and in such inferior [lower] courts as the Congress may from time to time . . . establish." The First Congress used this constitutional power to set up a system of federal courts. The Judiciary Act of 1789 established what has grown into one of the great court systems of the world.

THE JURISDICTION OF FEDERAL COURTS

The Constitution grants the federal courts jurisdiction in a wide variety of cases. **Jurisdiction** means the authority to judge and administer the law. Listed below are the kinds of cases that are brought to trial in federal courts:

1. Any person accused of disobeying any part of the Constitution, including all of the amendments, is tried in federal court.
2. Anyone accused of violating a treaty of the United States is tried in a federal court.
3. Anyone accused of breaking laws passed by Congress is brought before a federal court.
4. Federal courts have jurisdiction when a foreign nation sues the government of the United States or a citizen of the United States.
5. American ambassadors and consuls are tried in federal courts if they are accused of breaking the laws of the country in which they are stationed.
6. Crimes committed on American ships at sea are tried in federal courts.
7. Crimes committed on certain federal property are tried in federal courts.
8. Any disagreement between states is tried in a federal court. Lawsuits between citizens of different states also come under federal jurisdiction.

However, the Eleventh Amendment provides that any lawsuit against a state brought by a citizen of another state or of a foreign country shall be tried only in state courts.

THE DISTRICT COURTS

At the base of our federal court system are the **District Courts.** There is at least one of these courts in each of the 50 states. Some of the larger states are divided into two or more federal court districts, each with its own district court. Today there are 94 federal District Courts in the United States and its territories.

The District Court is the only federal court in which jury trials are held. These District Courts have **original jurisdiction** in most federal cases. That is, most federal cases are heard first in a District Court. District Courts do not have **appellate jurisdiction.** That is, they do not hear cases that have already been tried in another court and then appealed.

These District Courts try cases in which a person is accused of breaking a federal law. District Courts also try cases that involve citizens of different states, or involve the United States government or the government of a state as a party in the case. (See exceptions under the Eleventh Amendment.) Congress gave these cases to the federal courts in the belief that they could serve as fair judges in such actions.

The Constitution is definite about where federal cases shall be tried. Article 3, Section 2 states, in part, that ". . . such trial shall be held in the state where the said crime shall have been committed. . . ." The reason for this provision is to make sure that the accused person receives a fair and convenient trial. The witnesses who will testify are usually close at hand, and no one has to travel long distances to be heard.

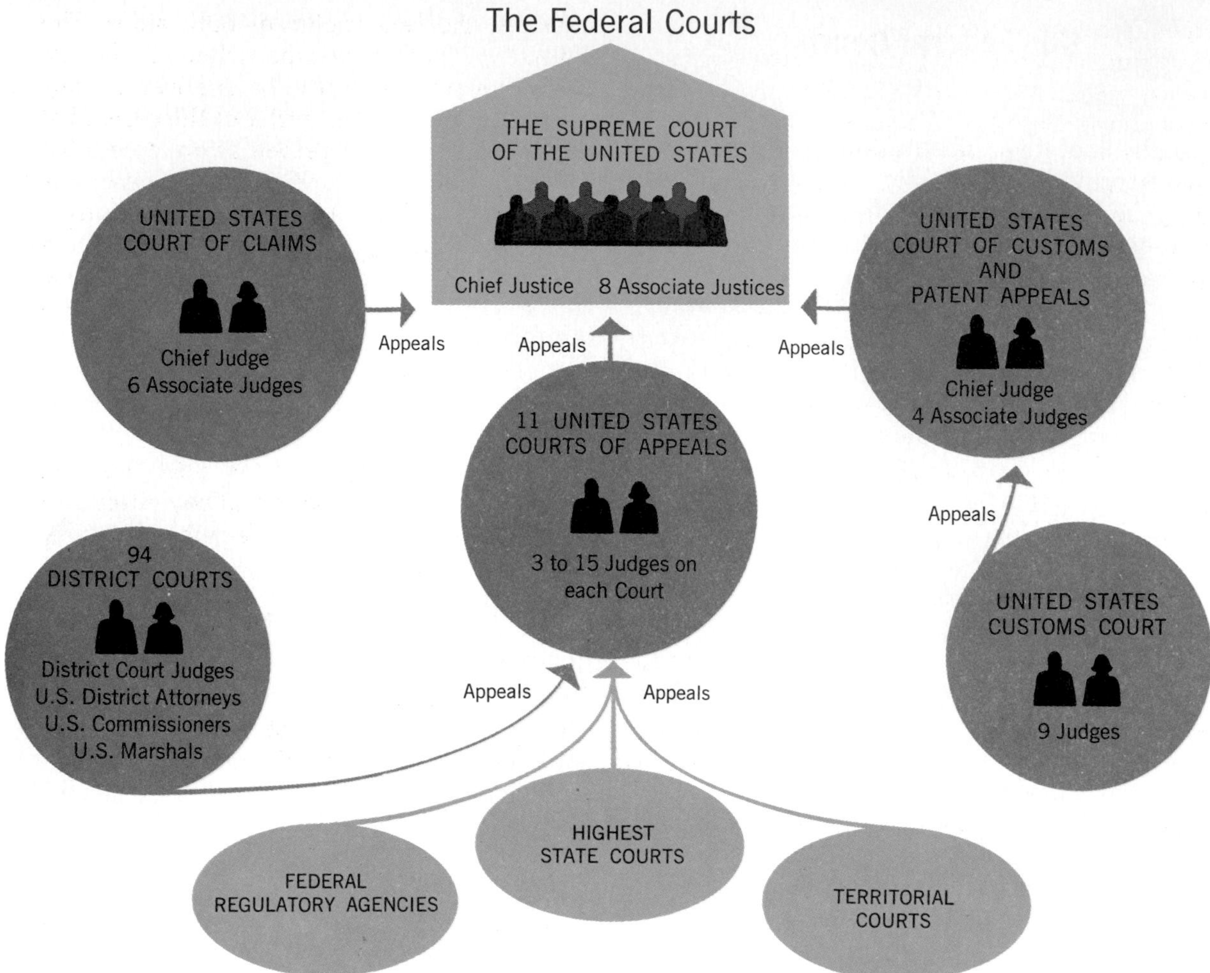

Furthermore, the jury will be familiar with the location of the crime, and it can judge the truth of the evidence more intelligently.

DISTRICT COURT OFFICIALS

Most District Courts are presided over by a single District Court Judge. In very busy districts, there may be a number of judges. District Court judges decide matters of court procedure, explain the law involved in the case to the jury, and fix the sentence if the accused person is found guilty by the jury. District Court judges are appointed for life and they are paid a salary of $42,000 a year.

Each District Court has a **United States Marshal,** who may appoint deputies for assistance. Marshals arrest persons accused of breaking federal laws. They also deliver official court orders called **subpoenas,** which require persons to appear in court. The United States Marshal also sees that the court's verdict is carried out.

Each District Court also formerly had a **Federal Commissioner** who heard the evidence against the accused person and decided whether the case deserved to be brought before a grand jury. These officials are being replaced by **United States Magistrates,** who do the work of the former Commissioners. But they also try certain minor cases without referring them to the grand jury. If the case comes to trial, the United States is represented by a **United States District Attorney,** who serves as the federal government's lawyer.

UNITED STATES COURTS OF APPEALS

If accused persons feel that some point in their favor was overlooked in the trial in the District Court or that they were not given justice there, they may appeal the case. That is, they may ask a higher court to review the way the District Court handled the case.

It would be impossible for a single court such as the Supreme Court to handle all the thousands of cases that are appealed each year. Congress realized this fact. As a result, it established courts called **Courts of Appeals.** These Courts of Appeals have appellate jurisdiction. That is, they review cases that are appealed to them from the District Courts.

There are 11 United States Courts of Appeals. Congress has divided the nation into ten large judicial districts known as **circuits.** The eleventh circuit is located in the District of Columbia. There is a Court of Appeals for each circuit. Each Court of Appeals has from 3 to 15 judges, and the senior judge serves as the chief judge. The judges of the Courts of Appeals are appointed for life, and their salary is $44,600 a year.

COURTS OF APPEALS REVIEW DECISIONS

Jury trials do not take place in the Courts of Appeals. When a case comes before a Court of Appeals, the judges review the evidence and make the decision. They examine the records of the District Court trial, and hear pleas by the lawyers for both sides. They call witnesses if needed, and carefully consider the legal rights of both sides. The judges do not determine whether the accused person is guilty or innocent. They are not holding another trial of the case. That is not their job. Their job is to determine if the person who appealed the case was granted the full legal rights during the trial.

At least three judges hear each case, and they reach their decision by a majority vote. If the Court of Appeals finds that justice was not done, it sends the case back to the District Court for a new trial. But if it agrees that justice was done, then it upholds the decision of the District Court.

The Courts of Appeals not only hear appeals from District Courts. They also hear cases appealed from the decisions of independent agencies that regulate commerce and industry. For instance, a railroad company that believes the fare rates fixed by the Interstate Commerce Commission are unfair can appeal to a Court of Appeals for a review of the Commission's decision. The findings of the Court of Appeals are usually final in such cases.

THE SUPREME COURT

The highest court in the land is the Supreme Court of the United States. The Supreme Court meets in Washington, D.C., and its decisions are final. There is no appeal from a Supreme Court decision.

The Supreme Court has the power to study and review any law passed by Congress. Before it may do so, however, someone must challenge the law and bring a case to court. After the case has passed through a District Court, and then a Court of Appeals, it may come before the Supreme Court. The Court itself decides whether or not it will hear a case. If it decides to hear the case, the Supreme Court may then decide whether a law is **constitutional** or **unconstitutional.** That is, it may rule whether a law passed by Congress goes beyond the powers granted to Congress by the Constitu-

Chief Justice Warren Burger of the Supreme Court of the United States is seated in the center in this recent picture of the nation's highest court.

tion. This power of the Supreme Court is called the power of **judicial review.** It allows the Supreme Court to check on the actions of Congress. The Supreme Court may also review and rule on the constitutionality of state laws.

The Supreme Court does more than just hear cases appealed from lower courts. It has original jurisdiction in all cases concerning ambassadors and ministers, and in most cases involving state governments. In cases in which the Supreme Court has original jurisdiction, the Court's decision is final.

JUSTICES OF THE SUPREME COURT

The size of the Supreme Court and the salaries of its **Justices,** or judges, are determined by Congress. There are nine Justices on the Supreme Court. The Chief Justice receives a yearly salary of $65,000, and the eight Associate Justices receive $63,000 each. Justices are appointed by the President and must be approved by the Senate. All justices are appointed for life, but they may be impeached for misconduct in office. If they are found guilty, they may be removed from office.

THE COURT OF CLAIMS

Congress also has set up a number of other federal courts to handle special types of cases. Cases involving property claims or contract suits against the government of the United States are heard in the Court of Claims. A Chief Judge and six Associate Judges hear such cases. When the Court of Claims hands down a decision against the federal government, the person bringing the suit is usually granted a sum of money. Congress then authorizes the payment of the claim.

THE CUSTOMS COURT

When an individual or a business firm brings certain goods from another country, import taxes, or tariffs, must be paid on them. People who are dissatisfied with the tax placed on their goods may take their cases to the Customs Court. The headquarters of this court is in New York City, but it hears cases in other large cities that are ports.

THE COURT OF CUSTOMS AND PATENT APPEALS

Cases appealed from the Customs Court go to the Court of Customs and Patent Appeals. Cases appealed from the actions of the Patent Office concerning inventions are also heard in this court.

TERRITORIAL COURTS

To bring justice to the people who live in the territorial possessions of the United States, Congress has established Territorial Courts. The people of the territories, as you will later see, possess most of the rights of United States citizens.

THE TAX COURT

Appeals concerning the payment of federal taxes are heard in the Tax Court. The Tax Court is an independent agency but has powers like those of a court. It hears cases in many different cities but its headquarters is in Washington, D.C.

CONSIDER AND DISCUSS

Identify. jurisdiction / District Courts / original jurisdiction / appellate jurisdiction / United States Marshal / subpoena / Federal Commissioner / United States Magistrates / United States District Attorney / Courts of Appeals / circuits / Supreme Court / constitutional / unconstitutional / judicial review / Justices / Court of Claims / Customs Court / Court of Customs and Patent Appeals / Territorial Courts / Tax Court

Review. 1. What is the purpose of the United States Courts of Appeals? 2. What original jurisdiction does the Supreme Court have? 3. How does the Supreme Court check on Congress? 4. If a New York resident breaks a federal law while visiting in Texas, in what district court will the case be tried?

Discuss. How does the Supreme Court fit into the system of checks and balances?

3 Our Federal Courts at Work

The First Congress of the United States, meeting in 1789, acted promptly to put the provisions of the Constitution into effect. They passed a **Judiciary Act** providing for a Supreme Court consisting of a Chief Justice and five Associate Justices. They also provided for 13 District Courts, and three Circuit Courts of Appeals. George Washington appointed John Jay as Chief Justice of the Supreme Court, and the work of the judicial branch of government began.

THE INFLUENCE OF JOHN MARSHALL

The early years in the history of the federal courts were spent in organizing, hearing cases, and taking care of the many details necessary to establish a new court system. Then, in 1801, President Adams appointed John Marshall as Chief Justice. In his 34 years as Chief Justice, John Marshall established the Supreme Court as a powerful

continued on page 105

CRIME CONTROL VS. INDIVIDUAL RIGHTS

WHAT DO YOU THINK?

How would you feel if the police entered and searched your home without any warning? What if you found out the police were listening in on all your phone conversations? What if you were arrested for a crime and kept in jail for months before you could defend yourself at a trial? Does this sound like a nightmare?

Suppose, now, that the police tapped the telephone of a suspected criminal. By this method, they learned about a big shipment of illegal drugs. Then they burst into the house and found a lot of drugs. They arrested the people in the house and kept them in jail until their trial. That way, the suspects could not go on selling drugs, or destroy evidence, or warn other criminals. Does this sound like good police work?

Crime is a serious and growing problem in the United States. More and more crimes are committed every year. What can be done to stop this trend? Will giving new powers to the police help to reduce crime? What price are we willing to pay for these new police powers?

In 1970, the Washington, D.C. Crime Act was passed. It gave police officers in Washington the right to enter a private home without knocking, or without identifying themselves or their purpose. In some cases, it allowed the police to tap telephones. And it allowed "preventive detention"—that is, holding accused persons who are "considered dangerous" in jail or some other place until their cases come to trial. Some people believed this law was a "model anticrime program that pointed the way for the entire nation." Others saw it as a "blueprint for a police state."

Critics of the D.C. Crime Act said that the price was much too high. This law, they said, destroyed some of our most basic rights as American citizens. It directly violated the Bill of Rights. How can we achieve law and order, they asked, if we undermine the Constitution itself? Can you see any conflicts between the police powers given by the D.C. Crime Act and the Bill of Rights?

The Fourth Amendment guarantees "the right of the people to be secure in their persons, houses, papers, and effects, against unreasonable searches and seizures." A search warrant can be issued only

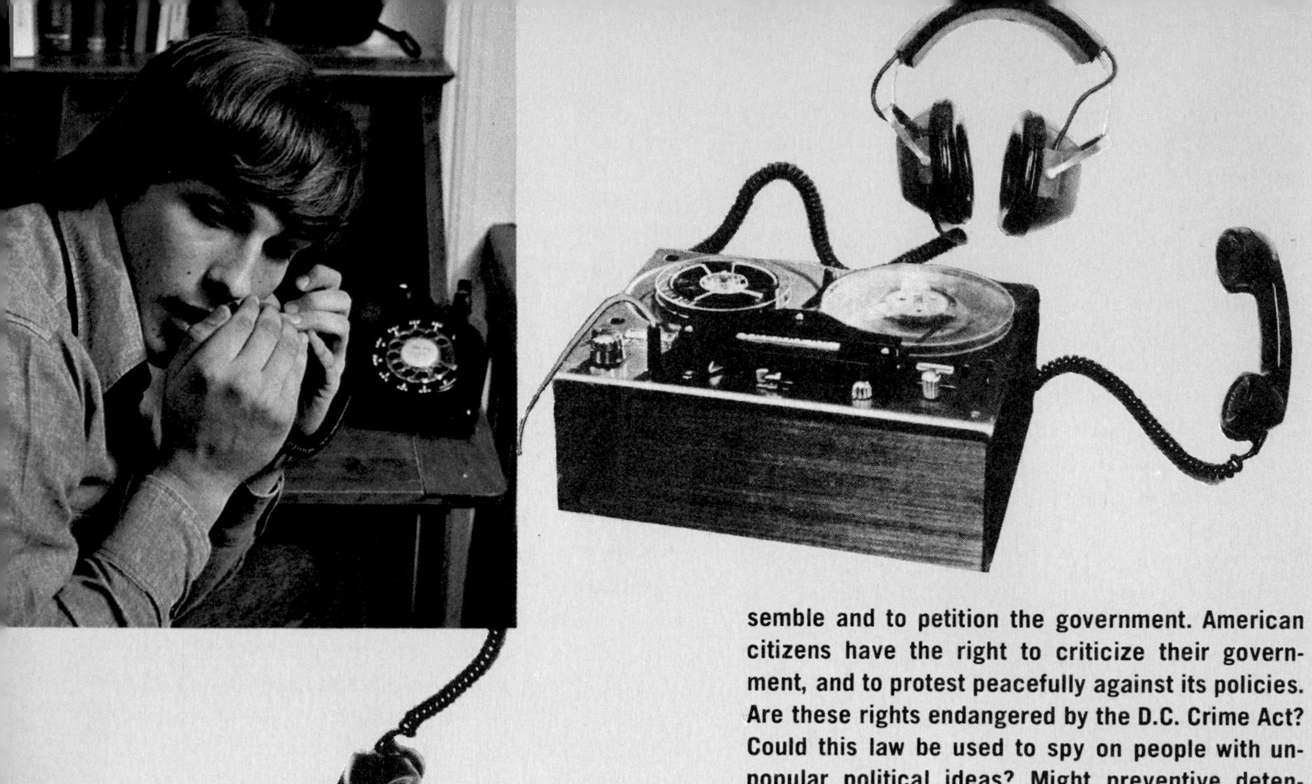

for a good reason. It should describe the place to be searched and the persons or things to be seized. Did the "no knock" right given by the D.C. Crime Act violate this right of privacy? Congress thought it did. In 1974 it changed the act. Since then police officers have had to obtain search warrants that identified the officers and stated the purpose of the search.

But what about the rest of the D.C. Crime Act? The Fifth Amendment guarantees that no one can "be deprived of life, liberty, or property, without due process of law." The Eighth Amendment provides for reasonable bail. Can people be kept in jail if they have not been found guilty in a court of law? In our system of justice, a person is considered innocent until proven guilty. Does "preventive detention" violate this principle?

The First Amendment guarantees freedom of speech and press. It guarantees the right to assemble and to petition the government. American citizens have the right to criticize their government, and to protest peacefully against its policies. Are these rights endangered by the D.C. Crime Act? Could this law be used to spy on people with unpopular political ideas? Might preventive detention be used to prevent people from expressing ideas considered "dangerous"?

Supporters of the D.C. Crime Act say that this law is aimed only at criminals. Law-abiding citizens, they say, have nothing to fear. What do you think? Might the police make mistakes? Can the police be trusted not to abuse their powers?

The writers of the Constitution were afraid of giving too much power to the government, including the police. They wanted to be sure that the rights of individuals were protected. Americans today are afraid of crime and violence. They look to the government to protect them. Does this mean that in order to make our communities safer we should give up some of our individual rights?

Many Americans believe that to weaken the Bill of Rights is to weaken our whole democratic way of life. They oppose laws like the D.C. Crime Act. Others say that the dangers of this law are greatly exaggerated. They believe that we must give the police a freer hand to deal with crime. What do you think? Is the D.C. Crime Act a good law? Or does this law threaten our rights too much? What additional information might you want before making a decision?

instrument for justice. In more than 500 decisions, John Marshall gave more power to the Supreme Court.

During his long term as Chief Justice, John Marshall established three basic principles of American law. In the famous case of **Marbury v. Madison,** John Marshall stated that the Supreme Court had the power to declare a law passed by Congress unconstitutional. This power was known as judicial review. The Court under Chief Justice Marshall also established the principle that laws passed by state legislatures could be set aside if they were against the Constitution. The third important principle was that the Supreme Court had the power to reverse the decisions of state courts. Over the years, the Supreme Court came to have the final power to decide what the Constitution meant. As Chief Justice Charles Evans Hughes once said, "We are under a constitution, but the Constitution is what the judges say it is."

CHECKING ON THE POWER OF THE SUPREME COURT

In these early years of our history, some Americans did not agree with the Supreme Court's decisions. Many of our nation's leaders felt that the Court was becoming too powerful. Thomas Jefferson was especially upset by the principle of judicial review. Jefferson said that Marshall made the Constitution "a mere thing of wax . . . which . . . [the Court] may twist into any form they please." Nevertheless, Jefferson could do nothing about the Supreme Court. In decision after decision, the Court interpreted the Constitution and broadened its meaning.

Was there nothing that could be done about the growing power of the Supreme Court? Was the Supreme Court really exceeding its powers? Let us take a closer look at what happens if the Supreme Court rules that a law passed by Congress is unconstitutional. As you know, this means that the law has no force. However, Congress may pass a new law that follows the Constitution and that the Supreme Court may uphold. In this way laws may be improved while the rights of people under the Constitution remain protected.

Another way to make a desired law constitutional is to change the Constitution. Let us see how this happens. In 1895, the Supreme Court declared that an income tax law passed by Congress was unconstitutional. They pointed out that the Constitution (Article 1, Section 9, Clause 4) states that direct taxes must be apportioned according to the population of each state. In other words, such taxes must fall evenly on all people. The income tax did not meet this Constitutional requirement, and was thus unconstitutional. However, in 1916, the states ratified the Sixteenth Amendment, which gave Congress the power to tax incomes. The income tax then became legal and constitutional.

THE SUPREME COURT CAN CHANGE ITS MIND

The debate over the Court's powers has been going on ever since Jefferson's time. Yet, some Americans forget that the Supreme Court has helped to make the Constitution a long-lived document. By interpreting the Constitution differently at different times, it has helped the Constitution to meet the demands of changing times. The Supreme Court is aware of changing social, political, and economic conditions. In reaching its decisions, it takes into consideration the state of mind of the people and the advancing ideas of justice for all.

Let us consider one example of the Court's changing attitudes to meet new needs. In the late 1800's, many southern states segregated their schools. That is, they set up separate schools for white students and black students. The states claimed that the schools were **"separate but equal."**

Many Americans claimed that segregated schools were unequal. They said that forcing students to attend separate, and therefore unequal, schools was a violation of the equal protection clause of the Fourteenth Amendment. This amendment provides:

> No state shall make or enforce any law which shall abridge [take away] the privileges or immunities [protection] of citizens of the United States; nor shall any state deprive any person of life, liberty, or property without due process of law; nor deny to any person within its jurisdiction the equal protection of the laws.

In 1896, the Supreme Court ruled, in the case of **Plessy v. Ferguson,** that providing separate but equal facilities for black Americans was not a violation of the Fourteenth Amendment. This decision became the legal support for segregation and the legal basis for "separate but equal" schools.

Then, in 1954, the Supreme Court heard the case of **Brown v. The Board of Education of Topeka.** In this case, the National Association for the Advancement of Colored People argued that segregated schools were not equal and therefore violated the Fourteenth Amendment, which guarantees equal protection. The Court considered the arguments on both sides. After almost six months of deliberation, Chief Justice Warren read the unanimous decision of the Supreme Court: Segregation in schools was unlawful and must be ended. Segregated schools were unequal, and therefore they violated the Fourteenth Amendment. The Court rules that schools should be desegregated "with all deliberate speed." The Supreme Court had reversed its earlier decision.

Federal troops sent by President Eisenhower escort black students into a high school in Little Rock, Arkansas, to carry out the Supreme Court order ending segregation in public schools.

THE PRESTIGE OF THE SUPREME COURT

Throughout its history, the prestige and dignity of the Supreme Court has grown. The Supreme Court justices, for the most part, have not become involved in politics and have not been influenced by favors or bribes. Most Americans believe the Court is an important part of our democratic system, for in most cases it has been the defender of the peoples' rights.

The decisions of the Supreme Court have not, however, been free of controversy. Some courts have seemed too liberal, and others, much too conservative. In the late 1930's, President Franklin D. Roosevelt attempted to change the nature of the Supreme Court by adding more judges to the Court. But the public outcry caused Roosevelt to drop his plan. Americans did not want to change the balance of power among the executive, legislative, and judicial branches set up in the Constitution. And they wanted the Court to remain free of political influence.

ENFORCING SUPREME COURT DECISIONS

Even though the debate over the Court's powers has continued throughout our history, it must be remembered that the Court's power is limited. The Court makes important decisions that affect American policy and American life. But it cannot enforce these decisions. The Court must depend on the executive branch to enforce its decisions. And the cooperation of the public is necessary if Supreme Court decisions are to be effective.

The desegregation of the schools is one example of the limits of Supreme Court power. Although the Supreme Court ruled against segregated schools in 1954, some American schools remain segregated. The Court's decision has not been completely realized because some Americans have refused to accept it.

On the other hand, the decisions of the Court often greatly influence American life. In recent years, decisions of the Supreme Court have made far-reaching changes in three areas of American life—voting, civil rights, and the rights of accused persons.

The Supreme Court made a number of decisions in the 1960's which greatly strengthened the rights of accused persons. For the most part, these decisions applied to the time immediately following a person's arrest. In the famous 1966 case of **Miranda v. Arizona,** the Supreme Court declared that the police must inform suspects of their rights before they may question them. They must inform them that they have the right to remain silent, that anything they say may be used against them, and that they have the right to have a lawyer present when they are questioned. If they are too poor to afford a lawyer, a lawyer will be appointed.

The Supreme Court also made several important decisions in the area of voting and representation in state legislatures and the House of Representatives. The "one man, one vote" decision was the most far-reaching of these rulings. According to this decision, election districts for choosing representatives to the Congress and state legislatures must be divided by population as equally as possible. This means that every citizen's vote must be equal in value and will result in genuinely representative government at both state and federal levels.

The third area in which the Supreme Court's rulings have had important results is in civil rights and civil liberties. The 1954 Brown decision against segregated schools has not completely ended segregation in American schools or American life. But the Court's decision struck a blow against segregation in America by suggesting that all laws that set up segregation were unconstitutional. The civil rights movement and civil rights legislation of the 1960's followed. Laws approving segregation were removed one by one. Laws guaranteeing the precious

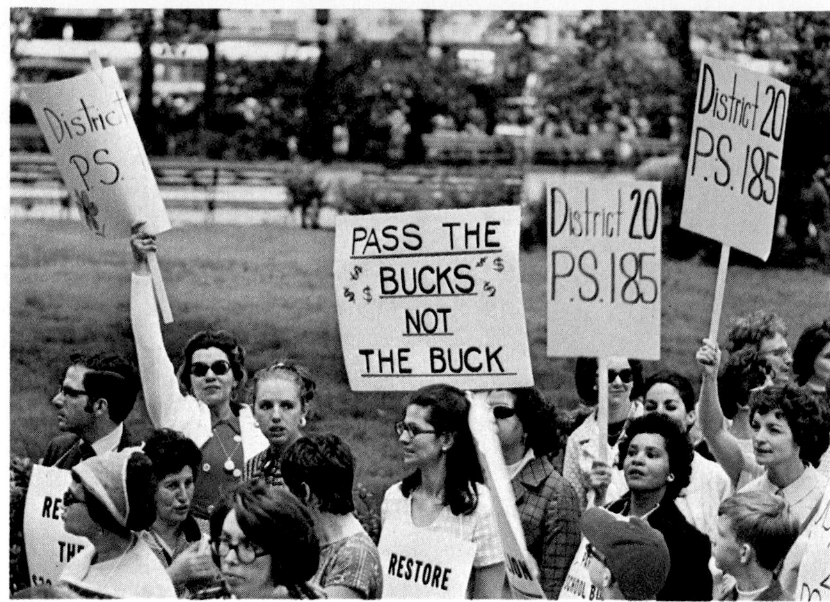

In recent years, some Supreme Court rulings have protected the rights of Americans to protest peacefully. These Americans are demanding more funds for education.

right of voting to black Americans were passed. By its action, the Court provided leadership in showing that the rights guaranteed in the Constitution applied to all Americans.

Recent Court rulings have extended the rights and freedoms, or civil liberties, of Americans. The Court has extended many freedoms, especially the meaning of freedom of speech. Some rulings have protected the rights of Americans to protest peacefully against actions of the government.

A CASE TO CONSIDER

In a 1969 decision, the Supreme Court upheld the right of school children to wear black arm bands to school to protest against the Vietnam War. The Court ruled that the five students involved in the case, ranging from 8 to 15 years of age, had the right to demonstrate peacefully during school hours. The Court said, "It can hardly be argued that either students or teachers shed [leave] their constitutional rights to freedom of speech or expression at the schoolhouse gate." Justice Fortas, speaking for the majority in the 7 to 2 decision, stressed the idea the Court was protecting peaceful protest that must not disrupt classroom activities.

Speaking for the minority—the two justices who did not vote in favor of the decision—Justice Black stated that the decision in this case opened up "a new revolutionary era of permissiveness . . . [when] students . . . will be ready, able and willing to defy their teachers on practically all orders."

There have been differences of opinion over the Supreme Court decisions in the areas of voting, civil rights, and the rights of the accused persons. These differences have been especially strong regarding the rights of accused persons and civil liberties. Some Americans have favored these decisions as further protection for the rights of Americans. Others have felt that the Supreme Court has gone too far. Some have felt that the Court's decisions protected criminals. Yet, others have said that they guaranteed justice to all Americans. What is the proper balance between the rights of the individual and the rights of society as a whole? This is a question we must each answer for ourselves.

CONSIDER AND DISCUSS

Identify. Judiciary Act / *Marbury v. Madison* / "separate but equal" / *Plessy v. Ferguson* / *Brown v. The Board of Education of Topeka* / *Miranda v. Arizona*

Review. 1. What three basic principles of American law were established by the decisions of Chief Justice John Marshall? 2. In what two ways can Congress make a law constitutional after the Supreme Court has declared the law unconstitutional? 3. Why did the Supreme Court change its decision in the case of *Brown v. The Board of Education of Topeka?* 4. What rights of the accused were established by the Miranda decision?

Discuss. How can the Supreme Court's decisions influence American life? Give examples to prove your point.

CHAPTER

Summary

The federal courts make up the judicial branch of our federal government. The job of these courts is to judge laws and to bring to trial those accused of breaking laws.

In the United States, we believe in the idea of government by law. But these laws must be enforced fairly. The federal courts not only enforce the laws, but also make sure that every accused person enjoys the Constitution's guarantees of a fair trial.

The Constitution gives the federal courts jurisdiction, or authority, to hold trials in a wide variety of cases and to judge these cases. Judges conduct trials in all the federal courts. Federal District Courts are the only federal courts in which juries are used.

In trials before federal District Courts, accused persons have the right to the judgment of their fellow citizens. Under certain conditions, convicted persons may take their cases next to the Court of Appeals, and perhaps even to the Supreme Court.

The Supreme Court is the highest court in the land. It hears appeals from lower courts, and its decisions are final. The Supreme Court also has the power of judicial review. That is, it hears cases brought to test laws and decides whether such laws are constitutional.

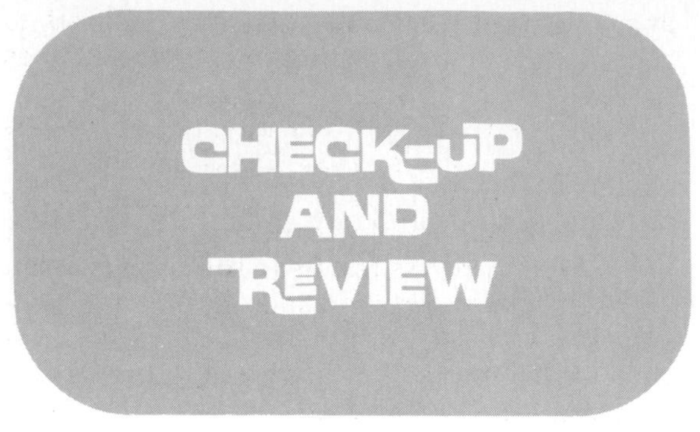

VOCABULARY

In the ten sentences listed below, the words in *italics* are *not* used correctly. They make each of the statements false. On a separate piece of paper, correct the sentences by putting in the words that make each statement true.

1. When a law is passed by a legislature, it is called *common law.*
2. The *grand jury* sits at the court trial of a case and hands down the verdict.
3. The federal *Courts of Appeals* have original jurisdiction in cases affecting ambassadors, ministers, and consuls.
4. The *Supreme Court* is the only federal court in which jury trials are held.
5. Cases involving claims against the government of the United States are tried in the *Customs Court.*
6. *Federal Courts* have jurisdiction when a citizen of a foreign nation sues a state of the United States.
7. The power of the Supreme Court to decide whether or not a law passed by Congress is unconstitutional is called the power of *original jurisdiction.*
8. A sum of money that has been deposited with the court to guarantee that an accused person will be in court at the time of his trial is called a *writ of habeas corpus.*
9. The Supreme Court of the United States is made up of one Chief Justice and *nine* Associate Justices.
10. Crimes committed aboard American ships at sea are tried by *state courts.*

CHECK-UP

Without looking at your text or your notes, try to answer the following questions. Then check with the text or your notes to see if your answers are correct.

1. What is the difference between statutory law and common law?
2. What are six rights that guarantee a person a fair trial?
3. Who sits on a trial jury? How are they selected?
4. What is the difference between "bail" and a "fine"?
5. What is meant by the term "appellate jurisdiction"?
6. What was the significance of the case of *Miranda v. Arizona?*
7. In what two ways can Congress make an unconstitutional law constitutional?
8. How does each of the following serve the District Court: United States Marshal, Federal Commissioner, United States District Attorney, petit jury?
9. In what court would you appeal a decision about your federal income tax?
10. Name three types of cases in which federal courts have original jurisdiction.

CITIZENSHIP AND YOU

The courts of the United States are one of the most important parts of our government. They guard your right to "equal justice under law." You and your classmates can learn more about them by participating in a variety of activities dealing with the courts and their functions.

1. Class Projects

Visit a federal court in your district. Arrangements for such visits are usually made by writing to the presiding judge.

Choose a court case that has been in the news media recently. Discuss the main points of the case and any problems the court lawyers or prosecutors may be having.

Invite a local lawyer, judge, or court official to visit your class and answer questions about court procedure.

2. Group or Committee Projects

A committee may prepare reports on "Famous Jurists You Should Know." Include such people as John Marshall, Roger Taney, Oliver Wendell Holmes, Felix Frankfurter, Charles Evans Hughes, William Howard Taft, Earl Warren, and others. The reports on these people may be made orally, presented in a series of picture stories, or distributed to the class members in the form of a mimeographed booklet.

A group may prepare a mock trial in which students play the roles of judge, lawyers, witnesses, and jury. Rehearsals for the trial will help to make it more real and meaningful.

3. Individual Projects

For a better understanding of the work of the Supreme Court, each student should read at least one Supreme Court decision. Copies of leading decisions will be found in I. Starr, L. Todd, and M. Curti (eds.), *Living American Documents* (Harcourt Brace Jovanovich), or R. Cushman (ed.), *Leading Constitutional Decisions* (Prentice-Hall).

Draw a map of the United States showing the location of the 11 Courts of Appeals circuits. Mark your own circuit in a special way to make it stand out.

CIVICS SKILLS

WEIGHING THE EVIDENCE

People often see things in different ways. How they view events or interpret facts is based on their attitudes. "There are two sides to every question" is an old warning against listening to only one side or point of view. Actually, there are often three or more sides to important issues. To form your own opinion, you must seek out all of the facts, opinions, and expert advice that you can find. Then the evidence must be weighed and a tentative evaluation reached, subject to change if more or different information becomes available.

In this text you will find a number of issues that face Americans today. These are important issues that will probably remain unsolved for some time. You will find opposing points of view on each of these issues. Read the points of view and consider each person's arguments. With which view do you most agree? Perhaps you disagree with both points of view and have still a third argument to present.

Come to class prepared to make a strong case for your conclusion. Listen to your classmates. Do their ideas on the subject differ from yours? Why? Have they some facts that you do not have? As the discussion proceeds, note how a majority of the class members are thinking. Does their thinking reflect something in their background or in the kinds of homes and communities from which they come? Is the majority always right?

Get into the habit of relating what you are reading, hearing, and observing to what you already know. How does the issue relate to what you have learned about government, the Constitution, and rights? Also be aware that some arguments may not be valid because all of the facts are not available. If so, try to get more facts. The more background you have, the more valid your conclusions will be.

PRACTICING YOUR CIVICS SKILLS

In "A Case to Consider" on page 108, you read about a Supreme Court decision that affected students who protested against the Vietnam War by wearing black arm bands to school. What were the main arguments the Court gave for and against the decision? Which side would you have voted for if you had been a member of the Court? What further evidence do you think you would need to reach a fair decision?

Now suppose that the students were carrying large banners to class in addition to wearing black arm bands. Would that fact change your decision? Why or why not?

CHAPTER
Introduction

> We, the people of the United States, in order to form a more perfect Union, establish justice, insure domestic tranquility [peace and safety], provide for the common defense, promote the general welfare, and secure the blessings of liberty to ourselves and our posterity [future generations] do ordain [order] and establish this CONSTITUTION for the United States of America.
>
> —Preamble to the Constitution of the United States

In the first five chapters of this book, you have studied about the people of the United States and the government under which they live. With this background of understanding, we are now ready to consider how the three branches of our federal government work together to meet the needs of the American people. Let us see what kinds of services the federal government provides.

Our national government was established in order to carry out the purposes stated in the Preamble of the Constitution. In this chapter you will learn how the federal government carries out these purposes:

1. To Form a More Perfect Union
2. To Establish Justice and Insure Domestic Tranquility
3. To Provide for the Common Defense
4. To Promote the General Welfare
5. To Secure the Blessings of Liberty

CHAPTER

6

The Federal Government Serves Its Citizens

1 To Form a More Perfect Union

In our nation's early years, the federal government had to face the problem of bringing the people of the 13 separate states together into a united nation. This seemed almost an impossible task. Travel between the states was difficult. It also took a long time because the few roads were only poor dirt roads that became muddy when it rained. Mail delivery was very slow. For example, it took weeks for a letter to get from Massachusetts to Georgia. Communication was difficult because of the many isolated settlements. How could such a scattered population be united under one central government?

THE FEDERAL GOVERNMENT HELPS UNITE THE STATES

From the beginning, the federal government realized that transportation facilities were extremely important to the new nation. American leaders knew that good roads and other forms of transportation were a basis of a united country. Transportation was needed to develop the nation and its resources, and it was necessary for the growth of agriculture and industry. American leaders also knew that a transportation system was needed for our defense, to enforce the nation's laws, and to collect taxes. As a result, the federal government soon became involved in helping to build roads and canals. In 1816, a new economic plan called the "American System" was passed by Congress. An important part of this program was the building of roads to tie together the industrial Northeast and the farm lands of the South and West.

As the years passed, the nation grew. From 13 states along the Atlantic seacoast, it stretched across the American continent to the Pacific Ocean. State after state was added. As the nation grew in land size and population, the federal government continued to provide a good transportation system. Often, the federal government and state governments worked together to build roads and canals.

The building of a good transportation system helped the nation to grow westward to the Pacific Coast. Roads, canals, railways, and steamboats helped make it possible for people in different parts of the nation to exchange products and ideas. They also made it possible for Americans to work together to build our nation.

HIGHWAY SYSTEMS HELP UNITE US

Today, our states are bound together by a modern highway system. These superhighways aid American business and commerce. They provide an efficient and inexpensive method of transporting raw materials and manufactured goods across the nation. They also help Americans to obtain many kinds of products. People can travel across our vast nation easily and quickly. Many of these roads also make it possible for Americans to live in the suburbs and drive to work in the cities.

The federal government has helped the states to build nearly 1.6 million kilometers (1 million miles) of roads. Among them is the national system of interstate highways which now cover 68,000 kilometers (42,500 miles). In addition, rural roads and city streets, built and paid for by state and local governments, total over 5.6 million kilometers (3.5 million miles). All of these roads help tie the nation together and aid in national defense.

THE FEDERAL GOVERNMENT AIDS OTHER TRANSPORTATION

From the time of the first railroads, the United States government has helped the railroad companies by **granting,** or giving, them land and money. The government decided to help the railroad companies because railroads were an important way of joining the nation together. Besides land and money, the government also gave the railroads contracts to carry the mail. The money paid to the railroads for this service helped to keep the railroads running.

In more recent times, the nation's railroads have had pressing money problems. Many railroads are in debt. And Congress is seeking ways to help make the railroads a profitable business once again.

Pictured below is an early Telstar communications satellite. These satellites have made international television possible.

The federal government has also aided the airline industry. Airlines have been granted mail contracts. In addition, the United States has helped with cash grants to help build modern airports. Huge sums have been granted to the aircraft industry to develop faster and larger planes for military and commercial use.

The movement of people and goods on the high seas is also aided by the government. **Subsidies,** or money grants, have been made to help build ships and port facilities and to keep the ships in operation. America's Corps of Engineers also aids water transportation in the United States by helping to improve waterways, harbors, and other facilities. Even with all this help, our merchant marine and passenger liners have found it difficult to compete with foreign ships. The higher wages paid to American sailors, and other costs, continue to make competition difficult.

In addition to aiding transportation, the federal government, through certain independent agencies, has helped to regulate the movement of goods and people:

The **Interstate Commerce Commission** helps to encourage efficient transportation by regulating rates and taking steps to improve railroad, truck, and bus service.

Another independent federal agency, the **Civil Aeronautics Board,** regulates the rates and services of airlines. Safety precautions are also enforced.

The **Federal Maritime Commission** of the Department of Commerce carries out Congressional provisions to aid marine interests.

The **Federal Highway Administration,** which is in the Department of Transportation, supervises the building and upkeep of federal highways and promotes highway safety.

"TO ESTABLISH POST OFFICES"

When the delegates wrote the Constitution, they realized that mail delivery was very important. Therefore, the Constitution gave Congress the power "to establish Post Offices and Post Roads." Throughout our nation's history, the postal service has expanded. Today, over 680,000 employees are engaged in delivering all the regular mail, airmail, special delivery letters, registered mail, and parcel post packages throughout the United States. Post offices also sell money orders and stamps. In addition, the postal service sees to it that the mails are not used for unlawful purposes.

Until 1970, the Post Office Department was one of the executive departments of our government. Its head was a member of the President's Cabinet. However, over the years, the department lost more and more money. The mails were slow, and there was much criticism of the postal services. As a result, Congress decided that the Post Office Department should become an independent government agency and be run on a businesslike basis. Congress set up the new independent agency in 1970.

This independent agency is called the **United States Postal Service.** Its aim is to make the mail service self-supporting and more efficient. But there are many problems involved in providing good mail service for 220 million people. The new Postal Service has not yet been able to insure prompt service. And it is still losing money.

HELPING PEOPLE TO COMMUNICATE

In addition to the mail, there are a number of ways in which Americans keep in touch with each other. Telephone, telegraph, radio stations, and television networks help to make up a vast communication system used by Americans. Congress has given the **Federal Communications Commission** the power to regulate this communication system in the public interest. The use of the air waves for radio and television broadcasts is organized to prevent conflict and confusion. Telephone and telegraph rates are subject to public accounting and control.

OTHER MEANS OF COMMUNICATION

A unified nation where all people may live in peace and harmony has been a goal of Americans ever since the beginning of our nation. Americans have relied on their government to provide services that help in achieving this goal. The government has helped provide transportation and communication facilities to join the nation together. In addition, a uniform currency, standards for banks, and banking procedures have helped to unify the nation. Later, a system of free education also helped to unite Americans. Today, the United States is a nation of diverse people who live together sharing a common heritage, a common language, and a sense of national unity and pride.

CONSIDER AND DISCUSS

Identify. grant / subsidies / Interstate Commerce Commission / Civil Aeronautics Board / Federal Maritime Commission / Federal Highway Administration / United States Postal Service / Federal Communications Commission

Review. 1. Why has the federal government set up a system of interstate highways? 2. What methods has Congress used to aid railroads, airlines, and shipping? 3. Why was the Post Office Department changed to an independent agency?

Discuss. In what ways can transportation and communication systems help to form "a more perfect union"?

2 To Establish Justice and Insure Domestic Tranquility

Under the Constitution, the power to regulate the conduct of citizens in the interest of their safety and well-being is shared by the state and federal governments. This power to regulate certain activities of the people is called **police power.** In the United States, most of the police power is exercised by our state and local governments. The federal government, however, does its share in helping to protect the lives and property of Americans.

THE FEDERAL GOVERNMENT'S POLICE POWER

This police power makes it possible for the federal government to carry out one of the purposes of the Preamble to the Constitution—"to insure domestic tranquility," or to secure the peace and safety of all our citizens. Some Americans fear the possibility of too much police power in the hands of the federal government. They fear that under certain conditions our nation might become a "police state" in which all actions of the people would be controlled by the federal government. The government would then be all powerful, and the liberties of the American people would be destroyed. We should keep such warnings in mind. But most Americans agree that the federal government usually has used the federal police power wisely to carry out the laws and protect the safety of Americans.

Let us look at some of the law enforcement groups and see how they work to protect law and order:

The **Federal Bureau of Investigation (FBI)** is the best known of the federal government's law enforcement agencies. The FBI is an agency of the Department of Justice. Its chief task is to investigate crimes that break federal laws. FBI agents are stationed throughout the nation, and they investigate such crimes as bank robberies, kidnapping, and spying. The FBI works closely with state and local police forces when criminals cross state borders. In the 1970's, investigations showed that the FBI had sometimes used unlawful methods, such as wiretapping and break-ins, to gain evidence. As a result, in 1976, the FBI was reorganized.

The **United States Secret Service** is a division of the Treasury Department. It performs two important services. Secret Service agents guard the life and security of the President, Vice-President, and other high officials. They also protect leaders of other nations who visit the United States. The Secret Service also arrests suspected counterfeiters—that is, people who make or distribute fake American coins or paper money.

The **United States Coast Guard** is responsible for protecting the safety of our nation's coastal waters. The Coast Guard keeps a constant lookout for all those who try to **smuggle** goods, that is, to bring products into the country in any unlawful way. The Coast Guard also keeps a lookout for icebergs and other dangers to shipping, and it helps ships in distress. The Coast Guard is part of the Transportation Department in peacetime, but it is part of the Navy in time of war.

OTHER FEDERAL POLICE AGENCIES

The **Drug Enforcement Administration** is a division of the Justice Department. It helps to enforce laws concerning the sale and purchase of habit-forming drugs. The Administration tries to make sure that the drugs will be used only for medicinal purposes.

The **United States Customs Service** is another division of the Treasury Department. It is familiar to most Americans who have left the country to travel abroad. This Service inspects all goods that travelers bring back from foreign countries. It prevents the importation of illegal goods. It also collects tariffs, or import duties, on goods brought in.

The **Immigration and Naturalization Service** of the Department of Justice makes sure that immigration laws are enforced fairly. The service also patrols our nation's borders to prevent persons from illegally entering the United States.

REGULATORY AGENCIES PROTECT AMERICANS

You have already read how the Interstate Commerce Commission and the Federal Communications Commission help protect our citizens by enforcing laws relating to interstate transportation and communications. These commissions and other independent agencies that enforce the laws passed by Congress are called **regulatory agencies.** There are several other regulatory agencies in the federal government.

The **National Labor Relations Board (NLRB)** is an important federal regulatory agency. When disputes arise between workers and their employers, the National Labor Relations Board may step in and require that the two groups sit down and settle their differences. The Board also can act to end certain practices by unions or management. In either activity, this agency tries to protect the public's interest as well as the rights of labor and management.

The **Federal Trade Commission (FTC)** acts to prevent unfair practices by business firms. It helps to protect Americans against false advertising and other dishonest practices.

The **Civil Aeronautics Board (CAB)** regulates America's commercial air transportation. It assigns routes to airlines and supervises rates and services. It also sets the rate the Postal Service pays for the carrying of mail by air.

The **Securities and Exchange Commission (SEC)** helps to enforce laws regulating the sales of stocks and bonds. In this way, it helps protect Americans when they invest their money in stocks and bonds.

THE USE OF FEDERAL TROOPS

From time to time in our history, federal troops have been sent into states to enforce the law. George Washington used soldiers to put down the "Whisky Rebellion" and force those who made whisky to pay the whisky tax. In more recent times, President

The President can send federal troops to help in an area that has been struck by a natural disaster. These troops are unloading food for hurricane victims in Mississippi.

Eisenhower sent federal troops to escort black students into a formerly all white high school in Little Rock, Arkansas. And President Kennedy sent troops to the states of Mississippi and Alabama to make sure that black students were allowed to attend the Universities of Mississippi and Alabama. President Johnson used troops to restore order in a number of cities where riots occurred in the 1960's.

When federal troops are needed to help restore order in a state, **martial law** may be declared. Under martial law, the rights and freedoms of the people may be restricted. A **curfew** is often put into effect, and no one is allowed on the streets after a certain hour. The government of the area is taken over by the military authorities until the end of the emergency.

FEDERAL AID IN EMERGENCIES

Federal troops may also be called out to aid an area which has suffered a natural disaster such as fire, earthquake, or hurricane. The troops help to rescue people, clear the area of debris, and assist the local authorities in any way possible.

The federal government also provides financial aid to areas struck by a natural disaster. The President may declare such a place a disaster area, and then federal funds may be sent in to help clear and rebuild the damaged areas.

Federal funds are also used to aid the unemployed, to furnish food for the hungry, and to set up programs to improve economic and social conditions. This kind of aid is offered to areas in need when industry has moved away, crops have failed, or for some other economic reason. Congress and the American people believe that such aid is necessary to establish justice and insure domestic tranquility.

CONSIDER AND DISCUSS

Identify. police power / FBI / Secret Service / Coast Guard / smuggle / Drug Enforcement Administration / Customs Service / Immigration and Naturalization Service / regulatory agencies / NLRB / FTC / CAB / SEC / martial law / curfew

Review. 1. In what kinds of cases do the federal law enforcement officers make arrests? 2. Name four regulatory agencies in the federal government, and tell how each serves American citizens.

Discuss. Do you think the federal government has always used its police power wisely to protect American citizens?

3 To Provide for the Common Defense

Until all people have learned to live in peace, the United States will need to be able to defend itself. In the mid-1970's, our nation had over 2 million people under arms. The annual military costs of the United States averaged over $90 billion. About 26 cents out of every dollar spent by the federal government went to provide for our national defense.

WHAT ARE OUR DEFENSE NEEDS?

Today, many Americans believe our nation needs to keep its defenses strong. They point to struggles taking place in various parts of the world as threats to our security. Many Americans believe we must have strong defenses to offset the growing power of such Communist nations as the Soviet Union and China. These Americans believe that the best way to prevent war is to keep our nation always prepared for war.

In recent years, however, some Americans have felt that we were spending too much money on building weapons. These Americans felt our nation's defenses were strong enough and that we should spend less money on weapons.

ORGANIZING OUR NATION'S DEFENSES

The President of the United States is responsible for defending our nation, and he is the head of America's military organization. The Constitution provides that the President "shall be **Commander-in-Chief** of the Army and Navy of the United States."

Congress has established the Department of Defense to assist the President in carrying out the duties in providing for the nation's defense. The head of this department, the Secretary of Defense, is a member of the Cabinet and advises the President on all matters of defense. Serving under the Secretary of Defense are the Secretaries of the Army, Navy, and Air Force. Acting on the advice of these officials and others, the President makes recommendations to Congress concerning our nation's security.

Congress itself has a number of important defense powers. Chief among these is the power to declare war. As representatives of the people of the United States, the members of Congress alone have the power to declare war against another nation. Congress also has the responsibility "to raise and support armies" and "to provide and maintain [support] a navy." Our nation's lawmakers must decide how large our armed forces are to be. They also must vote funds to buy the weapons and other kinds of equipment our military forces need. Today, defense spending for a single year is greater than all the money spent by our federal government during the first hundred years of its existence.

PLANNING FOR THE NATION'S DEFENSE

To see that the billions of defense dollars are put to the best possible use, Congress has established several defense agencies. The President, who must supervise the entire defense program, appoints those who head the defense agencies. These agencies give valuable advice to the President.

continued on page 123

Our National Priorities

WHAT Do YOU THiNK?

The United States is one of the richest countries in the world. Even so, our resources are limited and our country still has some difficult problems to solve. More than 26 million Americans live in poverty. The crime rate is rising rapidly. The problems of pollution plague us. Many large cities are in trouble. And many Americans receive poor health care. Is something wrong? Are we really using our national resources in the wisest possible way? Or do we need to change some of our national priorities?

Priorities are the choices we make in tackling our problems. Which of our national needs are really the most important? Which problems should we try to solve first? These priorities are usually measured in terms of money. How much of our tax money should we spend on exploring outer space? on cleaning up polluted rivers? on providing jobs for the unemployed? on building up our armed forces? on finding a cure for cancer? Should we spend more money in the future on some of these things? Can we spend less money on others?

The chart at the right shows how our tax money is actually spent. What priorities does this graph show? Do you agree with our present priorities? Or should we spend more money on some things and less money on others?

Here are some Americans' ideas on which programs should be cut back. Some Americans believe that we should reduce military spending. They point to existing stockpiles of nuclear bombs, missiles, planes, and guns. Why, they ask, do we need to keep spending such huge amounts of money on more weapons? Also, they say, too much money is wasted on faulty weapons, unfulfilled contracts, and general inefficiency. Finally, they argue, the most serious threats to our nation's future are not military. They are poverty, pollution, and many other problems right here at home.

What do you think of these arguments? Is too much of our tax money going to the military? Would our national defenses be weakened by a cut in military spending? Do you need to look at how the money in the military budget is divided before you can make up your mind? How much goes to salaries? to weapons development? to other areas?

Other, smaller programs have also been suggested as areas where budget cuts could be made. Some people have been critical of the space program, for example. They feel we have spent too much money on moon landings and probes of Mars. Do you think the space program should be given a lower priority? What government programs would you cut back to provide money for new priorities?

What do you think should be our highest national priorities? How should we divide up the money collected in taxes in the future?

Some people believe that our first concern must be with the environment. If we have no clean air to breathe or water to drink, nothing else will matter. We must work to preserve the natural wealth and beauty of America for ourselves and our children. Do you think the federal government ought to spend more money on these problems?

Another problem that affects us all is health. Some people believe that good health care ought to be a right of all Americans, rich or poor. Do you think the government ought to provide some sort of health insurance for all citizens? Certain diseases, especially cancer, require a great deal of research

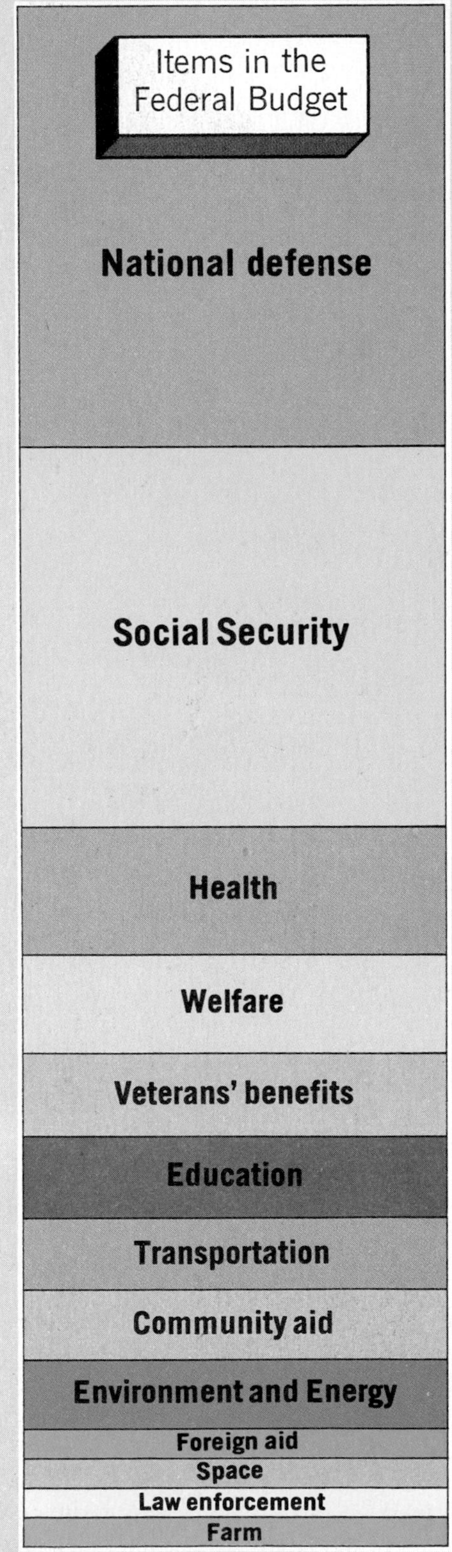

Items in the Federal Budget

National defense

Social Security

Health

Welfare

Veterans' benefits

Education

Transportation

Community aid

Environment and Energy

Foreign aid

Space

Law enforcement

Farm

if cures are to be found. Do you think tax money should be used for this kind of research?

Some people say that in a country as rich as ours, poverty can be eliminated. The federal government, they suggest, could guarantee a minimum income for all Americans. This would stimulate the economy as a whole, give children a better start in life, and possibly reduce crime. What do you think of this idea? Should we give a higher priority to eliminating poverty?

Another serious problem involves the services that are provided by local government. These important services include police and fire protection and public schools. They may also include garbage collection, public transportation, snow removal, and many other services. Local governments are finding it difficult to provide all these services with local property taxes. Do you think the federal government should use some of its tax money to help support local governments?

If you could write a budget for the nation, what would you choose as our national priorities? Keep this question in mind as you read more about our country and its problems. See if your own priorities are changed by new information.

THE NATIONAL SECURITY COUNCIL

A great deal of the President's advice on foreign policy and military matters comes from the **National Security Council.** This top-ranking group makes the plans for the defense of our nation. The members of the National Security Council are the President, the Vice-President, the Secretary of State, and the Secretary of Defense. Note that all these members are civilians. In this way, our national defense policy is not in the hands of the military. This acts as a check on the power of the military in the United States.

THE JOINT CHIEFS OF STAFF

The members of the National Security Council depend upon the **Joint Chiefs of Staff** for information about military matters. The Joint Chiefs of Staff consist of the Army Chief of Staff, the Chief of Naval Operations, the Air Force Chief of Staff, and the Commandant of the Marine Corps. One of these officers is appointed as Chairman of the Joint Chiefs of Staff by the President. The Joint Chiefs are the principal military advisers to the President and the Secretary of Defense, as well as to the National Security Council. They watch over the organization of America's armed forces and plan the wisest use of our military strength in case of war.

THE CENTRAL INTELLIGENCE AGENCY

The National Security Council receives information from the **Central Intelligence Agency (CIA).** The purpose of the CIA is to gather information about the military and political activities of foreign nations. In recent years, this agency has been criticized for interfering in the governments of other nations and for acting independently of Congress and the President. It has also carried out activities within the United States, which it does not have the authority to do. As a result, in 1976, Congress took greater control over the CIA.

TRAINING OUR MILITARY LEADERS

To train officers for the armed forces, Congress has set up four academies, or colleges. Army officers, you recall, attend the United States Military Academy at West Point, New York. The United States Naval Academy is located at Annapolis, Maryland. The Air Force Academy is at Colorado Springs, Colorado, and the Coast Guard Academy is at New London, Connecticut.

Candidates for the various academies must be between 17 and 22 years of age. They must be unmarried and of good character. Candidates are nominated by the Representative from their district or by one of the Senators from their state. Usually four candidates are named for each vacancy or opening. All candidates must have good high school records. They must also pass a series of scholastic and physical tests. The successful candidate receives a free four-year college education leading to a Bachelor of Science degree and, upon graduation, becomes an officer in one of the services.

In 1976, women were admitted into all the service academies on an equal basis with men. When they graduated, they were eligible to serve as officers in the armed forces.

SERVING IN THE ARMED FORCES

Throughout most of our history, the armed forces have depended upon volunteers. The first large-scale compulsory military service system, or **draft,** was used in 1917. Almost 3 million men were drafted under this first **Selective Service Act** to fight in World War I. American men were drafted again in 1940 under the first peacetime draft in American history. And most of the men who fought in World War II were drafted. Because of the tensions that developed after World War II, the Selective Service Act of 1948 was passed. This draft law remained in operation until a new draft law was passed in 1967. Under the draft regulations of the early

1970's, each male citizen of the United States had to register, or sign up, for military service. He had to register at his local draft board within five days of his eighteenth birthday. Draftees were called into service by a yearly **lottery**—a chance selection of birth dates. Young men were called into service in the order that their birth dates were chosen. Each young man could be called only during the one year in which he was 19.

THE DRAFT—PRO AND CON

In the 1960's, the draft became an important issue in the United States. Many Americans wondered if the draft should be kept, changed, or done away with.

Those who favored the draft agreed that no system of selective service could be completely fair. But they said that the draft was a good way to meet the needs of the armed forces. They argued that the civilian soldier always had been the backbone of our fighting forces. And they said the draft built patriotism, provided career training, and showed the nation's will to defend itself.

Americans who were against the draft system said that it promoted militarism, and took away people's right to plan their lives. They claimed that volunteers made better soldiers. Critics also said that the draft was unfair and wasteful because only a few of the many millions of people who registered were ever drafted.

When American involvement in the Vietnam War ended in 1973, the draft ended. America switched to an **all-volunteer army.**

The *U.S.S. Constellation,* pictured here, is one of America's 15 attack aircraft carriers. It is armed with guided missiles, and can carry 85 planes on its deck.

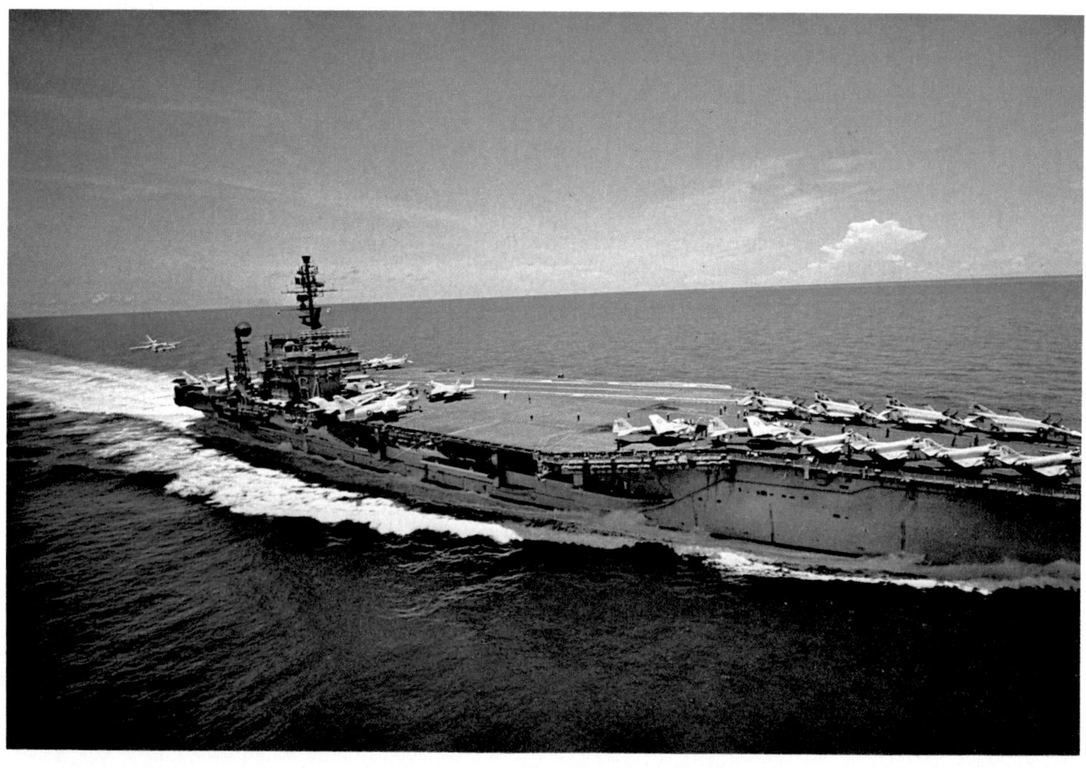

THE ALL-VOLUNTEER ARMY

By the mid-1970's, the armed forces of the United States had been organized on an all-volunteer basis. The volunteer armed forces had more than 2 million people. Of these, about 100,000 were women. The emphasis was on efficiency and readiness to do whatever military job needed to be done.

To attract young people with the right qualifications, the armed forces offered higher pay and good benefits. For example, the salary for a private or a seaman in the late 1970's was nearly $400 a month. After four months of service, they were eligible to receive a pay increase. Each member of the armed forces gets 30 days paid vacation each year. In addition, there are clothing allowances, medical and dental care, and cost-of-living allowances for married persons. And qualified men and women may gain college credits, attend Officers' Candidate School, or try for an appointment to a service academy.

Because of the all-volunteer service, the armed forces emphasize education and training in job skills that can be used when a person leaves the armed forces. For those who decide to make the military their career, there are bonuses of up to $2,000 for reenlisting and good pensions after 20 years or more in the service.

CONSIDER AND DISCUSS

Identify. Commander-in-Chief / National Security Council / Joint Chiefs of Staff / Central Intelligence Agency / Selective Service Act of 1917 / draft / lottery / all-volunteer army

Review. 1. What are the chief powers of Congress concerning defense? 2. How much money is spent each year for defense? 3. Where are the officers of the armed forces trained?

Discuss. Why is it important that the American armed forces be under the control of civilian officials?

4 To Promote the General Welfare

Our federal government performs many services and activities that play an important role in our daily lives. Some of these activities are intended to assist each of us. They are government services designed to promote the welfare, or well-being, of all American citizens. In addition, the federal government provides many services that are intended to meet the special needs of groups of citizens.

YOU AND THE FEDERAL GOVERNMENT

The activities of the national government have a direct effect upon your life and on the lives of all Americans every day. The doctor who cared for you when you were a child probably received advice and information from the **Public Health Service.** The baby foods you ate were tested by the **Food and Drug Administration** to make sure they were pure. If you took a trip on a bus or a train to visit relatives living in another state, the **Interstate Commerce Commission** helped to make sure that you received good service and were charged fair rates.

The federal government is also interested in you as a student and as a young American. The **Office of Education** furnishes information to your school on ways to provide the best education for all students. Federal funds help to support programs of education in your school. When you telephone your friends, the Federal Communications Commission is behind the scenes making sure you receive efficient service. This same agency also helps to guard the airwaves so that you can enjoy radio and television programs.

When you plan a summer vacation, the services of the federal government go along with you. The United States Postal Service helps you get information about places you might like to visit. It also carries the postcards you write to friends and relatives. The automobile in which you ride (or your train, plane, boat, or bus) is made of metal mined under the supervision of the **Bureau of Mines.** You can travel freely from state to state, and the federal government guarantees that your rights will be respected everywhere you go. You may visit America's great national parks or historic monuments, which the government operates for all Americans to enjoy. Even if you travel to a foreign land, the services of the Department of State will follow you. It will give you a passport to travel abroad, and it will help you if you have a serious problem while traveling abroad.

THE WORKER AND THE FEDERAL GOVERNMENT

More than 87 million persons are employed in the United States. These workers have rights which are carefully protected by the federal government. Congress has passed laws to help American workers, and has set up agencies to carry out the provisions of these laws.

The **Fair Labor Standards Act** fixes the minimum wage, or the lowest wage that workers may receive. It also puts a limit on the working hours of most workers. The right of workers to join a union and to bargain with their employers is enforced by the **National Labor Relations Board.** The Department of Labor helps to encourage good working conditions in factories and offices by requiring safety devices and safe practices in industries engaged in interstate trade.

The federal government affects the lives of American workers in other ways, too. Congress has passed **workers' compensation laws.** These laws provide that workers will receive weekly payments if they are hurt on the job and cannot work. Like all Americans, workers must pay taxes to the national government. The government requires the

In this picture, a meat inspector is checking the grade and quality of beef. This is only one of the ways that the federal government works to keep our food safe and pure.

employer to withhold a certain amount from each worker's paycheck to help pay the worker's contribution to the **Social Security** program, which pays workers a regular sum each month when they retire. The employer also pays into the worker's Social Security account. In addition, the employer must pay into an **Unemployment Insurance** account, so that workers receive money if they are out of work.

BUSINESS OWNERS AND THE FEDERAL GOVERNMENT

The prosperity of the American nation is based upon the right of individuals to work for themselves or others in a business and to make an honest profit if they can. The system of freedom in business is known as free enterprise, or capitalism. It is based upon free competition, in which each business firm tries to make a product that people will want and that will outsell similar products.

The federal government encourages American businesses to provide the public with the goods and services that they want. At the same time, the government enforces laws to prevent dishonest business people from cheating the public or practicing unfair competition in doing business.

In Chapter 14, you will learn more about how our nation's businesses operate. But a few examples here will show you some of the many ways in which the federal government affects American businesses. The exact time when the workday starts, for instance, is based upon the official time set up by the **United States Naval Observatory.** Workers in many factories and offices punch in on a time clock which was patented by its manufacturer in the **United States Patent and Trademark Office.** The measurements used to define the size and weight of items produced and used by business firms are set up by the **National Bureau of Standards.**

The Department of Commerce furnishes business firms with information that helps them plan what kinds of products to make and decide how many they need to sell. The freight rates for shipping goods by train, truck, or plane are regulated by the Interstate Commerce Commission. And, like the individual citizen, business firms also have to pay their share of taxes to help meet the cost of government services.

Business people enjoy considerable freedom to own and operate their factories and offices as they see fit. At the same time, they must practice fair business methods.

In the past, some business companies have joined together and become so big and powerful that they forced smaller companies out of business. Then the big company began to charge high prices for its products. Congress decided that these practices were not in the best interests of the nation. Therefore, Congress passed antitrust laws forbidding companies to join together in one large firm, called a "trust," if such a merger would create a **monopoly,** or control over a product so that there is no competition.

RESEARCH AND THE FEDERAL GOVERNMENT

The United States government encourages research that aids business and improves the lives of all citizens. Products such as electronic calculators, digital clocks, microwave ovens, new types of plastics and paints, and better television sets are all the results of government-sponsored research.

Who does this research? Some of it is carried out by scientists working in the various executive departments—such as Agriculture, Interior, Defense, and Health, Education and Welfare. Other research is done by universities, private research firms, individual scientists, and large industries using federal grants of money. In a recent year, over $3 billion in federal funds was granted to colleges and universities for research. This money was used for such vital projects as space research, agricultural research, weather and environmental studies, astronomy, oceanography, earthquake research, and chemical analysis of foods and drugs. These research efforts help our nation remain a leader in industrial and technological advances.

THE FARMER AND THE FEDERAL GOVERNMENT

The welfare of farmers is the main concern of the Department of Agriculture. It does research on many farm problems to help the farmer. Among the problems it studies are methods of fighting crop-killing insects, ways of developing new and better types of crops, improved methods of farming, and the use of new labor-saving farm machinery. Agents from this department also help the farmer to solve many practical farm problems.

The federal government also has helped farmers by passing laws to help them get fair prices for their crops. And the government pays farmers to practice soil-conservation methods. Special federal banks have been set up to lend money to farmers at low interest rates. The **Federal Crop Insurance Corporation** aids farmers if floods, drought, or any other disasters ruin their crops.

This federal aid to farmers costs large amounts of money. The money to pay for these government programs is furnished, of course, by the taxpayers. For this reason, the farm programs of our federal government are reviewed by Congress and debated at nearly every session. In deciding how best to use public funds to aid agriculture, our nation's lawmakers must answer certain questions. Will a particular farm bill help most American farmers, or will it benefit only a small number of farms? Is this bill the best way to encourage better agriculture? These and other questions must be answered each time farm legislation comes before Congress.

In this laboratory run by the Department of Agriculture, scientists are testing the effects of pollution on plants. These testing laboratories are just one of the ways the Department helps farmers.

WAR VETERANS AND THE FEDERAL GOVERNMENT

Of special concern to all Americans are the war veterans who fought to defend our nation. The **Veterans Administration** is an independent agency of the federal government that assists the men and women who served in the armed forces. The Veterans Administration administers the **G.I. Bill of Rights,** which was passed by Congress after World War II, and renewed after the Korean conflict and during the Vietnam War. This law provides for government-guaranteed loans for veterans to enable them to pay for college education, or to buy homes, farms, or businesses.

The Veterans Administration provides hospitals in which veterans may receive medical care. In addition, disabled veterans may receive special training to prepare them for jobs. The **United States Employment Service** helps veterans and others to find jobs. The **Civil Service Commission** allows veterans preferences, or advantages, in taking examinations for government jobs. An honorably discharged veteran has five points added to the score on some Civil Service examinations. A disabled veteran gets an extra ten points, and is given first choice when there is a government job opening.

CONSIDER AND DISCUSS

Identify. Public Health Service / Food and Drug Administration / Interstate Commerce Commission / Office of Education / Bureau of Mines / Fair Labor Standards Act / National Labor Relations Board / workers' compensation laws / Social Security / Unemployment Insurance / United States Naval Observatory / United States Patent and Trademark Office / National Bureau of Standards / monopoly / Federal Crop Insurance Corporation / Veterans Administration / G.I. Bill of Rights / United States Employment Service / Civil Service Commission

Review. 1. How does the federal government serve you? 2. Give examples of the ways workers, business people, and farmers are helped by the government. 3. Why are "trusts" against the law?

Discuss. In what ways do the activities of the federal government affect your daily life?

5 To Secure the Blessings of Liberty

Changing times call for changes in our government. But how can the Constitution, which was written in the age of sailing ships, secure the blessings of liberty in our jet age? The answer is that the writers of the Constitution were wise enough to plan a government that could be changed to meet new conditions.

Under the Constitution, the President can recommend whatever program of action is needed to meet new conditions. Congress has the power to change old laws and to make new laws when needed. The Supreme Court may make new decisions in the light of changed conditions.

But what happens if a needed law or change in government is forbidden by the Constitution? Does this mean that the law or the change can never be made? No! In such cases, the Constitution itself may be changed by the people of the United States through their elected representatives. Such changes in the Constitution are called **amendments.** How are amendments to the Constitution made?

HOW AMENDMENTS MAY BE PASSED

The process for amending, or changing, the Constitution is set forth in Article 5 of the Constitution of the United States. This ar-

Ways in Which the Constitution May Be Amended

- An amendment may be proposed by a two-thirds vote of both houses of Congress and approved by the legislatures of three fourths of the states.
- An amendment may be proposed by a national convention called by Congress at the request of two thirds of the state legislatures and approved by the legislatures of three fourths of the states.
- An amendment may be proposed by a two-thirds vote of both houses of Congress and approved by ratifying conventions in three fourths of the states.
- An amendment may be proposed by a national convention called by Congress at the request of the legislatures of two thirds of the states and approved by conventions in three fourths of the states.

ticle provides that an amendment may be proposed, or started, in two ways. The first way is to have Congress propose an amendment by a two-thirds vote in both houses. Since a two-thirds vote in Congress is difficult to obtain, this means that members of both houses must make sure the change is really necessary.

The second way of proposing an amendment to the Constitution has never been used successfully. But it could be used if Congress should refuse to propose an amendment that the American people believed was necessary. Under this method, the legislatures of two thirds of our states can ask Congress to call a national convention to propose an amendment.

After an amendment has been started in one of the two ways described above, it also must be ratified, or approved, by the states. The amendment may be ratified in one of two ways. It may be sent to the state legislatures, and if three fourths approve, the amendment is passed. Or the amendment may be sent to **state ratifying conventions** elected by the people of each state to consider the amendment. If the conventions in three fourths of the states vote for the amendment, it is passed. The method of ratification must be described in each proposed amendment. If the amemdment is ratified in either of these two ways, it becomes a written part of the Constitution.

THE AMENDMENTS TO THE CONSTITUTION

In more than 180 years, only 26 amendments have been added to the Constitution of the United States. These amendments may be summarized as follows.

THE BILL OF RIGHTS

As you will recall, the first ten amendments (the **Bill of Rights**) were added to the Constitution in 1791. These ten amendments were passed as a group in order to guarantee many of the rights and liberties of the American people. The Bill of Rights was added to our Constitution to make it clear that the American people had not given up any of their traditional rights or freedoms when they established a new and stronger government under the Constitution. (The Bill of Rights is described in Chapter 2.)

Since the passage of the Bill of Rights, Amendments 11 through 26 have been added, in order to make various changes in our system of government. These amendments may be summarized as follows.

THE ELEVENTH AMENDMENT

The Eleventh Amendment was added to the Constitution in order to give state courts the right to try lawsuits brought against a state by citizens of another state or by citizens of a foreign country. The original Con-

Freedoms Guaranteed by the Bill of Rights

FREEDOM OF RELIGION

Freedom of worship.

Freedom to belong to any religion, or to none.

No official religion may be established.

FREEDOM OF THE PRESS

Freedom to print books, newspapers, and magazines.

No one may print falsehoods or writings that harm our citizens.

FREEDOM OF PETITION

Freedom to urge our governments to pass laws.

Freedom to ask our governments to take certain actions.

RIGHTS TO EQUAL JUSTICE

All persons accused of a crime must receive fair and equal treatment in a court of law.

FREEDOM OF SPEECH

Freedom to express ideas and opinions.

No one may use this freedom to speak falsely in order to harm or to injure other citizens.

FREEDOM OF ASSEMBLY

Freedom to hold meetings.

Meetings must be peaceful and obey local laws.

FREEDOM AND SECURITY OF CITIZENS

No unlawful search may be made of our homes.

Right to bear arms to protect ourselves.

No troops may be stationed in our homes.

stitution gave the federal courts the right to try such cases. The Eleventh Amendment gave back to the states a power that the original Constitution had taken from them.

THE TWELFTH, TWENTIETH, TWENTY-SECOND, AND TWENTY-FIFTH AMENDMENTS

These amendments deal with the office of President and Vice-President. The Twelfth Amendment cleared up a misunderstanding in the election process by requiring members of the Electoral College to cast separate votes for the President and for the Vice-President. The Twentieth Amendment changed the opening date of new sessions of Congress from March to January. This largely eliminated the time served by **lame duck** members of Congress defeated in the November election. It also provided that the President's term begin on January 20 instead of March 4, as planned in the original Constitution. The Twenty-second Amendment placed a limit of two terms on the number of times a President may be elected to and serve in office. The Twenty-fifth Amendment provides clear procedures for filling the office of President or Vice-President if either dies, is seriously ill, or cannot serve for some other reason.

THE THIRTEENTH AND FOURTEENTH AMENDMENTS

These amendments were ratified after the Civil War. They were intended to give black Americans the same rights as those enjoyed by white Americans. The Thirteenth Amendment outlawed slavery in the United States. The Fourteenth Amendment granted full citizenship to black Americans. Also, it goes on ". . . nor shall any state deprive [take from] any person of life, liberty, or property, without due process of law; nor deny [refuse to give] to any person within its jurisdiction [authority] the equal protection of the laws." This part of the Fourteenth Amendment was intended to protect all citizens, but especially black Americans, against unfair actions by state governments. It protects them just as Amendment Five of the Bill of Rights protects citizens against such actions by the federal government.

THE SIXTEENTH AMENDMENT

Before the Sixteenth Amendment was ratified in 1913, Congress could not collect taxes on a person's income. The costs of government were increasing, and new sources of revenue were badly needed. This amendment allowed Congress to pass an income tax law. As a result, income taxes soon became the main source of funds for the federal government.

THE SEVENTEENTH AMENDMENT

This amendment gave to the American people the right to elect United States Senators directly. According to the original Constitution, Senators were to be elected by the legislature of each state. This practice was followed for many, many years. In time, however, many Americans came to feel that the voters should elect Senators directly, in the same way that they voted for members of the House of Representatives. The Seventeenth Amendment, which gives the American people this right, became a part of the Constitution in 1913.

THE EIGHTEENTH AND TWENTY-FIRST AMENDMENTS

The Eighteenth Amendment has an especially interesting history. It came about as a result of many people's concern with the issue of liquor, or alcoholic drinks. A third political party, the **Prohibition Party,** urged the federal and state governments to pass laws to discourage drinking. Finally, in 1919, those who were against the use of liquor succeeded in having the Eighteenth Amendment passed. The Eighteenth Amendment forbade the "manufacture, sale, or transportation of intoxicating liquors within . . . the United States. . . ."

By 1933, the people of the United States decided to **repeal,** or cancel, the Eighteenth Amendment. Congress proposed a new amendment, and ratifying conventions met in the states to ratify the new amendment. The Twenty-first Amendment repealed the Eighteenth Amendment. It also gave the authority to control alcoholic drinks back to the states.

THE FIFTEENTH, NINETEENTH, AND TWENTY-THIRD AMENDMENTS

The right to vote, or suffrage, is one of the most important possessions of free people in a democracy. The struggle to gain the right to vote for all Americans was not easily won. It is a struggle that still goes on. Much progress has been made, but it required constitutional amendments to obtain this precious right for certain groups. The Fifteenth Amendment, ratified in 1870, states, "The rights of citizens of the United

States to vote shall not be denied or abridged [lessened] by the United States or any state on account of race, color, or previous condition of servitude." The amendment gave black Americans the right to vote.

The Nineteenth Amendment, ratified in 1920, granted women the right to vote. This right was won only after a long, hard struggle. It was led by courageous women such as Lucretia Mott, Elizabeth Cady Stanton, Susan B. Anthony, and Carrie Catt. They argued that women should not be second-class citizens. They also wanted the Declaration of Independence to read "that all men and *women* are created equal." In 1869, Wyoming became the first state to give women the vote. By 1912, six states had granted the vote to women. The suffragists, those who fought for the right of women to vote, finally won in 1920, when the amendment was ratified.

The Twenty-third Amendment was ratified in 1961. It gave those who live in the District of Columbia (Washington, D.C., the nation's capital) the right to vote for President.

THE TWENTY-FOURTH AMENDMENT

The fixing of voting qualifications in federal and state governments and the conduct of the elections is one of the powers reserved to the states. However, the states must respect the provisions of the Constitution concerning these matters.

Following the Civil War, some states established a requirement that all persons must pay a special tax, called a **poll tax,** in order to vote. Many Americans believed that this tax was aimed at the poor, and

The movement to gain the right to vote for women began in the 1800's. Although women such as those pictured here held marches and demonstrations for many years, women did not gain the right to vote until the Nineteenth Amendment was ratified in 1920.

especially at black Americans, to discourage them from voting. As a result, opposition to this tax increased until finally, in 1964, the Twenty-fourth Amendment was passed. This amendment forbade people to use the poll tax as a qualification for voting in federal elections. In 1966, the Supreme Court ruled that the poll tax is unlawful as a qualification for voting in state elections.

THE TWENTY-SIXTH AMENDMENT

The most recent amendment to the Constitution was ratified in 1971. This amendment reduced the minimum, or lowest, voting age in federal, state, and local elections to 18 years of age. Previously, the minimum voting age had been 21. Amendment Twenty-six was designed to give young Americans a greater voice in government.

A Twenty-seventh Amendment to the Constitution was proposed in 1972. It guaranteed equal rights to women and men. Thirty-eight states had to ratify the proposed amendment by March 22, 1979 in order for it to be adopted.

CONSIDER AND DISCUSS

Identify. amendments / state ratifying conventions / Bill of Rights / lame duck / Prohibition Party / repeal / poll tax
Review. 1. What are the ways in which an amendment to the Constitution may be proposed and passed? 2. Which amendment was repealed? Why? 3. Why was the Seventeenth Amendment necessary?
Discuss. How have the amendments to the Constitution helped to make the United States more democratic?

CHAPTER
Summary

Our federal government was to carry out the purposes of the Constitution. These purposes are stated in the Preamble.

Our nation's government helps "to form a more perfect union" in many ways. Two examples are seen in the way it helps to promote commerce and communication between people.

Our federal government insures "domestic tranquility" by using its "police power." It works with state governments to enforce laws.

Our government also provides for "the common defense." The President and the Congress work together to keep our nation strong.

Our federal government is busy in its efforts "to promote the general welfare," or the well-being of all Americans. It acts to protect our health and safety. And it aids business people, workers, farmers, and all other citizens.

One reason why our federal government has met the needs of Americans lies in its ability to change. The Constitution can be amended. Court decisions can increase freedoms. Congress can pass new laws.

VOCABULARY

Can you find the right word or phrase to answer each of the following questions? Copy the questions in your notebook, and place the correct answer after each question.

1. Who is the Commander-in-Chief of the armed forces of the United States?
2. What branch of our national government has the power to declare war?
3. What top-ranking groups make the defense plans for our nation?
4. What law provides money payments for a worker who is injured on the job?
5. What single word is used to describe America's free enterprise system?
6. To which government department would you write to obtain a passport?
7. When a large firm gains control of all or most of a business so that there is no competition, what is it called?
8. What bureau of the government controls television broadcasting?
9. What amendment was repealed when the Twenty-first Amendment was passed?
10. What organization supplies the individuals who guard the life of the President?

CHECK-UP

The following questions will help you to summarize and review the material in this chapter. Read each question carefully, decide upon your answer, and then check with the text to see if your answer is correct and complete.

1. What are the chief powers of Congress in regard to national defense?
2. What is the purpose of the Central Intelligence Agency?
3. What are some of the services that the federal government provides for you?
4. How does the national government help business, labor, and the farmer?
5. How do Amendments Five and Fourteen protect property owners in our nation?
6. What organizations carry out the police powers of the federal government?
7. What is the difference between a drafted army and an all-volunteer army?
8. How does the Seventeenth Amendment give the people a greater voice in the government?

CITIZENSHIP AND YOU

Our national government works actively to provide for the common defense, to promote the general welfare, and to secure the blessings of liberty for all Americans. The activities listed below suggest things you can do to help increase your understanding of how the federal government does its work.

1. Class Projects

Each member of the class may bring in a newspaper clipping showing a current activity of the national government. The class secretary or the teacher may draw a chart on the board with these headings: "National Defense," "General Welfare," "Securing Liberty." As each student explains the government activity described in the clipping, the secretary lists the activity on the board under the heading it best illustrates. When the chart is completed it should contain good examples of the numerous government services.

2. Group or Committee Projects

A committee may report on "The Training of Officers for the Armed Forces."

Another group may gather a classroom library of pamphlets and other materials on career opportunities in the armed forces.

Several students may interview local leaders to find out whether any of the programs in the community are sponsored by the national government.

Organize a panel discussion around the topic "Federal Regulation of Business Firms: Too Much or Too Little?"

3. Individual Projects

Carry out one of the following projects, and share your findings with the class:

Read the Fifth and Fourteenth amendments to the Constitution of the United States. Explain how these amendments protect each American citizen.

Using the *World Almanac* or similar reference books, find out the names of the present members of the Joint Chiefs of Staff.

Draw a cartoon showing how the United States protects its citizens abroad.

CIVICS SKILLS

EXAMINING PRIMARY AND SECONDARY SOURCES

In your study of civics, everything you read will be either a primary source or a secondary source. Primary sources are sources from the period in which an event took place. They include eyewitness accounts, letters, reports, diaries, official records, speeches, newspaper and magazine articles, documents, and other contemporary evidence. Primary sources help social scientists to reconstruct events that took place in the past and to understand them better. The Declaration of Independence and the Constitution are examples of one important kind of primary source—documents.

Secondary sources are sources from a later period—after an event has taken place. Often, they interpret an event's significance and make value judgments about the event and the people involved. Secondary accounts sometimes use primary sources as evidence. Your civics textbook is an example of a secondary source.

Both primary and secondary sources are important in your study of civics. Primary sources will enable you to examine evidence at first hand. They will help you gain an immediate impression of an event. Secondary sources will give you insight into how people interpret and analyze events. They will also help you to see how people's attitudes and values affect their interpretation of events.

PRACTICING YOUR CIVICS SKILLS

Try to decide which of the following are primary sources and which are secondary sources.

1. The Preamble to the Constitution.
2. Benjamin Franklin's autobiography.
3. An account of the Whisky Rebellion in an old newspaper from 1794.
4. A biography of George Washington.
5. The Bill of Rights.
6. A magazine article written last year about the Whisky Rebellion.

Make a list of some of the advantages of using primary sources as evidence. Then make a list of some of the possible disadvantages. Do you think primary or secondary sources are more important? Why?

State and Local Government

CHAPTER

Introduction

On August 21, 1959, President Dwight D. Eisenhower declared Hawaii to be the fiftieth state in the Union. Some 8,000 kilometers (5,000 miles) away from our nation's capital, the people of Hawaii received the long-awaited news with great joy. In the streets of Honolulu, the capital city of the new state, bands began to play "The Star-Spangled Banner," and "Hawaii Ponoi," the state song. Sirens, bells, and horns were sounded to celebrate the day, and thousands of people paraded in the streets. They lighted bonfires, built from logs that had been sent to Hawaii from each of the 49 other states. The greeting "Aloha, citizen" filled the warm summer air.

Hawaii was now a full-fledged state of the United States. The new citizens of Hawaii entered the federal union as equal citizens, enjoying the same rights and privileges as all other Americans. What are these rights and privileges? Just what does it mean to be a citizen of one of the 50 states of the United States?

How do state governments serve their citizens? How do state governments govern their citizens? How are state governments similar to the federal government? What are the citizens' responsibilities toward their state? You can find the answers to these and other questions as you read this chapter and study these topics:

1. The States of the United States
2. State Lawmakers
3. State Governors
4. State Courts

CHAPTER

How State Governments Serve Their Citizens

1 The States of the United States

If you look up the word **state** in your dictionary, you may find that one of its meanings is "a group of people occupying a definite territory, organized under one government, and not subject to control from the outside." This description fits independent nations, such as France or Brazil or Burma. But what about the 50 states of the United States?

OUR STATES AS UNITS OF GOVERNMENT

The states in our nation are not independent, nor are they free from outside control. Our 50 states are part of our federal union, and they share their powers with the national government. Why, then, do we use the word *state* in describing Pennsylvania, Alabama, Colorado, Washington, or any other of the 50 states?

When our country began, the 13 states did indeed act like small nations, or states. Under the Articles of Confederation, you may recall, each state issued its own money, regulated trade crossing its borders, and often treated neighboring states as though they were foreign nations. For a while, it looked as though America would be divided into 13 small, weak nations.

But at the Constitutional Convention the delegates worked long hours to establish a better form of government. The 13 states agreed to give up some of their powers in order to form "a more perfect union." The resulting form of government, as you recall, is called a **federation,** or **federal union.**

What powers were given to the federal government, and what powers were retained by the states?

THE DIVISION OF POWERS

The new national government—the federal government—was given the power to regulate trade between the states, to conduct foreign affairs, to print and coin money, to set up a postal service, and to build an Army and a Navy.

But the states also kept important powers for themselves. The Tenth Amendment to the Constitution provided that "The powers not delegated [given] to the United States by the Constitution, nor prohibited by it to the states, are reserved to [set aside for] the states respectively, or to the people."

According to the Constitution, then, our states are units of government that have considerable power to govern the people who live within their borders. Why, then, do we call these 50 large units of government states? We do so because of tradition and because in many ways our states are powerful and independent. Although the states divide the powers of government with the national government, the states are important and have real power. The states are close to the people, and state governments provide many important services.

FROM 13 STATES TO 50 STATES

The 13 original states became part of the United States when they approved the Constitution. Most of the other states that were added later, however, were once territories of the United States. A **territory** is an area, governed by the United States, that is eligible to become a state.

By the **Northwest Ordinance** of 1787, Con-

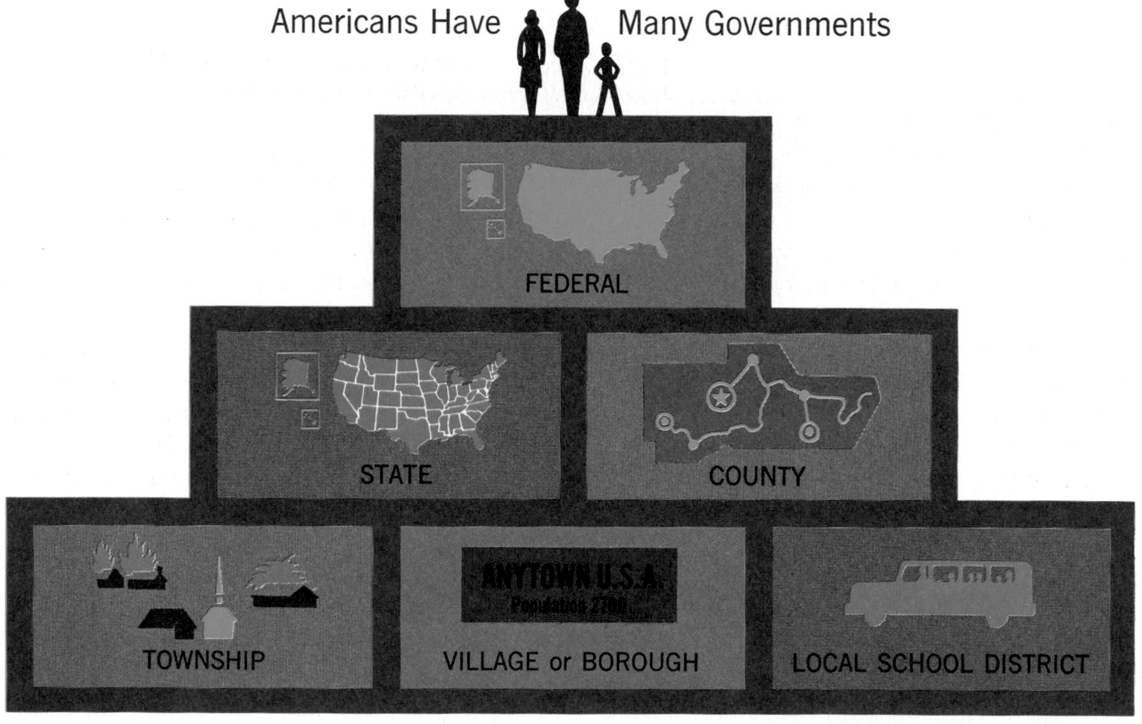

gress provided for a way to add these territories to our nation as new and equal states. A territory usually passed through five stages before it became a state.

1. At first, it was governed by a territorial government made up of officials appointed by Congress.

2. When the population of the territory reached 5,000 male settlers old enough to vote, the voters had the right to elect the members of their own lawmaking body.

3. When the population of the territory grew to 60,000 or more voters, the territory was eligible to become a state. The territory lawmakers sent a petition to Congress asking to be organized as a state.

4. If Congress agreed that the territory was ready to be considered for statehood, it passed an enabling act, requesting the people of the territory to draw up a constitution, or plan of government.

5. After a state constitution was drawn up and approved by the people of the territory and by Congress, Congress then voted to admit the territory as a new state.

STATE CONSTITUTIONS

Each of our 50 states has its own constitution. Your own state constitution probably interests you most of all, and it is worth careful study. This written plan of your state government contains the rules of how the government of your state is to be organized and how it is to carry on its work. Most state constitutions are long and complex, but they usually contain the following parts.

1. A preamble, or a beginning, which states the basic ideas and ideals on which the state government is founded.

2. A bill of rights, sometimes called a declaration of rights, listing the freedoms guaranteed to all citizens of the state.

3. An outline of the organization of the state's government, with the duties of the executive, legislative, and judicial branches carefully spelled out.

4. Provisions for elections, including qualifications for voting that must be met by the citizens of the state, as well as rules about how elections are to be conducted.

5. Provisions for managing state affairs, including education, keeping law and order, building highways, regulating business, and raising money by means of taxes.

6. Methods of amending, or changing, the state constitution, and a list of the amendments passed.

Most state constitutions have been amended many times. This has been necessary because the powers and duties of state governments have changed greatly since their constitutions were first written. During recent years, a number of states have drawn up new ones. States that have adopted new constitutions since 1970 are: Illinois and Virginia (1970), North Carolina (1971), Montana (1972), and Louisiana (1974). A new constitution is usually drawn up at a state constitutional convention by delegates elected by the people.

THE STATES AS GOOD NEIGHBORS

In joining the Union, the states agreed to work together in harmony. One way they promised to cooperate is stated in Article 4, Section 1 of the Constitution of the United States, which states, "Full faith [belief] and credit [acceptance] shall be given in each state to the public acts, records, and judicial proceedings [court decisions] of every other state."

The **"full faith and credit" clause** makes certain that each state will accept the decisions of courts in other states. If a court in Texas, for instance, decides that one of its citizens owns a certain piece of land, the other states will accept this legal decision. Another example of the "full faith and credit" clause is the acceptance of the official records of other states. A marriage certificate or a birth certificate issued by any state is accepted by all other states.

States work together in other ways, too.

As more settlers moved into the Northwest Territory, the number of states continued to grow.

They share information on wanted criminals, for example. If a prisoner escapes from jail in Utah and flees to Colorado, the Governor of Utah can ask the Governor of Colorado to have the Colorado authorities apprehend and return the prisoner. This method of returning escaped prisoners is called **extradition.**

THE STATES AND THE FEDERAL GOVERNMENT

Since the 50 states and the federal government share certain powers, and in other cases have separate powers, they must work together. What are some of the ways in which the federal and state governments join together to provide services that Americans require?

The Constitution of the United States, in Article 4, Section 4, promises that "The United States shall guarantee to every state in this Union a republican form of government. . . ." A republican form of government is one in which the people elect their own representatives to carry out the work of the government. Every state, as it joined the Union, has been required to provide for a republican form of government in its state constitution.

Article 4, Section 4, of the Constitution also promises that the United States government will "protect each of them [the states] against invasion." As a result, the national government has strong military forces to defend the states and the nation against attack. In addition, the Constitution says that the federal government must stand ready to help any state put down "domestic violence." An example of domestic violence might be rioting in a town when a mob has gotten out of control. The Governor may call on the National Guard of the state if local police cannot control the disorder. In extreme cases, the state legislature, or the Governor, may ask the federal government for assistance.

The federal and state governments share

the costs of furnishing a number of services to the American people. Federal and state governments work together to build highways, to assist jobless workers, to give relief to the needy, and to aid in the conservation of natural and human resources. Working together, state and national governments assist the blind, provide low-cost lunches for school children, offer job training for the handicapped, and carry out slum clearance programs. These are some of the important ways state governments and the national government work together to serve the American people.

CONSIDER AND DISCUSS

Identify. state / federation / federal union / territory / Northwest Ordinance / "full faith and credit" clause / extradition

Review. 1. What are some of the powers reserved for the states? 2. What are the stages by which a territory becomes a state? 3. What are the six parts of most state constitutions? 4. Give examples of federal and state cooperation in your neighborhood.

Discuss. Do you think state governments should be given more power? Why or why not?

2 State Lawmakers

Each state has a lawmaking body elected by the people of the state. In 26 states this lawmaking body is called the **Legislature.** In Montana, North Dakota, and Oregon, however, the lawmaking body is called the Legislative Assembly. In Massachusetts and New Hampshire the official name is the General Court. Other states call their lawmaking body the General Assembly. In this chapter we shall use the general term, **state legislature.**

STATE LAWMAKING BODIES

Nebraska has a one-house (unicameral) legislature. In all the other states, the legislature is bicameral (divided into two houses). The larger of the two houses is called the **House of Representatives** or sometimes, the House of Delegates. The smaller house is known as the **Senate.**

The members of both houses of a state legislature are elected by the people of the state. Each member represents the people who live in a particular district of that state. The division of the state into districts is determined by the state constitution. Orginally, the upper house (Senate) of the state legislature usually had one Senator from each county, or from each Senatorial district into which the state was divided. However, the counties or districts were often unequal in population, and sparsely populated areas of the state often had as many Senators as heavily populated areas.

In 1964, the United States Supreme Court ruled that all state electoral districts must be equal in population—or as nearly equal as possible. This was the famous "one man, one vote" ruling. Since this ruling, most of the states have set up election districts of equal population.

QUALIFICATIONS AND TERMS OF STATE LAWMAKERS

Members of a state legislature must be citizens of the United States. They must live in the state and district which they represent. In most states a state Senator must be at least 25 years of age, and a Representative (or Delegate) must be at least 21 years of age. Some states, though, have lowered the age to 21 for Senators and to 18 for Representatives. In Texas Senators must be at least 26. Salaries differ greatly from state to state. New York pays its legislators $32,500 a year. But in New Hampshire they receive only $200 every two years.

In most states, Senators are elected for four-year terms. State Representatives usually serve for two years. In Alabama, Louisiana, Maryland, and Mississippi, Senators and Representatives both serve four-year terms. Some other states have a two-year term for the members of both houses. The Senators who serve in Nebraska's one-house legislature serve for four years. In all states the members of the legislature can run for reelection and may serve any number of terms.

HOW STATE LEGISLATURES ARE ORGANIZED

By the late 1970's, the legislatures in 35 states met in regular sessions every year. The legislatures in 14 states met once every two years. California has a two-year session that meets during the entire time. In other states, a session might last from 20 days to six months or more. The Governor, or sometimes the state legislature, may call "special sessions" to meet emergencies.

At the beginning of the session, the presiding officer and other leaders are chosen. Committees are appointed. In 31 states there is a Lieutenant Governor who presides over

How the Powers of Government Are Divided

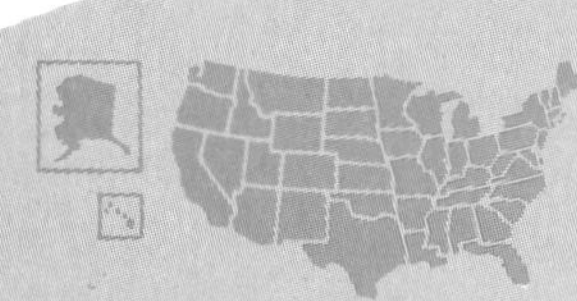

FEDERAL GOVERNMENT POWERS

- To regulate foreign trade and commerce between the states
- To coin and print money
- To conduct foreign relations with other nations
- To establish post offices and roads
- To raise and support armed forces
- To declare war and make peace
- To govern American territories and admit new states
- To pass naturalization laws and regulate immigration
- To make all laws "necessary and proper" to carry out its powers

POWERS SHARED by Federal and State Governments (Concurrent Powers)

- To collect taxes
- To borrow money
- To establish courts
- To enforce laws and punish lawbreakers
- To provide for the health and welfare of the people

STATE GOVERNMENT POWERS

- To regulate trade within the state
- To establish local governments
- To conduct elections
- To determine qualifications of voters
- To establish and support public schools
- To incorporate business firms
- To license professional workers
- To keep all the "reserved powers" not granted to the federal government nor prohibited to the states

the Senate. In the other states, the Senate chooses its own presiding officer. Members of the lower house in all states choose their own presiding officer, who is usually called the **Speaker.**

After choosing the presiding officers, the state legislature organizes its committees. In the upper house, committee members are chosen by the presiding officer or by all the members of the house. In the lower house, the Speaker usually appoints the committee members.

HOW STATE LEGISLATURES PASS LAWS

The lawmaking process in state legislatures is similar to the procedure followed in Congress. Almost every step you studied in the making of federal laws (Chapter 3) is followed by state legislatures. Here is a brief summary of the way in which a bill becomes a law in a state legislature.

1. A bill is introduced. Any member of either house may introduce a bill, or proposed law. It is first handed to the clerk, and it is given a number. The presiding officer reads the title of the bill aloud and sends it to the appropriate committee.

2. The bill in committee. In due time, the committee begins to consider the bill. The committee listens to various witnesses and then questions them to obtain the necessary information. The members may discuss the bill for many hours. Then the committee meets behind closed doors and votes on the bill. It may vote to pass the bill, to change it, or to kill it. Or the committee may "pigeonhole" the bill and not consider it at all. Only a few states require that a state legislature committee must give a report on every bill it considers.

3. The bill reaches the floor. If the committee approves the bill, with or without amending it, it sends the bill back to a full meeting of the house. Then the bill is read aloud for the second time, this time line for line. The members of the house now begin to debate the bill. Each part of the bill is discussed. Amendments, or changes, may be offered, and if passed they become a part of the bill.

After a third reading, usually by title only, the members vote on the bill, often without further debate. A few legislatures save the debate for the third reading. If the bill fails to pass, it cannot be considered again until changes are made. A new bill must be drawn up, introduced by a member, and approved by a house committee. Bills that are passed are signed by the presiding officer and sent to the other house.

4. The bill in the second house. When the bill is introduced in the other house, it is read by title, given a number, and sent to committee. If the bill survives the changes, hearings, and debates in this committee, it is sent back to the floor of the second house. Here it is read two more times, debated, perhaps changed again, and then voted upon.

Bills that pass one house and fail in the second house are dead. If both houses of the legislature pass a bill in the same form, the bill is then sent to the Governor to be signed. If both houses pass the bill, but in different forms, the bill is sent to a conference committee.

5. The bill in conference committee. When the second house changes a bill, as it often does, then the first house must approve the changes or send the bill to a **joint conference committee.** This committee is made up of members selected from both houses who must try to reach a compromise, or agreement, which will be acceptable to both houses. Usually the two houses accept the compromise bill worked out by the conference committee. This final version of the bill is then voted on by each house.

6. The bill is sent to the Governor. The final step in making a state law is to send the bill to the Governor to be signed. States differ in the amount of time they give the Governor to reach a decision on a bill, but it

Our State Governments

THE VOTERS ELECT

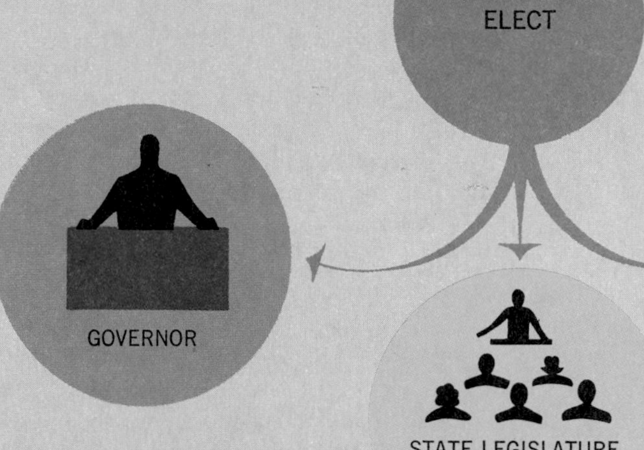

STATE COURTS*

STATE EXECUTIVE DEPARTMENTS

TREASURER

SECRETARY OF STATE

AUDITOR

ATTORNEY GENERAL

SUPERINTENDENT OF EDUCATION

DIRECTOR OF PUBLIC HEALTH

+

OTHER STATE AGENCIES

THE STATE SUPREME COURT

HIGHER STATE TRIAL COURTS
Courts of appeals
Superior courts

STATE TRIAL COURTS
County courts
District courts

LOWER STATE COURTS
Justice court
Magistrates court (police, municipal)
Traffic court
Domestic relations court
Juvenile court

*In most states the judges of most state courts are elected by the voters, but in some states some of the judges are appointed by the Governor or the legislature.

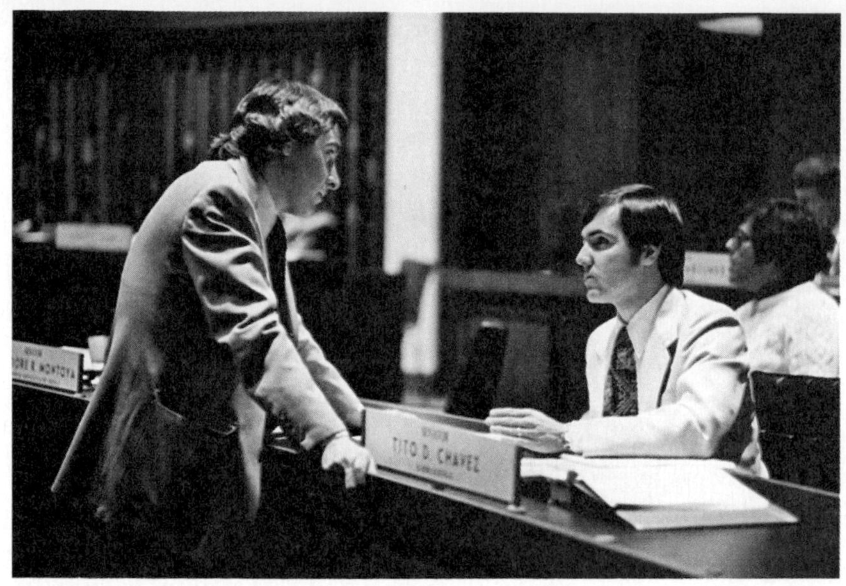

A state legislature passes laws for each state. Here, state Senator Tito Chavez of New Mexico talks with another lawmaker at a hearing.

usually is about five days. If the Governor signs the bill within this time, it becomes a law. If the Governor holds the bill longer than this and does not sign it, the bill becomes a law without the signature.

In all states except North Carolina, the Governor may veto a bill he or she does not wish to sign. In 43 states, the Governor may veto part of money bills. The Governor's veto is final unless, in most states, two thirds of the members of each house pass the bill again over the veto. If the Governor vetoes the bill after the session has ended, the legislature cannot pass the bill. However, several states require that such a veto must be reconsidered at the next session.

THE RESERVED POWERS OF THE STATE

You may remember that the Tenth Amendment to the Constitution sets aside, or reserves, to the states and the people all powers not specifically granted to the federal government. These **reserved powers** make it possible for each state to pass important legislation for its people. What are the powers of government that are reserved to the states?

State governments are responsible for conducting our system of elections. States decide most of the qualifications for voting in elections. Of course, they must respect the federal Constitution's provisions about voting. States also set up the methods for conducting all local, state, and national elections. In this way, our federal system of government depends upon the states to see that the American people are given the opportunity to elect their own representatives.

Another important function of state governments is education. The power to establish and maintain schools belongs to the state government. In general, states set up local school districts which operate public schools. The federal government may offer certain kinds of aid and advice. But the states have the power to decide what kinds of schools they will have. However, state school regulations cannot conflict with the Constitution, or with the rulings of the Supreme Court.

State governments have control over all

local governments within their boundaries —cities, towns, townships, and counties. Local governments get their powers from the states. States have many other reserved powers. The states make laws concerning marriage and divorce. They regulate traffic on the highways. State laws also deal with health, safety, welfare, and the regulation of business within their borders. What other reserved powers can you think of?

CONCURRENT POWERS

The states also share many powers with the federal government. Such shared powers are called **concurrent powers.** Just because the federal government was granted certain powers in the Constitution does not mean that state governments do not also have these powers. Unless a power is forbidden to the states by the United States Constitution, state governments may exercise that power.

A good example of a shared, or concurrent, power is the power of taxation. Both the federal government and the state governments have the power to tax. They both collect many kinds of taxes to carry on their activities. State governments raise money by taxing gasoline, liquor, cigarettes, real estate, income, and personal property. The money raised through state taxes is used to pay for education, highways, health and safety programs, relief and welfare, and many other activities of the states.

CONSIDER AND DISCUSS

Identify. Legislature / state legislature / House of Representatives / Senate / Speaker / joint conference committee / reserved powers / concurrent powers

Review. 1. What are the qualifications for members of state legislatures? 2. How does a bill become a state law? 3. Give several examples of reserved powers.

Discuss. Describe some of the concurrent powers shared by our federal and state governments. Why must these powers be shared?

3 State Governors

Like the federal government, each state has a system of checks and balances. Indeed, the pattern of state government is very much like that of the federal government. However, it has been only in this century that Governors have become the chief executives of their states in more than just name in many states.

THE POWERS AND DUTIES OF GOVERNORS

As chief executives of their states, **Governors** may appoint a number of officials with the approval of the state Senate. Some top officials, however, are elected by the people, and Governors have little control over them.

Only the state legislatures can pass laws. But the Governors play an important part in proposing new laws. Governors usually appear before the state legislatures at one of the early meetings. There they outline laws they think should be passed. From time to time, they talk to leaders of the legislature urging them to pass bills.

Since the Governors are the heads of their political parties in the states, state Senators and Representatives pay close attention to what they say. State officials know that the Governors can aid them during their next election campaigns. They also know that if they pass bills that the Governors oppose, the bills may be vetoed.

In most states, one of the Governor's most important responsibilities is to draw up a budget for the state. The budget is a plan of income and spending. A **budget director** or a

budget bureau aids the Governor. Long hours are spent in figuring out the amount of money the state will need during the next one- or two-year period, and the taxes that will be required to meet this need. The completed budget is given to the legislature for approval.

GOVERNORS CARRY OUT THE LAWS

After the legislatures have passed laws, it is the responsibility of the Governors to put them into force. If the legislatures pass new tax laws, for example, it is the duty of the Governors, through their assistants, to issue orders that will determine the way in which these taxes are collected. The orders that set up methods of enforcing laws are called **executive ordinances.** Almost every law passed by the legislature requires such executive orders.

The Governors have many other powers. The heads of the state police force and the state militia answer to them. In times of an emergency, such as a flood or a hurricane, the Governors may call out the National Guard to

The Powers and Duties of the Governor

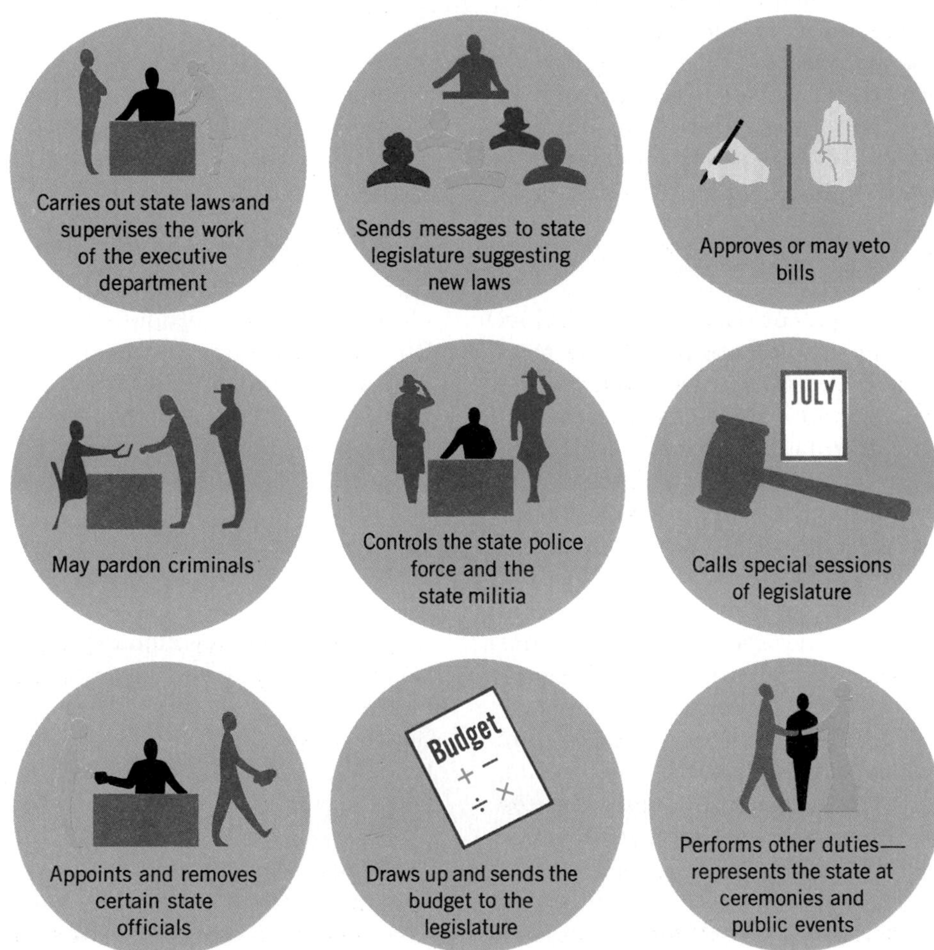
Carries out state laws and supervises the work of the executive department
Sends messages to state legislature suggesting new laws
Approves or may veto bills
May pardon criminals
Controls the state police force and the state militia
JULY
Calls special sessions of legislature
Appoints and removes certain state officials
Budget
Draws up and sends the budget to the legislature
Performs other duties—represents the state at ceremonies and public events

A Governor is the chief executive officer of a state. Here, Governor Ella T. Grasso of Connecticut waves to supporters.

help keep order. They also have the power to pardon, or free, certain prisoners, although a state pardon board advises them in such cases.

QUALIFICATIONS OF GOVERNORS

The chief executive of each state, the Governor, is elected by the people of the state in a statewide election. According to the constitutions of the states, candidates for Governor must be (1) citizens of the United States, (2) 30 years of age or older (a few states allow persons 25 years of age to run for Governor), and (3) residents of the state for a certain number of years.

The salaries of the Governors vary considerably among the states. The Governor of New York, for example, receives $85,000 a year. The Governor of Arkansas receives only $10,000 a year. In most states, Governors are given an official residence at the state capital, where they and their families live. And in most states, Governors are given an allowance for expenses.

Governors serve a four-year term of office in 47 of the states. They serve a two-year term in 3 states. In a number of states, Governors cannot serve for two terms in a row.

OTHER STATE EXECUTIVE OFFICIALS

At election time, the voters of the states elect a number of officials in addition to the Governors to help run the state governments. The following officials are the more important members of the states' executive branches. In most states, these officials are elected by the voters. But in some they are appointed by the Governor.

The Lieutenant Governor. This official becomes head of the state executive branch if the Governor dies, resigns, or is removed from office. The **Lieutenant Governors** often serve as presiding officers of the state Senate. Because they are not members of the Senate, they cannot vote except to break a tie. All but 11 states have Lieutenant Governors.

The Secretary of State. This official keeps the state's records, issues charters to cities and corporations and carries out other duties described in the state constitution. Only

Alaska and Hawaii do not have Secretaries of State. In states which do not have a Lieutenant Governor, the Secretary of State serves as Governor if the Governor dies, resigns, or is removed from office.

The Attorney General. This official takes care of the state's legal business, or matters concerning the law. If any state officer wants advice about the meaning of a certain law, the **Attorney General** gives it. The Attorney General, or an assistant, represents the state in court when the state is involved in a lawsuit. The Attorney General may also assist local officials in the prosecution of criminals.

The State Treasurer. This official is in charge of handling all state funds. The **State Treasurer** receives all tax money and issues all state checks or other payments. This official collects and pays out all public funds as provided by state law.

The State Auditor. This official is sometimes called the **Auditor-General** or **Comptroller.** The Auditor makes sure that no public funds are paid out of the state treasury unless payment is authorized by law. Usually the Treasurer cannot pay any bills without a written order signed by the Auditor. This order to pay out money is called a warrant. The Auditor also examines the state's financial records from time to time to make sure they are correct.

The Superintendent of Public Instruction. This official is sometimes known as the **State Commissioner of Education.** The Superintendent's chief duty is to carry out the policies of the State Board of Education (which in some states is known by other titles). The State Board makes regulations, under state law, that govern the various local school districts of the state. The members of this board and the Superintendent of Public Instruction are elected in some states. In others, they are appointed by the Governor. The Superintendent is in charge of the distribution of state funds to the local school systems according to the law.

THE GOVERNOR'S CABINET

In some states the officials we have just learned about are a part of the Governor's Cabinet. In other states they are not considered members of the Cabinet unless they are appointed by the Governor. Like the President's Cabinet, the Governor's official advisers are heads of the executive departments of the state government. Most states have a Department of Justice (headed by the Attorney General), a Department of Labor, a Department of Agriculture, and a Department of Highways. In addition, there is a Department of Safety containing the state police. The Department of Public Works is responsible for all public construction projects in the state except highways.

STATE EXECUTIVE AGENCIES

In recent years, our state governments have had to meet many new problems. A number of new agencies or departments have been set up to help take care of these problems. These agencies are in the executive branch of our state governments. They are sometimes called boards, commissions, or departments. Usually these agencies are headed by state officials appointed by the Governors. They are also responsible to them. In some states, however, the heads of the agencies are appointed by the state legislature. They are responsible directly to the legislature.

Among these state boards or commissions is the State Board of Health. Its Director enforces health laws and recommends measures for the improvement of the health of state citizens. The Board of State Welfare supervises programs of aid to the poor, the unemployed, and the handicapped. The Civil Service Commission is in charge of the employment of people who work for the state. Other state agencies administer state laws on agriculture, highways, and conservation. They also regulate banks, public utilities, and insurance.

STATE GOVERNMENT EMPLOYEES

As our state populations grow in size, more and more state employees are needed to carry on the work of state governments. Large numbers of state employees are found in the Highway Department, with its construction and work crews. The State Board of Health employs a large number of doctors, nurses, and inspectors. Many clerks, stenographers, accountants, typists, and other workers are needed in the executive agencies and departments of state government.

Most state employees get their positions through the **state civil service commission.** State examinations are given regularly to hire qualified workers. There are other state jobs which are not under civil service. These jobs are filled through recommendations of political party leaders and office holders. Such jobs often go to those in the party who have helped in some way in the election campaign. However, most state government jobs are under civil service. And they are open to any qualified citizen.

State universities provide the opportunity for higher education at a reasonable cost.

CONSIDER AND DISCUSS

Identify. Governor / budget director / budget bureau / executive ordinances / Lieutenant Governor / Secretary of State / Attorney General / State Treasurer / Auditor-General / Comptroller / State Commissioner of Education / state civil service commission

Review. 1. Name three important duties of the Governor. 2. What services do state agencies perform for the citizens of the state?

Discuss. Should all state employees get their jobs through the state civil service? Why or why not?

4 State Courts

Each state government has the power to keep peace and order within its boundaries. It exercises this power through all three branches of state government. The legislature passes laws to provide for the welfare and safety of the people of the state. The executive branch sees that these laws are put into effect. The judicial branch—the state court system—has the job of judging, or interpreting, the meaning of these state laws and punishing those who break them.

THE WORK OF THE STATE COURTS

State courts handle many different kinds of cases. If a person is involved in an automobile accident that requires a legal settlement, the case is tried in a state court.

A dispute between two neighbors over the boundary line between properties will be settled in a state court. Every day, state courts hear hundreds of cases, ranging from traffic violations to robbery and murder.

State courts handle two types of cases—criminal cases and civil cases. **Criminal cases** are those in which the person on trial is accused of breaking a state law. In such cases a lawyer for the state presents the evidence against the accused. He or she represents the people of the state because breaking a state law is a crime committed against the people of the state. Serious crimes such as burglary, kidnapping, or murder are called **felonies.** Less serious offenses such as traffic violations, disorderly conduct, or violation of health laws are **misdemeanors.**

Civil cases involve a dispute between two or more individuals. If one person claims that another owes him or her money, for example, and asks a state court for help in collecting the money, the case would be a civil case. Another example of a civil case might be a large corporation's lawsuit against another firm for not carrying out its part of a business contract. In a civil case, the state court must judge who is right and must award damages in the case.

HOW OUR STATE COURTS ARE ORGANIZED

The organization of state courts varies from state to state. But three types of courts are found in most states: lower state courts, state trial courts, and higher state courts.

1. Lower state courts. In the early years of our history when most Americans lived in farming areas or in small towns and villages, it was common for them to elect one of their neighbors as a **Justice of the Peace.** Usually these officials were not trained in the law. They were often school teachers, carpenters, or farmers. The Justice of the Peace depended on common sense in settling disputes in the community.

Justices of the Peace are still found in most rural areas and small towns, and some large cities. This official presides over a **Justice Court,** and tries misdemeanors and civil cases involving small sums, usually of $100 or less. For misdemeanors this official can hand down fines or short jail sentences.

In our larger towns and cities there are lower courts that are usually presided over by an elected judge. These lower courts are called **Magistrate's Courts, Police Courts,** or **Municipal Courts.** They are courts for city dwellers. All cases are heard by the judge and not by a trial jury. But the decision of the judge may be appealed to a higher court.

Many large cities have set up other lower courts to handle special matters. **Traffic Courts,** for example, hear cases involving traffic violations. **Domestic Relations Courts** hear cases involving family disputes, neglect of children, separation of married couples, and sometimes, divorce cases. **Juvenile Courts** hear cases involving young persons under 18 years of age.

In these special lower courts, judges with special legal training are usually in charge. These judges conduct hearings without a jury. They are usually more interested in getting at the cause of the trouble and preventing further difficulty than in handing out fines or jail sentences. Judges in Juvenile and Domestic Relations Courts work closely with social workers to help families who are in trouble. The decision of the judge in serious cases may be appealed to a trial court where there is a jury.

2. State trial courts. Serious criminal and civil cases are handled in state **trial courts.** Trial courts are also known as **Courts of Record** because a complete record is kept of the proceedings in each case. All cases are heard by a jury, and a trial judge presides. In about three fourths of the states, the judges are elected by the people of the county or district in which they serve. All the constitutional guarantees of a fair public trial are followed in these courts.

About one third of our states have trial courts called **County Courts.** The County Court is located at the county seat, which is the center of county government in most states. The Court holds sessions at regularly fixed dates. In other states the trial courts are called **District Courts.** There are also **Circuit Courts** where the judge travels a circuit from one county to another to hold court.

Larger cities usually have several trial courts. Sometimes one of the courts hears only civil cases. Another hears only criminal cases. Other names for trial courts in some states are **Appellate Courts, Superior Courts,** or **Courts of Common Pleas.**

3. Higher state courts. If a person has any grounds for believing that his or her case was not handled fairly in a trial court, that person may appeal to a higher court. The usual basis for such appeal is that the trial judge violated one of the rights to a fair trial guaranteed to all citizens by the Constitution of the United States.

The highest court in the state is usually called the **State Supreme Court.** The judges who sit on this court hear cases on appeal in much the same way as does the Supreme Court of the United States. The State Supreme Court judges are elected in most states. But in some states they are appointed by the Governor with the advice and consent of the state Senate. The decision of the State Supreme Court is final unless a federal law or a constitutional issue is involved. Then the case may be appealed to the Supreme Court of the United States.

When hearing an appeal, the State Supreme Court does not conduct a new trial. Instead, the judges of the State Supreme Court study the record of the trial of the lower court, hear the arguments of lawyers, and decide the case by majority vote. The judges must decide whether the trial in the lower court was carried on in such a way that the person on trial was guaranteed all the rights under the Constitution.

In some states, the State Supreme Court is kept so busy that **State District Courts of Appeals** have been set up to help lighten the burden on the State Supreme Court. These courts rank just below the State Supreme Court. In the District Court of Appeals, as in the State Supreme Court, there is no jury trial. Arguments are heard by groups of judges.

OUR OVERCROWDED COURTS

There have been many proposals in recent years for the reform of our state court system. These state courts are overburdened with work. So many cases come before them that the court calendar often runs a year or more behind schedule. It is not unusual to find automobile accident cases that have waited for two to three years for a court settlement.

In many of our largest cities, the jails are crowded with persons who have been accused of crimes, who may or may not be guilty, but who are kept in jail awaiting trial. Some have waited for more than a year. They have remained in jail because they do not have the money to post bail. They have not been brought to trial because there are so many cases ahead of them.

This backlog of cases makes it impossible to fulfill the constitutional guarantee of a speedy public trial. Most Americans point to three causes for this situation. First, there is more court work than ever before, and not enough judges to handle the increasing caseload. Because of our increased population, there are more crimes committed and more lawsuits. Second, trials are long and slow. The very guarantees that protect us often cause trials to take a long time. Third, some courts are not conducted in an efficient manner. For example, some courts do not open until 10 a.m. and they adjourn, or close, at 3 p.m. Judges call frequent recesses, or breaks in a trial. Lawyers sometimes use delaying tactics. Many Americans say that courts have not kept up with the times.

They suggest the courts use modern business techniques such as computers to make court work more efficient.

Many cases never go to trial. They are taken care of quickly by **plea bargaining.** That means that the accused person is allowed to plead guilty to a lesser offense than the original charge. Because of this, the accused person receives a lesser penalty than if there had been a trial and a guilty verdict had been given. Plea bargaining keeps the court cases rolling along by saving time. But the guilt or innocence of the accused person is not proven.

The conditions in our courts are serious. Their improvement is an issue well worth the concern and attention of every American citizen.

CONSIDER AND DISCUSS

Identify. criminal cases / felonies / misdemeanors / civil cases / Justice of the Peace / Justice Court / Magistrate's Court / Police Court / Municipal Court / Traffic Court / Domestic Relations Court / Juvenile Court / Trial Courts / Courts of Record / County Courts / District Courts / Circuit Courts / Appellate Courts / Superior Courts / Courts of Common Pleas / State Supreme Court / State District Courts of Appeals / plea bargaining.

Review. 1. What courts do most states provide to bring justice to their people? 2. Why do we have special courts for young people? 3. Why do states have Supreme Courts?

Discuss. Should an accused person be allowed to plea bargain? Why or why not?

CHAPTER

Summary

Each of our 50 states has its own state government. The state government manages the internal affairs of the state. Like the federal government, the state government is based on a written constitution.

In the Constitution of the United States, many powers are left to the states. The states have power over public education, elections, highways, and setting up local governments. The states share with the federal governments such powers as taxation, law enforcement, and the protection of the health, safety, and welfare of the people.

State governments have legislative, executive, and judicial branches. Most of the states have a two-house legislative (lawmaking) body similar to Congress. And the process of passing state laws is similar to that of putting federal laws through Congress.

The Governors of the states are the executive officers of the state government. They see that state laws are carried out. Governors are aided in their work by the heads of the state's executive departments.

State courts judge state laws and bring to trial those accused of breaking state laws. The court system in the states includes Justice Courts, Trial Courts, Courts of Appeal, and the State Supreme Court.

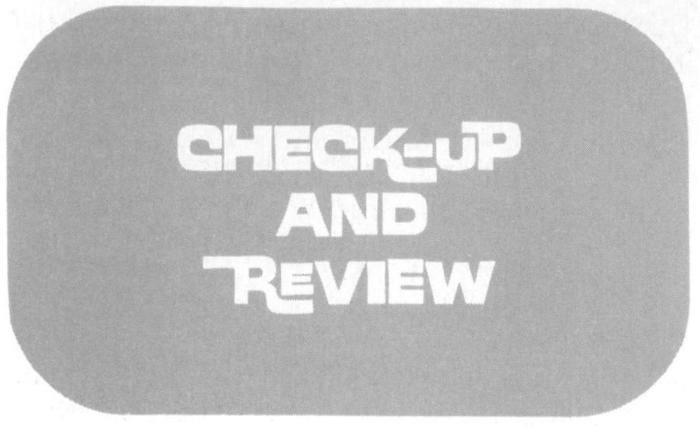

VOCABULARY

Listed below are a number of words that you have learned in your study of state government. Copy the words in your notebook, and after each word explain its meaning.

state	Governor
extradition	Lieutenant Governor
concurrent powers	State Trial Court
reserved powers	State Supreme Court
Comptroller	legislature
felony	Attorney General
misdemeanor	territory
veto	Justice of the Peace

CHECK-UP

The following questions will help you to direct your attention to some of the most important ideas in this chapter. Write down your answers, and come to class prepared to discuss them.

1. What is a state in the United States?
2. Can you name some of the powers reserved to the states?
3. What are the main parts of most state constitutions?
4. How do our states show "full faith and credit" to other states?
5. What are "concurrent powers"? Give several examples.
6. Trace the process by which state laws are made.
7. How does each of the following officials serve in the state government: Governor, Secretary of State, Treasurer, Auditor?
8. What is the state civil service? How does it help to make state government work more efficiently?
9. How are federal and state courts alike? How are they different?
10. What are some of the weaknesses in our courts?

CITIZENSHIP AND YOU

Since state government affects your daily life in many ways, you need to learn all you can about it. You and your classmates will want to explore your state government and share your findings through oral, written, and graphic reports. Below are some suggested activities.

1. Class Projects

Plan to have the class visit the state capital. If possible, make your visit when the state legislature is in session. Arrange to meet the state senator or delegate from your district and discuss the bills the legislature is considering. Remember, the better you plan, the more worthwhile your trip will be. Observe and take notes during your visit. Follow up your visit with discussion and further reading. Don't forget to write a letter thanking those who helped to make the trip possible.

Hold a mock session of the state legislature in your classroom, with various students playing the roles of delegates and officials. In some states, mock assemblies are held in the state capital, with boys and girls from all parts of the state attending as delegates. If anyone in your school has participated in one of these mock sessions, invite him or her to tell the class about it.

2. Group or Committee Projects

Make a large chart of your state government. Include the executive, legislative, and judicial branches of government. Try to make the chart as clear as possible.

Draw a large map showing your state's election districts.

Make a bulletin board displaying articles, drawings, pictures, and cartoons about the government of your state.

Have a committee interview a state legislator and report back to the class.

A group of students can visit a state court and report to the class on their experiences.

3. Individual Projects

Members of the class may investigate and report to the class on one of the following topics:

Voting Requirements in Our State
The State Budget
Our State Constitution
Our State Flower, Flag, and Motto
Recent State Laws
Our State Courts
Our State Senators

CIVICS SKILLS

USING THE DICTIONARY

During your study of state government, you learned a number of important words such as *concurrent, felony, extradition,* and *unicameral.* Most of the words were explained in the text, but some may need to be clarified further. It is a good idea to look up such words in the dictionary. Good dictionary skills will help you to read more intelligently and to express your thoughts as clearly as possible.

In order to make good use of the dictionary, you should be familiar with what it can do for you. Turn to a good dictionary and examine it. The words are arranged in alphabetical order. After each word you will find its meaning and preferred pronunciation. Many dictionaries also provide information about cities, important people in history, abbreviations, and foreign words and phrases.

You will find many activities involving dictionary skills at the end of each chapter in this book. Here are some suggestions that will help you develop good dictionary skills:

1. Get a good dictionary of your own and use it constantly.

2. Use new words. Make them a part of your own vocabulary.

3. Tell someone about a new word you have learned. By sharing your information, you help to make the meaning clear in your own mind so that you will remember it longer.

4. Be curious. Explore new subjects and new words. Don't be afraid to ask questions. If someone uses a word that you do not know, find out what it means. Then use the word yourself when you have a chance and add it to your vocabulary.

5. Work to improve your use of English. Put your ideas in writing. Learn to express yourself. Revise what you have written. Try to express your ideas clearly by using the exact word you need.

PRACTICING YOUR CIVICS SKILLS

Use your dictionary to look up the underlined words in the paragraph that follows. Then rewrite the paragraph using your own words in place of the words you looked up. For example, in the first sentence the words <u>bailiff</u> and <u>defendant</u> are underlined. You might change the sentence to read "In a visit to a court we saw an official who had charge of prisoners bring in the accused person."

In a visit to a court we saw a <u>bailiff</u> bring in the <u>defendant</u>. The <u>judge</u>, a dignified woman, then came in and took her place at the <u>bench</u>. The court clerk read the <u>charge</u> which was filled with legal terms. We learned that the man was accused of <u>grand</u> <u>larceny</u>, which is a <u>felony</u> in our state. The defendant, through his <u>attorney</u>, <u>waived</u> a jury trial. The <u>prosecuting</u> <u>attorney</u> and the defense attorney then approached the bench. After a <u>conference</u> they and the defendant went into the judge's <u>chambers</u>. We were told later that by <u>plea bargaining</u> the accused had pleaded guilty to petty larceny, which is a <u>misdemeanor</u>, and he received a light sentence.

CHAPTER

Introduction

Local governments were our first governments. The primitive tribe that chose the strongest person to be its chief and the oldest leaders to form a council was establishing local government. It was seeking a better, safer life.

In the same way, the first English settlers who landed at Jamestown, Virginia, in 1607 soon realized they needed rules and leaders. At first, the settlers at Jamestown had to look out for themselves. They searched for gold, and had to find their own food and provide their own shelter. As food supplies began to run low, and as the colonists faced hunger and disease, they saw that they needed to work together if the colony was to survive. The colonists formed a council to make laws for the colony. They chose Captain John Smith as president of the council to see that the laws were carried out. This government at Jamestown was the first local government in America.

Today, local government is still the first and most important government in our lives. It protects our lives, our safety, and our homes, and it helps to keep our environment clean. Local government provides us with schools, libraries, and other important services. We can see the work of our local government every day, and if it fails to do a good job it affects each of us directly. In this chapter we shall read about local governments and the work they do, as we study these topics:

1. The Many Units of Local Government
2. Town, Township, and Village Governments
3. City Government
4. How Our Governments Work Together

CHAPTER

8

How Local Governments Serve Their Citizens

1 The Many Units of Local Government

Local government has grown as America has grown. As the American people settled in counties and rural communities, in towns and cities, and in suburbs, they set up local governments. The American people have found that good local governments make their lives easier, safer, and more pleasant. These local governments in the United States include counties, parishes, towns, townships, villages, boroughs, cities, and some with other names. The activities of one or more of these governments affect you every day of your life. They perform many important services for you.

HOW LOCAL GOVERNMENTS ARE ESTABLISHED

All local governments are established by and receive their powers from the state governments. State constitutions provide that the state legislatures are to set up a government for each village, town, county, and city within the state borders. If the people of a town or city wish to change the way their local government is organized, or operates, they must ask the state legislature to allow them to do so. State governments, however, give their local units of government considerable power to manage their own affairs.

Most local governments are incorporated by the state. That is, they are organized by the state and receive **charters,** or plans of government, from the state legislatures. These charters give local governments certain legal powers and authority to govern their own affairs. Local governments have the authority to tax their own citizens, to keep law and order, to own property, to sue and be sued, and to have the same rights in courts as do individuals.

WHY WE NEED LOCAL GOVERNMENT

The people who live in each local area or community depend upon local government to serve them in many ways. We take for granted such conveniences as running water in our homes, sidewalks, trash collection, roads, and good sewage systems. A great deal of planning on the part of local officials was necessary to make such conveniences possible. Only when something goes wrong with local services do we appreciate them.

All these services depend upon a well-run local government. Some of the services, like electricity and public transportation, may be provided by privately owned companies. But local government is very much concerned that these services are economical and well regulated.

It might be possible for each person working alone to provide all the services that local governments provide. Each person might bury trash in the backyard or hire someone to haul it away. Each person might be able to guard against fire by keeping a fire extinguisher handy. But life would be more difficult if each person had to do all these things alone. The people in American communities find that by working together they can secure better and more efficient services than by working alone.

LOCAL AND STATE COOPERATION

Local governments work hand in hand with state governments in order to make our communities better, safer places in which to live. Many of the laws which govern local communities are passed by state legislatures. These laws, along with laws passed by local lawmaking bodies, are called **ordinances,** and are usually enforced by local government.

What are some of the state laws that are enforced by local governments? One of these is the election law. Elections are carried on according to state law. But the polling places and the officials who supervise them are provided by local governments. Another example is the law having to do with weights and measures in the stores. For example, in most states the scales on which a butcher weighs meat must come up to certain standards of state law. Yet this law is often enforced by local inspectors. The police departments of our local governments enforce both state laws and local ordinances.

OUR COUNTY GOVERNMENTS

In many states the largest unit of local government is the county government. Most of our states are divided into **counties.** These counties help to carry out state laws. They also serve as court districts. And they conduct elections. In Louisiana these local units are called **parishes.**

Alaska has no counties. And while Connecticut and Rhode Island have counties, they are geographical areas only, without county governments. Most counties in the New England states are judicial districts. In these areas, the functions of county governments usually are performed by towns.

The county form of government began in the Southern colonies. In this region, agriculture was the main industry and the population was scattered. Tobacco, rice, indigo, and cotton plantations were often located long distances from each other. In these Southern colonies, the county form of government, borrowed from England, seemed well suited to the settlers' needs.

County Government

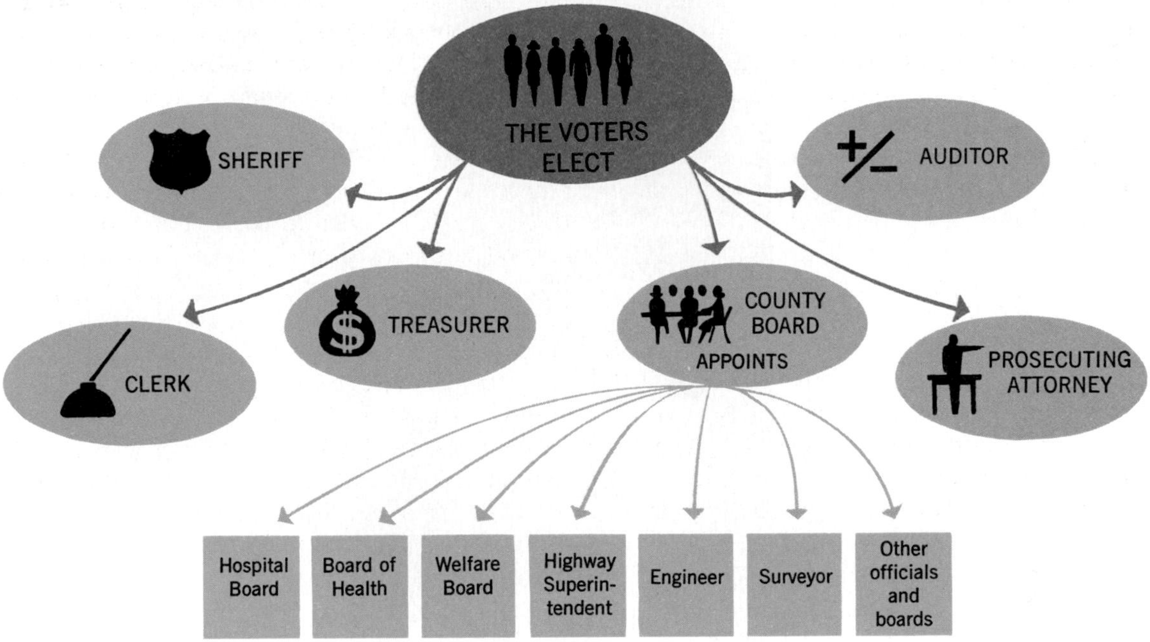

THE VOTERS ELECT

SHERIFF

AUDITOR

CLERK

TREASURER

COUNTY BOARD APPOINTS

PROSECUTING ATTORNEY

Hospital Board

Board of Health

Welfare Board

Highway Superin-tendent

Engineer

Surveyor

Other officials and boards

Each Southern colony was divided into a number of counties. The plantation owners in each county met regularly in some central, easy-to-reach town, which became known as the **county seat.** At these meetings, the plantation owners passed the laws of the county government. The chief official in this early form of government was a **Sheriff,** a name borrowed from a similar official in England. The Sheriff's job was to see that the county laws were enforced.

Today, in states where counties are important, county government serves two main purposes. First, the county governments help the state government in collecting various state taxes, supervising elections, and enforcing state laws. Second, county governments serve the people by providing them with roads, schools, and libraries, with health and welfare services, and with law enforcement.

The number and size of counties vary from state to state. The large state of Texas has 254 counties, while Delaware has only 3. In all, there are slightly more than 3,000 counties in the United States.

COUNTY OFFICIALS

At the head of a strong county government is a group of officials elected by the voters. This governing group is often called the **County Board.** Other official names for this group are **County Commissioners, County Council, Fiscal Court, County Court,** or **Board of County Supervisors.**

The County Board may pass local laws regulating health and safety. It may collect taxes on real estate or personal property in the county. The County Board also supervises county buildings such as the courthouse, the jail, and the library.

In many counties there is no single leader at the head of the executive branch of the county government. Instead, there are several county officials, each with separate

The police in our communities enforce many laws passed by state and local governments. Here, a traffic control officer makes sure that drivers obey the city traffic laws.

responsibilities. These officials are elected by the people of the county.

The **Sheriff** enforces the law. He or she selects deputies to help in law enforcement. The Sheiff arrests lawbreakers, and carries out orders of the courts. In many places, the Sheriff has charge of the county jail.

The **County Clerk** keeps a record of the actions and decisions of the County Board. The Clerk also keeps records of births, deaths, marriages, and election results. Usually he or she tells the public of all laws and regulations passed by the County Board.

The **County Treasurer** takes care of the county's money. The Treasurer sees that no money is spent unless the County Board approves it. Sometimes the Treasurer collects taxes. But often counties elect a **Tax Collector** to do this job.

The **County Auditor** examines the county financial records and sees that these official records of taxes received and money spent are kept properly.

The **County Prosecuting Attorney** represents the state government in county trials. He or she is also known as the **District Attorney** or **State's Attorney.**

The number of county officials varies from state to state. Even in the same state, some counties have more officials than other counties. Some counties have as many as 70 officials. They include the sealer of weights and measures, a veterinarian, a purchasing agent, a public defender, the park commissioner, public health nurses, and the coroner.

THE RISE OF THE COUNTY EXECUTIVE

As the population of areas outside of the cities has grown, there has been a demand for better county government. With the approval of the voters and of the state legislature, a number of counties have reorganized their governments. Many have established the position of **County Manager** or **County Executive.** This official is usually hired by the County Board to carry out the work of the county government. In some places this person is elected by the voters. The County Executive's duties are to supervise the work of the county government and to put it on a businesslike basis. This type of county government places the responsibility in the hands of a single executive.

CONSIDER AND DISCUSS

Identify. local government / charters / ordinances / county / parishes / county seat / Sheriff / County Board / Sheriff / County Clerk / County Treasurer / Tax Collector / County Auditor / County Prosecuting Attorney / County Manager

Review. 1. How are the local governments in our states established? 2. What powers do local governments have? 3. What services do local governments provide? 4. Name the principal county officials.

Discuss. In what ways does local government directly affect your life?

2 Town, Township, and Village Governments

Although counties are the largest of all the units of local government, they are not always the most important. In a number of states, the counties serve only as districts of the state for the purpose of conducting elections. In these states the real work of local government is carried on by other units of government. And in all of our states, counties must share the job of local government with other units of government. What are these other units of local government? There are several of them: towns, townships, villages and boroughs, cities, and special districts.

TYPES OF GOVERNMENT IN THE COLONIES

The town form of government began in the New England colonies. The settlers in each New England colony received a grant of land from the English king. On this land, the colonists established small towns in which they built their homes and their churches.

At the edges of the towns, the colonists established their farms. Every day, they left their homes and worked on the farms. The colonists considered these outlying farms to be part of their towns. Later some of the settlers moved to the farms outside the towns. But as long as these farms were located within the town limits, the people who lived on them were counted as members of that town. Thus, the New England towns stretched out into the countryside as counties did in other settlements.

In New Amsterdam (later New York) the settlers set up a village government. Only the village itself, which included the homes of the settlers as well as other buildings, belonged to the village government. The outlying parts of the settlement were not considered part of the village, and they later came under the county government. As other settlers pushed farther west, they settled in other communities. Some of them called their settlements **towns.** In Pennsylvania settlements were often called **boroughs.** Thus, many different names were used for these small settlements.

EARLY TOWN GOVERNMENT IN NEW ENGLAND

The people of the early New England towns worked out a simple yet effective form of local government—the **town meeting.** All

At town meetings, town business that concerns all the people or a large majority of them is discussed and then voted on. The town meeting pictured here took place in a New England town.

the people who lived in a town, as well as those who lived on the surrounding farms, met together regularly in the town hall. At these public meetings, the citizens of the town talked over their problems and decided how they should be handled.

Every citizen had a chance to speak on any question. After all opinions had been heard, the people at the meeting were asked to vote on the question. In this way, each citizen had a direct vote in the government. The New England town meeting was a form of **direct democracy.** A number of the less heavily populated towns of New England still carry on their business in this way. Town meetings are also held in a number of states in the Middle West. How is a typical town meeting conducted in the United States today?

THE TOWN MEETING TODAY

In New England towns, the regular town meeting is usually held in the spring. A warrant, or notice of the town meeting, is posted in various parts of town well ahead of the meeting. It is the official notice of the time of the meeting, and it lists the town business to be discussed.

On meeting day, the voters gather in the town hall. Before the meeting gets under way, the town elections are held. Some towns, however, wait until after the meeting to hold elections. The voters elect several (usually three or five) officials, called **Selectmen.** These men or women manage the town's affairs during the period between regular town meetings. The voters also elect the other town officials, including a town clerk, members of the school committee, a tax collector, a tax assessor, and fish and game wardens. Some towns elect these officials on a separate election day rather than at the town meeting.

Before or after the elections, the voters discuss the town's business. They elect a **moderator** to preside over this part of the meeting. The Selectmen who have been in office for the past year report on their activities. The Treasurer gives the financial report, explains the debts the town has incurred, and asks the meeting to vote to pay these debts. Then comes a discussion of town business for the coming year. The voters may be asked to give their opinions on such matters as street lighting, the building of a new school, purchasing more snow removal equipment, improving a town road, or a proposed increase in the tax rate. After the discussion ends, a vote is taken on each item. Voting is usually by voice vote, but on important issues the townspeople stand to be counted.

THE REPRESENTATIVE TOWN MEETING

The town meeting form of government works well in areas of small population. There it is easy for all the voters to gather at one central place. But as the population of many towns has grown in recent years, some New England towns have had to make changes in the form of their town meetings. One change which has worked well is the **representative town meeting.** In this type of town government, the voters elect representatives to attend the town meeting and to make decisions for them. This system is also known sometimes as the **limited town meeting.**

EARLY TOWNSHIP GOVERNMENTS

In the Middle Atlantic states (New York, Pennsylvania, New Jersey, and Delaware), counties were divided into smaller units of local government called **townships.** These townships served many of the same purposes as the towns in New England. Townships were responsible for maintaining local roads and rural schools, and for looking after the poor.

As county governments grew in the Middle Atlantic states, township governments became less important except in rural areas. In time, these states developed a form of local government called **county-township government.** In this mixed form of local government, the county and township officials work side by side to help the people to govern their local affairs.

A stronger type of township developed in those Middle Western states that were carved out of the old Northwest Territory between the Ohio and the Mississippi Rivers. As you may recall, in 1785 Congress worked out a system of surveying, or measuring, this vast area. According to the system, the Northwest Territory was divided into areas 9.6 kilometers square (six miles square) called **congressional townships.**

These early congressional townships were *not* units of government. They were only divisions of land. As settlers from New England moved into this territory, they set up governments similar to the town governments they had known in the states from which they came. The new units of government became known as **civil townships.** Sometimes a civil township occupied the same area as a congressional township, but usually it took in more territory.

TOWNSHIP GOVERNMENT TODAY

Today, townships exist in 21 states—mostly in the Middle Atlantic and Middle Western states. They provide government for rural areas. Towns or villages that are located within the boundaries of a township have been granted their own forms of government by the legislature.

Township governments differ somewhat from state to state. Usually the township is

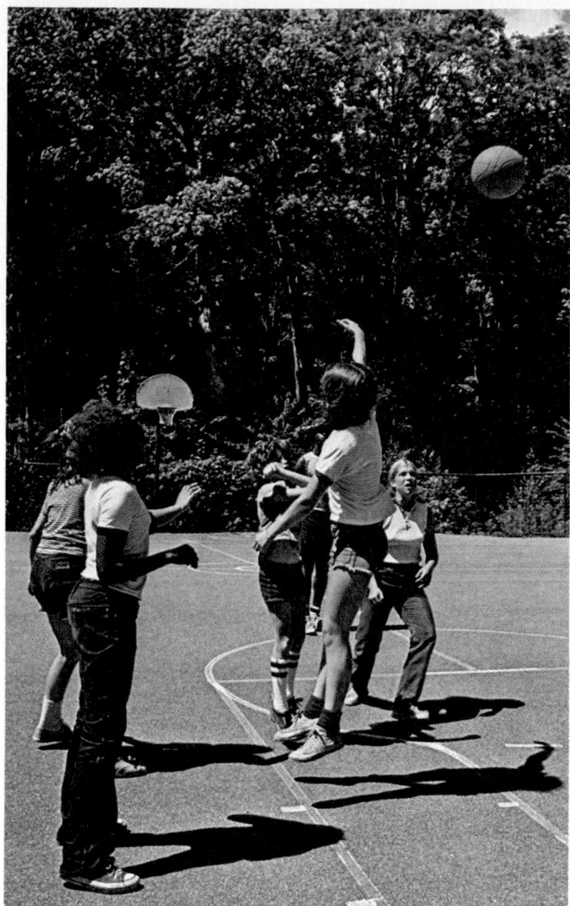

These young people are playing basketball at school. School districts are an example of special districts set up by the state.

headed by a chairperson or **Township Supervisor** who is elected by the voters. The voters also elect a **Township Board of Commissioners** or **Board of Trustees,** who make the laws or regulations for the township. There is usually a Township Clerk, who keeps the official records of the township. Law is enforced by **Constables,** and minor cases are tried by the Justice of the Peace. Most townships also elect an assessor, a treasurer, a collector of taxes, and school board members.

SPECIAL DISTRICTS AND SCHOOL DISTRICTS

Often, people living in a certain area within their local unit of government have a special need not shared by others living within the area. In such cases, the people may go directly to the state legislature and ask that the legislature grant them a charter to set up a **special district.** For example, in a farming area in a part of a large Western county, the farmers may wish to have irrigation water for their crops. To pay for the pipes, ditches, and other equipment to supply this need, the state legislature may set up an irrigation district. This special district has no other purpose than to supply water and to tax the lands at a rate sufficient to pay the costs. All other local government services remain in the hands of the county.

Thousands of special districts have been formed in states for the purpose of meeting the special needs of the people in various localities. Some of these special needs are sewage disposal, fire protection, police protection, water supply, parks and recreation centers, library service, public transportation, and gas and electric systems. The legislature usually provides for an elected or appointed commission to handle the details of the special district.

The most common special districts are those set up by each state to provide local schools. There are more than 15,000 **school districts** in the United States. Each of these districts has its own governing body called the **Board of Education.** They employ an executive, usually called a **Superintendent of Schools,** to manage the day-to-day operation of the schools.

VILLAGE AND BOROUGH GOVERNMENTS

Village government is another unit of local government. When rural communities grow to a population of 200 to 300 people, their inhabitants often find that they have problems that require them to work and plan together. As a result, they may decide to organize their community as a **village** or **borough** and to set up their own local government.

The request to establish a village or borough government must be sent to the state legislature. If the legislature approves, it permits the village or borough to establish its own government. The village government may be given the power to collect its own taxes, to pave its streets, to set up a fire company and a police department, and to provide other services.

The village or borough is often governed by a three- to nine-member **council,** or **Board of Trustees.** The voters also elect an executive called the **Chief Burgess,** or **President of the Board of Trustees,** to carry out the laws. This person is also sometimes called the **Mayor** of the village.

In small boroughs or villages, most of the local officials serve on a part-time basis, since there is not enough village business to occupy them full time. However, there may be a full-time clerk, a constable, a street commissioner, and an engineer.

If the population of a village or borough becomes large enough, the people may ask the legislature to grant the community a city charter. The number of people needed to qualify as a city varies from state to state. But many states require a population of 2,500 people before a state charter is granted. You will learn more about city governments in the next section of this chapter.

CONSIDER AND DISCUSS

Identify. town / borough / town meeting / direct democracy / Selectmen / moderator / representative town meeting / township / county-township government / congressional township / civil township / Township Supervisor / Board of Commissioners / Constables / special district / school district / Board of Education / Superintendent of Schools / village / Chief Burgess

Review. 1. Why is the New England town meeting called a form of "direct democracy"? 2. Why are county governments less important in New England than in the South? 3. What are the main purposes served by township governments? 4. What advantages might a rural community gain by becoming a village?

Discuss. Some people think that there are too many units of local government and that this makes it difficult to have good government. What do you think? Why?

3 City Government

More Americans live under city government than under any other unit of local government. Because a city usually has a large population crowded into a small area, it has more difficult problems than other units of local government. The city government has to handle a variety of problems dealing with health, education, and safety. It must keep traffic flowing smoothly through neighborhood streets. City police patrols and squad cars must be on the alert to prevent crime. City garbage and trash collections must operate efficiently. Street lighting, paving, water supply, traffic signals, crossing guards, sewage systems—all these and hundreds of other services are the daily business of city governments.

Besides providing such services, city government helps to provide cultural activities that are an important part of city life. Cities help to support libraries, museums, parks, and botanical gardens. City government often contributes to universities, hospitals, musical groups, and art galleries.

Many city governments encourage architects to design buildings that make the city more beautiful.

THE ORGANIZATION OF CITY GOVERNMENT

City governments, like all other local governments, are established by state legislatures. Most state constitutions require that a community grow to a certain size before it can become a city. When the population of a community reaches that size, the people ask the state legislature to grant it a charter. A **city charter** is like a constitution. It contains a plan of government, and it sets forth provisions for the city government and outlines the powers granted to it.

City governments differ in the way they are organized. In general, there are three main kinds of city government. They are (1) the mayor-council government, (2) the commission government, and (3) the city manager government. You will want to learn which form your city has and how it operates.

THE MAYOR-COUNCIL CITY GOVERNMENT

In the mayor-council form of city government, the lawmaking body is called the **City Council.** The chief executive of the city government is the **Mayor,** who sees that city laws, or ordinances, are enforced. The Mayor and the members of the City Council are elected by the voters of the city. Their term of office varies, but in most cases it is either two years or four years.

Under the mayor-council government, the city is divided into districts called **wards.** Each ward elects one member of the Council. In some cities, though, the people of the city elect a number of **council members-at-large** (from the entire city or area). Almost all City Councils are unicameral. That is, they have just one house.

In addition to electing the Mayor and the Council, city voters elect other officials, including a treasurer, judges of the municipal courts, a city attorney or solicitor, and tax assessors. Other officials, either elected or appointed, are the heads of such departments as police, fire fighting, traffic, water, welfare, parks and playgrounds, civil defense, housing, licenses, and purchasing.

THE WEAK-MAYOR PLAN OF CITY GOVERNMENT

During the early years of our nation's growth, the American people were slow to grant strong powers to their mayors. The experience of colonists with English governors who did not listen to the people's wishes made Americans fear officials who might be too strong. For this reason, some cities developed the **weak-mayor plan.**

Under the weak-mayor plan of city government, the City Council checks the Mayor's powers. For example, the Council may appoint the heads of all city departments. These heads report directly to the City Council. In addition, the Mayor must obtain the consent of the Council in order to spend money or take other actions. The weak-mayor plan often results in conflicts between the Mayor and the Council, with the result that important city work often does not get done in these cases.

THE STRONG-MAYOR PLAN OF CITY GOVERNMENT

In recent years, most mayor-council cities have made their governments more efficient by following the **strong-mayor plan** of city government. Under the strong-mayor plan, the Mayor is given more responsibility for running city affairs. The Mayor is also given increased power.

The strong Mayor appoints most of the city officials and can also dismiss them if they do not do a good job. The Mayor is also given the responsibility of drawing up

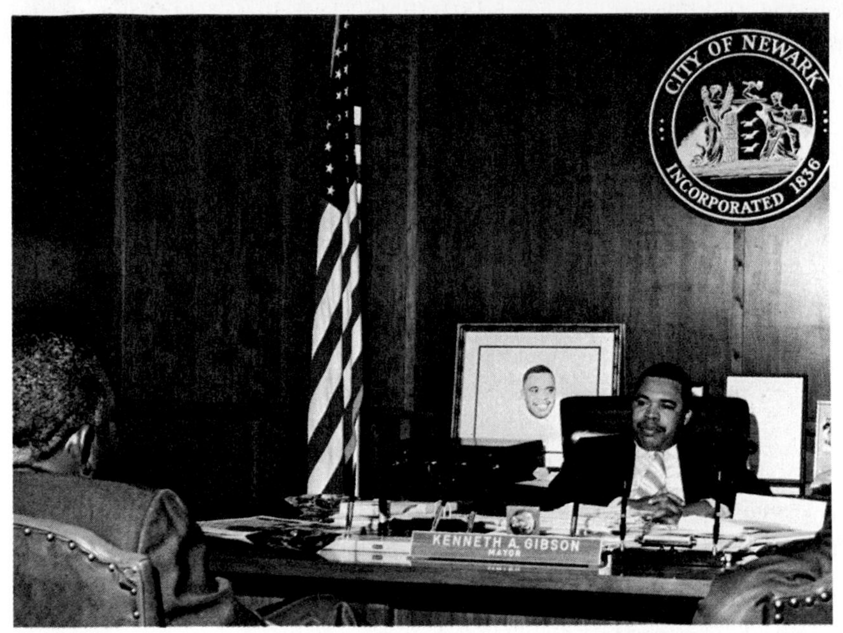

The Mayor of a large city often has a busy day. Here, Mayor Kenneth A. Gibson of Newark, New Jersey, meets with aides in his office.

the city budget. When the Council has approved a budget, the Mayor is responsible for seeing that the city's money is spent properly. Under this plan, the Mayor takes the lead in carrying on the city's business. The Mayor has the chief responsibility for the city's government. It is difficult for the Mayor to make excuses or to blame the Council or other city officials for weaknesses in the city government.

One possible disadvantage of this strong-mayor plan is that sometimes an inefficient Mayor may misuse power. As a result, some cities have given up the mayor-council form and have turned to other types of city government.

THE COMMISSION PLAN OF CITY GOVERNMENT

A new form of city government grew out of a hurricane which struck Galveston, Texas, in 1900. A huge tidal wave swept across the city, flooding homes and businesses and causing millions of dollars in damages. Nearly 7,000 of the city's 37,000 residents lost their lives. The city's Mayor and Council were unable to handle the disaster. Yet something had to be done at once.

Leading citizens in Galveston asked the state legislature for permission to set up a new form of city government. It was called the **commission plan.** Under the plan the city was governed by a **Commission** consisting of five people. Each **Commissioner** was put in charge of a department of city government. The Commissioner was given the power to run the department as a business would be run. The new commission plan met the emergency in Galveston. And it worked so well that it became the form of government in that city for the next 70 years. Other American cities also copied this commission plan of government.

THE WORK OF THE COMMISSION

Under a commission government, a city is governed by a Commission elected by the voters. The size of this city Commission

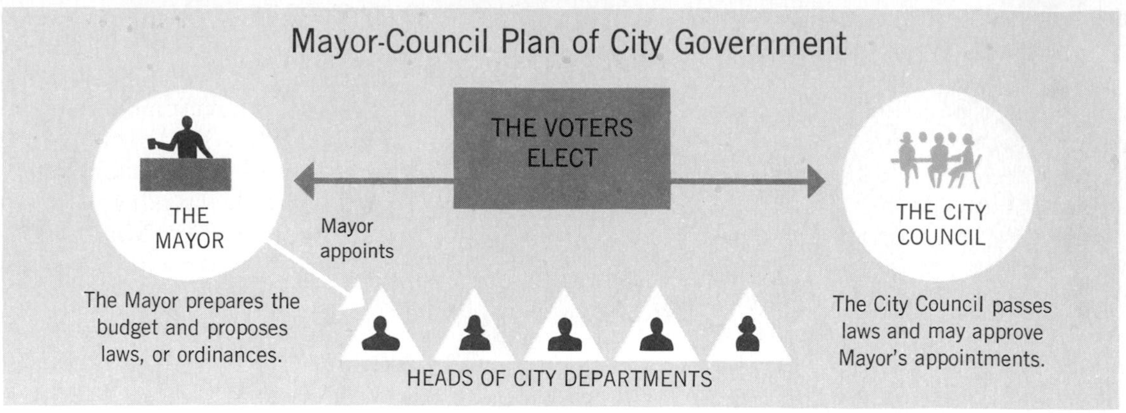

Mayor-Council Plan of City Government
THE VOTERS ELECT
THE MAYOR
Mayor appoints
THE CITY COUNCIL
The Mayor prepares the budget and proposes laws, or ordinances.
HEADS OF CITY DEPARTMENTS
The City Council passes laws and may approve Mayor's appointments.

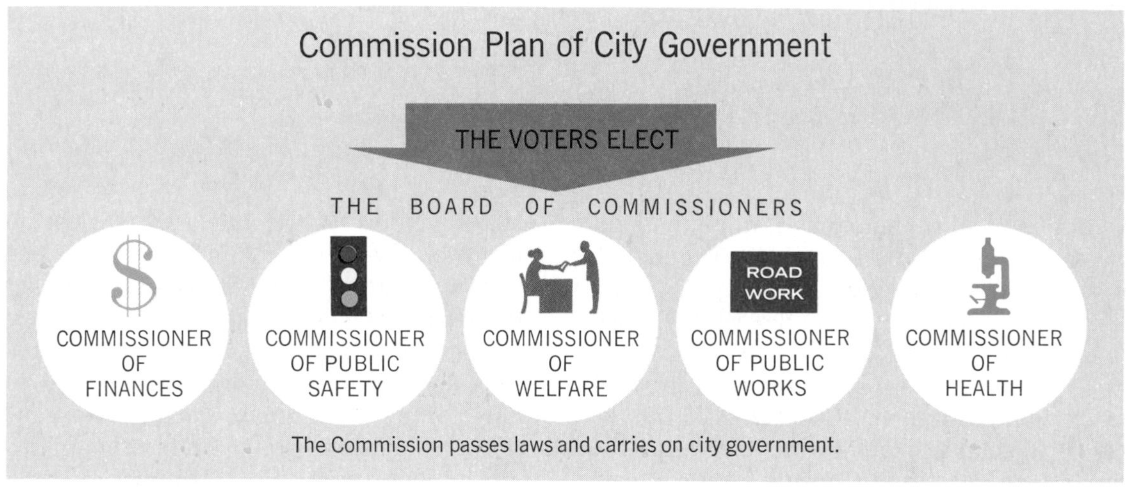

Commission Plan of City Government
THE VOTERS ELECT
THE BOARD OF COMMISSIONERS
ROAD WORK
COMMISSIONER OF FINANCES
COMMISSIONER OF PUBLIC SAFETY
COMMISSIONER OF WELFARE
COMMISSIONER OF PUBLIC WORKS
COMMISSIONER OF HEALTH
The Commission passes laws and carries on city government.

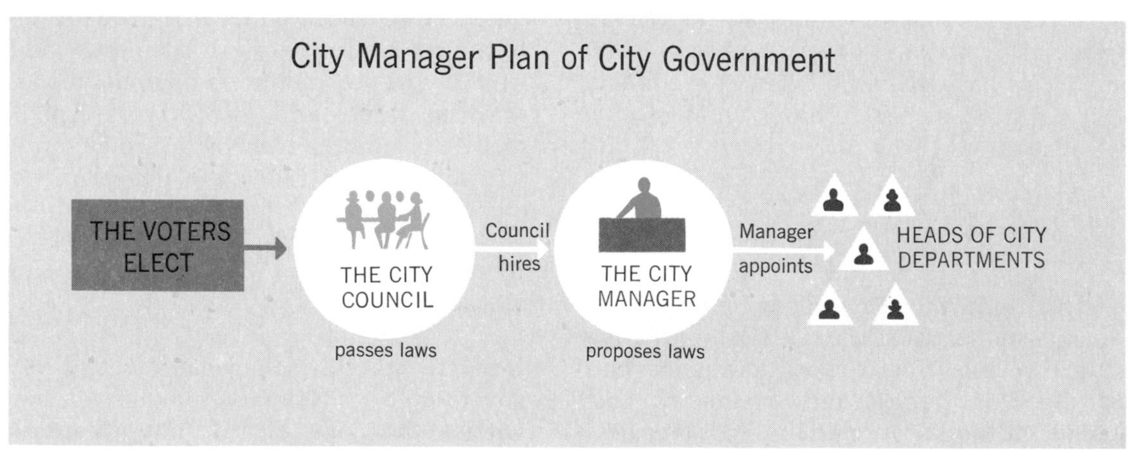

City Manager Plan of City Government
THE VOTERS ELECT
THE CITY COUNCIL
passes laws
Council hires
THE CITY MANAGER
proposes laws
Manager appoints
HEADS OF CITY DEPARTMENTS

varies from three to seven, but usually it has five members. The Commission is the city's lawmaking body as well as its executive body. The Commission passes the city's ordinances, and each Commissioner is in charge of an important city department.

One Commissioner usually is the head of the department of safety, which includes the police and fire fighters. Another Commissioner is in charge of public works, and must see that the city has an adequate supply of pure water and that the streets are kept clean and in good repair. A third Commissioner is in charge of the city's finances, including tax collections. Another Commissioner heads the welfare department, which supervises the care of the poor, the aged, and the unemployed. The health department is under the supervision of another Commissioner who is in charge of city hospitals, clinics, and health inspectors. The city's schools are supervised by the Board of Education, not by a Commissioner.

The Commissioners meet as a group to make the city laws. But they enforce the laws as individual Commissioners. Each Commissioner carries out the laws as they apply to the department. Either the voters or the Commissioners choose one of the Commissioners to be Mayor. The Mayor has no special powers. Except for presiding over meetings of the City Commission, the Mayor has the same powers as other Commissioners.

In some cases, the commission form of city government has had certain disadvantages. The voters sometimes found that it was not possible to elect officials who knew how to run a department of the city's government. Then, too, there are activities of city government that can come under several departments. Sometimes Commissioners disagree about who should handle these activities. Because of these possible weaknesses in the commission form of city government, some cities have turned to another form of city government—the city manager plan.

THE CITY MANAGER PLAN

In 1908, Staunton, Virginia, was the first city to set up a form of government known as the **city manager plan.** Under city manager government, the voters elect a **City Council** to act as the city's lawmaking body. The Council then hires a **City Manager,** who carries out the city's business and enforces the city laws. The City Manager is the city's chief executive, and appoints the heads of the departments. They report directly to the City Manager. Under this system, the city is run much like any big business firm by specially trained people.

Where do cities find good City Managers? A small city may turn to a university in which courses in city management are taught. They interview graduates and hire one to run the city. Or the city may choose as its Manager an engineer who has worked on city projects. A business person who has been active in community affairs may also be chosen. A large city often hires someone who has a good record as Manager of a smaller city, perhaps in another state.

Since City Managers are hired by the Council to serve the city's needs, they must do a good job or the Council may dismiss them. City Managers are appointed, not elected, so that they will not take part in party politics or be under any political pressure. In this way, the City Manager is given a free hand to run the city government efficiently and economically.

The city manager form of government, too, has some disadvantages. In some cases, city manager government may not be suited to a city's needs. Some large cities, such as Cleveland, Ohio, have tried the city manager plan and found that it did not work well for them. Some of our smaller cities find that they cannot afford the salary required to hire a good Manager. And some cities believe that they are better governed when the voters elect the officials who are to run the city's government.

CONSIDER AND DISCUSS

Identify. city charter / City Council / Mayor / mayor-council government / wards / council members-at-large / weak-mayor plan / strong-mayor plan / commission plan / Commissioners / city manager plan / City Manager

Review. 1. What is the difference between the weak-mayor plan and the strong-mayor plan of city government? 2. What are the advantages of the commission plan of city government? 3. If your City Council was looking for a City Manager, where might they be able to find one?

Discuss. Which plan of city government do you favor? Why?

4 How Our Governments Work Together

You live under at least three levels of government—local, state, and national. If each of our levels of government paid no attention to the work of the other governments, life would become difficult and mixed up. City governments might pass city laws that went against state laws. State governments might ignore federal laws and do whatever they wished. No citizen could be sure which set of laws to obey.

HOW POWERS ARE DIVIDED AMONG OUR GOVERNMENTS

Fortunately, under our federal system of government, the powers of each level of government are clearly defined and understood. The Constitution of the United States is the "supreme law of the land." All levels of government must obey it.

Our state constitutions, in turn, set up rules which govern the people of each state. These state constitutions must not, of course, take away from the people any of the rights guaranteed in the federal Constitution.

Local units of government, such as counties, townships, villages, and cities, have their powers defined for them by the state legislatures. These powers are explained in their charters. In this way, each of our governments has its work to do. And each is given the powers to do it.

WHY OUR GOVERNMENTS WORK TOGETHER

Many of our nation's problems call for cooperation among local, state, and national governments. Consider, for example, the way in which America's modern highway system was built.

Back in colonial days, the building of a road was considered a local project. If the people of any town wanted a road, they had to build it themselves. As towns spread westward, each county undertook to build connecting roads. The county called upon the local farmers and townspeople who needed the road to supply the labor or to provide money to hire workers.

These early roads were often terrible. They were twisting and rutted, dusty in dry weather and muddy after a rain. But these roads were cheap to build and easy to keep repaired. The local units of government could easily handle the job of planning and paying for such roads.

As our nation grew, highways were needed to connect the East with the growing West. As a result, Congress voted to have the federal government build some main roads to the West. The most important of these early roads was the **National Road** (or Cumberland Road). It started at Cumberland, Maryland, and went as far west as Vandalia, Illinois. For a long time, however, most roads throughout the United States

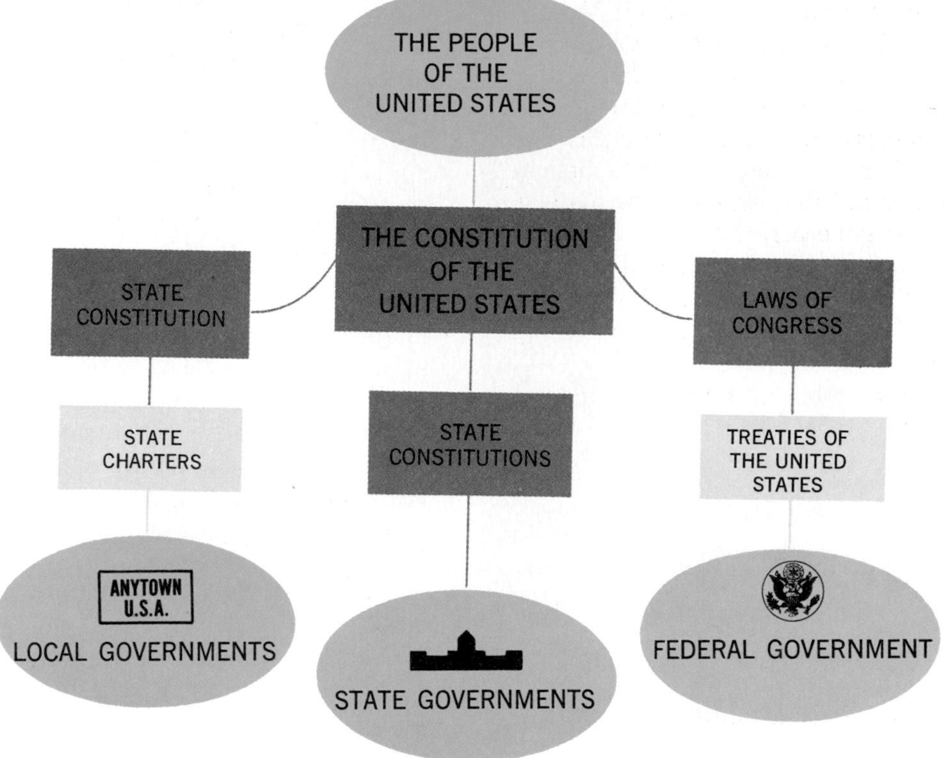

were built by local governments or by private companies that collected a **toll,** or fee.

When the automobile was invented, it became clear that new and better roads were needed. No longer was road building a local problem alone. Motorists needed new highways that would stretch across their home state and connect with roads in other states.

STATE AND FEDERAL GOVERNMENTS COOPERATE IN ROAD BUILDING

Late in the 1800's, even before automobiles were in common use, the state of New Jersey was the first to use state funds to help its counties improve their local roads. Massachusetts went a step further in 1894 when it began to build a statewide highway system. Other states soon followed the lead of New Jersey and Massachusetts and set up state highway departments to build main roads. Today, most well-traveled roads are built and maintained by the state. State governments spend many billions of dollars each year to build and improve roads and to keep them safe.

The federal government has an important role in our states' road-building programs. It helps to pay a large part of the cost of new state highways. It does so because good roads contribute to the welfare of all our citizens. The **Interstate Highway System** planned by the federal government now connects all parts of the country and is being extended and improved. It is a joint project of the federal and state governments. The states plan the routes and supervise construction of the roads. But the roads must meet

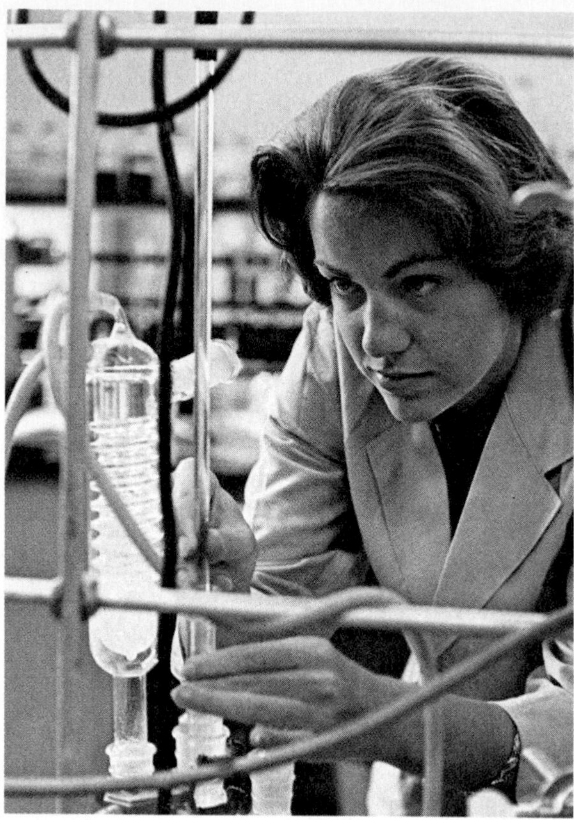

The FBI helps state and local police by giving them information from their laboratories and fingerprint files.

federal requirements. The federal government pays 90 cents of every dollar of the cost. This money comes from a Highway Trust Fund to which motorists contribute when they pay taxes on gasoline.

The federal government also assists state and local governments in building other highways, bridges, and tunnels. The states receive more than $6 billion in federal funds each year for such purposes.

OTHER WAYS IN WHICH GOVERNMENTS COOPERATE

Our federal, state, and local governments work together in many other ways. Local and state police officers work together with the Federal Bureau of Investigation. They help each other in trying to capture criminals. Most states have crime laboratories where services also are used by local police officials. State and local police may obtain helpful information from FBI files, such as the fingerprint files. Criminals arrested and convicted by local governments are often sent to prisons and reformatories maintained by state governments.

The stores and business firms in your own neighborhood must obey many state laws to promote good business practices. The safety of the men and women who work in local factories or mines is aided by state inspectors who see that safety regulations are obeyed. State bank inspectors help to keep your savings safe. Insurance companies in your locality are also supervised by the state to protect policy holders and to see that claims are settled promptly and fairly.

State governments also serve local communities by setting up state licensing boards. These boards give examinations and issue licenses to doctors, dentists, lawyers, engineers, nurses, and accountants. This service helps to make sure that communities have qualified professional workers.

LOCAL, STATE, AND FEDERAL COOPERATION IN EDUCATION

Public education is one of the most important fields in which the various levels of government cooperate to serve the public. State governments grant funds to localities to help them operate their schools. State boards of education provide helpful services for local school districts and see that they obey state laws. Actual control of the schools, however, is left to local boards of education, who know the needs of the students in their schools.

The federal government cooperates by helping with special funds for schools. Schools with a large number of students from poor areas receive special federal aid to enrich the educational program. The federal government also supports research in education and assists the states with programs to make education more up to date.

OTHER FEDERAL AID PROGRAMS

The federal government also provides state and local governments with funds to help them carry out certain important programs. Such programs include public assistance to the aged, the blind, the disabled, families with dependent children, and medical and financial aid to the poor. These funds are called **grants-in-aid.** They must be used for specific programs. Also, the programs must meet the standards set by the federal government.

The governments that receive this money promise to match the sum with their own funds. That is, for every dollar received from the federal government, the state or local government must also put up a dollar. However, the number of programs are based on the state's ability to pay. For example, a poor state might pay only 25 percent of the costs of a program. The federal government would pay the other 75 percent.

But what about other pressing financial needs facing state and local governments? In 1972, Congress passed a **Revenue Sharing Act.** This act provides over $6 billion a year to state and local governments. The funds may be used without federal controls for programs they feel are needed.

CITY GOVERNMENTS WORK TOGETHER

Today's speedy transportation and rapid communication have brought our cities much closer together than they used to be. They face many common problems. The **United States Conference of Mayors** meets regularly so that the mayors of our cities may compare problems and their solutions. Some of the problems that may be discussed at a conference are: how to get more money for police, what to do if fire fighters go on strike, what to do about air pollution, and how to deal more efficiently with garbage collection.

As neighboring cities grow closer together they share many problems. Take, for example, the many villages and townships that make up Nassau County on Long Island, New York. As the population of this area grew from 300,000 in 1947 to nearly a million and a half in 1970, one community merged into the next in an almost continuous line. The officials of the various cities in the county realized that close cooperation by all Nassau County cities was becoming an absolute necessity.

For greater efficiency and better service, the officials of the various localities got together and agreed that their communities should combine most of their services and share them. As a result, fire alarms are now answered by the fire departments of several neighboring cities. Local schools are shared in order that students may attend schools offering special courses that they need. The costs of trash collection, water, and other services are shared. Only the police departments are maintained separately by the various towns, but even here Nassau County communities cooperate closely.

GOVERNMENTS ALSO COMPETE

Although government cooperation is growing, governments also compete with one another. The various levels of government often compete for taxes. For example, a family may have to pay income taxes to both state and federal governments. But they may also have to pay a sizable real estate tax to one or more local governments.

States compete with each other to attract industry. They offer businesses lower taxes, a good supply of labor, good highways, and favorable laws to encourage industry to move to their state. Cities compete for trade and industry in similar fashion.

The federal government and federal laws sometimes seem to interfere or compete with local laws and customs. The federal government may challenge the election procedures in a state or locality if such procedures conflict with federal law.

Our combined system of federal, state, and local governments is complex. It would be surprising if there were not instances of conflict. As our population and our industries grow, the problems we face will increase. Only by working together can we make our democracy work.

CONSIDER AND DISCUSS

Identify. National Road / toll / Interstate Highway System / grants-in-aid / Revenue Sharing Act / United States Conference of Mayors

Review. 1. Why is the federal government interested in better roads? 2. How does a state use its licensing power to aid localities? 3. How does the federal government aid schools? 4. Give examples of the way governments compete with each other.

Discuss. How does your local government cooperate with other communities?

CHAPTER Summary

Each of us is directly affected by our local government. The governments of our cities, towns, townships, and counties take care of many of the practical needs of our lives. They provide fire and police protection, a water supply, a sewer system, trash removal, street lighting, and other necessary services.

County governments serve the common needs of people over a fairly large area. In some states, more and more power has been given to the towns and cities, and the counties serve mainly as election districts.

Town meetings still serve much of New England and some parts of the Middle West. The rapid growth of population, however, has caused larger New England towns to set up representative town meetings.

Town and township governments in many areas work with the county in governing and in providing services to their communities. Special districts provide for specific needs of people, often in rural areas. Sewage systems, water supply, and local schools are problems handled by these local governments.

City government has had to meet many special problems in recent years. Some cities have kept the mayor-council plan of government. Other cities have turned to the commission plan or are using the city manager plan of government.

In solving their mutual problems, the levels of local government in the United States have learned to cooperate. But many pressing problems also cause competition and conflicts that need attention.

VOCABULARY

Write a paragraph summary of the main ideas in this chapter. In the first paragraph use the following words:

county	County Board
county seat	Auditor
Sheriff	County Manager

The second paragraph should contain the following words:

town meeting	representative town meeting
Selectmen	township
moderator	special district

In the third paragraph, the following words should be used and explained:

Mayor	wards
Commissioner	City Council
City Manager	charter

CHECK-UP

Write out brief answers to the following questions and come to class prepared to discuss each of your answers.

1. In what ways do local governments affect your daily life?
2. What are some of the legal powers of incorporated towns?
3. Why have representative town meetings been used in some New England and Middle Western towns?
4. Has the spread of our population into the suburbs increased or decreased the importance of county government? Why?
5. Why might the problem of trash disposal lead to the formation of a special district?
6. Why is it said that city government is probably the most important unit of local government in present-day America?
7. What are the three principal forms of city government? How are they alike? different?
8. Why might a small city be more likely to have a mayor than a city manager?
9. How do federal, state, and local governments cooperate in road building?
10. Can you give an example of a way in which several cities might cooperate for the good of their citizens?

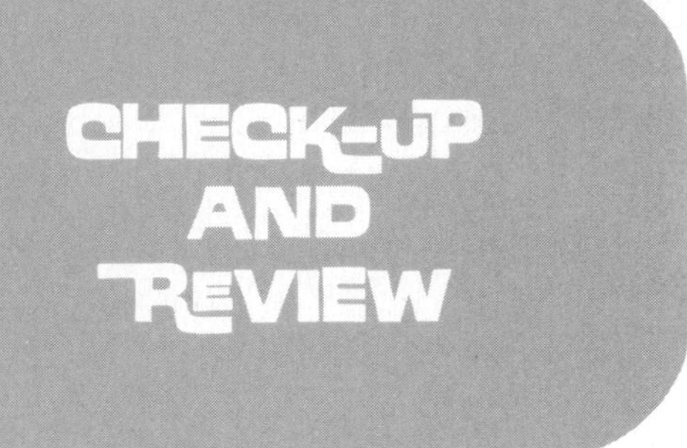

CITIZENSHIP AND YOU

As you study local government you will want to learn more about your own county, village, town, or city. Get to know the government closest to you. Here are some valuable projects.

1. Class Projects

Your class may cooperate in a local "clean-up, paint-up" campaign. Or your class may volunteer to take part in an anti-littering campaign. Ask your local chamber of commerce how you can help in programs of this kind.

Field trips to various parts of town, such as the city hall, police station, fire department, and other points of interest, will help you to get to know your community better.

Invite the mayor, a council member, or some other local official to talk to your class and explain how your community is governed.

Conduct an open-forum debate on this topic: *Resolved,* That the city manager form of government is better than the mayor-council government for our city. Get the facts first, then present a point of view to support the side you take in the debate.

2. Group or Committee Projects

Take a series of photographs of interesting places in your community. Prepare a display of your finished pictures.

A committee may make an appointment to interview a local official. Be prompt, be prepared with good questions, and give a report of the interview to the class.

Prepare a map of your town. Consult census reports and other sources. Use special colors to show how the population has grown since the year 1900.

3. Individual Projects

Interview your parents or other adults to learn what local taxes they pay. For what are these taxes used?

Prepare a scrapbook of articles and pictures showing special problems in your community. Sections of the scrapbook may be devoted to such topics as government, crime, transportation, safety, sanitation, water supply, schools, and elections.

Read a book on local history and report to the class the main facts about the founding and growth of your community.

CIVICS SKILLS

EXPLORING YOUR COMMUNITY

Exploring your own community's history and government can be an interesting and rewarding experience. In every community, there are many opportunities to learn from first-hand experience. Because these opportunities are so close to you, they are sometimes overlooked. Take a new look. Many of the subjects discussed in this chapter can be observed.

One of the first steps in exploring your community is to make a general survey of its main features. In a class discussion, you and your classmates may share your knowledge of local things worth seeing. After making a preliminary list, do some research to add features with which you may not be familiar. Read what has been written about your community. Interview some community leaders or older citizens who may know interesting facts about local geography, history, and government. Share these findings with the class.

Discussion, reading, and interviewing are important parts of a community survey. But nothing takes the place of first-hand observation. Visit places of historic interest, business offices, government buildings, and other interesting places. Such visits may be made by the entire class, or by small groups, or by individual students. Some members of your class may be able to visit business firms where their parents work and report back to the class.

Your class will get the most out of its field trips if it makes careful preparations for them in advance. Necessary permission to visit should be obtained ahead of time so that the visit will be expected and welcome. Learn as much as you can about the place to be visited before you start out. Then you will know better what to look for. Think about the questions you want to ask. Take notes on important things you learn. You may wish to make sketches or take photographs. (You should get permission first.) Ask questions and show a real interest.

After the trip, follow it up by discussing your findings with your classmates. Prepare a display of pictures, sketches, and other material gathered on the trip. Do some further reading about some of the new things you learned about your community during your trip.

PRACTICING YOUR CIVICS SKILLS

Prepare a scrapbook or a bulletin board display of articles and pictures showing special areas of concern in your community. Sections of the scrapbook or of the bulletin board may be devoted to such topics as government, crime, transportation, safety, sanitation, water supply, schools, and elections.

Identify the type of government that your community has. Then construct a chart showing the government officials in your community and the responsibilities of each offical. How are these responsibilities important to your well-being?

After you have made a thorough study of your community, imagine that you were able to make any changes you wanted in order to make it a perfect community. First, make a list of all the problems you saw in your community. Then, try to decide how you would go about finding solutions to these problems. Besides solving community problems, what other changes would you make in your community to make it an ideal place to live?

UNIT
FOUR

The Citizen in American Government

CHAPTER

Introduction

Are you ready to vote? The Twenty-sixth Amendment to the Constitution of the United States gives you the right to vote when you are 18 years of age. In a few years, you will be faced with the decision of casting your vote intelligently for national, state, and local officials. Your vote will help to choose the leaders of our nation and to determine the way billions of dollars are spent. National and local policies will be determined in part by you.

Before the Twenty-sixth Amendment was passed in 1971, most states set the minimum age for voting at age 21. However, many Americans, including Presidents Eisenhower, Kennedy, Johnson, and Nixon, urged that the voting age be lowered. Those who favored lowering the voting age argued that young people were maturing faster and were better educated than ever before. They were better prepared to vote at age 18 than their parents had been at 21. Others argued that a person who is old enough to be drafted at 18 and asked to fight for our country is old enough to vote.

To make your vote count most, you should become actively involved in government and politics. Joining a political party and working to elect candidates you believe in is one excellent way to participate. How does one go about joining a political party and influencing its actions? How can an individual make his or her vote count most? These and other aspects of elections and voting will be considered in this chapter, as we study the following topics:

1. Our Two-Party System of Politics
2. Political Parties in Action
3. The Right to Vote
4. Nominating and Electing Our Leaders

CHAPTER

9 Electing Our Leaders

1 Our Two-Party System of Politics

Nowhere in the Constitution will you find any provision for political parties. They are not an official part of the organization of our government. Anyone who has lived in America at election time, however, knows that political parties are a very important part of our democratic way of life.

THE PURPOSE OF POLITICAL PARTIES

A **political party** is an organization made up of a large group of citizens who have similar ideas on public issues and who work to put their ideas into effect through government action. To achieve their purposes, political parties try to get the voters to elect those whom the party favors to public office. Parties also work hard to get laws passed that they favor.

In the United States, political parties are voluntary. All citizens are free to join the party of their choice. Or they may decide not to join any party. Those who join a political party usually do so because they agree with most of that party's ideas and the ideas of its candidates. Of course, not all members of a party agree on every issue. If members are in serious disagreement with a party on important issues, they are free to leave the party. They may then join another party or decide not to belong to any party.

Most Americans of voting age belong to

a political party. As members of a party, they can join with other citizens to try to put their party's ideas to work in our local, state, and national governments. Political parties play a large role in helping the American people to govern themselves.

WHY WE HAVE POLITICAL PARTIES

Why do we have political parties in the United States? The reason is simple. Political parties offer a practical way for large numbers of people with similar ideas to get things done. Political parties are concerned with **practical politics.** This means that the parties are concerned with what actions governments should take. Everyone's life is affected by practical politics. When you complain about the high cost of living, you are taking a practical interest in politics. If you just complain, however, you are not very effective. But if you join with other citizens who agree with you, you can make your voice heard in a way that gets results.

Political parties perform other very important services. They nominate, or select, candidates for public office. **Candidates** are the men and women who run for election to the offices on the various levels of our government. Most of the people who serve in public office in the United States have been elected to their offices as candidates of political parties. They ran for election because they were selected by their party. It is not impossible, but it is very difficult, for a person to run for office without the support of a political party.

Political parties also take positions on public issues. They try to get laws passed. Before a Presidential election, each party draws up a **platform.** A platform is the program that the party promises to support if its candidates win the election. During the election campaign, each party tries to convince

How Political Parties Serve Our Nation

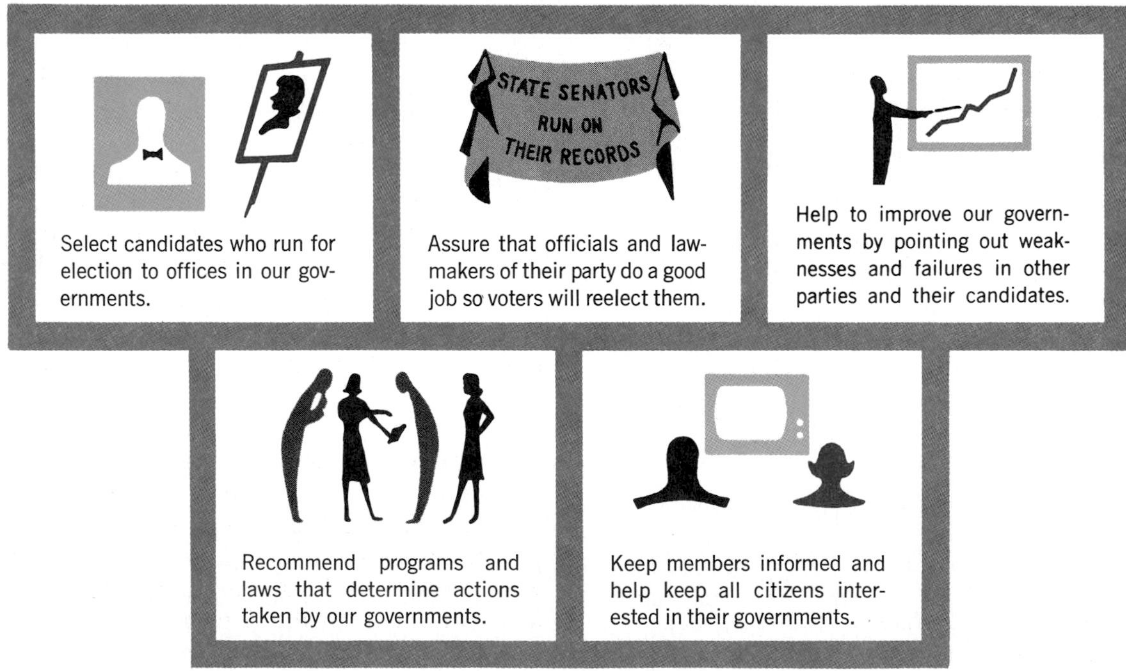

STATE SENATORS
RUN ON
THEIR RECORDS
Select candidates who run for election to offices in our governments.
Assure that officials and lawmakers of their party do a good job so voters will reelect them.
Help to improve our governments by pointing out weaknesses and failures in other parties and their candidates.
Recommend programs and laws that determine actions taken by our governments.
Keep members informed and help keep all citizens interested in their governments.

Thomas Jefferson (left) and Alexander Hamilton (right) were leaders of our first political parties.

the voters that its platform offers the best program.

After an election, the winning candidates become the leaders of our government—the ones who make and carry out our laws. The political party to which these leaders belong tries to make sure they do a good job in order that the party's candidates will win again at the next election. The party whose candidates lost will be watching for any weaknesses or mistakes the new leaders may make. This party also will be quick to inform the public if the winning party's candidates do not keep their campaign promises after they are elected.

HOW OUR TWO-PARTY SYSTEM STARTED

The history of political parties dates back to the early days of the republic when our government first began to operate under the Constitution. The first political parties began during President Washington's administration. Those who favored a strong national government became known as **Federalists.** Those who favored limiting the power of the central government were called **Anti-Federalists.**

Alexander Hamilton became the leader of the Federalists. He proposed policies that would make the federal government strong. Thomas Jefferson, the leader of the Anti-Federalists, opposed Hamilton and the Federalist party. Jefferson and the Anti-Federalists tried to limit the power of the federal government.

As President Washington watched these two different viewpoints lead to the establishment of political parties, he became worried. He feared that the growth of parties would weaken the new nation. In his Farewell Address as President he warned his fellow Americans of the dangers that might result if parties were established.

But Washington's warnings were soon forgotten. Political parties became a lasting part of government in the United States. There was one period, which you may remember from your study of American history, called the "Era of Good Feelings" (1817–25). Then we had only one strong political party. The rest of the time, however, our nation had two strong political parties.

THE BEGINNING OF THE DEMOCRATIC AND REPUBLICAN PARTIES

The present **Democratic Party** began in 1827, when Andrew Jackson broke away from the party started by Jefferson. Jackson believed that the federal government had fallen into the hands of the wealthy and was being run for their benefit. Jackson was determined that the federal government should represent the frontier settlers, the farmers, the city laborers—the common people. He was elected President in 1828, and the Democratic Party he established began its long history.

The present **Republican Party** began in 1854. In that year, several small groups that opposed the policies of the Democratic Party joined together. The party was started by people who were against slavery and opposed the spread of slavery into the territories. In 1860, the candidate nominated by the then new Republican Party, Abraham Lincoln, was elected President.

THE ADVANTAGES OF A TWO-PARTY SYSTEM

For over 100 years, the Democrats and the Republicans have been our two major political parties. Beginning with Jackson, the Democrats have elected a total of 13 Presidents who, up to 1980, served for a total of 70 years. The Republicans, starting with Lincoln, have had 16 Presidents who, until 1980, served for a total of 71 years.

These figures show that our two major political parties have had almost equal strength. This **two-party system,** as we call it, has worked remarkably well. When one party fails to please a majority of voters, there is another strong party ready to take over. The newly elected party often tries new programs and policies in dealing with the nation's problems.

If we had more than two strong political parties, all of about equal strength, no one party would be able to win a majority of votes. In order to run the government, then, two or more of the political parties would have to work out a compromise and agree to work together. This agreement between two or more political parties to work together to run the government is called a **coalition.**

Coalition governments, however, have certain disadvantages. Often the political parties disagree and the coalition breaks apart. This makes the government and the country weak. Some of the nations of Europe have this multi-party system. France and Italy have had great difficulty in governing themselves because of the many small parties. However, in the Netherlands and other nations this system has worked well.

ONE-PARTY DICTATORSHIP GOVERNMENTS

In countries with more than one political party, the voters have a choice. They may decide which party to join and which party to vote for. But in many other countries governments have been based on a one-party system. These governments are controlled by a single, all-powerful party. All other political parties are forbidden by law. Such countries are sometimes called **dictatorships,** because a single political party controls the government and dictates, or commands, and the people must obey.

Italy, under Mussolini, and Germany, under Hitler, had such governments. Today, the Soviet Union, the People's Republic of China, and most communist countries are run by a single party. Chile and Angola are also examples of dictatorships with one political party. Americans have traditionally opposed dictatorships, because such governments do not allow freedom of thought and action to their people.

THIRD PARTIES IN THE UNITED STATES

Besides the two strong political parties in America, there are also a number of minor political parties. In the national elections, there are always several candidates who have been nominated by these minor political parties. These minor parties are called **third parties.** At certain times in our history they have had great influence.

In 1912, Theodore Roosevelt was denied the nomination of the Republican Party. As a result, he left the Republican Party and started a third political party called the Progressive Party. Roosevelt ran for President as the nominee of this party. He was not elected. But he took away enough votes from the Republican candidate, Taft, to permit the Democrat, Woodrow Wilson, to win.

At other times in American history, third political parties have proposed new ideas that were opposed at first by the major political parties, but were later adopted. For example, in the late 1800's, the Populist Party was formed by a group of Americans who favored several new ideas. One of the most important of these ideas was the election of United States Senators directly by the voters. The leaders of the two major parties favored the election of Senators by state legislatures as provided in the Constitution. When Populist ideas began to find favor with the American people, some of these ideas were taken over by the major parties. In time, some of these ideas, including the direct election of Senators, were put into effect.

RECENT THIRD-PARTY TRENDS

Minor political parties have been active throughout most of the nation's history. They continue to nominate candidates. Now, candidates of the Socialist Party, the Communist Party, and others appear on the ballot. Usually, they receive very few votes.

In the late 1960's, one minor political party, the **American Independent Party,** played an important part in national elections. George C. Wallace, Governor of Alabama from 1963 to 1967, formed the party and ran as its candidate in the 1968 Presidential election. Some people feared that he would win in enough states to prevent either of the two major-party candidates from winning. This did not happen. Wallace received 9.9 million popular votes, but only 46 electoral votes. In 1972 he returned to the Democratic Party.

CONSIDER AND DISCUSS

Identify. political party / practical politics / candidates / party platform / Federalists / Anti-Federalists / Democratic Party / Republican Party / two-party system / coalition / dictatorship / third parties / American Independent Party

Review. 1. What purposes do political parties serve? 2. How do third parties help our democracy? 3. What are the chief advantages of the two-party system?

Discuss. What are some of the issues on which Republicans and Democrats disagree?

2 Political Parties in Action

In order to work effectively, a political party must be well organized. It must have leaders, committees, and workers who are able to carry out the party's program in the community, in the state, and throughout the nation. The party must also be able to raise money to pay for its expenses. The party must nominate its candidates for office and plan its campaign to get these candidates elected. There are a hundred and one details that have to be given careful attention.

Today, our two major parties operate the way they do because their members have worked out these procedures over the years. Interestingly enough, both major parties are organized in much the same way.

PARTY COMMITTEES AND THEIR JOBS

The party's planning is done through a series of committees. Each political party has a National Committee, a State Central Committee, County Committees, and City Committees. Each of these party committees is headed by a chairperson. The members of these committees are usually elected by the party voters at election time. Sometimes, however, the committees are chosen at meetings of party leaders. These meetings of party leaders are known as **caucuses.**

The largest of the party committees is the **National Committee.** Membership on this committee carries great distinction. Until recently, it consisted of one National Committeeman and one National Committeewoman from each state, each territory, and the District of Columbia. In the 1970's, both parties enlarged the membership of their committees. Members may be chosen in three ways. They may be elected by a state convention, by a statewide election, or chosen by the State Central Committee. The Chairperson of the National Committee is chosen by the party's Presidential candidate.

Each political party has a **State Central Committee** to supervise the party's operation within each of the 50 states. The Chairperson of the State Central Committee is one of the party's most prominent members in the state. He or she is often a member of the National Committee.

At the local level there are the **County** and the **City Committees. Township Committees** are sometimes found in rural areas. Members of local committees come from each election district or precinct. They are chosen in an election by party members. The chairperson of the committee, elected by its members, is the local party leader.

Each county or city is divided into precincts or election districts. Each of these usually has its own committee. Known as the Precinct Committee or Election District Committee, this group and its chairperson are important, especially at election time.

WHAT THE COMMITTEES DO

The National Committee does most of its work in the year of a Presidential election. It selects the city in which the **National Convention** is to be held. It sets the date and draws up rules for the convention. During an election year, the National Committee publishes and distributes literature and arranges for campaign speakers. It also helps the Presidential candidate to plan and conduct the campaign.

The State Central Committee represents the party organization in each state. Just like the National Committee, it is busiest at election time. The State Chairperson works with the members of the State Central Committee to keep up a strong state organization and to maintain party harmony. The committee works to raise money for campaigns and to help candidates win in elections.

The party's success or failure often depends on what the local committees and their leaders do. The county or city committee is responsible for conducting all campaigns on the local level. It raises money for the party and the party's candidates. Through the local chairperson it makes recommendations for political appointments and for candidates for office. A strong local chairperson may stay in office for many years and become powerful in the party.

How Our Political Parties Are Organized

NATIONAL COMMITTEE

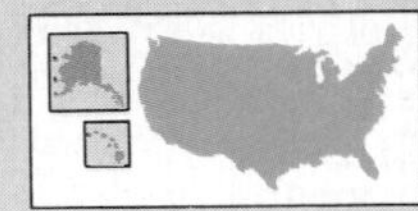

STATE CENTRAL COMMITTEES

COUNTY COMMITTEES

CITY COMMITTEES

WARD COMMITTEEMEN AND COMMITTEEWOMEN

PRECINCT CAPTAINS (LOCAL COMMITTEEMEN AND COMMITTEEWOMEN)

THE AMERICAN VOTERS WHO ARE MEMBERS OF THE PARTY

THE LOCAL PARTY ORGANIZATION

To make voting easier for our citizens, each city is divided into **wards** or **election districts.** In larger cities, these wards are divided into voting **precincts.** The voters in each precinct vote at the same place, called a **polling place.** The rural precinct may cover large areas of countryside while a precinct in a crowded city may cover just a few blocks. The party leader in the precinct is called the **Precinct Captain.** The Precinct Captain encourages all voters to get out and vote for the party's candidates.

At election time Precinct Captains are very busy. They round up volunteers to hand out the party's campaign literature. They see that pictures of the party's candidates are displayed in local shops and on neighborhood billboards. Precinct Captains may arrange to have disabled voters driven to the polling place. They also see that party workers telephone voters, urging them to cast their votes for the party candidates. The Precinct Captains are also busy between elections getting to know the people in the neighborhood.

POLITICAL PARTY FINANCES

The cost of running for political office, especially for offices in the federal government, is very high. In the 1972 Presidential election campaign, the Republicans spent $62 million to elect their candidate. The Democrats spent $46 million. This money was used to pay for office rent, for secretaries, for printing posters and handbills, for traveling expenses, and for radio and television broadcasts. After the campaign, Congress decided to pass legislation to keep campaign spending within reasonable limits and to prevent any questionable campaign practices.

The Federal Election Campaign Act, which was passed in 1974 and amended in 1976, provided that candidates trying to win their party's nomination for President would receive

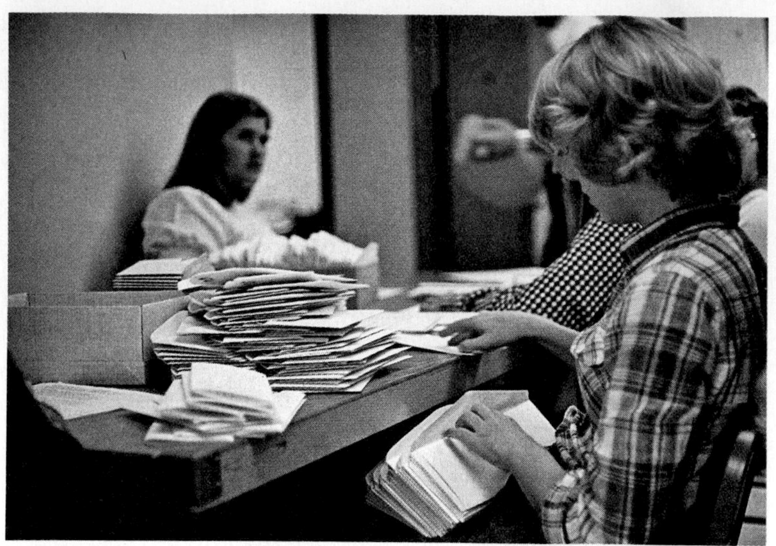

Many young Americans take an active part in politics. These teenagers are doing volunteer work for the candidate they support. Can you think of other kinds of work that young people can do in politics?

federal matching funds to help them run their campaigns. This money comes from an election fund provided by those who indicate on their income tax forms that they wish to contribute one dollar of their taxes for this purpose. To be eligible for federal matching funds, candidates must limit their spending in nomination campaigns to $10 million. Up to $5 million of this amount comes from federal funds. The candidates must match this amount with their own funds. After winning their party's nomination, candidates of the major parties receive $20 million in federal funds to run their election campaigns. They are limited to spending this amount. Candidates of minor parties receive funds after the election, based on the number of votes they get.

Where do candidates and political parties get the funds they need to match federal funds and to meet additional expenses? They get them from private contributions, from interested groups, and from candidates' personal and family funds. But what of the danger that those who contribute large amounts will receive special favors from the party in power? The Federal Election Campaign Act tries to meet this danger in several ways. Each candidate must report the name of each person who contributes $100 or more. Individuals may only contribute $1,000 to candidates before they win the nominations and $1,000 after they win the nomination. Organizations may only contribute $5,000 to any candidate. And candidates who receive federal matching funds can not spend more than $50,000 of their own money. The provisions of this law are enforced by a Federal Election Commission.

YOUNG PEOPLE AND PARTY WORK

More than ever before, young people are becoming interested in politics. Beginning with the Presidential campaign of 1968, high school and college students in large numbers started working for the candidates of their choice. In every campaign since, more and more young people are becoming actively involved.

The variety of their activities is enormous. The candidate's office needs to be staffed, telephones must be answered, messengers are needed, literature and buttons need to be distributed. In addition, workers are needed to go from door to door to explain the candidates' stands on the issues. They can also encourage people to register to vote, and to vote. On election day, young people can help voters get to the polls by babysitting and by furnishing rides to the elderly or the handicapped. There are many opportunities for young Americans to help the candidates they support get elected.

CONSIDER AND DISCUSS

Identify. caucuses / National Committee / State Central Committee / County Committee / City Committee / Township Committee / National Convention / ward / election district / precinct / polling place / Precinct Captain

Review. 1. How are political parties organized? 2. How does the Precinct Captain serve the party? 3. How can a high school student become active in politics?

Discuss. Do you think it is a good idea to have laws regulating the amount of money candidates can spend in elections? Why or why not?

3 The Right to Vote

Today, you are a full-fledged citizen of the United States. When you reach the age of 18 you will have the right to vote in national, state, and local elections. Your right to vote is very important, because it is the way you can most directly affect the way our government is run. No right is more important to you as an American than your right to vote.

STATE QUALIFICATIONS FOR VOTING

Each state has the right to decide qualifications for voting in state elections, as long as it respects the Constitution's provisions about voting. The Constitution forbids any state to deny a citizen the right to vote because of race, color, or sex. To insure this, Congress passed the **Voting Rights Act of 1965.** This act authorized the Attorney General of the United States to appoint federal examiners to register voters in areas where states denied them the right to vote because of race or color. An extension of this law, passed in 1970, prohibits any state from using **literacy tests,** or reading tests, as a requirement for voter registration.

Many states deny the right to vote to certain persons who they believe are not eligible to vote. In many states, a person who is convicted of a serious crime loses the right to vote. Most states also deny the right to vote to mentally ill persons confined in hospitals. And persons who are not citizens (aliens) are not allowed to vote.

REGISTERING TO VOTE

When a person goes to the polls to vote, how do the officials know that he or she is a qualified voter? Most states make sure of this by requiring all voters to register ahead of time. However, a few states—for example, Iowa—only require people who live in cities to register. When you register, you give your name, address, date of birth, and other information that would show that you meet the qualifications for voting.

Almost all states have **permanent registration.** This means that you must register only once as long as you live at the same address. Some of these states, however, provide that a voter who does not vote in a certain number of elections must be dropped from the roll of voters. A few states still have **periodic registration** in some or all areas. This means you must register before each election or regularly at some interval to remain a qualified voter. To register, a citizen usually goes to the city hall or to some place set up for this purpose. When you have registered, your name will be placed on the voters' list. You may be given a card showing that you are a registered voter.

When you register to vote, you may be asked to register as a member of the political party of your choice. You may change your party membership at a later date by registering again. You may also choose to register as an **independent voter,** and not become a member of a political party. However, if you do not register as a member of a party, you may not be able to vote in the primary elections.

PRIMARY ELECTIONS

Two separate elections are held regularly in most states. The **primary election** comes first, before the **general election.** The primary election, usually held in the spring, gives voters a chance to choose the candidates from each party who will run for office in the general election.

There are two types of primary elections, the open primary and the closed primary. In the **closed primary,** only the voters who are registered in the party can vote to choose the party's candidates. Most states use the closed primary. So in most states only registered Democrats can vote for Democratic candidates and only registered Republicans can vote for Republican candidates. Those who register as independent voters cannot vote in the closed primary.

In the **open primary,** voters may vote to choose the candidates of either party, whether they belong to that party or not. They can vote only for the candidates of one party, however.

In both types of primary elections, the candidate who receives the highest number of votes is the winner. In some states, especially in the South, there may be a runoff election between the two leading candidates to decide the winner. The winning candidate in the primary election then becomes the party's candidate in the general election.

What about the independent candidates who belong to no political party but wish to run for office? They cannot, of course, be party candidates in a primary election. An independent candidate who can get enough supporters to sign a petition, however, can have his or her name printed on the ballot in the general election.

Independent candidates do not get elected as often as regular party candidates. But they do win some elections. It is even possible for a person to be elected to an office when his or her name is not printed on the ballot. In some states, space is included on the ballot to "write in" the name of a person the voter prefers. It is difficult to get elected by **write-in votes** but it does happen.

NOMINATION BY CONVENTION

In some states, political parties nominate their candidates in convention. A **convention** is an official meeting of a party. The people who attend and vote in the convention are elected as delegates by the various committees in the state's political organization. In a state convention the county and city committees select the delegates. In a national convention the state committees select the delegates.

GENERAL ELECTIONS

Congress has set the date for the general elections of the President and Congress as the first Tuesday following the first Monday in November. A Presidential election takes place every four years, and Congressional elections occur every two years. Most general elections for state officials are also held in November. Since the President and members of Congress are elected in even-numbered years, most states elect their state officials in odd-numbered years. But elections are held at different times in different states.

On election day, the American voter faces

a great responsibility and privilege of citizenship. The voter must make a choice among the candidates of the various parties. In many local elections, third parties may be strong, or write-in candidates may be well worth considering. Even in national elections the choice is never simple. The intelligent voter has studied hard to find the best candidate. He or she has read newspapers and magazines, listened to the candidates on radio and television, and talked about the candidates with other people.

As voters enter the polling place, they may see several neighbors at work. They are acting as **inspectors,** or **poll watchers.** Each party has its own poll watchers to see that the elections are conducted fairly.

VOTING—IN THE PAST

During the first part of the 1800's, voting in the United States was by **voice vote.** Voters announced aloud to the election official the name of the candidate for whom they wanted to vote.

This system of voice voting made it possible to influence the way a person voted. Suppose a person's boss was standing in line. The boss could hear how the employee voted and might discharge the employee who did not vote the way the boss wanted.

In 1888, a new system of voting was adopted. A printed **ballot** was used. This is a paper containing the names of the candidates and a place for the voter to mark a choice. This ballot was marked in secret, so that no one knew for whom a person voted. This method of voting is called the **Australian ballot** or the **secret ballot.** It helped to make American elections fairer and more honest.

VOTING—TODAY

More and more often, the voter today is using a **voting machine** instead of a paper ballot. Most states use voting machines either statewide or at least in some area of the state. The voting machine itself is a large, curtained booth. The voter enters the booth and pulls a lever to close the curtain. On the front of the voting machine, the voter sees several rows of small metal bars or levers with the name of a candidate under each lever. A party's candidates are all on one row.

The voter may vote a **straight ticket**—that is, vote for all the candidates of one party. Or the voter may vote a **split ticket**—that is, vote for some of the candidates of both parties. When the voter has finished, he or she pulls back the lever which opens the curtains. This action automatically records the vote in the machine and shifts all the levers back into position so they are ready to be pulled down by the next voter.

The voting machine provides a fast and easy way of voting in secret. It is also pos-

This poll watcher checks the voting booth as each person enters to vote.

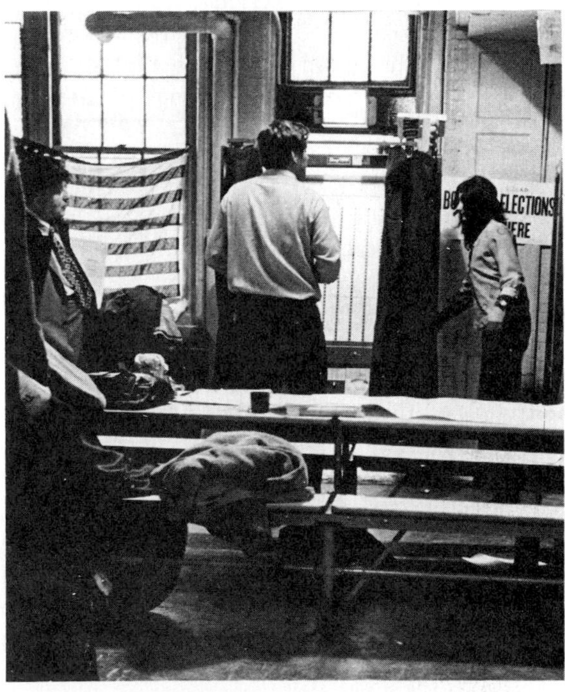

sible to know election results much more quickly since voting machines keep a running count of the votes cast for each candidate. When the final vote is cast, election officials open the voting machine and read the total vote for each candidate.

On election day the polls are usually open from early in the morning until evening. In many states, election day is a public holiday so that there is no excuse for failing to vote. In other states the law provides that all employers must give time off during the day to any employee who wishes to vote.

CONSIDER AND DISCUSS

Identify. Voting Rights Act of 1965 / literacy test / permanent registration / periodic registration / independent voter / primary election / general election / closed primary / open primary / write-in votes / convention / poll watchers / voice vote / Australian ballot / voting machine / straight ticket / split ticket
Review. 1. What are the usual state qualifications for voting? 2. How is the states' control of elections limited by the Constitution? by Congress? 3. Explain the difference between primary and general elections.
Discuss. If you were registering to vote and were asked your choice of political parties, would you register as a Democrat, a Republican, or an independent voter? Why?

4 Nominating and Electing Our Leaders

The election of the President and Vice-President of the United States is an exciting and important event. By studying this election in detail, you can learn a great deal. You especially learn how elections are carried out at all levels of American government.

"A HAT IN THE RING"

Every four years our nation is stirred to a high excitement as the time for the Presidential election draws near. Americans like a good, hard-fought battle. And the election of the President is one of the best. Most Americans eagerly follow the election campaign as newspapers, radio, and television report about it.

Long before election day, the two major parties begin to prepare their forces. The National Committee of each party meets to decide where the party's **national nominating convention** will be held. The men and women of the Committee begin to make arrangements for the convention. They decide on the speakers to be invited and plan ways of raising funds for the campaign.

Leading party members who hope to be candidates begin to make speeches which will make them better known to the public. At an appropriate time, some of these candidates announce that they intend to run for the highest office in the land—the Presidency. In the language of politics, they "throw their hats in the ring."

CHOOSING CONVENTION DELEGATES

In each state, members of each political party choose **delegates,** or representatives, to go to their party's national nominating convention. During the 1970's, Presidential primaries grew in importance. In 1976, the majority of the Democratic and Republican delegates at their party conventions were selected by Presidential primaries. The District of Columbia and 29 states held Presidential primaries. And all but four of these states held **Presidential preference primaries.** In preference primaries, voters indicate which candidate they prefer, or want, the delegates to vote for at the convention. In some states, the candidate who gets the most votes wins all the delegate votes from that state. In other states, each candidate gets some of the delegate votes based on the proportion of primary votes received. In still other states, the primaries only indicate the voters' preference. The delegates may vote as they wish at the convention.

In states that do not hold primaries, the delegates are chosen by the state's party leaders in state or local party conventions. Or they are selected by state committees.

Each state sends to the national nominating convention twice as many delegates as the total number of Senators and Representatives that the state elects to Congress. The state of Alabama, for example, has two Senators and seven Representatives in Congress. Consequently, it is entitled to send 18 delegates to the national convention. Each state is also entitled to send additional delegates if the party's candidate won in that state at the last Presidential election. Both parties use complicated formulas to choose extra delegates. States also send alternates who vote when regular delegates become ill.

THE NATIONAL NOMINATING CONVENTION

The party's national nominating convention is held during the summer of each Presidential election year. On the opening day of the convention, a series of exciting events begins to occur. The delegates from each state are seated throughout the great convention hall. Sometimes there are rival delegates who claim to represent the regular party organization of their state. The **Credentials Committee** of the convention must then decide which delegation to seat.

Bands play, convention delegates walk about talking to one another, the temporary chairperson of the convention raps for order. Later, the permanent chairperson takes over. This person was selected by the National Committee beforehand from among the party's prominent members. A **keynote speaker** then addresses the delegates.

Then the convention gets down to business. The **Platform Committee** presents the party platform. This written statement outlines the party's views on important issues and sets forth a proposed program for our nation. This is the program the party promises to put into operation if its candidate is elected. After strong and sometimes heated debate, the platform is voted on and adopted by the delegates.

CHOOSING THE PRESIDENTIAL CANDIDATE

The convention now tackles its most important item of business—choosing the party's candidate for President. As the roll of the states is called, selected delegates come to the platform to **nominate,** or name, the candidates favored by the delegates. Each nominating speech is followed by one or more seconding speeches. After the nominating speeches, there may be a demonstration in support of the nominated candidate. The band plays. Delegates who favor the candidate jump up and parade about the convention floor, waving signs and carrying pictures of the candidate. In recent years, some Americans have criticized nominating conventions for having a circuslike atmosphere. At recent conventions, attempts have been made to place a time limit on demonstrations. But it is hard to control political enthusiasm.

Some of the candidates named are favorite sons. **Favorite sons** are party leaders who are popular in their home states. These men and women usually are state Governors or Senators. In most cases, favorite sons have little chance of being nominated for the Presidency.

Why, then, do states nominate favorite sons? Sometimes the name of a favorite son is presented to honor the state's party leader. In other cases, states name a favorite son in order to delay a decision on which of the well-known candidates they will support. These delegates vote for their favorite son on the first ballot. Then, in later ballots,

Before our modern system of communications, candidates had to rely on personal tours, newspapers, and trucks such as this one to reach the public. What can you learn about the Presidental campaign of 1916 by reading the signs on this truck?

they usually switch their votes to one of the leading candidates.

Not all states, of course, nominate candidates. There may be a total of half a dozen or more candidates nominated. Many of these nominees will have run in Presidential preference primaries. When the political party has a President in power who is eligible to run again, the convention almost always nominates this person for a second term. In fact, often no other candidate is placed in nomination at the convention.

After all the candidates have been placed in nomination, the balloting begins. A roll call of the states is taken, and each state delegation votes for the candidate it favors. When a candidate receives a majority of the votes of all the delegates at the convention, the candidate is declared the Presidential nominee. Sometimes, one of the candidates is nominated on the first ballot. When no one candidate is strong enough to win a majority, many ballots may be taken. Supporters of the leading candidates may meet with state delegations to try to win them over. In some cases, agreements might be made. For example, one state might agree to switch its vote for the presidential candidate in return for support for its own candidate for Vice-President.

When a candidate wins a majority of the delegates' votes, the huge auditorium is filled with noise and excitement. The delegates cheer and demonstrate to show their enthusiasm for the candidate who is to represent the party in November.

The delegates turn next to the nomination of the Vice-President. Vice-Presidential candidates often are chosen for their vote-getting ability or because they are from a part of the nation whose support the party needs. They must be well qualified to be President since they are next in line for the Presidency if the party wins the November election. The Presidential candidate usually has the strongest voice in deciding who the Vice-Presidential candidate will be.

THE ELECTION CAMPAIGN

Under the general direction of the National Committee Chairperson, the election campaign gets underway soon after the convention ends. One of the most widely used methods

An important part of an election campaign is getting to know the candidates' ideas. Here, Jimmy Carter, the Democratic Presidential candidate in 1976, gives a speech. Today, such speeches are heard nationwide over radio and television.

of campaigning is a personal-appearance tour by the Presidential candidate. Jet planes make it possible for a candidate to criss-cross our nation many times in an election campaign. In this way, candidates may make many speeches in many places in a relatively short time.

Television is another effective campaign device. Millions of Americans watch and listen as the candidates discuss their ideas and programs. As a result, Americans are able to get to know the candidates and to hear their ideas.

ELECTION DAY

The actual campaigning ends on the night before election. Even so, election day itself is a busy one for party workers. They are busy telephoning and urging citizens to vote.

Between 75 million and 80 million Americans go to the polls to vote in a typical Presidential election. Many millions more could vote, but for some reason or other they do not. Some have not registered. Some say they were not able to get to the polls for personal reasons. Others claim they were too busy. Some say that it was too much trouble to vote, or that their one vote would not make any difference. These Americans have had no voice in choosing their leaders and the direction of the nation.

On election night, most Americans watch the election returns on television. They are able to hear complete details of all the political races across the United States. Because of the time difference, the first election returns come from the Eastern states. Gradually the election returns start coming from the Western states. The last reports come in from California, Hawaii, and Alaska. Many Americans stay up late until they know who won. Sometimes the final results are not known until the early morning.

THE ELECTORAL COLLEGE

In a Presidential election, American voters do not vote directly for the President. They vote for men and women called **electors,** who will cast the official vote for the President. These electors' names may or may not appear on the ballot. A vote for the Demo-

continued on page 198

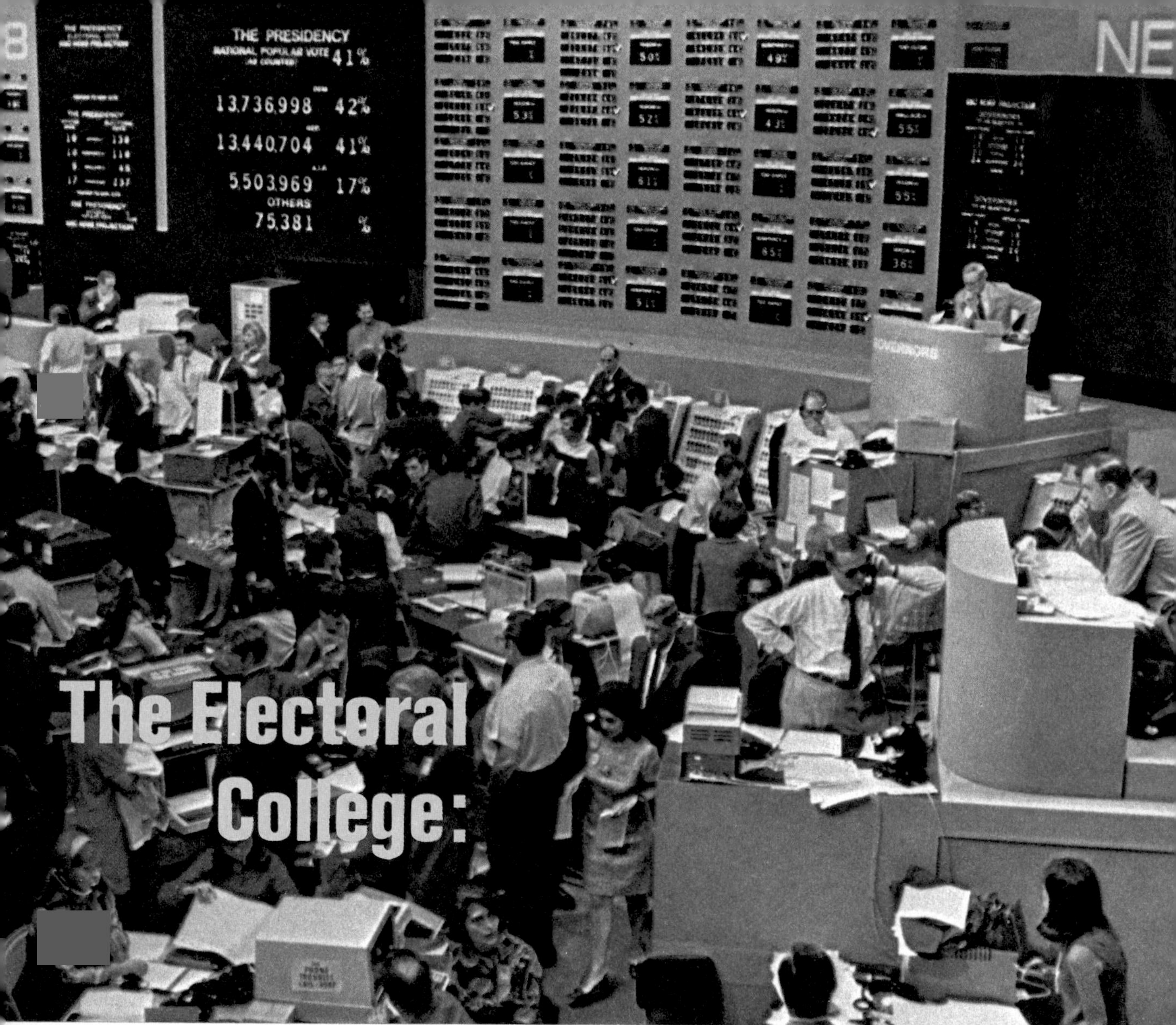

The Electoral College: Relic or Safeguard?

Suppose you are running for Student Council President. You receive more votes than anyone else. Then another candidate is declared the winner. How could this happen?

It could happen if your school constitution is modeled after the United States Constitution. Suppose that you vote for Student Council President by rooms, just as Americans vote for President by states. Imagine that each room has one electoral vote. The candidate who gets the most votes in a room receives its entire electoral vote. Other candidates who get some votes in the same room get no credit at all for these votes. Can you see how it is possible for a candidate to win the most popular votes, but not get the most electoral votes?

This is the way our Electoral College system works in choosing the President of the United States. Why do we have this system of indirect election? Is it a good system, or should it be changed?

WHAT DO YOU THINK?

The writers of the Constitution did not believe the President should be chosen directly by the people. Most people, they felt, would not know enough about the candidates to make a wise choice. Instead, the voters in each state were to choose well-known people as their special representatives, or electors. These electors would use their own judgment in deciding on a Presidential candidate.

This system soon began to work very differently. As you know, political parties began to nominate candidates for President. Electors were pledged to a particular party's candidate. By voting for one party's electors, people were really voting for the candidate of their choice.

The Electoral College system of today still differs from a direct popular election of the President in at least three ways:

1. It is still possible for an elector to vote for a different candidate than the one he or she was pledged to support. This actually happened as recently as 1968.

2. The voting is still by states. The candidate who wins in each state gets *all* of that state's electoral votes. As we have seen, a candidate who does not get the most popular votes can still win a majority of electoral votes and be elected. This actually happened in 1876 and in 1888.

3. If no candidate wins a majority of electoral votes, the final choice is made in the House of Representatives. In this case, the candidate who ran second, or even third, could become President. This has not actually happened since 1824. In 1968, when there was a strong third-party candidate, many people were afraid it might happen again.

Many people now believe that the Electoral College system is out of date, and even dangerous. They want to replace it with a direct, nationwide election for President. Other people believe that the Electoral College system is basically a good one. They think it provides important safeguards that ought to be kept.

What are the arguments in favor of direct election? Supporters claim it would be the most democratic way of choosing a President. Every vote would count exactly the same, whether the voter lived in Alaska or New York. The results would be known immediately and definitely. It would no longer be possible for a second-choice candidate to become President.

Are there any problems or dangers in the idea of direct election? Opponents say it would weaken our federal system. The separate states would no longer have a part in choosing the President. The traditional balance between large and small states would be upset. A candidate could be elected by winning almost all the votes in one part of the country and almost none in another part.

Defenders of the Electoral College also claim that it works better in close elections. Many times in our history, a candidate has won a clear majority of electoral votes, even though the popular vote was very close. With a big spread in electoral votes, they say, there is less danger of disputes over the outcome. For the same reason, some add, there is less temptation to cheat.

Supporters of direct election say the only honest way of deciding a close election is to count the actual votes. A President should not be able to claim a big majority, if he really won by only a few popular votes. As to cheating, they say, the temptation is much greater if a few extra votes can swing a state's entire electoral vote.

What do you think of these arguments? Would you support a Constitutional amendment to do away with the Electoral College? If so, how should Presidential elections be organized? If not, are there any ways of improving the present Electoral College system?

cratic candidate is actually a vote for the Democratic electors. A vote for the Republican candidate is a vote for the Republican electors. Each state has as many electors as it has Senators and Representatives in Congress. In addition, Washington, D.C., has three electoral votes.

In each state, the electors gather in the state capital on the first Monday after the second Wednesday in December. The electors of the political party whose candidate received a majority of the votes in the state in the November election cast all the state's electoral votes at this December meeting. If the Democratic Presidential candidate won a majority of the state's votes in November, then it is the Democratic electors who cast the state's **electoral votes.** If the Republican candidate won, then it is the Republican electors who gather at the state capital to cast the official vote.

The votes cast by the electors then are sent to the President of the Senate in Washington, D.C. On January 6, following the Presidential election, both houses of Congress gather in the hall of the House of Representatives. The votes of the **Electoral College,** as the whole group of 538 electors is called, are opened and officially counted. The candidate who receives a majority of the electoral votes is declared President of the United States.

If no Presidential candidate receives a majority of the votes in the Electoral College, then the President is to be chosen by the House of Representatives from among the three leading candidates. If no candidate receives a majority of votes for Vice-President, that official is to be chosen by the Senate from among the two candidates with the highest electoral votes. As you may know from your study of American history, this method has seldom been used.

The Electoral College was originally set up in the Constitution because those who planned our government were uncertain just how successful the people of the new republic would be in picking wise leaders. You will re-

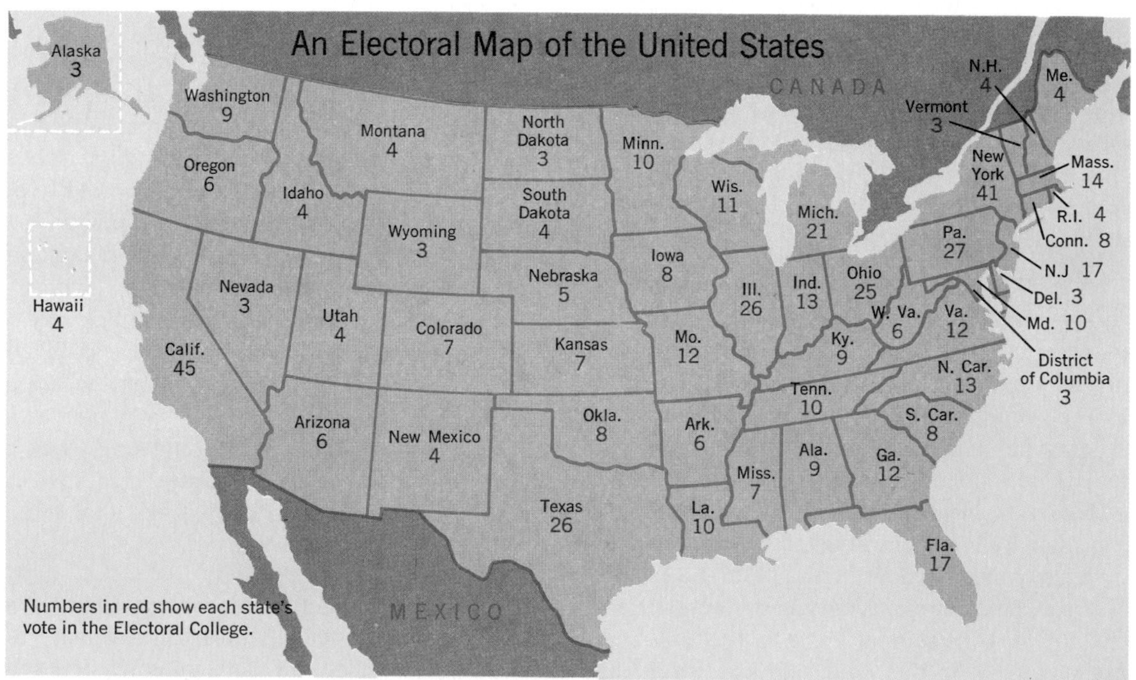

call that they also provided for members of the Senate to be elected by state legislatures rather than directly by the people.

In recent years, many plans have been proposed for a system of direct election by popular vote to replace the Electoral College. Many Americans favor the direct election of the President and Vice-President. Others favor keeping the present system. The House of Representatives in 1969 approved a proposed amendment to the Constitution to substitute direct election by the people for the present electoral system. By the late 1970's, the Senate had not yet acted on this amendment. And, of course, before it could become part of the Constitution, it would have to be ratified by 38 states.

CONSIDER AND DISCUSS

Identify. national nominating convention / delegates / Presidential preference primary / Credentials Committee / keynote speaker / Platform Committee / nominate / favorite son / electors / electoral votes / Electoral College

Review. 1. How are delegates chosen to attend the national nominating convention? 2. How can a voter get to know the Presidential candidates? 3. How many electoral votes does each state have?

Discuss. Do you think there should be a national primary to choose the candidate for President of each political party? Why or why not?

CHAPTER
Summary

Elections are important and exciting events in our national life. Election day is the time when the voters choose the leaders of their governments.

Although political parties are not mentioned in the Constitution, they have become an important part of our system of government. Political parties choose the candidates who run for office and become our leaders. Political parties offer a practical way for persons to work together to put their ideas and programs into effect in our government.

Today, America has a strong two-party system. The Republican and Democratic parties are organized on the national, state, and local levels. Both parties work through a series of committees to get their candidates elected.

American voters may belong to either party, or they may decide not to join a party. In any case, voters are free to vote for any person or party they wish. The Constitution provides that the states set most of the qualifications for voting, subject to the restrictions set by the Constitution and by Congress.

The Presidential election, held every four years, is a dramatic event in American history. Americans follow closely the party nominating conventions, the election campaign, and the election results.

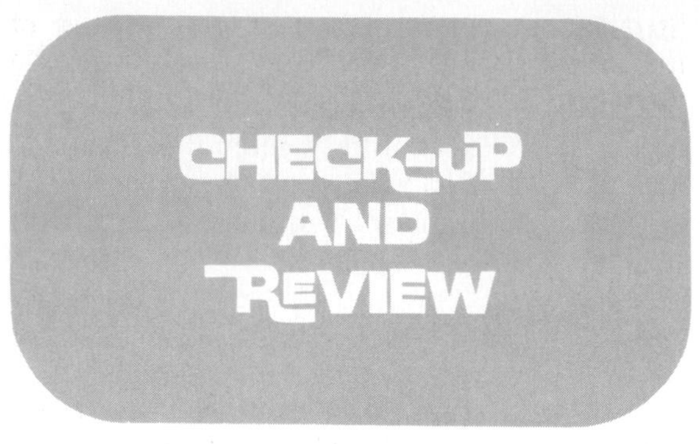

VOCABULARY

One of the best ways to learn new words is to practice using them. Copy the following words in your notebook. Beside each word write a sentence using the word to show its meaning in civics.

nominate	precinct
Democrats	caucus
Republicans	primary
registration	general election
ballot	Electoral College
platform	poll

CHECK-UP

The following questions call for you to express your own ideas on several important topics. Think about each question and come to class prepared to give your opinion, backed up with facts.

1. Why do we have political parties in the United States?
2. How is your life affected by practical politics?
3. What are the main advantages of the two-party system?
4. How have third parties served our nation?
5. How are the major political parties organized in the United States? What part does the local committee member play in the party's organization? How can voters influence their party's policies?
6. How are political parties financed? For what purposes do political parties spend money? Why should each member contribute to the party?
7. What are the usual qualifications for voting in elections? What is meant by the expression "If you don't register you can't vote"? How can the right to vote be lost?
8. What is the difference between a primary and a general election? Why is it important to vote in the primary?
9. Describe the way in which a Presidential candidate is chosen by a political party.
10. How has television influenced Presidential election campaigns?

CITIZENSHIP AND YOU

Political parties and elections at all levels will have more meaning to you if you take an active part in them. The time to start is now. Here are some activities on which you and your classmates can get started at once.

1. Class Projects

Hold a mock election, complete with speeches, posters, and campaigning. If a state, local, or national election is going on at this time, base the mock election on the real one. It will be interesting to see how the results of the class election compare with the actual election results.

Some civics classes have taken the leadership in conducting a schoolwide mock election. Often local government officials will provide the school with a voting machine to use in the school's election.

2. Group or Committee Projects

Committees may gather information and report to the class on such topics as "What are the qualifications for voting in our state?" "Are there third-party activities in our locality?" "Which party won in our state in the last national election?"

3. Individual Projects

Interview your parents and other voters to get their reactions to the following question: What is your opinion of any third parties that are active locally?

Find articles giving various points of view on the Electoral College system.

Attend a political rally or other meeting of voters and report to the class on what you observed.

CIVICS SKILLS

READING THE NEWSPAPER

Each day, newspapers report on important national and world news, and tell what is going on in your own community. To be an informed person, you should develop regular newspaper-reading habits. You should practice them throughout your lifetime.

The first step in learning to get the most out of your newspaper is to look through it carefully. Get to know how it is organized and where the various features are located. Find the index. This is usually on the first or second page. It lists all of the newspaper's features and tells you what page each is on. Now find the location of important national, international, and local news. Learn to recognize the editorial page, the feature columnists, the financial reports, and other worthwhile features.

You should also know something about the point of view of the newspaper you read regularly. Does it always support Republican or Democratic candidates at election time, or is it politically independent? Is it conservative, liberal, or middle-of-the-road in its editorial policy? You may check on your local paper's coverage of the news by comparing its treatment of events with the way the same events are treated in national news magazines and on television broadcasts.

As you study the various topics in this civics textbook, watch for examples in the news of things you are learning. Share your findings with the class.

PRACTICING YOUR CIVICS SKILLS

Use the following to make an analysis of your newspaper:

1. What is the name of your newspaper? Where is it published?
2. Make a list of all the sections in your newspaper. Which ones interest you most?
3. Are the pages in each section numbered separately? Or is the newspaper numbered consecutively like a book?
4. Where is the index? the editorial page?
5. Is your newspaper published daily? Is there more than one edition a day?
6. Name at least two columnists who write for the newspaper several times a week.
7. Feature stories are not like straight news stories. They entertain, appeal to the emotions, or discuss topics of interest. Are the feature stories in your newspaper scattered throughout? Or are most of them in one part of the paper?
8. Which features of the newspaper always appear in the same place?

Pick an issue in your community that local political parties are interested in. Check your newspaper every day for several days to see what news articles, editorials, or cartoons say about the issue. Then answer the following questions:

1. What did you learn about the issue?
2. Did you learn anything about political parties that is not covered in Chapter 9?

CHAPTER
Introduction

The many activities of government cost money—huge sums of money. Our federal government alone spends more than $400 billion a year. State and local governments spend many more billions of dollars. Where does this money come from? It comes from the American people who must pay for the services they receive. Nearly half of every dollar earned by American workers and businesses goes to the federal government in the form of taxes.

What is this money spent for? In the late 1970's, the federal government spent from $80 billion to over $100 billion each year on national defense. Veterans' benefits cost over $18 billion. Space research and technology cost another $4 billion or more. The Department of Health, Education, and Welfare spent about $128 billion. Most of this money went back to American citizens in the form of social security and welfare payments. In addition, many billions of dollars were needed by the federal government to help states and local areas. It helped them build highways, housing, and community redevelopment projects, and to pay for the many other programs and services.

The money the taxpayers give does not cover the enormous costs of government. As a result, the government borrows money from the people, from banks, and from other sources. This borrowing adds to the national debt, which rises each year. In 1960, the national debt was over $290 billion. Since then, it has more than doubled. The interest on this debt is many billions of dollars each year. And it must be paid.

The costs of government keep rising. And we pay for them with our taxes. As taxpayers and citizens, we have a responsibility to make sure that our government spends our money wisely. In this chapter, you will learn more about government spending and taxes as you study these topics:

1. Why Our Government Costs Have Increased
2. Many Kinds of Taxes
3. Managing Our Nation's Money

CHAPTER

10

Paying the Costs of Government

1 Why Our Government Costs Have Increased

Each year our federal, state, and local governments spend huge amounts of money. In many cases, our governments find that they must spend more than the amount that they receive from taxes. One important reason why our governments cost so much money today is that our nation has a larger population than ever before. This growing American population requires many services. Another reason is that during the past 50 years, the activities of our government have increased enormously. Americans have also asked our governments to provide many more services over the years.

INCREASING SERVICES AND INCREASING COSTS

Our local governments provide the American people with police, fire fighters, public health programs, schools, paved streets, sewers, trash removal, parks, playgrounds, and many other services. Our state governments provide highways, state police, aid to public schools, unemployment insurance, health service, welfare, and many other services. The federal government provides for our nation's defense. And it aids business, labor, and agriculture. It provides agencies to protect the public's health, aids in highway construction, and serves its citizens in hundreds of other ways. Americans demand these services and they must be paid for.

RISING COSTS OF GOVERNMENT SERVICES

The cost of government also has gone up in recent years because of the rising cost of living. Today's dollar will not buy as much as a dollar did in past years. In addition, the services and programs of our federal government have grown much larger and more costly.

In 1913, a single two-lane highway cost a few thousand dollars a mile. Today, this distance on a six-lane superhighway, with overpasses and cloverleafs, costs about 1 million dollars. The cost of defense, too, has risen sharply. In 1913, our nation's defense dollars were spent largely for supporting soldiers and their field supplies. Today, we spend billions of dollars on missiles, nuclear submarines, jet fighter planes, nuclear-powered aircraft carriers, and radar and electronic communication systems. Also, salaries for the armed forces are rising.

THE HIGH COSTS OF WAR

Our federal government has been forced to spend enormous sums of money on wars. It costs many billions of dollars to fight a war. Therefore, during every war, the federal government must borrow billions of dollars from the American people. As a result, each war has caused a great increase in our nation's debt. Americans are, in this way, still paying some of the costs of the Spanish-American War, World War I, World War II, the Korean conflict, and the Vietnam War.

Another very costly expense of our federal government is the money required for the care of America's war veterans. All veterans who need hospital care are provided with such care. And those veterans who are old or unable to work receive pensions. Nearly five cents out of every dollar that the federal government spends is spent for veterans' care.

Why the Costs of Our Federal Government Have Increased

220 Million
106 Million
1920
1978
America's population has grown.
BREAD
30c 59¢
Prices have increased, and the cost of living has risen.
The national debt has grown rapidly and requires huge interest payments.
Our federal government now provides more services.
Large sums are spent for America's defense.

How the Federal Government Spends Its Money

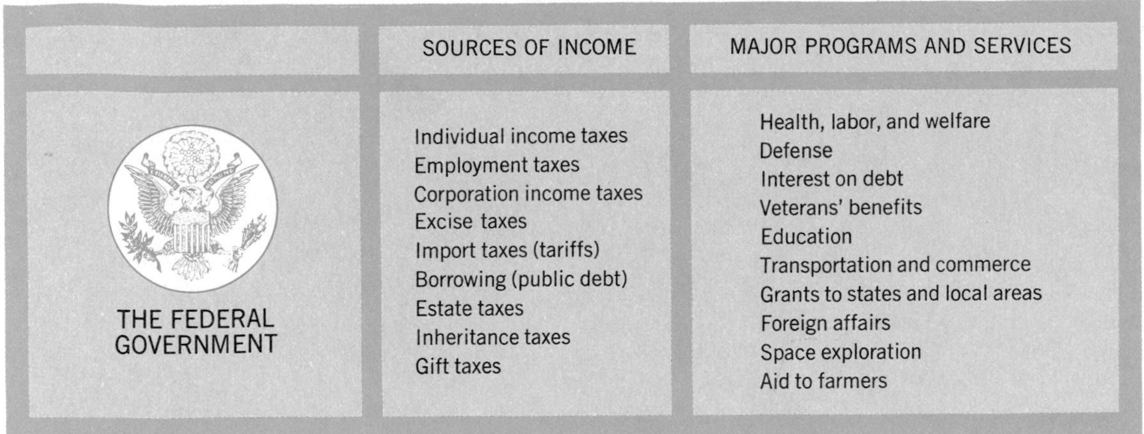

SOURCES OF INCOME
MAJOR PROGRAMS AND SERVICES
THE FEDERAL GOVERNMENT
Individual income taxes
Employment taxes
Corporation income taxes
Excise taxes
Import taxes (tariffs)
Borrowing (public debt)
Estate taxes
Inheritance taxes
Gift taxes
Health, labor, and welfare
Defense
Interest on debt
Veterans' benefits
Education
Transportation and commerce
Grants to states and local areas
Foreign affairs
Space exploration
Aid to farmers

WHAT CAN BE DONE ABOUT THE INCREASING COSTS OF GOVERNMENT?

Many Americans complain about the high costs of government. It is understandable that they should do so. All citizens have the right to expect that their government will spend their—the taxpayers'—money wisely.

Today, Americans are paying more in taxes than they ever did before. As the cost of living has gone up, taxes at all levels of government have also risen. Government costs, just as family living costs, have continued to rise. For example, it costs the government more for salaries and supplies. The money for these increased costs has to be collected in taxes.

Since there are so many demands placed upon our governments, government officials are constantly faced with difficult decisions. What government programs need money most? What programs will bring the greatest benefits to the people? The first thing that government officials do is to list the government activities that need money, listing them in order of their urgency and need. This is called establishing **priorities.** Programs at the top of the list have high priority. Programs lower on the list have lower priority. Our government officials try to spend funds for those high on the list. Programs of very low priority may have to be left out. In recent years, there has been much debate over our priorities.

THE PURPOSE OF TAXES

All of our American governments—federal, local, and state—raise most of the money to pay for services and programs by collecting taxes. A **tax** is a payment of money that citizens and businesses are required to make in order to help pay for the costs of government. A tax is compulsory. That is, citizens have to pay it whether they want to or not.

Taxes generally serve two purposes. The most important purpose is to raise money, or **revenue,** with which to pay for government expenses. The second purpose is to **regulate,** or control, some activity. How are taxes used to regulate activities?

Taxes on imports, for example, are sometimes fixed at a high level. Their aim is not to raise large sums of money but to discourage imports in order to encourage business activity in our own country. High taxes on cigarettes and alcoholic beverages, too, are partly intended to discourage their use.

continued on page 208

PAYING YOUR FAIR SHARE OF TAXE$

WHAT Do YOU THINK?

Who pays for government and all its services? We do—the people. All of us are taxpayers. If your state has a sales tax, you already pay this tax every time you buy something. When you start to work, you will most likely have to pay federal income tax. In most states, there is also a state income tax. These income taxes will take a big piece out of every paycheck you earn.

Most Americans are willing to pay their fair share of taxes. But what if you had to pay more income tax than some millionaires? In 1970, for example, there were at least 106 people with incomes over $200,000 who paid no federal income tax at all. How is this possible? Is there something wrong with our tax system?

Tax reform has become a big issue in recent years. In particular, critics have attacked certain "loopholes" in the federal income tax.

These loopholes, it is said, provide ways for rich people to avoid paying their fair share of taxes. The criticism caused the national government to revise the tax law in 1976.

First, let us look at some of the loopholes. Whom do they benefit? How much do they cost the taxpayers as a whole?

1. "Capital gains" are the profits made by selling certain property, including stocks. Only half of a taxpayer's long-term capital gains are taxed. And only a minimum tax may have to be paid on the other half, depending on the individual case. This loophole costs the taxpayers, in terms of tax money lost, almost $6 billion a year.

2. The interest earned on state and local bonds is not taxed at all. This loophole benefits only the very top income brackets. People with incomes of over $1 million avoid an average of $36,000 each in taxes. The total cost is over $1 billion in lost taxes.

3. A special "depletion allowance" is deducted from the taxes of people who make their money from oil and other mineral resources. This, too, benefits a small number of very wealthy people. The tax revenue lost amounts to $465 million from individuals, and over $2 billion from oil companies.

What are the reasons for these special tax benefits? Should they be eliminated?

The capital gains tax and the oil depletion allowance are called tax "incentives." Incentives are rewards that encourage people to act in certain ways. These tax loopholes have encouraged people to invest money in our economy, and especially in oil drilling. Many people believe these tax incentives are necessary to help our economy grow, and to meet our need for more oil.

Other people believe that the cost is higher than the benefits. Most investment, they argue, would take place anyway. Above all, they believe it is wrong for people with lower incomes to pay a higher rate of tax than wealthier people. In effect, they say, these tax privileges are a form of "welfare" for the rich. What do you think they mean? Are you in favor of closing these loopholes?

Tax-free bonds help state and local governments. People will buy these bonds at a low rate of interest because of the tax saving. By not collecting a tax, the federal government helps keep down the cost of local borrowing.

This kind of help is very important to state and local governments. But is a tax loophole the best way? Suppose these bonds paid a higher rate of interest and were taxable—just like private company bonds. The federal government could simply give the tax money back to the states and cities, to pay for the higher interest costs. Experts tell us that the extra tax revenue would more than pay for the higher interest.

Many other special benefits are written into our tax laws. We can subtract certain costs of owning a home, for example. Tax benefits to homeowners are almost $10 billion a year. Contributions to charities, which also may be deducted, cost almost $5 billion a year.

Many people believe that these tax benefits are good for the country. Others say they are unfair. Tax benefits to homeowners, for example, cost more than the yearly budget of the Department of Housing and Development (HUD). Would it be better to close this loophole, and add the money to HUD's budget instead? Would the money be distributed more fairly this way?

The Tax Reform Act of 1976 eliminated many of the loopholes. It did this mainly by limiting the amounts and kinds of deductions that people could take. It especially affected those who invest in certain kinds of partnerships, and those who pay over $10,000 a year in interest. Among others who were affected by the law were some business owners, and people who work at home. But even with these and other changes, loopholes remained in the tax system.

If we eliminated every single tax loophole, good or bad, federal revenue could increase as much as $77 billion a year. Or, to collect the same revenue as now, tax rates could be much lower—perhaps ranging from 7 to 44 percent, instead of 14 to 70 percent. Of course, this would also eliminate all the incentives and special benefits now built into our tax system. Do you think this would be a good idea? Should we keep some tax "loopholes," and eliminate others? Which ones? The answers will have a direct effect on you—the taxpayer of the future.

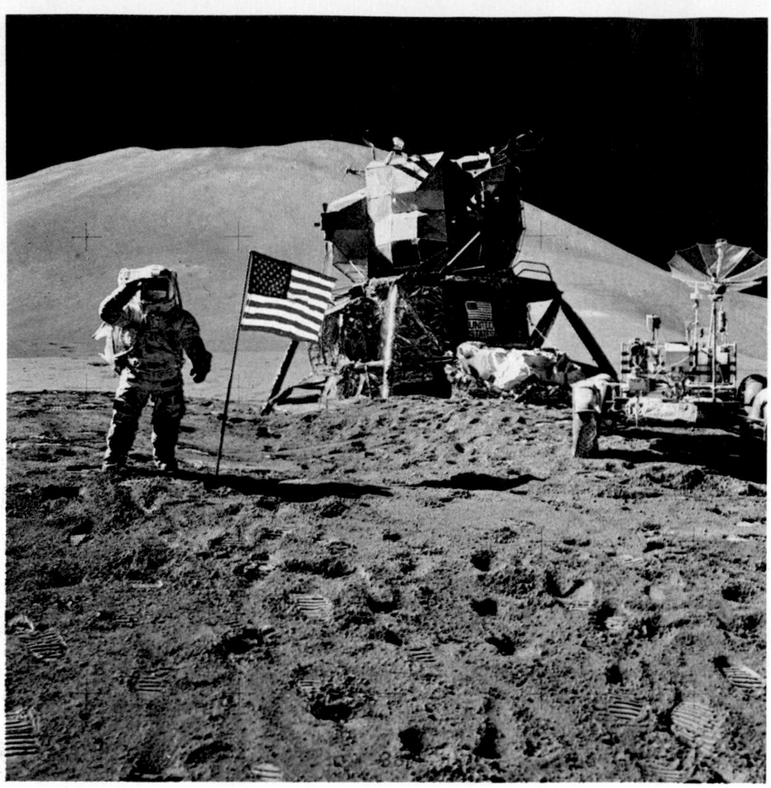

Government costs keep rising each year. Part of this increase goes to pay for government services and salaries. Part also goes to pay for such programs as space research, including the moon landings.

SOME RULES OF TAXATION

Our governments try to follow certain rules, or principles, when they set up taxes. They follow these rules to try to make taxes as fair as possible for all our citizens. What are these principles of taxation?

1. Taxes should be based on our ability to pay. That is, taxes should not be so high that they are difficult for many people to pay. In order to make it possible for all citizens to pay, income taxes are lower for those citizens with low incomes and higher for those with high incomes. Other taxes, such as sales and real estate taxes, are at a fixed rate for all citizens within a given area, but are set at a reasonable level that all can pay.

2. A tax should not be easy to avoid. If some people can avoid, or not pay, a tax while others have to pay, the tax is not fair. A local real estate tax, for example, is difficult to avoid because the house is there for the tax assessor to see.

3. Taxes should be easy to pay. Americans want to pay their taxes quickly and easily. Therefore, most taxes can be paid in person at a nearby government office or can be paid by mail. A large part of some taxes is taken out of workers' paychecks before they receive their checks. These taxes are withheld by employers and are sent by the employers directly to the government.

4. Taxes should be collected at a convenient time. Suppose that all taxes had to be paid right after the Christmas holidays when many people have bills to pay. Most Americans would find that paying taxes at that time was particularly difficult. Therefore, our governments try to collect taxes at a time when it is easier for citizens to pay them. In addition, the United States government tries to make it easier for citizens to

pay certain taxes by collecting part of the total tax each month instead of requiring that the entire tax be paid in full all at one time.

OTHER METHODS OF RAISING REVENUE

Other means of raising money for governmental needs include **fees, fines,** and **payments for special services.**

Governments raise money by charging fees, or small payments, for various licenses —hunting licenses, dog licenses, marriage licenses, and so forth. State governments raise large sums of money from the fees they charge for drivers' licenses and automobile license plates.

Money paid by a citizen as a penalty for breaking certain laws is a fine. Fines add to the funds of local governments, especially. Such fines are those for parking, for speeding, for jaywalking, and for violating the building code.

Governments provide special services that are paid for directly by those who use these services. The federal government sells timber from national forest reserves, and it sells electricity from certain federal dam projects. Those who receive this timber or this electric power must pay for it directly. State governments collect payments from drivers who use certain toll roads and bridges. Local governments sometimes install parking meters to collect payments from those who wish to park their cars on the street.

GOVERNMENT BORROWING

Although our governments raise most of their funds through taxes, their needs are sometimes so great that they must **borrow** money. A large project, such as a school, a bridge, or a stadium, costs so much to build that it usually cannot be paid for fully out of the government's income in any single year. As a result, the government must borrow money from its citizens by selling bonds. This money is then paid back, with interest, over a number of years. In recent years our federal government has spent more money each year than it takes in. As a result, our nation is in **debt** for more than $600 billion.

One of the ways governments raise money is by charging fees for licenses. A marriage license bureau collects money by issuing licenses to people wishing to marry.

CONSIDER AND DISCUSS

Identify. priorities / tax / revenue / regulate / fees / fines / payments for special services / borrowing / debt

Review. 1. What are some of the reasons for the high cost of government? 2. What are the two main purposes of taxes? 3. What are some of the principles that are followed to make taxes fair for all citizens? 4. Why does the government have to borrow money?

Discuss. Some Americans believe that we have too many different kinds of taxes. Do you think it would be better if we just had to pay one kind of tax? Why or why not?

2 Many Kinds of Taxes

When we walk on a sidewalk or drive on a paved street, we are enjoying a government service that has cost a great deal of money. When we watch telecasts of American spaceships circling the planets, we are watching an important government research program that costs billions of dollars each year. How are these and the other services and programs of our governments paid for? Our taxes are the most important source of money used to pay for our local, state, and national governments.

PROPERTY TAXES

At one time, most of the revenue, or money income, for our governments came from property taxes. Today, property taxes are collected mainly by local governments. They are the chief source of income for many local governments. **Property taxes** are taxes collected on two different kinds of property, real and personal.

Real property consists of land and buildings. **Personal property** includes such things as money, stocks, bonds, jewelry, clothing, and furniture. Since it is more difficult to determine the value of an individual's personal property, most governments use the property tax to cover only real property. If personal property is taxed, the rate is usually very low.

The property tax is based upon the value of the property owned by the individual. To determine this value for tax purposes, local governments depend upon local officials called **tax assessors.** These assessors visit the property and make a judgment of its value. Usually property is assessed, or valued, at a lower figure than its actual market value, or its price in a sale.

When the tax assessors complete their work, the local government adds up the assessed value of all the property in the locality. The local government then figures the total amount of money it needs to raise by the property tax. It divides this amount by the total assessed value of property in the town. The quotient is the **tax rate.**

To see how this works, take the example of a small town that needs revenues amounting to $100,000 from its property tax. Suppose that the total assessed value of property within the boundaries of the town is $3 million. To figure out what property owners will pay, we divide $100,000 by $3 million. This gives us a tax rate of $.03 on each dollar, or $3 on each $100 of assessed property value. This 3 percent tax rate means that a house and land assessed at $10,000 will be taxed at the rate of $300 a year.

In many of our states, public schools are supported by a local tax on property, sometimes called a **school tax.** The school tax is collected by the town, village, county, or school district in which the school is located and it is turned over to the local school board. In most cases, public school districts also receive aid from the state government to help pay the cost of schools.

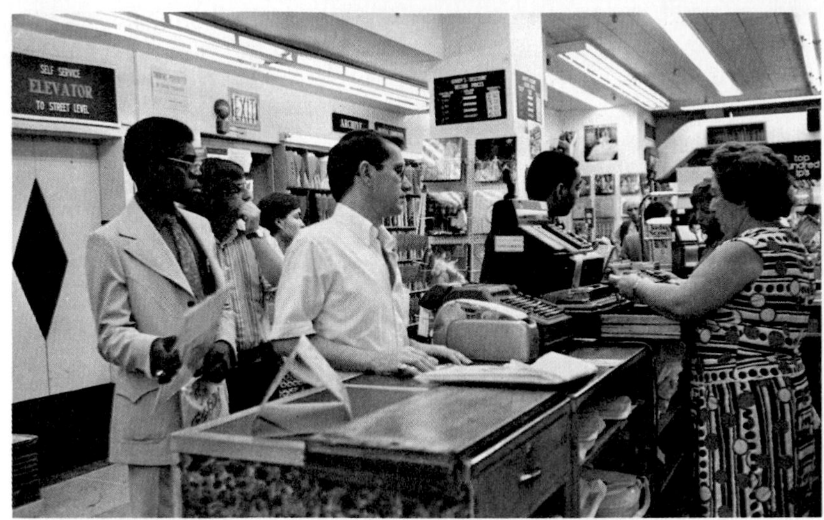

Most state and city governments raise money through sales taxes. These people will have to pay a tax on the records they are buying.

THE SALES TAX

Most of our state governments and many city governments now have a sales tax. The **sales tax** is a tax collected on most things Americans buy when they shop in their local stores. Sales tax rates have been going up in recent years. In some places, the tax is as high as seven or eight cents on each dollar spent.

The sales tax is collected by stores directly from the customer. Stores then send the sales tax money to the state treasurer or the local tax collector. Some states return part of the state sales tax to town and city governments to help them meet their expenses.

EXCISE TAXES

Excise taxes are collected by the federal government and some state governments. The **excise tax** is collected on certain services and articles produced and sold in the United States, usually on "luxury" items. It is similar to a sales tax. Some of the items on which excise taxes are collected are tobacco, alcoholic beverages, gasoline, lubricating oils, and air travel.

TARIFFS, OR IMPORT TAXES

The United States government collects import taxes on many products imported from foreign countries. This import tax is called a **tariff,** or sometimes a **customs duty.** In the early days of our nation, the tariff was one of the largest sources of income for our federal government.

Today, however, the United States usually uses tariffs to regulate trade rather than to raise money. There are two reasons why **protective tariffs** are levied on certain goods by the United States government. First, some of our industries need protection against foreign competition. Many foreign countries can manufacture goods at a far lower cost than they could be manufactured in the United States. Lower manufacturing costs would allow those goods to be imported and sold here for far less than an American manufacturer would have to charge. American industry would lose business, and some American workers might lose their jobs. A tariff on the imported product raises its price, making it as expensive as, or more expensive than the American product. Although tariffs protect industry, in some cases they hurt American

Taxes that our government collects on imported goods are called tariffs. In this picture, a ship carrying products made in foreign countries docks in San Francisco, California.

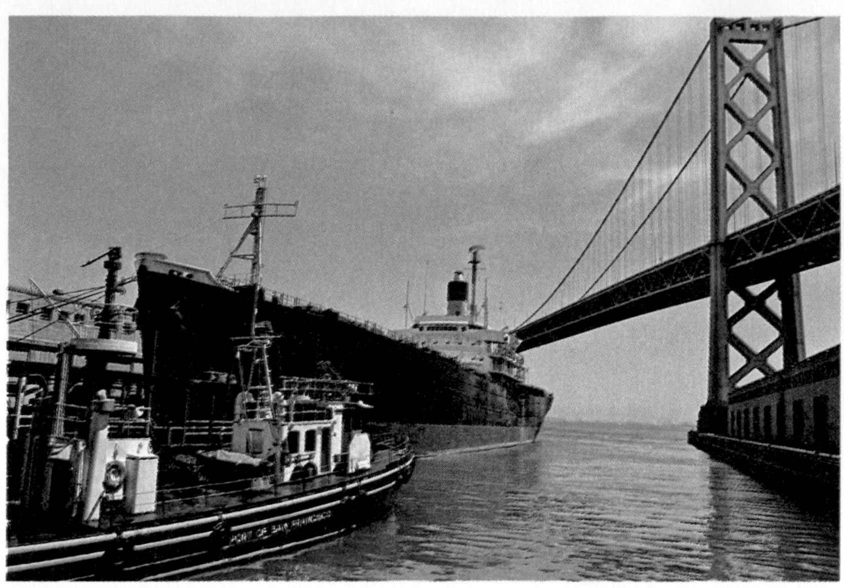

consumers by raising the prices they must pay for certain products.

The second use of the protective tariff is to protect an industry whose goods are needed for the nation's defense. It is for this reason that our government places protective tariffs on chemicals, aircraft, and ships. In this way, the government helps our nation to provide for its defense needs.

PERSONAL INCOME TAXES

The largest source of revenue for our federal government is the **personal income tax.** It brings in billions of dollars each year. The amount of income taxes that people have to pay changes. Congress changes tax rates when it wants to help the economy. It also does so to encourage or discourage some kinds of spending or to improve the tax system.

How does our tax system work? In 1976, for example, all Americans under 65 years of age who earned $2,450 or more a year had to file income tax returns. Persons over 65 had to file returns if they made $3,200 or more. The federal tax is not based on a person's total income. It is based on the amount left over after certain amounts have been subtracted.

All taxpayers are allowed to deduct, or subtract, $750 for each dependent—each person they support in the family. For example, a working father claims himself, his spouse, and children as dependents. A working mother does the same. If, for instance, there were five members in the family, the taxpayer subtracts $3,750 from the total income. In other words, the taxpayer does not pay tax on $3,750 of the income earned.

Taxpayers also can subtract certain expenses, such as money given to charities, taxes paid to state and local governments, interest on money borrowed, and business expenses. The amount left over after all subtractions have been made is called the **taxable income.** This is the amount on which income tax is paid.

The tax rate that individuals pay depends upon the size of taxable income. People with large incomes pay at a higher rate than those with small taxable incomes. In 1976, a taxpayer who had a taxable income of only $500 paid at the lowest rate—13.6 percent, or $68. But a taxpayer with a taxable income of over $100,000 paid at the highest rate. This person paid $50,090 plus 70 percent of all income over $100,000.

American taxpayers must fill out and mail their tax forms on or before April 15 each year. But most taxpayers do not pay all of their income tax at the time they file tax returns. For all except self-employed workers, income tax payments have already been taken out of each paycheck by their employers, who forward the tax money to the federal government. Filling out the tax forms helps taxpayers to see whether they owe more money or whether they will get back some of the tax money withheld by their employers. The system of paying taxes in small payments each payday makes it easier for most Americans to pay their personal income taxes.

The income tax is a very successful means of raising money to support government. All but a few of our state governments also collect a personal income tax. Each of these states has its own personal income tax law and fixes its own income tax rate. Some cities have also established a **payroll tax,** which is a form of income tax. For the payroll tax, the employer deducts a certain percentage of each employee's pay and sends the money to the city tax collector. This tax rate is usually the same for everyone. Payroll tax rates, as well as the state income tax rates, are much lower than those for the federal income tax.

CORPORATION INCOME TAX

The second largest source of income for the federal government is the **corporation tax.** It also is an important source of income for our state governments. This tax is not based on the total income received by the corporation. The tax is based on a corporation's profits only. Corporations also may deduct certain amounts from their taxable income. For example, they may deduct for invest-

How State and Local Governments Spend Their Money

	SOURCES OF INCOME	MAJOR SERVICES
STATE GOVERNMENTS	Federal government General sales tax Personal income tax Cigarette, gasoline, and liquor taxes Corporation income tax Inheritance tax Licenses and fees	Education Public welfare Highways Health and hospitals Police Public building programs
ANYTOWN U.S.A. LOCAL GOVERNMENTS	Federal and state governments Property tax School tax Licenses and permits Fines Amusement taxes Personal property taxes	Schools Public welfare Fire and protection Health and hospitals Utilities Streets and roads Sewage systems Parks and playgrounds Libraries

ment in new machinery, research, and for certain kinds of losses. After such deductions, the corporation pays federal taxes on its taxable income at the rate of 20 percent for the first $25,000, and 22 percent for the second $25,000. Corporations that make over $50,000 pay $10,500 plus 48 percent of the amount over $50,000. The federal government collects between $30 billion and $45 billion each year from corporate income taxes.

ESTATE, INHERITANCE, AND GIFT TAXES

When a person dies, the heirs may have to pay several taxes on the real estate, money, and personal property that are left behind. First, there is the **estate tax.** This is a federal or state tax on all of the wealth that a person leaves. After exemptions are taken out, large estates are taxed at a varying rate. The heirs will have to pay between 18 to 70 percent, depending upon the size of the estate that they receive.

Then there is a state tax on the share of the estate an individual inherits, or receives. Be sure you understand the difference between the two taxes. The estate tax is based on the value of the entire estate before it is divided. The **inheritance tax** is based on the amount an individual receives as a share of the estate.

Even a gift of money may be subject to a tax by the federal government. A **gift tax** return must be filed by any person receiving a gift of more than $25,000 in one year. When the total lifetime gifts reach a certain sum ($47,000 in 1981), taxes must be paid at a rate of 18 to 70 percent.

CONSIDER AND DISCUSS

Identify. property tax / real property / personal property / tax assessor / tax rate / school tax / sales tax / excise tax / tariff / protective tariff / personal income tax / taxable income / payroll tax / corporation tax / estate tax / inheritance tax / gift tax

Review. 1. Which of our governments uses the property tax to collect most of its income? 2. How do we pay a sales tax? 3. Is anything ever taxed more than once? Give an example. 4. How does a protective tariff work? 5. How does an estate tax differ from an inheritance tax?

Discuss. Do you think protective tariffs are a good idea? Why or why not?

3 Managing Our Nation's Money

One of the most important jobs of the various governments in the United States is to manage the public money wisely. As you know, our local, state, and federal governments collect and spend many billions of dollars each year. Therefore, our governments have set up separate divisions to handle public funds. In addition, each of our governments checks on the way public funds are spent.

COLLECTING PUBLIC MONEY

Each of our governments has a department that collects taxes. In the federal government, income taxes are collected by the **Internal Revenue Service (IRS).** The IRS is an agency of the Department of the Treasury, and it has branches throughout the nation. Tariffs on imports are collected by the Customs Service, another division of the Department of the Treasury. State and local governments have their own tax collection bureaus.

After tax money is collected, it is sent to the treasuries of the various governments. The tax funds of the federal government are handled by the **Treasurer of the United States.** It is the Treasurer's job to see that

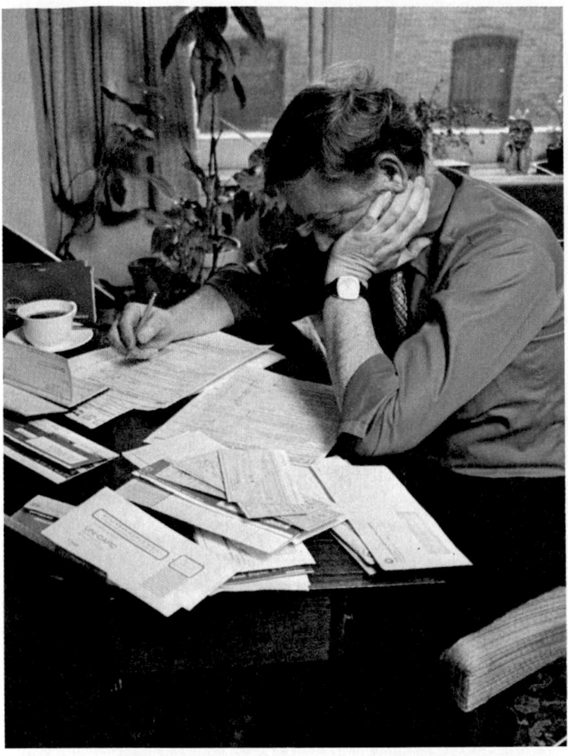

This taxpayer is going over the facts and figures before filling in his income tax form.

all federal tax money is kept safe and that it is paid out only as authorized by the Secretary of the Treasury. The Secretary of the Treasury may spend money only when authorized to do so by Congress.

In our state and local governments, the official who acts as the "watchdog of the treasury" is the **Comptroller.** Comptrollers have a job similar to that of the Treasurer of the United States. These state and local officials have the job of seeing that public funds are spent only as authorized by the state legislature or the city council.

PLANNING GOVERNMENT SPENDING

All governments have budgets. A **budget,** you will recall, is a plan for raising and spending funds. The budget lists the amount of revenue, or money income, as well as the sources from which this revenue will be collected. It also lists the expenditures, or money to be spent, for various public purposes. A budget usually covers the government's operations for one year.

The chief executive of each of our governments is responsible for drawing up the budget. In a village, town, or city, the Mayor, City Manager, or other executive officer plans and draws up the budget. In most state governments, the Governor prepares the yearly budget of the state's spending and income. Budget planning in the federal government is the responsibility of the President with the help of the Director of the Office of Management and Budget. In a local school district, the Superintendent of Schools is charged with this responsibility.

After the budget of the federal government is prepared each year, it is published in book form. Each year this huge budget book contains hundreds of pages, listing thousands of separate items.

The job of planning the budget for our federal government is so complicated that the President must have help. For aid in this task of planning federal revenue and expenditures, the President turns to special advisers.

THE OFFICE OF MANAGEMENT AND BUDGET

This important agency makes studies of our nation's economy. It then forecasts the amount of tax income the government will receive in the coming year. The Director of the Budget, who heads the Bureau of the Budget, requests each of the executive departments of the federal government to make a careful estimate of how much money it plans to spend the following year.

The Director then brings all these estimates together and submits them to the President. Priorities are established for the various items. Some may be cut in order to

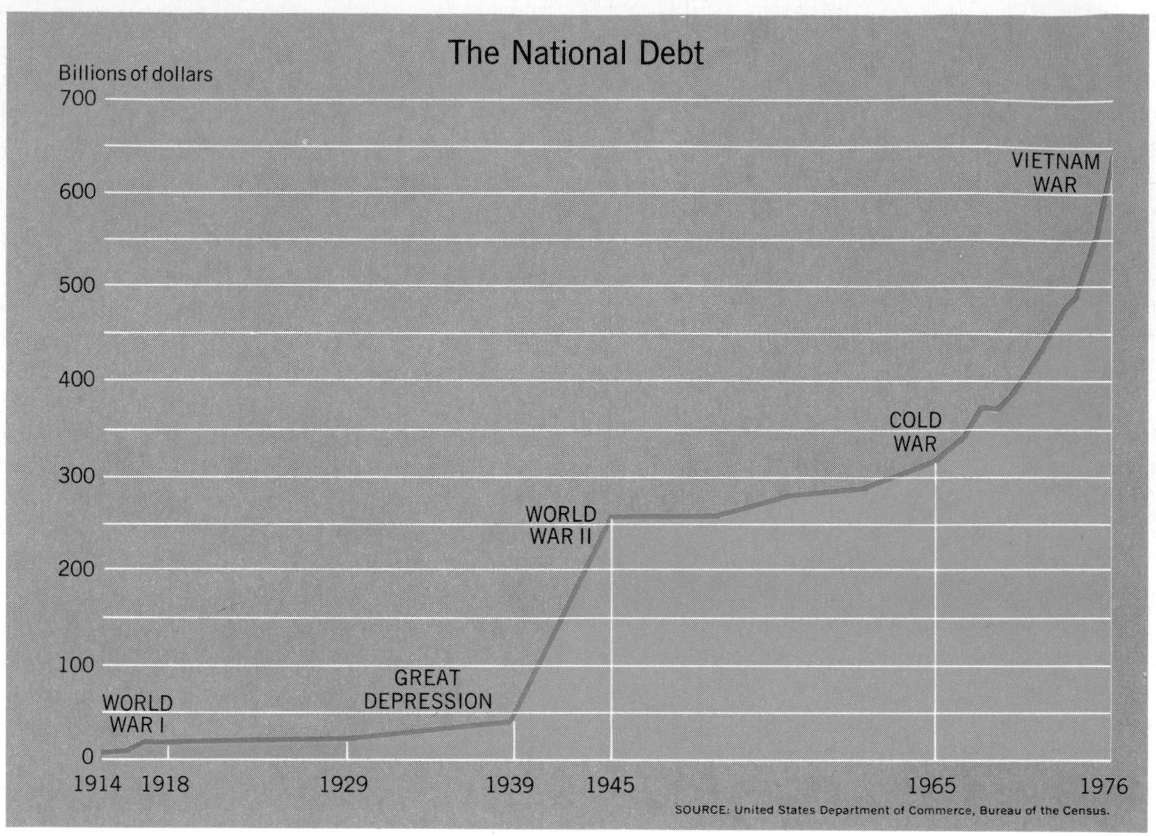

bring the total expenditures closer to estimated revenues. When the budget is in its finished form, the President sends it to Congress, along with a message explaining the budget and urging that it be passed.

PUBLIC MONEY IS A PUBLIC TRUST

Handling government money is very complex. It is also of extreme importance to the nation's welfare. It is necessary to keep careful records, or accounts, of how every dollar is spent and where it comes from.

To make sure that public funds are spent according to law and can be fully accounted for, all governments provide for an audit of their account. An **audit** is a careful examination, or study, by a trained accountant, of every item of income and expenditure. The auditor checks to make sure that every cent is accounted for and that every expenditure was properly authorized.

The expenditures of local governments are usually audited by a department of the state government. Expenditures of local school districts are examined by auditors from the State Department of Education, or by an independent auditing firm. In our state governments, the audit is usually made by an independent agency of the state under the direction of the Comptroller. All federal expenditures are checked by the General Accounting Office, an agency of the legislative branch of the federal government.

RESPONSIBILITY FOR PUBLIC FUNDS

The responsibility for public funds is divided among the three branches of government. The executive branch must propose a budget, or plan the spending. The legislative branch must approve the budget before any public money can be spent. The head of the executive branch must see that the money is spent according to the budget's plan. The courts in the judicial branch settle disputes over the collecting and spending of the public money.

In the federal government, the President recommends how public funds may be raised and how they may be spent. But only Congress has the power to raise funds and to spend them. All bills to raise revenue must begin in the House of Representatives. The House closely studies each bill to raise revenue because it knows that the American people want their tax dollars to be spent wisely. Appropriation bills, or bills to spend money, go through the same steps that you studied earlier when you learned how bills become laws.

State and local governments have similar safeguards for raising and spending public funds. In a number of instances, however, certain expenditures on the local level are voted on directly by the people of a community. For example, a proposal to raise money by issuing local government bonds must be approved by the voters.

BALANCING THE BUDGET AND BORROWING

When a government budget is **balanced,** the amount of the revenue equals the amount of the expenditures. That is, the amount of money received equals the amount of money spent. Sometimes a government budget is not balanced, however. When its budget is not balanced, the government's expenses usually are greater than its income from taxes and other sources. This shortage of income is called a **deficit.** A government may, however, receive more income than it planned, so that its revenues exceed its expenditures. This excess, or extra, income is called a **surplus.**

Deficits, or shortages, in a government budget must be made up by borrowing. Governments obtain **short-term loans** by borrowing from banks enough money to tide them over for a year or less. **Long-term borrowing** is usually done by issuing government bonds.

A **government bond** is a certificate stating that the government has borrowed a certain sum of money from the owner of the bond. The government promises to pay interest on this money, and it also promises to repay the full amount of the loan on a given date. These bonds, issued by our local, state, and federal governments, are looked upon as good investments. Issuing bonds is the usual way of financing large-scale expenditures such as public buildings, bridges, stadiums, and the like.

THE PROBLEM OF THE FEDERAL DEBT

The federal government has borrowed huge amounts of money in recent years to try to balance its budget. To do so, it has issued several kinds of government bonds. You may be familiar with one of these kinds of bonds—savings bonds.

Everyone who owns savings bonds or other federal bonds has loaned money to the government. Each year the government must pay interest on these bonds, and some of the bonds themselves must be paid off. These payments add to the high cost of government and also add to our national debt. By the late 1970's, the national debt had climbed to more than $600 billion.

How large a debt can our federal government owe? By law, the federal government can borrow only as much as Congress votes to permit. To enforce this law, Congress has established a **debt limit** for the federal government. The federal government must keep its borrowing within this debt limit unless Congress votes to raise the debt limit to a higher sum.

The whole subject of taxes, public funds,

and the federal debt is a difficult one for many Americans to understand. But the well-being of the American nation depends on how wisely our governments handle public funds. If wise policies of raising and spending money are to be followed, the citizen must make an attempt to understand these subjects and vote for intelligent, responsible leaders.

CONSIDER AND DISCUSS

Identify. Internal Revenue Service / Treasurer of the United States / Comptroller / budget / audit / balanced budget / deficit / surplus / short-term loans / long-term borrowing / government bond / debt limit

Review. 1. Describe the process of preparing the federal budget. 2. Name some of the safeguards that protect the raising and spending of public funds. 3. What are appropriation bills? 4. How do governments borrow money? 5. Why does the United States have a high national debt?

Discuss. Do you think governments should always have a balanced budget even if some government services must be eliminated? Or do you think governments should be able to go into debt and continue to provide these services? Why?

CHAPTER Summary

Government costs money. This money must be provided by our citizens. Each of us shares the cost of government, and this cost is rising every year.

As our population has increased, the costs of the services of government have increased. Wars, highway programs, space exploration, veterans' benefits, welfare programs, and interest on the debt have added to the costs we must pay. Money for our government is raised by taxes, fees, fines, special payments, and borrowing.

There are many kinds of taxes. Americans pay taxes on incomes, property, purchases, imported goods, corporation profits, gasoline, cigarettes, and many other things. Our federal, state, and local governments all collect a share of these taxes.

Our nation's money is important to all citizens, and it must be managed wisely. There are agencies to collect this money, and others to see that it is spent properly. The executive branches of our governments work closely with the legislative branches to plan government spending and money raising.

Our governments also borrow large sums to help pay their expenses. This borrowing has created a large national debt. This public debt is a problem that concerns all Americans. As taxpayers, we must help to pay this debt as well as the current costs of our governments.

VOCABULARY

Write a three-paragraph summary of the main ideas that have been presented in this chapter. In the first paragraph use the following words:

taxes	revenue
fees	borrowing
fines	debt

In the second paragraph use the following words:

property taxes	tax assessor
tariff	sales tax
income tax	excise tax

In the third paragraph use the following words:

Comptroller	expenditures
budget	audit
priorities	deficit

CHECK-UP

Test yourself by answering each of the following questions. Discuss your answers with other members of your civics class.

1. Why are the costs of government increasing each year?
2. What are some of the ways in which governments raise money?
3. What two main purposes do taxes serve?
4. Can you give four rules for good taxation?
5. What is the difference between real property and personal property?
6. Describe the way the sales tax works.
7. What are the two purposes served by a protective tariff?
8. What is the largest source of revenue for the federal government?
9. Can you list the steps by which a government budget is prepared and passed?
10. What safeguards protect the public money at the federal level?

CITIZENSHIP AND YOU

Learn more about how Americans pay the costs of government by taking an active part in one or more of these activities.

1. Class Projects

Participate in an open-forum debate on this topic: *Resolved,* That the sales tax is unfair to people with small incomes.

Join with your classmates in listing on the chalkboard the many kinds of taxes paid by citizens in the United States. Be sure you can explain how each tax works.

Invite a local income tax expert to tell your class about some of the problems faced by the average taxpayer each year.

As you listen to the income tax expert, jot down questions you would like to ask. Also, write down any points the expert makes that you do not understand or that you would like to know more about. During the discussion period after the talk, ask your questions. Raise the points about which you would like to receive more information.

2. Group or Committee Projects

A group can present a sociodrama in which each member plays the role of a different taxpayer. One student may represent the owner of a small business, another a farmer, another a corporation executive, another a worker, and so on. Let each student tell about the taxes he or she pays and the problems he or she faces. The drama can be summarized by a student representing the average citizen. This person will explain the services that the government provides with the funds raised by the taxes.

A small committee may prepare pie charts showing the budget of the United States government for the current budget year. Two pies should be shown, one to indicate the sources of income and the other to show how the money is spent.

A photography committee may present a series of pictures showing projects and services in your community or area that are paid for with tax money.

3. Individual Projects

Obtain a state or federal personal income tax form and fill it out for an unmarried taxpayer making $10,000 a year. With average deductions, how much income tax will the taxpayer have to pay?

Express your ideas about taxes and taxation by drawing a cartoon. Ideas for such cartoons may be obtained by studying the ways similar topics are handled by cartoonists in local papers.

CIVICS SKILLS

WRITING EFFECTIVELY

By applying your writing skills to civics, you can learn to be more exact. As you put your thoughts into writing, they will tend to become clearer and more complete. Here are some suggestions for the practice of good writing skills.

1. Learn to make brief but helpful notes as you read and listen.
2. Prepare well-organized notes for use in your reports and discussions. Learn to use your notes to improve the way you present your ideas to others.
3. Write clear, interesting summaries or briefs setting forth your points of view on the subjects you are studying. Get into the habit of backing up your opinions with as many facts and examples as you think you need.
4. In an essay-type question, organize your ideas in outline form on an extra piece of paper. Then use this outline as a guide in writing your answer.
5. Use the new words you are learning in your civics class. Be sure you include them in your written report, in the notes you make in class and in any summaries you write for yourself.
6. Try from time to time to summarize the main ideas in the day's lesson. Write an outline or a short paragraph.
7. Remember that the way to learn to write well is to begin to write. Practice your writing skills as often as you can.

PRACTICING YOUR CIVICS SKILLS

Choose one of the following forms of writing: essay, letter, poem, outline, script for a motion picture or television presentation, short story. Then use that form to express your views on some aspect of taxation.

The editorial is another form of written expression. An editorial is an article in a newspaper or magazine in which the editor gives an opinion on some subject. Imagine you are such a person. Write an editorial giving your views on whether or not high tariffs are needed to protect American industries.

UNIT
FIVE

Citizenship in the Home, School, and Community

CHAPTER
Introduction

In the first four units of this textbook, we have learned how different governments of the United States – national, state, and local – are organized to carry on our public business. The individual citizen can have considerable influence in our democracy. Much of the success of our form of government depends upon the way each person carries out his or her powers and responsibilities. Where is the citizen educated in the ways of democracy? In this unit we shall study the influence of the family, the school, and the community upon our way of life.

During the world's long history, human beings have developed many *institutions*. Institutions are organized, customary ways of doing things. One of our most important institutions is the home or family.

The *family* is a group of people, united by ties of marriage, blood, or adoption, who share the same home. The family provides the individual with the basic needs of food, clothing, and shelter at a time when he or she is dependent upon others. Also, from being together, the family members develop and share certain customs and traditions. One of the traditions the individual learns about in the family is what it means to be a citizen.

In this chapter you will learn more about the family and its influence, as you study these topics:

1. The Changing Family
2. Modern American Families
3. Your Family and You

CHAPTER 11
Citizenship and the Family

1 The Changing Family

The people who settled America brought with them strong family ties and a belief in the importance of a good family life. Each colonial family was different from its neighbor in some ways. But colonial families had much in common. From these early beginnings came an American way of life that to some extent still exists.

THE TRADITIONAL FAMILY

The first census of the United States, taken in 1790, showed the average family to have about four children. Many families were larger. At that time, our country was largely **rural** and most Americans lived on farms. Each child was a welcome addition to the family, for there was plenty of work to do on the farm. Older boys worked with their father. They learned how to plow the soil, plant seeds, harvest the crops, care for the animals, repair barns and fences, and do the many chores necessary on a small farm. The mother taught the daughters to sew and cook, to make soap, and to do the other heavy household chores that kept the family going.

Life on the early American farm was hard. Often the work was almost backbreaking. Sometimes farm children worked from sunrise to sunset, with little time for play or education.

About a hundred years ago, most American families lived on farms much like the one pictured above.

The early farm family was the basic work unit that produced most of what the family needed in order to survive. The contribution of each family member was necessary to keep the family and its work going. The family depended on all its members to do their part. Because of this need to work together, there often developed a cooperation and a strong spirit of family pride.

THE CITY FAMILY

One hundred years ago, eight out of every 10 Americans lived on farms or in rural regions. Today only one in 24 Americans live on farms. The rest of our population is concentrated in cities or suburban areas. This movement of Americans away from the farms to the cities and suburbs has resulted in fundamental changes in family life.

During the years of the 1800's, remarkable progress in science and technology took place. Because of these discoveries, large factories were built in many **urban**, or city, areas. These factories needed many workers. At the same time, the development of farm machinery meant that fewer people were needed to work on the farms. Farm families began to move to urban areas to seek jobs in the factories.

City families were no longer able to spend as much time together as the early farm families. The city family no longer worked together as a team, the way the early farm family had. The father no longer worked alongside his sons. Instead, he left home early in the morning to go to work, and he did not return until late at night. The younger children usually were left at home with their mother. But older children of 12 to

14 years of age were sent to work long hours in factories.

Today, city and suburban families are usually smaller than the farm families of the past. The city family averages fewer than two children. Children no longer work in factories. They spend much of their time at school. Fathers often commute long distances to work. Housework has become easier because of modern inventions, so many mothers now also go to work. Nearly half of the women between 16 and 64 years of age are employed outside the home. Three out of five of these working women are married and living with their husbands. As a result of these changes, the city family does not need to work together as the farm family of the past did.

In many ways, American family life is easier and more pleasant than it was a hundred years ago. American families today generally are better educated and more prosperous. Most of them live in better homes and are better fed and better clothed. They are healthier and have a great deal more free time in which to enjoy themselves. But, in recent years, American families have also experienced a few problems.

FURTHER CHANGES IN THE MODERN AMERICAN FAMILY

More American families have had trouble staying together than in the past. The divorce rate in the United States has increased in recent years. More will be said about this subject in the following section.

The family was once the main influence in the lives of children. Many other influences have become important for children today. Schools are taking on part of a child's education that was once thought only the job of the family. Children are now very much influenced by young people of their own age. And television has become an important factor in their lives.

Throughout history, there has always been a split between parents and children as the children grow older and more independent. The modern world is changing rapidly. And children are now growing up in a world very different from the world in which their parents grew up. Therefore, the split between parents and children has widened. It has been called a **generation gap.**

A different problem that has developed in recent years is that of older people in the United States. In the past, it was quite common for grandparents to continue living with or near their children and grandchildren. Now, many families move so often and such great distances that grandparents less often live with or near their families. Also, with advances in medicine, many more people are living to an older age. Since most older people no longer work and often are not close to their families, they can feel lonely or unwanted.

The increased number of families in which both parents work has brought up the problem of how their children are to be taken care of. This question is especially important when the children of working parents are of preschool age. The issue of day care for these children and how it should be provided has been hotly debated.

A few people have given thought to and tried different kinds of family styles, such as the commune. In a commune, a number of adults and children live together in a large group. Work and care of the children is shared among the adults.

The American family has gone through many changes in recent years. Yet despite a lessening of family closeness and communication, it remains the most important influence on children in our society.

CONSIDER AND DISCUSS

Identify. institution / family / rural / urban / generation gap

Review. 1. Why did so many of the early settlers of America welcome large families?

2. In what ways has family life changed in recent years?

Discuss. Why do we have so many working mothers in our society?

2 Modern American Families

There are many different kinds of families in the United States today. There are city families, suburban families, small town families, and farm families. Some families are rich, and some are poor, but the great majority are middle-income families.

In America there are families in which the husband works and the wife stays home to look after the house and children. There are homes in which both parents work. There are homes where just the wife takes care of the children because the father has died or the parents are divorced, or living apart. Some children have lost both parents and live with other people or in orphanages. Because of the many different kinds of American families, there is no such thing as the typical, average American family.

THE FAMILY SERVES THE NATION

The American people depend upon the family to perform many important functions.

1. The family insures the future of our nation. To provide for the healthy growth of our nation, we must have future generations of citizens. The family is looked upon as the place where children should be raised as securely and happily as possible.

2. The family trains us in citizenship. The family has the responsibility of helping chil-

The family is the most important "community" in the United States. One of the family's important roles is to educate family members. Here, a mother helps her children to read.

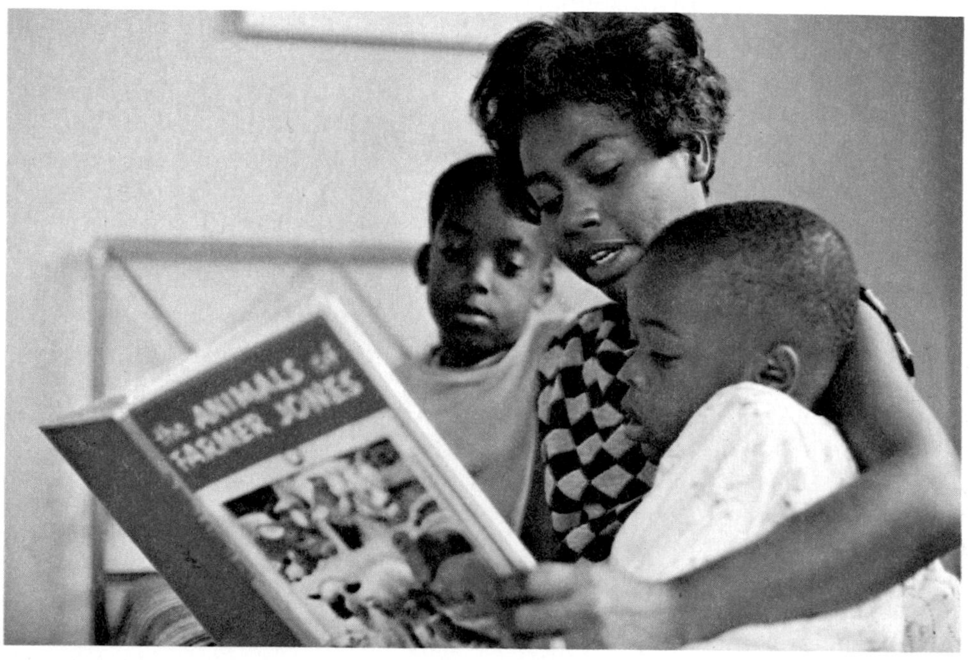

dren learn to respect the rights of others and to understand what their responsibilities as useful citizens will be.

3. The family helps us to manage money. The family earns and spends money to provide food, clothing, and a place to live for its members. The family should encourage children to learn how to manage money, how to save, and how to share financial responsibilities.

4. The family educates its members. We learn many more things from our family than we sometimes realize. It is in the home that children learn to walk, to talk, to dress themselves, to wash their faces and brush their teeth, to get along with others, to play safely, and to share in the work of the household.

5. The family teaches us good behavior. The child's earliest ideas of right and wrong are taught in the home. We learn how to behave from the members of our family.

STATE LAWS ABOUT MARRIAGE

Because the family is so important to our nation, a great many laws have been passed to protect the family. These laws have been passed by state legislatures because the right to regulate marriage laws is one of the powers of the state government.

The more than 2 million marriages that take place each year must meet laws set up in the state in which they are performed. State laws, for example, have established the earliest age at which young people may marry. Most states require that a young man and woman be at least 18 years old to be married without parental consent. In many states, boys and girls may be married at 16 if they have the consent of their parents, and of the court in a few states. Some states allow people to marry at younger ages. New Hampshire, for example, permits marriage with parental and court consent if the boy is 14 and the girl is 13. The average age

This couple is being married in a church. In most states, before the ceremony could take place the couple would have to apply for a marriage license and meet other requirements.

at which young people married in the late 1970's was between 23 and 24 years for men and between 21 and 22 years for women.

About half of our states require a **waiting period** of two to five days from the time a couple applies for a marriage license until the license is issued. This waiting period allows the couple to "think it over." And it is intended to discourage hasty marriages. All but a few of the states also require that a young man and woman applying for a marriage license must take a **blood test** to show that they are in good health.

All states require that marriages must be performed either by officials such as a Justice of the Peace, a judge, or a mayor, or by a minister, priest, or rabbi. Witnesses must be present at the ceremony to testify that a legal marriage was performed.

STATE LAWS PROTECT FAMILY MEMBERS

When the marriage ceremony is completed, the newly married couple is considered a family unit. Husband and wife now have certain rights guaranteed by law. If the rights of the husband or wife are neglected, the courts may be asked to step in. Usually, cases of nonsupport, desertion, and other marital differences are tried in a **Domestic Relations Court.**

Children, too, have certain legal rights as members of the family. If a child is not given the proper care by the parents, the law can step in to protect the child. In a few cases, if parents cannot take care of a child, a state court may take the child from the parents and place the child in a **foster home.** The state pays the foster parents to care for the child.

If the child's parents die, a judge may appoint a relative or close family friend to act as a guardian to look after the child. A **guardian** is a person appointed by a state court to care for individuals who are not yet adults, or who for some other reason are unable to care for themselves. In many instances, parents or guardians may themselves be held responsible for the child's actions if the child breaks the law.

STATE LAWS ABOUT SEPARATION AND DIVORCE

Marriage is a legal act recognized by law. A marriage can be officially ended only by the action of a state court. The court can end a marriage by granting a divorce or a legal separation.

If a married couple finds that they cannot get along together, they can take their problems into a state court. The judge will hear both sides of the argument and make a decision. In some cases, the judge may decide that a **separation** is the best answer. This means that the marriage is to continue, but the couple will separate and live apart. The husband must usually continue to support the wife and children during the period of the separation. In cases of separation, it is possible for the couple to return to living together.

THE PROBLEM OF DIVORCE

Divorce is the final, legal ending of a marriage. Each state makes its own laws concerning divorce. Most states make it difficult to obtain a divorce by limiting the causes for which divorces are granted. Some grounds for divorce are desertion, non-support, mental and physical cruelty, frequent drunkenness, frequent use of drugs, insanity, conviction of a serious crime, and adultery. In most states, courts have ruled that a divorced woman may receive a regular income from her former husband. These payments, called **alimony,** usually end if the woman marries again.

Divorce has greatly increased in recent years. Over 1 million marriages end in divorce each year. Over 40 percent of all marriages in the United States end in divorce.

Some Americans believe that the best way to cut down on the number of divorces is by passing stricter marriage laws. Others believe that more thoughtful marriages would result in better family life and lead to fewer divorces. Among other things, they point out that one of the best answers to the divorce problem lies in better education of all young people before they enter into marriage. Many schools now have courses in marriage and family relations to prepare young people for a happier married life.

There are also some Americans who favor less strict divorce laws. California has made it easier to get a divorce in that state. Some Americans believe that it is not healthy for children to live with two parents who are not getting along. They believe it is better for these parents to separate or divorce and work toward a new arrangement.

Our national, state, and local governments are concerned with the stability of the home and family. Laws are passed to protect marriage partners and their children. Funds are voted to keep families together and to aid in child care and family welfare. Laws, however, cannot do the whole job. The best way to guarantee a happy family life is to encourage family members to share and to work together for the good of the family group. The responsibilities of marriage are serious and important not only to the family members but also to the nation.

CONSIDER AND DISCUSS

Identify. waiting period / blood test / Domestic Relations Court / foster home / guardian / separation / divorce / alimony

Review. 1. Name some state laws regulating marriage. 2. How does the state protect children? 3. What is the difference between separation and divorce?

Discuss. What do you think are the obligations each family member has to every other? What do you think are the characteristics of a good and healthy family life?

3 Your Family and You

A home is more than just four walls, a roof, floors, windows, and doors. Through the years it has come to mean a special place where the family lives together in safety and in comfort. The word **home** means the familiar place that members of the same family share.

The ideal home is warm and secure. But no family can ever live up to the ideal all of the time. Any group of people living together will disagree at times and need to find ways to solve their differences.

Conflicts can occur between parents and children or between brothers and sisters. These disagreements require members of the family to make compromises, to give a little and to take a little. One of the signs of a well-adjusted family is that members of the family are able to work together to find solutions to the irritating problems of everyday living before they grow into big, emotional crises.

GOOD CITIZENSHIP AT HOME

Using common sense and considering another person's viewpoint help to prevent serious family trouble. Remember that each member of the family is a person worthy of respect. Each person has rights. If someone's rights are respected, that person is more likely to respect the rights of others in return.

The members of a well-adjusted family try to be sincerely interested in one another's activities. One important time to share discussion about what everyone has been doing throughout the day is at the dinner table.

Even family disagreements can bring benefit to the individual members. Arguments, if kept in hand, can teach you how to present your ideas effectively and help you to understand the other person's point of view.

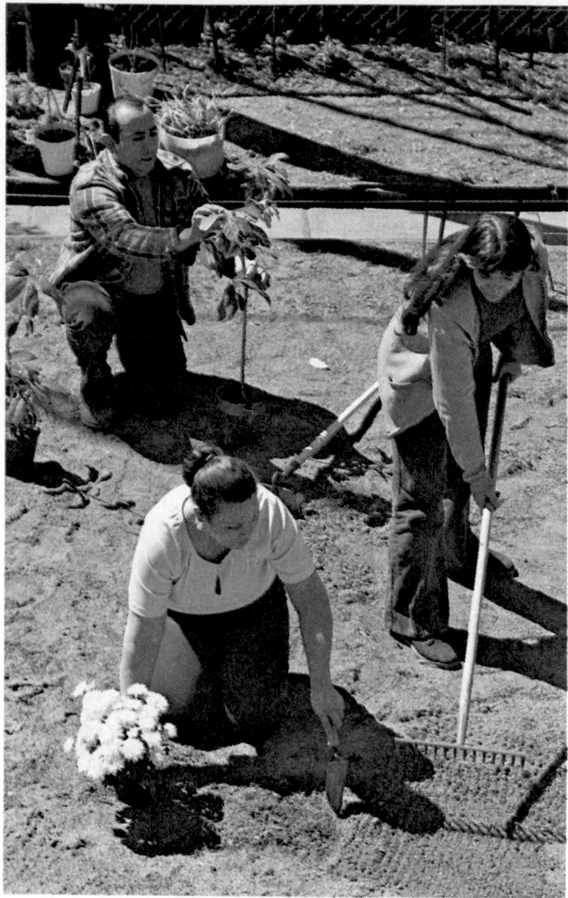

All the members of a family should share in the responsibilities and work of the family.

Talking over ideas with others teaches understanding and aids in the art of getting along with other people.

THE PROBLEM OF FAMILY FUNDS

One problem in many families concerns the way the family should spend its money. Mother and dad worry about earning enough money to pay for all the things the family wants. They are concerned about the best way to feed and clothe the family on their funds. The children in the family want money for school lunches, transportation, supplies for hobbies, tickets to school events or to the movies, as well as for many other things that seem very important at the time.

There are just so many dollars to be divided among the members of the family. When everyone cannot have everything he or she wants, compromises must be worked out. Doing one's share in handling family funds is an important opportunity. Learning to manage money now will be valuable to children when they become adults.

THE FAMILY BUDGET

Most families operate on some kind of a budget. The very thought of a budget scares some people. When they think of a budget, they picture a complicated bookkeeping system with row after row of figures. They also believe that it usually means "pinching pennies" and denying good times to all members of the family.

A budget should not scare anyone. A budget is simply a plan for spending the family's money. In fact, if a budget is carefully thought out and then put into action, it can reduce the family worries about money matters.

No one else can tell you and your family how to budget its money. They may make suggestions and help to explain a little about handling money. But your family's own special interests and needs require that your family work out its own spending plan.

The first step is to gather facts. Then make a workable plan based on these facts, and cooperate in carrying it out. The starting point in all budgets is the total amount available to spend. Most families have a fixed amount of income. And they must keep their spending and their savings within this income.

First of all, you would have certain **fixed expenses.** These are expenses that occur regularly and must be paid. There would be rent on an apartment, or mortgage payments on the house. There is also the cost of food. This is one of the most important items in the budget. There may also be such regular payments as insurance and telephone bills. With the remaining money you could pay for amusements, clothing, medical expenses, and other items. You would probably want to set some money aside for savings. A plan would help you to spend this money wisely.

PREPARING FOR THE FUTURE

You can help your own family to follow its budget plan. One important way is to help prevent waste in your home. Try not to ask for things that upset the budget. Talk to your parents before you agree to do things that cost money. Don't insist upon doing things your family cannot afford.

If you receive a regular allowance, or earn some money on your own, draw up your own budget. Decide upon the amount you need for transportation, lunches, and other fixed expenses. Then, if you can, set aside some money for future expenses or emergencies.

Remember, too, that your home is the best place in which to learn about home management. Handling money is just one skill you will need for the future. By learning to get along with your family, you are preparing yourself for the day when you manage your own home.

CONSIDER AND DISCUSS

Identify. home / fixed expenses

Review. 1. Why do families have budgets? 2. How can you help your family manage its finances?

Discuss. What are some ways you can try to be a good family member?

CHAPTER

Summary

The American family is the foundation on which our nation's future depends. It is the group in which young citizens learn valuable lessons that stay with them the rest of their lives.

As our nation has changed, so has family life. We have changed from a nation of farm families who provided for many of their own needs, to a nation of city dwellers who depend on others for most of their needs. Families are smaller. And more women work outside of the home. In spite of these changes, many aspects of family life are still the same.

Most American families are well fed, well clothed, and have good housing. However, there are still many families in our land who do not have these advantages. This is one of the problems that concerns our nation.

There are other problems, too, that we must consider. Among these are nonsupport, divorce and various marital difficulties in the home. Local, state, and national governments are working in many ways to find solutions to these problems.

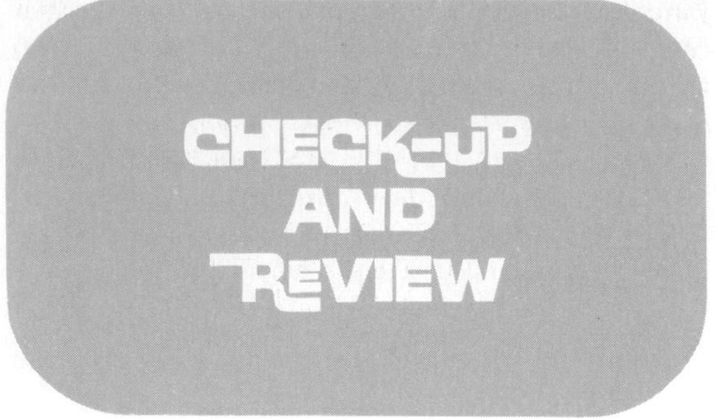

VOCABULARY

Study the following pairs of words. Tell how the words in each pair are related and how they are different.

institution	—	family
farm family	—	city family
separation	—	divorce
waiting period	—	blood test
fixed expenses	—	budget

CHECK-UP

Below are several questions that will help you increase your understanding of American families. Discuss your answers in class. See what you can learn by sharing ideas.

1. What do you think is a good definition of the word *family*?
2. Compare traditional American farm life with modern city life. How are they alike and how are they different?
3. Name five ways in which the family serves the nation.
4. What are some of the laws that protect the home and the family?
5. Why do most states have a waiting period before a marriage license is given?
6. What are some of the ways in which we can practice good citizenship in the home?
7. What is a budget? How does a budget help in the management of a family's income?
8. How can each member of the family help in managing the family budget?
9. What are some of the possible solutions to the problem of divorce?

CITIZENSHIP AND YOU

Join your classmates in studying the place of the family in American life. Here are some suggestions for projects to help in your study.

1. Class Projects

The United States Bureau of Labor Statistics has worked out tables for family budgets. Here is the table for a family of four with a yearly income of about $10,000.

Food	30.8%
Housing	19.4%
Taxes and social security	14.1%
Clothing and personal care	10.6%
Medical care	8.5%
Transportation	7.3%
Other family needs	4.8%
Insurance, job expenses, gifts	4.5%

On the class chalkboard, work out a monthly budget for this family. Show how much may be spent for each item.

2. Group or Committee Projects

A bulletin-board committee may prepare a display called "Good Citizenship Begins at Home."

Reading committees can read and report on such topics as "Famous American Families," "Poems and Songs About Home," and "Family Life in Other Lands."

Form an interview committee to talk with ministers, marriage counselors, judges, and police officers. Ask this question: "How Can Home Life Be Improved in Our Community?" Report on these interviews to the class.

Have members of the class set up several situations that can cause difficulties in families. Then have different members of the class play the roles of family members—father, mother, sister, brother. Each group should develop a different solution. That way the class can see the possible ways different people would deal with the situations. Afterwards, the class can discuss which is the best way to handle each situation.

3. Individual Projects

Your own ideas about good family citizenship will become clearer if you write them down. Try putting your ideas into essay form. Good titles for such essays might be "The Ideal Family" and "My Home in 1990." Several essays may be read and discussed in class.

CIVICS SKILLS

USING THE LIBRARY

Making good use of your school library and public library is one of the skills that will help you in all your schoolwork. This chapter of your civics text discusses a number of topics that you could investigate further in the library. Some of the topics you might look up and read about are: "The Origin of the Family," "Marriage Laws," "Home Life in Other Countries," "Divorce in America," and "Care of Orphans."

It is a good idea to become thoroughly acquainted with at least one library. Quietly explore the library. Locate such important features as the card catalog, encyclopedias, and other reference books. Study the location and general arrangements of books, magazines, and newspapers.

When you want to look up a book, go to the card catalog. There books are listed in three ways: by author, title, and subject. Books on the home, family, marriage, and budget will be found under the first initial of each word. A number is given to each book, and the books in the library are arranged according to these numbers. With this number you can find the exact section of the library to locate the book you want.

Using the library can be like going on a treasure hunt. The first book you locate may not have the precise information you need. But it may list other books that will provide your information.

PRACTICING YOUR CIVICS SKILLS

Go to the card catalog of the library and find the number for the latest edition of *The Statistical Abstract of the United States.* Locate this book in the library and use it to answer the following questions:

1. What is the library number of this reference work?
2. How many marriages took place in the United States in the latest year given?
3. Are there more unmarried males or females over the age of 18 in the United States?
4. Out of every 1,000 persons in the United States who have been married, how many have been divorced?

CHAPTER
Introduction

A Senator of the United States is preparing a speech. A surgeon is about to begin an operation. An auto mechanic is preparing to repair a sports car. What do these persons have in common? They are about to show the practical effects of their education.

If they have really profited from their education, the Senator will make an effective speech, the surgeon may save a life, and the auto mechanic will keep the car running safely and smoothly.

The future of our nation depends, in large part, on our system of education and the way it affects citizens. America's schools and colleges need to help train our citizens to meet the challenges of a complicated, rapidly changing world.

Today, almost every occupation requires some special training. The progress our nation must make in science, social science, engineering, and technology depends upon a supply of well-educated persons prepared to contribute to these fields. The way to success in every occupation and career is through study, training, and hard work. This is true whether the occupation is in stenography, nursing, carpentry, medicine, law, or banking.

In this chapter you will study about America's schools and the opportunities they offer you. You will also consider the best ways to make use of your school years as you study these topics:

1. The American School System
2. The Best Education for You
3. Developing Skills in Thinking

CHAPTER

12 Citizenship in School

1 The American School System

There are about 60 million students enrolled in public and private schools and colleges in the United States. The cost of running these educational enterprises in the late 1970's was over $130 billion a year. Over 3.2 million teachers are engaged in the day-by-day tasks of education. Why are the people of the United States willing to put all this money and effort into education?

THE PURPOSES OF EDUCATION

The American people are proud of the progress and achievements of their educational system. There are two main reasons for this great interest.

1. Schools exist to aid in the development of each individual American citizen. From the earliest days of our nation, the American people have placed great value on the importance of the individual. The first purpose of education is, therefore, to serve the individual citizen. All people should be given the opportunity to study and to learn in order to develop their talents and abilities. The Declaration of Independence sets forth the American belief "that all men [and women] are created equal, that they are endowed by their Creator with certain unalienable rights, that among these are life, liberty, and the pursuit of happiness." As a result, Americans believe that all citizens should be given equal

This picture of a one-room schoolhouse was painted in 1871. How have American schools changed since that time?

chances, through education, to make the most of themselves.

2. Schools aid in the development of the American nation. The welfare of all the American people depends upon the willingness and the ability of all individuals to use their talents so that they may contribute to the welfare of the entire nation. The aim of education is to teach Americans how to make an important contribution to various groups. It stresses the need for good citizenship in our nation. Our schools try to show how the welfare of each citizen and the welfare of the country depend on all Americans learning to work together for the common good.

HOW OUR SCHOOL SYSTEM CAME INTO BEING

The present American system of education has been growing for over 300 years. The first important step was taken in Massachusetts in 1647 when a law was passed requiring all towns to set up schools. The purpose of this requirement was to make sure that all children learned to read the Bible so that they would not fall into evil ways. This law provided that every town of 50 families or more was to hire a schoolteacher to be paid out of town funds. By doing this, the act moved the responsibility for schooling from the home to the community as a whole.

In many of the other colonies, however, the education of the young was neglected. The children of the wealthy were sent to private schools or were provided with tutors. But the children of poor parents often were put to work at an early age and were given little or no schooling. It was not until the first half of the 1800's that leaders such as **Horace Mann** began to achieve the goal of free public schools for all children. This system, however, did not include black Americans. Many of them were slaves, and by and large, they received no education.

Many Americans in those days were opposed to free public schools. Some taxpayers thought that it was unfair to make them pay for the education of other people's children. Owners of private schools claimed that free public schools would ruin their business. Certain church-supported schools claimed that education should be under the control of the church and the home.

By the time of the Civil War, the struggle for free, public, tax-supported schools was beginning to be won. Most Northern states and a number of Southern states had set up public school systems. But these school systems were usually limited to elementary schools, known as "common schools." There were only 55 public high schools in the whole United States in 1850. It was not until the period after the Civil War that a system of free, public secondary schools, or high schools, began to be set up in our states.

THE EDUCATIONAL LADDER

Most Americans spend a large part of their lives getting an education. There are many different levels to the American system of education.

NURSERY SCHOOLS

Many American children attend nursery school. The **nursery school** is usually a private school attended by children 3 and 4 years of age. In these schools, the child learns to play and get along with other children. Families in which both members work often send their children to nursery schools. Most nursery schools are private. But some American communities support nursery schools as part of their public school system. The federal government also grants funds for preschool programs in some communities.

KINDERGARTENS

The word **kindergarten** is German and it means "a garden for children." Many public school systems start with kindergarten classes for 5-year-old children. Kindergarten children spend a year learning how to get along with others, and preparing for first grade.

School and College Enrollment

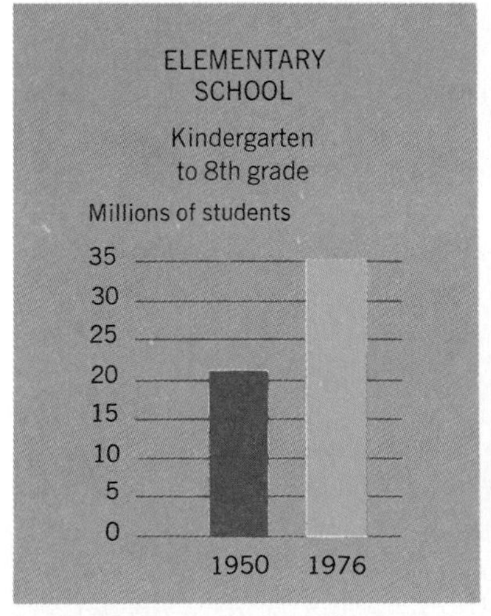

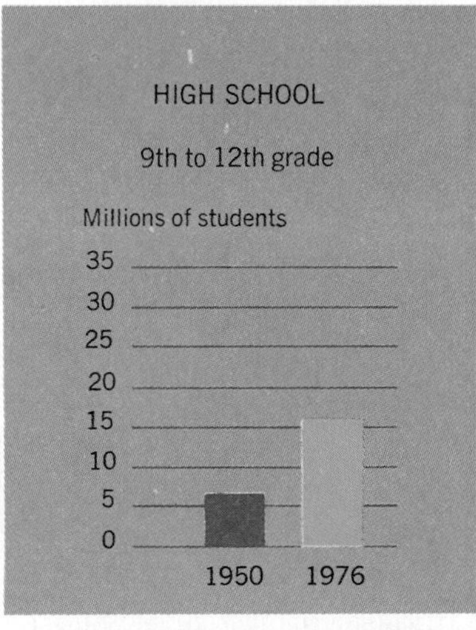

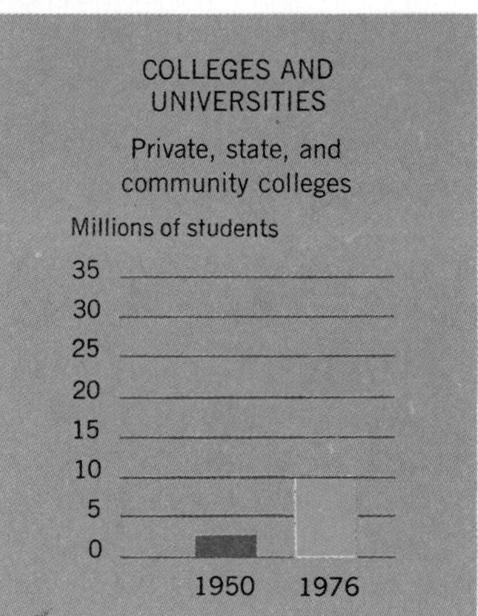

SOURCE: United States Department of Commerce, Bureau of the Census.

ELEMENTARY SCHOOLS

Elementary schools, which children enter as first-graders at the age of 5 or 6, teach the fundamentals of education—reading, writing, and arithmetic. The curriculum is also enriched by such subjects as history, geography, science, health, art, music, and physical education. Children attend elementary school from five to nine years, depending upon how the school system is arranged.

JUNIOR HIGH SCHOOLS

Junior high schools usually contain grades 7, 8, and 9. Some school systems have given up junior high schools in favor of Middle, or Intermediate, Schools, which usually include grades 5 or 6 through 8.

HIGH SCHOOLS

Public **high schools** admit students who have successfully completed the first eight or nine grades. There are generally three kinds of high schools. **Academic high schools** prepare students for college. **Vocational and technical high schools** enable students to learn a trade or occupation. And **comprehensive high schools** offer college preparatory work as well as vocational courses. About 85 percent of all American boys and girls of ages 14 through 17 are enrolled in public high schools.

JUNIOR COLLEGES

The growing demand for higher education is being met in part by two-year **junior colleges,** sometimes called community colleges. They are often supported by taxpayers and offer courses free or at low tuition to local high school graduates. Courses include training for technical fields, forestry, home economics, and business. Many junior college graduates transfer to four-year colleges or universities.

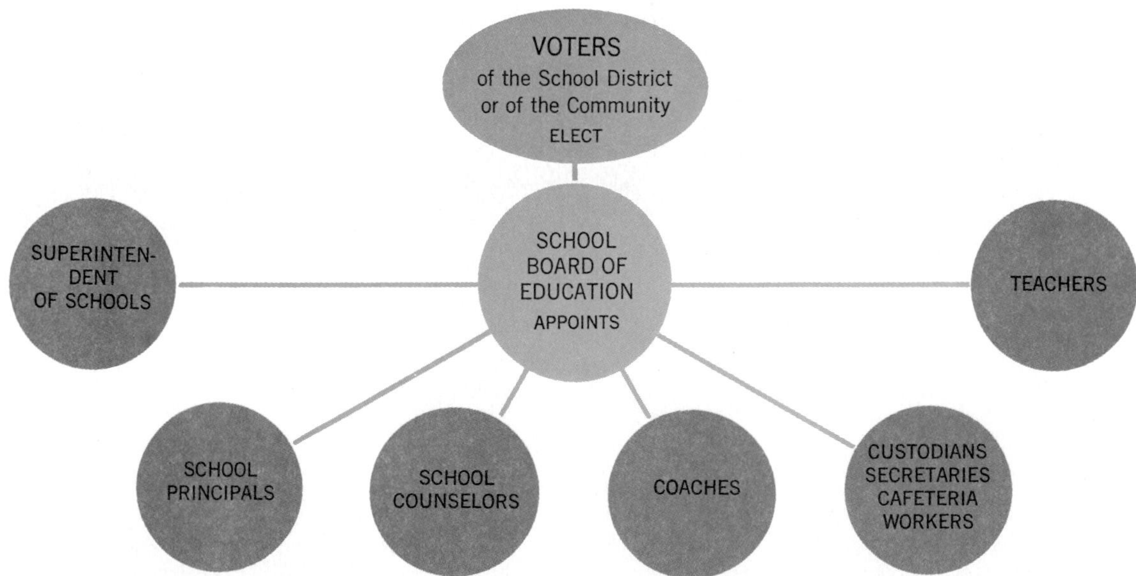

School districts are special units of local government. In some states, however, schools are dependent upon city, town, or county government. Local school boards are usually elected, but are appointed in some cities and counties.

AMERICAN COLLEGES AND UNIVERSITIES

Altogether there are some 2,700 colleges and universities in the United States. Most are coeducational. That is, they are open to both men and women students. They range in size from small **colleges** with only a few hundred students to large institutions with up to 100,000 students or more. About one third of all colleges are supported by state or local governments.

Some institutions of higher learning are called **universities.** A university includes one or more colleges, each of which offers studies in some professional field of learning. A university may have a college of medicine, a college of dentistry, a college of engineering, and a general liberal arts college. After graduation from a college, the student may go on to **graduate school** to work for an advanced degree.

SPECIAL SCHOOLS

Americans believe in equal opportunities for all citizens. They have, therefore, set up special schools and classes for the blind, the deaf, and the physically handicapped. In addition, there are schools for emotionally disturbed children and retarded children. Also, some communities provide special education opportunities for gifted children. In recent years the trend has been to place children from special schools back into regular schools.

There are also schools for adults who wish to extend their education or make up education they missed. The classes are usually held at night.

AMERICAN VALUES IN EDUCATION

Our school system has developed as it has because the American people value education highly. Some of the traditional values that have developed over the years are:

1. Public education should be free. There should be no hidden charges to prevent any citizen from receiving a good education at public expense. Public education in the United States costs local taxpayers well over $100 billion a year, including educational expenditures by the federal government of about $20 billion.

2. Schooling should be equal and open to all. No one should be discriminated against because of race, religion, or financial status. This value is still a problem for the American school system, and is discussed in the following section.

3. The public schools should be free of any creed or religion. The schools of the United States are open to all Americans regardless of their religious beliefs. The Su-

The "Ladder" of American Education

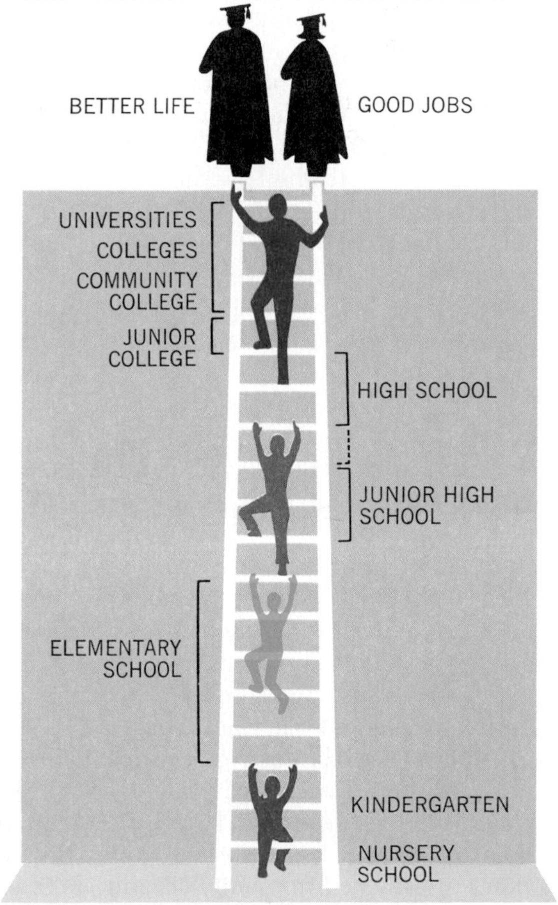

BETTER LIFE
GOOD JOBS
UNIVERSITIES
COLLEGES
COMMUNITY COLLEGE
JUNIOR COLLEGE
HIGH SCHOOL
JUNIOR HIGH SCHOOL
ELEMENTARY SCHOOL
KINDERGARTEN
NURSERY SCHOOL

preme Court has held that no special prayer or Bible reading shall be required. However, religious schools (sometimes called parochial schools) are permitted outside of the public school system.

4. Public schools are controlled by the state and local governments within which they are located. Local school boards run the public schools under laws passed by the state legislature. The State Board of Education assists the local schools, but does not give orders to the district board. The United States Office of Education also assists with advice and information. But the actual control is located in the local school district, where the people know the local situation.

5. Attendance at school is compulsory. Parents cannot decide to keep their children out of school. Each state compels the attendance of young people, usually between the ages of 7 and 16.

6. Schooling should be enriching and not just confined to the fundamentals. Most Americans believe that schools should be places where young people can grow in body, mind, and spirit. Athletics, clubs, social events, and creative arts are a part of each person's education. Schools should be lively places where individuals are encouraged to develop to their greatest potential.

PROBLEMS OF TODAY'S SCHOOL SYSTEM

The American school system faces certain problems today. In 1954, the Supreme Court ruled that students cannot receive equal educational opportunities when they attend public schools in which students are segregated, or separated according to race. This ruling has led to bitter controversy. The best way to integrate school systems and provide equal educational opportunities is a question that has not yet been resolved.

Court-ordered busing of students to achieve integration has been tried in some areas. In some places it has worked well. But in others it has led to violence and defiance of court orders by parents, students, and other people.

There are other important problems that challenge America's schools. Many of them are caused by lack of money. Some school systems are overcrowded and in poor condition. They need to improve their school buildings. They also need modern classroom equipment and other aids to learning.

Such problems must be solved if our educational system is to serve Americans well in the future.

CONSIDER AND DISCUSS

Identify. Horace Mann / nursery school / kindergarten / elementary school / junior high school / high school / academic high school / vocational and technical high school / comprehensive high school / junior college / college / university / graduate school

Review. 1. What are the two main purposes of education in the United States? 2. Why were early schools established in Massachusetts? 3. Why were free public high schools slow in developing in the United States? 4. What are the principal steps in the American educational ladder?

Discuss. Which of our educational values have not been fully achieved? Why not?

2 The Best Education for You

Luck has been defined as being in the right place at the right time. What we sometimes forget to add is that the lucky person is also able to see opportunities and to make good use of them. This is true in school and in studying, too. You must be alert in order to take advantage of the opportunities that are offered you in school. What are these opportunities?

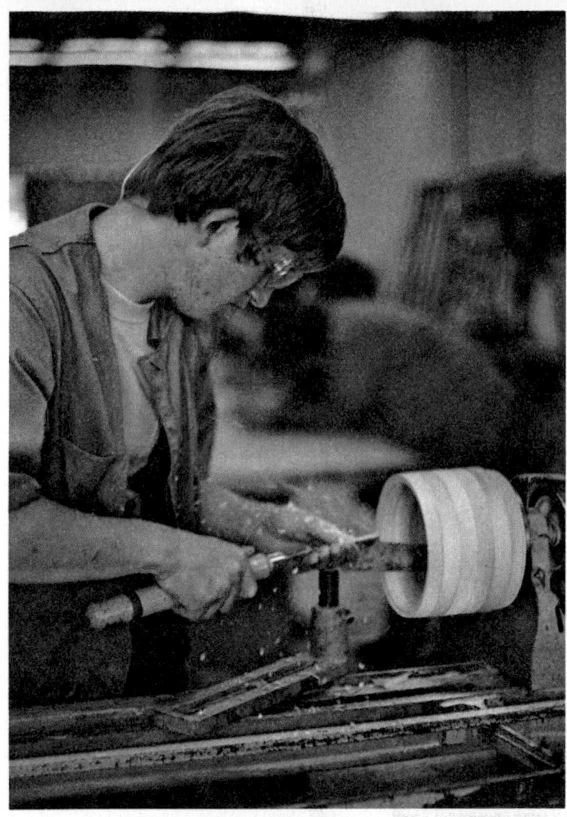

This student is learning new skills in the school shop. This experience may help him choose a career, or it may lead to an interesting lifelong hobby.

WHAT YOUR SCHOOL HAS TO OFFER YOU

Some years ago, a group of teachers and school officials stated the goals of education that American schools should try to achieve. The statement that they prepared is called **"The Seven Cardinal Principles of Secondary Education."** As you study these goals, or principles, try to think how your school works to achieve each of them. Ask yourself if you are taking advantage of the opportunities offered under each heading.

1. Using fundamental learning skills. One of the main goals of our schools is to teach each student the skills of reading, writing, and arithmetic. In addition, schools teach certain other skills that help students to learn and to study. These learning skills include skill in oral communication, skill in organizing and expressing ideas, dictionary and research skills, and the ability to read and interpret maps, graphs, charts, and cartoons. All students can use these skills to great advantage in many different courses in school.

2. Health education. Most schools offer a program in health education to teach students to develop good health habits. Health education usually includes programs of physical activities, including sports and athletic programs. Every student can benefit from the school's health education program. The theory and the practice learned in school will help you to take good care of your health and to keep physically fit in the years after you leave school.

3. Learning to be a good family member. Good citizenship begins at home. To become a good citizen, you must learn to cooperate with the members of your family. You must contribute your share around the house and be considerate of other family members. Many of your school activities require you to work together with other students. This cooperation furnishes good practice in helping you to work together with members of your family.

4. Training for your life's work. Your school provides the educational foundation on which special job training may be based. Your school also tries to help you prepare for job opportunities after you graduate. Employers want well-educated workers, and schools make it possible for you to become a desirable employee. It is up to you to take advantage of your education in order to prepare for the job in which you can contribute most to your nation and in which you will find the greatest satisfaction.

5. Active citizenship. To help you to become a good citizen, your school seeks to develop your interest in your community. It teaches you about the history of your nation,

its institutions, and the problems it faces today. Using many class and school activities, your teachers do their best to develop in you a sense of loyalty, love of country, good judgment, and a willingness to do your share.

6. Wise use of leisure time. Your school tries to teach you to enjoy good books, art, and music so that they may enrich your life. Your teachers encourage you to take up interesting hobbies and to take part in school activities such as athletics, dramatics, the glee club, or band.

By encouraging you to undertake such activities, your school is trying to help you to find a hobby or special interest that you will be able to enjoy now and in the future. In this way, your school helps to prepare you to make good use of your spare time.

7. Considerate behavior. Your school tries to teach students to adapt to accepted standards of behavior. It tries to develop in all students a feeling of consideration for their classmates, their teachers, parents, friends, and all members of the community.

GETTING THE MOST FROM YOUR SCHOOL CAREER

If you are to make the best use of the opportunities that your school offers, you will need to remember the goals that your school is trying to reach. Your years in school are very important years in your life. The success you enjoy in school and the study and learning habits that you develop will help to determine the kind of person you will be later in life. What kind of study and learning habits should you try to develop?

One of the first and most important study habits that all students must learn is the wise use of time. The well-organized student finds time in his or her daily schedule for study, for school activities, for exercise, for relaxing, and for the proper amount of sleep. Just as your family budgets its money, you will find it wise to budget your time. Work out a daily schedule for your more important activities, and form the habit of getting things done on time.

Activities such as a school band give students a chance to develop their individual talents.

HOW TO STUDY

Study your schoolwork in a careful and concentrated way. Have a regular place to study, where it is quiet, and where there is good working space and proper light. Have the materials you need close at hand.

Take notes on your reading. You will soon

find that writing down important ideas will help you to understand them and will fix these ideas in your mind. Make sure you understand your assignment before you start. Then determine to do the best job you can.

Your textbooks are written to help you to learn quickly and efficiently. Here are some hints to help you get the most out of your textbooks.

1. Learn how to use the **study aids** in the book. Refer to the table of contents, index, glossary, maps, charts, and picture captions.
2. Note the chapter title, the section headings, and the other subheadings within the chapter. They give you clues to the most important ideas.
3. Read through the assignment carefully, noting topic sentences and summarizing paragraphs.
4. Reread the assignment, this time making written notes on the important ideas and facts.
5. Turn to the questions at the end of each section of the chapter, and see if you can answer each one. If you find a question you cannot answer, turn back to the page in your textbook where this subject was discussed and find the correct answer.
6. Some people find a card file valuable. They build up a file containing definitions, formulas, important facts, and answers to key questions. These cards are especially good for review when preparing for a test.

TAKING PART IN CLASSWORK

When you come to class, bring the material you will need in order to take an active part in the day's lesson. The student who wants to learn is not afraid to ask questions. The questioning frame of mind can lead to answers. Pay careful attention to what is being taught in class. Think about the lesson. Learn to form your own ideas and opinions. If you fall behind or fail to understand a part of a lesson, ask for help.

HOW TO DO WELL ON TESTS

When it comes time for a test, go over your notes carefully. Some students find it helpful to have some classmate ask them questions that might appear on the test. This helps them to discover whether they really know the material. They want to discover what information they need to spend more time on. When taking the test, it is good to read over each question carefully before attempting to answer it. Look over the entire test to see how many questions there are and how much time should be spent answering each question. If there is time left at the end of the test period, read over your answers and check carefully to see that you have answered each question.

TAKING PART IN SCHOOL ACTIVITIES

School is more than just classes, homework, tests, and class projects. **Extracurricular activities** (activities in addition to classes), such as school clubs, choir, band, sports teams, cheerleading, dances, and social events are also a part of your education. You can learn a great deal from such activities. You may learn interesting skills or to express yourself in new ways. You may also make many new friends.

Extracurricular activities add to your fun in school. At the same time they help you to develop your own special abilities and interests. Some students are satisfied merely to "get by" in school. These students forget that they are cheating themselves.

CONSIDER AND DISCUSS

Identify. "Seven Cardinal Principles of Secondary Education" / study aids / extracurricular activities

Review. 1. What are the seven goals of education? 2. What good study habits are suggested in this chapter? 3. What are some ways to prepare for tests? 4. Why are extra-

curricular activities included in the school program?
Discuss. Why are your school years important to your future?

3 Developing Skills in Thinking

One of the main purposes of education is to help people learn how to think. The dictionary tells us that to **think** is to form ideas in the mind. This sounds simple enough, but how do we form these ideas?

THINKING AND LEARNING

We think mainly with facts. When faced with problems, thinking people consider all the possible solutions they know about. They then decide which solution seems best to them. How do we obtain the facts with which we do our thinking? We learn them.

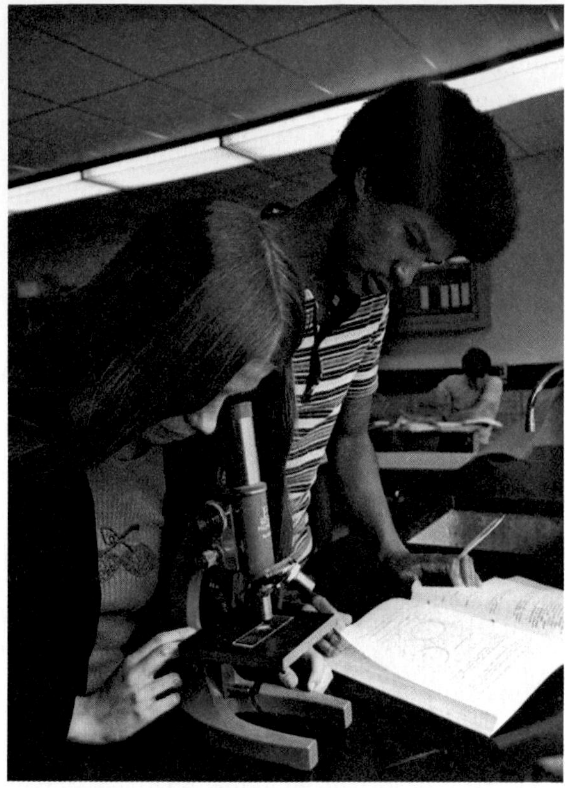

Books are only one of the tools of learning. Here, a student examines plant life under a microscope.

HOW WE LEARN

Almost everything we do—the way we act, think, pass along information, even the way we show emotion—is learned. People learn in many ways. But all learning is the result of some kind of **experience,** or things that happened in the past.

The simplest kind of learning is the result of experience that involves the motor nerves—those nerves that control our muscles. A person who touches a hot stove will jerk back the hand because of the pain. Next time, that person will avoid hot stoves. But suppose that while the person was reaching for the stove, someone said "hot" in a sharp tone. In the future, if near a hot stove, the person will draw back a hand whenever someone says "hot" in a sharp tone. This kind of learning is called **conditioning.**

Much of our behavior, or the way we act, is conditioned. People learn to do things because they expect to be rewarded or to gain satisfaction. Children, for example, will wash their hands before meals if they expect praise, a favorite dessert, or a hug. They will continue to behave in the desired way if they are rewarded occasionally. Behavior that is repeated often usually becomes a **habit**—an action that is performed automatically.

People also learn by copying, or imitating, others. Young children imitate their parents and other members of the family. They try to act and think like them. They repeat their parents' opinions and habits. As adults, people often imitate their friends and others they admire.

LEARNING IN SCHOOL

Much of what we know is also learned by looking and listening. Every day of our lives we learn through our senses and take in different kinds of information. But in our complex society, there is so much information that it has to be organized, or arranged in groups, in order to be usable. A large part of the organized information we learn is taught to us in schools and through books.

Besides facts, schools teach students how to make the best use of information by comparing and analyzing facts, by putting them together, and then drawing conclusions. We are also taught where to find information.

Our ability to learn depends upon our maturity, experience, and intelligence. It also depends on how motivated we are. Motivation is something within people that arouses and directs their behavior.

HOW WE THINK

Thinking is a complex process. It involves our awareness, understanding, and interpretation of what we see and know. We think when we solve problems by considering all the solutions we know. Every time we make a decision we solve a problem.

But sometimes we try to find an answer to something and cannot come up with it, no matter how hard we try. Then, suddenly, the answer will spring to mind. This is called **insight.** The answer seems to come out of nowhere. Actually, it comes to mind only after we have studied the problem and ruled out several possible answers. Without realizing it, people often take what they know about something else and apply it to the subject they are studying.

Occasionally, our solutions are original. The ability to find new ways of thinking and doing things is called **creative thinking.** Everyone can think creatively. We have other thinking abilities, too. Our abilities to reason, to question, and to weigh information are all ways of thinking.

FACT OR OPINION

It is important in clear thinking to distinguish between what is a fact and what is a personal **opinion,** or judgment. To illustrate, a newspaper reporter may write that a famous actor "angrily pounded on a neighbor's door until it was broken." The fact that the door pounding took place can be proved. Several eye witnesses may have seen it. But was the actor really angry? This is the reporter's judgment. The actor may have pounded on the door, not in anger, but to get a lot of publicity. A person's feelings, such as anger or happiness, are difficult to check or measure accurately. It is important, therefore, to know whether you are dealing with a fact or an opinion.

WHO INFLUENCES YOUR THINKING?

No one can do our thinking for us. But other people do help to determine what we think. Sometimes we are influenced by some well-known person we admire. We often listen carefully to what a famous person says. Our fathers and mothers, teachers, and friends also have a great influence on our opinions.

Sometimes people think and behave in certain ways because they are members of particular groups in our society. In judging a labor dispute, for example, an employer may tend to have a different opinion from that of a worker. Few persons are able to be impartial, or completely fair, to all sides all of the time. People sometimes have opinions that are biased, or that favor one side. All of us have certain fixed feelings, or **prejudices.** Prejudices are opinions that are not based on careful and reasonable investigation of the facts. We must be careful not to be ruled by our prejudices, or by those of others.

Propaganda Methods

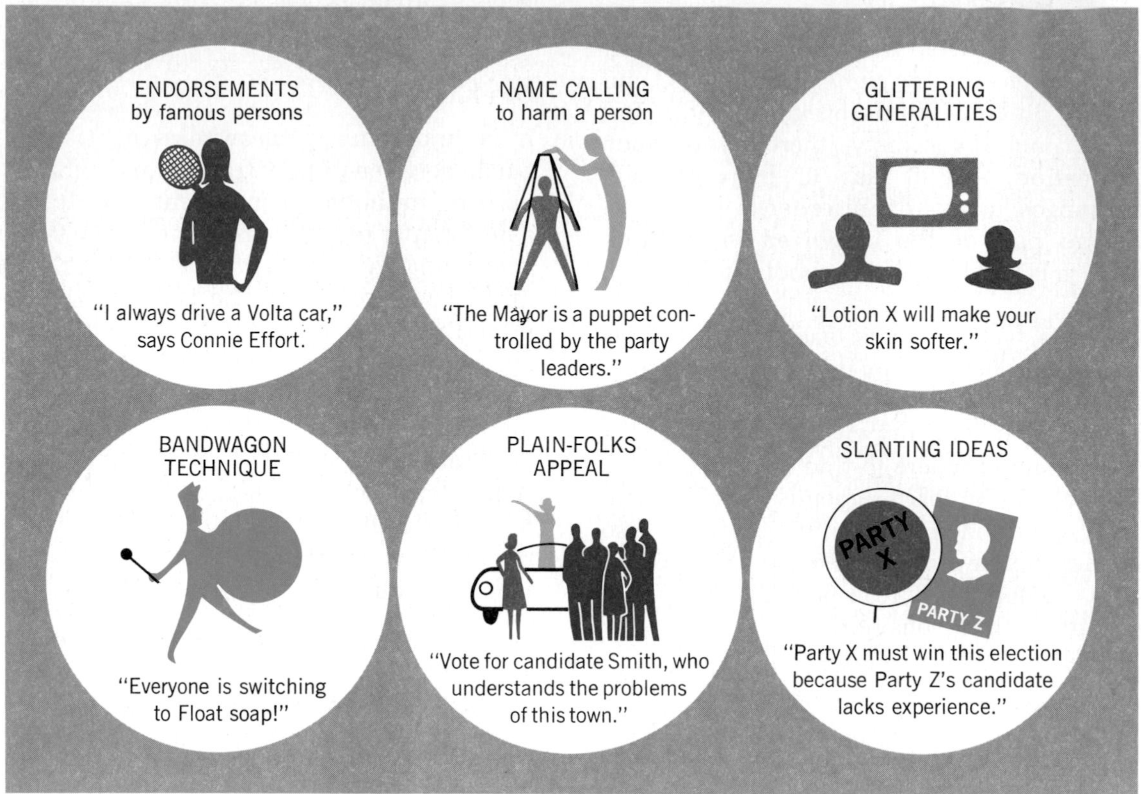
ENDORSEMENTS
by famous persons
"I always drive a Volta car," says Connie Effort.
NAME CALLING
to harm a person
"The Mayor is a puppet controlled by the party leaders."
GLITTERING GENERALITIES
"Lotion X will make your skin softer."
BANDWAGON TECHNIQUE
"Everyone is switching to Float soap!"
PLAIN-FOLKS APPEAL
"Vote for candidate Smith, who understands the problems of this town."
SLANTING IDEAS
PARTY X
PARTY Z
"Party X must win this election because Party Z's candidate lacks experience."

THINKING FOR YOURSELF

If most of your opinions come from other people, then you are probably not doing enough of your own thinking. In that case you should probably try harder to examine the facts and make up your own mind. A democracy can only work if its citizens are willing to think for themselves, and not simply accept what others tell them.

If you want to think for yourself as much as you can, you should study the way you make decisions and form judgments. Thinking for yourself depends upon knowing all the facts about a certain problem, listening to other people's opinions, distinguishing between facts and opinions, and then finally selecting from all you discover to form your own judgment.

LEARNING TO UNDERSTAND PROPAGANDA

Every day we get ideas from many different sources: newspapers, magazines, comic books, posters and billboards, radio and television programs. But many of the ideas we get from these sources have been directed at us for a purpose. Somebody is trying to get us to do something—to buy something, to believe something, or to act in a given way. Ideas that are used to try to influence us are called **propaganda.**

PROPAGANDA TAKES TWO FORMS

When propaganda ideas are presented as facts and their sources are kept secret, they are called **concealed propaganda.** Concealed propaganda tries to fool you without letting you know that it is trying to influence you.

Sometimes concealed propaganda is relatively harmless. For example, press agents may make up interesting stories about television stars to give these stars publicity in newspapers and magazines. But at other times concealed propaganda may be used to create harmful impressions. A photograph may be taken in a certain way or may be retouched to make a political candidate look bad. Or false rumors may be spread in order to harm someone.

Revealed propaganda is much more common in America. In revealed propaganda, readers or listeners are aware that someone is using ideas to influence them. Almost all advertising is revealed propaganda. You know when you see most advertisements that somebody wants you to buy something or to believe something. Television or radio commercials are direct appeals to the public to buy various products. During an election campaign, political parties may run commercials on television to get voters to support their candidates. But these commercials must be clearly labeled as paid advertisements.

The civics chapter you are now reading also contains revealed propaganda. It is openly spreading the idea that all students should work hard to try to improve their thinking.

METHODS OF PROPAGANDA

Propaganda experts sometimes use cleverly designed half-truths to mislead you. Some of these propaganda methods are hard to spot. Others can be easily seen through by those who know how to recognize them. What are some of these propaganda methods?

1. Endorsements. People who write advertisements are creating propaganda. They understand the way people think and act, and they use their knowledge to help sell services and products. Advertising writers know, for instance, that the American people admire well-known sports heroes. Therefore, they pay famous athletes to endorse, or approve, their product.

They know that if a football hero says that he drives a certain automobile, many people will believe that the automobile must be good. These people like their football hero so they will trust his judgment. But

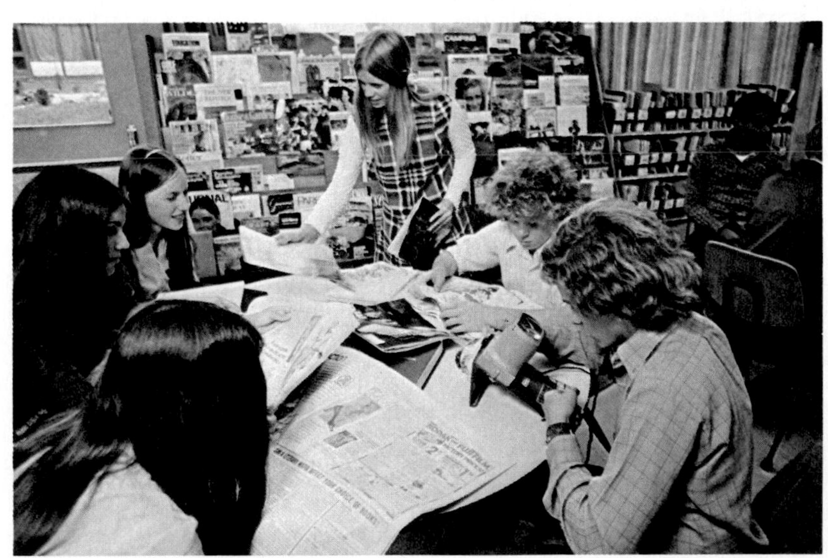

These students are looking at newspapers and magazines in their school library. What kinds of propaganda are they likely to find?

people who think for themselves know that this endorsement by a great athlete proves very little. A football player may be the greatest passing quarterback of all time, but this does not make him an expert on automobiles.

2. The bandwagon technique. Those who write propaganda know that if you say something often enough and loud enough, a great many people will believe it. If you can win some people over to your ideas, then in time more and more will come over to your side. This is known as the bandwagon technique of propaganda. "Everybody's doing it! Get on the bandwagon!" This method of propaganda appeals to people's desire to do what their friends and neighbors are doing.

3. Name calling. Another propaganda trick is known as name calling. This is the use of an unpleasant label or description to harm a person, a group, or a product. The use of terms such as "coward," "traitor," and the like, without showing any proof, is an attempt to make us think of a person in uncomplimentary terms.

Name calling is sometimes used to harm political candidates. During an election campaign, name calling may be used on both sides. You may hear that some candidate favors "reckless spending" or that another is "opposed to progress." The question to ask oneself is, What proof is given?

4. Glittering generalities. Another method to influence people's thinking is the glittering generality. This method uses words that sound good but have little real meaning. Many advertising slogans are glittering generalities. For example, such a statement as "It contains a miracle ingredient," has little meaning. This propaganda technique often uses such words as home, mother, country, freedom, patriotic, and American, because most people in our country approve of what these words stand for.

5. Plain-folks appeal. At election time, many candidates describe themselves as plain, hardworking American citizens who understand the problems of the average American family. This plain-folks appeal is designed to get votes. Candidates work hard to show the people that, as one of them, they can best represent the interests of the average citizen. It is important to investigate candidates' programs to see if they really would represent the average citizen.

6. Slanting ideas. Another propaganda method is known as slanting ideas. This method uses words in a certain way in order to favor a product, an idea, or a candidate. Newspapers, for example, may give front-page attention to the activities of the candidates they favor. The other political party and its candidates may be given smaller headlines or be reported only on the inside pages. The news is slanted to favor one party over the other.

CENSORSHIP VERSUS THINKING FOR YOURSELF

If it is easy to fool many people by using propaganda methods, why doesn't our government regulate what is printed in newspapers, books, and magazines? And why doesn't it control what is said over radio and television? The reason this is not done is that Americans believe in freedom of speech and freedom of the press.

If Americans could say and print only what government officials permitted, then we would have government control of speech and the press. This kind of control is called **censorship.** It is usually found in nations headed by a dictator who wants no criticism. Complete control of speech and press also prevents the people from expressing ideas against the government.

Freedom of speech and press allows the American people to learn a variety of ideas and views. No government official can censor, or control, what Americans say. Copies of speeches, newspaper articles, books, or magazine stories do not have to be approved by the government before they can be published. Our freedom of the press is guaranteed by the Constitution of the United States.

The fact that Americans are free to express themselves does not mean that they have the right to say or to print anything. They do not have the right to print or say something that is untrue in order to injure someone. There are laws against **libel,** that is, against printing false information in order to harm a person. Anyone who believes that some newspaper or speaker has tried to harm him or her with untruths may sue in court and collect damages if he or she wins the case. In this way, Americans are protected against those who misuse the freedom of speech and press.

Free speech and a free press give the American people the opportunity to discover for themselves the facts that they need to form their opinions. In return, citizens have the responsibility of using these facts intelligently in making their own judgments.

CONSIDER AND DISCUSS

Identify. think / experience / conditioning / habit / insight / creative thinking / opinion / prejudices / propaganda / concealed propaganda / revealed propaganda / endorsement / bandwagon technique / name calling / glittering generality / plain-folks appeal / slanting ideas / censorship / libel

Review. 1. How can we learn through experience? 2. What is the difference between an opinion and a fact? 3. Give some examples in which the different methods of propaganda are used.

Discuss. During time of war, certain news may be censored. Why? Is this fair?

CHAPTER Summary

The American educational system has developed in many ways during the history of our country, and it continues to grow. The American people value a free public education for all.

Your school tries to teach many worthwhile things. It teaches students the fundamental skills of learning. It offers a variety of subjects. Education also prepares you to be a good citizen in your family and in the nation.

One of the most important skills you learn in school is the ability to read well and to understand what you read. Schools also help people to become better able to think clearly and make judgments. One must learn to study the facts, and to distinguish facts from opinions, before making a judgment.

In learning to think for yourself, you need to consider how opinions are formed. You must be aware that many people are trying to shape your thinking. You need to be able to recognize propaganda—both concealed and revealed. You should be able to identify the various methods that are used to influence your opinion and your judgment.

CHECK-UP AND REVIEW

VOCABULARY

Below is a list of words that appear in this chapter. Copy these words in the vocabulary section of your notebook and write definitions beside each.

kindergarten	prejudice
university	experience
compulsory	propaganda
education	censorship
think	extracurricular

CHECK-UP

Write the answers to each of the following questions and be prepared to defend your answers in class.

1. Why is active citizenship considered one of the major aims of American education?
2. Why is it important for students to "budget" their time?
3. Why are maps and charts especially useful as study aids?
4. What extracurricular activities in your school do you find most important and enjoyable?
5. What are some of the ways in which we learn?
6. Why are facts important in forming judgments?
7. What are some of the methods used in propaganda?
8. Give examples of the ways in which television commercials use various propaganda methods.
9. Why is censorship necessary for dictators?

CITIZENSHIP AND YOU

Here are some activities you and your classmates may find interesting. These activities can also add to your learning about "School Citizenship."

1. Class Projects

Visit a local newspaper plant. Find out how news is gathered and printed. Talk to the editor and ask about some of the problems of censorship and propaganda.

Participate in an open-forum debate on this topic: *Resolved,* That schools try to teach us a wise use of leisure time.

2. Group or Committee Projects

Appoint a committee to make a study of the advertising appearing in a local newspaper. Have the committee report the results of this study to the class. They should pay particular attention to the propaganda methods used, the amount of space devoted to advertisements, and the kinds of things that are advertised.

A small group may interview school officials, parents, and local business people to gather their opinions on the importance of education. Quotations from these persons may be put on a chart entitled "What the Public Thinks of Our Schools."

3. Individual Projects

Read a book about American education and write a report about the book.

Draw a cartoon to illustrate the importance of good thinking.

Make a time budget, or schedule, for your day. Include in your schedule a regular time for study, recreation, meals, travel, work, household chores, and sleep. Try to follow this budget and see if it helps you to improve your study habits.

CIVICS SKILLS

SUMMARIZING

Chapter 12, "Citizenship in School," describes the American school system and the importance of education for you. It suggests a number of ways in which you may get the most out of your education. Can you find the main ideas in the chapter and then state them in a few short paragraphs? If you can, then you have learned to summarize. This ability to sum up, or to state the main points clearly and briefly, is an important civics skill.

Summaries may be prepared for a number of purposes. The purpose of the summary will help to determine the form it will take. You may, for example, prepare a summary to help you report to the class on something you have read or on an interview you have conducted. This kind of summary will include an introduction that gives the name of the author and the title of the book. It will also give the name of the person interviewed and his or her position. The summary will then list the main points in the book's contents, or the highlights of the interview. Finally, this type of summary will contain your own reaction and your evaluation of the importance of the material you are presenting.

If you are preparing a summary of a textbook chapter to help you get ready for a test, you will probably use a different form. The summary of the chapter might consist of a series of statements. Each statement sums up a main point in the chapter. Each statement may also have supporting facts listed below it. Or the summary might consist of an outline of the chapter, using the headings and subheadings which appear in the chapter. The exact form will depend on what seems to help you the most.

In any summary, you will first need to be sure you understand and remember the main facts. Second, you should arrange these facts in logical order so that you can present them in a way that other people can follow easily. Then you can write the summary in paragraph form if it is to be handed in. Or you can make the summary in brief note form if it is for your own use. If the summary is to be reported in class, it is usually made in note form – perhaps on index cards. Practice your summarizing skills and use them for better reports, to review for tests, and to fix important facts in your mind.

PRACTICING YOUR CIVICS SKILLS

Go to the magazine section of your school or public library. Find a magazine or newspaper article on a current problem in education. Read the article. Then make a summary of its main points. Bring your summary of the article to class and be ready to give your reactions to the author's ideas.

Read the feature on "Becoming an Adult: Freedom or Responsibility" on pages 260–262. Use your summary skills to answer the following:

1. What arguments are presented in favor of making 18 the legal age of adulthood?
2. What arguments are presented against making 18 the legal age of adulthood?
3. What is your opinion on lowering the legal age of adulthood to 18? Give your reasons.

CHAPTER

Introduction

There are very few people in the world who do not enjoy being with other people. Almost everyone finds life easier and more interesting when they can share it with others. We also need other people to provide us with goods and services that we cannot provide ourselves.

The settlers in early America found that it was easier to live near other people. They needed neighbors for protection. Their lives often depended upon a neighbor's help. The early pioneers also found that working together was an absolute necessity. Building a barn or harvesting crops often required help from others. Social affairs were more enjoyable when neighbors got together to have fun. Even learning was more worthwhile when families got together to hire a teacher and start a school.

Ever since America began, and indeed ever since the beginning of human history, people have lived and worked together. Long ago, people created an institution known as the community. Like the institution of the family, which you studied in Chapter 11, the community plays a vital part in American society.

By the word *community,* we mean a group of people having common interests, who live in the same area and who are governed by the same laws. The people in a rural area, small town, or city neighborhood are members of a community. They each have certain common interests, live under the same government, and are governed by local laws. In this chapter you will learn about community citizenship as you study these topics:

1. Many Kinds of Communities
2. Communities Have Many Purposes
3. Citizens Serve Communities

CHAPTER

13

Citizenship in the Community

1 Many Kinds of Communities

From the beginning, American settlers tried to pick out locations that had natural advantages for their settlements. Farmers were attracted to the fertile river valleys, and later the plains. Those interested in trade and commerce knew that a place with a good harbor would help them to build up a prosperous trade. A natural dam site along a river would provide power for mills. A bend in the river provided a good landing place for riverboats. Even today, a sunny climate, sandy beaches, or snow-capped mountains may encourage the growth of a tourist center or a retirement community.

CROSSROADS SETTLEMENTS

As American settlers moved farther inland, they often settled where two main roads crossed. Such a **crossroads** was generally a good place to sell supplies to travelers. An enterprising settler might build an inn at the crossroads. A blacksmith found business good for shoeing horses and repairing wagons. Farmers came to this small settlement to trade. In time, the crossroads settlement grew and became a thriving city.

COMMUNITIES AS TRANSPORTATION CENTERS

Our young American nation depended largely on rivers, lakes, and oceans for means of transportation. In this way, the waterways of America helped to determine the location of our cities. The largest cities in the American colonies were deep-water ports on the Atlantic Coast. Boston, New York, Philadelphia, and Charleston were such cities.

Most of our large inland cities grew up at lake ports or along major rivers. St. Paul and Minneapolis, Minnesota, for example, are located at easy-to-reach stopping points on the upper Mississippi River. New Orleans prospered because it was at the mouth of the Mississippi River, where goods coming down the river were reloaded onto ocean-going vessels. These cities became important **transportation centers** because of their location on major bodies of water.

The coming of the railroad also helped our cities to grow. After 1840, for the most part, railroad lines were built to connect various parts of our nation. They soon contributed to the further growth of our towns and cities. Railroads also created new cities. Inland cities that were not on rivers or lakes grew up as railroads provided a new and speedy method of transportation. Indianapolis, Dallas, and Denver grew prosperous on busy railroad lines.

Today, Americans depend heavily upon highways for transportation. New communities grow up along these highways. Out in the open countryside, land is less expensive than in the city. On this land new industrial plants are built without the need for railroad or water transportation. Trucks carry the goods over modern highways. New communities grow up around these plants to house the workers and provide services for them.

RESOURCES AND CLIMATE HELP COMMUNITIES GROW

America is a country with rich natural resources. It has a temperate climate in which vigorous activity is possible. We have broad, navigable lakes, rivers, and a long coastline that furnishes many good ports and harbors. We also have vast stretches of fertile soil, enough rainfall, good pasture land, and abundant forests. Beneath the soil are rich deposits of metal ores, petroleum, coal, and uranium. Chapter 23 deals with how we must be careful not to be wasteful and reckless in using our natural resources.

Climate and natural resources have aided the growth of many American communities. Duluth, Minnesota, for example, is a port on Lake Superior. It owes much of its growth to the great iron deposits located nearby in the Mesabi Range.

It was Southern California's pleasant cli-

This village in New Hampshire is a good example of a rural community. Most of the residents live, work, and shop in the small, closely knit community.

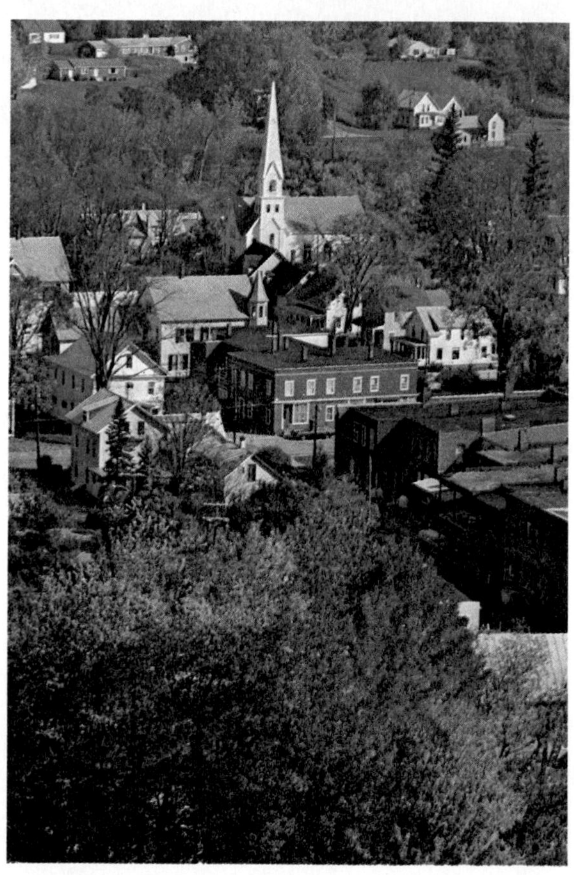

mate that attracted a large number of people. Not only is the California climate pleasant to live in, but it is also favorable for a wide variety of crops.

Many New England communities were settled near waterfalls. The early textile mills needed water power to turn machines that spun thread and wove cloth. Many settlers in the Middle West moved there because of the rich, fertile soil—one of nature's most important resources.

AMERICA'S RURAL COMMUNITIES

As we travel along America's highways we see a wide variety of communities. One way to classify and recognize communities is by their size.

The smallest American community is the **rural farm community.** In most parts of the United States, when you travel through the countryside you pass farm after farm. In Pennsylvania, for example, you will see farms on which a variety of crops are grown. These farms usually raise some pigs, cows, and chickens and are called "mixed farms." In Wisconsin, you see a large number of "dairy farms," or farms that produce milk and milk products. Farther west in Wyoming, you will see large "ranches," or farms that specialize in raising cattle or sheep.

In the South, you will pass tobacco farms and cotton farms. West of the Mississippi River, you will see large wheat farms. In the Imperial Valley of California, there are farms that grow fruit and vegetables for city markets. In Hawaii, you will see sugar-cane and pineapple plantations.

In the late 1970's there were about 2.7 million farms in the United States. Some farms are near others. Or they are near main highways or roads. Yet other farms are isolated and are a long distance from their nearest neighbors. The people who live on farms make up America's smallest kind of community—the rural farm community.

There is also another kind of rural community—the **small country town.** It has a population of less than 2,500 people and is located in a rural area, usually near open farmland. Most of these country towns serve as places where the farmer can buy supplies and where rural people can shop, go to the movies, and attend church. They are also marketing centers for farm crops.

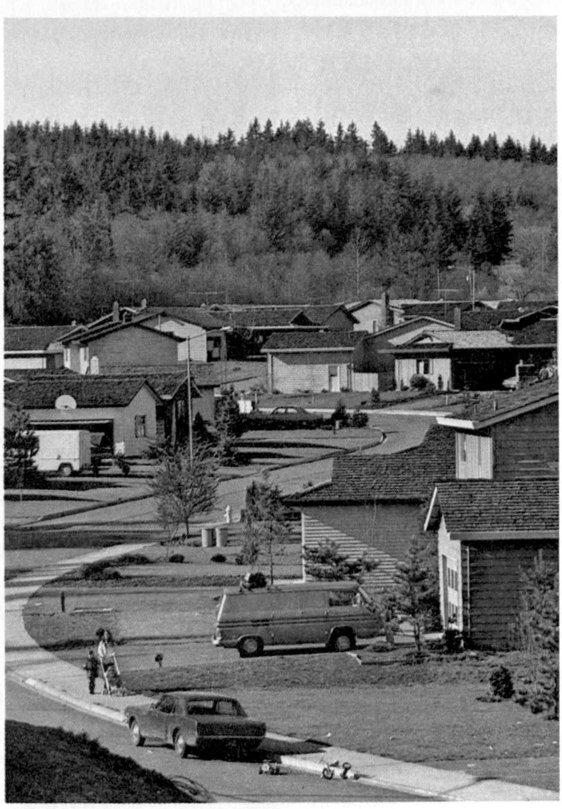

The residents of this suburban community look to a nearby city for jobs, shopping, and entertainment.

SUBURBS

The **suburb** is a town, village, or community located on the outskirts of a city. The people who live in the suburbs often work in the city. Each morning they travel from their homes to their city offices or other places of employment.

There are several reasons why many

The Los Angeles metropolitan area spreads out far in all directions. It includes many different kinds of neighborhoods, shopping areas, big office buildings, hotels, restaurants, theaters, and sports stadiums.

Americans wish to have their homes in the suburbs outside a large city. Many suburbs are smaller in size than the city, and some people like life in a smaller community. Other people want their children to grow up in a community where there are more open spaces, trees, and places to play. They want to have a larger house with a backyard. Other families want to get away from city crowds, and away from the noise and the traffic of big-city life. The suburbs make it possible for such people to live away from the city even though they earn their living in the city. But suburban towns have been growing rapidly in recent years and are beginning to experience some of the problems of urban living.

URBAN AREAS

Suburbs and all other towns and cities of 2,500 or more people are called **urban areas.** Urban communities vary a great deal in size. For example, in the mid-1970's the census listed the town of Linden, Alabama, which had a population of 2,620, as an urban community. It also listed New York City, with a population of over 7 million.

Seven out of every ten Americans today live in urban communities. Those who live in the large cities have nearby the theaters, fine restaurants, museums, and other cultural advantages that cities offer. They enjoy the hustle and bustle of city living. Recent studies show, however, that the suburbs are growing faster than the cities. More than half the urban population lives outside the central cities. A number of large cities actually showed a loss in population.

METROPOLITAN AREAS

Certain American cities such as New York City, Chicago, and Los Angeles have become so large that each one is known as a **metropolis.** If you fly over a metropolis, you will find it very hard to tell where the giant city ends and the surrounding towns and suburbs begin. The fact is that there really is no dividing line. Instead, the settled area seems to have no end. For this reason, a big city and its surrounding towns and suburbs are referred to as a **metropolitan area.** The metropolitan area of Chicago, for example, includes several fairly large cities in Indiana, such as Gary, Hammond, and East Chicago.

There is evidence that someday soon several of our metropolitan areas, particularly those along the Atlantic coast around Boston, New York, Philadelphia, Baltimore, and Washington, will grow into a single, endless metropolitan area stretching hundreds of miles. A new name has been given to this type of giant urban area. It is a **megalopolis.**

CONSIDER AND DISCUSS

Identify. community / crossroads settlement / transportation center / rural farm community / small country town / suburb / urban area / metropolis / metropolitan area / megalopolis

Review. 1. How do natural resources help to determine the kind of community a settlement will be? 2. How have highways affected the settlements of America? 3. Why do some people prefer to live in the suburbs? 4. Why do others prefer city life?

Discuss. Would you prefer to live in a rural or an urban community? Why?

2 Communities Have Many Purposes

At the beginning of this chapter, a community was defined as "a group of people having common interests, who live in the same area and who are governed by the same laws." What are some of their "common interests?" And how does the community serve its people?

LIVING AND LEARNING IN A COMMUNITY

One of the most important things that communities do is to teach us how to live and work together. Our first lessons in living together with others are learned in the home. Our family, as a small community, teaches us important lessons in sharing. Then as we grow up, we learn from neighbors, schoolmates, and friends. The people of our communities teach us to talk and to behave the way we do. They teach us values. The food we like, the kind of person we want to be when we grow up, and a hundred other things are learned by living with the people of our community.

COMMUNICATION IN COMMUNITIES

Most of us continue to learn as long as we live. Almost every day we share information with others about a great many things. This passing along of information and ideas from one person to another is known as **communi-**

cation. One reason why people live in communities is to be able to communicate easily. The problems people face seem to be made easier if they can talk them over with someone else. Life is also more pleasant if we can hear about the latest happenings in the neighborhood and learn new ideas from others.

Every community has a number of important means of communication. We have already mentioned the most common one—conversation. Such modern inventions as the telephone, the telegraph, and radio and television have increased our ability to learn and to share our information with others. We also communicate in writing through letters and postcards.

One of the most important of all means of communication is the newspaper. Newspapers tell us about happenings all over the world. They also give us news of our own communities, such as births, marriages, and deaths. Books and magazines are other important means we use to communicate ideas and facts.

COMMUNITIES HELP US TO ENJOY LIFE

One important reason why we have communities is that people enjoy the company of others. In nearly every American city and town there are motion picture theaters, bowling alleys, skating rinks, golf courses, and other places of recreation open to the public. Many of our larger cities have professional baseball, football, hockey, and basketball teams whose games are eagerly followed by sports fans.

Many recreational facilities are maintained at public expense. Taxes are used to support public playgrounds, athletic fields, picnic grounds, tennis courts, and public golf courses. There are also worthwhile activities sponsored by groups of citizens who

Community members often share an interest in sports. The "home team" might be a major league baseball team, a local bowling club, or the high school basketball team.

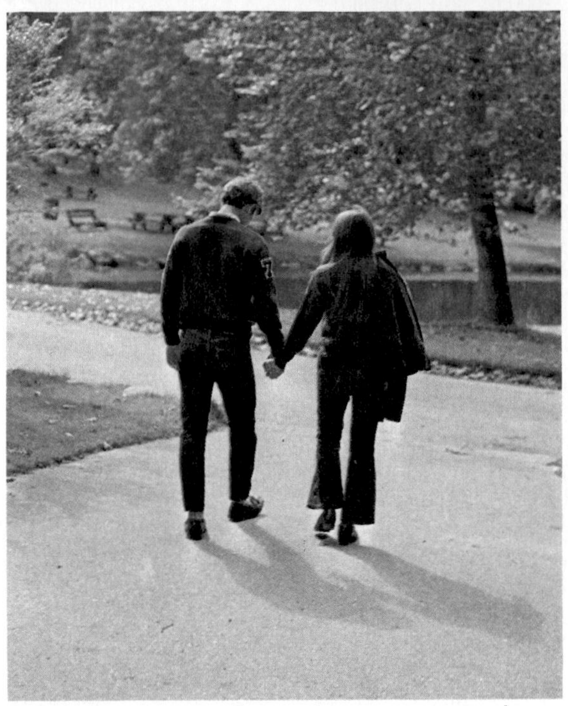

How can community parks and playgrounds help make life more pleasant for people of all ages?

are willing to volunteer their own time and money. The YMCA and YWCA, the YMHA, the Boy Scouts, the Girl Scouts, Campfire Girls, and the 4-H Clubs are examples of groups that help the members of the community to enjoy playing and learning together.

COMMUNITIES HELP US TO USE OUR FREE TIME

Many communities have learned to take advantage of an unusually good climate or geographical location. They have promoted and developed these advantages not only for their own residents but also to attract tourists. Lake communities and seaside towns have developed boating, water skiing, and swimming as special attractions. Rural communities have made the most of the hunting and fishing opportunities in their areas. Some other communities have featured skiing, horseback riding, and hiking.

There are several purposes served by good community recreational facilities.

1. Good recreational facilities provide worthwhile ways for Americans to use their leisure time. Young people have something interesting and healthful to do.

2. Good recreational facilities help all members of the community to keep physically fit. Well-run swimming pools, playgrounds, and recreation centers encourage good health habits and help members of the community to build healthy bodies.

3. Recreation often benefits the mind as well as the body. A recreation center may help us to develop new interests and hobbies. A community stamp club or coin club can teach us a great deal about history and geography.

4. All of us benefit from good recreation by relaxing and just having fun in the company of others. **Recreation** helps all of us to "re-create" ourselves—to feel like new people.

COMMUNITIES PROVIDE MANY SERVICES

One of the reasons communities have been established is to provide services to their citizens. There are certain things that the people of a community, working together, can do more effectively than each one can do separately. A good police force helps to insure our safety. Fire protection is a worthwhile community service. The public school is another valuable community service.

People living as neighbors have also found that they need pure water, an efficient sewer system, regular trash removal, and dependable gas and electricity. Sometimes the people of a community join together and vote to have services furnished to them by their local government in return for the taxes they pay. In other cases, some of the services are provided by private companies.

Continued on page 263

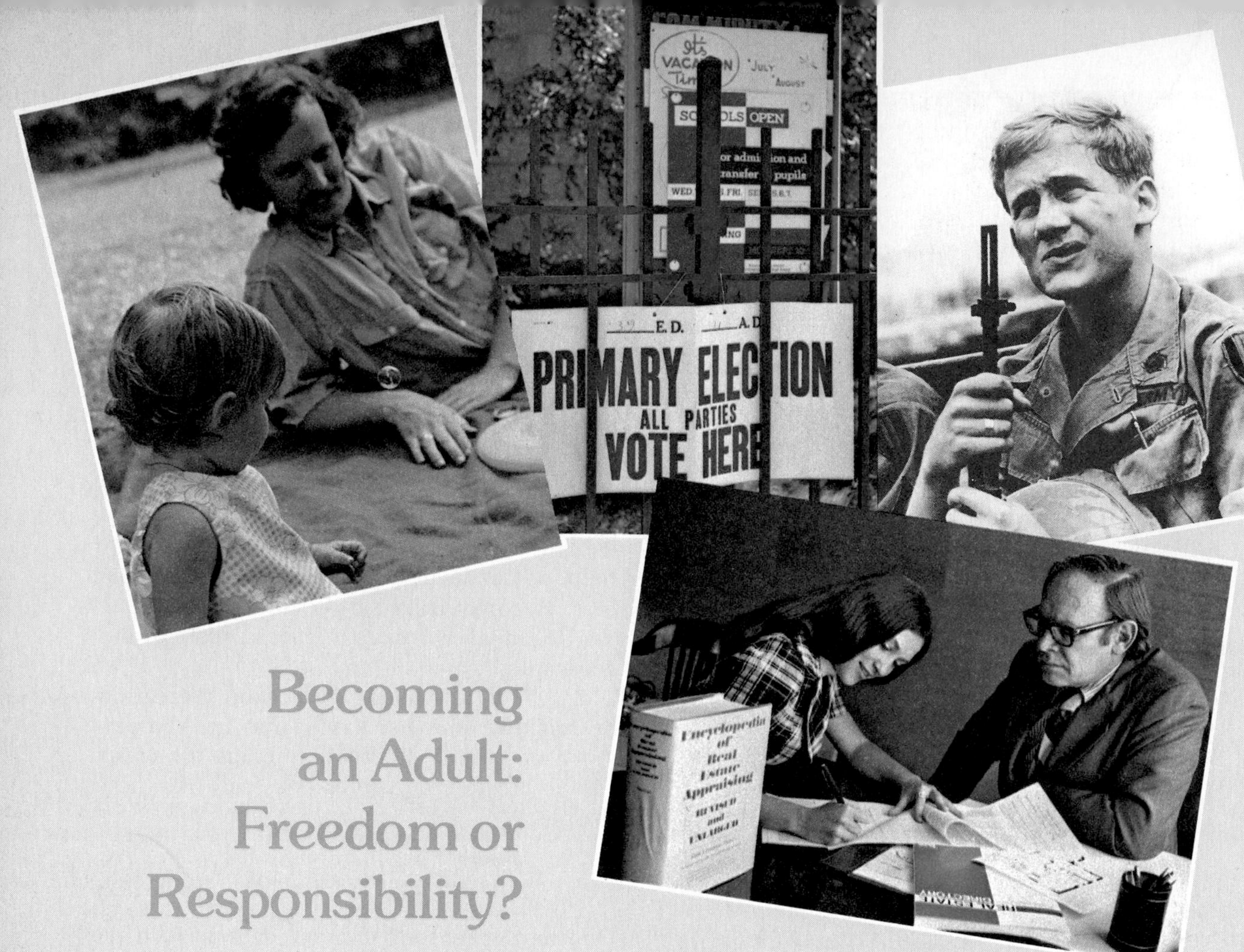

Becoming an Adult: Freedom or Responsibility?

WHAT Do YOU THINK?

Before 1971, a young man living in the United States could be drafted and sent into a foreign land to fight, and possibly to die, for his country. Yet in most states he was not considered old enough to vote. How could a citizen be sent to fight, without having a voice in his own government? This was one of the questions that led to the passage in 1971 of the Twenty-sixth Amendment, which lowered the voting age to 18 in all national, state, and local elections.

But the Twenty-sixth Amendment left many questions unanswered. Is the 18-year-old man or woman too young to sign a contract? Should a parent's signature be necessary before a young couple can rent an apartment or take out a loan? If 18-year-olds are old enough to vote, can they still be legally considered "children" in other respects? At what age does a person become a full-fledged adult member of the community?

These questions have led a number of states to change their laws, lowering the legal age of adulthood from 21 to 18. Other states have lowered the age for some purposes, but not for all. Still other states are considering whether or not to change their laws. What do all these changes mean for the young person of today? What effect might they have on you in the next few years? What effect might they have on your community?

The lowering of the voting age brought many young people into politics. About 10.5 million people between the ages of 18 and 21 became eligible to vote for the President for the first time in 1972. During the spring and summer of that year, many of them worked for various candidates for the Presidency.

Changes in the rules of the Democratic Party opened up its National Convention to many different groups, including young people. As a result, 21 percent of the delegates to the Democratic Convention in 1972 were under 30. In contrast, only 4 percent of the delegates had been under 30 in 1968. Although the Republican Convention still had only 3 percent of voting delegates under 30 in 1972, thousands of young Republicans flew to Miami Beach in Florida to take part in the events of convention week.

In the election of 1976, both parties encouraged young people to run as convention delegates. New rules of the Democratic Party, however, ended the quota system set up in 1972. Therefore, fewer young people attended the Democratic Convention. But young people continued to be interested in politics. Many of them joined campaign organizations and worked to elect both Democratic and Republican candidates in the election of 1976.

Young voters have become important not only in the Presidential election, but also in state and local elections. In some communities, especially those with a college or university, the youth vote has helped to decide an election. People under 21 have begun to run for local offices themselves. A 19-year-old was elected mayor of Newcomerstown, Ohio. Another 19-year-old was elected mayor of Ayrshire, Iowa. An 18-year-old was elected to the school board in Bremerton, Washington. Candidates under 21 also have been elected to city councils, county boards, and other local offices.

The new political power of young people has forced state legislators to reconsider the legal status of those 18 to 20 years old. Are they adults? Are they children? For what purposes should they be considered adults?

What does it mean if the age of adulthood is lowered to 18? It means that 18-year-olds become legally responsible for all their own actions. Their signatures are binding on contracts. They can buy a car, rent an apartment, open a charge account. They—not their parents—are responsible for paying their own debts. They can get married without their parents' consent. They can be tried for crimes in a regular criminal court. They can be sued in a civil court. They can be called to serve on a jury.

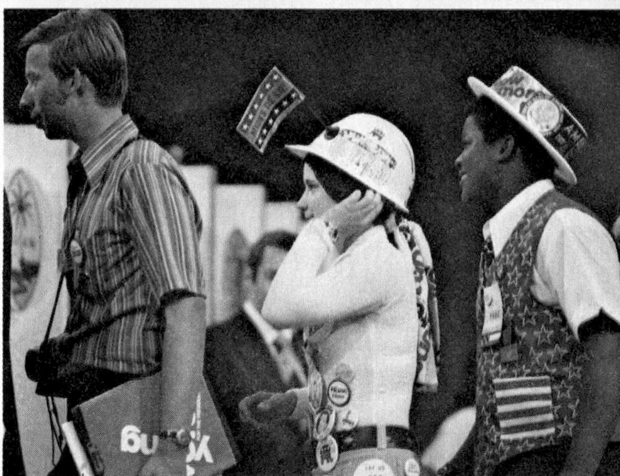

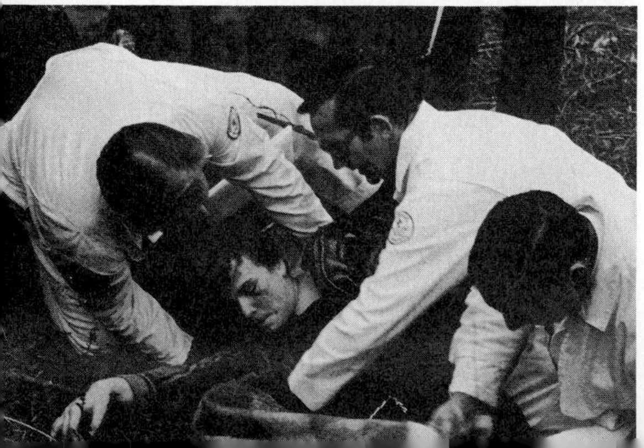

They can inherit money. In short, they have all the rights and privileges—and all the duties and responsibilities—of adults.

Those who favor lowering the age to 18 point to the young soldier, the young voter, the young officeholder. They note that many 18- to 20-year-olds are earning their own living. Some are already married and may even have children of their own. Others are living away from home, attending colleges and universities. These people, they say, should not be treated as children. Some 18-year-olds may be irresponsible—but so are some people over 21. The line must be drawn somewhere. If Americans can vote at 18, they argue, then they should be considered citizens in all other respects, too.

Other people see many serious problems in the idea of "adulthood" at 18. As more young people stay in school, many of them need their parents' support until age 21 or beyond. Should these people be granted—or forced into—full adult responsibilities? If their parents are separated or divorced, should their fathers' support payments stop at age 18? Various social-service and welfare benefits would also stop when a child reached 18. Some people are also worried that there will be increased auto accidents among young people. Others fear that there will be an increase in early marriages, possibly unwise, if there is no need for parental permission.

States have begun to change some of their laws affecting young people. For example, people may now marry at 18 without the consent of their parents in all but five states for women and 11 states for men. Many of the states that have changed their laws have reported one or another of the problems mentioned above. Often the problems are made worse by the differences among states. Young people may cross from one state to another to get married, for instance. But after returning to their own state, they may find that opinions about their legal rights and responsibilities differ.

How do you think the new laws will affect you? your community? Do your state laws treat 18-year-olds as adults? Is this true in all cases, or are there some exceptions? What do you see as the main advantages of adult status? What are the disadvantages? Do you think you will be ready for the responsibilities of adulthood at the age of 18? On balance, do you think it would be better to treat 18-year-olds as adults in every way? for some purposes, but not all? or only for voting?

Why We Live in Communities

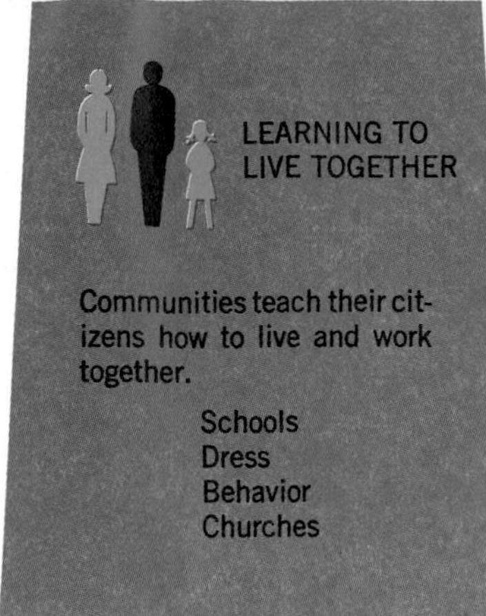

LEARNING TO
LIVE TOGETHER
Communities teach their citizens how to live and work together.
Schools
Dress
Behavior
Churches

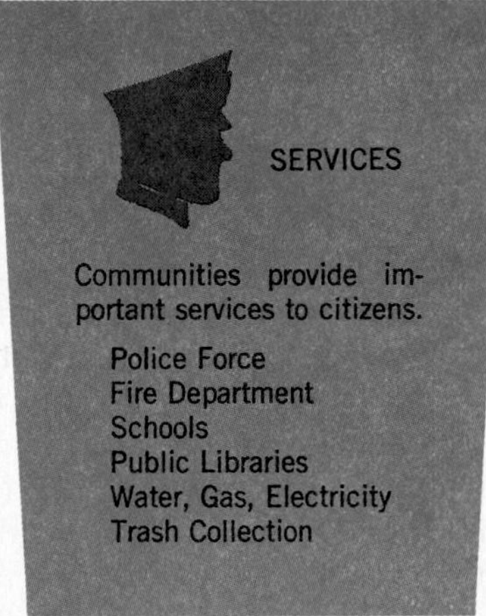

SERVICES
Communities provide important services to citizens.
Police Force
Fire Department
Schools
Public Libraries
Water, Gas, Electricity
Trash Collection

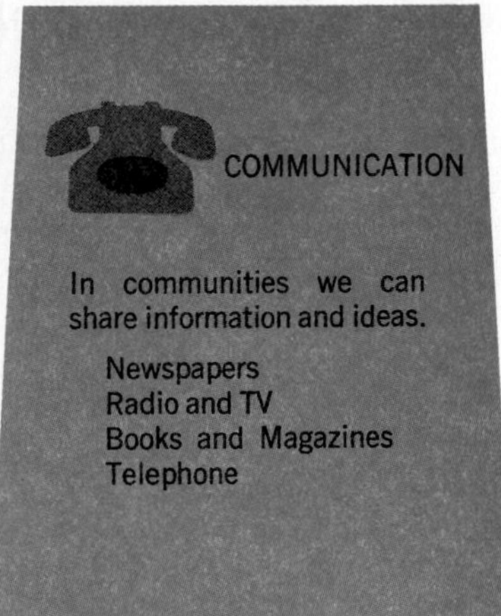

COMMUNICATION
In communities we can share information and ideas.
Newspapers
Radio and TV
Books and Magazines
Telephone

SHARING FUN
In communities we can enjoy being with other people.
Bowling, Tennis Courts
Public Playgrounds
Golf Courses, Theaters
Sports Teams
YMCA, YWCA

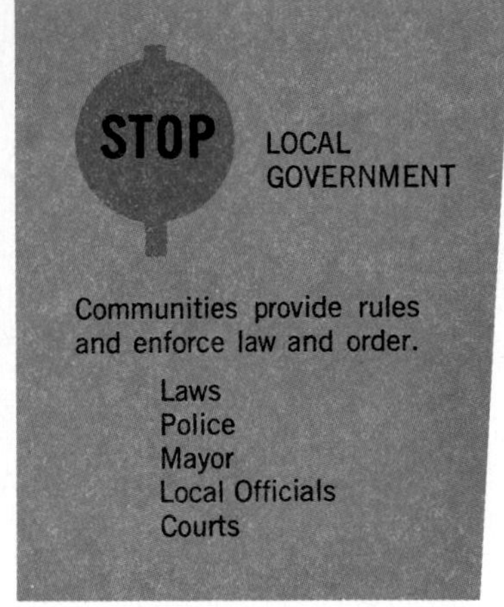

STOP
LOCAL
GOVERNMENT
Communities provide rules and enforce law and order.
Laws
Police
Mayor
Local Officials
Courts

COMMUNITIES PROVIDE LOCAL GOVERNMENT

American communities of all sizes serve their citizens by providing local government (see Chapter 8). When people live together, some kinds of laws and regulations are needed. Suppose that several neighbors get into an argument over where the boundary that separates their land is located. If there were no laws or local government, they might use force to settle their difficulties. Fortunately, our communities provide a local government with courts, judges, and law enforcement officers to help us maintain good order in our neighborhoods.

CONSIDER AND DISCUSS

Identify. communication / recreation
Review. What are some of the purposes that communities serve? 2. Describe four ways in which community recreation facilities help citizens.
Discuss. If you lived alone on a desert island, what community service would you miss most? Why?

3 Citizens Serve Communities

Communities depend upon **cooperation.** They serve many purposes for their citizens, but in return their citizens should serve them. Some citizenship services are compulsory. The members of the community must obey the laws or pay the penalty. They must pay taxes, observe traffic regulations, and conduct their business in an honest fashion. The young citizen must attend school. In most matters of everyday living, however, communities rely upon their members to regard the rights of others because it is the right thing to do.

YOUR COMMUNITIES

Each of us lives in many communities, profits from their services, and owes certain obligations in return. The obligations at home of cooperation and respect for family members have already been mentioned. This cooperation should also extend to people in your immediate neighborhood. Citizens also should feel responsible for the larger communities they live in.

FACING COMMUNITY PROBLEMS

Every community faces problems that must be solved if life in that community is to be as pleasant as it can be. In Chapter 21 we shall consider in detail some of the serious problems of urban living that trouble our nation. For now, we would urge an interest in local problems in whose solution every citizen can share.

HOW AMERICANS IMPROVE THEIR COMMUNITIES

Groups of concerned citizens are doing something about their problems. Take the example of Las Vegas, New Mexico, a town of about 15,000 people. For years, Las Vegas streets were rundown and its sidewalks in need of repair. The town had few recreation centers. But the citizens of Las Vegas, young and old alike, were proud of their community. And finally some of them decided to act to improve Las Vegas.

The Mayor headed the community's new improvement program. A new gymnasium was added to the high school. A community swimming pool was built. The young people of the town began to feel that Las Vegas was a good place to call home. As streets and sidewalks were rebuilt, the town began to take on new signs of life. Several new projects were planned to continue Las Vegas' program of improvement.

Each year other American communities face their problems and do something about them. The citizens of Decatur, Illinois, undertook a program to improve their downtown areas, to end slums, and to reduce traffic jams. Decatur cleared and rebuilt a large part of its business district. In similar fashion, the industrial city of Worcester, Massachusetts, established a successful new program of better schools, playgrounds, museums, and homes for the aged.

The atomic energy town of Richland, Washington, won national praise for the work of its efficient police and fire departments. The people of Bloomington, Minnesota, took steps to prevent their water supply from becoming polluted by building a $16 million sewage and water system. These citizens did something about their community problems.

PITTSBURGH'S IMPROVEMENT PLAN

Shortly after World War II, the people of Pittsburgh, Pennsylvania, took a critical look at their city, and they were not pleased with what they saw. The smoke from the steel mills and factories was so thick that Pittsburgh was known as "the Smoky City." The traffic jams were awful. The central city was

A cable car provides a dramatic view of Pittsburgh's "Golden Triangle." This modern downtown area is the result of careful planning and large-scale public funds.

rundown, and the appearance of the city left a lot to be desired. Community leaders agreed that parts of the city would have to be torn down and rebuilt. Other sections of the city would need to be repaired and renewed.

The people of Pittsburgh agreed that improvements were needed. They voted to spend the necessary money, and soon work began. Architects planned whole new sections of the city. At "the Golden Triangle," where the Allegheny and the Monongahela rivers meet, many new modern metal and glass skyscrapers were built. Some of these were office buildings. Some were buildings to house the city government. Others were "civic center" buildings to provide recreation for Pittsburgh citizens.

Pittsburgh took advantage of its prosperity and built anew. It took advantage of the pride that its residents felt for their community. In this way, Pittsburgh worked out the answers to many of its problems. The city began a successful campaign that greatly reduced the amount of smoke in Pittsburgh's air. Two-level roads were built along the river to speed traffic through the city. A new water system was planned to take care of the city's increasing water needs. Parks and recreation centers were built, and soon more were being planned for the future.

Today, Pittsburgh is still hard at work to improve itself and solve its problems. Like most communities, it is proud of what it has already done. But its citizens also know that their city must continue to plan and build and change if it is to meet their needs.

GOOD CITIZENS MAKE GOOD COMMUNITIES

Right now you are an active member of your local community. You attend its schools and enjoy its parks and playgrounds. You are protected by its police and fire departments. You depend upon it to provide you with many other services. Tomorrow, you may work in this community and raise a family there. It is important, therefore, that you be a good citizen in your community.

Each member of a community has certain duties and responsibilities. Take one example—that of doing one's share in keeping the community clean. **Littering** is a problem that costs communities millions of dollars each year—each of us can do something about it now. Learn the facts about your community, its government, its problems, and its opportunities. Take pride in your community, and practice good citizenship wherever you are.

CONSIDER AND DISCUSS

Identify. cooperation / littering

Review. 1. What are some of the problems communities face? 2. Why was Pittsburgh known as "the Smoky City"? 3. What steps did Pittsburgh take to solve its problems?

Discuss. How can you and your classmates help to make your community a better place in which to live?

CHAPTER
Summary

America is a nation of many communities. Communities differ greatly in size and population. But they have many common problems wherever they are located—in rural or in urban areas.

Communities serve many important purposes. They help us to enjoy living with other citizens, to get a good education, and to earn a good living. The prosperity of a community depends upon its location, its climate, its natural resources and industrial possibilities, and its hard-working citizens.

Pittsburgh, Pennsylvania, illustrates how our communities are meeting their problems through a planned program of improvement. Pittsburgh, like other cities, has attracted many different industries, improved its transportation system, and built a cleaner and more beautiful city.

Much work remains to be done in America's cities and towns. Many of our communities still have rundown slums, traffic tie-ups, parking problems, water shortages, and a large number of serious problems. As good citizens, all of us have a duty to study our community's problems and support efforts to solve them.

VOCABULARY

Write two paragraphs in which you summarize the main ideas in this chapter. Include the following words in your paragraphs, and underline each word as you use it.

community	metropolis
rural	megalopolis
urban	communication
suburb	recreation

CHECK-UP AND REVIEW

CHECK-UP

Write brief answers to each of the following questions, and come to class prepared to discuss your answers.

1. What are some of the reasons people live and work in communities?
2. What are some of the different kinds of communities in the United States?
3. Can you find the following facts in this chapter: What is the population of New York City? How large must a place be before it is considered an urban area?
4. Name three ways in which your community serves you and helps to make your life more pleasant.
5. What are some advantages of living in the suburbs?
6. What are some advantages of living in the city?
7. What are some of the problems that face our modern communities?
8. What are four ways in which recreation facilities help you?
9. What are some ways in which you can make your community better?

CITIZENSHIP AND YOU

You will have a better appreciation of your community and what it means to you if you and your classmates take an active part in community affairs. Look around you, study your community's problems. Then help to do something about them. The following activities will help you to get to know your community better.

1. Class Projects

Make a survey of your community. Find out about the people and the facilities in your locality.

One way to approach such a community survey is to divide the class into committees. Each committee may investigate and report on a certain part of community life. There may be committees on community history, local government, businesses and jobs, schools, recreation, natural resources, taxes and spending, traffic control, and housing.

The committees may obtain their information by examining official reports, reading local newspapers, interviewing local officials, studying books about the community, referring to maps of the area, taking field trips. Following these and other leads is like being a detective who is going after all the facts in a case. The committees should keep records of their findings and write reports about them.

There are several ways in which the different committees may share their findings with the class as a whole. One way is to prepare an exhibit that will display the findings of each committee. Another way is to have a panel discussion in which the chairperson of each committee reports to the class.

2. Group or Committee Projects

The class activity suggested above calls for work by a number of committees. In addition, a photography group may prepare an exhibit of pictures of the community.

A materials committee may gather maps, posters, pamphlets, and other materials from agencies of local government, from the chamber of commerce, and from local industries. These materials may be displayed on the bulletin board.

3. Individual Projects

A student gifted in art may draw or paint a community scene.

Local community scrapbooks may be kept by individual students.

A student who is interested in newspaper work might prepare a story on some aspect of community life. The story should be written in the style of a reporter, whose job it is to inform the public.

Prepare a bar, line, or picture graph showing facts about some feature of your community.

CIVICS SKILLS

SPEAKING AND DISCUSSING

The activities in this and other chapters call for discussion, reports, panels, and other forms of oral expression. The ability to speak clearly and forcefully requires practice. It is an important skill, since much of your life is spent in communicating with others. You will be able to get your points across if you begin now to develop your speaking skills. Below are some suggestions that will help you to make your practice more effective.

1. Get the facts first. Come to a discussion with information that is reliable and as complete as you can obtain. Be ready to give the sources of your information.

2. Use the civics vocabulary you are learning in these chapters. The exact use of the right words will strengthen your statements and make them clearer.

3. Be friendly and courteous during discussions or debate. Be ready to stand up for your viewpoint, but do it politely. In class discussions, address your remarks to the whole class and not just to one or two individuals.

4. Listen carefully to the other students' ideas. Do you agree or disagree with them? Ask questions about points you do not understand. Be sure you understand other points of view before you agree or disagree.

5. You will be more effective if you learn to speak informally rather than reading your notes or reports. If you must use notes, use them as reminders of the main points you wish to make. Learn to glance at your notes rapidly, and try not to depend on them too much. An exception comes when you wish to give an exact quotation. Then it may be effective to read it word for word, giving the source and perhaps the date when it was said or written.

6. Above all, practice. Take advantage of the opportunity that your civics class offers to try out your ideas and put them into words.

PRACTICING YOUR CIVICS SKILLS

Choose the type of community—rural, suburban, or urban—that you would like to live in. List your reasons for choosing this type of community. Then in a class discussion, present the reasons for your choice to the class.

Look around your community to discover any serious needs that you think must or should be met in the next few years. Some possible examples are housing, schools, hospitals, streets and highways, recreational facilities. Hold a panel discussion in class to discuss these needs and how they might be met.

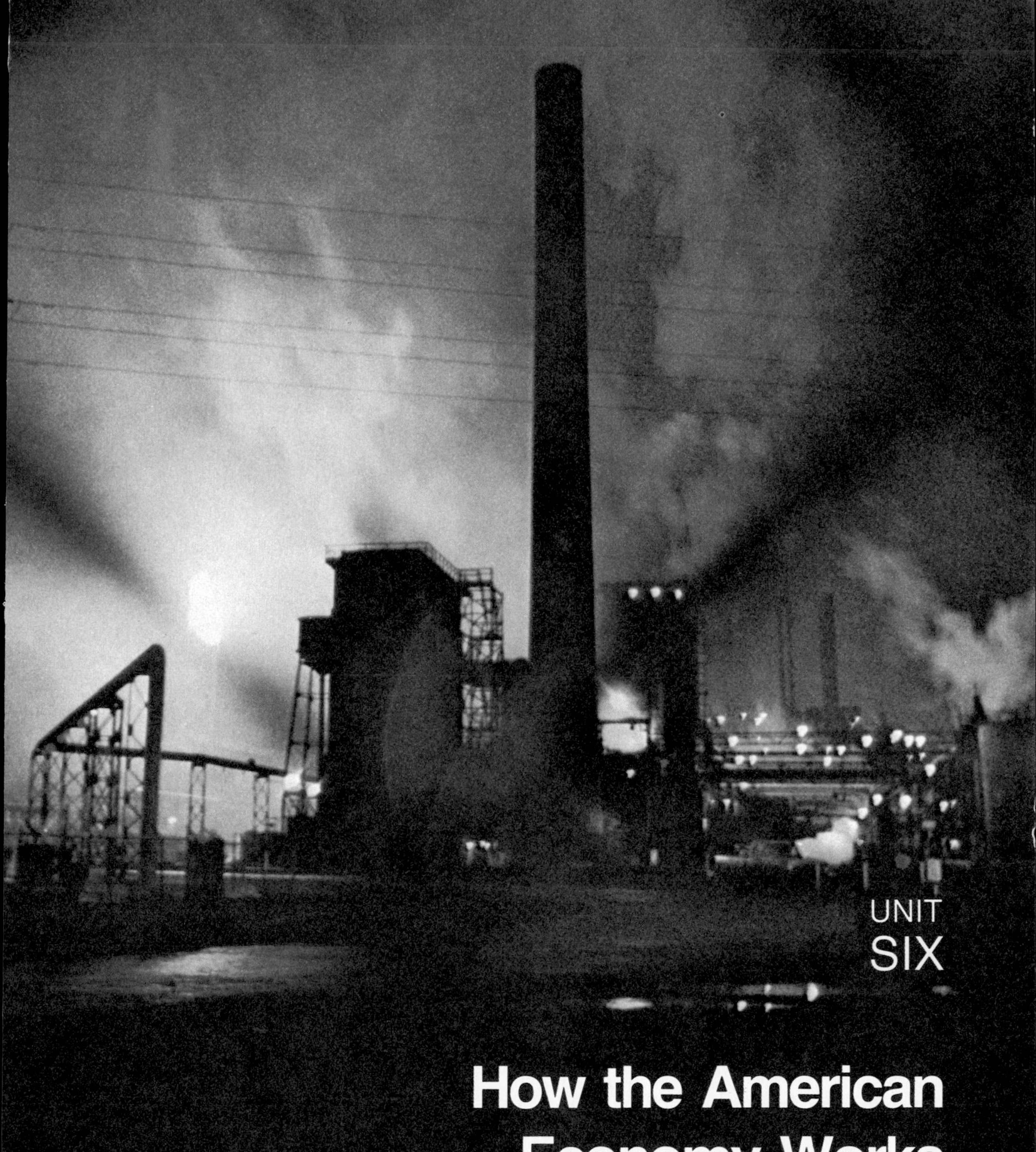

UNIT
SIX

How the American Economy Works

CHAPTER
Introduction

The United States is one of the richest countries in the world. Most Americans enjoy a high standard of living. Most of us take for granted our automobiles, color television sets, washing machines, air conditioners, and abundant food. On the average, we have more money to spend, and more articles to buy for our money, than the people of any other nation. Our economic system produces more goods and services than any other in the world.

What makes all of this possible? There are a number of reasons for our economic success. First of all, America is a land of great natural resources. Timber, minerals, energy resources, a good climate, and fertile soil have been ours in abundance. In addition, we have energetic and inventive people. They have taken our resources and turned them into needed and desirable products. And our system of government has encouraged private enterprise. It has protected the right of individuals to own private property and to make an honest profit. Finally, the United States has developed an economic system that has made it possible for the American people to find work and to make a financial success of their lives.

A country's *economic system,* or *economy,* is its method of caring for the physical needs of its people. It includes the production and distribution of goods and services, buying and selling, jobs, money, and savings. Our economic system has worked well. But like all systems, it has its problems. Millions of Americans who want jobs cannot get them. Many Americans still live in poverty. And our natural resources have been carelessly used, and even destroyed. These problems worry many Americans. In order to solve these problems and to make our economic system work even better, we must understand our economic system. In this chapter we shall examine this system as we study these topics:

1. How the American Economic System Works
2. How American Business Is Organized
3. How Business Decisions Are Made

CHAPTER

14

Our American Economic System

1 How the American Economic System Works

The American government, as you have learned, is based upon certain principles of freedom. We enjoy free speech, a free press, and freedom in our religious beliefs. We vote in free elections. Individuals in America can do as they choose if they do not interfere with the freedom of others. That is why our country is called a free country.

OUR ECONOMIC FREEDOMS

We also enjoy certain economic freedoms that are important to all of us. Because of these freedoms our economic system, or economy, is called a **free economy.** Let us examine some of these economic freedoms.

Freedom to buy and sell in an open market. Americans are free to buy and sell whatever they want. The American shopper can go from store to store looking for the best quality goods at a fair price. If the price a seller asks seems too high, the buyer is free to go somewhere else to buy the product. Producers are free to sell goods and services at prices they think buyers will pay. If people do not buy a product or service, the producer is free to change the price that is charged or to sell something else. This exchange between buyers and sellers who are free to choose is known as the **free market.**

Freedom to compete. Business firms in the United States compete with one another for

Freedom in Our American Economy

customers. That is, each business firm tries to get people to buy what it has to offer. Because customers are free to buy where they want, **free competition** allows them to show what goods they favor every time they make a purchase. If they do not buy a product, producers will make something else or go out of business. Therefore, producers make what they think the public will buy.

Freedom to earn a living. American workers are free to compete for the best job for which their training qualifies them. They also may bargain with their employers for higher wages, better benefits, and better working conditions. They are free to leave their jobs and find better ones. Or they may go into business for themselves.

Freedom to earn a profit. Why do people start businesses? They expect to make a **profit.** That is, they hope to make more money than it costs to run the business. People also **invest** in, or lend their money to, businesses and governments in hopes of making a profit. They invest in articles of value for the same reason. All of these people use the money they have saved to make more money. This is called the **profit motive.** Without it our free economic system would not operate.

Freedom to own property. Americans have the right to own and use their own land, personal belongings, and other kinds of property. The free market and free competition would not work if we did not also have private ownership of property. All Americans are free to do as they like with their own money. They may spend, save, or invest it. They may buy buildings, land, tools, and machines. These forms of property are called **means of production** because they are used to produce goods and services. Americans may start their own businesses and earn profits from them, if they can. They may employ others to work for them. They have the right to profit from their ideas and inventions. They can protect this right by copyrighting their ideas and patenting their inventions. The right to own and use property of all kinds is guaranteed in the Constitution.

THE FREE ECONOMY IN ACTION

In our nation, millions of different businesses, large and small, are at work producing all kinds of goods. Yet there is no person or group of people who decide how many automobiles, vacuum cleaners, loaves of bread, or comic books will be produced all over the United States. Every business firm is free to make its own decisions about what and how much to produce.

About 96 million Americans are engaged in the many kinds of jobs needed to produce our goods and services. Yet there is nobody who decides how many people should be steel workers, how many should be school teachers, how many should be truck drivers, or how many should be dentists. Each American is free to enter any career for which he or she is qualified.

Without anyone to supervise the process, enough goods of different kinds do get produced. Only rarely are there real shortages. Most of the time enough people, with the right training, provide needed goods and services and get them to market for people to buy.

SUPPLY AND DEMAND

One reason our free economy works so well is that it responds to the **law of supply and demand.** Mainly, it is this important force that determines the prices of goods. How does it work? Sometimes the supply of a product is greater than the public's demand for it. That means that there is more of a product on the market than the public is willing to buy. When that happens, the price of the product tends to drop. When the demand for a product is greater than the supply, the price often rises.

Let's use radios as an example of the way in which the law of supply and demand works. If manufacturers make more radios than can be sold in the market, the price may have to be lowered in order to sell them. Even at the lower price all of the radios may not be sold. As a result, fewer radios will be manufactured and the supply of radios on the market will decrease. But soon, people will need to replace their old radios. Or they may want to buy newer models. For whatever reason, the demand rises. Because the supply of radios is so small, the price may be raised and all of the radios will be sold. Manufacturers also will begin to make more radios to fill the demand.

This young couple is choosing new furniture. Because of the free competition in our economy, Americans have a wide variety of products to choose from.

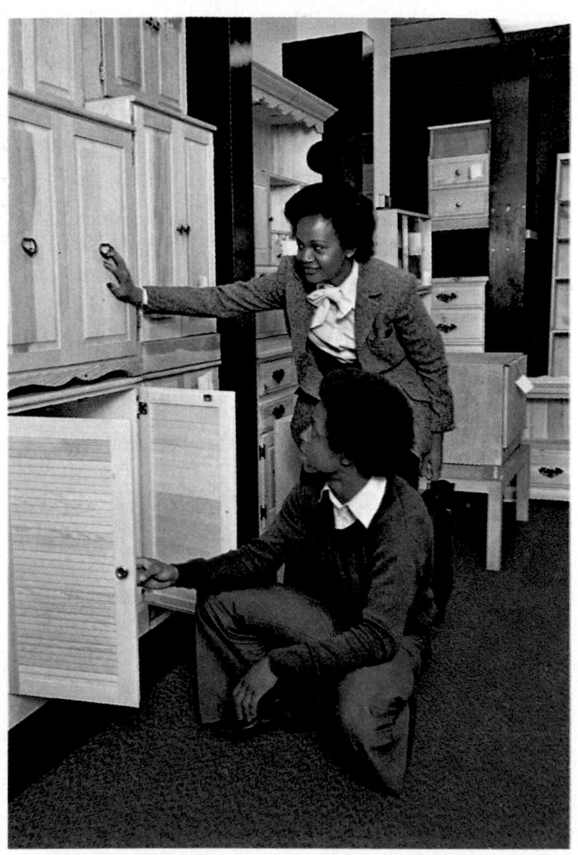

It is important to understand the workings of supply and demand, because in our economy this principle affects prices, wages, interest rates, stocks, and every other thing that has a price.

WHAT IS CAPITALISM?

Our American economic system is sometimes called **capitalism.** Another name for it is the **capitalistic system.** The money that Americans invest in a business is called **capital.** If they do not spend all their money on living expenses but, instead, save it to buy buildings, machines, and other means of production, they invest it. Capital is not only the money that people invest. It is also what people buy with it—land, buildings, machines, or anything else that means they own part or all of a business. Anyone who owns such things is a **capitalist.**

The tools owned by an independent electrician are capital. The electrician had to save in order to buy them. And the tools are used to produce things people want or to provide services people want. The machines that turn out automobile bodies are part of the capital of an automobile manufacturing company.

As you can see, the electrician is a capitalist on a small scale. The automobile manufacturer is a capitalist on a large scale. But if you own a few shares of stock in an automobile company, you are also a capitalist. These shares of stock mean that you own part of the company. You (or someone) had to save the money to invest in this stock. You did not spend the money to pay for living expenses or for fun.

People work, and they also invest in order to get ahead financially. Because many people are doing this, our economy produces the vast number of products that we all enjoy. New and better products are constantly being offered for sale. Business people who supply the American people with the products and services they want, at a price they are willing to pay, usually make a profit. And so, our capitalistic system works for the benefit of the American people as a whole.

OUR FREE ENTERPRISE SYSTEM

All American business people are basically free to run their own businesses in the way they think is best. They do not depend upon some government official to tell them how to do it, as business managers do in the Soviet Union, for example. Americans depend upon their own enterprise—that is, their own ability and energy. For this reason, our economic system is sometimes called a **free enterprise system.** Freedom in our economy permits enterprising business people to enjoy success and profits.

American business owners also take many risks. They are free to earn profits. But they are also required to take the losses if they make mistakes. They may produce a new product and find that customers do not want it. Or they may produce their products inefficiently and have to charge too much for them. If they make mistakes, they may be forced out of business. If their businesses fail, they may lose all their capital. As a rule, only efficient businesses succeed in our economic system.

THE RISE OF BIG BUSINESS

From their earliest beginnings, American businesses have been privately owned and run for the profit of their owner or owners. During the first hundred years of our nation's history, most businesses were small. But even then, some shippers, importers, and manufacturers became wealthy. It was not until the late 1860's that big businesses began to develop in the United States. These businesses benefited from America's new technology. For example, they used machines that were powered by steam or, later, by electricity. By placing these machines in factories where great numbers of workers were employed, businesses were able to produce large quantities of goods. The owners made huge profits. But some owners, hoping to pile up great fortunes and to gain economic power, used unfair business practices, such as trusts and monopolies.

TRUSTS, MERGERS, AND MONOPOLIES

Unfair business practices harm our free economy. They may interfere with the free market. Or they may affect the prices that everyone has to pay for goods and services. Therefore, it is important to know something about these practices.

One of the unfair methods that big business owners once used was to get together with other business owners to form a **trust.** That is, several companies in a similar business placed their stock in the hands of a group of trustees. They agreed that they would no longer compete with one another. Instead, they would divide the business among themselves. In this way, they could control prices. And in time, they could take control of an entire industry.

Another unfair practice used by big business was to combine with or buy out companies in the same business. If the combined company, or **merger,** became powerful enough, it could control an entire industry and charge what prices it pleased. It would then be a **monopoly.** A monopoly is a company that controls all or a large part of the total supply of a product or service.

Suppose that a large coffee company decided to lessen its competition by buying up all the small coffee companies or by forcing them out of business. The large coffee company might do this by lowering its prices below the cost of production. Soon all the other companies would have to lower their prices to stay in business. Every coffee firm would be selling coffee at a loss. Because the big company has more capital than the small companies, it can stand to lose money longer than they can. The small companies would be forced to sell out, merge with the big company, or go out of business altogether.

The big company would now be a monopoly. It alone would produce all the coffee on the market. And it could sell this coffee at a high price. Since there would be no other companies selling coffee, people would have to buy the high-priced coffee from the big company or do without it.

THE GOVERNMENT AS REFEREE

The referee of a basketball or football game sees that the teams observe the rules. In the same way, the federal government enforces rules that prevent business firms from using unfair practices. Congress passes the rules, and the executive agencies carry them out.

To prevent monopolies like the imaginary coffee company just described, Congress has passed antitrust and antimonopoly laws. The Sherman Antitrust Act of 1890 was passed to help prevent monopolies. It was strengthened by the Clayton Act of 1914, which forbade practices that would lessen competition. The antitrust division of the Justice Department and the Federal Trade Commission are responsible for enforcing these laws.

In recent years, the government and the American people have been trying to decide whether to regulate business combinations known as **conglomerates.** A conglomerate is formed when a large, powerful company buys businesses that produce, supply, or sell a number of different goods and services. For example, a conglomerate may control communication systems, insurance companies, hotel and restaurant chains, car rental businesses, and others.

The government watches mergers carefully to make sure that conglomerates do not gain too much control over an industry or part of the economy. If a conglomerate gains so much power that it threatens our free economy, the government may have to step in as a referee.

COMPARING ECONOMIC SYSTEMS

Over the past 100 years, our economic system has grown large, interconnected, and complicated. As a result, our national government now acts as referee and makes other economic decisions. Because the government makes more economic decisions than it once did, some economists now describe our system as a **mixed economy.** But it is still correct to call it a free economy or a free enterprise economy because most economic decisions are still made by individuals.

In an economy like that of the Soviet Union, the opposite is true. Most economic decisions are made by government officials who head huge planning agencies. Individuals are left with only a few decisions to make. People are told how much they can buy. The government decides what the price is to be. Workers are told what jobs they must take. And young people are told what jobs to train for. The government manages nearly everything.

For these reasons and others, we say that the leaders of the Soviet Union have established a **command economy.** In this type of economy, the government completely controls, or commands, the nation's economy. The government is all powerful. It owns almost all the capital, tools, and means of production of the Soviet Union. It tells the managers and workers in factories and on farms how much they must produce each year. If they do not produce as much as they are told to, their wages may be reduced or they may be sternly reprimanded.

CONSIDER AND DISCUSS

Identify. economic system / free economy / free market / free competition / profit / invest / profit motive / means of production / private property / law of supply and demand / capitalism / capitalistic system / capital / capitalist / free enterprise system / trust / merger / monopoly / conglomerate / mixed economy / command economy

These workers are employed by a machine tool factory in the Soviet Union. They work for the government, which runs all of the country's businesses.

Review. 1. What are some of our economic freedoms? 2. Why is competition important in our free economy? 3. How does the law of supply and demand work? 4. How does the United States government regulate business?

Discuss. What are the principal advantages of our free enterprise system? Can you think of any disadvantages?

2 How American Business Is Organized

About 100 years ago, a young clerk in a small New York town decided to try out a new idea for increasing his store's business. Gathering several small items from the store's stock, he placed them on a table near the entrance. Then he put up a sign on the table that read, "Everything on this table, 10 cents each." Customers who came into the store to buy thread or sugar began to stop at the table to purchase a bag of clothespins, or an eggbeater, or some other item that caught their eye. Business in the store began to show a good increase.

The young man then decided to open his own store, and to sell only five- and ten-cent items. Unfortunately, his new store was not a success. He lost all of the money that he had saved and borrowed to start the business. He did not give up, however. Instead, he borrowed the money he needed to buy new goods and to start over again. This time his business was a success.

The young man with the new idea was Frank W. Woolworth. With the profits from his new business, he soon opened another store, and then another and another. When he died in 1919, Woolworth had established 1,300 five-and-ten-cent stores in the United States and Canada.

Woolworth became a wealthy man because he had a good idea, and because he had the enterprise and business ability to make it succeed. Success stories like his encourage many Americans to go into business for themselves.

THE SINGLE PROPRIETORSHIP

There are over 13 million business firms in the United States today. Over 10 million of them are small businesses owned by one person. These are gas stations, grocery stores, beauty shops, drug stores, and other businesses that serve people who live nearby. These small businesses, owned by one person, are called **single proprietorships.**

You probably already know some of the advantages of going into business for yourself. Single proprietors are their own bosses. They alone decide what they will sell, the hours the businesses will be open, and how the businesses will be run. Because they are the owners, they take all of the profits.

On the other hand, there are disadvantages to being a single proprietor. Owners have to furnish all the money needed to rent or buy the buildings their businesses use and the tools and other equipment needed to run them. If they require help, they have to be able to pay the salaries of employees. Owners are hard-working people. They can hire others to help them. But they alone are responsible for the success or failure of their businesses. If their businesses fail, proprietors must face the losses. Workers may lose their jobs. But proprietors may have to sell everything they own to pay their business debts.

THE PARTNERSHIP

In the United States each year, many small businesses are being started while others are going out of business. Some small businesses fail because the single proprietor lacks enough capital or lacks the business

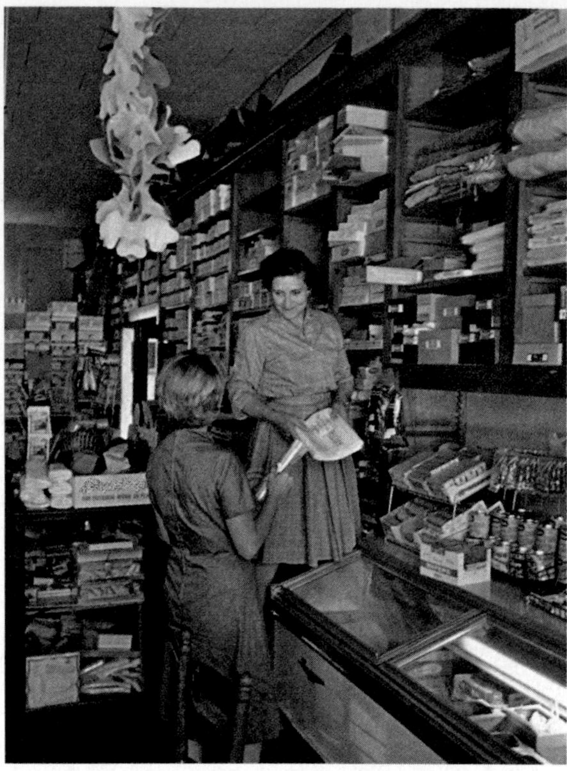

This general store in North Carolina is typical of the small businesses owned by a single proprietor.

ability to earn a good profit. For such reasons, the owner of a small business sometimes seeks another person to become a part owner of the business. They then form a **partnership,** which gives the business firm a greater amount of capital and a better chance of success. In a partnership, there is more than one person to provide capital, to share responsibility, to furnish ideas, and to do the work. The partners also share the risks. If the business should fail, the partners share responsibility for the debts of the business.

Any two or more persons can form a business partnership. Usually they sign an agreement setting up the partnership. But unwritten partnership agreements are legal and are recognized by a court of law. There are a few large and wealthy American businesses that are organized as partnerships. However, most partnerships are small.

You often can recognize a partnership from the name of a business firm: Smith and Jackson, Contractors; Hubbard and Reilley, Accountants; Cortes, Clark, Bernstein, and Brown, Attorneys. If the abbreviation "Inc." does not appear after the names, the business is probably a partnership. "Inc." is an abbreviation, or short form of, "incorporated." It means that the business is organized as a corporation.

THE CORPORATION

Just what is a corporation? Establishing a big business in America requires large sums of money—to buy land, to build offices and factories, to purchase tools and machinery, and to employ workers. For this and other reasons, a big business can seldom be set up by an individual or even by a number of partners. A different form of business organization is commonly used. This form of business organization is called a **corporation.**

1. Corporations raise money by selling stocks, or shares, of ownership. Each share of stock represents a part of the ownership of the corporation. The people who buy these stocks are called **stockholders.**

Suppose a new corporation is organized with a **capitalization** of $1 million. That means it has the legal right to accept this much money in the form of capital from investors. It could do this, for example, by selling 10,000 shares of stock at $100 a share. Each purchaser of a single share would own one ten-thousandth of the company. When profits are divided each year, each owner of a single share would get one ten-thousandth of the profits. Some stockholders own several shares. A few major stockholders may own many shares. Each stockholder receives a share of the profits in proportion to the amount of stocks owned. Corporation profits that are paid to stockholders are called **dividends.**

2. The corporation receives its right to operate from a state government. The state grants the business firm a **charter** of incorporation. This charter recognizes the corporation's right to carry on business, to sell its stock, and to receive the protection of state laws. In return, the company must obey state regulations in regard to its organization, the reports that it must make public, the taxes that it pays, and the way in which it sells its stock to the public.

3. The directors of the corporation are elected by the stockholders. Every corporation is required by law to hold at least one meeting of its stockholders each year. All stockholders have the right to attend this meeting and to speak—even if they own only one share. At this annual meeting, the stockholders elect a **board of directors.** They may also vote on major changes in the corporation's business. Each share of stock entitles its owner to one vote. Major stockholders therefore cast most of the votes. The board of directors, representing the stockholders, meets from time to time during the year to make important decisions about the affairs of the corporation.

4. The board of directors chooses those who manage the corporation from day to day. These top **executives** of the corporation are elected by the board of directors. They include the president of the company, vice-presidents, secretary, and treasurer. The president usually picks the other major assistants. Together, all of these officials are called the **management** of the corporation.

Corporations, as you have read, are owned by the stockholders. The money received from the sale of stock becomes the corporation's capital. The purchase of shares gives the stockholders the right to receive a part of the company's profits.

But what if the business fails? Are the stockholders responsible for paying the corporation's debts? No! The most that stockholders may lose is what they paid for their stock. This is the great advantage of the corporation as a way to gather together large amounts of capital. If the corporation fails, owing many debts, neither the stockholders nor the officers are responsible for its debts. If a corporation goes out of business, its assets (property and other valuables) are sold. The money raised from this sale is then used to pay off the debts.

PREFERRED AND COMMON STOCKS

A corporation may issue two kinds of stock—preferred stock and common stock. Owners of **preferred stock** take less risk when they invest their money. As long as the company makes a profit, they are guaranteed a fixed dividend every year. The corporation must pay these dividends to the preferred stockholders before other stockholders are paid their dividends. Because preferred stockholders take less risk, they do not usually have a vote in the company's affairs. They are owners, but they have no voice in managing the company.

Owners of **common stock** take more risk when they invest their money. They receive dividends only if the company makes good profits. Why, then, would anyone want to risk buying common stock? There are three main advantages in owning common stock.

1. If the company's profits are high, owners of common stock may receive higher dividends than owners of preferred stock.

2. If the company's profits are high, the market price, or selling price, of the common stock usually increases. This means that stockholders can sell their shares, if they wish, for more than they paid for them.

3. Common stock owners have a vote in electing the board of directors and in deciding certain company policies.

CORPORATION BONDS

Even with the sale of preferred and common stocks, corporations sometimes need additional large sums of money in order to expand operations. In such cases, the most common method that corporations use is the issuing of **bonds.**

The issuing of bonds is a method of borrowing money. Bonds are certificates stating how much the original purchaser paid. They also give the percentage of interest on this amount that the corporation will pay the bondholder each year. The company must pay the interest on its bonds before it pays dividends to stockholders. This interest must be paid whether the company earns any profits or not.

If the company cannot repay the money borrowed from bondholders by the date stated on the bonds, then the holders of the bonds may take over the business. They may close the corporation and sell its property to raise the money owed them. Or they may decide to keep the business in operation, perhaps with new management. They may do this in the hope that the corporation soon will be able to pay back the bonds.

The corporation is the most common form of business organization for most of America's large companies and for many smaller ones. The corporation is a permanent organization. It is unlike proprietorships and

How a Corporation Is Organized

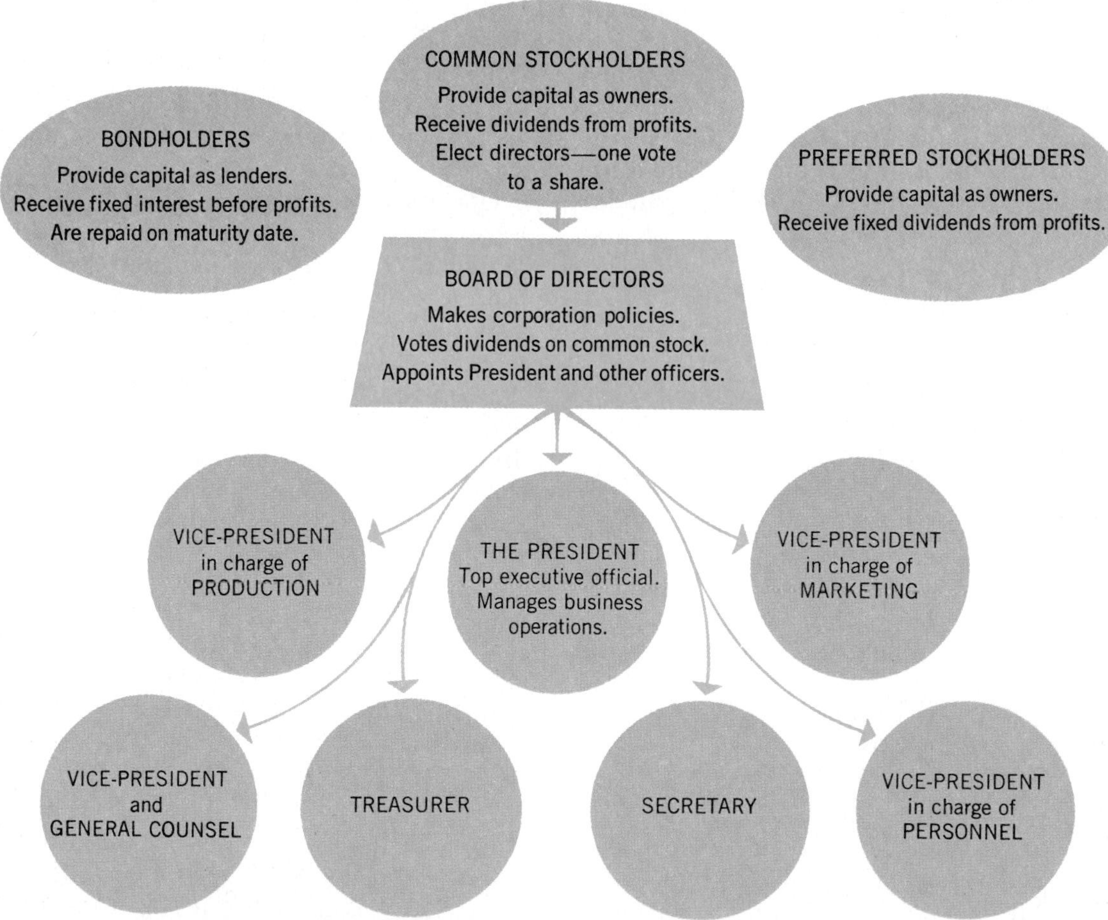

partnerships, which end when their owners die. Modern corporations play a vital part in our American economy.

CONSIDER AND DISCUSS

Identify. single proprietorship / partnership / corporation / stockholders / capitalization / dividends / charter / board of directors / executives / management / preferred stock / common stock / bonds

Review. 1. What are the principal advantages and disadvantages of the single proprietorship? 2. Where does a corporation get its money? 3. Why do people invest in stocks? 4. Why is the corporation form of business best suited to large industries?

Discuss. Would you rather work for someone else or own your own business? Why?

3 How Business Decisions Are Made

All Americans who run a business, whether they are individual proprietors, members of a partnership, or managers of a great corporation find that their business success depends mainly upon decisions they make about the use of four things: (1) land, (2) capital, (3) management, and (4) labor. These are called the **factors of production.**

PRODUCTION REQUIRES LAND

Suppose that Maria Morano, a hard-working young woman, decides to start a bakery business. She will need a place to conduct her business. That is, she needs land. Every business enterprise requires land.

To an economist, the word **land** includes more than just a place to locate a store, a factory, or an office. It also includes all the natural resources that come from the land. The wheat that is used to make flour for Maria Morano's bakery comes from the land. The wood for her bread racks grows on the land. All of the raw materials that are needed to produce goods of all kinds come from the mines, fields, and forests that are a part of the land.

Our nation's total supply of actual land, as well as of raw materials, is limited. In some places land is so scarce that there are many businesses in every city block. People who wish to start new businesses must make decisions about their location. Maria Morano, for example, must decide whether or not to own the property on which her business will be located. She can buy either a piece of land with a building on it or land on which she can build. Or she can pay rent for one. **Rent** is what a person pays to use land or other property belonging to someone else.

Rents and land prices are higher in crowded business areas where land is scarce than in less densely populated areas. Maria Morano must decide which location will give her the most profit. If she pays a high rent or price for land, she will be nearer customers. If she goes to the edge of town where land or rent are cheaper, customers will have to travel farther to get to her bakery. Maria Morano must also make decisions about the kind, quality, and costs of the flour and other raw materials she will use.

PRODUCTION REQUIRES CAPITAL

Maria Morano will also need equipment such as mixers and ovens. She may rent her equipment. Or she may buy it on the installment plan. If she has enough money, she may buy it more cheaply by paying cash. As you can see, Maria cannot go into business without money. Her decision to rent or buy equipment will depend on how much capital she has available, and how she wants to use it. Capital, you recall, is money used to pay for tools and other means of production.

How will Maria Morano find the capital she

The Four Factors of Production

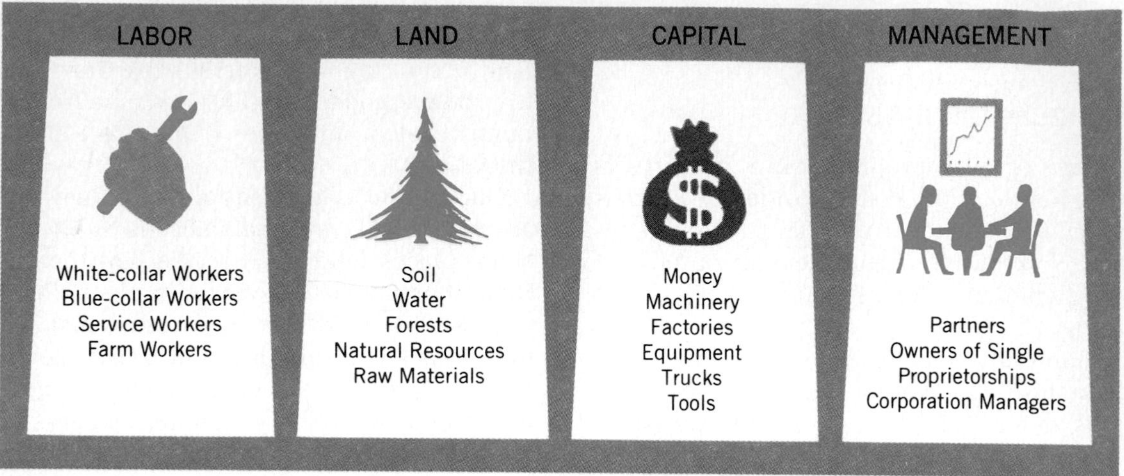

needs? Perhaps she will decide to go ahead alone and set up her business as a single proprietorship. To do so, she must have saved some money as capital. If she does not have enough, she may ask the bank for a loan. If the bank officials decide that Maria is a good **risk,** they will give her a loan. They will think she is a good risk if they conclude that she has good ideas for a business and is likely to pay back the loan. If Maria takes out a loan, she will have to pay the bank **interest.** Interest is what is paid to a bank or a person for the use of their money.

Perhaps Maria will decide instead to seek a partner or several partners who are willing to invest in the bakery business. Or she may decide to set up her business as a corporation and sell stock to raise capital. She would do this if she decided to go into the bakery business on a large scale.

PRODUCTION REQUIRES GOOD MANAGEMENT

All business owners must make such decisions as these. Then after the business has started, they must make decisions about how to distribute the product, how much to charge, whether to hire more people, and many others. Decisions of this kind make up the principal work of management.

Those who operate businesses are called **managers.** The group of managers of a single business, you will recall, is called its management. Their decisions will determine whether the business will succeed. If management makes the wrong decisions, the business may fail. If management makes wise decisions, the business will prosper.

When managers make decisions, they take risks. If business people did not take risks, the average standard of living in America would not be so high. Because Thomas Edison and other business people took risks, for example, Americans were among the first people to enjoy the benefits of electricity. Because Henry Ford and others took risks, Americans had the first low-priced, mass-produced cars. Because David Sarnoff and hundreds of others took risks, Americans enjoy radio and television networks.

These people were successful. Their decisions turned out well. But many other business people were not successful. Why are Americans willing to take such business risks?

MANAGEMENT AND PROFITS

Management takes risks because it hopes to produce profits. What are profits and how are they determined?

The money that a business firm receives from the sale of its goods or services is called **gross income.** Out of gross income, the firm must pay the **costs** of making and distributing its product. The cost of materials and supplies used in the business must be paid. Rent must be paid. If the business owns its own land and buildings, property taxes must be paid. Machines wear out. So money must be put aside to repair machinery or replace it. If the business has borrowed money, interest must be paid. Wages must be paid to workers. Salaries must be paid to those who manage the business. Even if proprietors own their own businesses and do all the work themselves, the salary they pay themselves is one of the costs of the business. Now, then, is there anything left?

If the business firm has been well managed, and if other conditions are right, there will be money left after all the costs have been paid. This amount that is left is called **net income.** What happens to this net income? Part of the firm's net income will go to pay federal and state income taxes. Some may be set aside in a bank to meet future business needs. The rest is profit. As you may recall, profit is what is left after all the firm's obligations have been met. In a corporation, profits are distributed among the stockholders as dividends.

PRODUCTION REQUIRES LABOR

The larger the business, the more workers it will need. As you know, a business hires workers and pays them wages. The word **labor** is used to mean the large group of workers who earn wages in business and industry. If Maria Morano does her own work, the amount of bread and rolls she can pro-

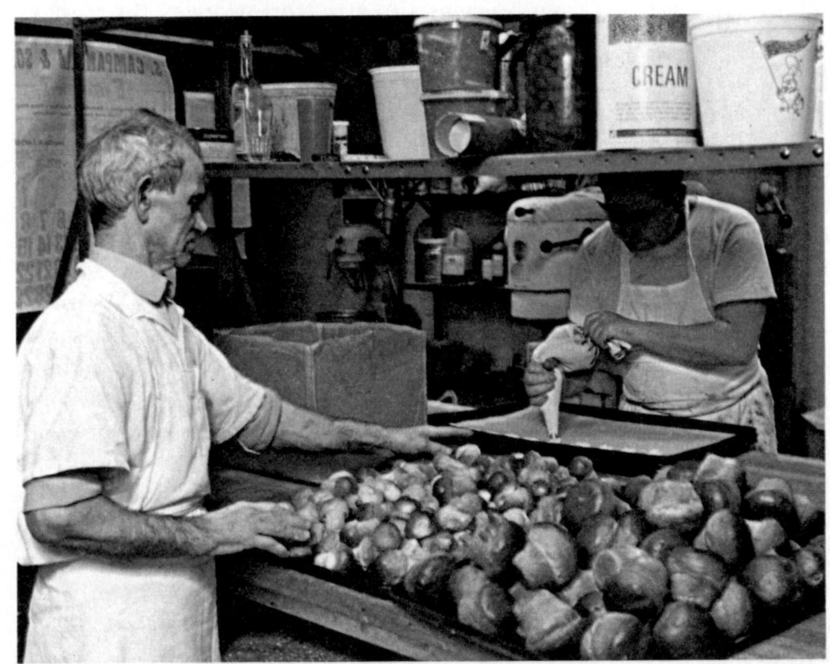

Like all businesses, this small bakery requires raw materials, capital, management, and labor. What evidence can you see of these four factors of production?

duce will be limited. If she hires more labor, her production will be greater. Her risk will be greater, too, because she must now make enough gross income to be able to pay wages. But her chances for profits from greater production will increase.

DIFFERENT KINDS OF WORKERS

Workers may be classified into several groups. The Department of Labor lists four major groups. You will read about them in detail in Chapter 18. Briefly, they are as follows:

1. **White-collar workers** are those who are self-employed or who do technical, clerical, or sales work. They also include professional workers and managers. Self-employed workers work for themselves. They include the proprietors of small and big businesses. One of the largest groups of white-collar workers is made up of clerical and secretarial workers. They include bookkeepers, clerks, typists, secretaries, stenographers, and others who work in offices, bank tellers, and mail handlers. Salespeople sell goods and services in stores. Or they represent their businesses to individual buyers, to other industries, or to governments. They include sales clerks, sales representatives, and insurance and real estate agents.

Professional workers and managers are the most highly educated of the labor groups. Professionals such as teachers, doctors, nurses, dentists, engineers, and lawyers usually have a college education and additional years of special study. Managers and administrators—those who run schools, other institutions, and businesses—also have a college education. Some have done graduate study.

2. **Blue-collar workers** are those who provide labor for business and industry. Many of these workers are employed in factories and in construction work. Some are skilled operators of special equipment, such as precision tools, welding equipment, and printing machines. Other blue-collar workers—for example, electricians, plumbers, and carpenters—are skilled in special crafts. People who operate transport vehicles, repair machines and appliances, handle freight, and work on roads are also blue-collar workers.

3. **Service workers** are those who perform services for the public. Included in this group are barbers, hair stylists, workers in private houses, guards, police officers, firefighters, dry cleaners, and waiters.

4. **Farm workers** are those who own, manage, and work on farms. They include the owners of small and large farms, paid farm workers, unpaid family members who work on farms, and farm managers and supervisors.

GOVERNMENT'S ROLE IN BUSINESS

As you may recall, government is important to American business. Our government does not tell business people everything they must do. But it does influence business in many ways. For example, government acts as a referee to make sure that big corporations do not destroy the competition of small businesses. Our Constitution protects the right of private property. National laws protect our free market. Other laws protect the right of business people to take risks to make profits.

Many agencies of the federal government help businesses. One of them, the Small Business Administration, helps small businesses as they compete in an economy dominated by large corporations.

The federal government acts as an overseer of our economy. This helps business, too. For instance, the Federal Reserve Board can raise interest rates on loans made by business if it thinks that the country's economy is rising too rapidly. This causes the economy to "cool off," or slow down. When business is too slow, the Federal Reserve Board can stimulate the economy by lowering interest rates. Business owners can then borrow money more cheaply to finance expansion.

Thus, we can see that government plays many roles in business. Even though we have a free enterprise system, our government helps keep the economy running smoothly.

CONSIDER AND DISCUSS

Identify. factors of production / land / rent / risk / interest / managers / gross income / costs / net income / labor / white-collar workers / blue-collar workers / service workers / farm workers

Review. 1. What are the four factors of production? 2. What are some of the kinds of workers in our economy? 3. In what three ways could Maria Morano organize her bakery business? 4. What is the relationship between good management and profits? 5. How may the federal government's policies affect production?

Discuss. If you were starting a new business, what are some things you would have to decide about your use of the four factors of production?

CHAPTER

Summary

The American economy, or business system, is based on ideas of personal freedom. Americans are free to choose their own jobs, free to work for others or to go into business for themselves, and free to buy and sell the goods and services they wish.

The American economic system is known as capitalism, or as a free enterprise economy. This means that it is based on a free market, free competition, private ownership of property, and the right to make a profit on business activities. Government does not tell business what to do. It acts as a referee to prevent unfair business practices. The free American economy based on capitalism is clearly different from a Communist system, like that of the Soviet Union, based on a command economy.

American business firms may be organized as individual proprietorships, partnerships, or corporations. Big business firms, or corporations, are owned by many people. These people own shares of stock in the corporations. The money they pay to buy the stock is the capital which the corporation uses to engage in business. Corporations also raise money by issuing bonds.

Business owners must make decisions about their use of the four factors of production—land (which includes raw materials)—capital, management, and labor. In the American economy, most of these decisions are freely made by business people as they seek to earn profits.

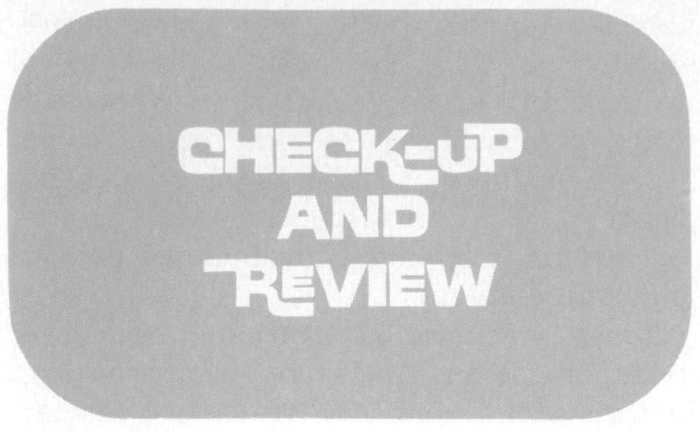

VOCABULARY

Many new words appeared in this chapter. "Our American Economic System." You will meet these words frequently in your study and in daily newspapers. List each of the following terms in your notebook, and beside each write a good definition.

economy	command economy
free economy	corporation
free market	stockholders
free competition	bonds
private property	single proprietorship
capitalist	board of directors
profit	land
free enterprise	capital
monopoly	labor
conglomerate	rent
trust	interest
partnership	risk
dividends	net income
management	merger

CHECK-UP

Answer each of the following questions and share your answers with your class during the discussion.

1. How would you describe our free enterprise economy?
2. How does the law of supply and demand help our economy work well?
3. What was the secret of F. W. Woolworth's success?
4. What is the advantage of a partnership over a single proprietorship?
5. If you wanted to establish a corporation, what steps would you take?
6. Would you rather own bonds, preferred stock, or common stock? Why?
7. What are the main features of America's free economy?
8. What are the main features of the Soviet Union's command economy?
9. What are the four factors of production?
10. Name four kinds of workers found in our economy.
11. How does our government aid and protect American business?

CITIZENSHIP AND YOU

The American free enterprise system is of great importance to each of us. We can learn more about it through research, reading, and projects. Below are some suggestions for interesting activities.

1. Class Projects

Hold an open-forum debate on the following topic: Are small businesses an important part of our free enterprise system?

Invite a local business owner to tell the class how he or she established a business. Ask the owner about labor relations, taxes, government regulations, and other problems faced by management.

Listen to a report by a panel on how the Soviet economy works. Discuss advantages of the American business system.

On a chalkboard chart, compare the ways in which decisions are made in the economies of the United States and the Soviet Union.

2. Group or Committee Projects

A class committee might visit a labor-union headquarters and interview union officials. Report to the class on the union's aims, methods, and achievements.

Conduct a survey of jobs and occupations represented by teenagers and adults whom you know. What goods do they produce? What services do they provide to the community? Make a report of your findings to the class.

Prepare a bulletin-board exhibit on "The American Way of Business."

3. Individual Projects

Prepare a written report on any one of the topics listed below.

Capitalism: The American Way
The Government as Business Referee
Legal Monopolies in the American Economy
The Story of a Great Corporation

CIVICS SKILLS

CRITICAL THINKING

The world of business is full of different viewpoints and ideas. For example, the statements made by factory owners about the causes of labor difficulties may be very different from the statements made by labor-union leaders. Which side is right? How can you make up your mind? How can you improve the quality of your judgments?

The answers to these questions are not easy. There is no simple way to learn the truth. The search for truth on any subject is long and hard. Indeed, experts on a subject often have to spend a lifetime to get near the truth. Yet all Americans must seek answers to problems that face them and their nation every day. How can we learn to think clearly in order to make up our minds?

The first step is to make sure that the problem or question is clear in your mind. You may find it helpful to write down the question to which you wish to find the answer.

Once the question is clear to you, you can begin to look for evidence that will help you to understand and judge the issues involved. What are the facts? It may surprise you to discover that there often are disagreements over the facts. One side says one thing and the other claims something quite different. In order to clear things up, you may need to go back to an original source. For example, what does the law actually say? What are the official figures, wages, and prices? What are the actual words that the person used in the speech?

In thinking through a problem, it is important that you learn to weigh all evidence. Are the facts used by the speaker or writer really the important ones you need to know? Are these all the facts you need to know, or are important facts still missing? In learning how to think clearly, you must learn to judge for yourself whether the given facts really fit the problem. You must also learn to judge which side of the argument the facts seem to support.

After you have weighed the evidence, you can reach your own judgment, or conclusion, about the truth. But try to keep an open mind. Remember that if new evidence is found, it may be necessary to change your judgment.

Sometimes there is more than one possible solution to a problem. In trying to decide which solution you favor, you may want to test how each solution might work. You may do this by mentally checking the facts against each possible solution. In some cases, you may actually try each solution in a real situation to see how it works.

PRACTICING YOUR CIVICS SKILLS

One of the important forms of business organizations in the United States is the conglomerate. Do some research and try to find out the chief advantages and disadvantages of this business form. After gathering the evidence, answer the following question: Is the conglomerate form of business a threat to our free economy? Why or why not?

Learn about the various candidates running for an office in your community. Read newspaper articles about the election and campaign literature prepared by the candidates. Compare their qualifications, ideas, and opinions. Then make a judgment on who is the best candidate based on the evidence you gathered. Present your opinion in class.

CHAPTER
Introduction

One of the outstanding features of the American economic system is its great ability to produce. In recent years, America has produced over $2 trillion worth of goods and services a year! This is more than any other nation in the world. The dollar value of what we produce is called the *Gross National Product (GNP).* It is figured out by adding up the dollar value of all the goods and services produced during the year.

Economists use the GNP to measure how well our economy performs. If the GNP rises year after year, the nation's economy is doing well generally. If the GNP for any one year falls, the economy probably slowed down during that year. This means that people did not have as much money to spend, save, and invest. There are also other ways of judging the productivity of an economy. The number of unemployed people, the number of business failures, and the tax income produced by the nation all help to tell us how healthy the economy is.

In this chapter you will take a closer look at the system of production that makes it possible for America to have such a high Gross National Product. You will also learn how our goods and services get to the people who want and need them. You will learn about some of the laws that protect consumers, and find suggestions about intelligent buying. These are the topics you will study in this chapter:

1. The American System of Mass Production
2. Marketing America's Goods
3. You, the Consumer

CHAPTER

15 How Our Goods Are Produced and Marketed

1 The American System of Mass Production

In recent years, the United States produced almost 9 million automobiles, trucks, and buses a year. Each year it produced over 39,000 new books and more than 16 trillion kilograms (36 trillion pounds) of meat. Every year, millions of other articles are made in America. What makes this huge production possible?

MASS PRODUCTION

There are many factors that make America capable of such enormous production. One is **mass production.** Mass production requires many large machines and vast amounts of power. Mass production means that huge amounts of goods can be made rapidly by machines to supply the needs and wants of America's large population. American inventors have developed machines that can make, or help make, almost any product you can think of.

One of the first inventors to make mass production possible was Eli Whitney. (You may remember him as the inventor of the cotton gin.) In 1800, Whitney signed a contract to make muskets, or guns, for the United States Army. Whitney promised to manufacture 10,000 guns in two years' time. This promise seemed impossible, because up to that time guns had been made by hand, one by one. To prove that he could

Foundations of Modern Mass Production

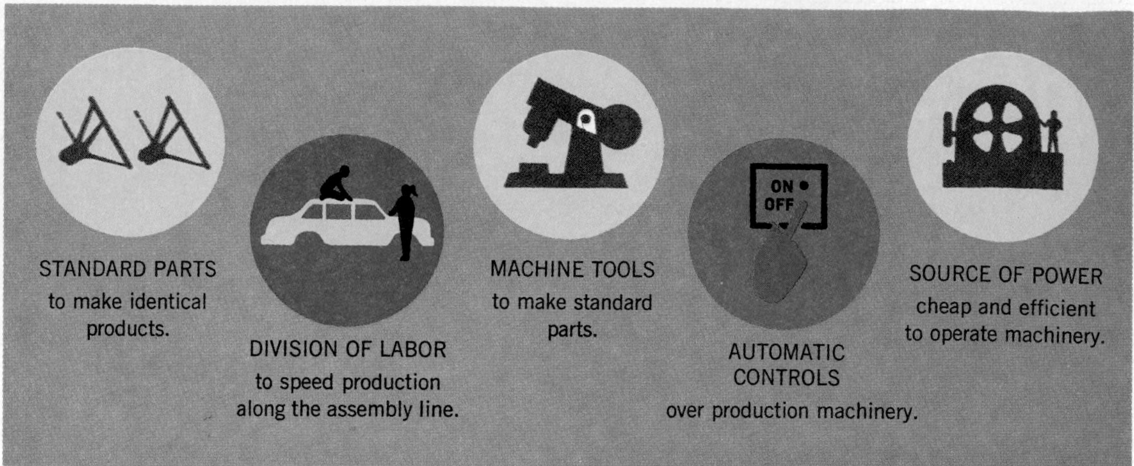

ON
OFF
STANDARD PARTS
to make identical products.
DIVISION OF LABOR
to speed production along the assembly line.
MACHINE TOOLS
to make standard parts.
AUTOMATIC CONTROLS
over production machinery.
SOURCE OF POWER
cheap and efficient to operate machinery.

keep his promise, Whitney agreed to show some government officials how he planned to make the guns.

From a box, he took ten gun barrels, ten triggers, ten stocks, and ten locks for exploding the powder. He asked the officials to choose one of each of these parts. Whitney then took the four parts and quickly put together a finished musket. To show that the parts were all alike he continued to put together muskets until all ten were completed. He had made ten identical guns from a box containing identical parts. And he was able to do this very rapidly.

Eli Whitney's methods have become the basis of all mass production, from radios and sewing machines to automobiles and giant tractors. What are these methods?

1. Use of machine tools. Whitney developed **machine tools,** or machinery carefully built to turn out parts that were exactly the same. Instead of boring each gun barrel by hand, for example, he made a machine that did nothing but bore gun barrels, all in the same way.

2. Use of standard parts. Each of Whitney's machine tools made parts that were exactly alike, called **standard parts.** That is, any Whitney gun barrel would fit any gun made by Whitney. Other parts were all alike and would fit any of the guns. This was a great advantage. If a part wore out, it could easily be replaced by a new standard part.

3. Use of division of labor. Barrels, triggers, stocks, and locks for Whitney's guns were made by different groups of workers, each operating a separate machine. No one worker made a whole gun. The whole job was divided among workers. In this **division of labor,** each worker was a specialist at part of the job.

The use of machine tools, standard parts, and the division of labor helped to increase production. The early machines used by Whitney and others were small and inefficient. Many machines used in factories today are enormous and highly efficient.

LARGE MACHINES REQUIRE GREAT POWER

For many years, Americans used the force of falling water, or **water power,** as the source of energy to operate their machines. Early factories were, therefore, located near streams. Dams were built to hold back water so that it could be released when necessary to turn water wheels. As these big wheels turned, their power was used to turn machines within the factory. Then a great change took place. James Watt, a Scottish engineer, invented a practical steam engine. This invention became more and more popular in the United States. Soon **steam power** began to replace water power.

Steam power continued to be the leading source of industrial power during the 1800's. In the 1900's, however, several new sources of power were developed. The **internal combustion engine** used the power released by exploding gasoline. It was often used to run small machines. But it was mainly used in the automobile. The source of power that really made modern mass production possible, however, was **electricity.**

Around 1900, the use of electricity began to spread. At first it was used mainly for lighting. As time went on, however, it was used in many other ways. American families now use electricity to run their toasters, fans, refrigerators, air conditioners, washers, dryers, vacuum cleaners, and radio and television sets. And today, nearly every American factory uses electricity as its source of power.

Most electricity is now generated by steam plants and hydroelectric dams. But the search goes on for even better sources of energy. The source of all energy is, indirectly, the sun. Scientists believe that someday soon it will be practical to use the energy of sunlight directly. **Solar energy,** as direct energy from the sun is called, has already been used to produce some electricity. It has been used in our space program, for example, to power satellites.

Another source of energy that is being used today is **nuclear energy.** This is the great force that holds atoms together. It can be released when atoms are split or combined. Large nuclear-generating plants are operating in many parts of the country. They are able to produce a great deal of energy from a small amount of fuel. But they also may pose a threat to humans and the environment. The more nuclear plants there are, the greater the chance for accidents. Many people worry about what might happen if for some reason radiation escaped from the plants.

MASS PRODUCTION IN AN AUTOMOBILE FACTORY

One of the best ways to understand modern mass production is to visit an automobile manufacturing plant. Suppose you were to go to Detroit, Michigan, to make such a visit. What would you see?

After you enter the Detroit automobile factory, it may take you a few minutes to get used to all the activity and noise. But as you look about, you begin to see how Eli Whitney's methods of manufacturing are still used by American industry.

As an engine block moves by, a team of workers goes to work on it. First, a huge machine tool bores 87 holes into the block, all in one operation. As the block moves along, workers fit pistons, valves, and bolts into the holes. And the block becomes an internal combustion engine. Other teams of workers fasten carburetors, ignitions, and other parts to the engine. One automobile engine after another is being made in this way, each exactly alike.

How does modern mass production use Whitney's methods? Think about what you have just seen in the automobile plant. You saw a machine tool used to produce identical parts—in this case, bored engine blocks for cars. You saw many examples of the division of labor. Each worker does a special job, and has become highly skilled. You saw many standard parts, such as valves, being used. Each valve fits exactly into a hole in the engine block. Each wire fits into a part where it belongs. Eli Whitney's ideas for making guns really started something important!

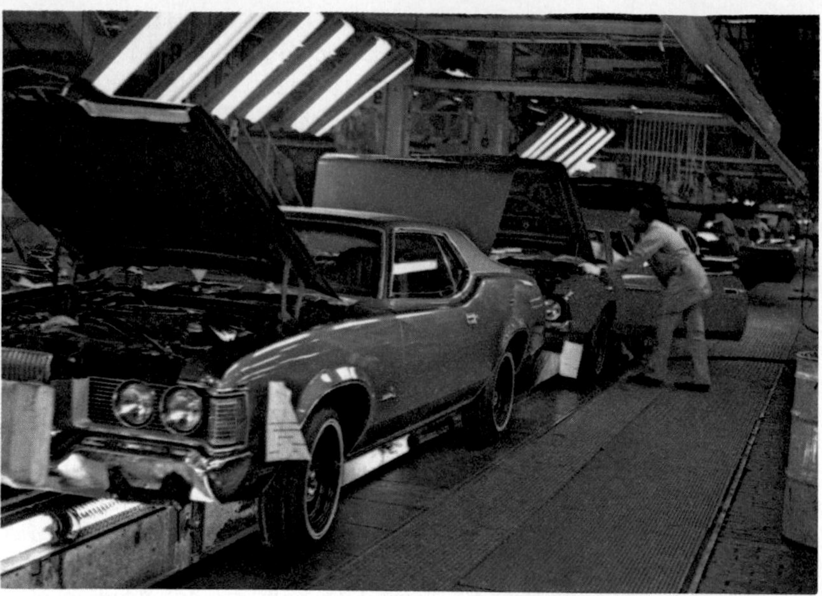

The assembly line of an automobile factory provides a good example of modern mass production. Here, workers are putting the final touches on automobiles.

PRODUCTION ON THE ASSEMBLY LINE

One feature of modern mass production is different from Whitney's day. That feature, which is used in almost every industry, is the **assembly line.** How does the assembly line work?

Let's watch it again in our visit to the automobile plant. Starting with just the frame, the car moves along on a large **conveyor belt.** The belt slowly moves many car frames at a time through the factory.

As the car frame moves along the assembly line at a slow speed, the four wheels are added to the frame. Then an engine, the transmission, the windshield, and a steering wheel and gears are added. Seats, door panels, and lights are put on next. The car moves on to the paint shop. There it is spray-painted and dried. It is finally driven off the assembly line and tested. The car is now ready to be shipped to an automobile dealer's showroom. There, customers may look at it, test drive it, and buy it.

But how do the various parts arrive at the assembly line just in time to become parts of the finished automobile? At the beginning of your tour, you recall, you saw an engine being made. This engine was not then on the main assembly line. It was on a side line, or **feeder line.** The engine's movement along the feeder line was timed so that the engine was completed just as the feeder line met the main assembly line. The engine was then lowered into place in the car from its overhead conveyor belt. In this way, feeder lines are used to assemble many parts of the car and bring them to the main assembly line exactly when and where they are needed.

Your imaginary visit to an automobile plant should have helped you to understand the mass production methods that are used in nearly all of America's large industries. Remember that the automobile industry, while important, is just one of our nation's large industries. Bread from Maria Morano's bakery is made in the same way. Flour and other ingredients are dumped into mixers from overhead bins. Conveyor belts running from the storage rooms supply the bins. After the loaf is shaped, it is carried on a conveyor belt through a block-long oven. By the time it reaches the other end of the oven, the bread is baked. The finished loaf travels through another machine that slices and wraps it. Still another machine packs loaves in boxes. A conveyor then transports the box to trucks for delivery to stores.

MASS PRODUCTION IN THE WORLD

Mass production was first developed in America, but it has now spread to other countries. European countries have made use of it for years. Japan has adopted and perfected methods of mass production. Japan can now produce certain kinds of goods more rapidly and at a lower cost than American industry.

The Soviet Union also uses mass production methods. But it has not been as successful as Japan. One reason may be that in the Soviet Union, as you may recall, the government controls the economy. Property is not privately owned. People are not free to start their own businesses as they wish. They also cannot decide what prices to charge, or the amount of goods and services to produce. This kind of command economy does not have the same incentives, or motives, that a free economy has. A free economy stimulates business people to take risks. When there is no incentive to make a profit by taking a risk, people may be less inclined to take risks. What, for example, was Eli Whitney's incentive? He invented a new method of production because he hoped to profit from it. So did all the other business people who adopted and perfected our system of mass production.

Business people must be quick to grasp new ideas. To continue competing, they must be ready to change from old ways to new ways. They must do this even if it means rebuilding factories and buying costly new machinery.

CONSIDER AND DISCUSS

Identify. Gross National Product / mass production / machine tools / standard parts / division of labor / water power / steam power / internal combustion engine / electricity / solar energy / nuclear energy / assembly line / conveyor belt / feeder line

Review. 1. What did Eli Whitney contribute to the American economic system? 2. What forms of power are used in American industry? 3. Describe the methods of mass production used in the automobile industry. 4. How does incentive affect the economy?

Discuss. From the worker's point of view, what are some advantages and disadvantages of mass production methods?

2 Marketing America's Goods

American industry and business produce goods and services that supply our needs. But production is only one side of supplying our needs. The other side is **distribution.** After goods are produced, they must be distributed to the people who want them.

Distribution also has two sides to it. One is **transportation.** Goods have to be transported from the places where they are made to the places where people can buy or use them. Getting people to buy the goods is called **marketing.** Americans have been inventive, in both transportation and marketing.

TRANSPORTING AMERICA'S GOODS

In such a vast land as the United States, transportation has always been important. Early in our history, the American people learned that a good system of transportation was necessary to bring together, or unify, the nation. As a result, young America went through a long period of road, canal, and railroad building. This made it possible for American businesses and industries to transport their goods to all parts of the country.

American industry was greatly aided by the growth of railroads. Railroads that fanned out all over the country helped to create a single huge market for products. Long freight trains rolled from coast to coast carrying raw materials, machine tools, standard parts, and countless goods and products. The railroads brought up-to-date products to every American city, to most towns, and within reach of all farms. They brought business people a means of rapid travel and communication.

RAILROAD TRANSPORTATION TODAY

The railroads were America's chief method of transporting passengers and freight for nearly a century. In the mid-1900's, railroads found it difficult to compete with other means of transportation—trucks, buses, automobiles, and airplanes. In the 1960's and 1970's, many railroads went bankrupt. It looked as if railroad transportation in the United States would come to a halt.

But railroads are an important part of our transportation system. They are needed to carry bulk cargo such as coal, steel, and grain. And they give people jobs. To try and save the railroads, Congress created a new national rail passenger system called **Amtrak.** It was organized with funds from the national government and began running in 1971. In 1976, Congress acted to save vast stretches of freight tracks in the Northeast. It sponsored **Conrail,** or the Consolidated Rail Corporation. Conrail combined several bankrupt railroads.

Some experts think that our railroads cannot become profitable unless they modernize. The tracks and equipment of many railroad lines are in poor condition. Also, our trains are not as speedy as more modern trains in some countries. For example, the Metroliner travels between New York and

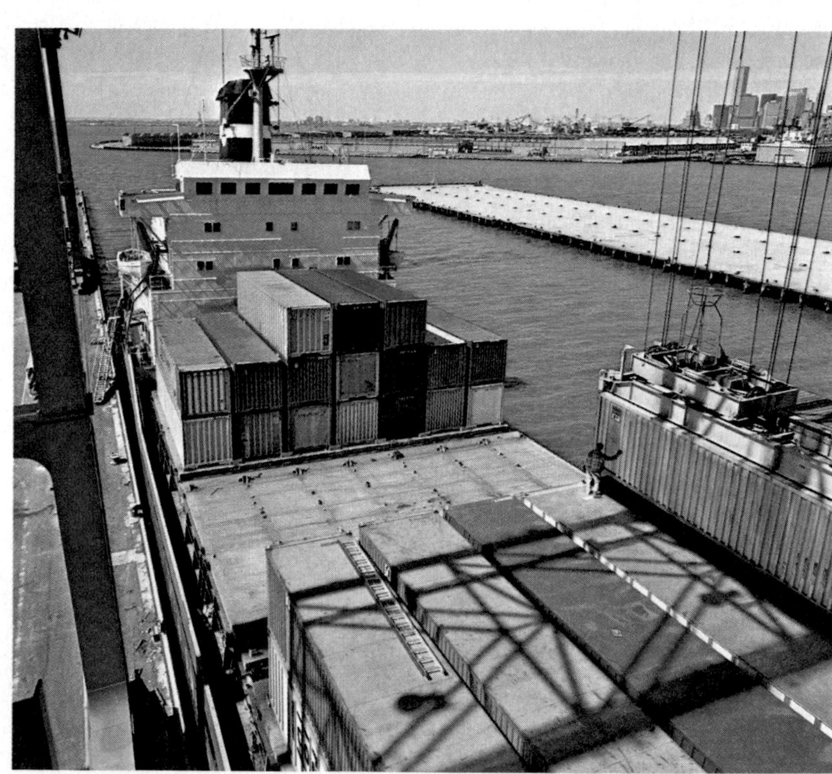

This modern ship carries its cargo in special containers. These containers can be lifted off the ship directly onto railroad cars or trailer trucks.

Washington, D.C., at speeds of up to 144 kilometers (90 miles) an hour. But modern trains in Japan, France, and Iran travel at speeds of 160 to 200 kilometers (100 to 125 miles) an hour.

AIR TRANSPORTATION

Today, railroads must compete with other forms of transportation. In passenger transportation, the airlines have grown rapidly. In 1950, railroads carried over 6 percent of the passengers traveling between cities. Airlines carried less than 2 percent. By the late 1970's, the airlines had over 10 percent of passenger traffic. The railroads had less than 1 percent. Modern research, equipment, and management methods have made America's airlines among the best and safest in the world.

Airlines now carry all first-class mail between American cities. They are also important in transporting freight. Airlines can transport all kinds of freight—from small packages to large industrial machinery, tractors, and autos—with great speed.

AMERICA'S HIGHWAY SYSTEM

The automobile is America's leading means of transportation. Private automobiles carry over 86 percent of all passengers—more than all other kinds of transportation combined. More than 134 million cars, trucks, and buses are registered in the United States. That is about one vehicle for every two persons.

Rapid highway transportation depends upon good roads. To speed motor traffic, our nation has built a great highway system. We now have more than 6.1 million kilometers (3.8 million miles) of roads. Some of them are **toll roads.** On these roads, drivers must pay a toll, or fee, to use them. Other roads are **freeways,** which are free of charge. More and more of the recently built roads are **limited-access superhighways.** Limited access means that cars can enter the highways only at certain points. Superhighways have several lanes and high speed limits. The Interstate Highway System built at public expense, is now nearly complete. It provides a network of highways that reaches every part of the nation.

Buses, cars, and trucks can be seen on our highways at all hours. Cars create the heaviest traffic. Large hired trucks carry 36 percent of the nation's freight. Another 24 percent is transported by private trucks. Heavy traffic on highways and roads has caused a number of problems. Among them are traffic jams, accidents, air pollution, and the heavy use of oil—a non-renewable resource. Among the steps that are now being taken to solve these problems are lower speed limits, non-polluting cars, smaller cars, and better mass transportation.

MASS MARKETING

Mass marketing means selling goods in large quantities. This kind of large-scale selling is well-illustrated by the modern **supermarket.** The supermarket is a huge store that sells hundreds of different kinds of products of nearly every brand. At first, the supermarket was mainly a food store. Now it also sells drugs, auto supplies, phonograph records, clothes, hardware, and many other products. The customer pushes a cart up and down the aisles, selecting articles from well-stocked shelves. When the customer has finished shopping, he or she rolls the cart to the "checkout" counter. There a cashier rings up the purchases on a cash register.

This type of marketing is called **self-service.** It is an efficient and inexpensive way to sell goods because it is labor-saving. Self-service is a fairly new method of marketing. Fifty years ago, storekeepers hired clerks to sell their goods. But storekeepers had to pay their clerks salaries. To make up for the money spent in salaries, storekeepers charged more for products.

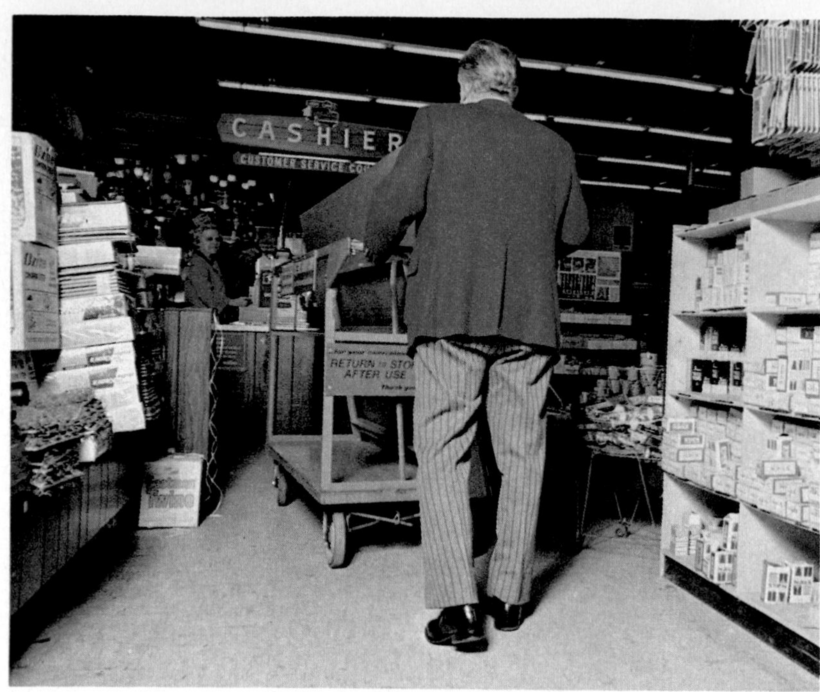

Many Americans today buy their food in supermarkets. Other kinds of supermarkets are becoming common, too. Here, a shopper selects the lumber and hardware supplies he needs, then takes them to the cashier.

Standard packaging also adds to the efficiency of the self-service system of marketing. Goods come from the factory already wrapped. Crackers, for instance, are sealed in "dual wrappers" and sold in boxes. Sugar comes in boxes or bags or different weights. Steaks, chops, and other meats are cut in popular sizes and wrapped in plastic. Years ago, crackers came in a barrel. They were weighed out for each customer. Sugar also was scooped out of a barrel. It was poured into a paper bag and weighed for each customer. Today few items have to be weighed or measured.

Another feature of mass marketing is the **one-price system.** This means that the selling price is stamped on every item. The one-price system was first used by Wanamaker's department store in Philadelphia more than 100 years ago. Now it is standard everywhere. Before the one-price system, customers often bargained with salespeople to try to get the price down a little. Imagine the amount of time a shopper would spend in buying the week's groceries if the bargaining system were used today.

SHOPPING MALLS AND SHOPPING CENTERS

An outgrowth of the supermarket has been the shopping mall or shopping center. This is a large cluster of stores, partly or completely surrounded by a large parking area. The center of the mall or shopping center is usually a food supermarket or a large department store. Nearby there will also be a drug supermarket, dry cleaner, hardware store, service station, restaurant, and a dozen or more stores and shops of other kinds. This is highly efficient marketing, because customers can drive in, park their cars, and buy almost everything they need. Because so many goods are being sold so rapidly in the shopping center, many stores can afford to sell them at lower prices.

CHAIN STORES AND SMALL RETAIL STORES

Many of the stores in a shopping mall or center are chain stores. A **chain store** is a store owned and operated by a company that has many stores. The company may purchase its goods directly from the factory or farm. Or it may own its own factory or farm. Because it buys or produces goods in large quantities, the chain can get its products at lower cost.

Many stores are independents. That is, they do not belong to a chain of stores. Many such stores are **specialty shops.** They sell only certain kinds of goods or offer a particular kind of service. They may sell special brands of women's clothing, or books of all publishers, or men's clothing.

These small, independent stores often offer special services that bigger stores usually do not offer. Their prices may be higher than those of larger stores. But some customers are willing to pay higher prices to get the special services. Small stores may take orders by telephone and deliver directly to the customer's door. They may sell on credit. That way a family can pay its bill once a week or once a month. Smaller stores often handle special products for which there is not a great demand. These locally owned stores are important to most communities. The business people who own and operate them make an important contribution to the prosperity of any community.

WHOLESALERS AND RETAILERS

Products often pass through several hands from the time they leave the factory and the time they reach the customer. A factory often sells goods in large quantities to a **wholesaler.** This business person owns a large warehouse where goods can be stored. The wholesaler sells to **retailers.** A **retail store** is one that sells directly to the public.

Wholesalers are often called **distributors.** They perform a service between the factory and the retailer. In the end, of course, the customer must pay for this service. Chain stores, large department stores, and supermarkets often have their own warehouses. Thus they have no need for distributors. And sometimes they can offer goods at lower prices to the public.

The distribution and marketing of goods, whatever methods are used, cost a great deal of money. Sometimes, it costs as much to market a product as it did to make it in the first place. Inefficient marketing adds to the price you pay for a product. Just as in mass production, efficiency in mass distribution reduces the prices of the things you buy.

ADVERTISING

Mass marketing of goods would not be possible without advertising. Advertising speeds up the movement of goods from factory to public. It tells people about new products, and makes some of them want to buy these products. Thus, in the competition between producers of similar products, advertising often makes the difference between the success of one product and the failure of another. Some people say this is bad. They say it would be better and less wasteful not to have so many products. Others say that competition among mass producers, mass marketers, and mass advertisers helps to keep quality high and prices low.

National advertising makes it possible for producers to sell their products all over the country. They do this by getting people to recognize their products by their **brand name.** This is called **brand identification.** When customers shop, they may choose a product with a brand name that they have heard about most favorably or most often. By using national advertising, small producers can grow into large, national producers. Thus, they can mass produce for a larger market at lower costs.

As producers, marketers, and advertisers go about their business, they sometimes do not tell the truth about their products—or not the whole truth. In the next section you can learn how to sort out the things they say and do. You can learn how you, as a consumer, can get good value for your money in the American system of mass production and mass marketing.

CONSIDER AND DISCUSS

Identify. distribution / transportation / marketing / Amtrak / Conrail / toll roads / freeways / limited-access superhighways / mass marketing / supermarket / self-service / standard packaging / one-price system / chain store / specialty shops / wholesaler / retailer / distributors / brand name / brand identification

Review. 1. What are the two sides of distribution? 2. How did the growth of our railroads affect business? 3. How are goods transported today? 4. Name some features of modern supermarkets? 5. What is the role of advertising in American business?

Discuss. What kind of store do you prefer to shop in—a supermarket or a small local store? Why?

3 You, the Consumer

Each of us is a **consumer,** or customer. A consumer is one who buys or uses products and services. As consumers, we play an extremely important part in the American free economy. Each year, America's business firms spend billions of dollars to get us to buy their products. They run advertisements in newspapers and magazines, on billboards and posters, over radio and television. They think up clever slogans that they hope we will remember. They know that some of us will buy the product whose slogan appeals to us. Often the slogan has nothing to do with the quality of the product.

Some shoppers are **impulse buyers.** They buy just because they see something they think they want. They like the slogan or the advertising skit on television. So they buy the product. They buy without thinking about the price or about the real usefulness of the product. Other people buy intelligently. Anyone can learn to buy intelligently.

LEARNING WHERE AND WHEN TO BUY

There are a number of ways in which consumers can get the most for their shopping dollars. For example, wise food shoppers study the food advertisements in the local paper. They find out which stores are having special sales. At certain times of the year, chicken may be priced very low. At other times, certain fruits and vegetables may be bargains.

By watching for sales, you can often buy suits, dresses, slacks, socks, shirts, blouses, neckties, and other articles at reduced prices. Some people never pay the full price for an article. They stock up when the price is low.

A low price on an item, however, does not always mean that the item is a bargain. Furniture, automobiles, television sets, and even houses are often advertised as bargains. But a bargain is not a bargain if it is something you cannot really use, or if it is poorly made. And it is not a bargain if the one you have is just as good as a new one.

HOW TO JUDGE PRICE AND QUALITY

Wise shoppers must be able to judge the quality of a product. They also must know how they plan to use the product. Out of the many goods and services available, shoppers must make sure that they choose those that are

This modern shopping center is located in California. Here a family can do all its shopping in one place. The attractive setting also makes it a nice place to meet friends and neighbors.

best-suited to their own needs. Many consumers solve the problem by shopping only at well-known stores that guarantee the quality of anything they sell. Others learn how to shop around at various stores and to look for real bargains.

Many people buy articles by brand name. They trust certain business firms. And they believe that all products bearing the brand names of these firms must be of good quality. This may or may not be true. Large, nationwide firms, as you have read, sell their products under brand names. They spend billions of dollars making consumers aware of these names. One way you can be sure of the quality of a product is to study its label carefully.

HOW TO STUDY LABELS

Labels are placed on foods, clothing, and other articles in order to protect you, the consumer. Our governments require that certain kinds of information be included in these labels to help consumers judge the quality of the products they wish to buy.

There are a number of federal laws on labeling. The Food, Drug, and Cosmetic Act requires that all packages of food, as well as drugs and some cosmetics, must state all of the things these products contain. The Wool Products Act requires that the label on clothing state how much wool it contains. Manufacturers must also state the name of the fabric in every garment, whether wool, cotton, or artificial fiber. They must also tell how to clean it. The Fur Products Labeling Act requires that a maker of a fur garment state from what animal the fur was taken and from what country the fur came.

Some of our state and local governments require that every package of meat must carry information about its contents. If it is hamburger, for example, it must name the part of the animal from which the ground meat comes. It also must state whether anything besides meat has been added. Some

Continued on page 303

Protecting the Consumer

A woman in Chicago, Illinois, bought a late-model used car for $2,500. Later, she found out that the engine block was cracked and the automatic transmission was faulty.

A family in Las Vegas, Nevada, bought a new color television set. A few months later, it shorted out and started smoking. The repairer told them it was put together badly, and some of the parts were missing.

A woman in Baltimore, Maryland, bought two pillows marked "washable." When she washed one, it fell apart in the washing machine.

Has anything like this ever happened to you or your family? Do you know anyone who has been "taken in" by a misleading advertisement, or a fast-talking salesperson? Try to give some examples of your own.

WHAT DO YOU THINK?

All of us are consumers. We buy the goods that other people produce and sell. We have the right to choose whichever products we want to buy, as long as we can pay for them. If a product sells well, it will make a profit. If people refuse to buy a product, the producers will lose money. They will have to stop making that product, or make it more attractive, or perhaps lower the price. In this way, our economic system is supposed to serve the consumer.

But how do we decide which goods to buy? Frozen foods are handy. But what is really in them? Are they safe to eat? Are they nutritious? Which brands are better? You like a certain pair of slacks. What are they made of? Will they shrink or fade? How long will they last? You go to buy a bicycle. You like its looks and the way it rides. But is it well-built? How safe are the brakes and the steering? Will it be in and out of the repair shop? Is it really worth the price? Your car breaks down. Does it really need a major overhaul? Or does it just have a loose wire?

Most consumers simply cannot answer questions like these. We cannot be experts on everything. Our choices are so wide. And today's products are so complicated. We are even more confused by the way things are packaged and advertised. We need information in order to make our choices. But most of our information is what the sellers want to tell us about their own products. Are they telling the truth? Are they telling the whole story? We are left at the mercy of advertisers, salesclerks, and repairers.

A number of laws have been passed to protect the consumer. The Pure Food and Drug Act and the Meat Inspection Act were first passed in 1906. They set up minimum standards of health and safety. The Federal Trade Commission was established in 1914. It helps to protect us against fraud and false claims. Most states also have laws to protect the public.

Congress passed a number of new laws in the 1960's and 1970's. The Truth in Lending Law requires that anyone who offers a loan or credit must state clearly the full cost. Many people used to pay huge amounts of interest without knowing it. The Truth in Packaging Law forbids misleading pictures or names on packages. A label cannot say "juice," for example, if it is only a fruit-flavored drink. The Auto Safety Law sets standards for all cars made in this country or imported. Congress also established the Consumer Product Safety Commission to prevent businesses from making products that can cause injuries.

Are these laws enough? Many people do not think so. They believe that the individual consumer is still at a great disadvantage. Companies can still get away with selling inferior goods and services. What can consumers do to protect their interests better?

Consumers around the country have begun to lobby their government for more protection. Ralph Nader, for example, wrote a book attacking car manufacturers for building cars that were unsafe. This started a whole campaign for auto safety. "Nader's Raiders," his group of active pro-consumer lawyers, have since become involved in many other consumer issues. Another active group is the Consumers Union. Its magazine, *Consumer Reports,* reports on its own tests of many different products and brands. Almost 2 million people buy this magazine.

What do consumer groups want? Above all, they want clear, honest information about the products

they buy. Only then can consumers make intelligent choices. They believe that the people who make and sell goods should be responsible for providing this information. Thus, for example, they want all ingredients to be spelled out on packages—including chemical additives. They want the nutritional content of all foods printed on the labels. They want food packages to be dated to show freshness—openly, not in a secret code. Some companies are beginning to do these things on their own. Do you think other companies should be required to do the same? Are these demands unfair to producers or sellers?

Consumer groups also want easier ways of comparing prices among different brands and sizes of the same product. A large supermarket, for example, might easily carry 25 brands of cereal in several different sizes. Suppose one brand cost 69 cents for 227 grams (8 ounces), and $1.05 for 425 grams (15 ounces). Another brand of cereal is 79 cents for 340 grams (12 ounces). Which box of cereal is the best buy? Imagine asking yourself this question about every brand and size on the shelf. Yet this is the kind of problem that is faced by consumers across the nation every day.

For this reason, many people favor "unit pricing." The unit price is the price of an item per pound, or any other standard unit. Thus, in the example above, the first box of cereal costs $1.38 cents per pound (454 grams). The second box costs $1.12 per pound, and the third box costs $1.05 per pound. Now can you tell which is the best buy?

In some places, supermarkets are required to post unit prices. Other supermarkets post unit prices anyway, as a service to their customers. Does your local supermarket or grocery store use unit prices? Does it seem like a good idea? Would it work for other kinds of stores? Why or why not?

A number of government agencies have been set up to help protect the consumer. These include the Consumer Product Safety Commission, and many state and local agencies. If you feel you have been cheated, do you know where to go for help?

How much control do consumers have over the quality of goods and services they receive? Should the government set stricter standards of quality? What other ways can you think of to strengthen the rights of consumers?

laws require **unit pricing.** That is, the price tag must show how much money a unit—a gram or an ounce, for example—is being asked. A can of peaches with 283 grams (ten ounces) in the can would be a better buy than a can at the same price with only 227 grams (eight ounces). Also, a can with fewer peaches and more syrup would not be as good a buy as one with less syrup and more peaches, even if the weight marked on the can was the same.

Unless people are able to read labels intelligently, the labels will be of no help to them. Beware of such a term as "highest quality." These words sound good. But they often have no real meaning. A label that states that a piece of clothing is "pre-shrunk" means little. The label does not tell you how much the piece of clothing is likely to shrink when it is washed. But if the label says "Sanforized," you know that it will not shrink more than 1 percent. The word "Sanforized" is a standardized term in the clothing industry that has this meaning.

SOME ORGANIZATIONS THAT AID CONSUMERS

Sometimes people find that a product has been falsely labeled or advertised. They or anyone who comes across any unfair business practices, should get in touch with the **Better Business Bureau.** There is one in or near most communities. This organization is ready to give advice and assistance to people who feel that they have been cheated or treated unfairly by a business firm.

The federal government also protects the consumer in a number of ways. The Federal Trade Commission has the power to bring to court any business firm that uses false or misleading advertising or false labeling. The National Bureau of Standards tests and grades many products. Manufacturers are required to give this information on their labels. The Department of Agriculture inspects and grades meat, poultry, and certain other foods sold in interstate commerce. The United States Postal Service sees that business firms do not use the mails to cheat the public. And, as you have read, the Consumer Product Safety Commission checks products to see if they will cause injuries.

A number of cities have also established Commissioners or Departments of Consumer Affairs. The duties of these officials are to publish consumer advice. They also warn business firms if they violate consumer laws. The firms are brought to court if they persist in cheating consumers.

There are a number of private organizations that help consumers. For example, there are consumer organizations that test and rate nearly every product the public buys. These organizations publish the results of their tests in magazines and special reports. Among such consumer organizations are Consumer's Research and Consumers Union. A trip to the library to examine their publications may help you to compare various brands of the same product. In this way you can learn which is the best buy and which is best for your own needs.

PAY NOW OR LATER?

When you buy something, you may pay cash. You also may charge it. Or you may buy it on the installment plan. Just what are the advantages and disadvantages in buying merchandise in these three ways?

The man or woman who pays cash is likely to be a careful buyer. Since the buyer must pay the full amount at the time of purchase, he or she is likely to think carefully before handing the money to the clerk. Also, a person with cash is sometimes in a better bargaining position than someone who has to rely on credit. He or she may be able to make a lower cash offer for some product or service just at the time when the seller needs some ready money.

On the other hand, suppose you find a real bargain on something that you need. But you do not have the ready money to pay for it. At such times, a charge account can be of help. A **charge account** is an easy form of credit that stores grant to many of their customers. A charge account can usually be obtained by people who have a steady job and who have a record of paying their bills on time. A charge account permits customers to make their purchases during the month. But they don't have to pay for them until the end of the month, or whenever they get the bill from the store.

If customers fail to pay the bill when it is due, the store may close their charge account. Such customers become bad credit risks. As a result, they may find it difficult to obtain a charge account somewhere else. Stores compare information about customers. This enables them to find out whether a person is a good credit risk.

PROS AND CONS OF CHARGE ACCOUNTS

There are advantages to using charge accounts. What are some of them?

A charge account makes it easy for you to keep track of what you have bought and what you paid for various articles. You do not have to carry large amounts of cash with you when you go shopping. If you have a charge account, it is easier for you to return purchases you decide you do not want. Charge account customers often receive notices of sales before the sales are advertised in the local newspapers.

Most important, when you have charge accounts and pay your bills regularly, you establish a good credit rating for yourself. A **credit rating** tells how well customers pay their bills. A good credit rating is valuable when you want to open other charge accounts, take out a bank loan, or buy a house.

There are also disadvantages in having a charge account. What are some of them?

Charge account customers often pick up the phone and order what they want without shopping around for the best values. They may buy things on impulse that they do not need. They may find themselves paying more for what they buy. Stores that sell for cash often sell for less because they do not have to hire clerks or pay for computers to keep charge account records. But, stores that allow charge accounts often charge interest on unpaid balances. If the bill is not paid by the due date (usually 10 to 30 days after the customer receives the bill), many stores add 1.5 percent of the unpaid balance to the bill. This comes out to an interest rate of 18 percent per year! The federal **Truth in Lending Law** now requires stores to print this kind of information on their bills.

BUYING ON THE INSTALLMENT PLAN

Another way that consumers can buy goods without paying the full amount in cash when they make their purchases is to use the **installment plan.** In this system of buying, the buyer uses cash to pay part of the purchase price. This is called the **down payment.** The buyer then pays the rest, called the **balance,** in small equal payments, or **installments,** over a period of weeks or months.

Automobiles, refrigerators, furniture, and other large items are often bought on the installment plan. The purchaser signs a written contract with the seller. The contract states how much the installment payments must be and how often they must be paid. It also states that the article still belongs to the seller. If the customer does not complete the necessary number of installment payments, the seller can take the article back, or **repossess** it. When this happens, the purchaser loses the article. He or she also loses the amount of money that has already been paid.

Buying an article on the installment plan increases its cost. In addition to the regular price, a **carrying charge** as well as interest on the unpaid balance is included in the installments. If you should ever think of buying something on the installment plan, you may find it cheaper to borrow the money from a bank. You can then pay cash for the article and pay the bank back in installments. This is called **installment credit.** Banks usually charge only interest, and not an additional carrying charge, for installment loans. The interest paid to the bank may be less than the combined carrying charge and interest under an installment-plan contract.

Whether you buy under an installment plan or installment credit, it is wise to make as large a down payment as possible for any article you buy. It is better to pay off the balance as quickly as possible.

CONSIDER AND DISCUSS

Identify. consumer / impulse buyer / unit pricing / Better Business Bureau / charge account / credit rating / Truth in Lending Law / installment plan / down payment / balance / repossess / carrying charge / installment credit

Review. 1. How can consumers shop wisely? 2. What is the possible advantage of buying brand names? 3. What can a label tell you? 4. What organizations help consumers get a fair deal? 5. What are the advantages and disadvantages of installment buying?

Discuss. If you were going to buy a used car, what steps would you take to make sure you were getting a good buy?

CHAPTER
Summary

The American system of mass production makes it possible for the American people to enjoy a high standard of living. This standard of living depends upon the variety of goods and services people can buy.

Mass production is made possible by large machines, standard parts, and division of labor. It needs great sources of power to run the machines. These elements of mass production are organized in an assembly line on which the products flow as they are manufactured.

Another essential feature of our free economy is mass marketing. Railroads, trucks, ships, and planes transport goods from factories, farms, and warehouses. They take them to places where consumers can buy them. Our mass marketing system includes many kinds of stores and service organizations. And it requires the labor of many workers.

As consumers, or customers, each of us has an important role to play in our economy. By knowing how to judge price and quality, and buying wisely, we help manufacturers and retailers to know how they can serve us best. By making use of the consumer organizations that serve us, and by learning the best ways to pay for goods, whether by cash or credit, we get good value for our money.

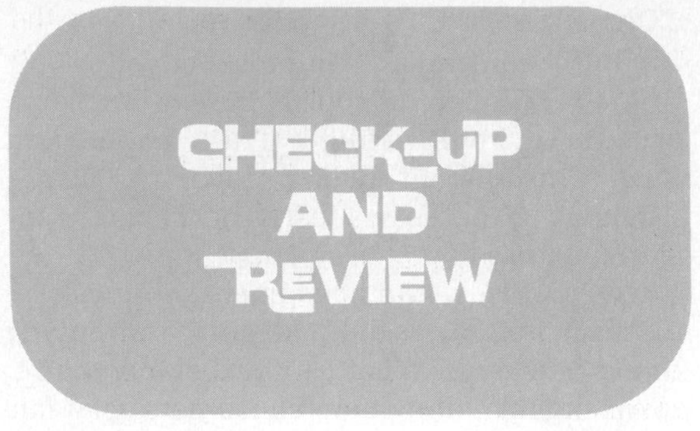

VOCABULARY

In learning "How Our Goods Are Produced and Marketed," you were introduced to a number of important words. Get to know these words better by using them in sentences. Write a sentence for each of the following words:

unit pricing	machine tools
Gross National Product	standard parts
mass production	assembly line
retail store	wholesale
distributors	consumer
installment plan	credit rating

CHECK-UP

Write out your answers to each of the following questions, and copy the questions and answers in your notebook.

1. What is meant by the term *Gross National Product*?
2. Why is Eli Whitney sometimes given credit for starting mass production?
3. How has our national system of transportation changed in recent years?
4. Why can chain stores sell articles cheaper than small local stores? How do some small stores stay in business?
5. How does the wholesaler serve our economy?
6. What is the danger in being an impulse buyer?
7. What are the main advantages and disadvantages in installment buying?
8. Give some rules for wise buying.

CITIZENSHIP AND YOU

Many features of the American business system can be studied in your own community. Others require investigation through research and reading. Below are some activities that will help you to understand our free economy.

1. Class Projects

Visit a state or local museum to find examples of early hand tools and machinery. What do they tell you about early manufacturing methods?

Invite a member of your local consumer agency to address the class. Have the speaker inform you about the agency's activities, and about some things consumers should be aware of when buying.

Hold an open-forum debate on this topic: *Resolved,* That installment buying is a danger to family finances.

2. Group or Committee Projects

Divide the class into committees to visit local industries, wholesale markets, retail stores, trucking firms, and the chamber of commerce. The committees should investigate and report on local methods of production and marketing. Some features that can be investigated are: mass production, distribution and marketing, self-service stores, standard packaging, the use of credit, and installment buying. The reports may be made in writing or by panel discussions.

A display of local products may be arranged. Each person contributing to the exhibit should be prepared to tell how his or her local product is manufactured. The source of the material used to make it, and the marketing methods used to get the product to customers should also be known.

3. Individual Projects

Cartoons may be prepared to show how the four factors of production come together to make a product or to provide a service.

Draw sketches or collect photographs for a bulletin-board display on the history of transportation in America.

On an outline map of the United States, show the principal highways, air routes, waterways, and railroads used in distributing goods.

Prepare a report on the contribution of one of the following to American economic growth: Henry Ford, Andrew Carnegie, John D. Rockefeller, Ellen Demorest, George Westinghouse, Thomas Edison, J. P. Morgan, F. W. Woolworth, Sara Hale, Eli Whitney, Cyrus McCormick, or Samuel Morse.

CIVICS SKILLS

WORKING IN GROUPS

In this chapter and in the other chapters of this textbook, activities have been suggested that involve groups and committees. Working with others does more than give you an opportunity to learn about a subject. It also gives you a chance to practice the skill of cooperation. If all the members of the group do their share and each member helps the others, more can be accomplished than if each member works alone. The same is true in many of the group activities that Americans carry on at local, state, and national levels. An important part of our American way of life is the skillful way in which our citizens work together for the common good.

Committees for some class activities may be made up of students with special abilities to get certain jobs done. Once the group or committee has been set up, it should be organized with a chairperson and a secretary.

The chairperson should be a student who is a good leader. The requirements for leadership vary as the group undertakes different activities. For example, a person with skills in art may be an effective group leader when the committee is arranging an artistic display. For another activity, some other member of the group might be a better leader.

One of the qualifications for secretary is the ability to express ideas clearly and correctly. A secretary must also be someone who can be relied on to do work promptly and neatly.

After a group has been organized, it should decide upon its goals. The group should agree on exactly what it wants to do. Then the job should be divided so that each member of the group is responsible for a certain part of the task. A time limit should be set for completing the project. And all members should try to meet their part of the assignment on time.

When all members have done their work as well as time will permit, the group can prepare its report. Try an interesting new way to report to the class. Illustrations, exhibits, tape recordings, chalkboard outlines, and charts will add to the group's report and help the class to learn from its findings. The group or committee should try hard to organize its material in a clear and logical way. There is real satisfaction in group work if it is done well.

PRACTICING YOUR CIVICS SKILLS

Have the class form several committees to visit local supermarkets. Each committee should visit a different supermarket. Committee members should see if the store uses unit pricing and if perishable products such as milk, meat, etc., are dated. They also should check prices for several food items such as carrots, cereal, applesauce, and others. Members should check to see if the store is kept clean, if shelves are well stocked, and if specials advertised in the newspapers are available. Each committee can prepare a report. The class can compare their findings on local supermarkets. Which store do you think is best? Why?

CHAPTER

Introduction

In this chapter you will read about a subject that is always interesting — money! Money is one of the most useful ideas ever invented by humans. Without it the high productivity of our modern economy would not be possible. The whole process of mass production, marketing, and consumption would grind to a halt. Without money, we would have to depend on *barter.* Barter was used in the early societies before money became the worldwide basis of trade.

Barter — swapping one product for another — was often difficult. Suppose that you are a shoemaker living in the early days when barter was the principal method of trade. You have more shoes than you can use because you spend most of your time making shoes. How can you obtain other things you need? You will have to swap shoes for them. You take several pairs of shoes and set out for the marketplace. You may need flour, bacon, a new shirt, a bolt of cloth to make into dresses, and a broom. When you get to the market, you find a tailor with shirts to sell. But the tailor does not want any shoes. Next you meet a miller. The miller has flour packed in huge sacks, when all you want is a small sack of flour. The miller is willing to trade a huge sack of flour for all of your shoes. After thinking it over, you agree to the trade.

You now try to trade flour for the things you want. You trade some of the flour for a broom. You meet a butcher who has a supply of bacon, but who doesn't want any flour. The butcher would like to trade some bacon for some pottery. So you hurry around the market place to find someone who has pottery and who needs flour. Then you return to the butcher and exchange the pottery for the bacon you need.

By this time it is late evening, and the market is closing. You are too tired to do anything about finding a bolt of cloth or a shirt. As you return home, tired and discouraged, you think there must be a better way of doing business. In this chapter, as you read about the following topics, you will learn how money, banking, investment, and insurance contribute to better ways of handling financial affairs.

1. Money and Credit
2. Banks and Banking in America
3. Saving and Investing
4. Insurance Against Hardship

CHAPTER

16 How Americans Manage Their Money

1 Money and Credit

At different times and in different places people have used many different things for money. Cows, pigs, guns, playing cards, hides, furs, olive oil, big stones, knives, tobacco, copper, iron, wampum beads, shells, rings, silver, and diamonds have all been used for money. During World War II, American soldiers stationed in Europe used chocolate bars for money. They used chocolate because in several nations the official paper money was worthless. Chocolate bars were valuable because people wanted chocolate and would accept it in payment for goods and services.

WHAT IS MONEY?

The use of chocolate bars for money helps you to understand what money really is. Money is something that sellers will take in exchange for whatever they have to sell. Buyers can exchange it for whatever they want to buy. **Money** is a **medium (or means) of exchange.**

To a banker, the term "money" may include checks, bank accounts, and other kinds of writing on pieces of paper. You will read later about some of these kinds of money. For now, start thinking about the "jingling money" and "folding money" that people carry in their pockets or purses. Another name sometimes used for these kinds of money is **currency.**

This is the casting platform where coins are made at the Philadelphia Mint.

Paper bills and coins do not get their value as means of exchange just because the government prints them or stamps them out of metal. Money in these forms has value only because it will buy something. For a nation's currency to be worth something, the nation's economy must produce something for its people to buy. One reason America can produce so much, as you read in Chapter 15, is that American citizens are able to buy what is produced. American currency is also valuable in the world's markets because America as a nation produces so much.

EVERY COUNTRY HAS ITS CURRENCY

Every nation has its own supply of currency. In all nations, currency is alike in four important ways. What are the four common features of currency?

1. Currency must be easy to carry and must take up little space. People must be able to carry it with them for everyday use.
2. Currency must be based on a system of units that are easy to multiply and divide. That is, it should not take too long to figure out the number of coins and bills needed to exchange for any article.
3. Currency must be durable, or last a long time. It should not wear out too quickly, or fall apart. People must be able to keep currency until they are ready to spend it.
4. Currency must be made in a standard form and be guaranteed by the nation's government. In this way, all people can be certain that their coins and bills will be accepted by everyone else in exchange for goods and services.

The currency used by Americans is issued, or made, by the federal government. All United States paper money and coins are considered **legal tender.** That is, the law requires that every American accept this money as payment in exchange for all goods and services.

UNITED STATES COINS

You may remember that one of the weaknesses of the government under the Articles of Confederation was its lack of a standard currency. The Constitution solved this weakness by granting to Congress the sole right "To coin money, regulating the value thereof . . . ." In 1792 a **mint,** or special plant where coins are made, was established in Philadelphia. There are now two other mints, in Denver and in San Francisco.

Coins are sometimes called "hard money" because they are usually made of hard metal.

Newly minted coins are being counted by a coin-counting machine at a government mint.

In the United States, five principal coins are used: pennies, nickels, dimes, quarters, and half dollars. These coins are parts of one dollar. A quarter is one-fourth of a dollar. Coins worth one dollar are also minted. But they have not been used often.

For years, the value of a coin was decided by the amount of metal it contained. A silver dollar, for example, would yield about a dollar's worth of silver when melted down. In the past, many Americans would accept only hard money. They thought it was more valuable and reliable than paper money. Today, about 1 percent of our total money supply is in coins. Coins are used mainly for small purchases or for making change. Further, there is no gold or silver in today's coins. The government stopped issuing gold coins in 1934. In 1965, all silver was removed from quarters and dimes. Five years later all silver was removed from silver dollars and half dollars. All coins are now made of an alloy, or mixture, of 75 percent copper and 25 percent nickel.

Why do Americans accept coins that are not made of gold or silver? They accept them because they have faith in the United States government. They know that the coins will be accepted as legal tender when they are presented at stores, banks, or elsewhere. They also know that the government has a supply of gold and silver **bullion,** or bars. It is kept in a depository at Fort Knox, Kentucky. This bullion is used to pay our debts with foreign nations. It also helps to strengthen our nation's financial position.

UNITED STATES PAPER MONEY

Almost all of the money issued by the government today is paper money. It is printed at the Bureau of Engraving and Printing of the Treasury Department, which is in Washington, D.C. All bills are printed there in denominations, or amounts, of $1, $2, $5, $10, $20, $50, and $100. Bills in denominations of $500, $1,000, $5,000, and $10,000 are no longer issued, although some of them are still around.

Today, nearly all of our paper money is in the form of Federal Reserve Bank notes. "Silver certificates" were once issued, as were "gold certificates" before 1934. This meant that the federal government promised at any time to **redeem,** or pay, the amount of the bill in silver or gold. But the government found that it does not have to make this guarantee to the American people for its money to be accepted by them.

CHECKBOOK MONEY

Very little of what is bought and sold in the United States is paid for in either coin or paper money—the currency you have been reading about. Many Americans make greater use of another kind of money. This is the money represented by checks. A **check** is a written and signed order to a bank to pay a sum of money from a checking account to the person or firm named on the check.

Most of our total money supply is in the form of bank deposits. Bank deposits are the figures in a checking account or savings account. These figures represent the amount of credit in a person's or business firm's account. **Credit** is what the bank owes the person or the firm. The person or business firm spends money out of this account by writing a check.

The check is just a piece of paper. It is not legal tender because it is not guaranteed by the federal government. But most sellers will accept a check that has been written by a responsible person or firm. The person or firm who writes the check has built up the account by depositing checks—such as paychecks, for example—from other persons or firms. Because of the wide use of this kind of credit, many people never see most of their money. What they mainly see is a row of figures the bank sends them. These figures tell them how much credit they have in their bank account.

CHARGE ACCOUNTS AND CREDIT CARDS

As you read in Chapter 15, a charge account is a method by which a store extends credit to its customers. Customers can walk into the store and buy an item. They do not pay for it at that time. The store adds the price of the item to their charge account. At the end of a month, the store sends them a bill. This is a list of figures telling them how much they owe for what they bought.

The customer writes a check, payable to the store, for this amount. The store deposits the check in its own bank, which sends the check to the customer's bank. The customer's bank subtracts the amount from the customer's bank account. It then sends its own check to the store's bank. No one has seen any currency. (Banks do not collect from one another check by check. They use large collection agencies that handle many checks.)

Credit cards, like checks, are a substitute for money. Credit cards are issued by banks and other business firms that specialize in this kind of service. People get credit cards by applying for them in much the same way as they obtain charge accounts. But in this case, hundreds, sometimes thousands, of stores and other businesses throughout the country will accept the credit card in place of currency or checks. The customer shows the card. The store charges the credit card company. The credit card company pays the store and charges the customer. The customer pays all the credit card charges in one check at the end of a month. Again, no currency has changed hands.

CREDIT IN BUSINESS

Credit is used instead of currency in most sales involving large amounts of goods. Wholesale grocers may order half a truckload of canned goods, for example. They promise to pay for this order at the end of the month or, sometimes, within 90 days. Because they have good credit, the wholesalers can get the canned goods right away. If they can sell the canned goods before their debt is due, they will have the money they need to repay their debt.

Credit gives wholesalers a chance to do a larger amount of business than they could do if they had to pay for the canned goods immediately. But credit is sometimes used unwisely. Suppose business people use credit more often than they should. When the time comes for them to pay their bills, they find themselves in trouble. They cannot pay the bills they piled up by using credit. Then their **creditors** —those they owe money to—may force them to sell their businesses to pay their debts.

CREDIT IN THE FAMILY

Credit can also be an advantage to the average American family if used wisely. Emergencies occur in most families. Or sometimes a product or service is needed immediately. The family washing machine, for example, may break down. A new one may be needed. If the family does not have the money (or the balance in the bank) to pay for it, a new washing machine can usually be obtained on credit.

If the family plans to pay for the machine within a few weeks, they need only **short-term credit.** On the other hand, the family may need several months to pay. If so, they will plan to pay a certain amount each month until the total has been paid. This **long-term credit,** as you know, is also called **installment credit.** Most American families use this kind of credit to make large purchases, such as homes, automobiles, or furniture.

Like some business people, families may use credit unwisely. Suppose that a family buys so many things on credit that it cannot afford to meet the payments. What will happen? The stores will take back their products. And the family will lose all the money it has already paid for the products. It is easy to see why a family must plan ahead when it uses credit.

CREDIT IN THE OVERALL ECONOMY

Credit, as you have seen, plays several important roles in the buying and selling that goes on all of the time in America's free market. It also plays an important role in the successful operation of the economy as a whole.

In a healthy economic system, the supply of money must increase or decrease in relation to the general condition of the economy. When production picks up and business is brisk, there must be plenty of money available. Otherwise, goods that are produced cannot be sold. Production would have to slow down again. Free-flowing money in the form of credit makes it possible for customers to buy whenever there are goods to be sold.

If there is too much money available when production slacks off, prices may go too high. That would happen because there would be more money to spend than there were goods to buy. Customers would try to outbid each other to get the limited supply of goods. But with our credit system, when production slacks off, banks extend less credit to customers. Buying slacks off.

Our American society is made up, for the most part, of honest people. As a result, the widespread use of credit has become possible as a means of exchange. If buyers and sellers could not trust each other, credit would not be possible.

CONSIDER AND DISCUSS

Identify. barter / money / medium of exchange / currency / legal tender / mint / coins / bullion / redeem / check / credit / credit card / creditor / short-term credit / long-term credit / installment credit

Review. 1. What are four common features of money? 2. What is checkbook money? 3. How does our system of credit work?

Discuss. How can a family use credit to its best advantage? Give some examples.

THE COMPUTER AND YOU
THE COMPUTER AND YOU

WHAT DO YOU THINK?

Imagine a huge central information storage center in Washington, D.C. In an enormous computer is stored all kinds of information about you, your family, and every other American. At the touch of a button, the computer will print out a complete "data profile" of you or anyone else. This would probably include your age, your family, your medical history, your school record, employment record, income, loans and bank accounts, the cars you own, insurance claims, and any arrests or other trouble in your past. It might also include your friends, the magazines you subscribe to, organizations you belong to, and many other kinds of information.

What do you think of the idea of a "national data bank" like this? Today's computer technology makes it quite possible. Some people think it would be a good idea to collect all this information and have it easily available in one place. Other people believe this would be extremely dangerous to our individual rights and freedoms.

Even now, various companies, government agencies, and credit bureaus have files on nearly every American over 18. A national data bank would carry all this information gathering a step further. Every American would be assigned a number at birth. This number would be used on everything—birth certificate, school files, driver's license, tax returns, charge accounts, library cards, personal checks, everything. The central computer would open a new "file" in its memory bank, under that number, when you were born. Then all of the information now collected by different government and private agencies—and more—could be recorded in this one central file.

The great attraction of this system is that it would be simple, central, and efficient. If an insurance company wanted to know your medical history or your driving record, for example, they could just punch in your number. The computer would immediately give them the information they needed. For this reason, it is favored by many companies, banks, and government agencies.

A central computer data system is also favored by many law enforcement agencies. They could have on file complete information on every citizen, with picture, physical description, and fingerprints. Clues in any criminal case could be fed into the computer to obtain a list of possible suspects.

National security officials also like the idea of a national data bank. The computer could store information about what people say and do. It could keep track of what organizations they belong to, who their friends are, and what meetings or demonstrations they attend. This would give any government agency a record of all citizens who might be considered suspicious.

Can you see any dangers in the idea of a national data bank? Does it threaten our right to privacy? What about freedom of speech and assembly? Would it give the government, and even private companies, too much control over our lives?

Some Americans are strongly opposed to the idea of a central computer data system. They see it as the perfect tool of totalitarianism, or dictatorship government. If government officials know all the details of our lives, how much privacy or freedom will we have left? Would people really feel free to speak their minds? Would they be afraid to be seen with certain people, or to borrow certain books from the library? Would they always have the feeling that someone is watching them?

Who would have access to all this information? How much does your employer or your bank have a right to know about you? Could a business competitor, or even a personal enemy, get access to your file? These are very serious questions. To many people, the whole idea of a national data bank sounds much too dangerous.

What about mistakes? Information fed into the computer might not be accurate. Or it might not tell the whole story. This is already a problem with credit bureaus today. Credit investigators do not have time to check the facts they are given. They accept what other people say about you. What if a bank teller looks up the wrong account? What if someone has a grudge against you? Mistakes can also be made when this information is coded and punched into the computer. Who would know? You could be denied a job or a mortgage on your house because of something in your file, and never even know why. You would have no way of defending yourself against "accusations" made by the computer.

How do you feel about a national data bank now? Does it still seem like a good idea? What safeguards can you suggest? Are these enough to protect the rights of individuals? Do you think the advantages of a central computer would be worth the risks? Or would the dangers of such a computer be too great?

2 Banks and Banking in America

A thousand years ago, money was a problem just as it is for many people today. In fact, money was almost as much of a problem for the rich as for the poor. People with money had a difficult time finding a safe place to keep it. If they carried a large amount of money with them, thieves might steal it. Even if they put the money in a secret hiding place in their homes, the money might not be safe.

HOW BANKING BEGAN

In most communities, however, there were people who kept their wealth strongly guarded. These people were goldsmiths who made articles out of gold and had strong safes. It became common for the goldsmiths to do their neighbors a favor by allowing them to keep money in their safes. Soon other people in the towns began to bring their money to the goldsmiths for safekeeping. Before long, local goldsmiths found themselves in the money-keeping business. And they began to charge a small fee for performing this service.

It was a natural next step for the local goldsmith to become a money lender. The townspeople who needed money began to come to the goldsmith for loans. They asked for money for their businesses or to help them meet emergencies. In return for the loans, they signed a paper promising to repay the money within a certain time. They also promised to pay an added sum called **interest** for the use of the money.

People who borrowed money had to give some guarantee that they would repay the loan. Borrowers who owned property had to promise to give it to the money lender if they could not pay their loan when it was due. Property that is used to guarantee that a loan will be repaid is called **collateral.**

These practices that were started by the early money lenders, as well as many other later business practices, developed into the banking system we know today.

WHAT IS A BANK?

Banks are among the most familiar buildings in every American town and city. But they are more than buildings. A **bank** is a business firm that deals in money and credit. A bank takes the deposits of some of its customers, usually in the form of checks and other kinds of credit. It makes loans to other customers, usually in the form of checks or of credits, to their checking accounts. By law, it always has more money on deposit than on loan. This extra money is invested. On these investments the bank may receive dividends or interest. In addition, it also gets interest from the customers to whom it makes loans.

If a bank is chartered to do business under state laws, it is a **state bank.** If it is chartered under federal laws, it is a **national bank.** In order to get a charter, a bank must have enough capital to do business. It also must operate in accordance with either state or national laws. Like other business firms, a bank has a board of directors, officers, and stockholders.

TWO KINDS OF BANKS

There are two main kinds of banks in America, savings banks and commercial banks. In the past, savings banks sought small, interest-paying accounts. Commercial banks stressed checking accounts. Today, however, the difference between these banks is not as great.

Savings banks put the deposits of their customers into savings accounts. In the 1970's, many savings banks began to offer checking services to their customers. These services were often free of charge.

The **commercial bank** puts the deposits of most of its customers in checking ac-

Most Americans find it necessary to use the many services provided by banks. Which bank services do you and your family use?

counts, which, as you know, form the basis for checkbook money. It then makes loans to businesses and individuals. Most commercial banks also have savings departments. And many have trust departments that help customers manage property and invest money. Many commercial banks now offer free checking services to people who keep a certain amount of money on account. Some also offer interest on checking account balances.

The money that depositors put in a checking account is called a **demand deposit.** That is, the account is payable on demand. This means that the bank must give depositors their money any time the depositors request it by writing a check.

The money that depositors put in a savings account is a **time deposit.** Depositors may be required to give the bank advance notice when they wish to withdraw their money. But most banks do not require advance notice of withdrawals from regular savings accounts. On certain types of time deposits, which pay higher interest rates, money may be withdrawn at the end of a 90-day period. In some cases it must stay in the account from two to six years.

From long experience, banks have found that only a certain number of depositors will want their money at any one time. Banks, therefore, keep enough money in reserve to pay the few who will want to withdraw it. The amount of reserve money that banks must keep is fixed by law.

GEORGE MCCLAIN GETS A BANK LOAN

What really happens when a person borrows money from a bank? Consider the example of George McClain, a young man who owns and operates a gas station. George needs $5,000 to purchase some new equipment. He goes to a commercial bank and asks to speak to one of the bank's officers. The bank official listens to George and tells him that the bank will probably make the loan. George must show that he is a good credit risk.

George then brings in his business records. They show that his gas station is a profitable business. He also points out that he owns his own home, a car, and a boat, and that he has no large business debts. In this way, George McClain convinces the bank that he will be able to repay the loan when it is due. The bank then agrees to make the loan and to consider George's house as the collateral, or guarantee, for the loan.

Many loans made by commercial banks are **short-term loans.** They are to be paid back in 30 days, 60 days, or 90 days. George McClain receives a short-term loan of $5,000, due in 90 days. However, George does not receive any currency or even a check. What he gets is a credit in his checking account. But he does not get the full $5,000 credit. The bank takes out, say, $100 in advance as the interest it is charging for the loan. George McClain receives a credit of $4,900 in his checking account. Taking out, or deducting, the interest on a loan in advance is called **discounting.**

After he receives his loan, George McClain buys his new equipment. He pays for it by check. His gas station can now offer better service. And George begins to take in more money. The equipment company, richer now by George's borrowed credit, uses the money to expand its business. In fact, with George's check and the checks of other customers coming in, the equipment company may borrow money from a commercial bank for its own expansion. In this way, credit circulates, or moves around, and grows throughout the American economy. Each transaction makes other transactions possible.

GEORGE MC CLAIN RENEWS HIS LOAN

What happens when the loan is due at the end of the 90-day period? If George's business has done well enough, he can now repay the loan. But suppose the new equipment was late in arriving, or business did not increase quite as fast as expected. George may have to go to the bank and ask that his loan be renewed, or continued, so that he will not have to repay it for another 90 days.

Usually a bank will renew a loan to a person like George McClain whose credit is good. George, of course, will have to pay interest again on the loan renewal. However, if the bank officials think that George has not done a good job of managing his business with his new equipment, they may decide he is no longer a good risk. They may refuse to renew the loan. In this case, George must find some way to repay the loan at once. In order to save his house, which is the collateral for his loan, he may have to sell his car and his boat. Or he may even have to sell his business. As you can see, a loan involves a risk both for the bank and for the person who borrows the money.

GOVERNMENT REGULATION OF THE BANKING SYSTEM

There was a time when banks were allowed to do business just about as they wished. They sometimes loaned money without enough collateral. They sometimes did not keep enough money in reserve. Under these conditions, rumors might spread that the bank was shaky. Sometimes depositors would start a **run on the bank.** When so many depositors withdrew their money that the bank had no funds left, other depositors lost their money.

In the early days of our nation, bank failures happened so often that the federal government finally stepped in with a plan to regulate banking. In 1913, Congress established the **Federal Reserve System.** It required all national banks to belong to this system. State banks might join if they wished, and many did.

THE FEDERAL RESERVE SYSTEM

By now, most American banks belong to the Federal Reserve System. It regulates banking in America. This is the way the system is set up. The nation is divided into 12 Federal Reserve Districts. There is one large Federal Reserve Bank in each district. The Federal Reserve Banks do not do business with individuals or business firms. They serve only the federal government and the banks that are members of the Federal Reserve System.

The Federal Reserve Banks serve two main purposes. First, the federal government uses these banks to handle its own banking needs. The Secretary of the Treasury deposits the funds of the United States government in these banks. Then the Secretary writes checks on the federal government's account, just as an individual does who has a checking account. The Federal Reserve Banks also handle the sale of bonds issued by the government. Most United States currency, both paper money and coins, is put into circulation through the Federal Reserve System.

Second, the Federal Reserve Banks provide important services to the state and national banks that are members of the Federal Reserve System. Member banks are required by law to set aside a part of their depositors' money. This is called their **reserve.** Each bank must deposit its reserve in the Federal Reserve Bank that serves its Federal Reserve District. The total amount of money that a bank may lend depends upon the size of its reserves on deposit in the Federal Reserve Bank.

The Federal Reserve System is managed by a Board of Governors. The **Federal Reserve Board of Governors** consists of seven members appointed by the President, and approved by the Senate, for a 14-year term. The Board of Governors makes most of the major decisions for the Federal Reserve System.

A healthy economy must have enough money and credit in circulation, but not too much. The Federal Reserve Board decides, from time to time, how large a part of their funds member banks must set aside in reserve. When the Board increases this amount, banks have less money to lend. When the Board decreases the amount of the reserve, banks have more money to lend. This makes it easier for business firms and individuals to get loans. In this way, the Federal Reserve System can act to slow up the economy when that seems wise. Or it can speed it up when it is needed.

CONSIDER AND DISCUSS

Identify. interest / collateral / bank / state bank / national bank / savings bank / commercial bank / demand deposit / time deposit / short-term loan / discounting / run on the bank / Federal Reserve System / reserve / Federal Reserve Board of Governors

Review. 1. How did the banking business start? 2. What is the difference between a state and a national bank? 3. Tell how a person obtains a bank loan. 4. How does the Federal Reserve System work?

Discuss. How do banks stimulate business?

3 Saving and Investing

Most of us want money in order to spend it. But we do not have to spend it right away. One of the features of money is that it can be kept and spent at some future time. Most people try to keep some money in case they have unexpected expenses. Keeping money by setting it aside is called **saving.**

WHY PEOPLE SAVE

Almost everyone saves, or tries to do so. A family tries to put aside money for their children's education or to buy a house. Many people save money for their retirement years. And most families save money to meet emergencies, such as medical and hospital bills, loss of a job, or other unexpected difficulties. Saving is a part of knowing how to manage money wisely. Individual American citizens together have nearly $90 billion in savings. There are, as you will read, several ways to save money.

Some kinds of saving make it possible for many Americans to get together enough money to pay for expensive items, such as vacations, clothing, and household appliances. True, the American credit system allows us to obtain expensive goods and services without paying cash for them. But even in our credit system, the customer often must make a fairly large **down payment.** The largest purchases most persons ever make are houses and cars. To buy a house, you must first pay a sizable part of the total cost as a down payment. Builders may advertise, "Only 10 percent down—pay the rest as rent." But 10 percent of the cost of a $35,000 house is $3,500. The average family has to save a long time to accumulate $3,500.

The used-car dealer may advertise, "No money down, drive it home today!" But without a down payment, the monthly payments on the car may be higher than the buyer can afford. The smaller the down payment, the greater the amount of interest. And the larger the monthly payments. The extra interest will also make the total cost of the car greater. No doubt about it, learning to save, and practicing saving throughout life, can be useful to a person or a family.

HOW PEOPLE SAVE

There are various ways to save money, of course. You can hide your money under a mattress, put it in a cookie jar, or keep it in a piggy bank. Most Americans find that there are better ways to save money.

1. Many Americans save by putting money in the bank. They put aside a regular amount each week in a savings account at a bank. Or, whenever they make extra

Different Ways of Saving

SAVINGS ACCOUNTS
Regular Savings Account
Christmas Club Account
Special Savings Accounts

STOCKS AND BONDS
Government Bonds
Corporation Stocks
Corporation Bonds

INSURANCE
Life
Automobile
Fire and Theft
Endowment
Accident

The New York Stock Exchange is one of the largest stock exchanges in the world. Orders to buy and sell stocks are carried out on the trading floor, shown above.

money, they put it in their savings account instead of spending it. The bank pays interest on money deposited in a savings account. By saving in this way, a person's money earns more money for him or her. The money is always there to be withdrawn when it is needed.

Similar to a savings bank is a **savings and loan association.** This institution pays interest on money that savers deposit. It lends money mostly to people who are buying houses. Another way to save is in a **credit association.** Many business firms have credit associations. There, employees can save regularly and, when necessary, borrow money at a low rate of interest.

2. Many Americans save by buying bonds. You probably remember that when you buy a bond you are lending money to the business or government that issues the bond. When the bond reaches maturity, you get the money back. In the meantime, your money is earning interest. Agencies that issue bonds include the United States government, many state and local governments, and large corporations.

United States government bonds, as well as the bonds of most states, localities, and corporations, are a safe form of savings. Bondholders receive regular interest payments. But one form of bond, the United States Savings Bond, is different. A government savings bond bought for $75 earns $25 in interest after seven years and nine months. The purchaser who paid $75 gets back $100. Meantime, the buyer's money is safe—as safe as the government itself.

3. Some Americans save by buying stocks. You read about common stocks and preferred stocks in Chapter 14. There are

regular organizations that buy and sell stocks for their customers. They are called **brokerage houses.** The officials they employ are called **brokers.** Each brokerage house is a member of a **stock exchange.** Millions of shares of stock are bought and sold every working day at the stock exchange. By getting in touch with a brokerage house, anyone can buy stocks. To buy stocks, however, people need a great deal of knowledge about the stock market, for there are both safe stocks and risky stocks.

People who buy common stocks are taking a chance that their investment will earn more money—perhaps much more—than it would earn in a savings account or a bond purchase. Annual stock dividends may be higher than interest payments would be. Also, if the value of a stock rises in the stock exchange, the customer may sell that stock, take a profit, and buy a new stock. But the stock may pay small dividends or none at all. And its value on the stock market may fall.

To reduce the amount of risk in stock purchases, some people buy shares in **mutual funds.** These funds are managed by people who are familiar with stock market conditions. The mutual fund managers buy many different stocks. Thus, the risk in any one stock is not so great. By buying a share in a mutual fund, the purchaser owns a small piece of a large number of stocks.

4. Many Americans save by buying insurance. There are many kinds of insurance. Some of them are, in part, forms of saving. A private life insurance policy, for example, may be "surrendered" for its cash value after a number of years. You will read about different kinds of insurance in the next section.

SAVINGS IN OUR ECONOMY

Saving by individual citizens is absolutely necessary in our free economy. What happens to the nearly $90 billion that Americans have in savings accounts, bonds, stocks, and other forms of saving? That money is used to help expand our nation's economy. You have read that continued growth of production is considered important to a nation's economy. How is continued growth of production made possible? Continued growth is possible only if factories and other means of production are continually expanded. How does this happen? The means of production expand only when there is capital available to pay for new factories, machine tools, and other **capital goods.** You read about capital as one of the factors of production in Chapter 14.

Where does capital come from? It comes from savings. Suppose you have $10. You spend $5 of it and put the other $5 in a bank. The $5 you spend represents goods that you consume. That is, you spend the money for something you want. Whatever you buy, you use it up. You consume it. But the $5 you put in the bank you do not consume. It is money that can be used for another purpose. It can be invested. The bank can use this money to make loans to business people who need funds.

Saving and investing are not the same thing. Money in a piggy bank is saved. But it is not invested. Money that you deposit in a savings account in a bank is both saved and invested. It is saved by you. And it is invested by the bank. When you buy stocks and bonds, or put money into your own business, you are both saving and investing. When you invest, you turn money into capital. What the money buys is not consumed. It is used to produce goods and services. Thus, investing money results in the production of goods and services. This production, in turn, results in the making of more money, or, profits, as you may recall.

The ability of the American people to save large amounts of money, and the ability of our economic system to invest this money, helps to keep America prosperous. The ability of our free economy to raise large amounts of capital has made it possible for America's business firms to build huge factories to turn out vast amounts of goods.

Business firms also save in order to raise part of their own capital. The managers of most corporations put aside a certain part of their profits before they pay dividends to stockholders. This money is then put back into their businesses in the form of new capital. This new capital helps businesses to invest in new machines or to expand their factories. It also helps businesses to establish new branches or to add new lines of products to what they already produce. This new capital for expansion is in addition to the money that is set aside to replace older buildings and equipment when they wear out.

MAKING SAVING SAFE

When people put their money into a bank, they want to know that their money will be safe. They want to know that they will be able to get it back when they ask for it. Also, when people buy stocks or bonds, they want to feel that they are not taking unnecessary risks. It is more risky to buy stocks than to buy bonds, as you know. And both are more risky than depositing savings in a bank.

Saving Keeps Our Nation Prosperous

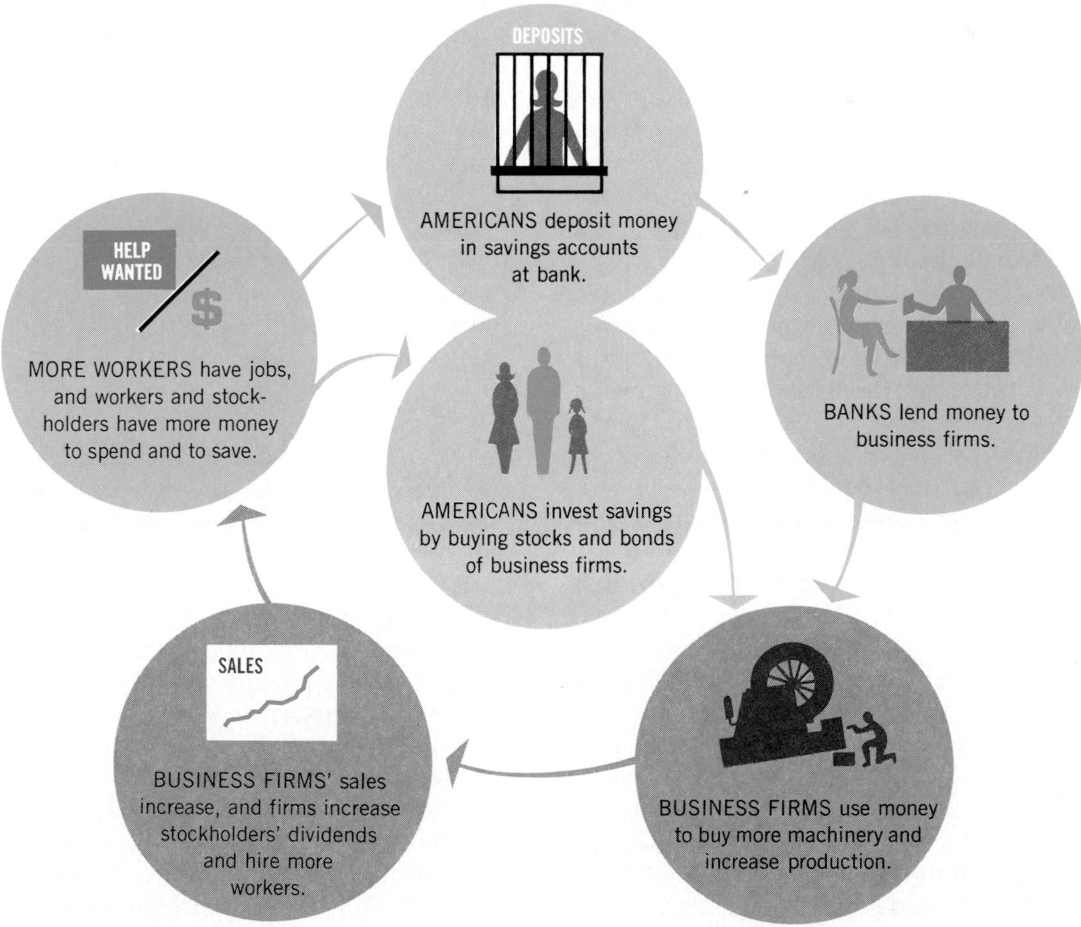
DEPOSITS
AMERICANS deposit money in savings accounts at bank.
BANKS lend money to business firms.
AMERICANS invest savings by buying stocks and bonds of business firms.
BUSINESS FIRMS use money to buy more machinery and increase production.
SALES
BUSINESS FIRMS' sales increase, and firms increase stockholders' dividends and hire more workers.
HELP WANTED
$
MORE WORKERS have jobs, and workers and stockholders have more money to spend and to save.

Even so, the purchaser of stocks does not want to take unnecessary risks. If a stock does not honestly represent a part ownership in the company issuing it, then the investor may be fooled and lose money.

For these reasons, our federal and state governments have passed laws to regulate the activities of those institutions that handle the savings of others. All banks must receive a state charter or a federal charter to operate. Our governments charter only banks that are properly organized and that have enough capital. After a bank is chartered, it is inspected regularly by state or federal officials. The bank's directors are held responsible for seeing to it that their bank obeys all banking laws. Also, you recall, all national and many state banks keep reserve funds in Federal Reserve Banks as required by the Federal Reserve Board.

In spite of these regulations, banks do sometimes fail. The officials of the bank may make unwise investments, and the bank is forced to close. What happens to the savings that people have deposited in a bank when the bank fails?

Most of such savings are now protected by the federal government. During the 1930's, many American banks closed their doors because business and industry were having difficult times. As a result, many depositors lost all or most of their savings. Congress then decided to take steps to protect bank depositors. It established a federal government agency that is called the **Federal Deposit Insurance Corporation (FDIC).**

You can tell whether your bank is a member of the Federal Deposit Insurance Corporation. It will say so on the window and in its advertising. Each bank that is insured by the FDIC contributes to an insurance fund held by the government. If any member bank fails, all depositors will be paid the amount of their deposits in the bank up to $40,000.

At about the same time that the FDIC was established by the federal government, the Securities and Exchange Commission (SEC) was given the responsibility for seeing that all offerings of stocks and bonds on the nation's stock exchanges were honest. At one time in our history, the public might be sold "watered-down" stock. This was stock that did not fully represent the value claimed for it. There were many other "stock dodges," or tricks, by which dishonest business people cheated the public. The regulations of the Securities and Exchange Commission have put a stop to such practices. The SEC constantly examines the practices of the nation's stock exchanges and of the brokers who buy and sell stock for the public.

All of America's savings organizations come under state or federal government supervision. Insurance companies are regulated by our state governments. Savings and loan associations are also regulated by state laws. Even company credit associations must allow government accountants to examine their books to be sure that they are being run properly. Since saving is so important to the prosperity of our nation, it is in the interest of the whole nation that individual savings be safeguarded.

CONSIDER AND DISCUSS

Identify. saving / down payment / savings and loan association / credit association / brokerage house / broker / stock exchange / mutual funds / capital goods / Federal Deposit Insurance Corporation

Review. 1. What are some of the reasons why people save? 2. What are some of the ways in which people save? 3. How do savings help business? 4. How does the federal government protect bank depositors? 5. Why do the state governments and the national government regulate lending agencies?

Discuss. A banker recently declared, "I don't see why I should have to pay FDIC insurance just because some bankers do not know how to run their business." Do you agree with the opinion of this banker? Why or why not?

4 Insurance Against Hardship

Life is full of risks and uncertainties. There is the chance of illness or accident. There is the possibility of losing one's job. A person's house could burn down or be destroyed by earthquake or flood. A motorist could be involved in an accident and be sued for thousands of dollars by someone injured in the accident. A father might die, leaving his widow with young children to support. And there is the uncertainty of old age, when one may not be able to work and earn a living.

Our economic system includes arrangements that protect people, at least in part, against such risks and uncertainties. These protections are called **insurance.** There is **private insurance** that individuals and companies choose to pay for. And, in the United States, there is insurance required by state and federal programs. This last type of insurance is called **social insurance.**

WHAT IS INSURANCE?

If you thought you might suffer a loss of $100,000 from some cause, would you be willing to pay a small sum—say $75 each year—just to make sure you didn't run this risk? That is what insurance is. It is a system of paying a small amount to avoid the risk of a large loss. The small amount that one pays for this protection is called the **premium.** Premiums may be paid yearly, or at regular times throughout the year. The large loss against which one is insured is called the **principal sum.** The contract that gives this kind of protection is called an **insurance policy.**

PRIVATE INSURANCE

There are many different kinds of private insurance companies. Altogether, they write insurance policies covering almost every possible kind of risk. Each company usually specializes in one or a few kinds of insurance.

How can insurance companies do what they do? How can they take such small amounts of money from people, yet pay them a large sum if hardship occurs to them? The reason is simple. Not everybody has a hardship. You may pay premiums on accident insurance all your life. Yet you may never collect a cent because you never have an accident. But you cannot be sure you will never have an accident. Most people consider it wise to buy insurance against such a risk.

A large insurance company has millions of policy holders who pay their small premiums regularly. Part of this money goes into a reserve fund. State laws specify how much of a reserve fund a company must maintain. The amount depends upon the kind of insurance the company issues, and the number of policy holders it has. When someone has a hardship of the type called for in the company's policies, payment of the principal sum is made out of the reserve fund. With millions of policy holders, there may be only a few thousand payments out of the reserve fund each year.

Except for money held in reserve funds, insurance companies invest the premiums they collect. They buy stocks and bonds, and make other forms of investment. The dividends, interest, and other income from these investments pay the expenses of these companies and earn profits for their shareholders. Their investments help provide the capital needed in our economy.

LIFE INSURANCE

One of the most valuable forms of insurance for a person to have is **life insurance.** The main purpose of life insurance is to provide money in case the policy holder dies early. In this way the family is protected from financial hardship. The person named in the policy to receive the money, in case of the policy holder's death, is called the **beneficiary.** It is wise for people to take out a life insurance policy when they are young. At an early age the premiums are smaller than at a later age.

Many different kinds of life insurance policies have been created by the insurance companies. Some, called **annuities,** provide retirement income for policy holders if they do not die early. People can take out **endowment policies** that pay the principal sum after a number of years. They can plan to receive the principal sum when their children are ready to enter college, for example. Business partners often take out life insurance policies on each other. In this way, if either dies, the other will have extra funds to run the business until another partner can be found.

INSURANCE AGAINST ACCIDENT AND SICKNESS

There are many forms of insurance that make regular payments to policy holders if they are injured in an accident or become too ill to work. **Accident insurance** may cover total disability or partial disability or both. Some policies cover all kinds of accidents—even breaking your leg from slipping on the soap in the bathtub. Other kinds of policies cover only accidents on "common carriers"—that is, on airplanes, trains, buses, and other means of public travel. In case of death, the beneficiary receives the principal sum.

Health insurance makes regular payments to policy holders when they cannot work because of illness not caused by an accident. Health insurance premiums are higher than accident insurance premiums because people are sick more often than they are injured.

Hospitalization insurance pays part of a policy holder's hospital expenses. Other insurance plans pay doctors' bills and other medical expenses. The familiar Blue Cross and Blue Shield are sponsored by the American Medical Association. The premiums for this kind of insurance are often paid in part by the policy holders and in part by their employers.

PROPERTY INSURANCE

For people who own a home, it is probably their greatest single investment. If the home should burn down, they would be financially ruined. For this reason, all homeowners carry some form of property insurance. **Fire insurance** is the most common form of property insurance. Americans take out fire insurance not only on their homes, but also on their factories, stores, offices, and other places of business.

Many homeowners take out what are called **homeowners' policies.** Such policies cover a person's home not only for fire, but for many other kinds of risk—windstorm, hail, flood, theft, burglary, and legal liability.

WHAT IS LIABILITY INSURANCE?

Suppose someone comes to your door on an icy day, and falls coming up the steps. As a result, the person breaks a leg and has to go to the hospital. You are legally liable, or responsible, because the accident happened on your property. No matter that you did not invite the person. No matter that you did not put the ice there. You might even have posted a sign by your door saying "Warning—Ice—Slippery." It makes no difference. You are legally liable for the injury to

How the Social Security Law Works

THE FEDERAL GOVERNMENT

administers

Retirement and Old-Age Insurance Program and Health Insurance Program

FEDERAL GOVERNMENT sets standards and makes contributions to

STATE GOVERNMENTS

administer and pay part of cost

Unemployment Insurance Program

Contributions by

Employer

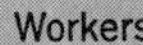

Workers

Self-employed workers

used for

Disability and Survivors' Payments

Retirement Payments

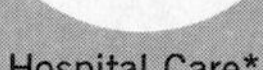

Hospital Care*

*A voluntary medical insurance plan also covers doctors' costs.

Contributions by

Employer

used for

Unemployment Insurance Benefits

Public Assistance Programs

Maternal and Child Health

Crippled Children

Child Welfare

Aid to the Aged

Aid to Dependent Children

Aid to the Blind

Aid to the Handicapped

Medical Assistance to the Aged

that person. He or she can sue you in court and collect payment called **damages.**

Liability insurance can protect property owners from high costs in cases of this kind. It can also save them the worry that something like this may happen.

AUTOMOBILE INSURANCE

The most common form of liability insurance is the kind that automobile owners buy to protect themselves. Automobile liability insurance covers automobile owners in case their cars kill or injure other people or damage property. Most automobile insurance policies also protect the owner from loss by fire and theft. Some states, such as New York, require all automobile owners to have liability insurance before they are able to register a car.

INSURANCE AGAINST DISHONESTY

Among the many kinds of private insurance are some that protect people against losses caused by burglars, embezzlers, and swindlers. Business firms, stores, banks, and homeowners carry burglary insurance. Banks and other businesses that deal in valuable documents carry forgery insurance. Forgery is the crime of falsely making or changing any check or other document. Companies that handle money pay to have their employees **bonded.** This means the company is repaid if an employee disappears with the company's money. Such policies also cover embezzling, which occurs when an officer steals from the company by making false entries in the company's records.

SOCIAL INSURANCE

The business failures of the 1930's caused much hardship and suffering among the American people. Many business firms and factories closed down. Millions of men and women lost their jobs. Banks failed, and thousands of persons lost their life savings. Money they had counted on for old age was gone.

To meet the problems of this troubled period, called the Great Depression, President Franklin D. Roosevelt and his advisers recommended many new laws. Congress passed most of them. Taken all together, these laws were called the New Deal. Some of the new laws brought immediate assistance to needy people. Some helped to get American business back on the road to prosperity. Some changed business practices that many people thought had helped bring on the Great Depression. Still other laws, looking to the future, offered protection to individual Americans against severe economic risks and hardships.

Government programs that are meant to protect individuals from future hardship are called social insurance. They take the idea of insurance that you have been reading about and make it compulsory for all, or most, of the nation's people. This way, almost everyone can receive its benefits.

An important program of social insurance was adopted by Congress and President Roosevelt in the Social Security Act of 1935. The act provides direct assistance to people who cannot work. As for people who can work, the act has two major parts: (1) Old Age and Survivors Insurance, and (2) Unemployment Insurance. In America these two kinds of insurance are often called **Social Security,** as you may recall.

OLD AGE AND SURVIVORS INSURANCE

The basic idea of Old Age and Survivors Insurance is this. During the years when workers earn money, they and their employers make contributions to a fund. This fund is called the social security trust fund. When workers retire, or if they become disabled and their earnings stop, they receive payments from the fund as long as they live.

If they die before retirement, their families receive payments. There is a payment for each child in the family under 18 years of age, and a payment for the widow or widower. Payments for children stop when they reach the age of 18. If they remain in school, the payments may continue until they are 22. The Social Security idea is a simple plan of paying a small amount each month while one works in order to get back cash benefits when they are most needed.

The monthly contributions under the Social Security Act are shared equally by workers and their employers. The contributions are actually a tax because they are compulsory. The program is compulsory because Congress wanted to make sure that as many Americans as possible would be spared some of the money problems they faced during the Great Depression. Since 1935, the program has been expanded from time to time. Coverage has been extended to workers in almost every industry, business, or profession. A person who is not employed by anyone, but who is a business owner or a member of a profession—a doctor, writer,

These older Americans are demonstrating to gain an increase in their Social Security payments. Does anyone in your family receive Social Security payments?

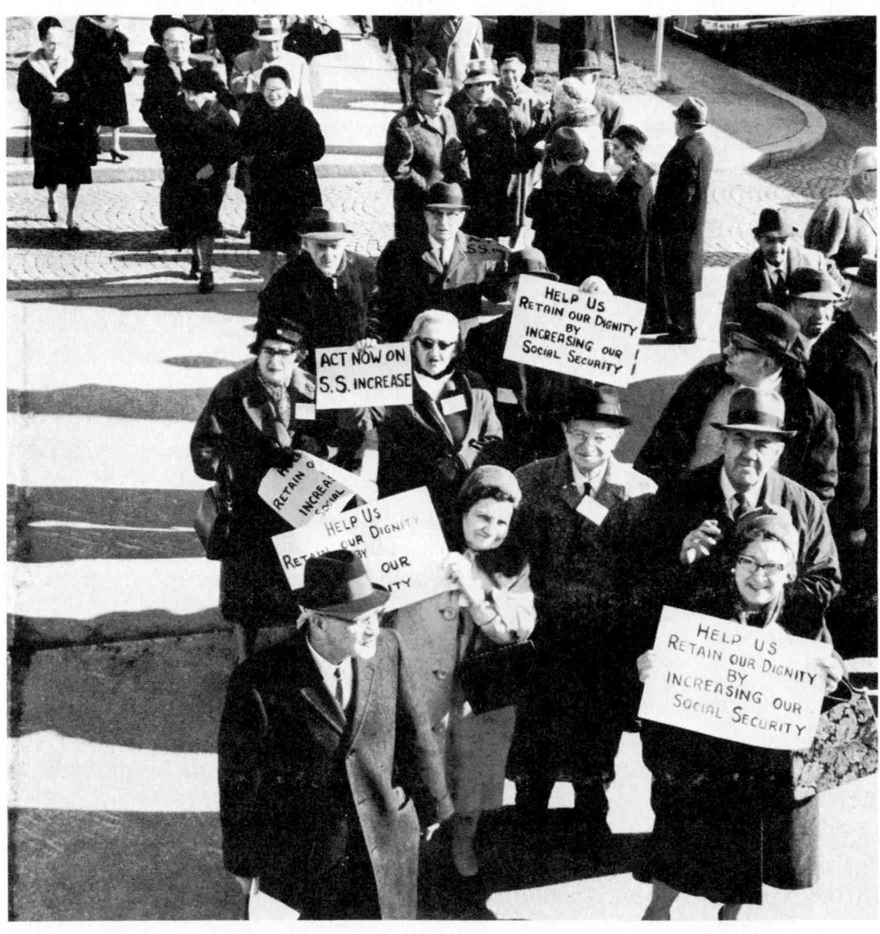

lawyer, or dentist—may also participate in the Social Security program. "Self-employed" people pay the whole contribution themselves.

Since 1935, the benefits paid by Social Security have gradually increased. So has the amount of the contribution. The amount that workers and their employers pay depends upon how much the workers earn a year. The amount workers receive upon retirement depends upon their average earnings over a long period of time. After retirement, the workers are paid a certain amount each month. Male workers also get an additional amount for their wives who are at retirement age. If the workers should then die, their wives continue to receive payments as long as they live. However, a wife who has worked and paid Social Security taxes is entitled to her own benefits. She may draw either her own benefits or part of her husband's—whichever is larger.

Benefits under Old Age and Survivors Insurance provide a cushion against the worst hardships caused by disability, death, or retirement of the wage earner. But the benefits are not large. Many people supplement their social insurance by buying private insurance of various kinds.

UNEMPLOYMENT INSURANCE

The problem of unemployment, or lack of jobs, was extremely serious when the Social Security Act was passed in 1935. At that time, between 12 and 15 million Americans were unemployed. Most of these people had lost their jobs because of the depression in the American economy. Most of them wanted to work but could not find jobs. The Social Security Act contained a plan for future difficulties of that kind—the unemployment insurance program.

Unemployment insurance operates in the following manner. When individuals lose their jobs they register at a nearby state employment office. Jobless workers report to the office to see if it can find them jobs. Businesses in the area call the state employment office when they have openings.

If they do not find a job right away, unemployed workers begin to receive unemployment benefits. The amount they receive a year varies from state to state. In most states, after waiting a week, jobless workers begin to receive payments. They continue to receive them until they find a job, or for 26 to 30 weeks at most. In areas of high unemployment, the payments are sometimes extended to 39 or more weeks. Unemployment benefits are not large. But they do help people to support themselves and their families while they are looking for work.

How is the unemployment insurance program paid for? Federal law requires all business firms that employ one worker or more to pay a tax to the federal government. During the 1970's, this tax was 3.2 percent of the first $4,200 paid to each employee in most states. An employer with a low unemployment rate may pay a lesser fee. States pay the unemployment benefits out of the sums collected by the federal government.

MEDICARE

The federal government has also set up programs to help Americans pay their medical expenses. In 1965 Congress passed the health insurance program known as **Medicare.** This program helps people 65 years of age and older to pay for hospital and nursing home care. The program also includes a voluntary medical insurance plan to help older citizens pay their doctor bills.

CONSIDER AND DISCUSS

Identify. insurance / private insurance / social insurance / premium / principal sum / insurance policy / life insurance / beneficiary / annuity / endowment policy / accident insurance / health insurance / hospitalization insurance / fire insurance / homeowners' policies / damages / liability insurance / bonded / Social Security / unemployment insurance / Medicare

Review. 1. Why is insurance important to the individual? 2. How can insurance companies cover a large risk for a small premium? 3. Name some of the principal kinds of private insurance and the purposes they serve. 4. In what major ways is social insurance different from private insurance?

Discuss. What kinds of insurance does the average American carry? Why?

CHAPTER
Summary

Money is a medium of exchange. We give it in return for goods and services. Modern money has no value in itself. We value it because the government guarantees it. We also value it because sellers will accept it in exchange for the things we want.

Very little of what is bought and sold is paid for by coins or paper money. Checks are written to pay for most of our trade. Banks play a key role in the process by paying by check. Banks are safe places in which to keep money. They also provide the checking service that transfers balances from one account to another when checks are written to pay for goods and services. Banks also aid business firms and individuals by making loans. In lending, a bank usually extends credit. The use of credit is very important to our economy.

The Federal Reserve System is an independent agency of our federal government. It regulates banking in our nation. Federal Reserve Banks are the banks for other banks. They help to regulate the use of credit in our economy by the amount of reserves they require other banks to keep on deposit. Federal Reserve Banks also are the banks in which the federal government keeps its funds.

When money is saved, it may be invested. That is, it may earn more money for the investor. Sometimes, however, the investor may lose the money if the investment is unwise. The money we put in savings banks is usually invested by the bank.

Our federal and state governments help to protect our savings and investments by regulating banks, insurance companies, and the sale of stocks and bonds. Insurance companies, as well as the federal government, issue policies that may help to protect us from most of the financial hazards of life. The forms of insurance include life, accident, health, hospitalization, liability, and unemployment insurance.

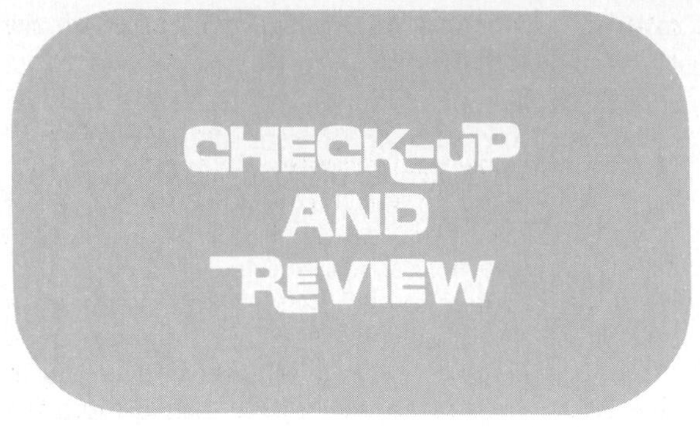

VOCABULARY

Listed below are a number of words that you have studied in this chapter. In your notebook or on a separate piece of paper, write three paragraphs using these words.

In the first paragraph, use and underline the following words:

barter	bullion
money	checks
coins	credit

In the second paragraph, sentences should contain these words:

collateral	Federal Reserve Bank
depositor	savings and loan association

These words should appear in the third paragraph:

saving	invest
insurance	capital

CHECK-UP

Try to answer each of the following questions fully without looking at your textbook. Then turn back to the book to check your answers and to see if you remembered most of the important facts and ideas.

1. What are four common features of currency?
2. What is the advantage of checkbook money over other forms of money? What is the principal disadvantage?
3. What gives our paper money its value?
4. How does credit help our American economy?
5. How is a bank chartered? What services do commercial banks and savings banks provide their customers?
6. What are some of the things that may happen to a dollar that is deposited in the bank?
7. Why is a Federal Reserve Bank sometimes called "a banker's bank"?
8. How does saving help to keep our economy prosperous?
9. How does the federal government help to make your bank savings safe?
10. How does insurance serve the individual? What are some important kinds of private insurance and social insurance?

CITIZENSHIP AND YOU

Here are some projects that will add to your understanding of money, banking, saving, investment, and insurance.

1. Class Projects

Discuss with your classmates your answers to the questions above in "Check-up."

Invite a banker to speak to your class about how the bank serves your community.

Hold a quiz show in which your class is divided into two equal teams. The teacher asks questions about money and banking of each team. If a team member cannot answer a question, then the next person on the other team may try to answer. Count one point for each correct answer. The quiz show ends after each team member has had a turn.

2. Group or Committee Projects

A group may prepare a picture chart explaining the four common features of currency.

Produce a sociodrama in which one student plays the role of the owner of a small business who comes to the bank for a loan. What questions will the business owner be asked? Under what terms will the bank give the owner a loan?

Prepare a map of the United States showing the 12 Federal Reserve Districts. Present this map to the class and explain how the Federal Reserve Banks serve their member banks.

3. Individual Projects

Write a brief essay setting forth a good plan for future savings. How much of your income do you plan to save? What would be a good way to invest your savings? What kinds of insurance will you probably pay for?

Prepare an oral report on the work of the Federal Deposit Insurance Corporation. Base this report on reading you have done.

Draw a poster or chart with a series of pictures showing some important events in the history of money.

Using statistics found in the *World Almanac* or a similar reference book, draw a graph entitled "Savings by Individuals in the United States." The graph may show growth of savings over a ten-year period. Or it may compare the ways in which people save.

CIVICS SKILLS

MAKING BOOK REPORTS

A number of the "Individual Projects" in this civics textbook have suggested reports on books. Book reports are required in many other classes. Therefore, making good book reports is a valuable skill to learn. A book report can be an interesting experience both for you and for the class.

A book report may serve several worthwhile purposes. First, it gives you an opportunity to share your findings with others. Second, a book report may stimulate others to read a book that has been found to be particularly helpful. Third, the book report may add facts, examples, and illustrations to subjects the class is studying. Fourth, new points of view and opinions often are introduced to the class.

In making a book report, remember to keep it brief. Don't try to relate all of the information or to summarize each chapter. Give the outstanding points made by the author. Describe some of the most interesting parts of the books so that others may want to read the book.

As you prepare your book report, keep your audience in mind. Take notes as you read. Then organize these notes to make them interesting to the class. Illustrate your report with quotations from the book if you find something especially worth quoting. Try, whenever possible, to summarize the author's main ideas. But make such summaries in your own words. Be sure, also, to give your reactions to what the author has written.

PRACTICING YOUR CIVIC SKILLS

Look through Chapter 17, "Our Economy Faces New Challenges," and choose a topic that interests you. Then go to the library and find a book that deals with this topic. Remember that you can choose several different kinds of books. For example, if you are interested in labor unions you might want to read a biography of a labor leader such as John L. Lewis or Samuel Gompers. If you are interested in the Depression, you could choose a novel that was written in the 1930's or about the 1930's, such as *The Grapes of Wrath* by John Steinbeck.

As you read, take notes on important ideas and interesting facts. Now organize your notes for an oral or written book report. Try starting your report with a startling or unusual fact. Try to tell the audience about the important ideas that the book contains. End your report by giving your own reaction to the book. Be ready to present your report to the class when the topic you chose is discussed in class.

CHAPTER

Introduction

The economy of the United States, the richest in the world, is filled with contradictions. While most Americans enjoy a high standard of living, some of our people live in poverty. Rundown city slums and shacks that lack heat, electricity, and running water stand in stark contrast to the city apartments and suburban homes of the middle class and the rich. The American economy, which in a single year produces over $2 trillion worth of goods and services, still has several million unemployed workers.

American farms produce record crops, yet there are people in our land who suffer from hunger. The stock market advances to new highs and then drops to new lows. Workers strike, wages go up. Yet prices rise and money buys less and less. Since World War II, the nation has spent so much on war and defense that there has not been enough money for many urgent needs at home. One great contradiction is that a nation with the wealth and know-how to send ships into space has not been able to solve the problems of poverty, unemployment, and inflation here on earth.

The problems and contradictions of American economic life are among the most important issues facing our nation. Our nation's leaders are well aware of how serious these problems are. During sessions of Congress, numerous bills are introduced to aid the poor, control inflation, assist the farmer, improve rural and urban housing, and stimulate employment. Many good laws have been passed, and some promising programs have been started. But, as you will learn, much more needs to be done before the problems of our economy are solved.

In this chapter you will consider four important challenges that face our economy:

1. Poverty in the Midst of Plenty
2. Problems of Labor and Management
3. The Farm Problem
4. Boom or Bust

CHAPTER

17 Our Economy Faces New Challenges

1 Poverty in the Midst of Plenty

Most people in the United States expect to live well. In this "Land of Opportunity," they believe that good jobs should be available to all who want them. They believe that wages and salaries should be high enough to enable workers and their families to eat and dress well, to live in comfortable homes, and to enjoy some of the **luxuries** that most Americans have come to expect.

A government report of the mid-1970's estimated that an average family of four living in a city or suburban area should have an income of nearly $6,000 a year in order to obtain the bare **necessities** of life. That meant that the family needed almost $6,000 each year just to pay for its food, clothing, and shelter.

THE MEANING OF POVERTY

What happens when a family's income is less than the minimum needed? The members of the family must do without certain necessities. Clothing must be made to last longer. The family may not eat as well as they should to stay healthy. Their housing may be below acceptable standards. When the family's income falls below minimum levels, they are in danger of hunger and cold. And many find it difficult just to stay alive.

People who do not have enough money

to afford the bare necessities of life live in **poverty.** They are the very poor. In the United States in the late 1970's, over 25 million Americans were living in poverty.

WHO ARE THE POOR?

There are some poor people in almost every part of our country. About 60 percent of the poor live in urban areas. Most of them live in inner-city areas. But there is poverty in rural areas too. Nearly half of all rural families are poor. Many Americans often do not see these poor people because their daily affairs do not take them into the inner city neighborhoods or into rural areas where poor people live.

The poor people are of all ages. Nearly half of them are under 21 years of age. They are the children of the poor. And their story is often sad. Born in poverty, they may drop out of school early. They may work only at low-paying jobs, if at all. Their own children may be raised in poverty. This passing along of poverty from one generation to the next is known as the **poverty cycle.**

Poverty is also one of the major problems of older people in our nation. Nearly 13 percent of the people over 65 years of age are poor. The payments made to them under our Social Security laws are not enough to live on.

The lower a person's income, the greater percentage of it he or she must spend just on necessities. Middle-class people spend about 65 percent of their incomes on necessities. But the poor must spend their entire incomes on them. Without sufficient income, poor people cannot take advantage of the "extra" benefits of American life. Most do not have adequate health care, educational opportunities, entertainment, automobiles, or television sets. They lack all the things that many people think of when they speak of the "American way of life."

The results of poverty are often boredom, hopelessness, and a loss of pride. Young people may turn to drugs or crime in an effort to escape from the world. The middle-aged poor know the worry of trying to get work and of not knowing where the next meal is coming from. They have trouble surviving from day to day. The elderly poor, instead of enjoying the so-called "golden years," often live them alone and in despair.

Poverty affects our entire economic system. People who might produce—and buy—goods and services do not do so. People who do work pay annual welfare bills of more than $25 billion in an effort to help the poor.

WHAT CAUSES POVERTY?

Among the causes of poverty are (1) lack of education or training for a job, (2) unemployment caused by changes in industry or slumps in the economy, (3) discrimination that denies job opportunities to a person because of race, religion, sex, or national origin, (4) misuse of an area's natural resources, and (5) old age, when people may have insufficient incomes along with illnesses that eat up life savings and take away the ability to work.

A visit to the poor section of almost any big American city shows examples of how the causes of poverty affect people. In the inner-city sections, one finds many black Americans and Spanish-speaking Americans who are poor. The percentage of unemployment is higher among these and some other minority groups than among other Americans. Such groups have suffered unfairly in many ways. Many cannot find jobs because they have not had the proper education and training. Many also have been excluded from certain kinds of well-paying jobs because of prejudice.

As one moves into rural areas—beyond the expressways and prosperous farmlands—a visitor finds many poor people. Among them are tenant farmers and sharecroppers, who do not own their own land. They pay a landowner for use of small pieces of land.

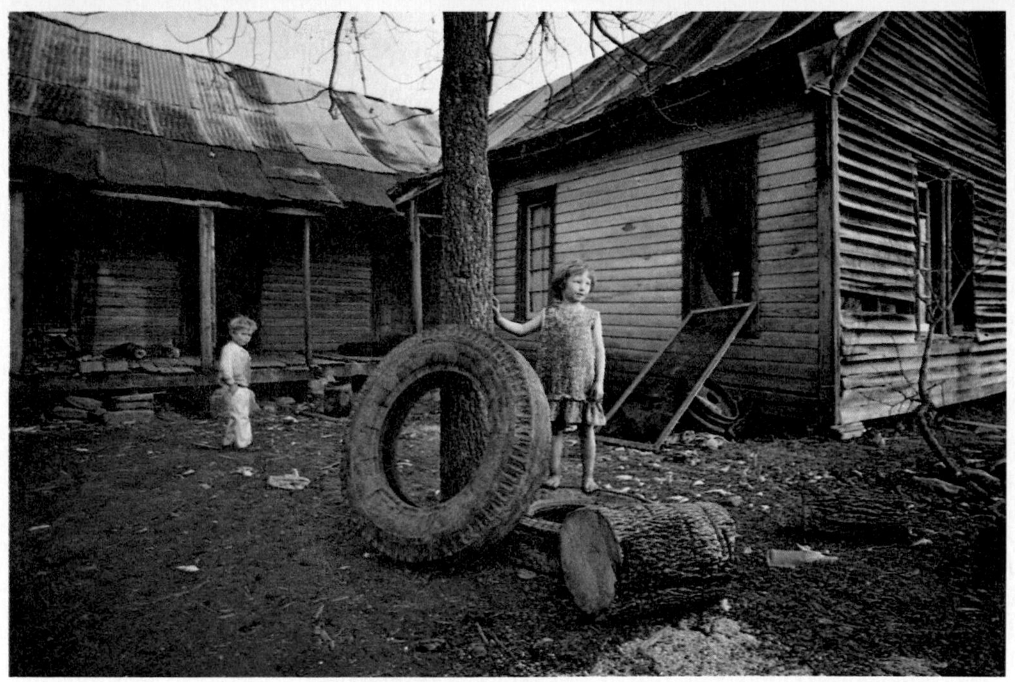

Over 25 million Americans live in poverty. One of the poverty pockets in the United States is located in Appalachia, where this picture was taken.

They pay either in cash rent or in a large share of the crops they grow. Many of these people who work on farms owned by others are among the poorest in our land.

There are also migrant farm workers. These are workers who move from place to place with the harvest season. They cut lettuce, pick grapes, tomatoes, apples, and peaches, and harvest other produce. Usually the whole family works. As a result, the children get little schooling. Even with all members of the family working, the amount they can earn is small. Untrained for any other work, they have generally had to take whatever the farm owners chose to pay them. Many migrant workers are Mexican Americans. During the 1960's the migrant workers began to demand higher wages and better working conditions. Under the leadership of such people as Cesar Chavez, who organized the United Farm Workers union, migrant farm workers began to make progress in their fight against poverty.

POCKETS OF POVERTY

Many parts of the United States have areas that are called **pockets of poverty.** Some of these areas have suffered from misuse of the natural resources of the region. One huge poverty pocket is Appalachia, an area that extends along the foothills of the Appalachian Mountains. It includes parts of ten states, from Pennsylvania to Alabama. Here, for many years, the people made a good living from good farm lands and from some of the world's richest coal mines.

Then the coal industry declined. Demands for coal decreased when people began to use more oil and gas as sources

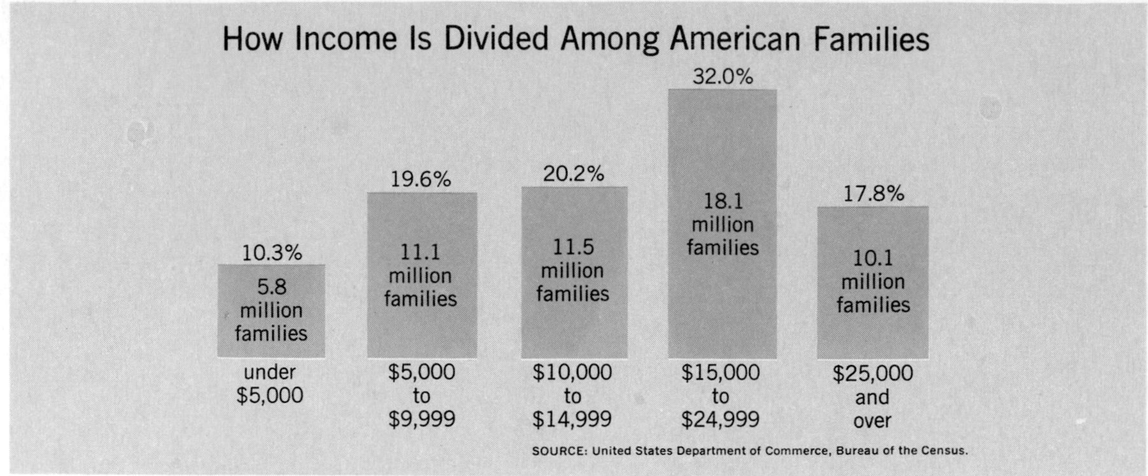

of heat and power. Many small mines were closed, throwing the miners out of work. **Technological unemployment** occurred when coal companies replaced miners with mining machines. In addition, much of the farmland in the area was damaged. The damage began with bad farming practices. It became worse when strip mining began in many areas. In strip mining, farmlands are torn up so that coal companies can easily dig out coal that lies near the surface. Over the years, the farmers and miners of Appalachia became among the poorest people in the nation.

Another pocket of poverty exists in the upper Great Lakes region. In this area, iron ore was once mined in great quantities. And timber resources gave work to many. As in Appalachia, the main industries of this region declined. And there was not enough new industry to give employment to those who had been left jobless.

Still other pockets of poverty exist on some American Indian reservations. Again and again throughout the history of our nation, the Native Americans were forced from their lands onto reservations. Their old ways of obtaining a living were destroyed. And many found it difficult to adjust to or to develop new ways of earning a living.

GOVERNMENT EFFORTS TO END POVERTY

The first massive efforts to deal with poverty in the United States came in the 1930's. This was the time of the Great Depression, as you may recall. About one third of the nation was living in poverty then. Under the leadership of President Franklin D. Roosevelt, Congress established a number of federal programs to help the poor. Projects were set up to provide work for many of those who wanted it. Welfare payments were made to those unable to work, including dependent children and handicapped persons. The Social Security program was started, as you know, to provide retirement benefits for the elderly and insurance payments for the unemployed. These programs and others helped to get the economy moving again and to reduce proverty.

But poverty did not begin or end with the Great Depression. Poverty has been a constant and serious condition in America. It exists even when the economy is in good general condition. For this reason, our government has continued to seek ways to eliminate poverty.

In the 1960's, President Lyndon B. Johnson placed this problem high on the list of important tasks for his administration. He declared a **War on Poverty.** At his urging, Congress created the **Office of Economic Opportunity (OEO).** Many programs were sponsored by this agency. One of them, the Job Corps, trained young men and women who had dropped out of school. The Head Start Program prepared young children for success in school. The Volunteers in Service to America (VISTA) provided trained workers to aid people in poor areas. The OEO no longer exists. But many of its activities are now conducted by the Department of Labor and two independent agencies—ACTION and the Community Services Administration. In addition, food stamps are available at low cost to poor families to help pay for their food. Medical aid for the needy, or **Medicaid,** helps the poor get medical services. Public housing bills have been passed to help eliminate slums.

THE WELFARE TANGLE

The most important aid to the poor comes from **welfare programs** of our federal, state, and local governments. Under these welfare programs, sums of money are given to the needy. In order to be eligible for welfare assistance, a family must have an income below the poverty level. The amount of aid varies from state to state. However, it averages less than $290 a month. Those in need must apply to their local welfare bureau. If they are found to be eligible for assistance, they receive regular monthly payments.

The welfare programs in our nation have been widely criticized. They are criticized by people on welfare for several reasons. Many people on welfare would rather have jobs and earn their own way. They object, also, because they must submit to interviews from time to time by public welfare workers, who have the right to ask them about private and personal matters. In addition, most families are unable to receive welfare if the father works. When the father is not able to earn money equal to, or better than, the welfare payments, he may decide to live apart from his family. He may even desert them so that they can receive welfare.

Many average citizens are also dissatisfied with the welfare programs. They believe that there are some people who receive welfare who do not deserve it, and others who do not receive enough aid. The programs are also extremely costly to the taxpayer. For these reasons and others, almost no one has been satisfied with the American welfare system. In the late 1970's, a number of new programs were being considered.

CONSIDER AND DISCUSS

Identify. luxuries / necessities / poverty / poverty cycle / pocket of poverty / technological unemployment / War on Poverty / Office of Economic Opportunity / Medicaid / welfare program

Review. 1. Even in times of national plenty, some people live in poverty. Why? 2. Why is Appalachia a pocket of poverty? 3. How did each of the following attack poverty: Franklin D. Roosevelt, Lyndon Johnson? 4. What are some of the criticisms of the welfare system?

Discuss. What do you think is the best way to help the Americans who are living in poverty?

2 Problems of Labor and Management

In the early days of our nation, many Americans were self-employed. They worked for themselves on small farms, or in small workshops, or in their own stores. Most businesses were small. They employed only a few workers, or wage earners. These wage

Continued on page 343

Poverty and Welfare: Is There a Way Out?

WHAT DO YOU THINK?

A woman in the suburbs was complaining to her neighbor:

> My husband works hard to earn a good living. We pay all our bills and try to save some money for the children's education. What happens? Our money is taxed away and given to people on welfare. Why should we support them? Let them go out and work for a living. Nobody deserves a free ride.

In a run-down area of a city, another woman was talking to her neighbor:

> My husband never could find a steady job. Even when he got work, it never paid enough to support me and the children. Finally, he just gave up. He figured we would be better off without him. What could I do? We had to go on welfare. Is it my fault we are poor? Is it the children's fault? The welfare people act as though we like living this way. I do the best I can for my kids. But they deserve a better break in life.

These are two sides of the welfare question. It has become a big issue in our country. Many people have strong opinions about welfare. What are some of the facts?

Here are some statements that you may hear people make. Do you know if they are true or false?

1. "Most people on welfare are black."
2. "Once people go on welfare, they never get off."
3. "Welfare mothers have lots of children, to get higher payments."
4. "Welfare benefits keep going up and up."
5. "The welfare rolls are full of fakes and cheats."
6. "A lot of people go on welfare to avoid working for a living."

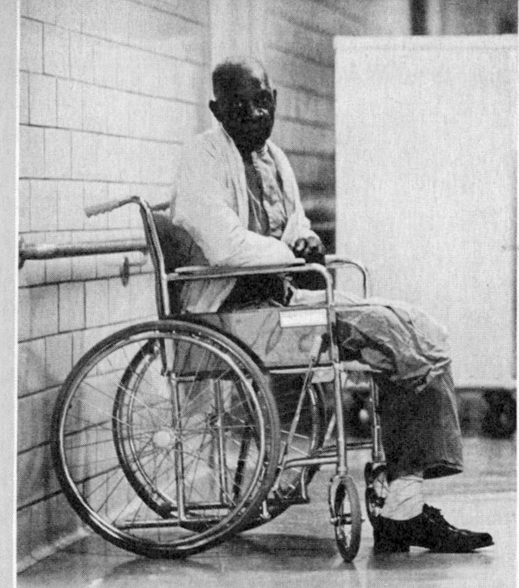

All of the above statements are false. Here are the facts:

1. About half of all welfare families are white. Most of the other welfare families are black or Hispanic.
2. The average length of time on welfare is less than two years.
3. The typical welfare family includes a mother and two or three children. The birth rate is about average.
4. Welfare payments have not gone up with the cost of living. In the past few years, many states have actually reduced welfare benefits.
5. The number of welfare cheaters is very small, less than half of 1 percent.
6. Most people on welfare are children, mothers, elderly, or disabled. Less than 1 percent are able-bodied men or able-bodied women without children.

Why do people go on welfare? Can they support themselves? Should they be supported by the taxpayers? What can be done to reduce the number of people on welfare?

Some people are simply unable to work for a living. They include the disabled and the very old. Most Americans agree that these people ought to be supported—perhaps by higher Social Security benefits. The real debate over welfare concerns the families—usually just mothers and children—who depend on the taxpayers for support. Why are these families not supported by the fathers? or by the mothers?

The usual reason seems to be that the father is unemployed or "underemployed." Many people cannot find work. Some people can find only part-time work. Other people work full time, but still earn too little to support a family. A man who mops the floors in an office building will probably never escape from poverty. He may wonder if it is even worth the effort. If he cannot provide for his family, he may leave them.

The mother faces the same problems—lack of jobs and low pay. In addition, she has the children to take care of. If she does earn any money, it is subtracted from the family's welfare check. Thus, a part-time or low-paying job is no help.

Can anything be done to solve these problems? A number of plans have been suggested.

Some people think that the answer is simply to take people off welfare and force them to work. In many states, people on welfare must sign up for jobs or job training. But there are never enough jobs for everyone, even after training. Most of the jobs that are offered pay below poverty level. Women must leave their children in a day care center—if one is available. The cost of job training and child care may be as high as welfare. This policy can also be abused. In some rural areas, for example, poor people have been forced to work at extremely low wages. Labor unions say that this is unfair to other workers. Some people even call it a form of slavery.

What do you think? Should people on welfare be forced to work for less than the minimum wage? Should mothers be forced to leave their small children at day care centers? Will this solve the problem of welfare? Will it take jobs away from other people? What rights do poor people have? Are they different from the rights of other Americans?

Other people say that the real answer is more good jobs. Most poor people want to work, they believe, if only they can earn a decent living. Unemployment figures show that millions of people are in fact looking for work. If private industry cannot provide enough jobs, they say, the government should. Surely there are enough useful jobs that need doing—if only we are willing to pay someone to do them.

Critics of public employment say that the government is already too big. They believe that employment should be left to the private economy. They also say that a program like this would cost the taxpayers too much. What do you think? Is government employment better than welfare? What other problems might it solve? Would it be worth the cost? Why or why not?

More jobs would help. But they cannot solve the whole problem. First, there will always be people who cannot work. Second, there will probably never be enough jobs for everybody. Third, some people may still not earn enough to support their families. What about these people?

Several plans have been proposed to replace the present welfare system. The basic idea of all these plans is to guarantee a minimum income for all Americans. It would apply to all poor families. If a family earned no money at all, they would get at least a minimum of support. If they earned some money, this support would be reduced—but not by the full amount. Thus, there would be a real gain for any money earned. If they earned enough money, of course, the government support would stop. Then the family would start paying their share of taxes. Does this idea sound like a good one? How would it be better than welfare? Would it be fair to the poor? to the taxpayer? Why or why not?

Many people think that welfare is the most serious problem in our country today. Other people say that the real problem is not welfare, but poverty. That is why they favor some form of guaranteed income. Can you think of any other ideas that might help to solve the welfare problem? Can you think of any other ways to help eliminate poverty?

earners usually worked side by side with the owner. They knew the owner personally. If they were not happy, they could speak to the owner and ask for better wages or improved working conditions. If the owner refused, they could quit their jobs. They could find work elsewhere because industry was growing and the nation was growing westward. There was little labor-saving machinery. Also, there were more jobs than workers most of the time. So, employers often found that they had to give their employees fair treatment.

During the years from 1800 to 1850, working conditions for many wage earners changed greatly in the United States. Large factories were built, using power machinery to make products. Many of these factories employed hundreds of workers, including men, women, and children. In these new factories, relations between employers and their workers were different. The factory managers and owners had no contact with the workers. The hours of work were long —12 hours or even 16 hours a day. Wages usually were low. Working conditions were often poor. But there was little that workers could do about them. As the western lands began to fill in, it became more difficult for dissatisfied workers to leave their jobs and start on their own.

THE RISE OF AMERICAN LABOR UNIONS

As American businesses continued to expand during the years from 1850 to 1900, the number of workers also increased. American workers now began to organize in groups to try to improve their wages and working conditions. These organizations of workers became known as **unions.** Several small unions had been established on a local basis earlier. But these local unions were not always successful in dealing with employers. Workers came to believe that they needed union organizations on a nationwide scale if workers were to become powerful enough to deal with employers as equals.

Between 1850 and 1900, the growing unions wanted the right to bargain with employers for better wages, shorter hours, and improved working conditions. As a result, the labor unions worked hard to show business firms that the best way for workers and employers to settle differences was by **collective bargaining.**

In collective bargaining, representatives of a labor union sit down with representatives of an employer and try to reach agreement. The terms of the agreement are put into a written contract. This **labor contract** is signed by both the employer and the officers of the labor union.

The labor contract spells out the wages to be paid to workers and the working conditions they are to have. The labor contract lasts for a fixed period of time. It usually is for one, two, or three years. When the contract nears its ending date, representatives of the union and the employer sit down again and bargain for a new contract.

METHODS USED BY LABOR

In the earlier days of union organization, collective bargaining often broke down. Sometimes employers refused to bargain at all. The **strike** was the chief method used by early labor unions to try to force business firms to bargain with them. That is, union members walked off the job if employers did not agree to meet labor's demands. Production then stopped and the company lost money.

What is to prevent a company from hiring other workers when there is a strike? The strikers try to prevent this by **picketing.** Picketing means that strikers walk back and forth, often carrying signs, in front of the factory or other place of business. By picketing, they try to keep other workers from entering by urging them not to do so. Any workers who cross the picket lines

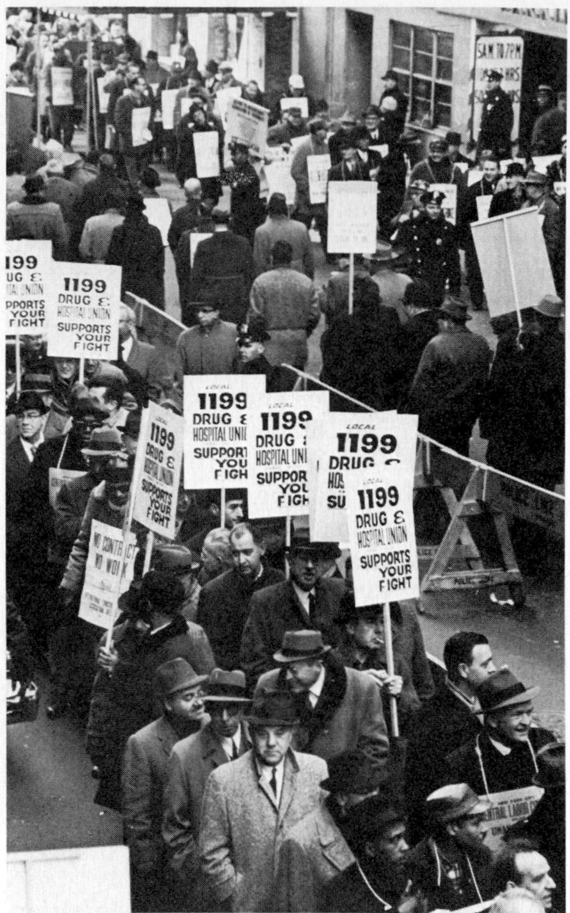

These workers are on strike because the union and the employer have not reached a satisfactory agreement on wages and fringe benefits.

and enter the factory or other place of business in order to return to work during the strike are called **scabs.** Sometimes fights have broken out between the strikers and scabs. The law now limits the use of scabs by employers.

Sometimes, instead of a strike, workers stay on the job but work much more slowly than usual. This union action is called the **slowdown.** Any kind of slowdown, or action short of a strike, is called a **job action.** The union, for example, may tell its members to follow all written orders to the letter, and to check and recheck. This job action slows down production and costs the company money. Sometimes it gains as much for the union as a strike would.

METHODS USED BY EMPLOYERS

Most business firms looked upon early labor unions as troublemakers. Therefore, business firms formed organizations of employers to oppose the growing power of labor. Sometimes employers hired **strike breakers,** or new workers, who were not members of the union. They took over the jobs of workers who were on strike. Private police were sometimes hired by employers to see that the picketing strikers did not prevent other workers from entering the plant. A period of conflict and struggle began between employers and labor.

Employers used other methods to fight the unions. They made up **blacklists** containing the names of those workers who were active in the labor unions. They sent these blacklists to all business firms and asked them not to hire anyone whose name was listed. Employers also found a way to fight labor slowdowns. They merely closed the factory and "locked out" the workers. The idea of the **lockout** was to prevent the workers from earning wages, so that they soon would be forced to go back to work.

THE CLOSED SHOP VERSUS THE OPEN SHOP

In the early days of labor organization, union leaders soon realized that unions needed money to succeed. To raise money, unions began to charge their members **union dues,** or fees. This money was used by the unions to pay their officials. During strikes or lockouts, it helped feed union members' families.

In order to succeed, the early labor unions knew that one of their chief jobs was to enroll every worker as a union member. As a result, it soon became the aim of the unions to establish a **closed shop** in every factory. In a closed shop, workers could not be hired unless they first became members of the union. The employers did not like the idea of a closed shop. They insisted upon an **open shop** in every factory. In an open shop anyone could be hired. Workers did not have to be union members or join the unions.

Much later, a third type of shop became popular, the **union shop.** In a union shop an employer can hire any worker, union or nonunion. But within a short period of time, usually about 30 days, new workers must join the union in order to keep their jobs.

The labor unions also asked that employers take the money for union dues out of workers' paychecks and turn these dues over to the union. Employers argued against dues checkoff, as it is called, because it would force them to collect dues for the union. However, dues checkoff is now a part of most union contracts with employers.

Sometimes employers tried to keep regular labor unions out of their businesses by organizing their own workers into **company unions** – unions sponsored by the companies. Labor leaders were opposed to these company unions because they were not independent.

THE AFL VERSUS THE CIO

Early unions were organized according to jobs or occupations. All members of the same skilled trade joined together in a **craft union,** or **trade union.** The carpenters throughout the nation, the plumbers, the bakers, the machinists, and so on, each had their own union.

In 1886 these craft unions formed a large organization called the **American Federation of Labor (AFL).** Under the leadership of Samuel Gompers, the AFL grew into a powerful labor group. Each craft union in the AFL had its own officers and its own local branches throughout the nation. Each craft union in the AFL worked to improve conditions in its own craft. But these craft unions joined with other unions in the AFL to strengthen their bargaining power.

As America's factories and businesses grew in size, some labor leaders believed that a new type of union should be formed. They thought unions should include unskilled workers as well as craft workers. These leaders pointed out that mass-production methods had weakened the importance of crafts. They insisted that all workers in each industry, such as steel, auto-making, and coal mining, should be members of the same union, no matter what kind of jobs they had. This is called an **industrial union.**

Industrial unions grew rapidly during the 1930's. Industry after industry – steel, auto-making, electrical equipment, rubber – was organized by labor leaders. Led by Walter Reuther and others, the industrial unions took members away from some of the craft unions. In 1936 the industrial unions formed one large organization called the **Congress of Industrial Organizations (CIO).**

Workers in many industries found it difficult to choose between the CIO and AFL. In many cases, the AFL or the CIO called a **jurisdictional strike,** or a strike to see which union group would represent the workers. The rivalry between the two large union organizations continued for many years. An agreement was finally reached in 1955. Then the AFL and the CIO joined together in a single labor organization, the AFL-CIO.

Today, the AFL-CIO is the largest American labor group. It has a membership of more than 16 million workers. But not every union belongs to this large combination of unions. The largest independent union is the International Brotherhood of Teamsters, Chauffeurs, Warehousemen, and Helpers of America (the Teamsters). It has nearly 2 million members. Other large independent unions include railroad unions and the United Auto Workers.

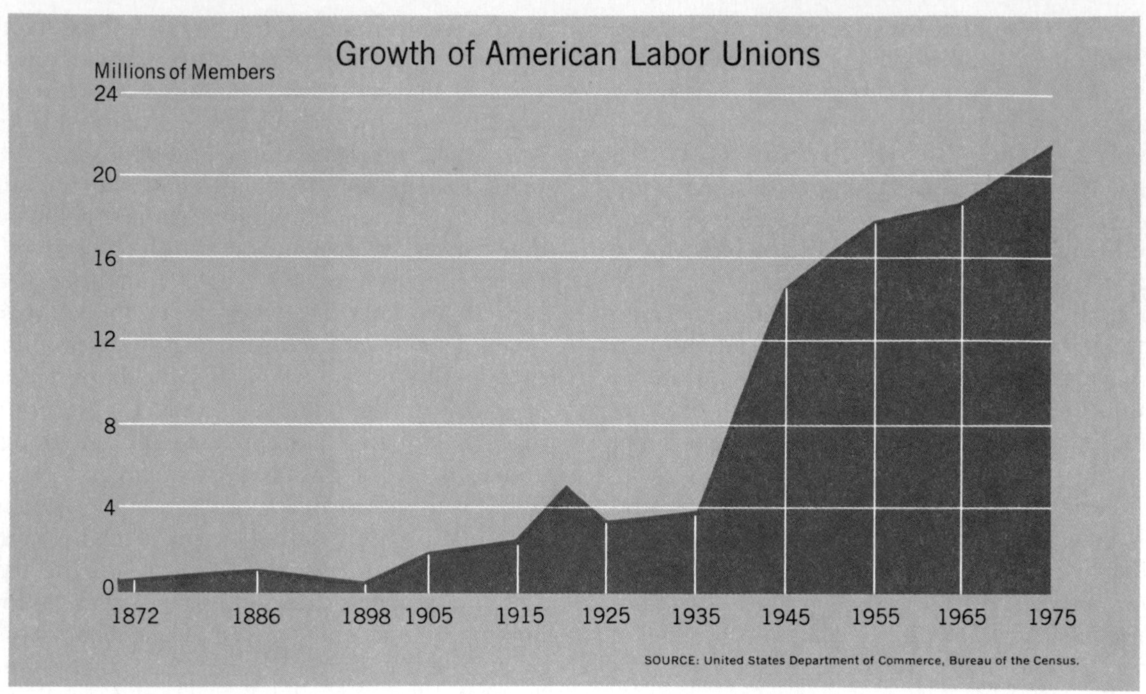

RECENT UNION ORGANIZATION

During the 1960's, the most successful new attempts to organize unions occurred among hospital workers and among the migrant farm laborers who pick grapes and harvest the produce of truck farms. For years these workers received very low wages. But union organization has brought some wage increases.

During the 1970's, the labor movement made gains among the men and women who work for our governments. There are laws that prohibit strikes against the governments. But some strikes by teachers, police, and other public workers have occurred for short periods.

CONGRESS PASSES LABOR LAWS

When workers go out on strike, the whole nation may suffer. For this reason, Congress has passed a number of laws to help workers and employers settle their disputes.

1. The National Labor Relations Act. This law, which is sometimes called the **Wagner Act,** was passed in 1935. It guarantees the right of all Americans workers to join the union of their choice. It also provides ways of settling disputes between unions and employers. An independent government agency, the **National Labor Relations Board (NLRB),** was set up under this act. It mainly judges the fairness of union and employer activities toward each other.
2. The Labor-Management Relations Act. This law, which is usually called the **Taft-Hartley Act,** was passed in 1947. It revised the Wagner Act in several ways. The Taft-Hartley Act allows the President of the United States to order any union to postpone a strike for 80 days when such a strike would threaten the national welfare. During this "cooling-off" period, a **fact-finding commission** may meet and recommend a settlement. At the end of the 80 days, however, the union may strike if no settlement is reached.

The Taft-Hartley Act also forbids the closed shop and condemns **featherbedding.** Featherbedding occurs when a union forces employers to hire workers who are not needed. In addition, the law enabled several states to pass **right-to-work laws.** These laws permit only the open shop in their states.

3. The Landrum-Griffin Act was passed in 1959 to prevent certain abuses by union officials. It prohibits persons with criminal records from serving as union officials for five years after their conviction. It also requires unions to file reports of their finances with the Secretary of Labor each year.

TODAY'S COLLECTIVE BARGAINING

Over the past 100 years, as you have seen, employers and workers have struggled, sometimes with the help of government, to work out new relationships. Employers have learned that well-paid workers are better able to buy the goods and services they produce. Union leaders and members have learned that strikes and other interruptions of production may be costly to them in lost wages and other benefits. Even so, in the mid-1970's there were more than 5,000 strikes a year, averaging 18 days each.

Today, when collective bargaining takes place, both sides must think about ways to increase productivity and protect reasonable profits. At the same time they must give workers reasonable wages and good working conditions. Their decisions have a powerful influence upon America's prosperity.

CONSIDER AND DISCUSS

Identify. unions / collective bargaining / labor contract / strike / picketing / scabs / slowdown / job action / strike breakers / blacklists / lockout / union dues / closed shop / open shop / union shop / company union / craft union / AFL / industrial union / CIO / jurisdictional strike / Wagner Act / NLRB / Taft-Hartley Act / fact-finding commission / featherbedding / right-to-work laws / Landrum-Griffin Act

Review. 1. Why did workers form unions? 2. What is the purpose of a strike? 3. How did employers fight strikes? 4. What is the difference between a trade union and an industrial union? 5. How does the federal government help labor and management?

Discuss. The strength of labor and management must be balanced. If either one becomes too strong, the nation suffers. Explain.

3 The Farm Problem

As you have read, many of America's poor people live on farms and in farming communities. They barely make a living from the land. But the United States also has large prosperous farms that are equipped with the latest farming machinery. They use scientific methods of raising crops. These farms are among the most productive in the world. It is largely because of them that most Americans eat so well.

In 1920, more than 30 million American people lived on farms. By the late 1970's, that figure had declined to about 8 million people. Yet during those same years the production of our farms increased enormously. Fewer and fewer people have been needed to produce more and more. In some ways this development has been good for the nation. But in other ways it has created problems.

FARMING HAS CHANGED

In the past, many farmers thought of farming not so much as a business but as a way to live healthfully in the open. They got great satisfaction from growing crops and raising farm animals. They enjoyed nature and liked the out-of-doors. Fifty years ago and more, it was common for the entire farm family to do the farm work. Most of what they produced was for their own use. They had a garden in which they grew their own vegetables. They had an orchard where they raised their own fruit. There was a wood lot where they cut their own stove wood. They raised chickens, hogs, and cows so that they had their own eggs, meat, and milk. If they had produce they did not need for themselves, they sold it. They used the money to buy whatever goods they needed that could not be produced on the farm. Most farmers owned only as much land as they and their families could manage.

This kind of family farming has been declining in the United States. There are still some families who live in the country, own their own land, and produce things for their own use. Among them are such groups as the Amish people of Pennsylvania. They live and work just about as their ancestors did 150 years ago. But few Americans today are willing to work so hard and to live without modern conveniences. On small, family-owned farms today, it is common for one or more members of the family to work in factories or offices in nearby towns or cities. The prices of things that these farmers need and want to buy are high compared to the money they get for their farm produce. As a result, few of them are now able to live by the old-fashioned farming methods they once used.

TODAY'S FARMS

Why is it now so difficult for the owners of small farms to make a living? The main answer is overproduction. With modern equipment,

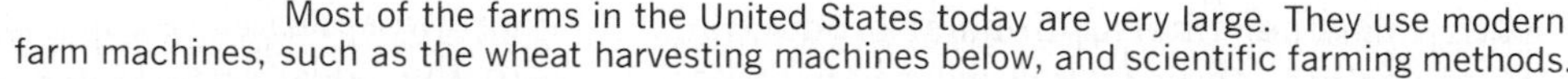

Most of the farms in the United States today are very large. They use modern farm machines, such as the wheat harvesting machines below, and scientific farming methods.

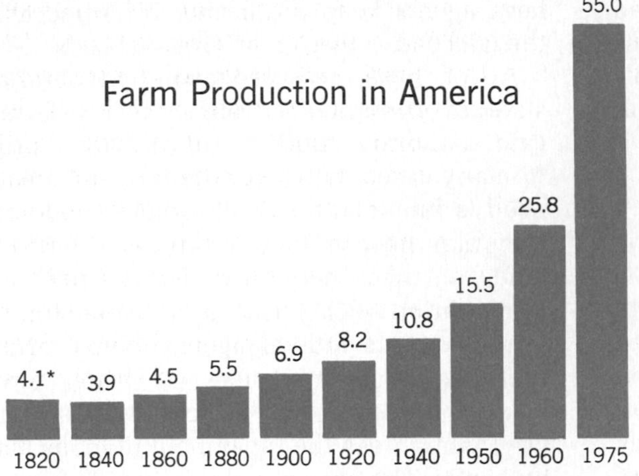

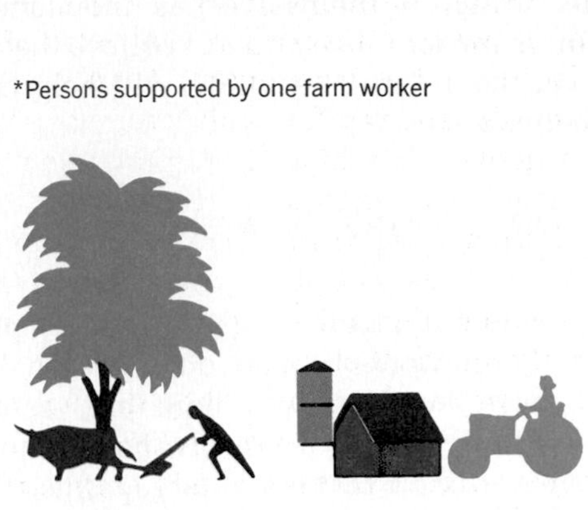

SOURCE: United States Department of Commerce, Bureau of the Census.

farmers in the United States can produce so much that the prices of farm products are usually low. This means that farmers, in order to make a good living, must raise and sell large amounts of their products. To do this, they need large farms.

The most efficient farms in the United States today are thousands of hectares in size. Such farms use the latest, most expensive machinery. Owners of small farms usually cannot afford to buy more land because the price of land is too high. The owners also are unable to afford the expensive equipment that is needed to operate large farms. One piece of machinery alone can cost over $40,000.

Only a few wealthy farmers operate the big, prosperous farms. Such farms are usually organized as corporations, and run as businesses. The owner or owners of such farms hire managers who have been trained in the nation's agricultural schools and colleges. Their farms use the latest machinery and the most up-to-date farming methods. Often these wealthy farmers own land in several different locations. Because of the large size of their operations, these farmers can make a profit even when prices of farm produce are not high. At the same prices, smaller farms will lose money.

FARMERS TRY TO HELP THEMSELVES

In some parts of our nation, the owners of smaller farms have gained benefits by forming **farmers' cooperatives,** or **co-ops,** as they are called. In a farmers' cooperative, many farmers join together to market their crops. This enables them to get the highest prices possible and cut the cost of marketing. Co-ops usually build grain elevators and other large storage places. There, members can store crops until the market price is favorable.

The farm cooperative can also purchase many things farmers need. Since it buys large amounts of these goods, it can get them at the lower wholesale prices. The success of cooperatives depends, of course, on how well they are managed and how effectively the members work together.

Some owners of smaller farms have also organized themselves into local unions. The members agree among themselves not to send their crops to market when they consider the price too low. By holding their produce, they hope to force the price up. In 1978, farmers even tried to strike. They demonstrated in the nation's capital. However, many nonunion farmers send all of their crops to the market. This makes it difficult for the farmers' union to succeed. In addition, many owners of small and medium-sized farms think of themselves as independent business owners. They do not believe that following the orders of a union will help them get better prices.

TENANTS, SHARECROPPERS, AND MIGRANTS

The owners of small farms have many problems. Farm workers who do not own land may have even more. There are, as you know, three groups of farm workers who are dependent upon owners of large farms. They are the tenant farmers, the sharecroppers, and the migrant workers.

About one eighth of all farmers in the United States rent their farms. If they pay their rent in cash, they are called **tenant farmers.** If they pay their rent by giving the owner part of what they grow, they are called **sharecroppers.** In either case, the farms they work are small. By the time they pay off the landowner, they usually have so little left that their families live in poverty.

Migrant workers, as you have read, move from farm to farm with the seasons, picking the crops on large farms for low wages.

HOW GOVERNMENTS AID THE FARMER

Local, state, and federal governments have understood for a long time how important the farmer is to America's welfare. When farmers' income is low, business in general suffers. Prosperous farmers help to keep America prosperous. The problem is to find a way to guarantee farm prosperity, especially for owners of small farms.

Most state governments and the federal government have programs designed to aid America's farmers. States have set up agricultural colleges to train future farmers. State agricultural experiment stations help to improve farming methods, to develop better seeds and insecticides, and to improve the breeding of farm animals. County farm agents keep the farmer informed about the latest advances in farming methods.

All of these measures taken by federal and state governments are designed to help farmers gain economic stability and to make a profit. In many cases, however, the farmers' greatest need is financial aid. To produce a good crop they may need money to buy seed, fertilizer, land, or machinery. The Farm Credit Administration (FCA) was established for this purpose. This federal agency helps farmers refinance their mortgages on better terms. It also lends money at low interest rates. Or it guarantees the repayment of loans made by banks. The agency especially aids farm cooperatives with long- and short-term loans for marketing and buying.

THE FARM PRICE-SUPPORT PROGRAM

The federal government has also tried to help farmers through programs that will keep the prices of farm goods high. Under one program, the government guaranteed farmers a certain price for their crops. The **support price,** as it was called, might be $2.00 a bushel, for example. Farmers who could get only $1.75 a bushel in the market, could take their grain to government storage houses and get a loan of $2.00 for each bushel. If the market price later went up, farmers could sell their grain and repay the loan. But if the price did not go above $2.00, farmers simply could fail to repay the loan. The government would keep the grain. (Some of it would be sold to foreign nations. And some would be used to feed hungry people in other lands.)

There were many criticisms of this program. The main one was that people had to pay for it twice. They paid through taxes to raise money for the program and through higher food prices. In addition, much of the money went to the owners of large farms. Small-farm owners received very little.

A new system was adopted in 1973, and it was extended in 1977. This system permits the government to set **target prices** for certain crops, such as wheat and corn. It also sets a lower loan price for farmers who need to take out a loan against a crop, much as under the old price-support program. Here is how the new system works. Suppose that the target price for wheat is set at $3.00 a bushel and the loan price at $2.25. If the market price is, say, $2.75 a bushel, farmers can sell their wheat at that price. The government will make up the difference between the target price and the market or loan price – whichever is higher. In this case, the government pays 25 cents a bushel. But farmers have to agree to limit the amount of land they use for crops.

Despite government aid, America's farmers continue to face problems. The gap between rich and poor farmers is still widening. Market prices are often too low. Problems such as these remain a serious challenge to the nation's economy.

CONSIDER AND DISCUSS

Identify. farmers' cooperatives / tenant farmers / sharecroppers / migrant workers / support price / target prices

Review. 1. Why are small-farm owners in financial trouble? 2. In what ways have farmers tried to help themselves? 3. How does the government help farmers?

Discuss. Do you think it is so important for small farms in the United States to survive? Why or why not?

4 Boom or Bust

Although Americans enjoy the highest standard of living in the world, our economy does not always behave the way we want it to. Sometimes we have a period of prosperity, called a "boom." During a boom, business is good. Jobs are plentiful. And profits are high. But then business slows down. Some companies begin to lose money, and many workers find themselves without jobs. The nation enters a period of hard times, or a "bust." This tendency to go from good times to bad, and then back to good times again, and so on, is called the **business cycle.**

THE PROBLEM OF INFLATION

One of the problems that often comes with a boom is **inflation.** Inflation means that the prices of most goods and services are rising. If your income is not rising fast enough, you will be able to buy fewer things. For example, suppose you work at various jobs during the summer to buy a new bicycle that is priced at $100. After earning the $100, you go to the store and find that the price is now $120. You are the victim of inflation. Your money buys less than before. Inflation is particularly bad for elderly people living on fixed incomes. Their incomes stay the same while prices go up.

Why does inflation accompany a boom? There are many reasons. During a period of prosperity, people have good jobs and high incomes. As people spend money, they push up the demand for goods and services. If businesses are already turning out goods as fast as they can, they will be unable to increase the supply. Prices will rise as customers compete with one another to buy scarce goods. Businesses will have to pay more for raw materials and transportation. Because jobs are plentiful at such times, business owners may have to increase wages in order to keep their workers and to attract new ones. Wages, costs of raw materials, transportation fees, rent, and interest on money borrowed are **costs of production.** When these costs rise, business firms may have to raise the prices of their products in order to pay the costs and still make a profit. These are just a few of the reasons why prices usually rise during a boom period.

This American family was one of the thousands of families who traveled across the United States in the 1930's on freight trains in search of work.

DEPRESSIONS AND RECESSIONS

Economists, the scientists who study our economy, speak of a period of hard times as a **depression.** During a depression, the number of people without jobs is high. People who are out of work do not buy many goods and services. As a result, many business firms must close down because they cannot make enough money to cover the costs of running the business. The whole economy slows down. That is, the nation produces fewer goods and services. Jobs become scarce. Teenage workers and people with few skills and little education are particularly hard hit. In a bad depression, even workers with a great deal of training and experience may not be able to find jobs.

The worst depression in our history occurred during the 1930's. This period is known as the **Great Depression,** as you may recall. The first sign of trouble came in October 1929, when the prices of stocks fell sharply. People who had paid hundreds of dollars for stocks found that they could sell them for only a few cents. Or they could find no buyers at all. Many banks failed. Depositors lost their life savings. By 1932, business was producing only half as much as it had produced in 1929. Thousands of firms were bankrupt. Farm prices were lower than ever before. By 1933, about 13 million people – nearly one fourth of America's workers – had lost their jobs. Most of these people had families to support. Unable to pay their mortgages, many homeowners lost their houses. Many farmers had to leave their land. In the cities jobless people stood in line for hours to get free soup. Children in classrooms sometimes fainted from hunger. These are only a few of the great hardships that people suffered during the Great Depression.

Sometimes the economy begins to slow down or stays in a decline for several months. Businesses fail, the number of people out of work rises, and profits decline. But things do not get so bad that we call it a depression. Instead, economists call this period a **recession.** Since the late 1930's we have had several recessions. The worst recession was in the mid-1970's. But we have not had another depression.

OLD THEORIES OF THE BUSINESS CYCLE

Before the Great Depression of the 1930's, most economists believed that the business cycle should be left alone. That is, they thought that the government should not step in and try to control inflation or to end unemployment. Most economists thought that the problems that come with the business cycle would cure themselves. If prices rose too high, people would stop buying goods and services until the prices came down again. Also, high prices would attract people to go into business. As a result, the supply of goods and services would increase. This would prevent prices from rising more.

Many economists also thought that recessions could not last very long. Workers who lost their jobs would soon be willing to accept lower wages. Therefore, businesses would be able to hire people for lower pay. Other costs of production would also be low. This would encourage businesses to produce more. As businesses expanded and increased their spending, they would help other businesses. Soon, new businesses would be started. The economy would improve. Salaries would be raised and more people would be hired. People would buy more, and so on. But then came the Great Depression, and the old theories did not seem to work.

GOVERNMENT EFFORTS TO AID THE ECONOMY

Wages were very low during the Great Depression. Millions of unemployed people were willing to accept any pay, no matter how low. But businesses did not hire them. Businesses also did not expand because there was no point in producing more goods when few people had enough money to buy them. To the surprise of the economists, the Great Depression did not end in a fairly short time. It went on year after year.

Finally, people were willing to have the government step in and do something to improve the economy. As you may recall, President Roosevelt established a program known as the New Deal. Under this program, unemployed workers were hired by the government to do useful work such as creating parks or building schools. Young people could join the Civilian Conservation Corps and work on projects to restore our forests and other natural resources. Homeowners and farmers could get loans to help pay their mortgages. You may remember from Chapter 16 that a Federal Deposit Insurance Corporation was set up to insure bank deposits. The Social Security system was established to give regular payments to elderly citizens and to help others in need. Unemployment insurance was created to provide workers with some money when they lost their jobs. All of this and other government spending helped get us out of the Great Depression.

Many of the measures established during the Great Depression remained in effect after the economy recovered. However, they have not solved all of our economic problems. We still have periods when business is slow. The number of unemployed people has remained high during both good and bad periods. And inflation continues to raise prices, so that it costs us more to live each year. Economists once believed that prices always fall during a recession. During the 1970's, however, we continued to have inflation, even during serious recessions.

GOVERNMENT AND THE BUSINESS CYCLE

There are several things the federal government can do to try to control the business cycle. For one, it can change its **fiscal policy,** or its program for taxing and spending. If the economy is going into a recession, the government can reduce taxes. Lower taxes give people more money to spend. Increased spending encourages businesses to produce more, which leads to the creation of more jobs. The government can also step up its own spending. It can buy more goods and hire more people to work for the government. It can build public projects such as bridges, dams, and hospitals. The government can also give larger payments to the unemployed, the poor on welfare, and the elderly.

Another way the government can try to control the business cycle is to change its **monetary policy,** or money policy. This policy is handled by the Federal Reserve System. As you may also remember from Chapter 16, Federal Reserve Banks serve as banks for other banks. They control the amount of money in the economy. If we are entering a recession, the Federal Reserve can increase the money supply by making it easier for banks to lend money to businesses at lower rates. This may encourage businesses to expand, thus creating more jobs and income.

If we are in a boom period, these actions can be reversed. When inflation becomes too high, the federal government can raise taxes and cut down on its spending. The Federal Reserve can make it harder for banks to lend money to businesses. This should decrease the amount of money in the economy.

At times, the government has used direct controls over the economy. In 1971, for example, a **wage-price freeze** was attempted.

Cartoons often comment on the nation's problems.
In this drawing, the cartoonist shows inflation as a monster eating up our dollars.

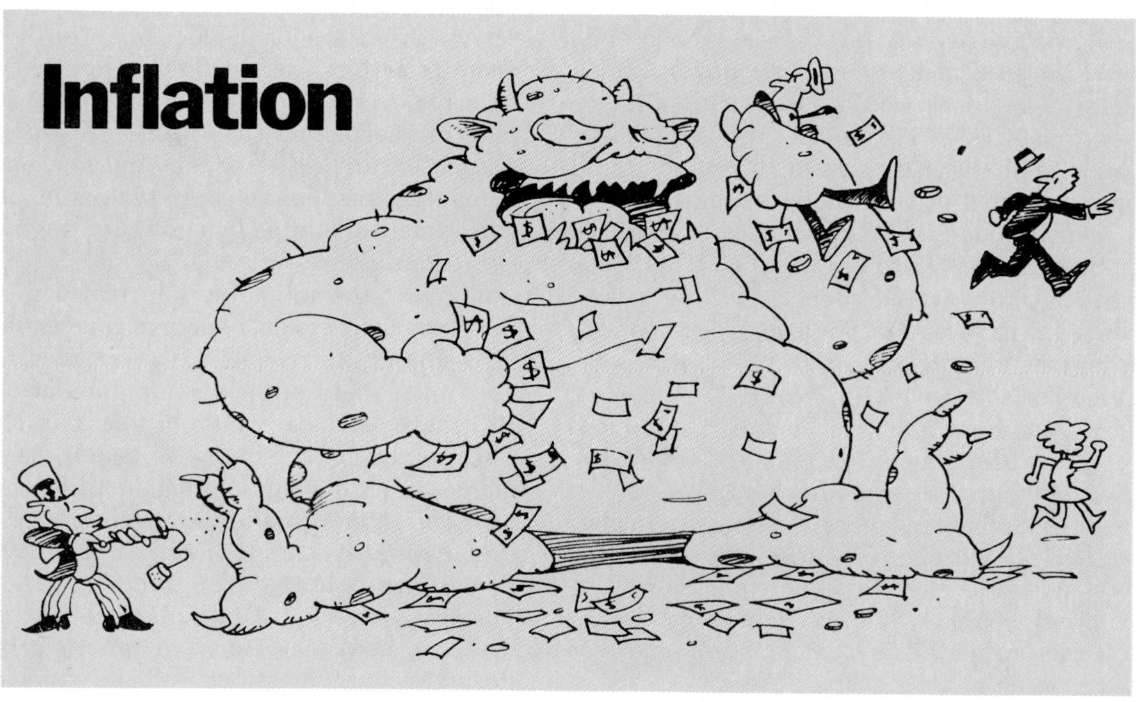

Most prices and wages could not be raised for several months, and then only a little. But the freeze was soon lifted because it did not work very well.

We have not yet learned how to control the economy. Some economists believe that it does not have to be controlled. They think that the government should keep out of the economy. They also believe that the programs begun under the New Deal have contributed to inflation. Other economists feel that the government can help the economy. They say that without government actions, inflation would have been worse than it is. They also say that government efforts have helped to prevent another Great Depression.

CONSIDER AND DISCUSS

Identify. business cycle / inflation / costs of production / economists / depression / Great Depression / recession / fiscal policy / monetary policy / wage-price freeze

Review. 1. What happened during the Great Depression? 2. How does government spending affect the economy? 3. How is inflation harmful? 4. What are some ways in which the federal government seeks to control the business cycle in the American economy?

Discuss. Is our country now in a period of inflation, depression, recession, or prosperity? Explain.

CHAPTER Summary

Our American economy is one of the most prosperous in the world. But there are problems that challenge our free enterprise system. One of these problems is poverty. Of our 25 million poor people, many are retired persons, migrant farm workers, unskilled persons, and minority group members.

Workers and management have trouble agreeing about wages and working conditions. Workers have formed labor unions in order to bargain with management. The federal government has passed laws to help labor unions and business management act fairly toward each other in bargaining and other relations.

Many of America's farmers have not shared fully in our nation's prosperity. Because of modern agricultural methods, fewer farmers are needed to produce larger crops. Many small-farm owners cannot compete with large farms. The federal government has found many ways to try to help farmers, such as farm subsidies.

Perhaps the most widespread problem facing our economy is the business cycle. When economic ups and downs are severe, everyone suffers. During depressions, workers cannot find jobs. During inflation, prices are so high that some people cannot afford what they need. Certain policies of our federal government are directed toward controlling these extremes.

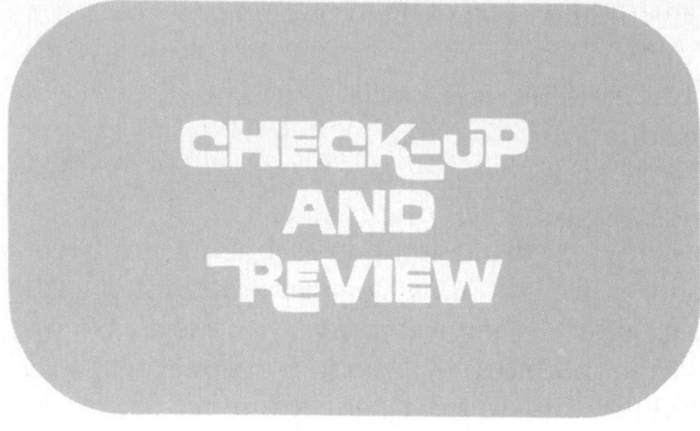

VOCABULARY

On a separate piece of paper, write the words that are listed below. Then read the numbered definitions that appear below the words. Choose the definition that best fits each word, and write the correct definition beside the word it matches.

poverty	inflation
depression	featherbedding
recession	welfare

1. Periods in our economy when prices increase greatly in a short time.
2. Forcing employers to hire workers who are not needed.
3. Periods in our economy when unemployment, business failures, falling prices, hardship, and poverty occur.
4. When people do not have enough money to afford the bare necessities of life.
5. Direct payments made to the needy.
6. Periods in our economy when there is a mild decline in the nation's business.

CHECK-UP

Write out answers to the following questions, and come to class prepared to take part in a discussion of the answers.

1. What is technological unemployment? Give several examples.
2. Why have people criticized the welfare system?
3. What steps can the federal government take under the Taft-Hartley Act when a strike threatens to harm the nation?
4. Why are some farmers not getting a fair share of the nation's income?
5. What steps has the federal government taken in recent years to help American farmers?

CITIZENSHIP AND YOU

You can learn more about the problems that challenge our American economy by taking part in some of the activities listed below.

1. Class Projects

The entire class can serve as a labor arbitration board. One student, acting as a representative of labor, appears before the board and presents labor's side of the case. A second student represents management and presents its side. The class then makes its decision in the case. If possible, each side should base its arguments on an actual case the class has studied.

If possible, have an official of a farm cooperative or of some farmer's group speak to the class about present farm problems.

Listen to a student report on economic depressions in the United States. Discuss steps that the federal government has taken to try to prevent future depressions.

2. Group or Committee Projects

Several members of the class may visit the nearest Internal Revenue Service office and interview the Director. Try to find out how many families in your area have incomes below the poverty level. Arrange for this visit by making an appointment in advance. Report to the class on the results of the interview.

Prepare a list or chart showing the labor disputes that have occurred in your community or a nearby city in recent years. How were the disputes settled?

3. Individual Projects

Collect newspaper articles about the cost of living, and report your findings to the class.

Draw a cartoon to illustrate some causes of disputes between management and labor.

Write an editorial on the farm problem. Include

your opinion of present programs to help American farmers.

Do some research on labor laws in your state. Does your state have a right-to-work law? If so, what does it say?

Read to the class the book report you prepared on the American economy as a project for Chapter 16.

CIVICS SKILLS

INTERPRETING PICTURES

There is an old saying that "one picture is worth a thousand words." This means simply that you can learn a great deal from pictures. Sometimes they can be better than words. Pictures can actually show you how people dressed in past times, what their houses were like, and the kinds of tools or machines they used. Pictures can also show you how something works. For example, a diagram can show you how a machine works.

You should study the pictures you see in your textbooks, newspapers, magazines, and elsewhere very carefully. They tell you much about the topics or subjects they show. But do more than take a casual look at the pictures. Study the main parts of the pictures and also the details. In your civics book, for example, you will find both photographs of actual events and paintings. You can learn a great deal by studying both kinds of pictures. To gain an idea of what you can learn, look at the photograph on page 337. What does it tell you about poverty? Does it also give you feelings about poverty?

Most people think that a picture only presents facts. That is, it shows things as they actually are. This is the common viewpoint that "the camera doesn't lie." But pictures are not just a representation of reality. They also express attitudes and opinions. Although photographs convey information about a subject, they often suggest an attitude toward an event or the people involved. Photographers select the details they want to emphasize. In some cases they may even omit important details. In this manner, they are presenting an interpretation of an event or situation. Look again at the photo on page 337. What details are emphasized? Would the picture be as effective without the children?

Paintings also express opinions. They express the artist's ideas and feelings about the subjects represented. Artists can show their ideas, attitudes, and feelings about people and events in many ways. The expressions that an artist puts on peoples' faces show his or her attitude about the people. The details that an artist chooses to highlight conveys his or her general view. For example, look at the painting on page 236. This is an idealization of an early school. It shows the artist's positive feelings about the school.

PRACTICING YOUR CIVICS SKILLS

Look carefully at the pictures on pages 142 and 224. What do they tell you about farm life in the 1800's? Now look at the picture on page 348. What does it tell you about modern farm life? How would you compare the farmers of the 1800's with modern farmers?

Look at the photograph on page 352. What details does the photographer emphasize? What expressions does the photographer show on the people's faces? What feelings does the photograph give you about the Great Depression? Do you think this is what the photographer intended?

CHAPTER

Introduction

Today's citizens must be prepared to find their places in a world where changes are taking place. The modern world is a world of astronauts, satellites, miracle drugs, computers, transistors, plastics, frozen foods, air conditioners, color television, microwave ovens, jet airplanes, and a thousand other wonders. And you may be certain that still more changes are on the way. What will these changes mean to you? What kinds of job opportunities will you find in this changing world?

In the early days of our nation—from 200 to 300 years ago—choosing a job was not difficult. In those days nine out of ten Americans lived and worked on farms. Only one American out of ten lived in a town or city and worked there. There were some job opportunities in our towns and cities. But their variety was limited. This situation was slow in changing. A hundred years ago there were still only a few hundred kinds of jobs among which to choose.

Today, of course, all this is greatly changed. There are thousands of different kinds of jobs open to Americans. You can see how the variety of job choices has increased! Another fact will help you to understand how rapidly job opportunities have increased in recent years. Nearly half of the jobs that this year's college graduates will obtain are jobs that did not exist when the graduates were born.

As one of the workers upon whom the future of America depends, you will want to find the job in which you can do your best work. And, from your point of view, you will be happiest and most successful if you are doing what you like doing and what you can do best. In this chapter you will study about the different jobs you may choose and the qualifications you will need for each of them. You will read about these topics:

1. The Challenge of a Career
2. The World of Work
3. Opportunities Unlimited
4. Learning More About Careers
5. Learning More About Yourself

CHAPTER 18 Careers for Americans

1 The Challenge of a Career

One of the most important things you will have to decide in your life is the kind of work you want to do. Work can be enjoyable. Or it can be unpleasant. The problem is to find the kind of work that best suits you and for which you are best suited. The happy worker is the person who has found a job that fits his or her special needs.

FREEDOM TO CHOOSE A JOB

Citizens of the United States have **freedom of job choice.** That is, they are free to choose the kind of job or occupation they wish to try to enter. No government official tells you where, when, and how you must apply for a job. This freedom of choice becomes important when you choose your career. It means that you may choose any kind of job that suits your interests, intelligence, and abilities. You need not follow the same occupation as your father or mother. Every young American is free to dream and to plan his or her own future. Young Americans are free to set their own goals. They are free to gain as much success in their jobs as their own abilities will allow.

The freedom of the individual to get the job that he or she wants is sometimes limited by the economic situation. During times of high unemployment, the individual may have to settle for less than a first choice in jobs. But a person still has the freedom to "make good" in the new job, to change jobs when the opportunity comes, or to save money and prepare for another job. These freedoms do not guarantee happiness or prosperity. But they do give each American a chance to find success in a job.

PERSONAL VALUES AND CHOOSING A JOB

The way in which young people use their freedom of job choice depends upon their **personal values** – the things they believe to be the most important in their own lives. A young person whose main purpose is to earn as much money as possible will seek an occupation that pays well. Another person may believe that helping others is the most important thing in life. He or she may feel happy only in following a career that is helpful to others. Such a person may become a teacher, a minister, a health worker, or a social worker. Personal values play a strong part in determining a person's choice of jobs.

Try to study the reasons why people work. It may help you to see why it is so important to find the job that will best meet your special needs. Perhaps you are thinking that the reasons are clear – most people work to satisfy their needs for food, clothing, and shelter. Many Americans, however, are not satisfied with meeting just these basic needs. They want more. They want a new automobile, a stereo record player, an automatic washer and dryer, and many other things that are now part of our high standard of living. And some day, they want to be able to retire comfortably.

In addition to the money a job pays, many people feel that a job should offer other rewards. They believe that a job should make them feel that they are doing something important. A job should also give them a chance to get ahead. Some people work largely from habit. They get into the habit of working at a particular job and find it a comfortable way to go through life. Others have a real desire to do something new and different. These men and women regard work as a challenge. They would not be happy in a routine job. Which of these ideas about work do you agree with?

THE BEST JOB FOR YOU

Every person must take a good, hard look at his or her own qualifications for different occupations before making a decision about a job. But how can a person try to decide which job is right for him or her?

With your abilities, talents, interests, and skills, there probably are many different jobs you can do. That is why it is sometimes hard to discover which job would really be best for you. However, as you begin to study about jobs, you may narrow your choice to those occupations that have a special appeal for you. But don't make the mistake of narrowing your choice too early. You may discover new and rewarding job opportunities as you get deeper into the subject and learn more about occupations that might interest you.

The most important step in deciding upon a career is to get to know yourself. Does this surprise you? Even though you may think you already know yourself quite well, you must now start to take another look at yourself. You must study yourself as honestly as you can to discover your abilities, interests, and skills.

If you think about it a minute, you can see why an honest study of yourself is useful when considering a career. It helps you to be practical and to understand your own strong points as well as your weaknesses. For example, if you are afraid of speaking before groups, you will have to overcome this fear if you want to be a lawyer or a teacher. Can you do it? Perhaps you can. Many people have. But be frank with yourself. Admit your weaknesses as well as your strong points. If you balance your job choices against your abilities and interests, you will be more likely to make a wise job decision.

HOW YOUR SCHOOL YEARS HELP YOU

To succeed in today's rapidly changing world, you will need the best education you can get. Employers want young men and women who read well, who write clearly, and who have learned as much as possible in school. Employers know that the educated person is easier to teach, is able to meet new situations better, and usually tries harder to get ahead in his or her job.

Getting a good education benefits everyone—you, your employer, and your country. And a good education more than pays back all your efforts and study. Among other things, your years of schooling pay off in hard cash. A study of American workers' earnings shows this interesting fact: During their lifetime, average high school graduates earn about $90,000 more than average high school dropouts. Education does not guarantee success. But it certainly improves your chances for earning a better income during your lifetime.

Some students find school difficult and decide to drop out. These **school dropouts** believe that if they quit school they will be getting a head start in earning money. But leaving school is the worst thing you can do if you really are interested in a good income. It is true that dropouts can begin to earn money sooner than students who remain in school. But most dropouts earn low wages, since they can obtain only the lowest-paying jobs. They do not have the education or the skills needed for most jobs.

Also, dropouts often find themselves without jobs. With every year that passes, a person who does not finish high school will find it harder and harder to earn a living. To make matters worse, the jobs that could once be done by unskilled workers are disappearing fast.

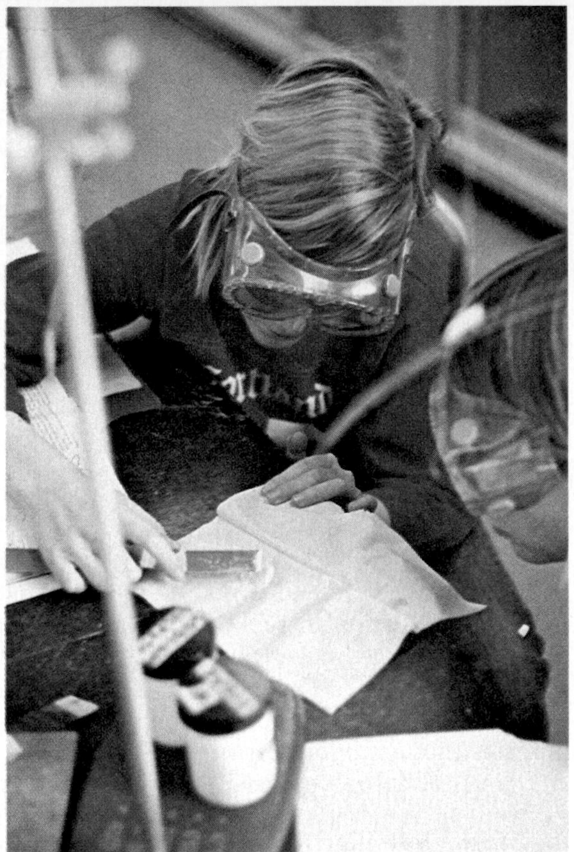

School training in special skills and trades may help prepare students for certain kinds of jobs.

THE KIND OF WORKERS EMPLOYERS WANT

Employers usually want persons who have a good general education. If special training is required in a certain industry, it is often given on the job. In looking for a secretary, for example, an employer wants someone who types and does neat work. The employer also hopes to find a person who can spell accurately, can follow directions, and who can develop skills on the job. When hired, the secretary is not expected to know much about the company's products. Such things can be learned on the job. The young person who is hired as a clerk in a grocery store may become the store manager if he or she has a good high school education and is able to solve practical problems. The employer knows that the young person can learn how to manage the store while working on the job.

The young man or woman who does well in a job is the one who builds on information and skills learned at school. The best way, therefore, to prepare for your future job—no matter what it may be—is to get everything that you can from your present school years.

BEGINNING YOUR CAREER CHOICE

You may be asking yourself: "Since American business is changing so rapidly, how can I be sure what job to prepare for and what kind of education to seek?" Fortunately, you do not need to make your job choice right now. If you stay in school, you have several years ahead in which you can study job possibilities that are open to you.

The first thing you need to do is to study various occupations and get some idea of the kinds of work they involve. Then you should consider the personal qualities that each occupation requires, such as originality, patience, or mechanical ability. Once you have done this, examine your own interests and abilities. Then see how well they fit in with different kinds of jobs.

Gradually, you will begin to focus in upon the best (or perhaps several jobs) that seem best for you. When you have made your first choice or choices of jobs, you will want to begin preparing for your career. The next four parts of this chapter will help you to begin thinking about the job you want to work at in the future.

CONSIDER AND DISCUSS

Identify. freedom of job choice / personal values / school dropouts
Review. 1. What freedom of choice has the American worker? 2. What are some of the reasons why people choose the jobs that they do? 3. Why is it unwise to become a school dropout?
Discuss. What kinds of things should you consider before choosing a career?

2 The World of Work

You are already familiar with many of the career opportunities in your community. When you have gone shopping, you have had a chance to see a number of workers in action. You have learned about jobs from your parents and friends. Perhaps you have worked at some part-time jobs. All of these experiences have helped you to become acquainted with the world of work. Now it is time to examine the various fields of work in a more systematic fashion.

Workers may be grouped into many different categories. These groupings may change over the years. According to the Bureau of the Census and the Bureau of Labor Statistics, workers today are generally grouped into four main categories. These are white-collar workers, blue-collar workers, service workers, and farm workers.

WHITE-COLLAR WORKERS

The largest group of workers in America today are the white-collar workers. White-collar workers are those who are in the professions, or who do technical, managerial, sales, or clerical work.

The professions. Jobs that require many years of education and training, and in which the work is largely mental rather than physical, are called professions. Included in this category are doctors, lawyers, architects,

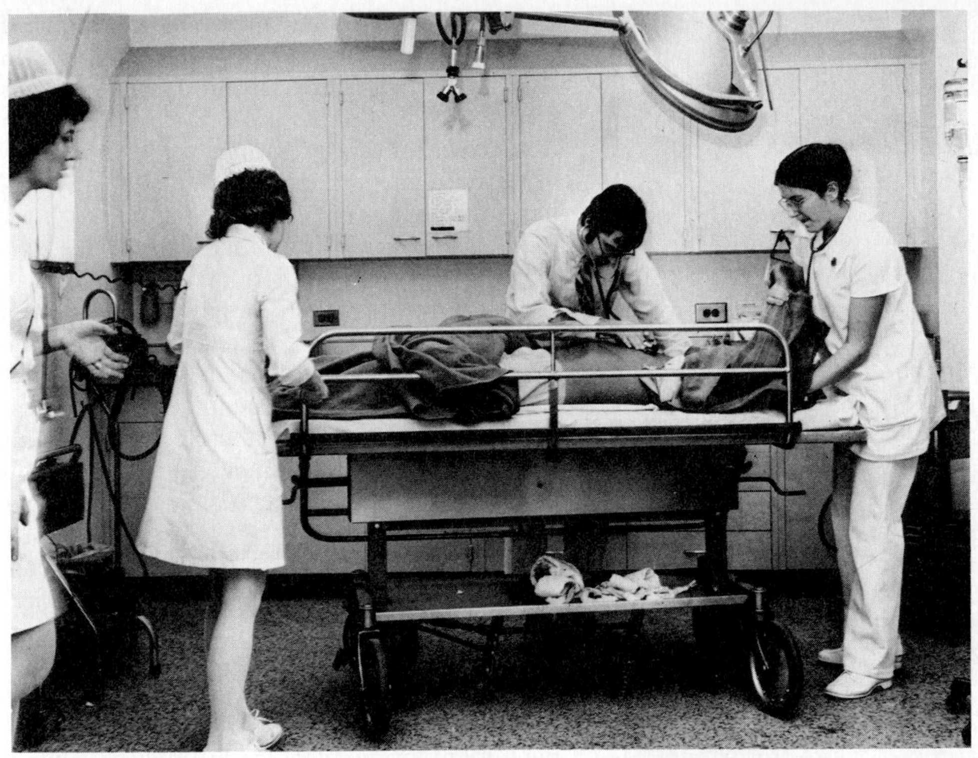

These doctors and nurses are treating a patient in the emergency room of a hospital. The profession of medicine requires long study but offers many rewards.

ministers, teachers, dentists, and others.

In the field of science, professional workers include chemists, biologists, botanists, geologists, and many other specialists. In the business world, there are professional workers such as accountants, economists, and engineers. Among the professionals in the arts are writers, painters, and entertainers.

As our economy has changed and grown, the demand for professional workers has also grown. Experts predict that by the mid-1980's, the number of workers in the professions will have increased by about 30 percent.

Technicians. The jobs done by technicians are similar in many ways to those of professionals. Among the best known of these highly skilled workers are medical X-ray technicians, physical therapists, dental hygienists, and medical laboratory technicians. Other technicians are employed in radio and television, motion picture, manufacturing, and computer industries.

A high school education is the foundation upon which the technician builds. Some technicians learn their skills on the jobs. But many of them must take special courses in colleges or in job-training schools.

Managers and executives. "Big business" in America probably will become even bigger in the years ahead. More experienced and well-trained people will be needed to manage business firms. The men and women who are in charge of large firms and corporations are known as managers, or members of management. They are also called executives because they are the people who execute, or carry out, the firm's business operations.

The owners of business firms know that

This skilled steelworker helps to produce many of the steel products on which American industry depends.

their success depends upon good management. They work hard to hire, train, and develop managers. Intelligent, hard-working executives are needed as heads of departments, branch offices, research divisions, and special projects. Government, too, needs executives to keep the nation's affairs running smoothly. In every community there are many opportunities for those who wish to manage grocery, dry cleaning, real estate, insurance, and other businesses.

A person with executive ability has very good chances for success in our free economy. But special training is needed if one is to become a successful executive. Today, many of our top executives are college graduates who studied management in university business schools. Many businesses also have their own executive training programs.

Many managers and executives are **self-employed workers.** They prefer to work for themselves. They take their own risks and hope to profit from their own efforts. Many self-employed workers are owners of small retail businesses, builders, and contractors. Managers and executives, however, are not the only self-employed people. Many professional workers, such as doctors, dentists, and lawyers, work for themselves, So, too, do many writers, painters, musicians, and other kinds of workers.

Clerical and sales workers. Clerical workers include typists, file clerks, secretaries, and stenographers. They do much of the paper work that is required to keep America's businesses and industries operating smoothly. The Department of Labor says that our nation will need many office workers in the years ahead, although some of their work is now done by computers, duplicators, and other modern machines and equipment.

Anyone who sells goods and services is a sales worker. Sales workers may be clerks in retail stores. They may sell from door to door. Or they may sell to other businesses, to institutions, or to governments. Sales workers are much in demand. Many of them get their training on the job. The skills they need do not require long periods of training, and may be learned by intelligent, hard-working individuals. Other sales workers, such as real estate agents, insurance agents, and specialized sales representatives often have college educations. Some must take special courses and pass state examinations.

BLUE-COLLAR WORKERS

Blue-collar workers provide labor for industry. They work in construction, steel, petroleum, transportation, manufacturing, mining,

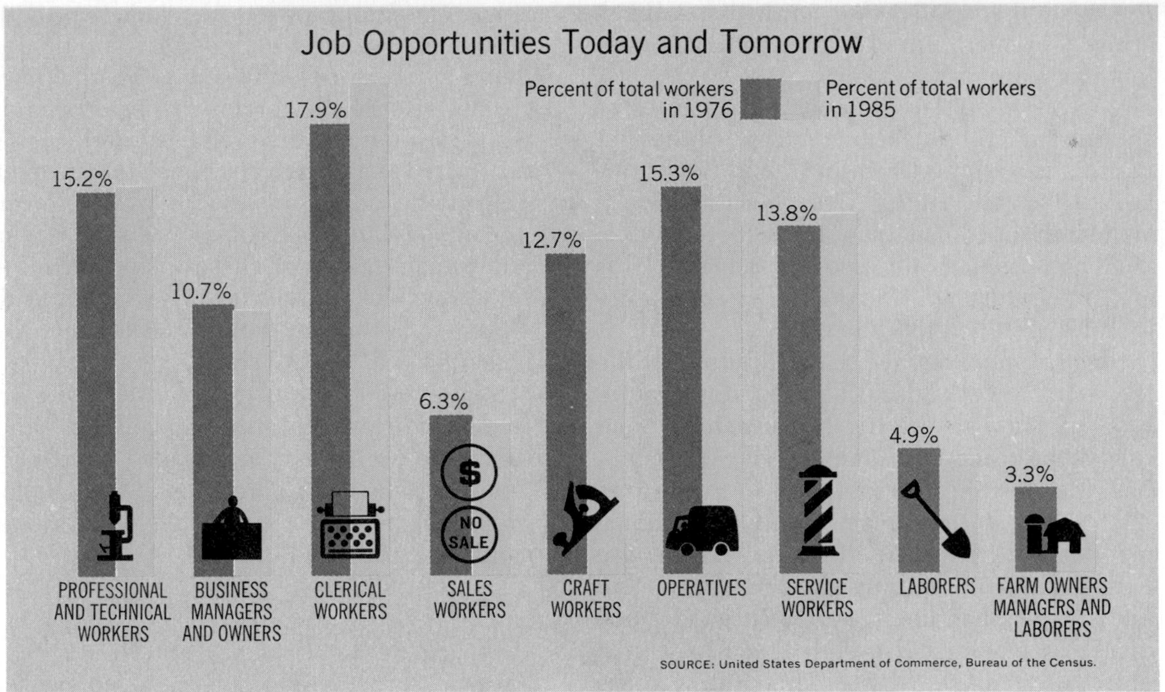

and many other industries. Since the mid-1950's, the number of blue-collar workers in America has decreased.

Craft workers. Craft workers are those in skilled occupations. They include: carpenters, electricians, machinists, bricklayers, roofers, plumbers, printers, bakers, auto mechanics, painters, patternmakers, repairers, and construction workers.

Workers in crafts, or trades, must be able to work skillfully with their hands as well as their heads. They must be good at practical mathematics. In many cases, they must have extra physical strength to do parts of their jobs. The most important requirement is good manual ability, or skill. That is, they must be able to do accurate and sometimes difficult work with their hands.

The usual method of training for a craft is for the new worker to serve an **apprenticeship**, or a fixed period of on-the-job training. An apprentice receives an income while learning the job. The usual length of on-the-job training is four years. Some industries and unions reduce the amount of apprenticeship time by giving credit for job-training courses completed in a high school or trade school.

When apprentices have learned their craft, they receive a "Certificate of Completion of Apprenticeship." After experience on the job, they may become master craft workers and receive the highest wages in their trade.

Each of the crafts has its own labor union. The number of people admitted into the crafts each year is limited by union rules, the needs of the industry, and the available supply of trained workers. Some craft workers, such as plumbers and electricians, must pass state examinations and receive licenses in order to practice their crafts.

The future holds many job opportunities for young people who can work with their hands as well as their heads, and who succeed in becoming skilled in the crafts. In the past, the crafts were worked at almost entirely by men. But now women have begun to enter many of the trades.

Operatives. People who operate machines or equipment in factories, mills, industrial plants, gas stations, mines, and laundries are called operatives. Other factory workers, such as those who inspect, assemble, and pack goods are also included in this group. Drivers of trucks, buses, and automobiles are operatives as well.

Many operatives get their training on the job. Their work usually does not require long periods of training because they often repeat the same task many times. The qualities that employers look for in operatives are dependability, good health, and some manual skill. Because a job does not require long periods of training does not mean that anyone can handle it. A really good truck driver or welder has a skill that was gained only after many years. This skill comes from practice, good judgment, and good physical coordination.

The jobs of some operatives face an uncertain future. The number of machine operators in American industry has declined as factories have become more fully automated.

Laborers. There are, and probably always will be, a number of jobs that call for little or no training. Workers without special skills are often employed to mix cement, carry bricks, dig ditches, and handle freight and other heavy loads. Workers who do this heavy physical work are called laborers.

There are fewer and fewer opportunities for laborers each year. Automatic power increasingly is replacing muscle power. More and more, machines are used to mix cement, dig ditches, load freight, and to do many other jobs requiring heavy manual labor.

SERVICE WORKERS

Today, one out of every seven employed Americans is a service worker. Service workers provide the public with some needed assistance. One group of service workers provides protection services. Included are fire fighters, police officers, detectives, and guards. Other groups of service workers are health service workers, such as nurses aides, orderlies, practical nurses, and private household workers. Yet another group of service workers is employed by business firms that sell services rather than products. These business firms are called **service industries.** They include dry cleaners, laundries, hotels, restaurants, barbershops, and beauty shops.

Some service industry jobs require a college education or job-training courses. Others teach the skills that are needed on the job. There are many opportunities in the service industries because much of the work they do cannot be automated.

FARM WORKERS

As you have read before, the need for farm workers has decreased greatly during this century. Anyone who owns, manages, or works on a farm, even an unpaid member of a farm family, is a farm worker. Today, only one out of every 30 workers is a farm worker. Experts predict that the need for farm workers will continue to decline.

CONSIDER AND DISCUSS

Identify. white-collar workers / professions / technicians / managers / executives / self-employed workers / clerical workers / sales workers / blue-collar workers / craft workers / apprenticeship / operatives / laborers / service worker / service industry / farm worker

Review. 1. What are the main categories of workers in America? 2. Why must those who enter the professions spend many years in training for their careers? 3. Why has the demand for laborers decreased? 4. What training must a worker have to become a master craft worker? 5. Name some service workers.

Discuss. Would you rather be self-employed or work for a large corporation? Why?

3 Opportunities Unlimited

Whether one is a member of a profession, a technician, a craft worker, a service worker, or a laborer, there are opportunities for advancement. Young men and women who graduate from a high school commercial course might start their careers as stenographers, filing clerks, or bookkeepers. Then, by attending special night-school classes, they might qualify for better positions. They might study accounting, for example, and learn how to keep business financial records. A skilled accountant is required by management as part of its business team. If young men and women have prepared themselves, they will be ready when the right opportunity presents itself.

GOVERNMENT JOBS

Our nation's largest employer is the United States government. Almost 3 million Americans work for the federal government, not counting those who serve in the armed forces. These **federal employees** work at every imaginable job.

They deliver our mail, care for war veterans, and protect against counterfeiting. They also run our national parks, forecast the weather, and inspect our food and drugs to make sure they are pure. Then, too, many thousands of clerks, typists, and secretaries are required to carry out the everyday business of the United States government.

To qualify for most federal jobs, those who apply must take a test. When government job openings occur, tests are announced. The jobs go to those who make the highest scores on the tests. These tests are usually called **civil service examinations.**

State and local governments also employ many different kinds of workers. Like federal employees, state and local workers usually are chosen by civil service examinations. Notices of government job openings in federal, state, and local governments are sent to school counselors. You may also see these notices on post office bulletin boards or printed in local newspapers.

OPPORTUNITIES IN THE ARMED FORCES

With more and more emphasis upon a volunteer army, careers in the military are being made more attractive. Salaries have been raised, and a greater choice of occupations is offered to men and women.

A high school graduate may receive technical training in the armed forces for such jobs as electronic repairer, telephone, radio, and radar operator and repairer, medical equipment technician, motor mechanic, surveyor, printer, medical technician, photographer, and many others.

Officer training has already been discussed in Chapter 6. To qualify for West Point, Annapolis, the Air Force Academy, or the Coast Guard Academy, one must be a high school graduate. Applicants must pass an entrance examination in English, American history, and mathematics. A high school diploma is also helpful in qualifying for most good jobs in the armed forces.

WORKERS IN HIGH DEMAND

The United States Department of Labor constantly studies job opportunities in our nation. Each year it reports where men and women are working and the jobs they are doing. This department of our federal government also studies the job needs of our nation. What workers are needed right now? What workers will be needed ten years from now?

In a study made in 1975, the Department of Labor estimated that through the mid-1980's job openings would be best in the following occupations:

Stenographers	Receptionists
Secretaries	Cosmetologists

Sales workers	Bank clerks
Bookkeepers	Truck drivers
Building custodians	Carpenters
Kindergarten and elementary school teachers	Accountants
	Computer operators
	Industrial machine repairers
Cooks and chefs	
Registered nurses	Social workers
Practical nurses	Private household workers
Engineering and science technicians	Construction workers

Keep in mind that the need for a certain kind of worker may be greater in some parts of the country than in others. The above study is for the nation as a whole. But local needs often result in an unusually heavy demand for certain kinds of workers.

Our nation will also need many professional and technical workers. Mathematicians, for example, are almost always in demand. So are law-enforcement officers and members of the armed forces. Also, remember that in all jobs there is a constant turnover because of promotions, job changes, or retirements. The well-prepared person will be ready to grab a job opportunity when it occurs.

EQUAL EMPLOYMENT OPPORTUNITY

In your study of career opportunities, you may have noticed these words in the classified advertisements in newspapers: "An Equal Opportunity Employer." This statement means that the employer does not practice discrimination against job applicants because of their sex, age, skin color, or ethnic background.

Congress passed the Civil Rights Acts of 1964 and 1968 to help end discrimination in hiring and in wage rates. These acts have opened up new job opportunities for women and for minority groups. An **Equal Employment Opportunity Commission,** appointed by the President, upholds the fair employment standards. Several states have similar laws, and commissions to enforce them.

Women are finally beginning to gain the right to be considered for any job. There are Congresswomen, women generals, women jockeys, women scientists, women cab drivers—indeed, few fields are not open to women today. In industry, job distinctions between men and women are breaking down.

The federal government employs thousands of women as clerks, secretaries, typists, personnel workers, and as specialists in many of the government's bureaus. Today, nearly all government jobs are open to women as well as men.

America's business firms are urging young women to study for scientific and technical

Computers are being used to help run more and more businesses. Many kinds of workers are needed to build, maintain, and operate these computers.

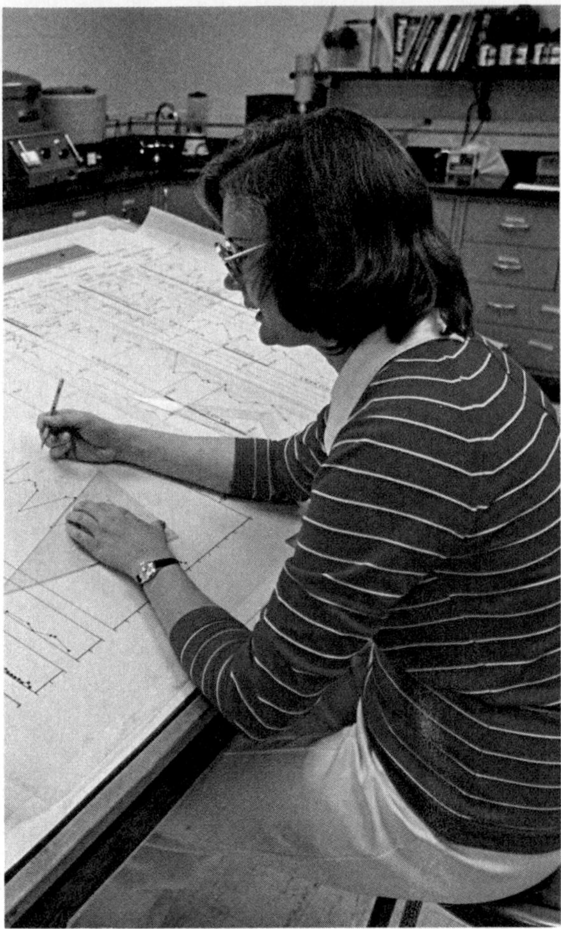

Many jobs require people with special training. This engineer is drawing detailed plans.

jobs that were once open only to men. The Women's Bureau of the Department of Labor has predicted that America's future needs for technical and scientific workers cannot be met unless more women are encouraged to enter these fields.

The profession of nursing is a field in which men as well as women are urgently needed. Many nursing positions are now open, and more will be open in the future in hospitals, public health agencies, nursing homes, industry, schools, doctors' offices, and the armed forces.

OPPORTUNITIES LIMITED

As you learned earlier in this unit, there are times when our economic system goes through a period of hard times. At such times a great many people are out of work. This unhealthy economic situation existed in the mid-1970's. Over seven million Americans were jobless.

Some of these unemployed persons lacked the new skills required in our economy. Some were out of work because the economy was not operating at full capacity. There were even some highly skilled scientists who lost their jobs when, for example, government spending on the space program was cut back. Engineers became house painters. Space scientists drove taxi cabs. Eventually, most of these people found jobs in which they could use their special skills. But in the meantime they underwent difficult periods of adjustment.

The young person studying careers should remember that there have always been periods of unemployment. It is wise to have more than one interest and, if possible, to develop skills in more than one area of work. You might want to consider job possibilities from the viewpoint of security before you make a final decision.

Further aspects of career choice will be considered in the next section.

CONSIDER AND DISCUSS

Identify. federal employees / civil service examinations / Equal Employment Opportunity Commission

Review. In what jobs will opportunities be especially good through the mid-1980's? 2. What qualifications must one have for a career as an army officer? 3. What is "An Equal Opportunity Employer"? 4. Why should a person studying careers consider the possibility of employment security?

Discuss. Would you rather have a low-paying, secure job, or a well-paying job with the risk of unemployment in bad times?

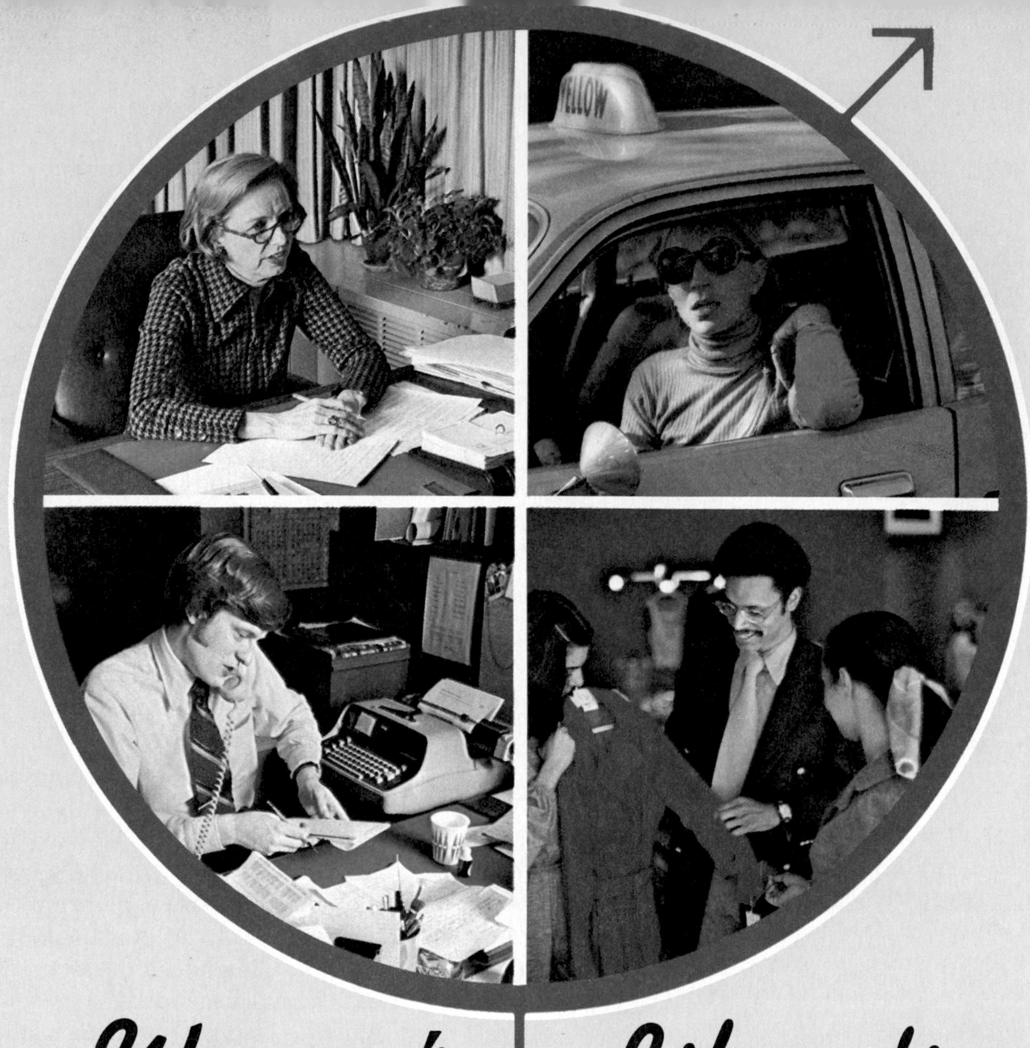

Women's Liberation

What factors will determine your career and the kind of life you live? Your abilities? Your education? Your interests? Yes, all of these. But what about your sex? If you are a girl, are your choices limited to only a few careers, including homemaker? Or do you have the same freedom of choice as a boy? If you are a boy and get married, will your wife have an independent career of her own? Or will she devote all her time to your home and children? Whether you are male or female, these questions are important to your future. They are all questions that have to do with Women's Liberation.

The Women's Liberation Movement of today has its roots deep in America's past. At the time of the Revolution, women like Abigail Adams urged that women as well as men should have a voice in their own government. But when the Constitution went into effect, only men had the right to vote. Beginning in the 1840's, a strong movement for women's rights grew. These women worked hard to gain the same basic rights as men—to own property, to go to college, to work at a profession, and above all, to vote. In 1869, Wyoming became the first state to grant women's suffrage, or voting rights. But it was not until 1920, with the Nineteenth Amendment to the Constitution, that all women finally gained the right to vote.

Does this mean that men and women are now equal in our society? Look around you. You will find very few women in Congress, or in the professions, or at the head of business corporations. Most of our doctors and dentists are men. The nurses who assist them are women. Most business executives and government officials are men. The secretaries who type their letters are women. On any job, the "boss" is almost always a man. We are so used to these differences between men and women that most people just take them for granted. But today, more and more women are beginning to ask "Why?"

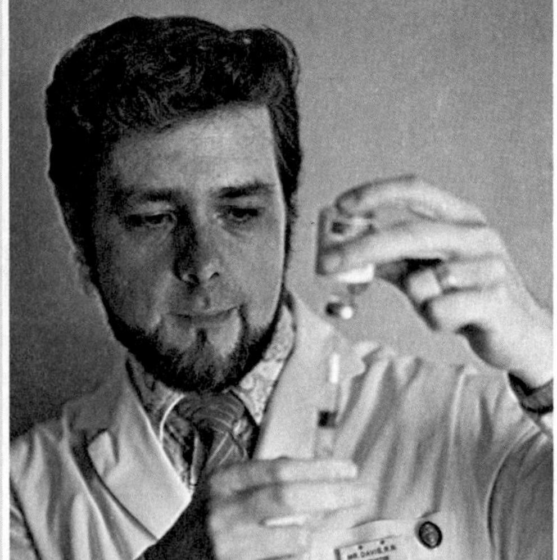

WHAT Do YOU THINK?

What do you think? Why are certain jobs held mostly by men? Is there anything wrong with this? Does "equality of opportunity" apply to women as well as men?

Many women trying to pursue a career have encountered sex discrimination. That is, some employers will not hire women for certain jobs, or will pay them less than men, or will not promote them to better jobs. Some colleges and professional schools admit very few women. Some unions and professional associations make it very difficult for women to join. Some businessmen's clubs do not admit women. In all of these examples, women are discriminated against simply because they are women.

The new campaign for women's rights has succeeded in getting Congress to pass the "Equal Rights Amendment." If ratified by the states, this new Constitutional amendment will guarantee that "Equality of rights under the law shall not be denied or abridged by the United States or by any state on account of sex." What do you think will be the effect of the Equal Rights Amendment? What changes will it bring about? What good effects will it have? Do you think it might have any bad effects? Explain your answer.

The Equal Rights Amendment and other laws will help to eliminate sex discrimination. But will these laws bring about full equality between men and women? Do you think men and women ought to be completely equal? Questions like these

have raised the most heated debate concerning the Women's Liberation Movement.

Some people have said that women simply do not have the intelligence or the energy to compete on equal terms with men. They are naturally dependent and need to be protected. What do you think of this argument? Do the boys in your class all get better grades than the girls? Do the boys work harder on class projects? Is there any evidence to support this theory of "male superiority"?

But there are other problems involved in careers for women, especially married women. Can a woman be a fulltime doctor or business executive, and still be a homemaker too? What if her husband's career takes them to a different part of the country? What happens when she has a baby?

Many supporters of the Women's Liberation Movement would say that these are all "male chauvinist" arguments. That is, they reflect the self-centered attitude of men. Why should a woman necessarily be a homemaker at all? Why shouldn't a woman hire a homemaker, just as an unmarried man might do? Or else the husband and wife could share equally in the household chores. And why should a family always be ruled by the husband's career? Marriage should be an equal partnership, they believe, and plans should be made to suit the best interests of both partners. What do you think of "equal marriage"? Is there any difference of opinion between the boys and the girls in your class?

The question of raising a family is perhaps the most important one of all. Supporters of Women's Liberation point out, first, that women today can choose if and when they want to have children. When a woman decides to have a baby, they say, she should be able to take a maternity leave, and then return to her career. These people say that motherhood need not be a full-time job, any more than fatherhood is. In many societies, children are taken care of by grandparents, older brothers and sisters, or nurses. What we need, they say, are more child-care facilities for working mothers. It is social custom, not nature, that insists on motherhood as a career in itself. Do you think they are right or wrong? Why do you say this?

There is no scientific evidence that can provide a sure answer to these questions. Each man and each woman must think about them and make his or her own decisions. But the Women's Liberation Movement is making both men and women sit up and think. Listen to the arguments on both sides. Perhaps you will want to change some of your own attitudes toward careers and marriage.

4 Learning More About Careers

As you read this chapter, you are probably discovering that you know a great deal more about careers and jobs than you thought you did. For one thing, in your earlier studies you have often read about the careers of famous men and women. However, no single book—even a book on careers—can give you all you need to know about various jobs that you will need before you can make a wise choice. You may have to spend a lot of time hunting in different places to get all the facts you will need in order to discover what would be the best job for you.

READING ABOUT CAREERS

One of the best ways to learn about jobs is to read the many books, magazines, and booklets on the subject. Explore your library, the newsstands, and any books you may have at home. Your local state employment office has a number of booklets about careers in your community. Usually, these booklets are free of charge. Since large business firms are always on the lookout for good employees, many of them put out interesting booklets that contain useful job information.

Reading about career opportunities in order to find a job field that interests you is like doing detective work. One clue leads to another as the job picture becomes clearer and clearer. You may find a clue in a book of fiction or in a biography. Then you may find another bit of evidence in a newspaper column or magazine article. In this way you act as your own detective in solving the problem of careers. As you read about jobs, of course, you must keep your own interests, needs, and abilities in mind. But you should also try to keep an open mind. You may discover a possible career that you never even thought about before.

WATCHING OTHERS AT WORK

Reading about jobs will help you learn many facts about them. But why not take a closer look by going out and observing job opportunities in your community? Through school-sponsored trips, you can learn a great deal about the jobs available in the factories, offices, and stores in your locality. One of your parents may be able to arrange for you to visit his or her place of employment. You can also learn about jobs by keeping your eyes open as you go about your daily affairs. Observe the work of bus drivers, police, teachers, salespeople, office workers, and others you meet each day.

You will learn more from watching people at work if you go about it in a careful way. Take notes on what you learn. Ask questions. Interview people who are working in jobs that interest you. Ask them to tell you what they like best and what they like least about their work. Talk over jobs that interest you with your parents, friends, and counselors. Discussing your ideas and trying them out on others will help make many ideas clearer in your own mind.

LEARNING BY WORKING AT A JOB

One good way to learn more about jobs is to go out and get a job. As a student, your work opportunities may be limited to part-time jobs and summer employment. You probably will take such jobs mainly as a way to earn some extra money. But you can also learn something from any job, no matter what kind of a job it is. Baby-sitting, for example, may lead you to think that you might like a future job in the nation's growing day care centers. If not, it will at least give you a chance to learn more about people. Baby-sitting can also help you to see why being prompt and dependable is important in any job. Being a newspaper carrier, a clerk in a supermarket, a gasoline station helper, or a movie usher are other

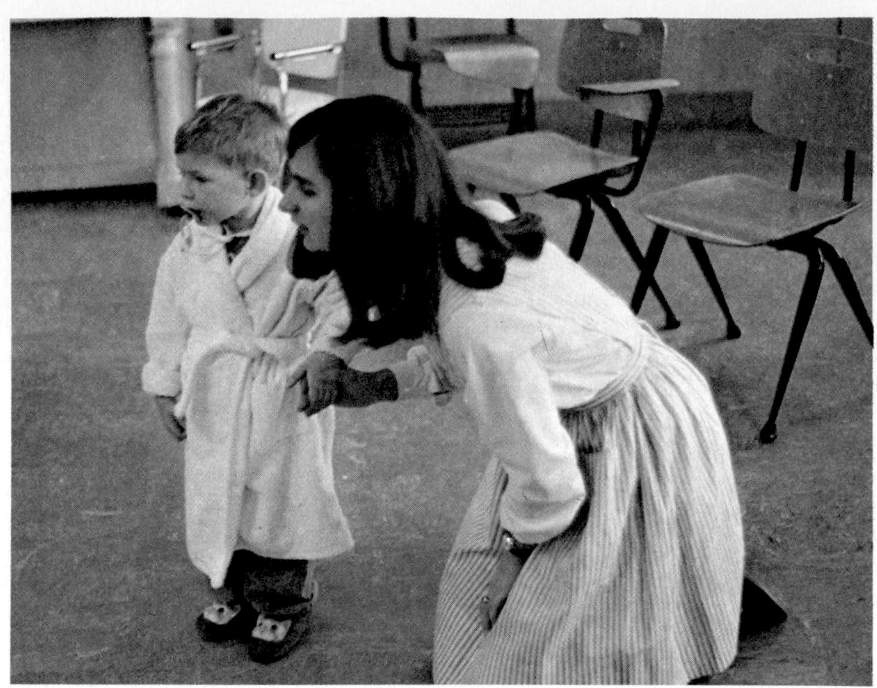

Volunteer work may offer opportunities to learn more about possible careers. This teenager works as a volunteer in the children's ward of a local hospital.

ways for you to get to know what work is really like.

Don't overlook your hobbies as an interesting way to find out more about what you like to do and what you can do well. Many people have turned their hobbies into their life work. Hobbies may also help you to learn whether you have special abilities. You can then begin to think about jobs that require abilities similar to those you use in your hobby.

Another good way to find out about your abilities is to take an active interest in school life. Try writing for the school newspaper. Manage a team. Serve on a class committee. Help decorate for school dances. Sell tickets for local affairs. These and other activities will give you a chance to see whether you enjoy writing, managing, selling, decorating, or some other skill that you may use later in a job.

JOB QUESTIONS TO ASK YOURSELF

As you consider your career choice, you can avoid guesswork if you will ask yourself these seven important questions. Your answers to them should help you to decide if you are making a wise choice of jobs.

1. What kind of work will I do in this job? Will I be working alone or with other people? Will I be working mostly with my hands or with my brains? What skills will I need to develop in order to do the job well? Does the job involve study and careful planning, or does it involve doing the same thing over and over again?

2. What personal qualifications are required? How important in this job are neatness, promptness, dependability, and a pleasant personality? Must I be able to follow directions? Will I be expected to give directions and to lead others? Does the job call for strong muscles?

3. How much education and training does the job require? Must I be a high school graduate? Is a college education necessary? Is a period of apprenticeship required for the job? If so, how long does it last? Is any specialized training required?
4. Are job opportunities in this field good? Are there many job openings now in this field? Is this a growing field of work? Will there be more openings when I am ready to look for a job? Is this the kind of job in which I can develop my abilities and move ahead, or is it a dead-end job?
5. What salary does the job pay? Is the starting salary only the first step toward a higher income in this job? What training must I have to receive salary increases? What other benefits, such as insurance, sick pay, on-the-job training, and pleasant working conditions are there? Will I be satisfied with the **salary range** (beginning salary, possible raises, and highest salary) that the job offers?
6. How do I feel about this occupation? Do I feel that this is a job worth doing? Will I be making a worthwhile contribution to the community? Will I be happy working with the kind of people who may be employees on this job?
7. In this kind of job, where will I have to live and work? Will I have to move to another part of the United States? Does the job require that I travel around a lot? Will I have to live in a large city? Are most workers in this field employed in factories, on farms, in offices, or in their own homes?

A SAMPLE JOB QUIZ

Why is it so important to ask yourself these questions—and to find the answers to them? You probably have guessed the reason. It is one of the best ways to find out whether the job you are considering is the right job for you.

Suppose that Janet Smith, a ninth-grade student, is interested in a job as a **medical technician.** The seven questions on this page and the next may help to provide her with the answers she needs to decide whether she really wants that kind of career.

Question 1. What kind of work will I do in this job?

Answer: Medical technicians usually work with doctors in the laboratories of hospitals and clinics, helping them to discover and to cure diseases. Medical technicians perform tests that help doctors to decide how to treat diseases. They take blood tests, for example, and report the results of these tests. They help to prepare various tests that doctors give patients to check for many diseases.

Question 2: What personal qualifications are required?

Answer: The medical technician must be a dependable, accurate person who is interested in science. She or he must be intelligent, careful, and able to follow directions. She or he must also have good eyesight and skillful hands.

Question 3: How much education and training does the job require?

Answer: At least three years of college are required, plus a year of special training in a hospital to learn laboratory procedures.

Question 4: Are job opportunities in this field good?

Answer: There is a shortage of medical technicians. Well-trained workers will have no trouble getting jobs. The work can lead to a job in medical research, to ownership of an independent laboratory, or to a job as a laboratory supervisor.

Question 5: What salary does the job pay?

Answer: The starting salary of a college-trained medical technician is about $9,500. Salaries increase with experience.

Question 6: How do I feel about this occupation?

Answer: Medical technicians do interesting and important work. They help those who are sick to get well again.

Question 7: In this kind of job, where will I have to live and work?

Answer: The medical technician works in hospitals, medical centers, private laboratories, clinics, and doctors' offices that are found in most communities. The worker can live anywhere within reach of the job.

The job quiz will help the person looking for a job decide whether to become a medical technician. It should also give you and the rest of your class a good idea of the work of the medical technician.

Using the seven questions listed above, you and your classmates can work out job quizzes for any occupations that interest you.

CONSIDER AND DISCUSS

Identify. salary range / medical technician

Review. 1. Where can you get information about careers? 2. How can a part-time job help you in choosing a career? 3. How are hobbies useful in deciding the kind of work you might like to do? 4. What are the seven important questions to keep in mind when considering a job?

Discuss. A girl in your class wants to be an artist. She knows that opportunities for artists are limited, and that only a few people manage to earn a living in this field. But she knows that those who do succeed may find it a very satisfying career. What advice would you give her?

5 Learning More About Yourself

Some jobs may interest you because they seem exciting and glamorous. Many young people think about becoming singers, actors, or professional athletes. But many of them finally discover that these jobs are too difficult or that they really are more interested in some other job.

Of course, if you decide that you have what it takes to be a success in one of these fields, then you should work as hard as you can to get into it. But if you honestly study your interests and abilities and discover you are more likely to succeed in some other job, you would be wiser to choose that job for your career.

To learn about yourself is not easy. It is difficult for most of us to look at ourselves honestly and to judge our own abilities and interests. But it is well worth the effort that it takes if we finally are able to get a true picture of ourselves. We must also learn how we appear, or seem, to other people. Often, other people can help us see ourselves as we really are.

There are several ways in which we can get to know ourselves better and to discover the kinds of persons we are. What are some ways in which we can learn to know ourselves?

PREPARING TO APPLY FOR A JOB

When the time comes to seek your first job, you will probably have to fill out a **personnel record form.** This printed form is a card on which you are asked to supply important information about yourself. Your personnel record form helps the employer to decide if you are the right person for the job. Large business firms have **personnel workers** whose job it is to hire new workers or to recommend them for employment. These personnel workers examine personnel record forms and interview people to find the best-qualified worker for a job opening.

You will probably find it helpful to practice filling out a personnel record form. Then when you apply for a job later on, you will know the kind of information you will be asked to give. You can practice writing out your personnel record in several ways. Perhaps you can fill out a real personnel form used by a local business firm. Or you may use a blank sheet of paper to outline important facts about yourself. Many students find it helpful to write short autobiographies including the chief facts about their lives. No matter which you choose, you will find it good practice to fill out a personnel form.

WHAT EMPLOYERS WANT TO KNOW

To prepare your own personnel record, you should know the kind of information that employers will want to have when you seek a job. In general, employers will want to know certain facts as follows:

1. Your Personal History. What do employers want to learn about you as a person? First, they want such facts as your name, address, and date of birth. Some may also want to know about your family. How many brothers and sisters do you have, and what are their ages? This will show whether you are an only child, the youngest or the oldest child, or one among many children. Employers sometimes want to know your father's and mother's occupations.

Each of these facts by itself may not seem important. But added together they help to tell the kind of person you are. Take a new look at these facts about yourself and see how they may help an employer to know and understand you.

2. Your School History. Your school record tells the employer a lot about you. List the subjects you have taken in the last two years and the grades you received in each. Then take a long, hard look at the reasons for these grades. What do grades mean? Perhaps you have high grades in English because you enjoy expressing yourself through writing. This may show that you should consider an occupation in which you can use your writing talent. On the other hand, you may have poor grades in mathematics. Does this mean that you should not even consider a job that requires mathematical ability? Not necessarily!

These young job applicants are checking a school bulletin board for jobs.

Grades do not always tell the whole story about one's interests or abilities. Some students with low grades in mathematics may just be finding themselves in this subject. Perhaps, they had trouble understanding number concepts in their earlier math courses. But after special effort, they are catching up in their studies. They may now be on their way to mastering math and getting higher grades. As you see, low grades in any subject are not necessarily a sign that the student cannot learn. Low grades often are a sign of lack of effort by the student rather than lack of ability.

Perhaps in listing your subjects and grades you should include a third column entitled "Reasons for the Grades." This column will help you in judging your own abilities and interests. It will also tell you how well you have used them up to now.

3. Your Health Record. Good health is an

important qualification for any job. In addition, some occupations require that workers have special physical qualifications. Sometimes good eyesight is essential. A medical technician, a surgeon, or a jeweler, for example, needs good eyesight. For this reason, you will want to examine your own health record and review your program for keeping fit.

There are many job opportunities, however, for persons with physical handicaps. The history of American business and industry is filled with stories of people who succeeded in spite of their handicaps. As just one example, Thomas Edison, the great inventor, was deaf. Yet his life was filled with outstanding accomplishments. A person may not be able to do anything about certain physical handicaps, but he or she can choose a job in which such handicaps are no drawback.

4. Your Outside Activities. Make a list of your hobbies, the school offices you have held, sports in which you take part, school organizations you belong to, and your part-time and summer jobs. After you have completed this list take another look at it. Does it show many different activities? What part of each activity did you like best? What part of your hobbies or part-time jobs did you enjoy most? This review can teach you much about your interests and abilities.

5. Your Special Interests. The things that interest you now may also point the way to the future. What are your present likes and dislikes? Do you favor indoor or outdoor work? Do you prefer working alone or with others? Do you prefer working with your hands or using your mind? Do you favor doing a variety of activities or performing the same activity over many times? Are you interested in being a leader, or are you a follower? Do you like to work on your own, or do you prefer to follow directions?

List all of your interests that you think might help you make a choice. Check back on the subjects you have liked best in school. Try to see if your interests have helped you do well in these subjects. Also review your hobbies and your part-time work activities to see what interests they may show.

STUDY YOUR TEST RECORD

Tests are another means of helping you to understand yourself and your abilities. Every test you take in school measures certain abilities. You have probably already taken tests that show how well you study, how accurately you remember what you read, how well you express yourself. It will be worth your while to go back over your test scores and consider the reasons for these scores. They should show your ability to do certain things. Here are some of the abilities that such tests seek to measure.

MOTOR SKILLS

Certain tests are used to determine how well people can use their hands—their **motor skills.** They measure how fast they can do things with their hands. They also check how accurately they do things. Certain other tests determine how well a person can handle and arrange small objects. You can understand why good motor skills are useful to a watchmaker or to a worker assembling small electronic equipment.

NUMBER SKILLS

One of the most common tests measures a person's ability to work with numbers quickly and accurately. Such **number skills** are essential to bookkeepers, carpenters, and accountants. Many scientists also need to be skilled in using numbers.

PERCEPTUAL SKILLS

How well can you picture things—that is, see them in your mind? In order to read a blueprint, for example, you must be able to picture in your mind the way a building will look when finished. You must be able to see depth and width in a flat drawing. The ability to think in this way is a part of **perceptual skills.**

LANGUAGE SKILLS

A teacher explaining an idea to students, a salesperson talking to a customer, and a parent showing a child how to draw all have skill in using language. The editor, the advertising specialist, and the executive in a business firm must be skilled in using written language. Many kinds of tests check this ability, called **language skills** or linguistic ability.

SPECIAL TALENTS

Some tests include sections that try to discover whether a person has artistic and creative talents. Sometimes there is also a section to measure one's ability to organize and present facts.

PERSONAL RELATIONSHIPS

There are tests to check on how well you handle personal relationships—how well you get along with others. This is an important skill in many jobs. Teachers should rank high in this skill. So should salespeople, social workers, receptionists, and other workers who deal with many people.

INTERESTS AND APTITUDES

There are certain other tests you take in school that can help you to know yourself better. These are called interest tests or **aptitude tests.** They are easy to take and reveal interesting things about you. Your teacher or counselor may help explain the results of these tests and the meaning that they have for you.

Such tests probably will not tell you the exact job you should have. No test can map out the future for you. What these tests are supposed to do is to help you discover your abilities and interests. Then it is up to you to match what you know about yourself with what you learn about various job opportunities.

By now you have probably made a good start on getting to know yourself better. As you study jobs that interest you, compare your opportunities with your abilities. Your present aim should be to choose a general field of work—a kind of work rather than a specific job. Leave the way open so that you can change to another kind of work if you need to do so. Remember, your present job choice may not be your final one.

Working on a school newspaper provides valuable experience for any career requiring good language skills.

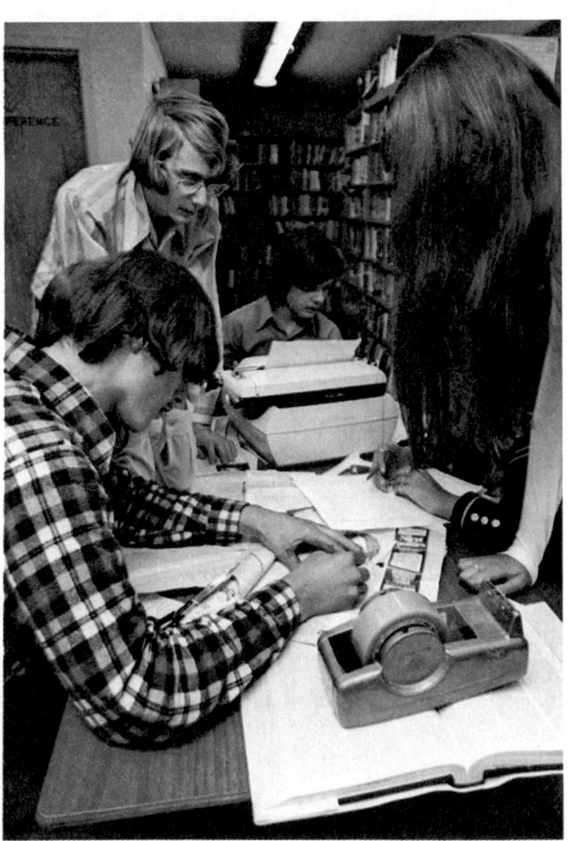

CONSIDER AND DISCUSS

Identify. personnel record form / personnel worker / motor skills / number skills / perceptual skills / language skills / aptitude tests

Review. 1. Why does an employer want a personnel record form filled out by job applicants? 2. Why is your school history important to an employer? 3. Why would an employer want to know about a job applicant's health? 4. How might one of your hobbies grow into a career for you? 5. What does an aptitude test reveal about a person?

Discuss. What information in this textbook has been of most value in helping you think about jobs? Why?

CHAPTER
Summary

All young Americans must plan for their jobs or careers in the world of work. There are many job opportunities for young people. But these opportunities keep changing. For this reason, you must get up-to-date information on jobs if you are to make a wise career choice.

In considering job opportunities, you should know about the work done by those in the professions, by managers, by technicians, by service workers, and by craft workers, operatives, and farm workers. You may also wish to consider businesses in which you can be self-employed, or careers in the armed forces, or jobs in government.

The choice of your career must be made by you. No one can make this choice for you. But there are certain general guides that you may find helpful. You can read widely about jobs, explore jobs in your community, interview workers, and work at a part-time job in order to gather all the information you can about job possibilities. The sample job quiz in this chapter should help guide you in searching for job information.

An important step in deciding upon a career is to learn more about yourself. Your personality, your school and health record, your special interests, your outside activities, and your work experience will be of interest to prospective employers. One good way to learn more about yourself is to examine the results of personal inventory and achievement tests taken in school.

You can prepare yourself now so that you will know what employers look for when hiring new workers. Get to know about jobs that are available, not only in your community but also throughout the country. Use your school years wisely, because the skills and knowledge you acquire in school will help you the rest of your life.

VOCABULARY

In the ten sentences listed below, the words in *italics* are used incorrectly. They make each of the sentences false. Correct the sentences by supplying words that make each statement true.

1. The *professions* are jobs that require little or no training.
2. The men and women who manage large business firms or corporations are known as *apprentices.*
3. Most *operatives* have special trades or occupations that require long periods of training.
4. *Self-employed workers* are workers who quit school in order to get a head start in earning money.
5. Large business firms have *medical technicians* to hire new workers.
6. The ability to read a blueprint depends upon one's *motor skills.*
7. *Service workers* include factory machine operators and laborers.
8. The widespread use of computers in business calls for skilled *executives* to repair them.
9. Dry cleaners, tailors, barbers, and beauticians are examples of *clerical workers.*
10. *Technicians* usually acquire their skills in a short time on the job.

CHECK-UP

Test your mastery of this chapter by answering each of the following questions:

1. What is meant by "freedom of job choice" in America?
2. What are some of the qualities that employers look for in their workers?
3. How does a person prepare for a career in a profession?
4. What is the difference between a craft worker and an operative?
5. What job opportunities are available to women in the United States?
6. What are seven important questions to ask yourself in considering any job?
7. Why are employers interested in knowing how well you did in school?
8. Why is your health record important to employers?

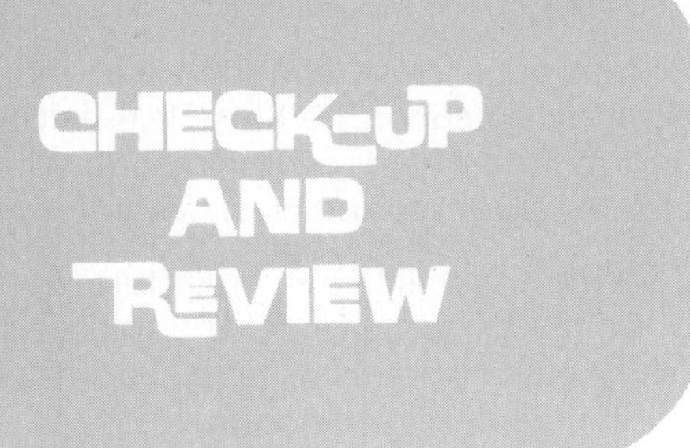

9. What are motor skills? number skills? language skills? perceptual skills?
10. What is the work of the Equal Employment Opportunity Commission?

CITIZENSHIP AND YOU

Your understanding of jobs and careers will be increased if you explore the job market in your community. The following projects are suggested to help you in this exploration.

1. Class Projects

Invite the school counselor to talk to your class about job opportunities in your community. Send the counselor a list of the questions you would like to have answered. Then the counselor will know which job interests to mention when he or she speaks to the class.

Other career experts in your community might be invited to speak to the class. They include personnel managers, employment agency interviewers, and college guidance counselors.

A group that has surveyed the employment opportunities in the local community may report to the class. The report may be in the form of a panel, an illustrated talk, or a dramatization of a young person in search of a job.

2. Group or Committee Projects

Prepare a bulletin board exhibit on job opportunities in the United States.

Interview business people, doctors, teachers, engineers, craft workers, and others to find out how they prepared for their work, the skills required, and the rewards and drawbacks of their jobs.

Collect pictures showing the many kinds of jobs done by American workers. The pictures may be arranged in a scrapbook, presented in a wall display, or shown to the class with a projector.

Construct a chart showing different kinds of jobs that may be listed under the following headings: White-collar workers, Blue-collar workers, Service workers, and Farm workers.

3. Individual Projects

Write an essay called "My Future Career." Gather the facts on a possible career for yourself. Then organize them into a presentation that describes the kind of work you would do, the training needed, the skills required, the salary and other rewards, and ways in which the job would help others.

Read and report on a biography of a noted American. Tell the part that his or her job played in bringing fame to the person.

Make a graph showing the growth of employment in your community over a number of years. You can use separate lines, bars, or parts of the graph to compare the growth of different kinds of jobs.

CIVICS SKILLS

INTERVIEWING

The subject of this chapter, "Careers for Americans," is an especially good one to use in developing interview skills. You will be able to learn a great deal about jobs you are interested in by talking to persons who are working at these jobs. Such interviews will be most useful if you prepare for them in advance and if you make good use of the information you learn from the interview.

Before going out on an interview, make sure you know what it is you wish to learn. Do some reading to prepare yourself for the interview. Then write down the questions you plan to ask. Decide what information and opinions you wish to gain.

Be sure to make arrangements for the interview in advance. Call or write for an appointment. Explain that the interview is a part of your class work. Be serious and businesslike. Make clear the kind of information you are seeking.

Arrive promptly for the interview. Dress neatly, just as you would if you were being interviewed for a job. Be polite when you meet the person to be interviewed. Tell the person the purpose of the interview and the various topics you wish to discuss. Listen attentively and, from time to time, ask questions. You may wish to take notes on the interview. But don't try to take down every word. Write down important thoughts and facts as reminders of what was said.

You may want to make arrangements in advance to use a tape recorder at the interview. Some people like to be interviewed in this way. Others do not. Therefore, be sure to get the person's permission before you use a tape recorder.

At the end of the interview, thank the person being interviewed and leave promptly. It is also a mark of courtesy to follow up the interview with a letter of thanks.

As soon as possible after the interview, organize your notes and write up your interview. You may wish to present it to the class in the form of a news story, as an oral report, or in question-and-answer form. The class will be interested in hearing what you learned from the interview. And you will have had an interesting and useful experience.

PRACTICING YOUR CIVICS SKILLS

A committee of students can arrange to visit the state's employment agency to find out what kinds of jobs are available and the qualifications and training necessary for these jobs. The committee may wish to interview several people at the employment agency. The committee should report what they learned about job opportunities to the class.

Choose a career that you are interested in. Then try to make an appointment with someone who works at this job. Perhaps your parents, teachers, or a guidance counselor may know someone whom you could interview. Make an appointment with this person and interview him or her to find out more about the career you are interested in.

UNIT
SEVEN

America in Today's World

CHAPTER

Introduction

On the desk of the President of the United States there is a bright red telephone. It connects directly with the leaders of the Soviet Union in Moscow. This so-called "hot line" is to be used only in case of the greatest emergency. If through some accident, for example, either nation launched an atomic missile toward the territory of the other, the phone would be used to warn the other side of the danger and to deny warlike intentions.

The fact that such a "hot line" is needed indicates the perils of international affairs in today's world. Hydrogen bombs with massive destructive power are stockpiled in a number of nations. An atomic war would spell the end of civilization. It is little wonder, then, that the world's leaders are seeking new ways to keep peace and to improve relations with their neighbors, near and far.

Much of the time and attention of many officials of the government of the United States is devoted to keeping the peace and to improving international relations. The President often meets with the heads of other nations in a conference to reach needed agreements. The Secretary of State may appear before the United Nations to appeal for a desired course of action. The Secretary of the Treasury may seek a new world monetary policy to aid international trade. At the same time, the Senate may be considering a treaty that will help keep the peace. In the House of Representatives, the Committees on Foreign Affairs, Armed Services, and Commerce may all be considering legislation that will affect our foreign relations. Working behind the scenes are hundreds of other officials gathering information, preparing agreements, seeking allies, and working toward better relations.

It is important that each citizen understands how our foreign policies work, for our lives and welfare may depend upon them. In this chapter we shall consider the following aspects of our foreign policy:

1. Conducting Our Foreign Relations
2. The Development of America's Foreign Policy
3. The United States in the United Nations

CHAPTER

19 Establishing Our Foreign Policy

1 Conducting Our Foreign Relations

The plans that our nation works out for dealing with other countries are called our **foreign policies.** The purpose of these policies is to maintain peace, trade, and friendship throughout the world. The way in which these policies are carried out and their success or failure affects our **foreign relations.** That means it affects the way we get along with the governments of other lands.

In carrying out its foreign policies, the United States depends upon a number of people. Government officials make contact with the leaders of other countries. Business firms carry on foreign trade and therefore affect our foreign relations. Even United States tourists traveling in other countries may influence the attitude of other people toward our nation. How does the United States plan our foreign policies?

THE PRESIDENT AND FOREIGN RELATIONS

The President of the United States is responsible for the conduct of foreign policies. Although he is aided by officials of the Department of State and other advisers, he must be responsible for the major decisions. Article II, Section 2 of the Constitution of the United States gives the President the following powers over foreign relations:

1. Military Powers. As Commander-in-Chief

of the Army and the Navy of the United States, the President makes recommendations to the Congress concerning the size of our armed forces and the kinds of weapons they shall have. He can also order troops, planes, and warships into troubled areas of the world. Only Congress can declare war. But the President, as head of the armed forces, can use American power to help keep the peace or to protect American lives and property overseas. However, the troops sent abroad must be recalled within 60 days unless Congress approves the action.

2. Treaty-making Powers. Formal agreements, or **treaties,** with other nations are a powerful factor in forming our international relations. With the advice and consent of the Senate, the President may make three kinds of treaties. **Treaties of peace** are agreements to end wars. Peace treaties spell out the terms for ending the fighting. They must be agreed upon by all sides in the conflict. **Treaties of alliance** are those in which nations agree to help defend each other in case of attack. **Commercial treaties** are those in which two or more nations agree to trade with each other on favorable terms. These treaties are also called **trade treaties.**

All treaties must be agreed upon by a two-thirds vote of the Senate. However, our nation sometimes reaches agreements with other nations that do not require treaties. The President of the United States may meet with the leader of a foreign government and come to a mutual understanding. This agreement is then announced in a joint statement to the people of their nations. Or the leaders may exchange official letters or notes in which they spell out an agreement. For the most important agreements on policy, however, a treaty must be signed.

3. Diplomatic Powers. The President, again with the approval of the Senate, appoints **ambassadors** to represent the United States in foreign nations. The President also receives the ambassadors from other nations to the United States.

The right of the President to receive ambassadors from foreign nations includes the power of **recognition.** That is, the President may decide whether to deal formally with the government of a foreign nation. To recognize a foreign government means to establish official relations with that government. Sending an American ambassador there and receiving their ambassador means that official recognition has taken place. The President may refuse to recognize a government whose foreign policies are considered unfriendly or dangerous to the United States. For many years, the United States refused to recognize the Communist government of the Soviet Union. Recognition was granted in the 1930's. Ambassadors were then exchanged.

Sometimes it is necessary to break off relations with a foreign nation. **Breaking off relations** means ending all official relations with a foreign country. In breaking off relations, the United States recalls our ambassador and the foreign nation's ambassador returns home. This is a serious move. It is made only when two nations are unable to settle a serious dispute. Sometimes it is a step taken just before war is declared.

Making foreign policy has become highly complicated and dangerous. As a result, the President now hires foreign policy experts to work directly with him in that important task. These policy-making experts are part of the Executive Office of the President.

THE DEPARTMENT OF STATE

The Department of State is the principal organization for carrying out the nation's foreign policy. It acts as "the eyes and ears of the President" in obtaining information upon which our foreign relations are based.

The Department of State is headed by the Secretary of State, who is appointed by the President with the approval of the Senate. The Secretary of State reports directly to the President and is assisted by a Deputy Secre-

The President of the United States is responsible for conducting the nation's foreign relations. Here, President Carter meets with leaders of Nigeria.

tary, Under Secretaries, and many assistant secretaries.

The Secretary of State advises the President and supervises the activities of America's ambassadors. The ambassadors are our nation's major representatives in foreign nations. They are appointed by the President with the advice and consent of the Senate. But they usually report to the Secretary of State. The ambassadors are stationed in the capital cities of most foreign nations.

In a few nations, America's representatives are known as **ministers.** Ambassadors and ministers, with their assistants, are members of our **diplomatic corps.** There are also **consuls** in many foreign cities to help American business people and travelers.

American ambassadors and ministers work for friendly relations with the countries to which they are assigned. They report to the Secretary of State on any events of importance that are happening in the nation in which they are stationed. Their reports are sent in secret code. Or they may be carried by special messengers called **couriers.** Sometimes, ambassadors or ministers will hurry to Washington to meet with the Secretary of State or the President on some special problem. Information obtained in this way helps the President and advisers to decide upon our policy and actions toward other countries. American consuls also send regular reports of business and trade conditions. These reports help American business firms plan their operations in foreign countries.

CONGRESS AND FOREIGN RELATIONS

The President leads our nation in dealing with world affairs. But Congress also plays an important role. For example, the Senate, as you know, must approve all treaties between the United States and other nations by a two-thirds vote. What happens if the Senate refuses to approve a treaty?

After World War I, President Woodrow Wilson wanted the United States to join the League of Nations. A provision for joining this peace-keeping organization was included as a part of the Treaty of Versailles that ended World War I. But a powerful group of Senators opposed membership of the United States in the League of Nations. These Senators succeeded in preventing a two-thirds majority vote in the Senate in favor of the treaty. As a result, the Treaty of Versailles was not approved. And the United States did not join the League of Nations.

It is very important that the President work closely with the leaders in both houses of Congress when deciding on foreign policies. The Senate Foreign Relations Committee and the House Committee on Foreign Affairs make important recommendations on questions of foreign relations.

Congress has another important power in foreign affairs. As you have read, both houses of Congress must approve all expenditures of public funds. The President may recommend that a loan be made to strengthen some nation. But unless Congress votes the money this policy cannot be carried out.

AGENCIES AID THE PRESIDENT

In carrying out the foreign policy of the United States, the President may call upon any department of the government for assistance. The Secretary of Defense and the Joint Chiefs of Staff may assist with advice about the movement of troops and the placement of military bases. The Secretary of Agriculture must keep the President advised concerning the availability of surplus foods that may be sent to a needy nation. The Secretary of the Treasury handles the financial transactions involved in foreign aid. The Secretary of Health, Education, and Welfare supplies information essential to medical aid for foreign lands. Other departments assist in their fields of specialization.

In addition to the help provided by the regular departments, Congress has established a number of specialized agencies to carry out aspects of our foreign policy. You are already familiar with some of these agencies from your study of Chapter 4. You will remember that the **Central Intelligence Agency** is responsible for gathering secret information essential to our national defense. It also helps to keep the President informed on political trends in various nations.

The **International Communications Agency (ICA)** helps to build better foreign relations. Its job is to keep the world informed about the American way of life and about American points of view on world problems. It does this through information centers set up in many cities of the world. The ICA also publishes booklets, distributes motion pictures, and sponsors the "Voice of America" radio programs. Its purpose is to help build good will and understanding abroad.

The **Arms Control and Disarmament Agency** seeks to prevent dangerous arms races. It does so by negotiating with other nations and seeking to reach agreements on arms limitations.

One of the more important of recent groups established to influence foreign relations is the **Agency for International Development (AID).** This organization makes loans and grants to developing nations. Since 1962, AID has provided over 40 billion dollars' worth of modern machinery, raw materials, food, fuel, medical supplies, and loans to help the world's peoples. AID also supplies money and technical assistance during emergencies resulting from floods, epidemics, earthquakes, and other disasters.

The fact that so many agencies and departments of government devote so much time to our foreign affairs indicates that foreign affairs are very important to us. How foreign affairs came to be so important will be considered in the next section.

CONSIDER AND DISCUSS

Identify. foreign policy / foreign relations / treaties / ambassadors / recognition / breaking off relations / ministers / diplomatic corps / consul / couriers / Central Intelligence Agency / International Communications Agency / Arms Control and Disarmament Agency / Agency for International Development

Review. 1. What is the purpose of our foreign policy? 2. What three types of treaties are made by the President? 3. How do ambassadors help to further our international relations? 4. How can Congress check on the President's activities in international affairs? 5. What are some of the government agencies that help the President carry out foreign policy?

Discuss. Do you think our country should give diplomatic recognition to Cuba, a Communist country? Why or why not?

2 The Development of America's Foreign Policy

In 1789, when George Washington became the first President of the United States, our nation was small and weak. The great nations of Europe looked upon the United States as an unimportant country. In fact, some of these European nations believed that the new American nation would not succeed. Since that time, the United States has grown into one of the world's leading nations. Our foreign policies have helped us to grow. As you will see, these policies have changed over the years to meet the changing times.

ISOLATIONISM

The new nation was deeply in debt and struggling to build its industries. It was also looking for solutions to many domestic problems. Most of the leaders of the new government felt that the United States should not take sides in European affairs. This belief that the United States should avoid involvement in foreign affairs is known as **isolationism.**

At no time in our history has the policy of isolationism been an easy one to follow. Even in the late 1700's, President Washington found it difficult to follow this policy. To the north of the United States was the British-owned colony of Canada, and a troubled border situation. To the south and west lay Spanish territory. It blocked American expansion westward and threatened American commerce on the Mississippi River. When American ships ventured out to sea, as they had to do to keep our trade alive, they were stopped and sometimes seized by ships of the British or French navy. At this time, Great Britain and France were at war. For several years it seemed that the United States might become involved in this war.

President Washington was able to avoid trouble with Great Britain by negotiating Jay's Treaty. This treaty seemed to settle many of the quarrels between the two nations. But it was unpopular in America. Pinckney's Treaty with Spain opened up the Mississippi River to American trade. Although war was avoided in these early years, troubles with other nations continued to plague the young nation. Staying out of the war in Europe was becoming more and more difficult.

During the administrations of John Adams and Thomas Jefferson, French and British warships continued to stop American ships at sea. President Adams avoided war and gained time through an agreement with the French. President Jefferson tried to avoid trouble by setting up an **embargo,** that is, by forbidding our ships to trade with Europe. This embargo was not popular because it brought hardship to Americans whose livelihood depended upon trade. When the embargo was lifted, American ships again ran the risk of being captured by British and French ships.

THE WAR OF 1812—A TURNING POINT

Negotiations, treaties, and embargoes failed to settle our differences with the warring nations of Europe. As a result, an increasing number of Americans felt that the only way to gain respect, freedom of the seas, and our rights as an independent nation was to go to war. Leading the demand for war were a number of young members of Congress known as **"War Hawks."** They pointed to Great Britain as the major enemy. Great Britain, they said, was stirring up the Native Americans on our western frontier, occupying forts on United States soil, and taking American sailors off our ships. This was the time, said the War Hawks, to take Canada and make it a part of the United States.

The War of 1812 with Great Britain ended in a **stalemate.** Neither side won a clearcut victory. However, the treaty of peace that ended the war settled disputed boundaries and other differences with Great Britain. Most important, the War of 1812 won a new respect for the United States among the nations of Europe. For 100 years following the conflict, the United States was able to stay out of European conflicts and to build up the nation at home.

THE UNITED STATES AND CANADA

The War of 1812 also marked a turning point in our relations with Canada. American attempts to invade Canada during the war had proved unsuccessful. After the war, Canada and the United States began to build forts along their border and to build fleets of warships on the Great Lakes. This was the kind of situation that could lead to border incidents and perhaps to war.

The leaders of both nations wisely decided to act to insure the peace. They met to talk over their differences and to sign a treaty of friendship. The result was the **Rush-Bagot Agreement.** This treaty provided that the two nations would settle their disputes with each other by peaceful means. As proof of their desire for peace, the two nations agreed that the boundary between the United States and Canada should not be fortified.

The friendly spirit of the Rush-Bagot Agreement has shaped our relations with Canada ever since. When difficulties arise, the two countries talk over their problems until they reach a workable agreement. In this way the two nations have joined in such outstanding projects as the St. Lawrence Seaway and the building of radar stations along the Arctic Circle, called the Distant Early Warning (DEW) Line. The DEW Line helps to protect both nations against any surprise missile attack across the North Polar region.

THE MONROE DOCTRINE

The course of our relations with Latin America, as well as with Europe, was set for many years by a doctrine announced by President James Monroe. A foreign policy doctrine sets forth a new policy of action with respect to other nations. It is a statement of United States policy, and it is not necessarily an agreement with any other nation.

The **Monroe Doctrine** grew out of events

in the early 1800's when the nations of Latin America had just won their independence from Spain. Spain and its European allies were determined that Spain should win back its American colonies. For a while, it looked as if Europe was about to interfere in the affairs of the new nations of Latin America. The United States government decided that our nation must take a strong stand to prevent the new nations of Latin America from being conquered again by Spain or any other European nation.

President Monroe used his annual message to Congress in 1823 to let the world know what the United States thought about this matter. He declared that any attempt by European nations to interfere in the affairs of any nation in the Western Hemisphere would be considered an unfriendly act by the United States. He promised that we would not interfere in European affairs, nor in the affairs of European colonies already established in the Americas. But he also declared that the Americas were no longer open to colonization by European nations.

President Theodore Roosevelt strengthened the Monroe Doctrine when he said that the United States would act as the police officer of the Western Hemisphere.

THE UNITED STATES AND LATIN AMERICA

The policy of action set forth in the Monroe Doctrine has guided our Latin American relations throughout the years. At first, the nations of Latin America welcomed the support of the United States. As "Watchdog of the Western World," the United States helped settle boundary disputes between Latin American countries. When certain European nations threatened to use force to collect debts owed by Latin American countries, the United States moved to prevent such interference.

The Monroe Doctrine was strengthened by Theodore Roosevelt in 1904. At this time, he declared that in the future the United States would take on the role of police officer of the Western Hemisphere. If Latin American nations were not able to manage their own affairs, the United States would step in. This policy became known as the **Roosevelt Corollary** to the Monroe Doctrine.

Americans in growing numbers then began to invest money in Latin American companies. When these investments were threatened by internal disorders, the United States sometimes sent troops to keep the peace. This policy became known as **dollar diplomacy.**

THE "GOOD NEIGHBOR" POLICY

In some ways, the actions of the United States in Central and South America helped the nations there. But these actions also stirred up bad feelings because they insulted the national pride of Latin American countries. Latin American leaders declared that the United States had turned from pro-

In this picture, President Woodrow Wilson is asking Congress to declare war against Germany in 1917. After World War I, the United States returned to its policy of isolationism.

tector to oppressor. As a result, the United States took steps to improve its dealings with Latin America.

In the 1920's the United States stated that the Monroe Doctrine would no longer be used to justify United States intervention in the internal affairs of any neighbor. In the 1930's, President Franklin D. Roosevelt announced a **Good Neighbor Policy.** This policy opposed armed intervention by the United States in Latin American affairs. Also, it emphasized friendly agreements.

As a result of the Good Neighbor Policy, the nations of the Western Hemisphere have joined together in an **Organization of American States (OAS).** The OAS works to strengthen the defenses of the Americas and to promote world peace. The United States and 19 nations of Latin America have also joined in an **Alliance for Progress.** The Alliance attempts to improve social and economic conditions in Latin America.

THE END OF ISOLATION

In 1914, when World War I broke out in Europe, the United States attempted to stay out of the conflict. President Woodrow Wilson announced a policy of **neutrality.** That is, the United States would neither aid nor favor either side. This policy was difficult to maintain. It became impossible when German submarines began to sink American merchant ships without warning and without regard to the safety of the passengers. In response to a war message by President Wilson, Congress declared war on Germany in 1917.

President Wilson stated that our aim in fighting World War I was to help "make the world safe for democracy." The victory of the Allies brought hope for a new era of peace. Woodrow Wilson centered his hopes in a new international organization called the **League of Nations.** The members of the League promised to solve their differences in a friendly fashion and go to war only as a last resort.

As you may recall, provision for joining the League of Nations was submitted to the American Senate as a part of the treaty ending World War I. But there were many Americans, including some powerful Senators, who feared that if the United States joined the League, the nation would be drawn into future European conflicts. The spirit of isolationism was still strong. And it helped keep the United States out of the League of Nations.

The beginning of World War II found the United States again in a neutral position. Neutrality Acts were passed in the mid-1930's forbidding the sale of arms to warring nations. In 1939, the United States did agree to sell arms, but only on a "cash and carry" basis. The arms had to be carried in foreign ships. Soon, the United States became the "arsenal of democracy," supplying arms needed by the Allies. But once again, our neutrality and the isolationist views of some Americans did not keep us out of war. The bombing of Pearl Harbor by the Japanese on December 7, 1941, shocked the American people. They realized that isolation in a worldwide conflict was not possible. The United States declared war on Japan and, soon afterwards, on Germany and Italy.

While World War II was still being fought, plans were being made for a post-war organization of nations to keep the peace. In 1945, the United States joined the people of three quarters of the earth in forming this organization. The promise and problems of this organization will be considered in the following section.

CONSIDER AND DISCUSS

Identify. isolationism / embargo / War Hawks / stalemate / Rush-Bagot Agreement / Monroe Doctrine / Roosevelt Corollary / dollar diplomacy / Good Neighbor Policy / Organization of American States / Alliance for Progress / neutrality / League of Nations

Review. 1. How did treaties help President Washington keep us out of war? 2. Why is the War of 1812 called a turning point in our foreign policy? 3. What are some of the steps taken by the United States and Canada to maintain friendly relations? 4. How has the Monroe Doctrine pleased and displeased Latin America?

Discuss. Why is the policy of isolationism difficult to maintain in today's world?

3 The United States in the United Nations

In 1941, President Franklin D. Roosevelt met with Winston Churchill, the Prime Minister of Great Britain, to discuss the aims of the Allies in World War II. The meeting was held on a ship in the Atlantic Ocean off the coast of Newfoundland. The agreement announced by these two great leaders was known as the **Atlantic Charter.** This document stated the following principles: (1) No nation should try to gain territory as a result of the war. (2) All peoples should have the right to choose the kind of government they want. (3) All nations should have the right to trade and secure raw materials. (4) The peoples of the world should be able to live without fear or want. (5) Nations in the future should not use military force to settle international disputes.

As World War II neared its close, the Allies, including the United States, were determined that the high principles set forth in the Atlantic Charter should guide the world to a postwar peace. In 1945, representatives from 50 nations met in San Francisco to establish an organization that would stress peaceful coexistence and cooperation. This organization was called the **United Nations.** Its purposes were set forth in the Preamble, or beginning, of its constitution, or **Charter.** The preamble reads in part:

We the people of the United Nations, determined

to save succeeding generations [the people of the future] from the scourge [evils] of war, which twice in our lifetime has brought untold [great] sorrow to mankind, and

to reaffirm faith [state our belief] in fundamental [basic] human rights, in the dignity and worth of the human person, in the equal rights of men and women and of nations large and small, and

. . . to live together in peace with one another as good neighbors . . . ,

have resolved to combine our efforts to accomplish these aims.

The United Nations was set up in 1945 to help the nations of the world work together to achieve peace. The headquarters of the United Nations, shown below, is in New York City.

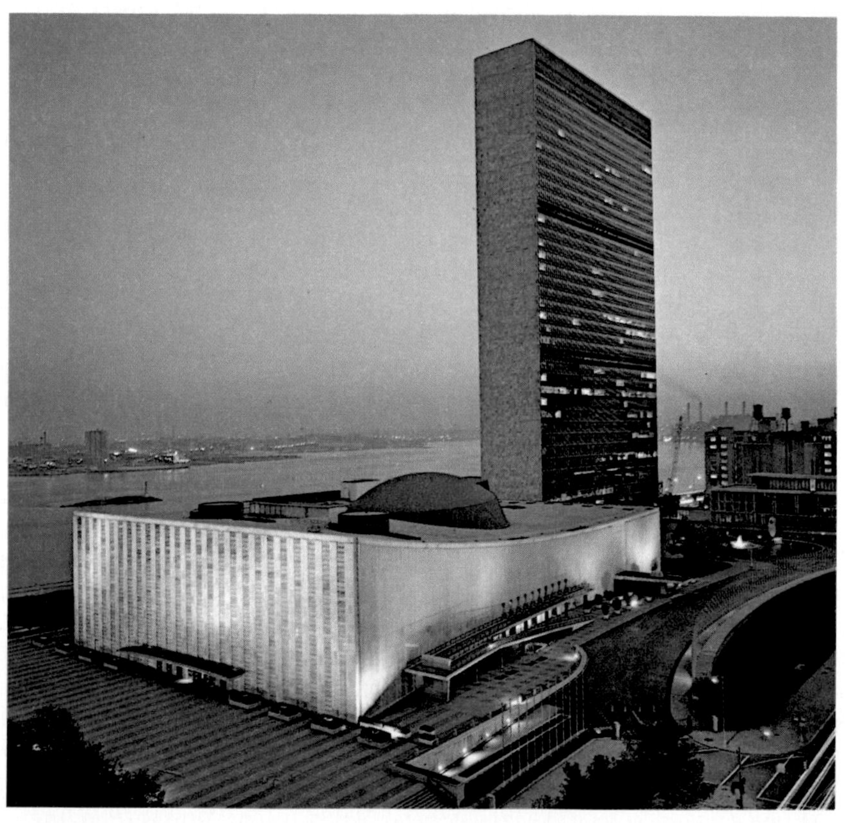

Organization of the United Nations

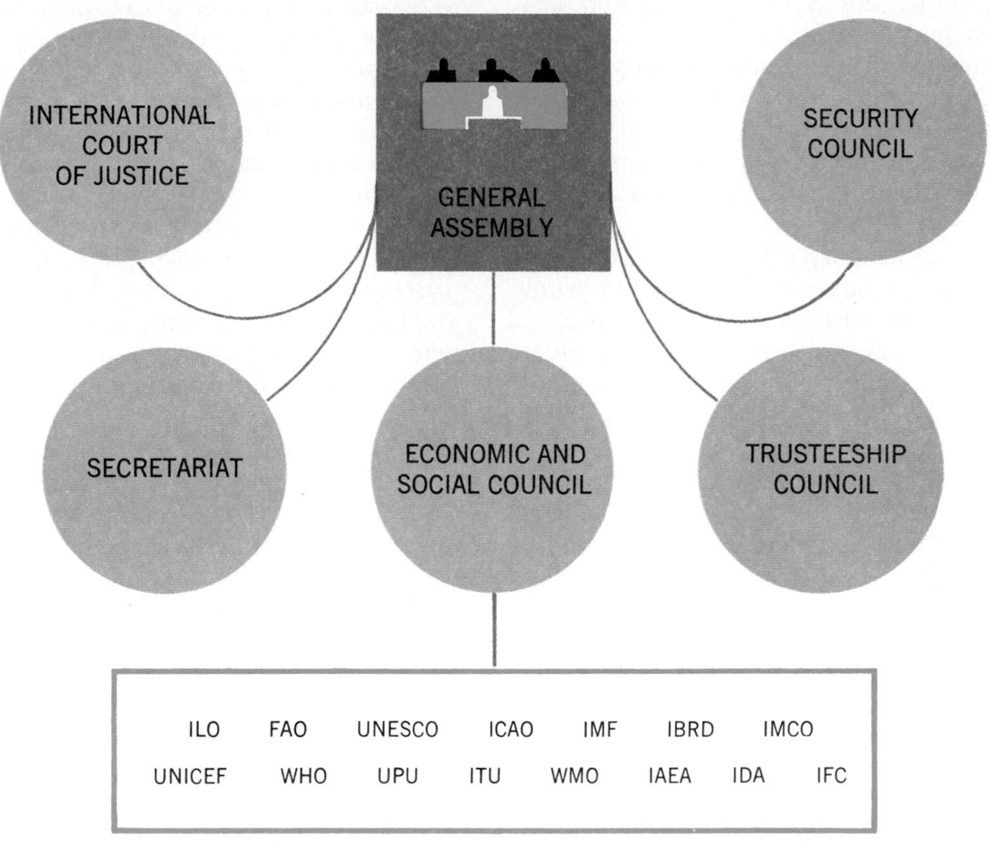

HOW THE UNITED NATIONS IS ORGANIZED

The Charter of the United Nations provides for six main divisions in the organization. These divisions are described briefly below.

1. The General Assembly. The body that discusses, debates, and recommends solutions for problems that come before the United Nations is called the **General Assembly.** Each member nation has one vote in the General Assembly. As more nations join the United Nations, the size of the Assembly increases. By the late 1970's, the membership had reached 149, with other nations wishing to join.

All important issues, such as decisions on matters concerning world peace, adding new members, or passing the budget, must be agreed upon by a two-thirds majority in the Assembly. Other issues are decided by a simple majority vote. The Assembly meets annually. Its sessions begin on the third Tuesday in September. It may be called into emergency session at any time. The Assembly elects its own president and makes its own rules of procedure.

2. The Security Council. The **Security Council** is the body mainly responsible for guarding the peace. It is composed of five permanent members and ten temporary members elected by the Assembly for two-year terms of office. The fifteen coun-

tries are each represented by one delegate. The permanent members are China, France, Great Britain, the Soviet Union, and the United States.

All measures that come before the Security Council must receive the vote of nine of the fifteen members in order to pass. But if one of the permanent members votes against the measure, it is automatically defeated, or vetoed.

To help prevent war, the Security Council may call upon quarreling nations to work out a peaceful settlement of their dispute. If any nation refuses to negotiate, or refuses the Council's offer to help settle the dispute, the Council may take action. It may call upon all members of the United Nations to break off relations and to end all trade with the offending nation. If all else fails, the Council may recommend that United Nations members use military force against the offending nation or nations.

3. The International Court of Justice. Member nations may take disputes over international law to the United Nations law court —the **International Court of Justice.** They do not have to do so, but many contesting nations have voluntarily agreed to come before the court.

This court consists of 15 judges from various nations who are elected by the General Assembly and the Security Council. The court's decisions are made by majority vote. The Court meets at The Hague in the Netherlands. It may be called upon by United Nations members to decide upon such matters as boundary disputes, debt payments, and interpretations of the meaning of the United Nations Charter.

4. The Economic and Social Council. The General Assembly elects representatives from 54 nations to serve as members of the **Economic and Social Council.** This group conducts studies of important topics such as the use of narcotic drugs, human rights, and international trade. It may then make recommendations, based on its studies. The recommendations are voted upon by the General Assembly.

5. Trusteeship Council. Certain islands and areas of the world that were once colonies are supervised by the **Trusteeship Council.** The Council assists these areas to prepare for self-government. The United States and other nations act as trustees and are responsible for the progress of the trustee areas. Trustees make an official report to the Council each year. The Council also sends missions to trustee areas to inspect conditions.

6. The Secretariat. The men and women who carry out the day-to-day activities of the United Nations are called the **Secretariat.** A staff of more than 9,000 clerks, typists, guides, translators, research experts, technicians, and others in its headquarters in New York City helps the United Nations to carry out the details of the organization's activities.

The Secretariat is headed by the Secretary-General of the United Nations, who is elected by the General Assembly for a five-year term. The Secretary-General is the Chief Executive of the United Nations. The Secretary-General prepares the **agenda,** or list of items to be discussed, at meetings of the General Assembly, the Security Council, the Trusteeship Council, and the Economic and Social Council. The Secretary-General is also responsible for carrying out the decisions of these bodies. The Secretary-General may bring before the United Nations any problems that may be threatening to world peace.

THE UNITED NATIONS DEPENDS UPON COOPERATION

The United Nations has no armed forces of its own. Without the cooperation of its members, it cannot keep the peace. There have been times when it has been able to obtain soldiers from its members to carry on a "police action." Usually, it relies upon moral persuasion, or a sense of obligation on the part of its member nations.

At meetings of the General Assembly, such as the one shown here, delegates from the member nations of the United Nations try to find solutions to world problems.

In other words, the United Nations is not a "super-government" that can force its will upon its members. Instead, the United Nations has become a kind of "town meeting of the world." There all nations have an opportunity to express their viewpoints about conditions that threaten the peace. In addition, specialized agencies of the United Nations have improved the lives of people in many parts of the world. What are some of these agencies and what do they do?

UNICEF

The hearts of all people go out to a sick or hungry child. At its first meeting, the United Nations decided to do something for the children of the world. It set up the **United Nations International Children's Emergency Fund (UNICEF).** All nations were urged to contribute to this fund to help feed and care for sick and hungry children anywhere in the world. Perhaps your school has helped to raise money for UNICEF. Such funds are used to supply milk, medicine, clothing, blankets, and other necessities to needy children. Children in more than 100 countries receive help from UNICEF.

WHO

The **World Health Organization (WHO)** is fighting a worldwide battle against disease. Malaria kills 1.5 million people each year. Many millions of the world's people suffer each year from such illnesses as influenza, heart ailments, tuberculosis, cancer, smallpox, and tropical diseases. These are the enemies that WHO is trying to conquer. The weapons in this battle are medicine, insect sprays, vaccines, sanitation programs, water purification, and health education.

FAO

The **Food and Agriculture Organization (FAO)** helps nations to grow more and better food for their people. The FAO has helped to develop a special kind of disease-resisting rice seed in India. It has introduced steel plows in developing nations. FAO experts are helping many nations with forest planting, soil conservation, irrigation, and improved farming methods.

UNESCO

The **United Nations Educational, Scientific, and Cultural Organization (UNESCO)** was established to extend educational opportunities everywhere. People who cannot read or write are often not able to learn about new and better ways of doing things. UNESCO has sponsored programs to set up schools in developing nations. This agency also promotes the exchange of students and teachers among countries. In addition, it encourages people to protect and develop their traditional arts and cultures.

IBRD

The **International Bank for Reconstruction and Development (IBRD),** sometimes called the World Bank, makes loans and gives technical advice to help nations improve their economies. It is helped by two other agencies, the International Development Association (IDA) and the International Finance Corporation (IFC). The IBRD has loaned more than $7 billion a year to developing nations of the world.

OTHER SPECIALIZED AGENCIES

The International Atomic Energy Agency (IAEA) was set up to promote the use of nuclear energy for peaceful purposes. When the world powers reach agreements about control of atomic weapons, IAEA has the responsibility of making sure that all signers of the treaty live up to its terms.

If you study a chart of the United Nations organization, you will see that there are many other specialized agencies. They include the International Labor Organization (ILO), which attempts to improve the welfare of the world's workers. There is also the World Meteorological Organization (WMO). It maintains a world weather watch to obtain data for long-range weather forecasting. The International Civil Aviation Organization (ICAO) promotes safety in air transportation. The International Monetary Fund (IMF) promotes world trade. Other agencies are the International Telecommunications Union (ITU), the Universal Postal Union (UPU), the World Intellectual Property Organization (WIPO), and the Inter-Governmental Maritime Consultative Organization (IMCO).

As you can see, the United Nations is a forum where nations of the world can talk over their problems. It also tries to improve conditions throughout the world.

ARGUMENTS FOR AND AGAINST THE UNITED NATIONS

Some Americans have been critical of the ways in which the United Nations sometimes works. They have become impatient when the Soviet Union has too often used its veto to keep the Security Council from acting. They point to the fact that the many small nations can outvote the large nations. They argue that the organization has failed to create a permanent police force to prevent military attacks and to stop trouble when it first breaks out.

On the other hand, many Americans believe that the United Nations is the world's best hope for peace. They point out that it has frequently been successful in leading disputing nations to the conference table. To the argument that the United Nations has not developed a good police force, they answer that such a force, over which we would have no control, would be unacceptable to our nation or to any world power. Those in favor of the United Nations claim that a forum where all nations can be heard, and which attempts to influence world opinion, is a good way to encourage world peace.

CONSIDER AND DISCUSS

Identify. Atlantic Charter / United Nations / Charter / General Assembly / Security Council / International Court of Justice / Economic and Social Council / Trusteeship Council / Secretariat / agenda / UNICEF / WHO / FAO / UNESCO / IBRD

Review. 1. What are the main branches of the United Nations organization? 2. How does the Secretary General serve the United Nations? 3. Give several examples of the specialized agencies and how they work. 4. What is meant by the expression "town meeting of the world"? 5. What are the major arguments that Americans use for and against the United Nations?

Discuss. Do you think the United Nations is doing a good job? Why or why not?

CHAPTER
Summary

The plan that our nation follows in dealing with other countries is called our foreign policy. The goals of America's foreign policy are peace, prosperity, and friendship. To keep the peace and to advance American interests, we send ambassadors, ministers, and consuls to represent us in other countries. We, in turn, receive representatives from other nations.

The President is responsible for conducting our foreign relations. He is aided by personal advisers and by the Department of State. They keep the President informed of events in other lands and help him carry out America's foreign policy. Congress, too, is concerned with foreign affairs because it must vote the money needed to carry out the nation's policies. The Senate must approve all treaties and the appointments of foreign representatives.

Through the years the United States has moved from a policy of isolationism to full cooperation with other nations. We have tried to establish friendly relations with our neighbors, north and south. In Latin America, we have changed our former policy of policing the continent to working together toward mutual helpfulness. Our world interests have involved us in two world wars. In the hope of being able to work with other nations to avoid another conflict, we have become a member of the United Nations.

The United Nations provides an organization in which nations may discuss serious problems and work out reasonable solutions. The specialized agencies of the United Nations work to serve the needs of the people of the world. The future of this world organization depends upon the willingness and ability of nations to work together in peace. World peace is a difficult goal to achieve. But most of the nations of the world hope that the United Nations will succeed.

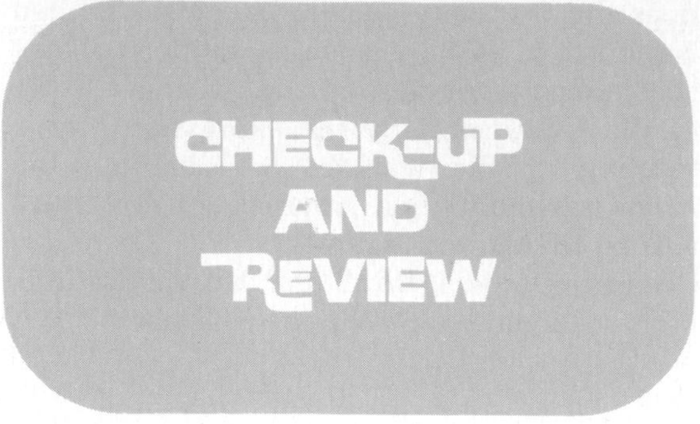

VOCABULARY

In learning about the foreign policy of the United States, you were introduced to a number of important words. To become better acquainted with such words, write sentences in which each of the following words is used properly.

alliances	isolationism
recognition	embargo
ambassador	Monroe Doctrine
consul	neutrality
courier	Charter
minister	Secretariat

CHECK-UP

Write out your answer to each of the following questions. Come to class prepared to defend your answer.

1. What powers over foreign affairs are given to the President by the Constitution?
2. How can Congress check on the President's powers in foreign relations?
3. What are the principal kinds of treaties that the United States makes with foreign nations?
4. What were the principal terms of the Rush-Bagot Agreement?
5. Why did the Senate refuse to ratify the Treaty of Versailles at the end of World War I?
6. Why was the Roosevelt Corollary resented by Latin American nations?
7. What are the main divisions of the United Nations, and how does each help to keep the peace?
8. What is the main job of each of the following United Nations agencies: UNICEF, WHO, UNESCO?
9. How can the United Nations enforce its decisions?
10. What are the principal arguments for and against a strong United Nations organization?

CITIZENSHIP AND YOU

Below are some activities that will help you to broaden your knowledge of the way the United States conducts its world affairs.

1. Class Projects

A number of schools have held successful mock meetings of the United Nations General Assembly. Each student takes the part of a different member nation. He or she expresses that nation's viewpoint on an important problem, such as admitting a new nation into the world organization.

In a general class discussion, make a list on the chalkboard of steps that led the United States from a policy of isolationism to a policy of international cooperation.

There are a number of good books on World War II. Read one of these books. Then discuss (1) what brought the United States into the war and (2) how the war influenced American foreign relations.

If a member of the class or a teacher has visited the United Nations, invite that person to describe the visit to the class. He or she may wish to illustrate the talk with slides or pictures.

2. Group or Committee Projects

Conduct a public-opinion poll to find out what people in your community think about the United Nations. Report your findings to the class.

A class committee may prepare a chart showing how the United States government is organized to conduct its foreign relations. The committee should then explain the chart to the class.

A group may prepare and present a mock broadcast of "The Voice of America." The broadcast may be aimed at Latin America. Its purpose may be to explain the attitude of the United States toward a current world problem.

A bulletin-board committee may help to introduce "Our Foreign Policy" by gathering pictures and news items showing world events in which our government is involved. The news clippings may be displayed around a map of the world, with colored strings from the clippings to the places on the map that they deal with.

3. Individual Projects

Prepare and present an oral report on one of the following people: Dag Hammarskjold, U Thant, Ralph Bunche, Harry S. Truman, Eleanor Roosevelt, Vijaya L. Pandit, George C. Marshall.

Draw a cartoon dealing with a current problem in our nation's foreign relations.

On an outline map of the world, show the locations of American troops in foreign nations. Come to class prepared to tell why the United States has soldiers in each of the locations.

CIVICS SKILLS

LEARNING FROM CARTOONS

As you study about foreign policy, you will find that newspapers and magazines often use cartoons to express points of view. Readers like to look at cartoons. And good cartoonists can express their views in an effective manner.

One of the best ways to learn from cartoons is to read the newspaper and news magazines regularly. In this way, you will know what is going on in the world. You may need this knowledge in order to understand what the cartoon artist is showing in the drawings.

Cartoons often use symbols. A person wearing a barrel instead of clothes is often used as the symbol for the American taxpayer. The figure of a tall man with a white beard and wearing a high hat, striped pants, and cutaway coat—"Uncle Sam"—is used to represent the United States. The Republican Party is represented by an elephant and the Democratic Party by a donkey. Get to know these and other cartoon symbols. Learn what they represent. If you find one you do not understand, ask your teacher, your parents, or a friend to help you interpret it.

A good way to learn more about cartoons and their meaning is to try to express your own ideas in cartoon form. Not everyone can draw well. But everyone can draw simple figures to get ideas across. Even stick figures can be effective. Keep your cartoons simple. Try for some humor, but stick to the subject you are trying to illustrate. Expiain your cartoons to the class, and listen to their suggestions for improvement.

PRACTICING YOUR CIVICS SKILLS

Each member of the class should bring to class a cartoon from a newspaper or news magazine. This cartoon should deal with some problem of foreign policy. Display the cartoons to the class on an opaque projector. What symbols are used? What real people are shown in the cartoon? What is the meaning of the cartoon? Do you agree or disagree with the point made by the cartoonist?

Bring in a number of cartoons on a subject that interests you. Some possibilities are: the Presidency, lobbying, health care, Congress, or the environment. Remember when studying the cartoons that they are expressing the artist's opinions in a humorous way. Then answer the following questions:

1. What opinion about the subject is expressed in each cartoon? How can you tell?
2. How do the opinions in your cartoons compare? Do they differ? How? Are they the same? How?
3. What is your opinion about the subject? Did any of the cartoons influence your opinion? Why?

CHAPTER
Introduction

A visit to the New York headquarters of the United Nations shows vividly the complexity of international affairs in today's world. Looking around the General Assembly, we are impressed by the large number of nations represented. Among the 149 members are a large number of nations that were not in existence when the United Nations was founded in 1945. In front of each group of delegates, often in traditional dress, are signs with the names of such countries as Maldives, Fiji, Lesotho, Bhutan, Djibouti, Surinam, and Qatar. Each of these small nations has one vote, the same as the Soviet Union, Great Britain, France, China, and the United States.

The great powers, especially the Soviet Union and the United States, seek the friendship and alliance of the smaller nations. Before an important issue comes up for a vote, there is much lobbying as the major powers seek to gain the votes necessary to decide the question in their favor. In today's world every nation is important and has an influence on foreign policy.

In United Nations debates, Communist countries and countries that are opposed to Communism often take opposite positions. Each group seeks to have its policies influence the actions of the international body. The floor of the Assembly becomes a forum for the expression of opposing points of view.

Just what is Communism, and why is the United States opposed to it? In this chapter, we shall consider the nature of this conflict of ideas and its effect upon American foreign policy. The topics around which this study will center are:

1. Communism and the Cold War
2. Communism and Containment
3. Seeking Peace Through Alliances and Aid
4. New Trends in American Foreign Policy

CHAPTER

20 Changing Foreign Policies for Changing Times

1 Communism and the Cold War

The ideas behind modern Communism come mainly from a German writer named **Karl Marx** (1818–1883). Marx lived at a time when the Industrial Revolution was spreading in Western Europe. The capitalistic factory system that arose at the time brought with it long hours and back-breaking labor for many workers. Factory owners grew rich and lived in fine homes. But the workers were poor and lived in dark, crowded, rundown buildings.

In 1848, Karl Marx and **Friedrich Engels** – the son of a wealthy factory owner – published a short book. It stated their ideas for a new economic system to replace capitalism and its unfair treatment of workers. This book, the **Communist Manifesto,** declared that in the future, in all nations, factories and business firms would be taken over by the workers (or the **proletariat,** as the workers were called). The workers in all nations would own or control the factors of production. All the land, capital, and labor would be theirs. Private individuals – capitalists, that is – would not be permitted to own or control the factors of production in order to make profits from them. Later these ideas were expanded by Karl Marx in another book called **Das Kapital** (from the German word for "capital").

The word **communism** comes from the Latin word "communis." This word means "sharing in common" or "belonging to all." According to Marx, the proletariat would run the government. Everything from raw materials to finished products would be owned by the government in the name of the workers. In the process of this change, capitalism would be overthrown, by force and violence if necessary. The workers would establish a "dictatorship of the proletariat" throughout the world. Marx hoped that eventually government itself would disappear.

RUSSIA ADOPTS COMMUNISM

The first nation in which the followers of Marx came to power was Russia. In the early years of the 1900's, Russia was still ruled by a tsar, or emperor, and nobles, as it had been for hundreds of years. The lives of the workers and the peasant farmers were never good. Often they were miserable.

By 1917, conditions in Russia under the tsar had become so bad that the people were ready for revolution. Russian armies were being defeated by the Germans in World War I. The people were starving. And they felt oppressed by the ruling classes. There was great unrest and widespread demand for change in Russia.

In March 1917, the tsar was overthrown. Reformers under the leadership of Alexander Kerensky took control of the government. The new rulers had terrible problems keeping order while trying to improve conditions.

A Communist extremist group, known as the **Bolsheviks,** believed that a Communist government was the only answer to Russia's problems. Led by **V. I. Lenin,** the Bolsheviks were determined to seize power. They attracted popular support with the slogan "land, peace, and bread." In the fall of 1917, the Bolsheviks seized most of the members of the Kerensky government. However, Alexander Kerensky himself escaped. The Bolsheviks set up councils (called **soviets**) of workers, peasants, and soldiers to carry out their program. Three years of civil war followed between the Red (Communist) armies and the White (anti-Communist) forces. The tsar and his family were executed. Many of the nobles were also killed. Finally, the Red armies were victorious in the civil war. Lenin and his Communist Party were in firm control of the Russian government. Russia now became known as the **Union of Soviet Socialist Republics (U.S.S.R.),** or the **Soviet Union.**

THE GROWTH OF THE SOVIET UNION

Under Lenin, the government owned and operated most of the nation's basic industries. It controlled iron and steel production, oil wells, coal mines, and the railroads. Some private enterprise was allowed, and capitalists from other nations were invited to in-

In this painting, Lenin is urging the Russian people to overthrow the government of the tsar.

In the Soviet Union, the government owns and operates the nation's industry and agriculture. The large government-controlled farms are called collective farms. Here, Soviet farmers are working on a collective farm.

vest in the Soviet Union's government-owned industries. The great estates of the nobles were divided up among the peasants. Some of these small farms were joined together into "collective farms" controlled by the government. Other farms were owned by independent farmers, called **kulaks,** who ran them as private businesses.

The Communist government of the Soviet Union had been in power only a few years when Lenin died, in 1924. He was succeeded by **Joseph Stalin.** A new, harsh era began. The Soviet economy was now based on government ownership of all industries, and government planning of all production and distribution. The kulaks lost their farms and many were killed. Their former farms were included in the system of collectives.

Stalin's rule and the new economic policies of the Communist government brought new hardships to many Soviet people. The standard of living remained low. The people lived under a strict dictatorship. It regulated not only their industry, but every aspect of their lives.

In time this planning did succeed in making the Soviet Union into a modern industrial nation. In 1912, Russia had ranked fifth among the industrial nations of the world. By 1950, the Soviet Union was in second place, surpassed only by the United States. Compared with the United States, however, Soviet living standards were still low. Factory workers and farmers were urged to work hard and make sacrifices while the nation built up its basic industries and its military forces.

THE SOVIET GOVERNMENT

The Soviet Union is made up of 15 states, called "republics." Each state has its own soviet, or council, that acts as its lawmaking body. Actually, each republic is given a

The Communist Party and the Soviet Government

Party level	Party organ	Government organ	Government level
ALL-UNION COMMUNIST PARTY CONGRESS	Central Committee POLITBURO AND SECRETARIAT	U.S.S.R. Presidium and Council of Ministers	U.S.S.R SUPREME SOVIET
UNION-REPUBLIC PARTY CONGRESS	Central Committee BUREAU AND SECRETARIAT	Republic Presidium and Council of Ministers	UNION-REPUBLIC SUPREME SOVIET
REGIONAL OR PROVINCIAL COMMITTEE	Party Committee BUREAU AND SECRETARIAT	Executive Committee	REGIONAL OR PROVINCIAL SOVIET
CITY OR DISTRICT COMMITTEE	Party Committee BUREAU AND SECRETARIAT	Executive Committee	VILLAGE, CITY, OR DISTRICT SOVIET

LOCAL PARTY GROUPS
There are 15.7 million Communist Party members in the Soviet Union. Party groups are set up in factories, offices, the armed forces, and in schools.

THE SOVIET PEOPLE
The voters—over 166 million Soviet citizens—formally elect members of various soviets, but the voters can vote only for the candidates named by the Communist Party.

limited voice in local matters. The laws for the nation are made by the **Supreme Soviet.** The Supreme Soviet, made up of representatives from the various republics, elects the **Council of Ministers.** These ministers run the main departments of the government, such as defense, finance, foreign affairs, industry, and agriculture.

The **Chairman of the Council of Ministers** is chosen by the Supreme Soviet. The Chairman is a powerful person. This position has been held by Stalin, Nikita Khrushchev, and Alexey Kosygin. The Chairman can also be removed by the Supreme Soviet, as Khrushchev was in 1964.

Only one political party is permitted to exist in the Soviet Union—the Communist Party. Its affairs are managed by a **Central Committee,** headed by a **Secretary of the Communist Party.** Stalin and Khrushchev served both as Chairman of the Council of Ministers and Secretary of the Communist Party. This made them very powerful.

After Khrushchev was removed, these two positions were separated and taken over by two people. When Kosygin became Chairman of the Council of Ministers, Leonid Brezhnev became Secretary of the Communist Party. The Secretary of the Communist Party is now the most powerful person in the Soviet Union.

The **Politburo** runs the Communist Party and develops its policies. It is made up of 11 top Communist leaders.

Only about six percent of the Soviet people belong to the Communist Party. At election time, only one group of Communist Party candidates is allowed to run for office. The people must vote either "yes" or "no" for the candidates. Very few people dare to vote "no."

THE SOVIET UNION BECOMES A WORLD POWER

In the late 1930's World War II, the terrible war that eventually involved the entire world, began. Adolf Hitler and his German forces destroyed the peace of Europe. In Asia, Japanese military leaders were determined to conquer their neighbors. Both of these nations endangered the Soviet Union.

By 1941, Germany had defeated France and placed most of Western Europe under its control. Suddenly Germany turned its armies against the Soviet Union. The Soviet troops fought bravely. But they were forced to retreat far back into their country. As they retreated, the Soviet soldiers burned crops, houses, factories, bridges, communications, and everything else that might be useful to the enemy. This "scorched earth" policy slowed the German advance and gave Stalin time to reorganize his forces.

Then nature came to the aid of the Soviet Union in the form of bitter winter weather. Hitler found that his lightning war, or "blitzkrieg," did not work well in below-zero temperatures. The war on the Russian front turned into a stalemate. In the summer of 1942, Germany renewed its offensive against the Soviet Union. By this time, the United States and its allies were supplying the Russians with needed military equipment. This helped the Russian defense. A large German army was forced to surrender at Stalingrad in February 1943. By 1943, events in other parts of the world were causing Germany to lose its advantage in the war.

The Soviet Union now took the offensive. While the Allies opened up a second front with their invasion of Western Europe in June of 1944, Soviet troops were moving across

The German defeat at Stalingrad, shown below, was an important turning point in World War II. This victory, in 1943, was won at great cost to the Soviet people.

May Day is an important holiday in many European nations. It is similar to Labor Day in the United States. In this picture, the Soviet people are celebrating May Day in a large and colorful parade.

Central Europe into Germany. When Allied troops reached the Elbe River, west of Germany's capital city of Berlin, they linked up with Russian troops. Soon afterward, Soviet armies entered the battered city of Berlin. With the fall of Berlin, the war in Europe ended on May 8, 1945.

THE COLD WAR BEGINS

When American soldiers and Soviet troops met at the Elbe River in Germany in 1945, they rushed forward to shake hands and pat each other on the back. They also exchanged friendly greetings. Hopes were high that the Soviet Union and the United States, allies in the war, would remain friends after the war. It was hoped that the Soviet Union would share the ideals expressed in the Atlantic Charter and in the Preamble to the Charter of the United Nations. Everywhere, people of all nations hoped that the world might now find a way to live in peace.

These hopes were soon shattered. During World War II, the Soviet Union occupied large parts of Poland and Rumania. After the war, in country after country in Eastern Europe, leaders of political parties opposed to Communism were jailed, forced to flee, or assassinated. Within a few years, Communist governments were set up in Poland, Rumania, Bulgaria, Hungary, Czechoslovakia, Albania, and East Germany.

In this way, the Soviet Union turned the nations along its borders into **satellite nations**—nations that take orders from Moscow.

Stalin and other Soviet leaders maintained that they were taking these actions so that Russia would never again be attacked by Germany or any other nation or nations of Western Europe. Leaders in the United

States and Western Europe thought that the Soviet leaders had more in mind than defense of their own country. They believed that the Soviet Union, with its great new military strength, would try to impose Soviet-dominated forms of government wherever it could. Only the fear of America's atomic bombs, some believed, prevented Soviet forces from trying to overrun all of Western Europe and Great Britain. At that time, only the United States had atomic weapons.

Thus, soon after World War II, much of the world was caught up in what was called a **Cold War.** On one side was the Soviet Union and its satellite nations. On the other side was the United States and other non-Communist nations. Both sides started using propaganda, spying, alliances, foreign aid, and all other methods of conflict short of actually starting an all-out war that might destroy the world.

Waging the Cold War while also trying to end it were the major problems of American foreign policy in the 25 or 30 years after World War II, as you will see.

CONSIDER AND DISCUSS

Identify. Karl Marx / Friedrich Engels / *Communist Manifesto* / proletariat / *Das Kapital* / Communism / Bolsheviks / V. I. Lenin / soviets / Soviet Union / Joseph Stalin / kulaks / Supreme Soviet / Council of Ministers / Central Committee / Politburo / satellite nations / Cold War

Review. 1. What were some of the ideas of Karl Marx? 2. How did the Soviet Union become a leading industrial nation? 3. What is the relationship between the government of the Soviet Union and the Communist Party? 4. How did winter weather aid the Soviet cause in World War II?

Discuss. What conditions in a country may lead people to adopt the ideas of Communism? Are there other ways to correct such conditions? What is the best way?

2 Communism and Containment

With the satellite nations of Eastern Europe under his control, Stalin also tried to increase Soviet power in the eastern Mediterranean Sea and the Middle East. He wanted an ice-free route for Soviet ships into the oceans of the world. He also wanted influence in the oil-rich lands of the Middle East. Troops from the Soviet Union occupied part of Iran, with its rich oil fields, during World War II. Instead of being withdrawn after the war, these troops were strengthened. A Communist Party was encouraged in Greece. Turkey was faced with a demand for a Soviet naval base within its territory. These southward thrusts of Soviet power were seen by the United States and other non-Communist nations as severe threats to their security and to world peace. American leaders felt they had to respond to the growing Soviet power.

THE POLICY OF CONTAINMENT

The President of the United States in the immediate postwar period was Harry S. Truman. He warned the Soviet Union that it must get out of Iran. He was successful. Stalin removed Soviet troops. President Truman then asked Congress to provide military equipment and economic aid to Greece and Turkey to help them resist Soviet influence. Because of this aid, Greece and Turkey did not become satellites of the Soviet Union. The success of America's aid to Greece and Turkey encouraged our government to give similar aid to other European nations. This policy of helping free nations to resist aggression became known as the **Truman Doctrine.**

The idea behind the policy adopted by President Truman came to be known as **containment.** The original purpose of this policy was to keep Soviet Communism from spread-

These children in Berlin wave at an American plane during the Berlin airlift. Planes loaded with food, fuel, and clothing supplied the city from June of 1948 to May of 1949.

ing. The forces of the Soviet Union were to be "contained" within the area in which they had been successful up to 1948.

THE BERLIN BLOCKADE

The next showdown between the United States and the Soviet Union came in 1948 in Berlin. At the end of World War II, Germany was divided into two separate countries. East Germany became a Communist nation. West Germany became a democracy. The city of Berlin, although located in East Germany, was not part of that country. It was occupied by troops of four countries—France, Great Britain, the United States, and the Soviet Union. Each nation controlled a part of the city. The non-Communist nations were given free access to the city over special land routes through East Germany. In June 1948, the Soviet Union closed these routes.

Stalin's strategy in closing the East German routes into Berlin was to force the non-Communist troops to leave and to make the city a Communist center. The German people living in the British, French, and American sections of the city—called West Berlin—were cut off from food, coal, and other necessities. They faced cold and starvation.

The United States and Great Britain took prompt action. They began a massive airlift of fuel, food, clothing, and other necessities. Airplanes were loaded with supplies and flown into the city. Day after day, in all kinds of weather, American and British planes landed in Berlin. More than 250,000 flights brought huge amounts of needed goods into West Berlin. The Soviet strategy failed. Stalin agreed to reopen the land routes.

COMMUNISM WINS IN CHINA

Before World War II, China's Nationalist government under **Chiang Kai-shek** was faced with two problems. One was the Chinese Communists, whose numbers had been growing. The other was Japan, which had invaded China in 1937. The Nationalists and the Communists united against Japan for a time. But after Japan was defeated in 1945, full-scale civil war broke out in China. In 1949, the Communists under **Mao Tse-tung** defeated the Nationalists, who fled to the island of Formosa (now called Taiwan), off the south China mainland. There they set up a government in exile. The Communists held the mainland, which became known as the **People's Republic of China,** or **Communist China.**

When the United Nations was formed in 1945, Nationalist China became a member, with a permanent seat in the Security Council. When the Nationalist government fled to Taiwan, it kept its United Nations membership with the support of the United States and other non-Communist nations. Membership was denied to the People's Republic of China. By the early 1970's, however, relationships among the world's nations had undergone many changes, as you will read. In 1971, the United Nations voted to expel Nationalist China and to give its membership to Communist China.

With almost 900 million people, or about one fourth of the total world population, the People's Republic of China has become a powerful nation. Mao Tse-tung, the Communist Chinese leader, was a strong follower of the ideas of Marx and Lenin. He interpreted these ideas and taught them to the Chinese people in ways that were suitable to their traditions.

Under Mao's direction, the entire nation underwent a revolution. The new Communist government tried to undo centuries of oppression by powerful rulers, warlords, landlords, and tax collectors. The people began to remake their lands, their agriculture, their industry, and their whole society.

THE KOREAN CONFLICT

As a result of an agreement reached after World War II, the peninsula of Korea, which juts out of eastern Asia into the Pacific Ocean, was divided into Communist North Korea and non-Communist South Korea. On June 25, 1950, the army of North Korea, equipped with Soviet weapons and aided by Chinese Communists, invaded South Korea in a surprise attack. A big question now arose for American makers of foreign policy. Would the United States apply the policy of containment to Asia, and come to the aid of South Korea?

The United States government, under President Truman, acted without hesitation. It called upon the United Nations to halt the invasion. The Security Council of the United Nations, with the Soviet Union absent, held a special session. It voted to send aid to the South Koreans.

Led by troops from the United States, 14 members of the United Nations sent combat forces to help defend South Korea. The Korean conflict lasted for three years. The fighting was difficult and bitter. But the United Nations troops finally forced the North Koreans and Chinese Communists to retreat back across the 38th parallel. This parallel is the dividing line between North and South Korea.

By July 1953, the Korean conflict had reached a point where neither side was able to win a clear-cut victory. Therefore, the two sides agreed that the Korean nation would remain divided into Communist North Korea and non-Communist South Korea. Tensions between the two Koreas have continued.

THE CUBAN CRISIS

The Cold War between the Soviet Union and the United States took a dangerous turn after 1949 when the Soviet Union began testing and developing atomic weapons. As each side increased its ability to destroy the other, along with most of the rest of the world, foreign policy in Washington and Moscow moved toward a "balance of terror." A severe crisis in the Cold War faced President John F. Kennedy in October of 1962.

The event took place on the island of Cuba, 144 kilometers (90 miles) from the American mainland. There, in 1959, **Fidel Castro** had led an army of **guerrilla** soldiers against Fulgencio Batista, the dictator of Cuba. Castro was successful and took over the Cuban government. In time, Castro set up a Communist government in Cuba.

In October 1962, President Kennedy was informed that the Soviet Union was building secret missile bases on the island. These missile bases, if finished, would have been a threat to a large part of the United States and to other parts of the Western Hemisphere, including the Panama Canal. President Kennedy immediately warned Premier Khrushchev of the Soviet Union that the United States regarded the missile bases as a danger to our nation's security. The United States could not permit this threat to continue, the President declared.

President Kennedy demanded that the Soviet Union remove its missiles from Cuba immediately. To force the Soviet Union to agree, President Kennedy declared that our nation was prepared to take whatever steps might be required, including the use of military force.

As a first step, the President announced that we would not permit the delivery of more offensive weapons—weapons of attack—to Cuba. The land, sea, and air forces of the United States moved into action to enforce this policy. The Navy sent destroyers to stop and search foreign ships bound for Cuba. Our Air Force flew over the waters of the Atlantic Ocean to locate and photograph ships on their way to Cuba. The Army mobilized in Florida. And the American naval base at Guantanamo Bay on the island of Cuba was strengthened.

As a result of this show of American military strength and determination, the Soviet Union backed down. It agreed to remove Soviet long-range missiles from Cuba and to take down the missile launching sites. From this time on, Soviet and American leaders understood the "balance of terror." They continued to pursue self-interests and to probe for each other's weaknesses. But they drew back several times from situations that threatened to develop into a third world war, which was certain to destroy much of the world.

INVOLVEMENT IN VIETNAM

American efforts to limit the spread of Communism led, in the 1960's, to serious involvement in the affairs of Southeast Asia. Before World War II, several small nations in Southeast Asia—Laos, Vietnam, and Cambodia—had been French colonies. When the Japanese forces were driven out at the end of World War II, France moved back into its former colonies.

Meanwhile, in Vietnam, a local government and army were being formed under the leadership of **Ho Chi Minh,** a Vietnamese Communist. The French and the Communists could not reach agreement, and war began. The French set up a non-Communist Vietnamese government. But by 1954, the Vietnamese Communists had defeated the French colonial forces in northern Vietnam. Under the Geneva Agreements of 1954, Vietnam, Laos, and Cambodia became independent. Vietnam, like Korea, was divided into a Communist northern half and a non-Communist southern half. The Geneva Agreements called for elections to be held throughout Vietnam in 1956 to reunite the country.

The government left behind by the French in South Vietnam was weak, inefficient, and often corrupt. Many of its officials were refugees from North Vietnam who did not understand the village people of South Vietnam. The promised elections were never held, partly because of fear that Ho Chi Minh and the Communists would prove too popular. Among the villagers were many who had been converted to the ideas of Ho Chi Minh and trained in guerrilla warfare. In the late 1950's, war broke out in South Vietnam. The Com-

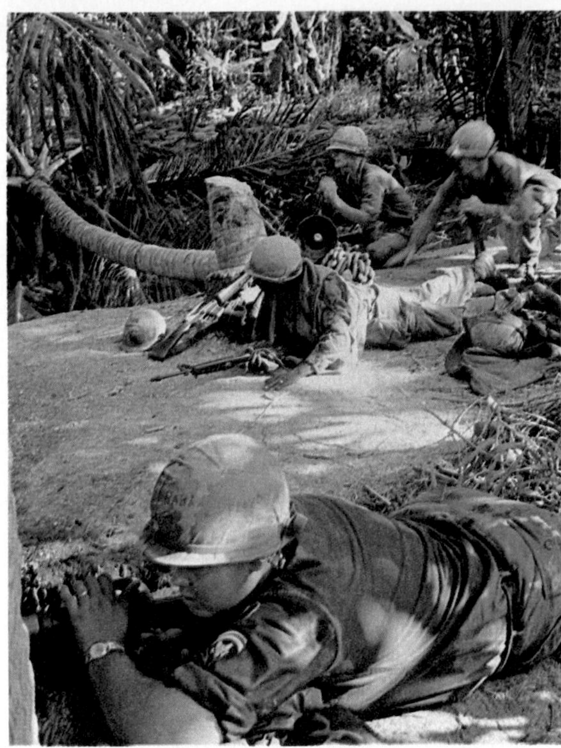

These American soldiers are in a "fire fight" on a road in Vietnam.

munist guerrillas, called **Vietcong,** seized large parts of the countryside and harassed the cities. They received troops, supplies, guidance, and other aid from North Vietnam. The North Vietnamese, in turn, received military supplies from the Soviet Union and Communist China. By this time, the South Vietnamese were getting aid and military advice from the United States.

To the American government, the situation in South Vietnam looked threatening. If South Vietnam fell to the Communists, other nations of Southeast Asia—Laos, Cambodia, and Thailand—might fall. American officials feared that Communism might then spread to the Philippines and Indonesia. But how should these new forces of Communism be contained? In 1962, President Kennedy sent 8,000 American soldiers to South Vietnam to serve as advisers and technicians, but not as combat troops. A year later this number was increased to 16,000.

THE UNDECLARED WAR

In August 1964, President Johnson reported to Congress that the North Vietnamese had attacked two American vessels patrolling the Gulf of Tonkin, off the coast of North Vietnam. Congress passed the **Gulf of Tonkin Resolution.** This resolution gave the President the power "to take all necessary measures to repel any armed attack against the forces of the United States and to prevent further aggression." It was not, however, a declaration of war by Congress.

American troops were soon sent into action in South Vietnam. They conducted "search and destroy" operations to try to rid South Vietnam of the Vietcong and North Vietnamese. Thousands of Americans were drafted and sent to fight. American aircraft bombed supply lines in North Vietnam and protected troops in South Vietnam. The war widened, battle deaths increased, and the cost of the war soared. By the time President Nixon came into office in 1969, over 500,000 American troops were in South Vietnam.

Perhaps no other conflict in American history brought more heated debate than our involvement in Vietnam. Those in favor of stronger military action argued that America's honor and position of world leadership were at stake. Opponents of the war maintained that its cost in lives and money was not justified. They said that the nation's leaders had involved America in a war without the consent of Congress. They argued that the money being spent on the war was needed to solve pressing problems at home. Some said that the United States had no business getting involved in Vietnam, that our security was not threatened there. As the fighting dragged on, dissatisfaction with the war grew. Students demonstrated and protestors marched on the nation's capital. Congressional hearings then were held to inquire into the war.

In his election campaign in 1968, President Nixon promised that he would bring the war to an honorable end. In the summer of 1969, he announced the policy of **"Vietnamization."** The plan was that the South Vietnamese were to be aided in preparing to take over the war. American troops were to be gradually withdrawn. But this plan was a disappointment to those who wanted to end the nation's involvement in Vietnam quickly. In 1970 the war was extended briefly into Cambodia. By 1972, American ground troops had been largely withdrawn. However, American air and naval forces continued to attack North Vietnam. In the meantime, representatives of the United States, North Vietnam, South Vietnam, and the Vietcong had been meeting in Paris.

In January 1973, a peace agreement was announced. After more than eight years of war, with almost 50,000 Americans killed, over 300,000 wounded, and at a cost of over $111 billion, the war came to an end for the United States. But despite the agreement, fighting continued in Vietnam. In 1975, the Communists launched a new offensive and South Vietnam fell. The Communists now ruled all of Vietnam.

CONSIDER AND DISCUSS

Identify. Truman Doctrine / containment / Berlin blockade / Chiang Kai-shek / Mao Tse-tung / People's Republic of China / Communist China / Fidel Castro / guerrilla / Ho Chi Minh / Vietcong / Gulf of Tonkin Resolution / Vietnamization

Review. 1. What was the purpose of the Truman Doctrine? 2. What broke the Berlin blockade? 3. Who won the Korean conflict? 4. How did President Kennedy deal with the Cuban missile crisis? 5. Describe America's involvement in Vietnam.

Discuss. In the 1960's, would you have supported or opposed American involvement in the Vietnam War? Why?

3 Seeking Peace Through Alliances and Aid

Since World War II, the United States has worked with the non-Communist nations of the world to assist their development and to help them resist aggression by Communist nations. Our government has treaty agreements with many non-Communist nations, promising them American support in case of Communist attack. It also has given these nations billions of dollars' worth of military and economic aid. American Presidents have met with leaders of the non-Communist nations to plan joint policies. They have also sought agreements with China, the Soviet Union, and other Communist nations to try to work out ways of living together peacefully.

TREATIES WITH OTHER NATIONS

As you know, one of the ways in which the United States conducts its foreign affairs is by signing treaties with other countries. Treaties, you recall, are written agreements in which our government promises to follow certain policies toward other nations. The President of the United States, as you know, must sign all treaties, and the Senate must approve them by a two-thirds vote.

OUR MANY ALLIANCES

Since 1945, the United States has followed a policy of establishing alliances with many nations of the world. It has alliances with many individual nations, such as Japan, South Korea, **Taiwan** (Nationalist China), and the Philippines. It has also established alliances with several large groups of nations. Two of these alliances with groups of nations are of special importance.

1. The North Atlantic Treaty Organization (NATO). NATO includes these 15 nations: the United States, Canada, Belgium, Den-

mark, France, Great Britain, Iceland, Italy, Luxembourg, the Netherlands, Norway, Portugal, Greece, Turkey, and West Germany. The purpose of NATO is to establish a united front against the threat of Soviet aggression in Europe and the Middle East. NATO members have agreed that "armed attack against one will be considered an attack on all." A joint NATO military command, called the Supreme Headquarters Allied Powers Europe (SHAPE), has been set up to plan military strategy for the NATO powers.

2. Australia, New Zealand, and United States Treaty Organization (ANZUS). The purpose of this treaty organization is to protect the mutual interests of the member nations in the South Pacific and to prevent the spread of Communism. Both New Zealand and Australia sent troops to fight against Communism in South Vietnam under this treaty.

In this picture, the Prime Minister of Great Britain is addressing a meeting of NATO leaders.

FOREIGN TRADE POLICIES OF THE UNITED STATES

Early in American history, our nation began to collect high import taxes on certain goods. These tariffs were intended to protect young American industries from foreign competition. They were called **protective tariffs.** Tariff rates were set high enough so that the prices that stores had to charge for imported goods were equal to, or higher than, the prices of similar goods made in the United States. A protective tariff helps American manufacturers. But it also means that American consumers must pay more for what they buy.

Many nations have used protective tariffs. This sometimes causes difficulties in relations between two nations. When an importing nation raises its tariffs, an exporting nation loses business. Sometimes, raising tariffs on one nation leads others to do the same. These "tariff wars" are bad for international trade.

To improve world trade, the United States and many other nations have joined in a **General Agreement on Tariffs and Trade (GATT).** This agreement helps to encourage **free trade,** or the elimination of tariffs and other trade barriers. We have also made **reciprocal trade agreements** with other countries, in which both sides agree to lower certain tariffs.

Congress has given the President power to raise or lower tariffs when it is believed the change will be in the national interest. This power makes it possible for the President to take prompt action in lowering tariffs when certain materials or products are in short supply and imports need to be encouraged. Tariffs may also be raised to discourage certain imports. A President may raise all tariffs and then work out lower reciprocal rates with individual nations.

Throughout Europe, homes, farms, and factories lay in ruins after World War II.

THE MARSHALL PLAN

Even before World War II ended, the United States joined with other nations in providing relief for people who were suffering because of war damage to their homes and industries. After the war, through the **United Nations Relief and Rehabilitation Administration (UNRRA)**, aid was given to people in all parts of the world. In Europe, where the heaviest damage occurred, it became clear that a different, long-range plan of economic aid would be needed. Hard times had followed World War II in the European nations. People were badly in need of food, clothing, homes, and jobs. In Western Europe, local Communist parties, supported by the Soviet Union, offered promises of a better life. There were fears that countries such as France would turn Communist.

In 1947, the United States Secretary of State, George Marshall, organized a plan to help the nations of Europe rebuild their factories, farms, homes, and transportation systems. Congress agreed that these nations needed American help. It granted $12.5 billion for aid under the **Marshall Plan.** Aid was offered to the Soviet Union and the other nations of Eastern Europe but was declined. Representatives of 16 Western European nations met in Paris and drew up a plan to rebuild their economies. By 1951, the economies of Western Europe had recovered to a remarkable degree. And Marshall Plan aid was ended.

THE POINT FOUR PROGRAM

President Truman, in his 1949 Inaugural Address, declared that the United States, as the richest nation in the world, should help raise the standards of living in other nations. As part of this program, he proposed that American experts in industry and agriculture should be sent to nations that requested such help. This aid proposal became known as the **Point Four Program.**

Under the Point Four Program, Americans were sent to help many nations. For example, American farm experts taught better methods of agriculture to farmers in Pakistan. Point Four experts taught Latin American nations how to control disease. Many African nations received help in building roads and industries.

THE PEACE CORPS

In 1961, President Kennedy proposed a new aid program called the **Peace Corps.** Its purpose was to send volunteers into countries that requested help. Peace Corps members worked directly with the people of these nations. They helped the people with everyday tasks and worked with them to build a better life. Peace Corps members helped to build roads, teach school, and aid in farming. They also served in medical clinics, and developed better ways of doing things that needed to be done.

This American Peace Corps worker is teaching in a school in Liberia. Has the Peace Corps helped to improve American relations with other nations?

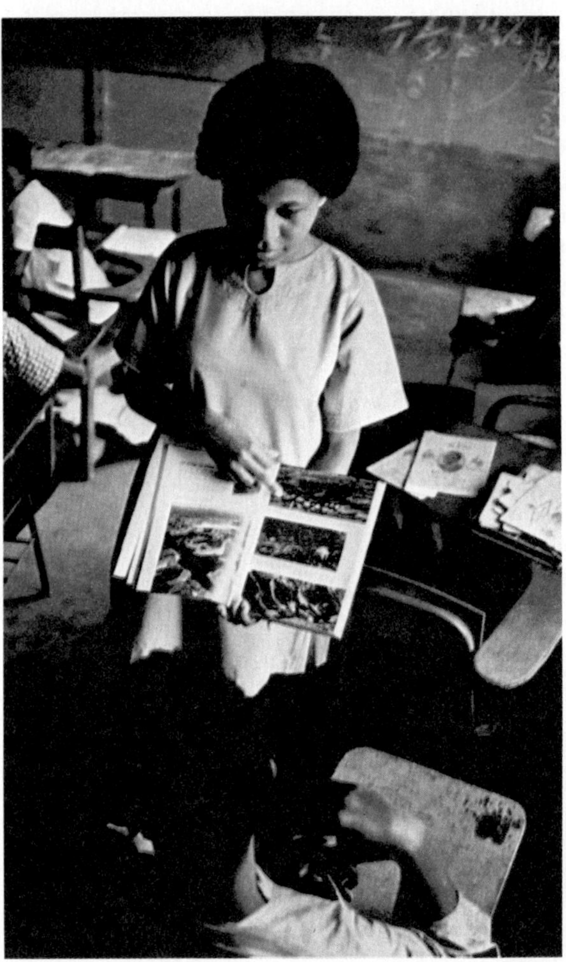

By 1970, about 10,000 Americans had served in foreign nations. Most of the volunteers were young men and women, although people between the ages of 18 and 70 were eligible. Volunteers received a small income from the United States government. This income permitted the volunteers to live as well, but not better than, the people of the nation in which they were working. By joining the Peace Corps, Americans showed that they were interested in the welfare of other people.

In 1971, the Peace Corps and other volunteer agencies were reorganized into a group called **ACTION.** The purpose of ACTION is to help all who want and need help, both at home and abroad. The Peace Corps has continued its work under this independent agency.

OTHER FOREIGN AID

Since World War II, the United States has given or loaned over $190 billion in aid to non-Communist nations. Some of this aid has been in the form of grants or gifts. But in recent years it has more often been in the form of low-interest loans. A large part of America's foreign aid is managed through the Agency for International Development (AID).

In recent years, about 1.3 percent of our federal budget has gone for foreign aid. More than 50 nations have received military aid to help them maintain their independence. Economic assistance has been given to help new nations in Africa and Asia become self-supporting. Foodstuffs, such as wheat, corn, and rice, have been sent from the United States to help feed the hungry people of the world.

THE FOREIGN AID POLICY

Should the United States continue to spend 1.3 percent of its federal income on foreign aid? Should it spend more? Should it spend less? Foreign aid has always been a controversial subject. There are many arguments for and against foreign aid.

Those who favor foreign aid point to the necessity for helping developing nations. If we do not, they say, these nations may turn to the Soviet Union or China for aid and thus come under Communist influence. And from a humanitarian point of view, they argue, our wealthy nation cannot watch people starve without offering to help. The foreign aid that we have given in the past, they say, has helped to build stronger nations and has contributed to world peace. They point out that most of the foreign aid money is spent by foreign nations to buy American goods and services. They also note that 1.3 percent of the federal budget is only a tiny fraction of the nation's Gross National Product.

Those opposing the present foreign aid policy claim that it is wasteful and that it takes money out of our nation. They also say that we should not bear so many of the world's burdens. Some critics believe that too much aid is in the form of military assistance. They question whether this kind of aid helps peace.

Another problem is that some of our foreign aid goes to countries that are dictatorships, or those that violate human rights. Some people say we should not aid such nations, even though they are anti-Communist.

Our future foreign aid policy may well determine the course of world history. Will the United States withdraw from world responsibilities, or will it find more effective ways to help its world neighbors? The answer calls for the best leadership America can provide. It also calls for concerned and informed citizens who will make their voices and views heard.

CONSIDER AND DISCUSS

Identify. Taiwan / NATO / ANZUS / protective tariffs / GATT / free trade / reciprocal trade agreements / UNRRA / Marshall Plan / Point Four Program / Peace Corps / ACTION

Review. 1. What is the main purpose of our strong alliances? 2. What is a "tariff war"? 3. What kind of work do Peace Corps volunteers do?

Discuss. What do you think our foreign aid policy should be in the future?

How the Peace Corps Helps Other Peoples

Helps to improve farming methods.
Helps build houses and roads.
Teaches new job skills, such as carpentry, bricklaying, and construction methods.
Teaches adults who lack education.
Helps to fight disease and to improve health standards.

4 New Trends in American Foreign Policy

In recent years the American people and their leaders have been rethinking foreign policy. Their problem was finding new foreign policies for a rapidly changing world. New policies were especially needed to meet developments among the Communist nations and among the newer developing nations.

THE SPLIT IN THE COMMUNIST WORLD

For a number of years after World War II, Communism seemed to be a single political and economic movement that threatened to take over the rest of the world. The Soviet Union controlled the countries of Eastern Europe and some of Central Europe. In Asia, the Soviet Union and China assisted North Korea in its aggression against South Korea. They also supported North Vietnam in its attempts to take control of South Vietnam. The Soviet Union backed Castro in Cuba and his attempts to spread Communism in Latin America.

As the years passed, however, it became evident that Communism was not a single, worldwide movement. In Central Europe, Yugoslavia was a Communist nation. But it refused to become a Soviet satellite. In the 1960's, the Soviet Union withdrew its support of the People's Republic of China when the two nations disagreed over policies for China's development. They then became enemies in a dispute over their borders. In Europe, Albania sided with China against the Soviet Union. The Communists of North Vietnam accepted aid from China and the Soviet Union. But the North Vietnamese made it clear that they intended to be independent.

DÉTENTE WITH THE COMMUNISTS

All of these events made it obvious that national pride was as important to Communist nations as it was to other nations. This evidence suggested to American leaders that there were possibilities for working out policies of peaceful relations between Communist and non-Communist nations.

The new explorations in foreign policy are sometimes called **détente** (from the French word for "easing," in this case the easing of tensions). President Nixon dramatized them in 1972 when he flew to Peking and Moscow to talk with the leaders of China and the Soviet Union. Out of these talks came new trade agreements and a freer exchange of journalists, scholars, and tourists. This also led to other opportunities to develop better relations. However neither side has given up its opposition to the political and economic system of the other.

LIMITING NUCLEAR ARMS

One of the most important results of détente has been progress in controlling the nuclear arms race. Earlier, in 1963, the United States and the Soviet Union had agreed in the **Nuclear Test Ban Treaty** to protect the earth's environment by testing nuclear weapons only underground. In 1968, they and 60 other nations signed a **Nuclear Nonproliferation Treaty** forbidding the spread of nuclear weapons to nations that did not already have them.

Strategic Arms Limitation Talks—known as **SALT**—began in the early 1970's. The first SALT agreement on limiting the number of offensive weapons was reached in 1972. It limited certain weapons to those already in existence or then being manufactured. Negotiations for more arms limitations have continued since then. They have made the danger of nuclear war seem more remote.

THE THIRD WORLD

During the 1960's and 1970's American foreign policy devoted increasing attention to a group of nations aligned neither with the Communist nor with the anti-Communist sides. These nations, located in Latin America, Asia, and Africa, are known as the **Third World.** Most of them formerly were colonies of Great Britain, France, Spain, Portugal, or the Netherlands. They won their independence in the years after World War II. Many need help in developing their economies. They are sometimes referred to as "developing nations."

Third World nations have a large part of the world's population. They also make up the largest group in the United Nations. Some of these nations have important natural resources. A main goal of America's foreign policy is to maintain friendly relations with them and to prevent the Soviet Union from gaining too much influence over them.

THE MIDDLE EAST

The United States has attempted to be friendly with all nations in the **Middle East**—Egypt and Israel and the other nations of Southwestern Asia. At the same time, however, the United States has been the chief supporter of Israel. Israel is surrounded by Third World Arab countries. It has fought four wars with these nations since its creation in 1948. The Arabs have received aid from both the United States and the Soviet Union. After the fourth Arab-Israeli war in 1973, oil-rich Arab countries tried to punish the United States and its European allies for supporting Israel. They did so by putting an embargo on oil to those countries. That is, the Arab countries refused to sell them oil.

The Arab countries ended the embargo in a few months. But the oil crisis showed how a powerful nation such as the United States can be dependent on Third World nations for important raw materials. The United States has encouraged negotiations between Israel and the Arab nations to bring peace to the Middle East.

SELF-DETERMINATION IN AFRICA

Another problem area is Africa. In the newly independent nations there, the majority of the population is black. These nations have sometimes resented their former white colonial rulers in Europe. At times it has been difficult for the United States to persuade these nations of its good will toward them.

The United States has been concerned that several African nations, such as Angola, Mozambique, and Ethiopia, have Communist-type governments. Some of them have become friendly with the Soviet Union. In South Africa and Rhodesia in southern Africa, most of the people are black. But they are ruled by white minorities. Both nations are rich in valuable resources such as chromium and uranium. As the blacks struggle to obtain equal rights, the danger of conflict involving neighboring nations becomes greater. Since the mid-1970's, America has encouraged equal rights for blacks through peaceful change.

RELATIONS WITH LATIN AMERICA

During the 1960's and 1970's, the United States was concerned that some Latin American countries had Communist governments or governments with undemocratic policies. By the late 1970's, conditions in Latin America had improved very little. The Communist government of Fidel Castro remained firmly in control in Cuba. Moreover, the Cubans were helping to spread Communism in Africa by sending Cuban troops to some nations there.

The United States was also concerned about the violation of human rights by some Latin American governments. It criticized those governments and threatened to reduce its aid. In 1977, six Latin American nations refused the aid in protest. Another issue that caused tension was the Panama Canal. The United States built the Canal during 1907–1914, and was given the right to control it forever. But the people of Panama wanted it under their control. In 1978 Congress passed two treaties that would turn the canal over to Panama in the year 2000. Many Latin Americans viewed the return of the canal as a sign of America's good will to its Latin American neighbors.

Student foreign exchange programs are one way to improve understanding between American students and students of other nations.

YOUR ROLE IN FOREIGN POLICY

The United States government listens to the opinions of its citizens on foreign policy. You are living during a time in which young Americans are becoming interested, more than ever before, in politics, social conditions, and international affairs. They are finding effective ways to express their interests and concerns about the issues of the day.

In many schools in the United States, students write letters to students in other lands. Many American schools go a step further and send funds to help support a child in a foreign land. Some American schools exchange a student from their school with a student from abroad. The foreign students who come here live with American families. They attend our schools and take part in our social life. These students learn about American democracy at first hand.

American citizens who send CARE packages abroad are helping to build friendship with other people. Church groups that send food, clothing, and money are demonstrating that Americans care about others. There are many opportunities for you, and for all Americans, to take part in such programs.

CONSIDER AND DISCUSS

Identify. détente / Nuclear Test Ban Treaty / Nuclear Nonproliferation Treaty / SALT / Third World

Review. 1. How did American thinking about Communism change between the late 1940's and the present? 2. What events caused this change in thinking? 3. What efforts have the United States and Communist countries made toward better relations? 4. What are some ways in which Americans can show friendship toward people in other lands?

Discuss. Are Third World nations important to the United States? Why or why not?

CHAPTER
Summary

After the end of World War II, the world was dominated by two opposing groups of nations. The Communist nations seemed set upon spreading their ideas and their form of government throughout the world. Democratic and other non-Communist nations opposed the spread of Communism.

A worldwide struggle between Communist and non-Communist nations, using every means short of all-out war, became known as the Cold War.

To resist Communism, the United States began a policy of containment. Our aim has been to resist the spread of Communism past its present borders. The Soviet Union tried to force the Allies out of Berlin by a blockade, which was broken by a great airlift of supplies. The policy of containment received another challenge when the Soviet Union and the People's Republic of China aided the North Koreans in their attempt to conquer South Korea. The troops of the United Nations, led by the United States, fought the Communists to a stalemate in Korea.

The Communist challenge was also met in Cuba when President Kennedy forced Premier Khrushchev, leader of the Soviet Union, to withdraw Soviet missiles from that island. In South Vietnam, our attempts to stop a Communist takeover resulted in the longest and most unpopular war in our nation's history, and eventually failed.

The United States has also sought peace through alliances, trade, and aid. Treaties of alliance have been made with many non-Communist nations. Trade agreements have been reached with a large number of countries. Aid to the economies of nations, through loans, grants, food supplies, and technical assistance, has helped them to build up their nations. Members of the Peace Corps have also helped to build friendship and understanding between our nation and others.

Since the 1960's, divisions within the Communist world have become evident. The United States and Communist nations have sought ways to achieve better understanding and reduce the danger of war. These explorations have resulted in new trade agreements and treaties limiting the use of nuclear weapons. Third World nations have gained importance. But political differences among some of them have caused wars and other conflicts. The United States has tried to maintain good relations with other nations, and it has encouraged peace efforts in many areas. Individual American citizens, especially young ones, must study foreign policy carefully and use their influence for the peaceful solution of international problems.

UNIT EIGHT

Improving Life for All Americans

CHAPTER

Introduction

In the early 1970's, the mayors of 12 large American cities met in New York City to discuss their common problems. They called national attention to the plight of big cities. But little did anyone guess that within a few years, the largest city in the nation would be on the verge of bankruptcy. In October 1975, New York City discovered that it did not have enough money to pay police, firefighters, sanitation workers, and other city workers. The city laid off about 60,000 city workers and cut many of its services. At first, the city government's appeals to the state and federal governments for help were turned down. Just in time, the school teachers of the city offered to use their pension fund to buy $150 million worth of city bonds to help the city out of the immediate crisis. Later, the state and federal governments loaned the city money under certain conditions.

The situation in New York City was not unique. The same thing was happening in other countries and in other large cities, some states, and smaller communities in America. Many state and local governments are not taking in enough money to pay for the services that they provide. What is the cause of this problem? Inflation is one cause. High wages is another. In addition, many cities have lost income as people and industries have moved from the cities to the suburbs and rural areas. New York City, for example, lost more than 400,000 people between 1970 and 1975.

These and other problems—pollution, crime, rundown areas, traffic congestion, and others—threaten the future of our cities. How can we save them? How can we improve the quality of life of our city dwellers? The problems of the cities are very great. Finding solutions will not be easy, as you will see when you read this chapter and study these topics:

1. Urban Growing Pains
2. Problems of Public Utilities
3. Problems of Urban Housing
4. Other Urban Problems
5. Planning for the Urban Future

CHAPTER

21 Problems of Urban Living

1 Urban Growing Pains

In Chapter 13, "Citizenship in the Community," you learned about different kinds of communities in our nation and the ways in which they serve their citizens. You were also introduced to some of the problems of community living. In this chapter, you will probe deeper into some of the serious problems of urban communities. These problems are important to all of us, for America has become more and more a nation of large cities. By the mid-1970's the metropolitan population of the United States was about 155 million. This meant that three out of every four Americans lived in and around cities. The fastest-growing cities were in Arizona, Florida, Texas, and Nevada. Regardless of where we live, urban problems affect each of us, and they must be solved.

WHY AMERICAN CITIES GREW

America began as a rural country with small, scattered settlements. At the time of the first census in 1790, the largest cities in the United States were New York City with about 33,000 people and Philadelphia with 28,000 people. Boston, Charleston, and Baltimore each had fewer than 20,000 inhabitants. All of these places had grown as port cities specializing in trade.

The 1800's saw a rapid growth in the size and number of cities in the United

States. By 1900, New York City had grown to a population of 3,437,200. Chicago was the second largest city, with a little over 1.6 million people. Philadelphia also had over a million people. Other large cities included St. Louis, Pittsburgh, Boston, Baltimore, Cleveland, Buffalo, San Francisco, and Cincinnati. All of these places had populations of more than 300,000.

Today, New York City has a population of more than 7 million people. In 1870, Los Angeles, California, was a small town of about 6,000 people. One hundred years later it had grown into a city of almost 3 million people. What caused this rapid growth of American cities? Here are some of the principal reasons for city growth.

1. The Industrial Revolution. The rapid growth of factories, especially in the years following the Civil War, brought many workers to the cities. Atlanta, Georgia, for example, with the opening of new mills and factories, grew from a population of about 37,000 in 1880 to about 65,000 in 1890. City jobs were plentiful in the years right after the Civil War, and even the most unskilled worker was welcomed.

2. Immigrant Workers. Millions of immigrants came to America in the late 1800's and early 1900's. Most of these immigrants settled in the cities. They crowded into poorer sections but were hopeful of working their way up the economic and social ladder.

3. Improved farming methods. During the agricultural revolution, farm machinery improved. This made it possible for fewer American farmers to provide more than enough food for the growing population of our nation. Unemployed farm laborers and younger members of farm families turned to the city for work and a chance to improve their lives.

4. Improved transportation methods. The development of modern transportation allowed American cities to expand their boundaries. The horse-drawn car, then the electric streetcar, commuter trains, buses, and subways, all helped cities to expand. With these services, people could live some distance from their place of work. But more than any other invention, the automobile aided the growth of our cities. With this invention, one could live off the main road and still get to many places with ease.

5. The lure of the city. To many Americans, the city has a strong appeal. Things are happening in the city that they want to be a part of. Fortunes can be made in the city. And there is a general air of excitement, of hustle, and of opportunity. Throughout our history, the lure of the city has drawn young people from the farms and small towns to swell the population of cities.

HOW AMERICAN CITIES GREW

Most of America's cities and towns were once small communities. They started as settlements located on a harbor, at the bend of a river, by a waterfall, or at the site of a frontier fort. Or they began where two well-traveled roads crossed. These communities were laid out according to patterns that met the needs of the times.

In most early towns, streets were narrow because they were built for use by a few horses and wagons. Often these streets were built to wind around steep hills or to follow the flat land along a river. The towns grew in an unplanned fashion. There was little idea of the amazing growth that was to take place in the future.

If you visit the older sections of many of our cities today, you will still find traces of the early towns. You may find narrow streets that wind in and out as they follow early wagon trails. Some of the streets of Boston are said to follow old cowpaths. These narrow streets were not designed for modern traffic.

But narrow downtown streets are just one of many problems that cities face because they have outgrown their original design. Through the years, cities have spread out from the spot where they began. As cities have expanded over the rural countryside, their growth has shown a typical pattern.

PATTERNS OF GROWTH

The growth of most American cities has been outward, away from the original center. If you were to draw a diagram showing how the typical city grew, it would look like a target. The old downtown area would be in the center. This center would be surrounded by several circles, each larger and larger as you go outward from the center. These circles would be irregular in shape and size. But generally they would follow the target pattern.

The old, central part of the city usually is now the downtown business center. Here you find older department stores, office buildings, factories, and warehouses. In some large cities, modern hotels and luxury apartment houses may also be located in the downtown section of the city. Although the city's business district often may be modern and well kept, areas in and around it may be rundown. The buildings in such areas are often old and in need of repair. Slum dwellings are often found in these areas.

The next circle outward from the downtown area is occupied by tenements, apartment buildings, or small private homes. These homes are often built side by side with little or no space between them. They sometimes have small backyards, but often no front yards. Also located in this circle are neighborhood shops and stores.

The next circle is sometimes called the **greenbelt.** Here are houses with yards and lawns, trees and shrubbery. This circle usually lies only partly within the city boundaries. It also extends beyond city lines, where it is called the suburbs. **Suburbs,** as you will recall, are the small, independent communities that surround a city. The people who live there have their own local government. But they also have

How Many American Communities Grew

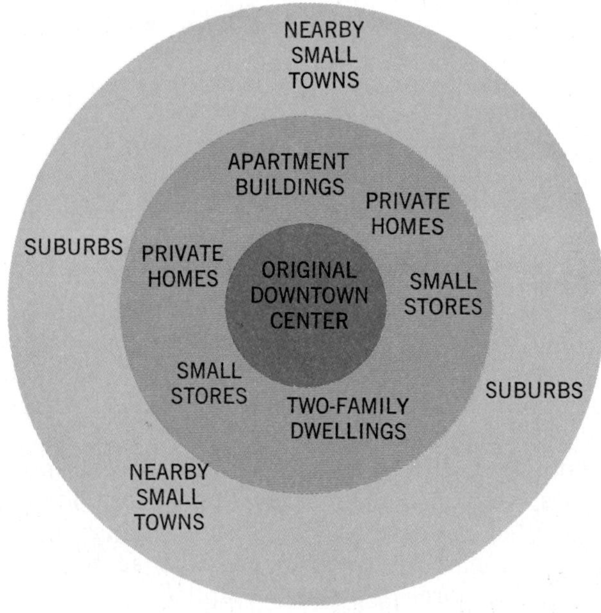

close ties with the city. Many of them work in the city and travel back and forth each day. Such travel from suburban home to city place of business is called **commuting.**

On the edge of the greenbelt is the **rural-urban fringe.** This is where the city meets the country. There are often farms and small towns in this area. City people sometimes go out into this area on holidays or vacations. The rural-urban fringe may lie from 80 to 160 kilometers (50 to 100 miles) from the city's downtown center.

FROM METROPOLIS TO MEGALOPOLIS

As you may remember, a large city with its surrounding area of suburbs and small towns is known as a **metropolitan area.** The Census Bureau lists cities of 50,000 or over, with their surrounding urban and suburban complexes, as Standard Metropolitan Statistical Areas. In 1976, there were about 272 metropolitan areas in the United States, an increase of 29 since 1970.

As metropolitan areas expand and grow outward, the rural areas between them become built up. Small towns become larger and larger. New housing developments extend into the rural-urban fringe. In some cases, whole new cities are born. Where forests and farms once stood, there are now stretches of almost continuous urban settlement. A growing area of overlapping cities like this has been given the name of **megalopolis,** meaning a very large urban area.

In the United States there are three such concentrations of people in which urban development is almost continuous. One occupies the area from Boston to Washington, D.C. This growing megalopolis, 965 kilometers (600 miles) long by 160 kilometers (100 miles) wide, contains about 49 million people. In other words, in less than 1.5 percent of the land area of the United States there live over 20 percent of our people. Another megalopolis stretches along the shores of the Great Lakes from Pittsburgh, Pennsylvania, to Chicago, Illinois. A third area extends from San Francisco to San Diego, in California.

In the older, central parts of some American cities, buildings are literally falling down.

From city to metropolis to megalopolis, the people of the United States have become more and more urbanized. With this urbanization has come a large number of problems. How, for example, can essential services such as water supply, trash removal, electric power, and mass transportation be provided for such great masses of people living so close together? You will examine such problems in the rest of this chapter.

CONSIDER AND DISCUSS

Identify. greenbelt / suburbs / commuting / rural-urban fringe / metropolitan area / megalopolis

Review. 1. Give five reasons why American cities grew so rapidly. 2. How did local geography help to determine the direction of city streets? 3. What are the main rings of city growth? 4. Where in the United States did megalopolises develop?

Discuss. What are the principal advantages and disadvantages of living in a large city?

2 Problems of Public Utilities

One of the principal purposes of government is to provide services to the people. Local governments provide a multitude of services such as police and fire protection and traffic control. They also supply schools, parks, and playgrounds. Local governments see to it that citizens have most of the public utilities they need. Local **public utilities** usually include street lighting, transportation services, sewage and trash disposal, electric and gas service, and water supply.

The larger a city is, and the more people it has to serve, the more important public utilities become. Imagine what chaos there would be in a large city if drinking water became unsanitary. Or suppose all forms of public transportation broke down or a complete and lasting **blackout** of electric current occurred. As our urban population grows and our cities expand, utilities must be planned to serve entire regions, rather than single communities. Providing public utilities for metropolitan areas or for a megalopolis is a serious and complicated problem.

UTILITIES SERVE THE PUBLIC

In our free economy, the public needs of the people have been met in a number of ways. Some public utilities are owned and operated as private business firms. Like other corporations, these utility companies are in business to make a profit. The telephone company is an example of a privately owned public utility that provides a needed service to the public. Other examples of privately owned public utilities are gas and electric companies, telegraph companies, railroads, and many bus lines.

Some public utilities are government owned and operated. Local governments, state governments, and sometimes the federal government may build and maintain public services. Government-owned utilities do not have to make a profit, like those operated by private business firms. Examples of government-owned utilities include subways, water supplies, and some bus lines. The United States Postal Service is an example of a government service that is organized like a corporation.

Throughout the United States, both private and publicly owned utilities are found. In many cities, essential transportation systems for large numbers of people are owned by the city. Most electricity and lighting are supplied by private companies. However, some states, like Nebraska, have state-owned public power utilities. The federal government also owns and operates some power agencies such as the Tennessee Valley Authority (TVA). The purpose of the TVA is to control floods as well as to supply electric power. In the Western states, many power-producing dams are operated by special districts.

WHAT IS A FRANCHISE?

Since public utilities provide services that are essential to the lives and well-being of the people, governments must see to it that utilities are operated in the interest of the public. One of the ways the city government assures good service is through the power to issue franchises. A **franchise** is a permit given to a private business firm. It gives it the right to run a public service.

Usually the city grants only one franchise for each service. This means that only the business firm that receives the franchise can sell this service. In other words, a franchise allows a private firm to run its service as a legal monopoly. This arrangement is efficient since it avoids the confusion of competition for a needed service. Imagine the confusion if there were two telephone companies serving the same street.

In return for a franchise, which grants a monopoly, a public utility company must agree to regulation by government. Before the franchise is granted, the company must prove to the government that it can give good service. The franchise can be revoked, or taken away, if the service is later found to be unsatisfactory. The rates that the utility charges its customers must be approved by the government. The utility cannot raise its rates without the approval of the government that issued its franchise.

All privately owned transportation companies, such as taxicabs, railroads, airlines, and intercity bus lines, must obtain franchises. In some instances, a city may issue a franchise if the private company operates only within the city limits. If city lines are crossed, a state transportation commission, or a similar state agency, issues the franchise.

THE ELECTRIC POWER PROBLEM

So great is the demand for electric power in our homes and industries that power companies must continually meet ever-increasing demands. New power-producing stations are being built. Others are being planned. A number of nuclear energy plants are now producing electricity. Still, the demand for electric power often exceeds the supply.

One method being used to help meet unusual demands is the **power grid.** Most of the power companies of the United States and parts of Canada are "hooked together" by interconnecting switches or junctions. Sometimes, the demand for electric power is greater than normal in one area. When that happens, the power company serving that area can tap into reserve power being generated by the power company in the area next to it. Sometimes power can be obtained from an area that is far away. On a map, these power-line connections look like a grid, or network.

In spite of the best efforts of the power companies, power failures sometimes occur. One night in 1965, there was a blackout that plunged most of the northeastern United States into darkness for several hours. Subways stalled, elevators stopped running, street lights went out, and electrical equipment shut off. A similar blackout occurred in the New York metropolitan area in 1977. These dangerous events emphasized the need for careful planning and development of adequate electric power.

SERVICES PROVIDED BY COMMUNITIES

Certain utilities and services are usually owned and operated by the local government. Often these services are available in return for taxes. Sometimes each household that benefits from the service pays a fee. Some of these important services are:

1. Water Supply. Communities must have water. Vast amounts of water are used every day in the United States. As our population has grown, communities have been hard pressed to maintain an adequate supply of water. New York City brings its water 200 kilometers (125 miles) from rivers and reservoirs in the Catskill Mountains. To bring huge supplies of water this long distance, New York City has bought up land areas for

reservoirs and has built pumping stations, filtration plants, and water mains. The expense of building and maintaining these facilities is paid for by the people of the city as part of their taxes.

2. Sewage Disposal. A great deal of the water used in our homes, stores, schools, and businesses is used to carry away sewage and other wastes. When a bathtub is emptied, for example, the dirty, soapy water must be disposed of in a quick, safe way. American cities have large systems of sewer pipes under the streets. But America's rapidly spreading population has placed a great strain on sewer lines. The movement to the suburbs has often outrun sewage lines. In many new housing developments, the sewage runs into private septic systems. Because of the runoff from these systems, surrounding grounds become saturated and nearby streams become polluted. There is hardly a community in America that does not pay increased taxes as new sewage systems are built.

3. Garbage and Trash Removal. The larger the city, the greater its problem of getting rid of waste material. Many sanitation workers, operating specially designed trucks, work throughout our large cities every day. They remove hundreds of tons of trash from private homes, apartment buildings, stores, and other places. Trash and garbage removal from private homes is usually paid for out of local tax revenues as a service to the taxpayers. Restaurants and hotels require more service. Therefore, they have to often pay for private garbage-removal services. Despite the efforts of sanitation workers, trash often litters the streets of American cities and creates an ugly, unsanitary condition.

Once the sanitation trucks have picked up the refuse, the city faces the job of getting rid of it. Some cities dump it far out in the ocean or in swampy places along the shores of oceans or lakes. A landfill method is used by some communities. The garbage and trash are taken to some isolated spot, dumped, and finally covered with soil. New, usable land areas are sometimes created by this method. Often the refuse is taken to a disposal plant to be burned. None of these methods is entirely satisfactory. Some of them have been questioned because they pollute the environment.

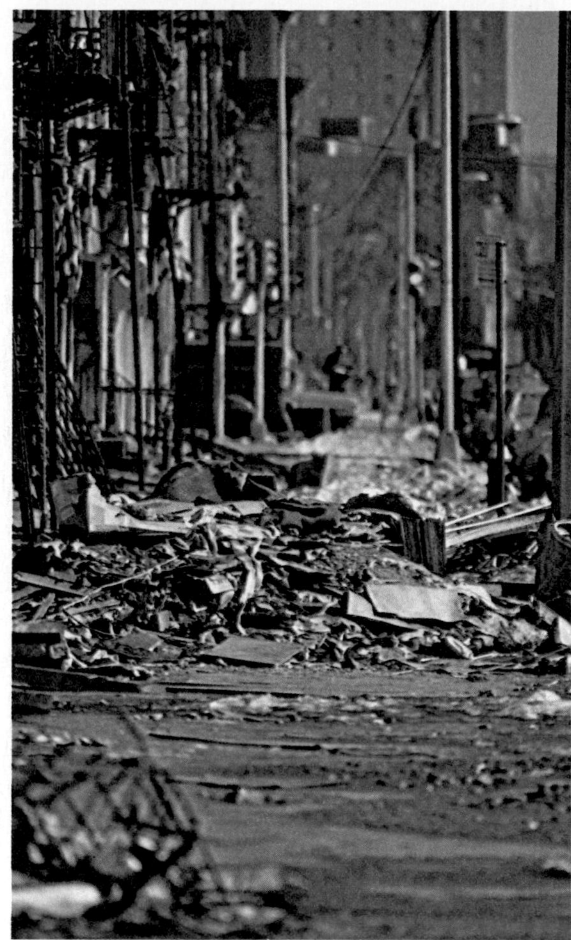

Trash removal is a problem in some cities. Poor neighborhoods usually get the worst service.

4. Public Transportation. An important service in cities is the providing of efficient means for moving their people. Our largest cities have rapid transit systems. Subways are usually community owned. Often they

City subway riders complain of overcrowding, poor service, and rising fares. Public transportation is a serious problem in many American cities.

operate at a loss. The loss is made up from taxes or from other publicly owned utilities that operate at a profit. Bus lines, either publicly or privately owned, are also often in financial difficulty. Many commuter railroad lines are losing money also. The federal government's Department of Transportation is trying to find ways to improve all aspects of our nation's transportation system.

OUR TROUBLED UTILITIES

Many public utilities of the United States are in deep trouble. Electric power companies set periods of restricted power usage. For example, during very hot summer days, the public is asked not to use air conditioners and other power-consuming appliances. Some gas companies refuse to take new customers because of a shortage of natural gas. Telephone service is often poor, with overloaded circuits, delayed dial tones, and long waits for service. The demand for water is so great in some communities that in the summer, lawns may be watered only on certain days. Railroads, bus lines, and subways are overcrowded. And the service is often inadequate.

What is the answer to the utility problem? Some people say that all utilities should be publicly owned. Others say that private ownership is best because it is more efficient. Whether publicly or privately owned, the future of public utilities depends upon wise management. It also depends upon decisions that must be approved by the voters of our communities.

CONSIDER AND DISCUSS

Identify. public utilities / blackout / franchise / power grid

Review. 1. Why are utilities important to a community? 2. How do city governments regulate utility companies? 3. How does the electric power grid work? 4. What are some of the utilities usually owned and operated by local governments? 5. What are some of the signs that public utilities are in trouble? Discuss. Do you think utilities should be publicly or privately owned?

3 Problems of Urban Housing

The cities of America contain some of the richest and many of the poorest people in the nation. A trip through any large city shows the great differences in the way people live. In the center of the city, on the fringe of office buildings, department stores, hotels, and theaters, there are rundown buildings. They are rotting from neglect and are almost unfit for people to live in. These are the slums. It is estimated that one in four of the people in American cities live in poor dwellings of this kind. Only a few blocks away may be luxurious apartment houses.

If one travels a little farther out, one may see single homes where middle-income families once lived. After these families moved to the suburbs, their homes were divided into apartments. Newcomers to the area and those who are fleeing from the slums now live here. This part of the city is sometimes called the **gray area.** It is becoming rundown and may be a future slum. Out beyond the gray area are better apartments and single homes. This mixture of city wealth and poverty is of concern to us all, for everyone is affected by it.

THE PROBLEM OF SLUMS

A **slum** is a dirty, rundown section of a city where families live crowded together in a few small, unpleasant rooms. Although slums are usually found in the central part of the city, they may develop in almost any area where there is crowding and where buildings are neglected.

Slums cost everyone money. The number of fires is greater in slum areas. This calls for more firefighters and fire-fighting equipment. More police officers are also needed to protect these areas. More of the city's money must be spent on health needs, welfare, and other services in slum areas than in any other part of the city. Yet slum areas pay less tax money to the city government than others. In this way, all of the people in the city help pay the costs of allowing slums to exist.

The people who live in the slums pay taxes of various kinds. But they also pay in misery. In these crowded areas there are high rates of disease and death. Compared with other sections of the city, there are higher proportions of school dropouts, juvenile delinquents, unemployed people, alcoholics, drug addicts, and criminals. Worst of all, there is a feeling of hopelessness, for slum dwellers often have no jobs and little hope for the future.

PLANNING TO END SLUMS

American cities have tried several plans to end slums. Some communities have tried replacing slum dwellings with **public housing projects.** These are apartment buildings built at public cost. The rents in these projects are low. And the apartments are open only to low-income families. The object of public housing projects is to improve the living conditions of the poor. But sometimes the projects also turn into slums.

Another plan to end slums calls for completely rebuilding the center of the city. Whole blocks of slums and other old buildings are torn down. Then, on this same land, groups of large, new, public buildings are constructed to form a **civic center.** Facilities are provided for business conferences, concerts, sporting events, and public exhibits.

Slums are ugly and dangerous places for children to grow up. The lack of decent housing is one of the most serious human problems of our inner cities.

Planners encourage private business to erect modern hotels, motels, and office buildings in this same area. The entire downtown section is carefully planned. It is given grassy areas and wide, well-lighted streets and sidewalks. Usually, near the civic center or elsewhere, such projects include better housing for former slum dwellers whose homes were torn down.

A third kind of community plan to end slums is to rebuild and repair the buildings in the area. Buildings that can be repaired are rebuilt by their owners. Sometimes the owners get financial help from the city. The houses and apartments are repaired and painted, and modern plumbing is installed. Buildings that cannot be repaired are torn down. They are replaced with new dwellings, or with parks and playgrounds. Streets are paved and lighted. Dirty backyards are cleaned up. Fences are torn down. And the open areas between buildings are cleaned and improved. Cities using this plan usually pass laws to enforce good housing regulations. They also set up housing courts to enforce the laws.

THE FEDERAL GOVERNMENT HELPS

Programs such as the ones you have just read about are called **redevelopment programs.** Under these programs, the central areas of some cities are being redeveloped and made attractive again. The programs are planned and carried out by local agencies, such as city or community planning commissions.

Sometimes a city will have an agency with a name like Commission for the Preservation of Historic Sites. This Commission identifies old buildings that should be preserved because of their historic value or because they are fine examples of architecture. Such places are restored and preserved to add to the attractiveness and interest of the city.

Redevelopment and preservation programs are costly. Sometimes land and old buildings must be purchased from their owners. Tearing down unwanted buildings is costly. Construction according to a new plan takes a great deal of money. The federal government has been one source of funds for this work. In 1949, Congress passed an act to aid urban redevelopment and renewal. This act, with later amendments, has helped many cities to rebuild run-down areas.

In 1965, the **Department of Housing and Urban Development (HUD)** was created by an act of Congress. This department is directly under the President of the United States. It has had the responsibility for channeling billions of federal dollars to the cities for redevelopment. Strict rules are laid down by HUD for the design and construction of projects it finances. Federal aid is more rapidly available to cities that draw up plans for the renewal of entire neighborhoods rather than just a building or two. Such programs have had considerable success in such cities as Baltimore, Philadelphia, New York, St. Louis, and San Francisco.

PRIVATE BUSINESS ALSO HELPS

Office towers, luxury-type apartment buildings, sports arenas, concert halls, hotels, and other buildings have been built by private industry on the sites of old slums. Corporations have been formed to undertake such redevelopment in the hope of making a profit. Some of the buildings in these projects have been noted for their outstanding beauty. Two of the most famous are the redevelopment in and around Lincoln Center in New York City and Kennedy Center in Washington, D.C. Other cities with outstanding urban-renewal projects financed largely by private funds include Pittsburgh, Boston, Denver, and Chicago.

Urban renewal projects, such as this one in New Haven, Connecticut, provide good housing for low- and moderate-income families. Urban redevelopment on a large scale will require a great deal of federal aid to the cities.

COMMUNITY BUILDING CODES AND ZONING LAWS

City governments have acted to prevent new housing problems, as well as trying to solve old problems. To prevent the development of new slums, cities have passed laws that builders must follow in making new buildings safe and attractive. Other laws require homeowners and apartment owners to keep their buildings repaired and comfortable. Such laws are part of a city's **building code.**

Every city and town has a building code. Before a new building may be started or remodeling takes place, builders must obtain a **building permit.** Their work is inspected at various times to make sure they follow the local regulations.

Zoning laws regulate the kind of buildings that may be put up in a particular area. Most communities are divided into zones. Some zones are set aside for houses only. Another zone may include houses, apartments, and small stores. Still another zone may allow factories but no homes. Zoning regulations protect residential areas from business, industry, or other activities that might destroy their residential values. To enforce such regulations, most city governments appoint or elect a **zoning board.**

SUBURBAN HOUSING PROBLEMS

If you go for a drive in the country, notice some of the things you pass. There will probably be new communities with attractive homes. But you may also pass old, run-down homes or poorly built stores. Other common sights may be gas stations, signs and billboards, junk yards, used car lots, and drive-in snack stands—all built without a well-thought-out plan. Such places may be called suburban slums. As suburbs have grown, some of them have had problems of water supply, trash removal, sewage disposal, increasing crime, and high taxes. Planning, building codes, and careful zoning can help prevent such problems.

CONSIDER AND DISCUSS

Identify. gray area / slum / public housing project / civic center / redevelopment program / HUD / building code / building permit / zoning laws / zoning board

Review. 1. What are some problems caused by slums? 2. What are some of the plans for ending slums? 3. How does the federal government aid urban renewal? 4. What is the purpose of zoning?

Discuss. Do you think that the federal government should help cities to rebuild? Why or why not?

4 Other Urban Problems

The best urban renewal and redevelopment plans are often handicapped when other problems get in the way. Crime and violence in a city may be so acute that the police force is the most expensive service in a city's budget. Problems of air or water pollution may be so serious that expensive, immediate steps must be taken to keep the city livable. Often, too, schools must be improved to give all children in the city a good education. All of these things cost money. But cities are short of funds. In the face of rising costs and the need for increased services, cities are losing many of their taxpayers. Where have they gone and why?

THE MOVE OF MIDDLE-INCOME FAMILIES

In recent years, more people have moved out of the central cities than have moved in. Most of those who move out of the city go to live in the suburbs. The census of 1970 showed that, for the first time in American history, more people lived in the suburbs and towns of metropolitan areas than lived within city limits. Cities such as St. Louis, Cleveland, Pittsburgh, Chicago, and Detroit lost population, while their suburbs gained. Only a few cities, such as Phoenix and Houston, showed gains in population.

Why are people leaving the cities? There are, of course, many reasons. Some people seek fresh air and sunshine, and houses with yards and trees. Others are afraid to live in the city. Crime in some cities is so bad that people are afraid to walk the streets at night. Those who move away from the city hope for a safer environment in the suburbs. Other reasons given by those moving out of the city include high taxes, loneliness, and pollution. Others seek better schools for their children, escape from the noise and bustle of the city, and the new jobs that are opening up in the suburbs as businesses move there.

This movement of people to the suburbs has had serious effects on American cities. For the most part, those who move are middle-class or upper-middle-class families. Many of these people still work in the city and use its services. But city governments often collect little or no tax at all from them. Furthermore, since the federal government's aid to cities is based upon their population, the cities lose federal aid when people leave. As people move out, cities lose federal aid for housing, schools, transportation, welfare, and other services. Cities also lose voters as people move to the suburbs. This means a loss of representatives in state government and in Congress. As suburban voters increase in numbers, they become more powerful in state elections.

THE TRANSPORTATION TANGLE

"Dirty, run-down, debt-ridden!" These are the words increasingly used to describe **mass transit** in our cities. Fewer passengers. Poorer service. Increased fares. What is causing the crisis in mass transit? Is there a remedy?

Transit officials point to the automobile as one cause. The movement of city workers to the suburbs has led many subways, buses, and railroads to extend their lines. But all too often the new mass transit lines lose money. Many suburban commuters prefer to drive their cars, even though expressways leading into the city are choked with traffic.

Rising payroll and maintenance costs on mass transit lines are another problem. Higher operating costs mean higher fares. And higher fares mean a further drop in the number of passengers. As service becomes worse, still other passengers take to the

Continued on page 443

Too many Americans travel to work by car, causing traffic jams, parking problems, and air pollution.

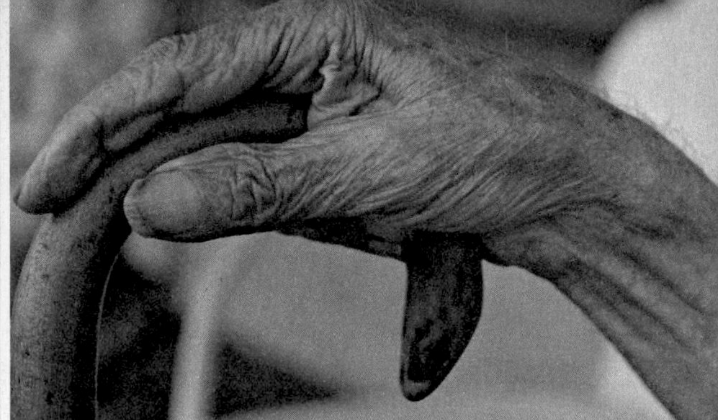

GROWING OLD IN AMERICA

WHAT DO YOU THINK?

Do you have grandparents or other relatives who are getting on in years? Do they live on their own, or with their children? In a retirement community, or in a nursing home? Are they burdened with any of the special problems—poor health, lack of money, boredom, loneliness—that affect many older Americans?

There are more than 22 million people in this country aged 65 and over—about one out of every ten Americans. Thanks to modern medicine, this group keeps growing. An American born in 1900 could expect to live, on the average, only 47 years. The average life expectancy of Americans today is over 70 years. Many people, of course, live much longer than this.

Many of these older Americans, or "senior citizens," live happy and healthy lives. But many others are in trouble. Why?

To some extent, the problems of older Americans are the results of changes in our pattern

of living. A century ago, when most Americans lived on farms, families were much bigger and more closely knit. As children grew up and got married, they did not always move away from home. Often they brought their wives or husbands to live on the family farm, where they had children of their own.

In these "extended" families, age was not a big problem. Everybody lived and worked together on the farm. As a man got older, he took on lighter chores while his son or son-in-law would do more of the heavy work. As a woman grew older, she might spend less time on her feet cooking. Instead she spent more time sewing or looking after the grandchildren. Young or old, family members contributed what they could and received whatever care they needed.

Our urban pattern of living today is very different. Most families today live in small houses or apartments. When the children grow up, they move away and start their own homes, often in a different city. Older people are now left on their own. At the same time, our modern economy has forced many of them to stop working at a certain age. When older people retire, their income suddenly goes down, and they must find new ways to spend their time. Failing health can make all these changes even more difficult to handle.

The old-age security provided by the rural extended family has largely disappeared. Can our modern urban society find new ways of providing for its senior citizens?

In recent years, retirement benefits under the federal Social Security system have been increased. The Medicare program now helps to pay the extra medical bills of senior citizens. Special housing projects have been built for the elderly. All these steps are important. But many problems still remain to be solved.

The first problem for many older Americans is money. How can older, retired people support themselves? Social Security checks alone are usually too small to live on. Many big companies

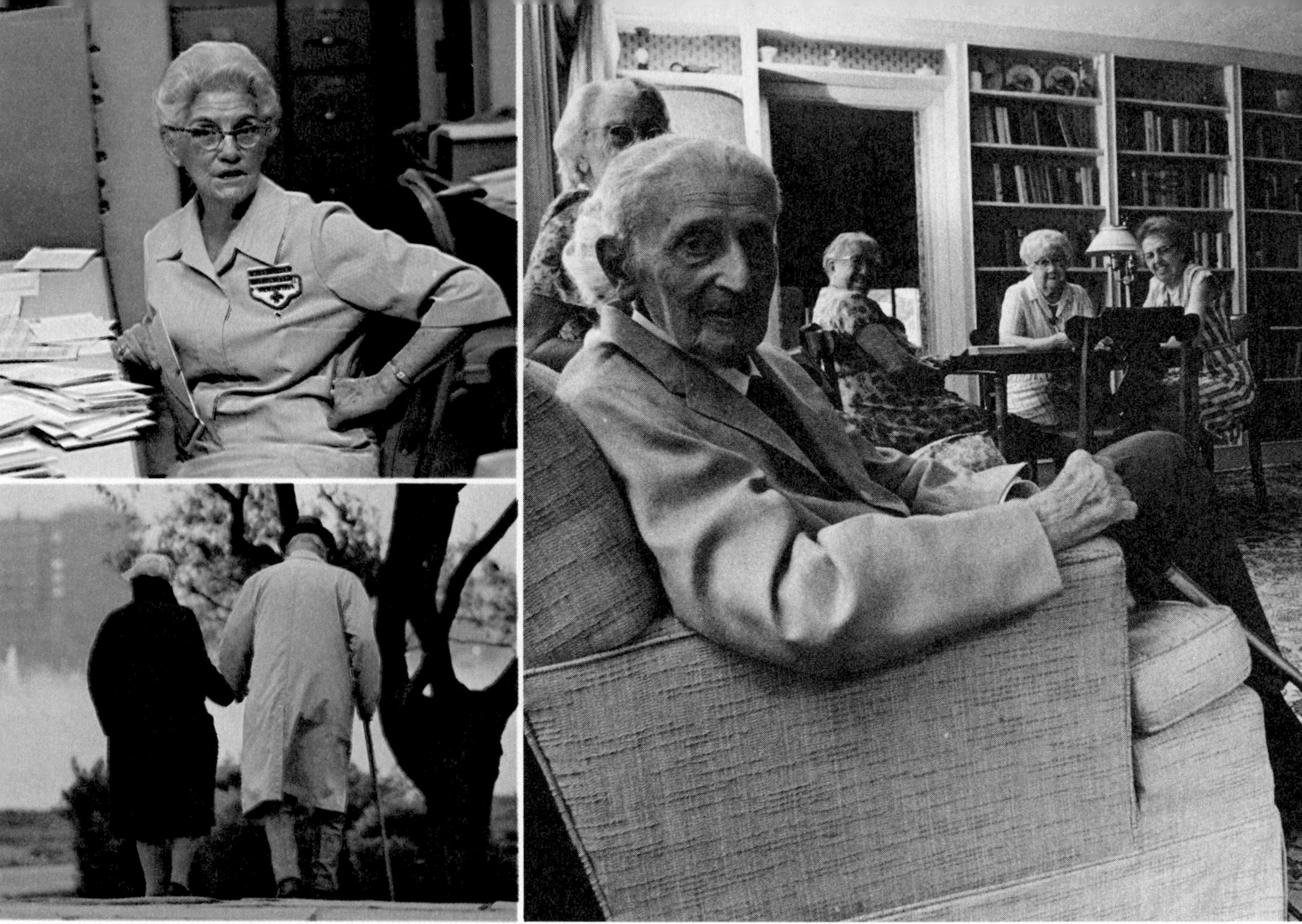

and labor unions have their own pension plans. Workers contribute to a pension fund during their working years, in order to receive monthly payments after they retire. But often workers lose their pension rights if they change jobs. Many workers have no pension plan at all. Without a good pension, or large private savings, many people must spend their later years in poverty.

How can this problem be solved? Should Social Security payments be increased yearly to keep up with the cost of living? Should we pass new laws to strengthen the pension rights of workers? Should we set up a national pension fund for all workers? What other ideas can you think of to guarantee a decent living for people too old to work?

Money is not the only problem, however. Many older Americans live alone, with little to do. They may feel unwanted and useless, with no purpose to their lives. These kinds of problems are perhaps the saddest of all. What can we do to help?

Retirement homes or communities are one possible answer. There are hot-meal services in some areas to provide better nutrition and companionship for elderly people who live alone. Neighborhoods or apartment buildings that include both older people and young families is another idea. In this way, older people would not be so isolated. They also might be able to babysit or do other part-time work for neighbors.

What do you think of these ideas? Do we have a special responsibility toward our senior citizens? Can you think of other ways to make life easier or more pleasant for older Americans? In 1978, a federal law changed the retirement age of many people from 65 to 70. How will this affect older people?

highways. Since 1950 the population of the United States has increased by about 70 million people. But the number of mass transit users dropped about 50 percent.

Different solutions have been suggested to cure mass transit problems. Most of them involve some degree of tax support. One proposal is to spend less on expressways, especially into cities, and more on mass transit systems.

Another proposal calls for doing away with all fares. Mass transit lines would be paid for with a weekly payroll tax of two or three dollars. The tax would be paid by all workers who live in the area served by the transit system. Supporters of this proposal say that citizens would leave their cars at home and use the mass transportation already paid for with their tax dollars. This would relieve pressure on the highways. It would also help to reduce pollution from automobile exhausts. Labor costs would be cut as no one would need to sell tickets or tokens, or to collect fares. Free transportation would attract visitors and shoppers, whose dollars would help the economy of cities.

Most cities look to the federal government to help rescue their failing transit systems. In 1970, Congress passed the **Urban Mass Transit Assistance Act.** The money that this law provided to improve facilities and equipment proved to be inadequate. As a result, in 1974 Congress passed another Mass Transportation Act. This act made more funds available for approved projects. Both these acts offered "matching funds," with the federal government providing two dollars for every dollar of local funds. With this help, some communities have begun to improve their mass transportation facilities.

Despite their many problems, mass transit systems are essential to every city. They are as vital as the highways, railroads, and airlines that connect the city with the rest of the nation and the world. They must be made to succeed if cities are to survive.

PROBLEMS OF THE INNER CITY

The movement of middle- and upper middle-income people outward from the center of the city has left an inner core of poor people. Many of them are black, Puerto Rican, or Mexican American. Along with slum housing, disease, and poverty, there are a number of special problems connected with the inner city that need urgent attention.

Welfare assistance. This is one of the great needs of the inner-city poor people. According to a report by the Department of Health, Education, and Welfare, about 13 percent of the people in ten of the leading cities is on welfare. The poor must be helped. But better ways must be found. Unemployment is a constant fact of life for many of the inner city's people. Many of them lack skills, and fewer and fewer job opportunities are open to them. In addition, many industries have moved out of the city and into the suburbs. **Industrial parks**—areas zoned for business and industry—have been set up in these places. These industrial parks have taken business and employment opportunities away from the city.

Schools. The schools in the inner city often have inadequate facilities. Also, the quality of education is often poor. Some teachers do not want to teach in the inner city because of the many problems. To improve the quality of education for the inner-city child, some communities bus inner-city children to better schools in other neighborhoods. Some attempts have also been made to bus children from the suburbs into inner-city schools. Supporters think this will bring about better integration and improve the quality of inner-city schools. Much controversy has surrounded this system of school **busing.** You can read about current aspects of the dispute in your daily newspaper.

Child care. Caring for the children of working mothers is another pressing problem in the slum sections of our cities. In some cases, the father is unemployed. The mother must find work or go on welfare. If the mother

City Problems

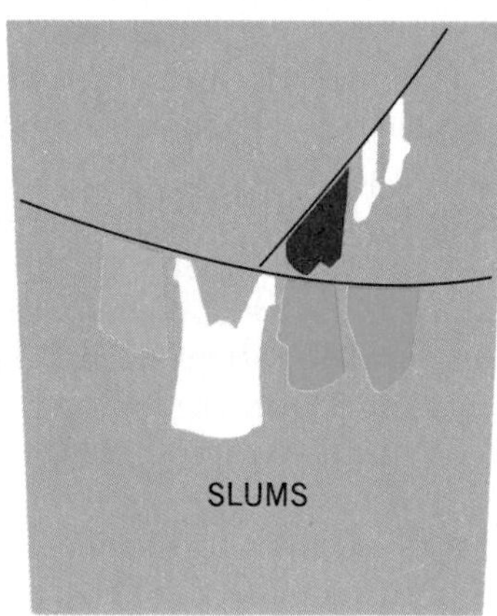

works, the children are often left in the care of relatives or neighbors. Or they are allowed to roam the streets. Sometimes these children are neglected and undernourished. They grow up without proper guidance and family love. Many cities are trying to set up **day care centers** where small children may receive proper care while their mothers work. Many of these centers for the care of children whose mothers work are supported by tax funds. It is hoped that they may help youngsters to grow up to be useful citizens.

Crime and violence. These are common in many slum areas. With little work, little hope, and a feeling of despair, people often turn to drugs for "kicks" or as an escape from their surroundings. They often steal to buy drugs. When people live in crowded, miserable conditions, violence is frequent. The slum sections of the cities have a large proportion of the nation's stabbings, shootings, and murders.

WHAT CAN BE DONE ABOUT URBAN PROBLEMS?

Solutions for our many urban problems are not easy. Much money is needed. But money alone cannot cure the city's ills. More jobs and job training would help. Better race relations would bring increased cooperation among the city's people. Better housing is a must. Can we develop plans to bring about these improved conditions? In the next section of this chapter, you will read about plans now under way.

CONSIDER AND DISCUSS

Identify. mass transit / Urban Mass Transit Assistance Act / industrial parks / busing / day care centers

Review. 1. Why have many people left the city? 2. How does the movement of people away from the city affect city finances? 3. What are some of the problems of mass transportation in the cities? 4. What are some of the problems of the inner city?

Discuss. Some city planners have suggested that no automobiles be permitted to enter the business section of any city. All those who come from the suburbs to work in the city would have to come by bus or train or subway. What do you think of this idea?

5 Planning for the Urban Future

What will the city of the future be like? Perhaps large parts of it will be turned into parks, playgrounds, and other open spaces. One suggestion has been to cover the entire city with a plastic dome so that the purity of the air, the temperature, and even the weather can be controlled. These may sound like impossible ideas. But groups of people are at work trying to save our cities, and desperate measures may be needed.

THE NEED FOR PLANNING

Americans are now aware of the mistakes that were made in building the cities of the past. Cities grew without much thought about their effect on the environment and the people who lived in them.

We are now trying to solve the problems of our growing cities with the help of planning commissions and similar groups that study the needs of our communities. Before a new express highway is built, for example, the route is carefully studied. Forecasts are made of traffic flow and what the new highway will do to street patterns. Plans are being made to substitute public transportation such as subways, commuter railroads, and buses for private automobile transportation. The effect of new buildings in the city and suburbs on the appearance and convenience of the whole metropolitan area is being carefully studied.

Most cities now have **community planning commissions** that work to improve urban conditions. Many counties and towns have similar agencies. Some large groups of cities and suburbs have **regional planning groups.** An example is the Regional Planning Association of New York. This group of private citizens has great influence because so many leaders of the region are members. The Regional Planning Association maintains a continuing study of New York City and the 22 county areas that surround it.

All of these groups employ planning experts. Among these specialists are traffic engineers, population specialists, economists, political scientists, landscape architects, and many other scientists who study the land and its uses.

PROBLEMS OF PLANNING

What are the problems of urban growth that occupy the attention of planners? You have already read about many urban problems. Let us consider some of the main problems that experts must try to solve.

1. Transportation. As you have seen, the automobile is now widely used as a means of transportation. However, the automobile is a very expensive form of transportation.

Most people, when they drive their cars to work, go alone. In addition to their costs for gasoline, oil, tires, tolls, and parking, there are public costs. On an expensive highway, for example, the space needed to accommodate 100 people, each in a separate car, is nearly 1.6 kilometers (1 mile) long. But only two railroad cars are needed to transport the same number of people. Automobiles may ruin other forms of transportation because they take their business away.

More and better commuter railroads seem to be the best answer to the increasing urban smog and monstrous traffic jams. As more and more people, in more and more private cars, come into the city, the situation will become worse. Some city planners favor keeping private cars out of certain sections of the city. To replace them with good public transportation would be expensive. But it may be the only answer.

2. Land Use. As land becomes more and more covered with buildings, land grows in value. It is important that we plan how to make the best use of urban land. In large cities, skyscrapers will probably increase in number and size. In New York City, for example, the World Trade Center rises 110 stories into the air. Its twin towers make it possible for each office to be open to daylight. The space over transportation terminals is being developed. Madison Square Garden in New York City is built over railroad lines. Better use of space underground is being encouraged. Many cities have developed underground parking spaces. And underground and covered shopping areas are being created.

Outside the city, land use is also of great importance. Space must be left for farms. Parks need to be set aside in forests, along shorelands, and in other remaining open areas. New suburban housing developments must be planned to allow for streets, trees, recreation areas, and public buildings, including schools.

3. Water Supply. The problem of water supply is linked to pollution. Experts say there is plenty of water in most parts of the United States. What we have not done is to take care of the available supply of water. Too much of it has been ruined for use by humans. New York City has had to go farther and farther into the Catskill Mountains to obtain enough water. Southern California obtains water from the Colorado River and from the Sacramento River, 708 kilometers (440 miles) away. Water has to be brought from such distances, in part because of the increasing demands for water. But also, in many places, water closer to home has been made unusable by the dumping of sewage and industrial wastes into streams and lakes. Plans for future water needs include adequate sewage disposal plants, the use of sea water, and better water collection facilities.

4. Cultural Activities. The city provides more diversity of culture, recreation, and entertainment than any other place where people live. In a large city one can hear music of different centuries and of many types. One can eat food from almost every country. The cultural background of the whole world may be sampled in the city's museums. People who live in large cities come from every race and national background.

Getting enough money for cultural activities is becoming more and more difficult as city budgets are strained to the breaking point. Libraries are cutting down on their hours. Municipal orchestras are in financial difficulty. Theaters are closing. These are signs of the deterioration in the cultural facilities of many cities. Such activities must enter into city plans and finances if cities are to keep their appeal.

METROPOLITAN AREAS PLAN FOR THE FUTURE

It is not surprising that the large city and its suburbs have many problems in common. Take the problem of transportation. The

Planning models like this one have been used to help decide the best locations for new office buildings, housing projects, a civic center, or parks and other recreational facilities.

streets of the city and the roads of the suburbs are a part of one system. In many cases, cities and suburbs have formed **metropolitan transit authorities.** These groups study the traffic problems in their areas and work toward their solution. Representatives from the city and from suburban communities are included in the transit authority. They cooperate on programs to solve traffic problems in the whole metropolitan area. Similar groups are developing plans to cooperate in solving other problems such as air pollution and waste disposal. Groups are also working to develop joint health services, parks, and recreational areas.

Among the metropolitan areas working on such programs are those around Detroit, New York City, Dayton, Kansas City, Peoria, Boston, and Los Angeles. Metropolitan cooperation is necessary to solve problems that overlap governmental boundaries. Sometimes several metropolitan areas face a common problem that is best settled by joint planning and cooperation. The metropolitan areas of Philadelphia, Trenton, and Wilmington have joined together to solve common problems.

Some Americans have suggested that this kind of informal cooperation should be replaced by a new type of government that would take in an entire region. If the state and local governments in an urban area united in a kind of federation—like the federal union that formed our present government—all might benefit. It will probably be some time, however, before our suburbs, towns, and cities will give up any of their powers. Nor will they easily agree to join into new regional forms of government.

CITY PLANNING AND THE CITIZEN

All of the citizens of the United States have a stake in plans for better cities. The city dweller will have a better place in which to live. The suburbanite who commutes to the city will be able to do so with greater comfort and speed. Farmers who sell their produce in the city will profit from a better-run city. Vacationers from small towns will find the city a more attractive place to visit. But plans may take a long time to work out. In the meantime, any city can be improved if its local citizens are interested in it. They can help to keep the city clean and to prevent pollution and waste. They also can support city officials as they struggle to solve urban problems. In many cities, people have formed block associations to improve the street they live on. These people have planted trees on their block and worked in many ways to improve their community. Such individual efforts can go a long way toward improving our cities.

PUTTING FIRST THINGS FIRST

Does it sometimes seem to you that there are so many urban and national problems that it is hopeless to think of solving them? In the 1960's, many Americans thought that way. In the early 1970's, however, some Americans became more optimistic. They believed that the nation was moving toward a better "system of priorities"—a better plan, that is, for putting first things first. But in the mid-1970's, many Americans became pessimistic again. What were the priorities that were changing? Why did Americans become optimistic, then pessimistic again?

First, in the early 1970's, people saw the possibility that the federal government might soon reduce the millions of dollars it had been spending on military affairs. They also saw that the great powers—the United States, the Soviet Union, and the People's Republic of China—were trying to find ways to live together more peacefully. Many Americans believed that if these changes occurred, there would be more federal tax money to help the nation solve its problems.

Second, many people knew that the federal government was studying the nation's system of taxation. Over the years, many people said, several unfair practices had crept into the tax programs. Some wealthy persons and large corporations had not paid their fair share of taxes. But with revision of the tax system, there would be more money available for solving America's problems.

Third, some people said that when the Vietnam War ended, less of our resources would be spent for military purposes. Then, the nation could direct more of its **economic resources**—raw materials, capital, and labor—toward building better cities, homes, transit systems, and other badly needed facilities. A large effort in this direction, some people said, could produce more jobs.

But things did not come out as people thought they would. The Vietnam War ended. The tax system was revised somewhat. And the United States improved its relations with the Soviet Union and the People's Republic of China. Yet, the urban and national problems remained. There were some new economic problems as well. As a result, many people became pessimistic again.

The Vietnam War ended in 1973. Soon after that, the United States went into a serious recession, as you may remember. Business slowed down. Many people lost their jobs. Inflation continued to raise the cost of living. In addition, Americans discovered that the nation's oil and gas supplies were low. Therefore, billions of dollars a day were spent to import foreign oil. That meant that every day billions of dollars left the country. Therefore, this money was not available for solving our problems at home.

The economy began to improve in 1975. But inflation, unemployment, oil and gas shortages, and urban problems remained. Experts could not agree on the solutions to these problems. Some Americans felt that the nation still needed to change its priorities. They said that the nation's tax system should be revised even further. Some also believed that Americans should cut down on their waste and on what they spend for luxuries. This would give people more money to spend on public goods and services. Then, these people said, the nation could solve its many problems, including its urban problems.

CONSIDER AND DISCUSS

Identify. community planning commission / regional planning groups / metropolitan transit authorities / economic resources

Review. 1. What kind of experts are employed by regional planning commissions? 2. What are some of the problems metropolitan planning commissions try to solve? 3. How can land areas in metropolitan areas be used more wisely?

Discuss. What problems in your local community need long-range planning? What problems do you think individuals could help solve by working together?

CHAPTER Summary

America has become a nation in which most people live in large cities or in the towns and suburbs of large metropolitan areas. Living in cities has both advantages and disadvantages. Among the advantages are cultural and economic opportunities. Disadvantages include slums, crowding, and crime.

The urban area has grown from a small town to a large city, to a metropolitan area. It finally grew to a kind of supercity called a megalopolis. Urban areas have grown because they became centers of industry and trade, attracting immigrants and people from farms and small towns.

To provide essential services for their people, cities have public utilities. Some of these utilities are publicly owned. Others are operated by private companies that have been granted franchises. In urban areas, the millions of people to be served have placed severe strains on electric systems, water supply, trash and garbage removal, and other essential services.

The city's housing problems threaten the health and safety of its people. The old centers of many cities have deteriorated. There, slums add to the city's problems. The federal government has contributed to housing developments to try to improve living conditions for city dwellers. There are also suburban slums that need attention.

The movement of middle-income people to the suburbs has left the city with reduced financial resources, a transportation tangle, and problems of politics and government. Many of the city's poor people must rely on welfare to supply their needs. Rundown inner-city schools trouble many people.

The future of our cities depends upon proper planning. Local and regional planning commissions must take bold measures to assure that the cities become proper places for people to live in.

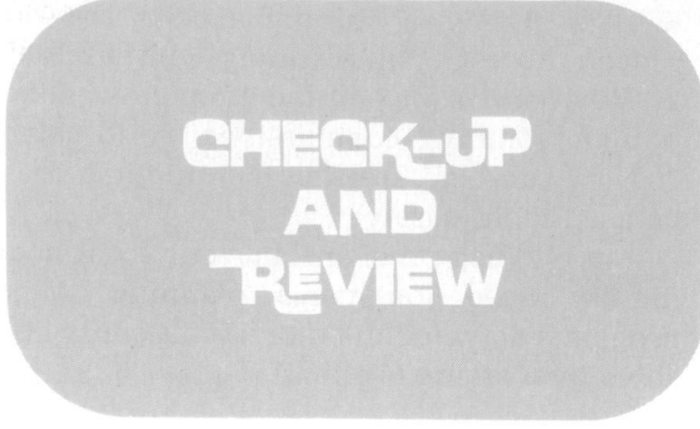

VOCABULARY

On a separate piece of paper or in your notebook, write the words that appear below. Then read the eight definitions that follow and choose the definition that fits each word. Write the definition beside the proper word.

suburbs	franchise
slum	metropolitan area
building code	transit authority
zoning	public utilities

1. Local laws and regulations governing construction of new buildings.
2. Services that are used by all the people of a community.
3. A government traffic board that tries to solve traffic problems in metropolitan areas.
4. A legal permit granting a private business firm the right to operate a public service.
5. A rundown city area where houses and apartments are overcrowded and need repair.
6. A large city of 50,000 or more people, plus the surrounding suburbs and small towns.
7. Dividing a city into areas and regulating the building that can go on in each area.
8. The small communities that surround a city.

CHECK-UP

Without looking in your textbook, write brief answers to each of the following questions. Then check your answers by rereading your textbook. Make corrections where necessary.

1. What are some of the problems that face modern cities?
2. Describe the way in which many American communities have grown from their downtown centers to the suburbs.
3. How did certain areas become slums?
4. What is the job of a regional planning commission?
5. Can you describe three methods of attacking city slums?
6. What are some of the services that communities provide their residents?
7. Why are some public utilities allowed to become legal monopolies?
8. What are some of the problems that arise in suburbs?
9. How do zoning laws help to make a better-planned community?
10. What are the principal arguments for and against private ownership of public utilities?

CITIZENSHIP AND YOU

Your understanding of the problems that American communities face today will be increased if you participate in individual and group activities. Here are some interesting things to do.

1. Class Projects

A number of groups may be appointed to study aspects of community life in your own city or town. Groups may study such problems as slums, the downtown business section, traffic, suburbs, and public utilities. The chairperson of each group may appear before the class. Instead of giving a formal report, he or she may answer questions from the class.

Another lively type of class discussion that your class may wish to try is the "buzz session." In considering a problem such as "The Need for Zoning in Our Town," the class may be divided into several informal groups of six to eight students. Each group conducts its own discussion of the topic for about ten minutes. The whole class then gets together again. Each buzz group reports its findings to the entire class.

2. Group or Committee Projects

This chapter on urban problems begins the study of Unit Eight, "Improving Life for All Americans."

It is a good chapter with which to begin a new bulletin-board display. The bulletin-board committee should strive for an eye-catching display of the main themes of the unit. It should have strong centers of interest and well-chosen illustrations to add information about the themes that are shown.

An interview committee may talk with community leaders about local problems. The committee may report the results of these interviews to the class.

A photography committee may take or look for a series of pictures of several areas and activities in the local community. Display them in class. Scenes should be included to illustrate many of the problems discussed in this chapter.

3. Individual Projects

Read about and prepare a report on the history and growth of your community.

Obtain a map of your local community. On it, show the location of important places, suburbs, and points of interest. You may want to redraw the map for your purposes.

On a bar graph, show the growth of population in your community during the past 50 years.

Using a local newspaper, clip out headlines and articles discussing local community problems. Display and discuss these clippings in class.

CIVICS SKILLS

DEBATING

The discussion of a controversial issue—a subject on which people hold strongly different views—may take place as a formal debate. The issue, or proposition, to be debated may be stated in the form of a resolution such as: *Resolved,* That one regional government should replace the many local governments in metropolitan communities. One team of debaters takes the *affirmative* view—favoring the proposition. The other team upholds the *negative* view—speaking against the proposition. Each debater is limited to a certain number of minutes of speaking time. There may be a *rebuttal,* or reply, in which one speaker on each side is given the opportunity to answer the arguments of the other side.

Another approach to discussion of important issues is the "open forum." Each member of the class who wishes to do so may speak briefly on the issue being debated. In this informal type of debate, many different points of view may be expressed.

To become a good debater, you must read as much as you can about the issue to be discussed. You must learn the basic facts, and learn how to use these facts in your argument.

As you read, take notes. If an expert on the subject, or some well-known person, has said something important on the topic, you may want to quote this person. Such quotations often strengthen your side of the debate. Gather facts and figures that support your point of view. Statistics are difficult to argue against.

In preparing for a debate, you may want to keep a card file of facts, quotes, figures, and other evidence. Referring to these cards may provide answers to the arguments of the other side.

Finally, arrange your arguments in logical order. Determine the main points that support your side of the debate. Then gather evidence to support your main points.

PRACTICING YOUR CIVICS SKILLS

A debate group may prepare and participate in a debate on the topic *Resolved:* That living in the city is more interesting than living in the suburbs. Or prepare a debate on this topic: *Resolved,* That one regional government should replace the many local governments in metropolitan communities.

If there is a political debate on television, the class should watch it and discuss the debating ability of each candidate. If a "live" debate is being held in your community, the entire class might attend.

CHAPTER

Introduction

Under the American form of government, as you know, elected officials write the laws that are needed in an orderly society. Enforcement of the laws is the duty of police forces of various kinds. But these forces must answer to elected officials, such as mayors, governors, and the President. Finally, there are courts of many kinds. They decide if a law has been broken and, if so, what the penalty or punishment must be.

In our rapidly changing society, Americans have had to rethink their attitudes and opinions about many laws, about the proper and effective role of police forces, and about the justice of courts, penalties, and forms of punishment. These questions are urgent because crime in America has been increasing rapidly. An average of 22 serious crimes are committed somewhere in our nation every minute of the day and night. Few people question that crimes against persons or property should be punished. However, they may disagree about the severity of the punishment or the treatment of prisoners.

There are many ways, as you will see, for Americans to protest against laws that they think are unjust and try to get them changed. The right of the people to protest in these ways is protected in the Constitution. Thousands of Americans exercised this right during the civil rights movement of the 1950's and 1960's. But this right is not protected if, in their protests, people commit crimes against persons and property, or break other laws that are necessary in an orderly society. In other words, nonviolent protest is a right of American citizens. Violent protest is not.

In addition to police forces, there are many other government officials in America who work to protect and promote the health and safety of individual citizens and of society as a whole. A new and growing problem for many of these officials, including the police, has been the rising abuse of drugs among Americans, especially young Americans.

In this chapter you will read about how Americans and their officials try to deal with such problems under the following topics:

1. Crime in America
2. Police Forces and Prisons
3. Dissent, Civil Disobedience, and Violence
4. The Drug Problem
5. Health and Safety

CHAPTER

22 Law Enforcement, Health, and Safety

1 Crime in America

The Federal Bureau of Investigation (FBI) of the United States Department of Justice gathers information about crime in all American states and localities. Each year the FBI publishes a report called *Crime in the United States—Uniform Crime Reports.* This report provides the most complete record we have of crime in our nation. It shows that since 1960, major crimes have more than tripled.

In the late 1970's, over 11 million serious crimes were reported each year in the United States. There was a murder every 28 minutes and a robbery every 85 seconds. A car was stolen about every half minute. On an average, 22 crimes take place every minute of every day and night. Crimes cost the public billions of dollars each year.

The FBI *Uniform Crime Reports* divides crime into two general categories—crimes against persons and crimes against property.

CRIMES AGAINST PERSONS

Crimes against persons are those that harm or end a person's life, or that threaten to do so. The worst of such crimes is, of course, murder. More than 20,000 murders are committed in the United States each year.

Most states define a **first-degree murder** as one that is planned and carried out deliberately. It may be punished by life imprisonment. A number of states have laws that permit some first-degree murderers to be executed.

A murder carried out on the spur of the moment, often in a fit of temper, is called a **second-degree murder.** It is sometimes called **manslaughter.** Punishment may lead to many years in jail.

The most common crime against persons is called **aggravated assault.** The term is used to describe any kind of physical injury that is done intentionally to another person. Such assault often takes place during the act of robbing a person. Its most common form is mugging or yoking, in which one robber throws an arm around the victim's neck from behind while another goes through the victim's pockets. In the late 1970's there were almost 500,000 cases of aggravated assault a year.

CRIMES AGAINST PROPERTY

The most common form of crime in America is stealing, or theft. **Burglary** involves forcible or illegal entry into someone's home or other property with the intention to steal. Over 3 million burglaries a year were reported in the late 1970's, or almost 27 percent of the crimes listed by the FBI.

Larceny is the theft of property without the use of forcible or illegal entry. If the property is worth over a certain amount (varying from state to state), the theft is called **grand larceny.** A theft under this amount is called **petty larceny.** Examples of larceny are theft of an outboard motor, stealing from a cash drawer, and shoplifting.

The theft of automobiles is the most common form of larcency. It is a serious national problem. Almost 1 million cars are reported stolen each year. Some are taken by organized gangs, who resell them or strip them and sell the tires, batteries, and other parts. But most stolen cars are taken by young people who drive them for a while, risking arrest, and then abandon them.

Robbery combines a crime against both property and person. It may be defined as taking something from a person by threatening the person with injury. The robber may demand "your money or your life" and back up the threat with a weapon. Over 400,000 robberies take place in our country each year. About 65 percent of them are done with firearms. A murder committed during a robbery, even if unplanned, is first-degree murder.

Another kind of crime against property is **vandalism,** or the willful destruction of property. The damaging of schools and other public buildings and property increased greatly during the 1960's and 1970's.

CRIME AMONG YOUNG PEOPLE

About one fourth of the people arrested each year are under 18 years of age. The FBI reported in a recent year that there were more than 1.5 million arrests of people in this age group. People under 18 are responsible for almost half of all auto thefts, nearly 10 percent of the murders, and over 40 percent of the burglaries and larcenies. During the 1970's, the rate of crime among young people jumped considerably.

Every state has special laws for governing young people. The ages to which these laws apply vary from state to state. Some states define **juveniles** as people under 16. Others set the age as high as 21. The average age for junveniles is under 18. Juveniles become **delinquents** when they are found guilty of breaking a law.

Young people, statistics show, do commit serious crimes. Often, they also commit minor offenses that bring them into conflict with society. For some of these offenses, the law is more severe on young people than it is on adults. Juveniles who stay out late at night, who constantly disobey their parents, or who repeatedly run away from home may be found to be delinquent.

When a person is found to be impossible for teachers and parents to control, that

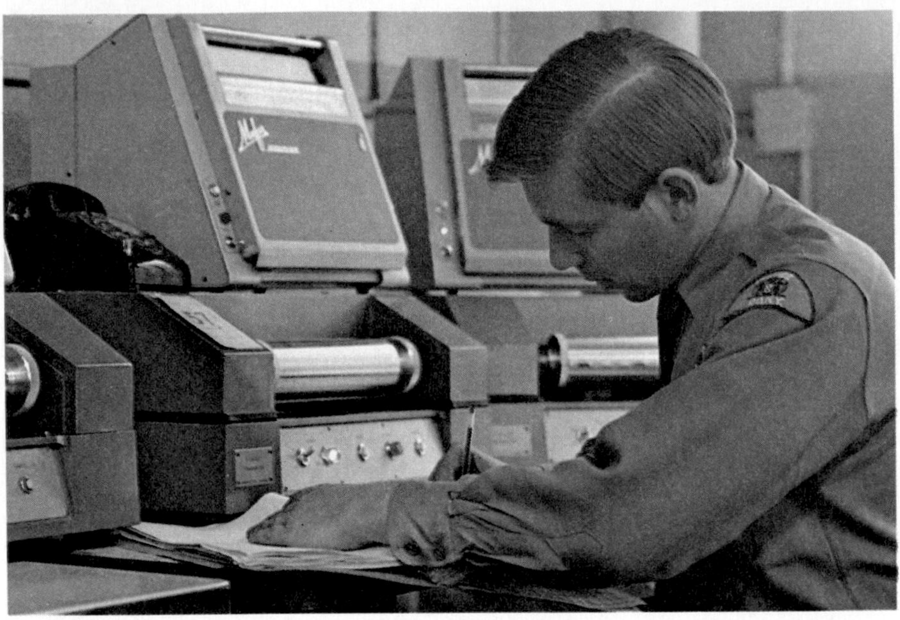

In recent years, the crime rate in the United States has been rising rapidly. This police officer is doing a fingerprint check to help solve a crime.

person is said to be **incorrigible.** After repeated instances of incorrigible behavior, a young person may be turned over to the juvenile authorities.

CAUSES OF JUVENILE DELINQUENCY

Why are some young people lawbreakers and incorrigibles, while most live law-abiding and useful lives? According to experts who have studied the problem, there is no single answer. All individuals are complicated. Their behavior, good or bad, may have many causes. Some of the more important causes of delinquency are:

1. Poor home conditions. Many juvenile delinquents come from homes where parents take little responsibility for their children. Often one parent is missing and the other works. Drunkenness in the home often drives the children into the streets, where they get into trouble.

2. Slums. The slum areas in our cities often have a higher rate of crime than other areas. Where people are crowded together in unpleasant living conditions, many young people are prone to get into trouble. Sometimes their actions are simply a search for thrills and adventure. There is some evidence, too, that they sometimes break the law in an attempt to "get even" with the community for the kind of life they have to live in the slums.

3. Membership in gangs. Some young people who get into trouble are members of neighborhood gangs. It is natural for a young person to want to be with a group and to take part in group activities. But when the gang turns against the community and breaks the law, it becomes a bad influence.

4. Dropouts and unemployment. When young people have nothing to do, no place to go, and no money to spend, they may be headed for trouble. A person who drops out of school is not necessarily headed for a life of crime. But facts show that an unemployed

young person, with little skill and training, often becomes a delinquent.

5. Alcohol and drugs. Almost every state has laws forbidding the sale of alcoholic beverages to anyone under 18 or 21 years of age. All states forbid the sale of habit-forming drugs to anyone who does not have a prescription from a doctor. Under the influence of alcohol or drugs, people often do things they would not do under normal circumstances. People on drugs, who may need from $25 to $100 per day to pay for their habit, often turn to crime—sometimes violent crime. You will read more about drugs later in this chapter.

6. Problems of mental health. Some young people get into trouble because of mental and emotional problems. They need help. Delinquents are often unhappy people. Deep down inside, they may be afraid of the world or feel that society is against them.

THE TREATMENT OF JUVENILE DELINQUENTS

Young people may be referred to the authorities by their parents if they are incorrigible. The school may refer them if they are habitual truants or troublemakers. Or they may be referred by the police if they are caught committing a crime. An investigation by a juvenile officer then follows. How serious is the offense? What do physical and mental tests show? What are their home conditions? What are their school records?

While this preliminary examination is going on, the juvenile may be released in the custody of parents, placed in a juvenile shelter, or held in a jail cell. But he or she must be dealt with according to the law. The Supreme Court has decided that juveniles have many of the same rights as adults. A juvenile who is arrested, for example, has a right to a lawyer, to a fair trial, and to be free from cruel and unusual punishment.

If, after a thorough hearing, the juvenile is found to be guilty as charged, a judge must decide what is best. Here are some of the things the judge may do: (1) place the delinquent on probation, (2) send the delinquent to a foster home, (3) commit him or her to a training school or reformatory.

Probation is a period during which a person guilty of an offense is given an opportunity to show that he or she can reform. The judge sets the provisions of the probation. For example, the judge may say to a delinquent, "I am placing you on probation. You will report to your probation officer and I will expect a good report about you. You will obey your parents and be in bed every night by eleven o'clock. You will make **restitution** for the damage you did. By restitution I mean that you will pay the costs as directed by your probation officer. If you do not behave yourself during your probation, or if you appear before me on any other charge, I will have to consider sending you to a House of Correction."

JUVENILE DECENCY

Most of America's young people are good citizens who stay out of serious trouble. They obey the law and the rules of society. **Criminologists**—scientists who study crime and the behavior of criminals—give the following suggestions to young people who want to avoid trouble with the law.

1. Do not get started on drugs. Those who try drugs often end up in criminal courts.
2. Get the best education possible. It will keep you busy, increase your chances for a job, and help you to face problems.
3. Avoid acts of vandalism. There are more effective and safer ways to express discontent or hostility.
4. Have the courage to say "no" when friends suggest illegal acts.
5. Live a full life, with plenty of physical activity and interesting hobbies. The person who is busy doing challenging things does not get bored and turn to criminal activities as an outlet.

CONSIDER AND DISCUSS

Identify. first-degree murder / second-degree murder / manslaughter / aggravated assault / burglary / larceny / grand larceny / petty larceny / robbery / vandalism / juvenile / delinquent / incorrigible / probation / restitution / criminologist

Review. 1. What are crimes against persons? against property? 2. Why are juveniles tried in special courts? 3. What are some causes of juvenile delinquency? 4. Describe what happens to juveniles when they are charged with breaking the law.

Discuss. What can your school and community do to help reduce juvenile delinquency?

2 Police Forces and Prisons

Our society depends upon cooperative citizens. It needs people who obey the law and who go about their daily tasks in a peaceful and orderly fashion. To help achieve this goal of "domestic tranquility," police forces have been established at local, state, and national levels.

THE ROLE OF THE POLICE

Efficient police forces have a number of aims. These are (1) to protect life and property, (2) to prevent crime, (3) to seek out and arrest those who violate the law, (4) to protect the rights of the individual, (5) to maintain peace and order, and (6) to control the flow of traffic on streets and highways.

It is not a police officer's job to punish lawbreakers or to decide who is guilty or not guilty. Deciding questions about guilt and punishment is the function of courts of law. Good police officers try to use their trained judgment about whom to arrest and on what grounds. They try to avoid the use of undue force, and to be patient in the face of insults and threats of personal injury. They try to act as peacemakers, advisers, protectors, and friends, as well as enforcers, in the never-ending struggle against crime. The modern policeman or policewoman must be a well-trained professional person, devoted to his or her duty, and skilled in the art of human relations. The job is not an easy one. It can also be a discouraging one because of overcrowding and other problems in the American court system. You read about these problems, and the need for court reform, in Chapter 7.

HOW OUR POLICE ARE ORGANIZED

A modern police force must be efficiently organized to take care of the complicated needs of present-day society. An understanding of the way in which an up-to-date police force operates will help us as citizens to cooperate in its activities.

1. A well-organized police force has headquarters control. In most places, the entire force is supervised and directed from a single headquarters. No matter where a crime happens, central headquarters can send police to the scene within minutes. To make this control possible, a modern police force has to have an up-to-date communications system and radio-equipped patrol cars.

2. A well-organized police force has a regular chain of command. All officers must know to whom they are responsible. They must also obey the orders they receive. At the top is the **police commissioner**, or chief of police. This executive is in charge of the entire force. Under the chief are police captains. Each captain is in charge of a major division of the department, such as the detective division, the division of traffic, and the homicide division. Under the captains are lieutenants in charge of platoons, and sergeants in charge of squads.

3. A well-organized police force has a group of well-trained men and women. The urban police officer today is often a specialist. There are traffic officers, patrol officers, detectives, communications specialists, laboratory technicians, narcotics investigators, and many others in a large, well-run police department.

4. A well-organized police department has a records department and a crime laboratory. The records department keeps information files on known criminals and the way they operate. These records are kept on punched cards. When the police are looking for a burglar who operates in a certain way, detectives feed these cards into a computer. The system quickly narrows down the number of suspects and makes it easier to find the guilty person. The crime laboratory uses scientific methods to uncover hidden clues, such as fingerprints, that will help to discover and capture criminals.

THE TRAINING OF MODERN POLICE OFFICERS

Modern police officers are carefully selected and trained. Before they are hired, they are fully checked and investigated. They must pass aptitude and intelligence tests, as well as civil service examinations or similar written tests. In addition, they must pass rigid physical examinations

Most cities require police officers to be high school graduates. In recent years, some cities have been seeking college graduates who think of police work as a good way to help their communities. In order to get the best men and women available, a community must be willing to pay good salaries. It must also be willing to make provisions for insurance, sick benefits, retirement pay, and aid to families of officers who are injured or killed in the line of duty.

New police officers attend special police academies. They learn about law, sociology, evidence, arrest procedures, and record keeping. They also receive on-the-job training that includes the use of weapons and other physical skills. They are taught how to deal calmly with the public, how to handle emergencies, and how to give first aid. Police officers must try to prevent trouble from taking place in their areas. When trouble occurs, they must be prepared to capture and arrest suspects, prepare reports for the courts, and appear in the courts as witnesses.

POLICE PATROLS HELP PREVENT CRIME

New police officers may begin their police career by "walking a beat." Many experts believe that **foot patrols** are an effective way to prevent crime, especially at night. Walking patrol officers can cover their territory carefully. Their job is to look into dark alleys, test doors to make sure they are locked for the night, and watch for suspicious persons or actions. To be really effective, the police force must be large enough so that all patrol officers on foot have a small territory. A city is safer if there is always a police officer nearby.

Most communities cannot afford all the foot patrol officers they need. They add to the strength and mobility of their force by using patrol cars. Radio-equipped police cars can be sent to any part of the city when trouble is reported or suspected. Cruising patrol cars often catch lawbreakers in action. Meanwhile, the fact that patrol cars are cruising through every section of the city helps to prevent crimes.

The main job of the police officer is to prevent crime. The well-trained officer knows the danger signs that invite crime—the burned-out streetlight, the open door, the broken window. By preventing crime, police officers save lives, money, and property. They also make the community a better and safer place in which to live.

When a crime is committed, the police officer's job is to round up suspects, collect evidence, and recover property whenever possible. Punishment of criminals, you recall, is not a part of the officer's job. Even if he or she catches a person in the act of breaking a law, the accused is entitled to a fair trial in court. Then, after the case has been heard, a jury of citizens, not the police officer, must decide if the person is guilty or innocent of the charge. If the person is found guilty, the judge decides the sentence.

PUNISHING LAWBREAKERS

There was a time when Americans believed that harsh punishment would prevent crime. Public whippings, chain gangs, and even public hangings were tried. Life in prison was made unpleasant in the belief that criminals would regret their crimes and decide never to return to prison. The harshest punishment was **capital punishment**—putting the criminal to death for serious crimes. It was hoped that such harsh punishment would discourage others from crimes.

The whipping posts, harsh prisons, and executions of the past did not prevent crimes. In fact, the old-style prison often made criminals worse. This problem still exists, especially in many prisons that are overcrowded. When first offenders are put in with habitual criminals, prisons all too often become schools for crime. Younger prisoners learn from older ones.

Overcrowding and other inhumane conditions have led inmates of many prisons to stage riots. One of the worst occurred at New York's Attica State Prison in 1971. Prisoners seized many guards as hostages and held them for four days. State police stormed the prison to put down the uprising. By the time it was over, 32 inmates and 11 hostages had died.

Many Americans have begun to question our prison system. Instead of training criminals to lead new lives, prisons often teach them more about crime.

NEW WAYS OF TREATING LAWBREAKERS

Improvement has taken place in the treatment of some prisoners in recent years. Up-to-date prisons have industries to teach prisoners useful trades. Some prisons offer a variety of educational programs, counseling help, and "rap sessions." Other efforts may also help the lawbreaker to learn how to live lawfully with others after leaving prison. But much money and effort must be spent before such reforms as these can be adopted in all American prisons.

Another recent change in the treatment of prisoners is the use of the **indeterminate**

sentence. When people are sentenced to prison, the exact number of years they must serve is not stated. They are given a minimum (least) number of years as well as the maximum (greatest) number of years that they may have to serve. They may be sentenced, for example, to serve a prison term of "from 6 to 10 years." If they behave well in prison, they will be released after the minimum number of years.

After serving only a part of their terms, prisoners may be eligible for **parole,** or release, on condition that they obey certain rules and keep out of trouble. A **parole board** studies each application for parole. Members of the board are provided with information about the prisoner by the prison psychologist, the doctor, guards, and other prison personnel. The parole board reviews the record, along with the prisoner's plans for a return to life outside of prison. On the basis of this information, parole may be granted.

When prisoners are paroled, they are released from prison and placed in the custody of **parole officers.** Their parole usually lasts until the end of the maximum part of their sentences. Until then, they report regularly to the parole officers.

The modern system of indeterminate sentences and parole is not a perfect system. But it does work reasonably well. Perhaps in the future, better ways will be found to help lawbreakers to change their behavior and to become useful citizens.

CONSIDER AND DISCUSS

Identify. police commissioner / foot patrol / capital punishment / indeterminate sentence / parole / parole board / parole officer

Review. 1. What are some of the functions of a police department? 2. What are four characteristics of the well-organized police department? 3. Name some ways in which police try to prevent crime. 4. How does a system of parole work?

Discuss. Do you believe that prisoners should be punished harshly or that they should be treated, as far as possible, like other Americans? Why?

3 Dissent, Civil Disobedience, and Violence

If American citizens believe that a law is wrong—that it requires them to do something they believe is not right—is there anything they can do about it?

EXPRESSING DISSENT

Under the American form of government, there are many things citizens can do. They can express their **dissent**—their disagreement with the law—in letters, phone calls, telegrams, or visits to their elected lawmakers. They can write books, articles, and letters to the editors of newspapers and magazines. They can make speeches.

Dissenters can also organize groups of people to bring pressures of several kinds upon lawmakers to change the law. A common method of pressure has been to organize a **demonstration.** The dissenters gather together and march in public carrying signs, singing songs, and making speeches. Demonstrations that are important and newsworthy are covered by television and shown to millions of people. If lawmakers do not respond to such pressures, Americans can work within political parties to elect new lawmakers who promise to change the law.

The right of the American people to express their dissent against laws in these and many other ways is protected in our state and national constitutions, provided only that the people do not break the laws while expressing their dissent.

CIVIL DISOBEDIENCE

Suppose that citizens have used some or all of these forms of dissent, but without result. Is there anything more they can do to change a law that they think is wrong?

There is a long and honored tradition in American society that citizens may commit acts of **civil disobedience.** They may disobey the law they object to, permit themselves to be arrested, stand trial, and perhaps be sent to prison. Their willingness to lose their freedom and to endure hardship, they hope, will make other people think harder about the opposed law. Perhaps others may join them in getting the law changed.

There are several famous acts of civil disobedience in American history. In colonial times, John Peter Zenger, a printer, broke British law by publishing articles that criticized the Royal Governor of New York. Zenger was arrested and tried. But the jury set him free. His case caused many Americans to think deeply about the importance of freedom of the press. They later insisted that this freedom be protected by the First Amendment to the Constitution. Just before the American Revolution, there were many other courageous acts of civil disobedience to unjust laws.

In the 1960's, Americans used nonviolent protest, such as marches, to gain equal rights for all.

Americans' understanding of civil disobedience was deepened after 1849. In that year Henry David Thoreau of Massachusetts published an essay called "Civil Disobedience." Years earlier, he had been jailed briefly when he refused to pay a tax that would be used to help finance the Mexican War. Thoreau believed that this war was immoral and might extend slavery. In his essay, he explained his belief that citizens should disobey laws that are contrary to their deepest beliefs.

CIVIL DISOBEDIENCE AND CIVIL RIGHTS

These early lessons about dissent and civil disobedience were in the minds of many Americans in the 1950's. At that time black Americans and white Americans joined in a struggle to gain black Americans their full civil rights. By civil rights we mean the rights guaranteed by the Constitution.

For centuries, black Americans had been treated as second-class citizens. Under slavery, they were property to be bought and sold with little thought for their rights as human beings. Black Americans were freed from slavery after the Civil War by the Thirteenth Amendment. They were made citizens of the United States by the Fourteenth Amendment. This amendment also forbade states to pass laws denying equal protection and privileges to any citizen. The Fifteen Amendment gave black Americans the right to vote.

Under the protection of these amendments, black Americans made some progress. But many white Americans viewed free black Americans with suspicion and fear. As a result, in the 1890's, laws were passed in some states to prevent black Americans from voting. Over the years the "separate but equal" principle arose. There were separate schools for blacks, separate drinking fountains, separate railroad cars, separate parks, and other separate facilities. Black Americans could not buy homes in certain sections of a community. They could not register at white hotels, nor eat in many restaurants. **Segregation,** or separation of black and white citizens, existed in the South as well as the North.

In 1955 a single act of civil disobedience spurred the movement that was to put an end to segregation. Rosa Parks, a black woman of Montgomery, Alabama, was arrested when she refused to give up her seat on a bus to a white person. Her act led the black people of Montgomery to organize a boycott of the bus company. It was led by a young, dynamic black preacher, Martin Luther King, Jr. After many months, the boycott succeeded. Montgomery changed its laws governing the seating of black people in buses.

In the years that followed, Martin Luther King, Jr., became a famous leader of the civil rights movement. He was put in jail many times for acts of civil disobedience. These acts, along with his eloquent writing and speeches, made many people, white as well as black, think about their attitudes toward civil rights for all Americans.

These Chicanos are demonstrating to gain greater rights and opportunities.

PROGRESS IN CIVIL RIGHTS

The goal of equal rights for all Americans has not yet been realized. But progress has been made. In 1954, the Supreme Court declared the "separate but equal" principle to be illegal. In the case of *Brown v. The Board of Education of Topeka*, the court ruled that segregation in public schools was a denial of rights to black citizens.

In addition, Congress passed several civil rights laws. These laws established six principles to guarantee the rights of black Americans and other minority groups. (1) The right to vote cannot be denied because of race or color. (2) Discrimination in public schools must end. (3) The right to work or to belong to a union shall not be denied because of race or color. (4) Any business open to the public, such as restaurants and theaters, shall be open equally to all people. (5) Public places of amusement such as parks and swimming pools shall be open to all people. (6) Discrimination in the rental or sale of houses is forbidden.

The voting rights of minorities were further strengthened by voting rights acts and by the Twenty-fourth Amendment to the Constitution. This amendment, passed in 1964, prohibits the use of poll taxes or other taxes as a requirement for voting in federal elections.

DEMANDS BY OTHER GROUPS

Encouraged by the progress made by black Americans, other minority groups began to seek equal rights and opportunities. Native Americans, Mexican Americans, Puerto Ricans, women, and others demanded an end to discrimination.

No group has faced more problems than the Native Americans. Many continue to live on government-run reservations. There they often suffer unemployment and live in poverty. Unlike other citizens, these Native Americans often do not have control over education, local government, and economic development. Moreover, they have had to struggle with federal controls and policies that keep changing. Partly for these reasons, some Native Americans have favored direct action to gain their rights. Other Native Americans have turned to legal means.

There are about 6 million Mexican Americans in the United States. Many of them are migrant workers who travel from farm to farm gathering crops. They are an important part of the nation's farm labor supply. Their work is hard, and the wages usually are low. Many other Mexican Americans work in cities. But they, too, often have low-paying jobs. A large number live in poor housing in **barrios**—the Spanish-speaking sections of large cities such as Los Angeles. To improve their lives, the Chicanos, as many Mexican Americans now proudly call themselves, formed labor unions. Cesar Chavez organized the farm workers. He asked all Americans to aid his efforts by boycotting, or refusing to buy, grapes and lettuce. The actions of Chavez and others helped many Mexican Americans. They began to obtain better working conditions and better wages. The Mexican Americans also demanded, and got, bilingual schools—schools in which subjects are taught in both Spanish and English.

The living conditions of Puerto Ricans also began to improve as their leaders learned how to make their power felt in large cities. Puerto Ricans demanded better job opportunities, better housing, and bilingual schools. Not all of their problems have been solved. But many Puerto Ricans now have jobs in all parts of our economy. You have read about the problems and gains of other groups earlier in the book. Some of the problems of Asian Americans are discussed in Chapter 1. The women's rights movement is treated in Chapter 18. All of these groups have tried to win their goals mainly through legal means and nonviolent action.

OUTBREAKS OF VIOLENCE

Over the years, most American law officials had learned how to deal peaceably with traditional forms of dissent and civil disobedience. In the 1960's, however, they faced a different problem when **riots** and other forms of violence broke out. Most of the riots took place in rundown sections of large urban areas. Few large cities were spared. It was reported that 239 riots occurred between 1963 and 1968.

These urban riots were not in the tradition of civil disobedience that you have been reading about. They were not in protest to specific laws and policies. Also, the rioters hoped to avoid arrest and punishment. The cause of the riots lay deep in the poverty, unemployment, and other evils in the slums. At one meeting of the National Council of Police Societies, it was pointed out that one of the most common causes of riots was that thousands of young people had nothing to do. Often teenagers who cannot get jobs become hostile. They tend to take out their anger by acts of violence.

The riots generally followed a pattern. A police officer making an arrest drew a crowd of bystanders. The crowd became unruly. Sometimes fires were started in stores where slum dwellers felt they had been cheated. Some stores were broken into and goods were stolen. Such stealing during a riot is called **looting.** Firefighters arriving to put out fires were often stoned or shot at. When the riots got out of control the National Guard was called in, and **martial law** was declared. Martial law is rule by the military powers and a suspension of civil liberties. A **curfew,** which ordered people off the streets after a certain hour, was often put into effect. Finally, order was restored.

ANTIWAR DEMONSTRATIONS

Not all of the riots and violence of the 1960's occurred in the slums. Some students in the nation's colleges became active in their resistance to the military draft, to the Vietnam War, and to college policies. Some protests were peaceful. But sometimes, buildings were burned or taken over, traffic was blocked, and college records were destroyed. In a number of instances, the National Guard was called out. The whole nation was shocked when, in 1970, students at Kent State University in Ohio and at Jackson State University in Mississippi were fired on by the National Guard. Several students were killed.

THE CHALLENGE THAT LIES AHEAD

In the 1970's, urban riots and campus disorders ended, for the most part. No one could be sure of all the reasons. Many people in the slums probably came to realize that they suffered most from the riots. New protections for the civil rights of minorities perhaps also helped. The Vietnam War ended. It was possible, too, that Americans had learned that violence in dissent does not attract followers to a cause. It repels them. Acts of civil disobedience need not involve crimes against persons or property.

To prevent violence and unrest all of us must work to eliminate poverty and discontent. Above all, it is our duty—as responsible citizens—to uphold the laws that guarantee equal rights for all Americans.

CONSIDER AND DISCUSS

Identify. dissent / demonstration / civil disobedience / segregation / barrios / riots / looting / martial law / curfew

Review. 1. What are some forms of lawful dissent in the United States? 2. What is meant by the principle of "separate but equal"? 3. Why was the decision in the Supreme Court of *Brown v. The Board of Education of Topeka* so important? 4. Name six principles of civil rights established by Congress.

Discuss. Were the acts of civil disobedience of John Zenger, Henry Thoreau, and Rosa Parks justified? Why or why not?

4 The Drug Problem

Widespread use of drugs has become a serious problem for people concerned with health, safety, and crime in American communities. We live in a fast-paced society where drugs are a part of everyday life for many people. There are drugs to help them sleep, drugs to keep them awake, drugs to curb the appetite, drugs to ease pain, and drugs to kill germs. The medicine chest in the average American home usually contains many different kinds of drugs. Some are harmless and others are poisonous.

People use drugs for three principal reasons. First, drugs are prescribed by physicians in the treatment of disease. When taken as directed, they are helpful to people. Second, drugs are used in self-medication. Depending upon the way they are used, they may be helpful or harmful. The third reason for using drugs is for excitement, a new thrill, to be sociable, to forget, or for "kicks." This third use of drugs is called **drug abuse.**

DRUG ABUSE

The improper use of drugs results in certain bodily changes. Some drugs cause a "high," or feeling of elation. Others result in depression or extreme drowsiness, and may lead eventually to sleep or unconsciousness. Some strong drugs, as you will read later in more detail, cause **hallucinations** in which the individual sees, hears, smells, or feels things that are not actually present. Under the influence of hallucinogenic drugs, people have stepped out of the windows of high buildings in the belief that they could fly.

Most of the drugs used by drug abusers are habit-forming. Continued use causes the users to become **addicts,** or slaves to the habit. Addicts are "hooked." They must have the drug or they suffer headaches and pains in the stomach, muscles, and bones. Addicts also require stronger and stronger doses of most drugs in order to get the effect they desire. The quality of drugs sold illegally by "pushers" is not regulated. Therefore, individuals may take too strong a dose, or overdose (OD), and "freak out." That is, they may lose their minds and have to be hospitalized. An overdose may also lead to death. In New York City, in a recent year, a powerful drug, heroin, was a leading cause of death among people between the ages of 19 and 35.

Much of the increase of crime in the United States is related to the illegal sale, possession, and purchase of drugs. Selling drugs without a license is against the law. In 1970, Congress passed a law making the illegal sale of drugs punishable by as much as a life sentence. The purchase or possession of certain drugs without a doctor's prescription is also a crime. In most states, possession of illegal drugs is a crime punishable by imprisonment of from five to ten years. People convicted of this crime lose some of their rights. They may be denied a passport, be barred from certain civil service jobs, and lose the right to vote. They also get a police record. This can mean, for example, that they may have difficulty in obtaining a driver's license.

A great many crimes are committed by drug addicts. Needing from $25 to $100 or more a day to buy illegal drugs, the addict often turns to crime. A large proportion of the crimes of mugging, purse-snatching, shoplifting, and burglary are committed by habitual drug users in search of money.

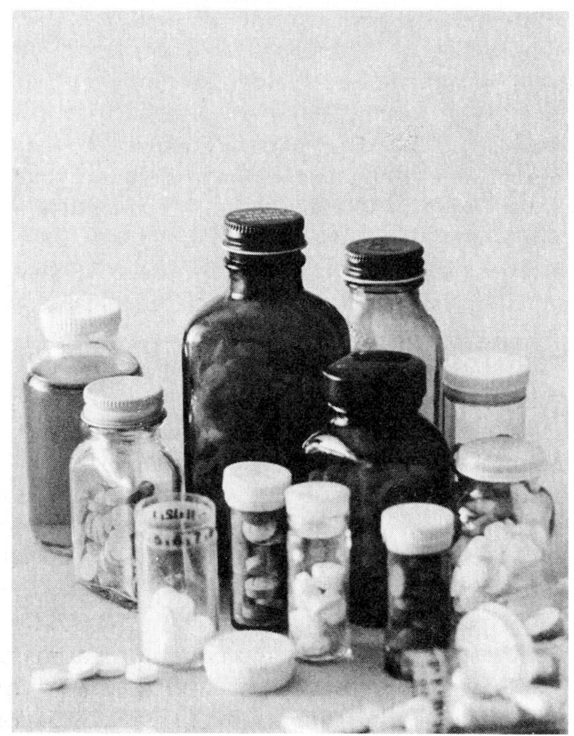

Drug abuse is a major problem today. Many of the drugs now being used are habit-forming.

WHY DRUG ABUSE?

According to the Drug Enforcement Administration in the United States Department of Justice, the number of drug addicts in the United States rose from 6,047 in 1966 to over 90,000 in the mid-1970's. It was also estimated that some 2 million Americans were experimenting with dangerous drugs. What were some reasons behind these startling statistics?

Scientific studies of drug use and abuse indicate that the first use of drugs is often social. At a party, someone brings pills or marijuana. Out of curiosity, and because it seems the thing to do, a person may try such a drug. For many, that is the end of it. But there is sometimes pressure to try something stronger. Some young people feel they will not be a part of the "crowd" if they refuse to try stronger drugs. Fearing they will be laughed at or not accepted by their friends, some young people try hard drugs. This has been the way many addicts started out.

Some people turn to drugs as an escape from life's problems. Psychologists tell us that such people cannot, or will not, face reality. They take drugs in order to dream —to intoxicate themselves so that they will not think about daily responsibilities. Instead of thinking about homework, jobs, and home obligations, such people worry about where their next "fix," or injection of dope, is coming from.

The abuse of drugs has also been encouraged by some people who claim that drugs will open up a beautiful new world of color and sounds. The mind, they say, will be expanded so that ideas and objects will be revealed in new and meaningful ways. To examine the actual effects of drugs upon the human nervous system, here are some facts that are known about them.

FACTS ABOUT DRUGS

The effects of a drug upon the human body depend on the nature of the drug. This can depend upon the amount taken, the way it is taken, and the physical condition of the person taking it. The fumes or powder of the drug are sometimes sniffed up the nose. Pills are swallowed. Drugs in liquid form, or dissolved in water, are injected under the skin ("skin popping"), or directly into the veins ("mainlining"). Marijuana and some other drugs are smoked or chewed. An objective analysis of leading drugs used by abusers shows the following effects.

Narcotics are used in medicine for the relief of pain. Among the most common are morphine, codeine, heroin, and methadone. Among illegal users, heroin (sometimes called horse, junk, or smack) is the most common of the narcotics. Heroin, a derivative of opium made from the poppy plant, gives the user a warm, sleepy feeling in which nothing matters. Side effects are loss of appetite, constipation, and a yearning for more. Heroin is habit-forming. Larger and larger doses are needed to give the user the desired effect. Stopping the habit is extremely painful. Hepatitis, a blood disease, is common among users who get careless about the cleanliness of the needles used for their injections.

Hallucinogens are the drugs that cause users to see, hear, and feel things that are not there. Among the drugs causing hallucinations are mescaline, LSD, and peyote. Perhaps the most common is LSD (d-lysergic acid), also called acid, trips, and Big D. This drug, made from chemicals found in fungus, often causes objects to take on unnatural colors, walls to move, and pictures to form in space. The hoped-for effect is a feeling of well-being in which laughter comes easily. But on a "bad trip" or "bummer," the images become threatening. Users thrash about in a highly nervous state and may injure themselves or others. LSD, although not habit-forming in a physical sense, may create a mental desire to repeat the trip again and again—always at the risk of a "bummer." There is evidence, also, that the use of LSD upsets the chromosomes of the body —the cells that determine hereditary traits.

Depressants include sleeping pills and other sedatives and tranquilizers that calm the nerves and help people sleep. When taken improperly, barbiturates—sleeping pills and tranquilizers—create a drunken condition in which the user staggers, stammers, and often becomes quarrelsome. Sometimes called Barbs, downers, reds, or feenies, these drugs are habit-forming. Withdrawal symptoms may be severe. More deaths are caused by overdoses of sleeping pills each year than by any other drug.

Stimulants are drugs that are used in medicine to relieve mild depressions or to control the appetite. They are sometimes used, with considerable danger, by truck drivers on long hauls, by students studying for examinations, and by athletes before a game, although it is illegal. The danger even in occasional use is that the mind and body do not get the rest they need.

Abusers say that stimulants, sometimes called bennies, speed, lid-poppers, and pep pills, give them a feeling of well-being and make them alert and active. But stimulants are habit-forming. Steady users become so dependent on the drugs that they care about nothing else. Large doses make users confused and anxious, and can also affect their vision. Prolonged use of stimulants can lead to actual brain damage.

Marijuana, made from the tops of the female Indian hemp plant, is an intoxicant. Its long-range effects are not yet clearly understood. Called pot, grass, weed, and Mary Jane, its effects, like those of most intoxicants, depends upon the user. It may bring on a dreamy, drowsy mood, loud laughter, or an anxious state of mind. It may also impair the judgment and make the user unsafe to be around, especially when driving.

THE PROBLEM OF ALCOHOL

Alcohol has effects similar to those of sedatives. Under its influence, the user may become talkative, loud, staggering, sick to the stomach, or merely sleepy. All states have laws prohibiting the sale of alcoholic beverages to persons under either 18 or 21 years of age. These laws are intended to protect young people from the unwise use of alcohol.

In the United States, many people take an occasional drink with friends or to relax after a day's work. But one in every 15 people who use alcohol becomes a problem drinker. Alcohol may be habit-forming. Also, excessive use results in physical damage. There are nearly 6 million Americans who are problem drinkers. These problem drinkers are called **alcoholics.** They suffer from a disease called **alcoholism.**

THE PROBLEM OF SMOKING

Since the early 1950's, scientists have studied the lives and health of people who smoke, especially those who smoke cigarettes. They have reported that smokers run great risks of lung cancer, respiratory ailments, and heart disease. So powerful was their evidence that Congress, in 1970, passed a law banning cigarette advertisements from television. A federal law also provides that every pack of cigarettes and every cigarette advertisement, shall carry a printed message. It says: "Warning: The Surgeon General Has Determined That Cigarette Smoking Is Dangerous to Your Health." As Americans have become more aware of its dangers, smoking increasingly has been banned or limited in theaters, planes, and other public places.

Whether you smoke or not will depend upon two things: (1) what you expect smoking to do for you, and (2) how you judge the arguments for and against smoking. Smoking is habit-forming. Once a person starts, it is difficult to stop.

THE CHOICE

Making decisions about whether or not to smoke, drink, or use drugs are more complicated for some persons than for others. In the case of smoking, or using alcohol, adult individuals must decide for themselves what their attitude will be. These are strictly personal problems, for the use of alcohol and tobacco is legal in most states.

In the case of drug abuse, the problem is also personal. But it is complicated by the fact that the user is breaking the law. The person who chooses the drug route may wind up in jail, in ill health, or dead. It may be difficult at times to say "no" to drugs. The choice may lie between being a part of the group and doing what one knows to be right. Decisions you make now may well become part of your future life style.

CONSIDER AND DISCUSS

Identify. drug abuse / hallucination / addict / narcotics / hallucinogens / depressants / stimulants / marijuana / alcoholic / alcoholism

Review. 1. What are the reasons some people abuse drugs? 2. What is the relation between drug abuse and crime? 3. What are the effects of the use of narcotics? hallucinogens? depressants? stimulants? marijuana? alcohol? tobacco?
Discuss. What are the arguments for and against the legalization of marijuana?

5 Health and Safety

In spite of its wealth and its extensive educational and medical systems, the United States is not as healthy a nation as it should be. There are many reasons why. Doctors tell us that we eat too much, drink too much, smoke to excess, exercise too little, and live at too fast a pace. Basically, better health depends upon exercise, good judgment, eating the right food, and the proper amount of rest. No one can manage these things for us. Individuals must assume responsibility for their own good health habits.

Yet the health of the individual is of concern to all of us. When workers become ill, production slows down. The drug addict who turns to crime endangers the peace of the community. The ill and elderly poor become responsibilities to their families and to local health resources. Persons with communicable diseases endanger those around them. For these and other reasons, the nation's health concerns all of us.

THE COMMUNITY GUARDS OUR HEALTH

Nearly every American city and town has a local **health department** to enforce rules of sanitation and cleanliness. It also offers aid in the prevention and cure of disease. This department keeps records of cases of disease and acts to stop disease from spreading. It may **quarantine,** or keep at home, any person who has an infectious disease.

The health departments in most cities have laboratories that test water, milk, and foods to make sure they are pure. They inspect all restaurants, diners, and other places that serve food to the public. They also inspect nursing homes, barber shops, and other places of business.

Most communities have local hospitals that are supported in part by local funds. A well-equipped hospital is an asset to community health, for it serves the sick and helps save lives. Some communities also have public clinics where medical care and prenatal care are offered free or at a small cost. Drug clinics offer help to addicts who want to stop taking drugs.

CARE OF THE MENTALLY ILL

Mental illness is one of the most serious health problems facing the American people. **Mental illness** is a sickness of the mind, and it is on the increase in America today. Mental illness can be due to severe emotional stress. Or it may result from the use of drugs and alcohol. Each year, over a half million new persons enter hospitals for the treatment of mental ailments. Many more receive private care.

All states, and many localities, have special hospitals to care for the mentally ill. There are also private hospitals that treat mental illness. The cost of treating patients in mental hospitals is high. The nation spends about $4 billion a year in this way. Even so, mental hospitals, especially public ones, are overcrowded and understaffed.

THE FEDERAL GOVERNMENT AND HEALTH

The federal government sponsors a variety of programs to aid the health of all citizens. The Department of Health, Education, and

Welfare (HEW) has charge of most of these health programs. This department gathers information about health problems and advises state and local governments. It also distributes federal funds to local programs.

One important agency of HEW is the **Public Health Service** of the United States. It carries on medical research, provides medical and hospital service in certain cases, and works with foreign governments to prevent the spread of disease. It maintains the largest medical library in the world. Three important agencies are under this Service. They are the Food and Drug Administration (FDA), the Health Services and Mental Health Administration (HSM), and the National Institutes of Health (NIH).

Federal efforts in the field of mental health are carried on by the **National Institute of Mental Health,** which is part of HSM. The job of the **Food and Drug Administration** is to see that all food and drugs offered for sale to the American people are pure and safe. It enforces the Food, Drug, and Cosmetic Act. This act requires that all new drugs must be tested and found safe before they can be offered for sale. It also requires that all food and drug containers must have labels listing their contents. The Meat Inspection Act also gives the federal government the right to inspect meat and poultry shipped from one state to another.

PAYING THE COSTS OF GOOD HEALTH

Health services are very costly and are going up every year. Average costs have more than tripled since 1965. Billions of dollars are spent each year for medical services—for medicines, hospital care, doctors' services, nursing, physical therapy, and other needs. State, local, and national governments contribute to some of these costs. Money is also raised through volunteer programs such as the Community Chest or United Fund, the Red Cross, the American Lung Association, and similar groups. Money is also contributed by foundations and by wealthy persons (philanthropists) who support hospitals and medical research. Most medical costs, however, are paid by individual patients. They either pay out of their own pockets or send their bills to a health insurance program.

PROMOTING SAFETY

Each year, more than 70 million Americans are hurt in accidents. Eleven million of these people must remain in bed for at least a day. About 100,000 die, and 400,000 are permanently disabled. A large percentage of the accidents that cause death or permanent disability take place at work. The rest occur on highways, in schools, on playgrounds, and in other public places.

During the 1970's, over 31 million accidents a year took place in American homes. Falls were the main cause of serious injuries in the home. Other causes of injury were fires, faulty household equipment, or the careless handling of equipment.

Nearly one third of all school accidents take place in school gymnasiums. They usually result from careless horseplay, not organized sports and games. Get to know your school safety rules, and follow them.

All Americans need to learn safety at play. Each year, thousands of Americans are killed and injured while they are "having fun." Good weather, especially over weekends, brings serious sunburn, broken arms and legs, cuts, and other injuries. Each year, over 6,000 persons in our country are drowned. Think of the tragedies that might be avoided if commonsense rules of water safety were observed.

SAFETY ON THE HIGHWAY

Most of the nation's serious accidents occur on streets and highways. Each year 47,000 people are killed and nearly 5 million are

Continued on page 473

HEALTH CARE: A Right or A Luxury?

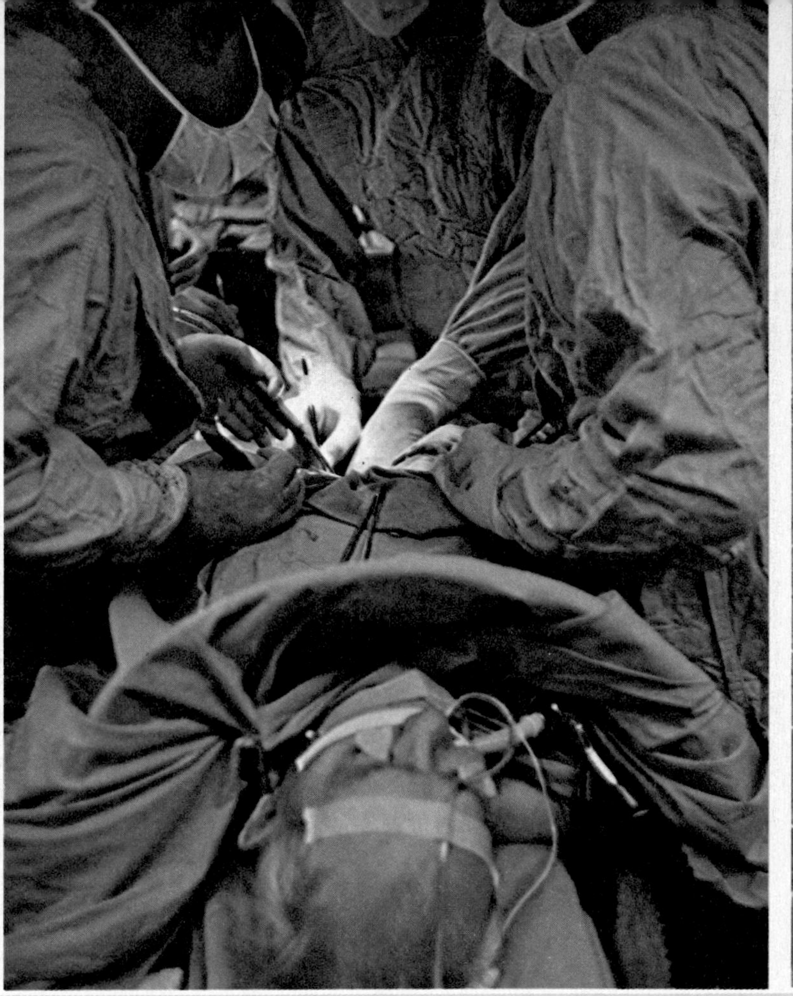

WHAT DO YOU THINK?

What would happen if you, or a member of your family, became seriously ill? Suppose you had to see several doctors, undergo many tests, and then have an operation. Suppose you had to spend a few weeks in the hospital. How much would all of this cost? Who would pay the bills?

An illness like this could cost many thousands of dollars. If your family has some kind of health insurance, at least part of the cost will be covered. But what about the rest? And what if, like millions of Americans, you have no health insurance at all?

The cost of medical care is very high, and rising fast. In the mid-1970's, Americans spent over $110 billion a year on their health—$500 for every man, woman, and child. This was almost three times what we spent in 1965, and four times the total for 1960. While the general cost of living has increased, the cost of medical care has gone up even faster.

How good a health care system are we getting for our money? One good measure of a nation's overall health is infant mortality—the number of babies who die in their first year. During the past 20 years,

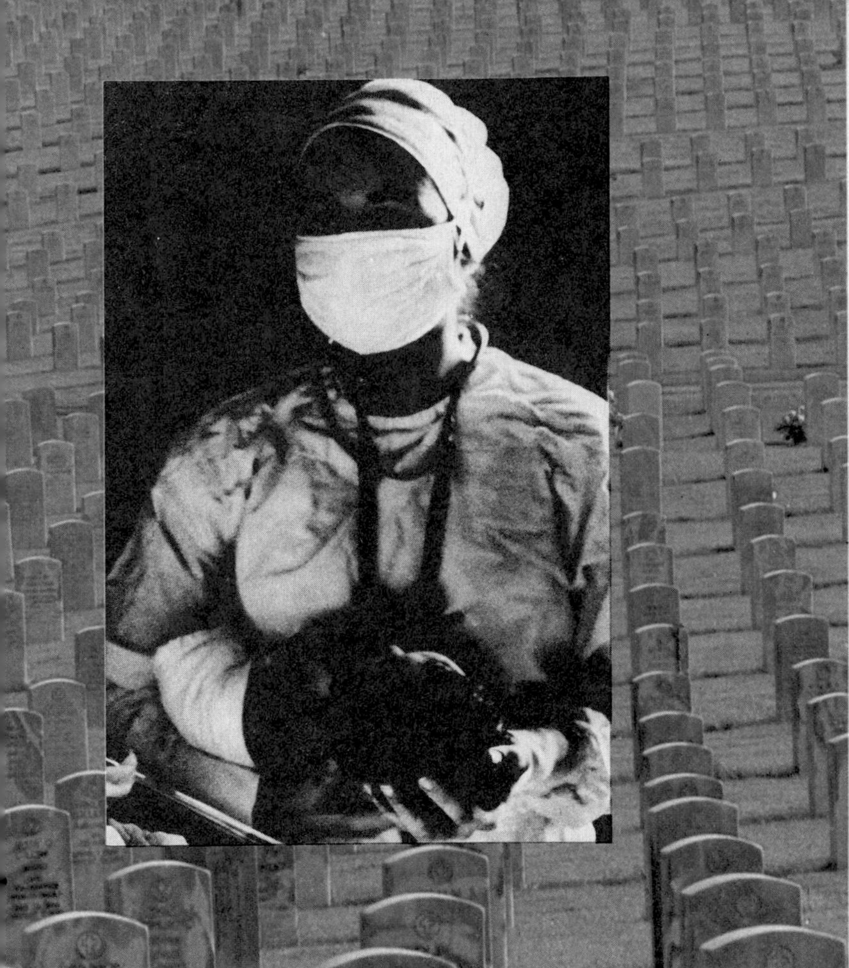

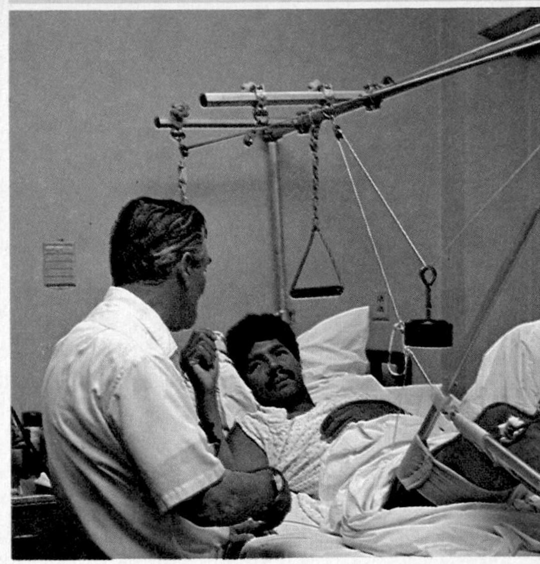

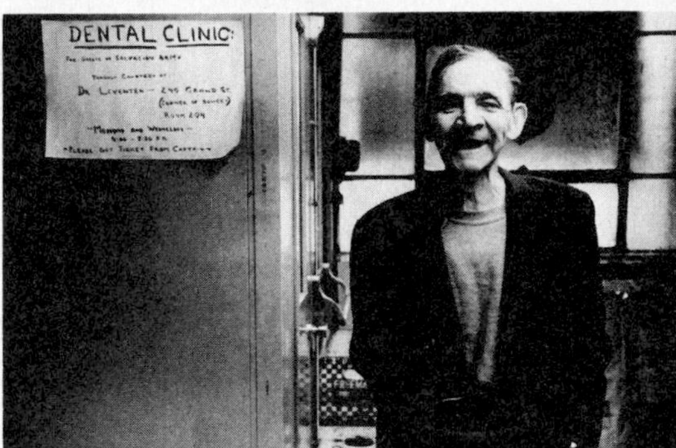

infant mortality, or deaths, in the United States dropped greatly as a result of scientific advances and better health care. But in the 1970's several countries had lower infant mortality rates than the United States. For the most part, however, there was only a slight difference between the rates of other countries and the United States. Figures show that we may not be the healthiest country in the world. But we are certainly one of the healthiest. What can we do to improve our health care even more?

Some people believe that our health care problems can be solved through insurance. Our system of health care, they believe, is basically a good one. The main problem is that not everybody can afford to take advantage of it. The answer, they believe, is some form of national health insurance.

A number of different plans have been suggested. One plan would use private insurance companies, with the government helping to pay some of the premiums. This plan would cover most employed people, for big medical bills. Another plan would provide total health

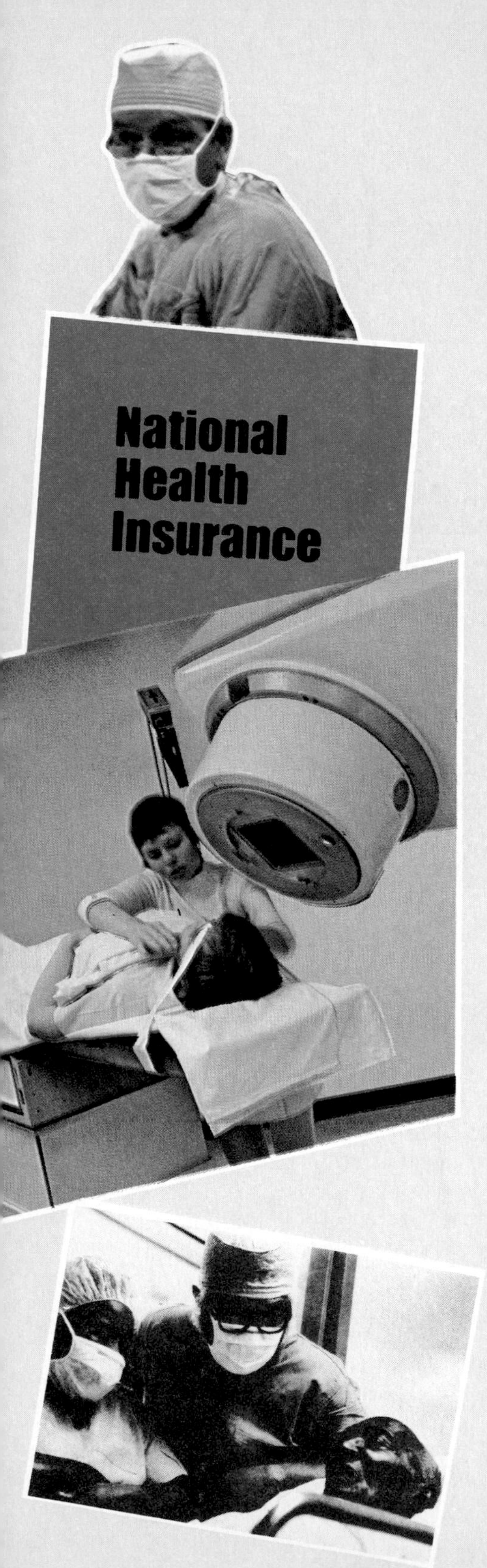

care for everybody. The government itself would provide health insurance. It would collect premiums and taxes to pay for it.

Does some kind of national health insurance seem like a good idea, or not? How might it help to improve our nation's health? What problems might be involved? Would you favor a full Health Security plan, or a more limited insurance plan? Why?

Some people think that our system of health care needs more reform. Medicare, for example, has been a big help for older Americans. But it has not done anything to lower costs, or to improve our health care facilities. In fact, costs have risen, partly because doctors and hospitals know the government will pay their bills.

How can health care be organized more efficiently? One plan that sometimes works well at the local level is the "prepaid group practice." These plans are set up by groups of doctors. A group sets up its own medical center, and agrees to share the costs and the income. Families join the plan by paying a yearly fee, like an insurance payment. In return they receive any and all health care they need. Instead of collecting individual fees, each doctor is paid a salary out of the group's prepaid fees. These fees also pay for their offices, equipment, and staff.

What are the advantages of a prepaid group practice? As a group, the doctors have lower costs than if they worked separately. They can afford facilities that would be impossible for an individual doctor. Members of the group benefit from the lower costs for facilities and care. However, in some cases, the groups have gone bankrupt because of increasing costs. Also, some groups have had to raise their fees, which has made their plans more costly.

Some systems of national health care use some of the ideas of prepaid group practice. In countries that have national systems like this, all citizens contribute to the cost of medical care through taxes. This money is used to support medical facilities and to pay doctors. Doctors receive a salary or a fixed fee for their services. All citizens have a right to whatever medical care they need.

Many Americans strongly oppose this kind of national health care system. They believe it would limit the freedom of doctors, and also of patients. These Americans admit that more people use health care in the countries that have these plans. But they point out that specialized medical care and research facilities often are not as advanced in these countries as in the United States. Some other Americans believe that doctors who oppose a national system are mainly interested in keeping their high fees.

What do you think? Try to find out about the health care systems of some other countries. What are the advantages of their systems? What are some of the problems? Do you think this kind of system would be good for the United States? Why or why not?

injured in accidents involving automobiles, bicycles, and public transportation such as buses. Most of these accidents could be prevented if drivers used more care.

With nearly 130 million drivers on America's roads, you may wonder that there are not even more accidents. The accident rate would be higher if it were not for safety belts, improved highways, police patrols, a lower speed limit, and the fact that most Americans are good drivers.

But traffic accidents can be reduced. One way is to require that all beginning drivers take driver-training courses before they are allowed to drive, as many states do. Another way is for all drivers to observe speed laws. The principal cause of accidents is speed. For this reason many states have introduced a **point system.** Any driver caught speeding is fined a certain number of points. After several speeding offenses, when a driver's points reach a certain total, his or her license is taken away. The point system works well because most traffic accidents are caused by about one third of the drivers. This group of drivers keep breaking traffic laws and causing accidents. They are a danger to the lives of those who drive with care.

AMERICA'S FIGHT AGAINST FIRE

Every year there are over 3,000 fires in the United States. This year, unless something happens to prevent it, about 6,000 people will die in these fires. The property loss will be over $5 billion.

What causes all these fires? The answer, in most instances, is carelessness. In the late 1970's, about 12 percent of building fires could be traced to the careless use of matches and to careless smoking. More than 11 percent of all fires were caused by faulty electrical equipment and bad wiring in homes and other buildings. Many fires were the result of faulty heating equipment and chimneys, sparks from fires, improper use of cleaning fluids, and faulty stoves.

THE WORK OF THE FIRE DEPARTMENTS

When a fire breaks out, prompt and dependable help must be available. We do not leave firefighting to chance or to the individual citizen. When faced with the danger of fire, the whole community must work together.

Local fire departments are organized in much the same way as police departments. In most cities, firefighters are selected and trained with great care. They must pass civil service examinations and be in good physical condition. Firefighters attend fire school for several months and then serve as "rookie members" of a fire company. They are trained to operate fire extinguishers, high pressure pumps, water towers, searchlights, and rescue equipment.

Firehouses are located in various parts of the city so that firefighters can quickly reach any area in which a fire may break out. In each firehouse, a crew of firefighters is on duty at all times. When anyone in the community pulls a fire alarm, the signal from the alarm box sends out a code that goes to the central office. The dispatcher at the central office reads the code and rings the fire alarm of the nearest firehouse. The central office also responds to fires reported by telephone or by police radio.

VOLUNTEER FIREFIGHTERS

In many small towns and suburbs of our nation there are too few fires to justify hiring paid firefighters. Therefore these areas rely on volunteers to work in their fire departments. In some communities there are a few paid firefighters and many volunteers.

Volunteer firefighters serve, not because they are paid to do the job, but because they have a sense of responsibility to their own families and to their neighbors. Volunteer firefighters take their work seriously and spend much time in training to fight fires. They develop pride in their records of service to the community.

Every year, fires kill thousands of people and destroy millions of dollars worth of property. Most of these fires are caused by carelessness.

THE COMMUNITY AND FIRE PREVENTION

The best way to fight fire, of course, is to prevent it. Communities do several things to reduce the danger of fire. Nearly all cities and towns hire inspectors to enforce local fire laws and to inspect buildings in search of fire hazards. These inspectors do not ordinarily go into private homes. Avoiding fire hazards in the home is the responsibility of each family.

Everyone should practice fire prevention. It saves lives and property. In a town with few fires, fire insurance costs less. If fires can be prevented, the cost of firefighting is reduced. As a result, more of the community's tax funds may be spent on other projects.

To remind citizens that fire safety pays, many communities have special fire-prevention campaigns. The President of the United States, has set aside a week in October as **Fire Prevention Week.** Schools, industries, churches, service organizations, and local government officials all emphasize the importance of preventing fires. The success of such campaigns, of course, depends on all citizens doing their part to prevent fires.

CONSIDER AND DISCUSS

Identify. health department / quarantine / mental illness / Public Health Service / National Institute of Mental Health / Food and Drug Administration / point system / volunteer firefighters / Fire Prevention Week

Review. 1. Why aren't Americans as healthy as they should be? 2. What are some things that local communities do to guard our health? 3. In what ways does the federal government help to guard the health of the American people? 4. Where do many of the accidents in the United States occur and why? 5. What are some of the causes of fire? 6. How can a community help to prevent fires?

Discuss. Do you favor a volunteer fire department or a paid fire department in your community? Why?

CHAPTER
Summary

It is natural that Americans want to protect themselves and others against crime. Such protection is one of the services that governments provide for their citizens. But crime has become a serious problem in America. In many large cities it is unsafe to walk the streets at night. The causes of crime are often rooted deep in the economic and social ills of the society. An attack on crime must also include a program of improving life for all Americans.

Juvenile delinquency is also a pressing problem, for it is often the beginning of a life of crime. Special courts deal with the problems of juvenile Americans, and special agencies of reform have been established. In order to enjoy decent, happy lives, young people need to learn the causes of crime and how to avoid them. They need especially to learn about drug abuse, which can easily lead to crime, broken health, and death.

The role of police officers in our society has become more urgent and complicated. In a good, modern police force, officers learn not only how to deal with criminals but also how to prevent crime and to "cool" situations that may lead to criminal activity. Many modern police officers want to be friendly, understanding members of the communities in which they work.

As our society has become more crowded and complex, Americans have developed different ways to protest unjust laws and situations. They also have learned the difference between nonviolent protest that can be helpful to society and violent protest that tears society apart. Nonviolent protest can attract followers. Violent protest repels them.

Police officers work closely with other government officials to protect and promote the health and safety of American citizens. There are many things that each person can and must do to safeguard his or her health and safety. Government officials are concerned with problems that threaten the health and safety of large numbers of people or of society as a whole.

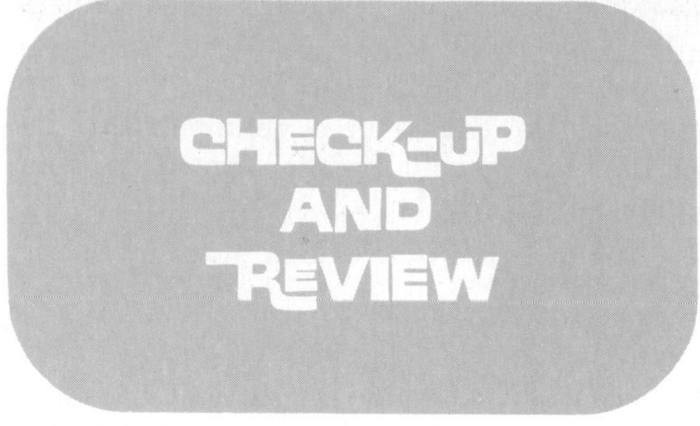

VOCABULARY

Copy the following words or phrases in the vocabulary section of your notebook, followed by definitions of each word or phrase.

crime	juvenile delinquency
parole	indeterminate sentence
dissent	civil disobedience
drug abuse	alcoholism
quarantine	volunteer firefighters

CHECK-UP

Think carefully about each of the following questions, decide on the best answer, and come to class prepared to defend your answer.

1. What is the difference between first- and second-degree murder?
2. What are the principal causes of juvenile delinquency?
3. What kinds of study and training are required for modern police officers?
4. What new policies toward the treatment of prisoners are now being tried in some parts of the United States?
5. What are some legal means that citizens can use to protest against unjust laws?
6. How does nonviolent civil disobedience differ from rioting?
7. How is the illegal sale, purchase, and use of drugs related to crime?
8. In what ways are the use of drugs, tobacco, and alcohol personal questions and in what ways are they public problems?
9. What are some ways in which our federal, state, and local governments try to protect the health of all citizens?
10. How can each citizen help to prevent fires in the home, in the community, and in towns and cities?

CITIZENSHIP AND YOU

There are many things you can do as a class, in groups, or as individuals to probe deeper into the important topics and problems you have read about in this chapter.

1. Class Projects

Each member of the class may bring a recent issue of a local newspaper to class. Using the newspaper as reference, the class may list on the chalkboard the kinds of crime that have been taking place in your local area. Discuss ways in which local officials and citizens might do more to prevent these crimes.

Participate in an open-forum discussion in which class members discuss causes of juvenile delinquency and what might be done to remove these causes.

Invite a public health official to give a talk on drugs in American society. In a class discussion following the talk, list on the chalkboard the main points made about the uses and abuses of drugs.

The entire class may visit a local police or fire station. During the trip, make notes about the training and work of police or fire forces. When you return to the classroom, discuss what you have learned and consider how each person may cooperate to help make these local services more effective.

2. Group or Committee Projects

A small committee might visit a local courtroom to observe an actual trial. Note the ways in which the rights of the accused person are protected. Report your observations to the class.

One committee might do research on one or more examples of nonviolent civil disobedience in the 1950's or 1960's. Another committee might do research on urban riots in the 1960's. Make reports to the class. Ask the class members to explain how the two kinds of actions differed.

A committee can visit and interview local Medicare officials. Report to the class on the kinds of work they do, the problems they face, and what local citizens might do to help solve these problems.

A committee may visit and interview a local fire official. Report to the class on what is said especially about the problem of false fire alarms.

3. Individual Projects

Prepare a report on one of the following topics: "Juvenile Delinquency in Our Town," "Drug Abuse in Our Town," "How Our Police (or Firefighters) Are Trained," "Health Care for Old People in Our Town."

Write an editorial setting forth your ideas about the way criminals are treated in the United States. Do careful research to support your ideas.

Do research and report to the class on how public health officials have prevented epidemics of severe diseases such as smallpox, tuberculosis, or polio. Include any evidence you find that people tend to become careless about preventing such diseases once the epidemics have ended.

CIVICS SKILLS

DISTINGUISHING FACT FROM OPINION

In order to analyze current issues, you must be able to distinguish between statements of fact and statements of opinion. A fact is something that is true or real and that can be proven. On the other hand, an opinion is someone's judgment or point of view. It is what the person thinks. Other people might agree or disagree with this opinion. But it is not something that can be proven one way or the other at the time. Sometimes, at a later time, we can see how certain opinions turned out to be correct judgments, while others did not.

Often, it is difficult to tell what is fact and what is opinion. You will frequently come across statements that appear to be factual. Yet, if you examine them carefully, you will find out they are really opinions. You should begin to discover ways to prove or disprove statements as factual. For example, you may have to go to an original source to check something you have read. Of course, it is not always possible to verify all statements. The important thing is that you begin to examine statements critically.

When you try to find proof that a statement is factual, several outcomes are possible. The statement is proven as a fact. The statement is proven false. The statement is shown to be a distortion of the truth. Or the evidence cannot be found to test the statement. Sometimes, people who are trying to influence others to follow a certain course of action may distort the truth in order to be persuasive. This is often the case in political campaigns. What the persons say seems to have the ring of truth. But upon closer examination their statements are found to be not entirely true.

PRACTICING YOUR CIVICS SKILLS

The following include statements of fact and statements of opinion. Read each statement carefully and decide whether it presents a fact or an opinion. Be prepared to support your choice.

1. Juvenile delinquents come from homes where one parent is missing.
2. Heroin is a habit-forming drug.
3. During the 1950's and 1960's, Congress established six principles for the rights of minorities.
4. Harsh punishments will prevent crime.
5. Foot patrols by police officers are an effective way to prevent crime.
6. Our national system of health care needs more reform.
7. Fire inspectors should inspect private homes.
8. An unfair action taken against certain groups is known as discrimination.

CHAPTER
Introduction

It was Christmas Eve. Astronaut James Lovell, halfway to the moon, looked out the window of his spacecraft. There among the stars he saw a round ball, a planet. One side of it was in shadow. But the other side was streaked with color—blue, brown, green, and white. It was beautiful. It looked, he said, like a "grand oasis in the vastness of space."

Lovell, with a grin, asked if this planet might be inhabited. The other astronauts laughed. Of course it was inhabited. It was the planet Earth. But in the vastness of space, the world we know looked small and lonely, surrounded by deep black sky. For the first time in history, humans could view the entire world from a great distance. The earth, thought the astronauts, is little more than a "spacecraft" among the stars. We are all riding on it, passengers together, dependent upon it for all the necessities of life.

The earth has been good to us. It has provided us with air to breathe, water to drink, food to eat, and all the many materials necessary to make our lives easier. Over the years, these natural resources have been taken for granted, as though they could never be used up. But now we know that the natural resources of the earth are not limitless. They need protection, especially from humans themselves.

Can we really use up the things that nature has provided for thousands of years? Indeed we can. We can burn all the fuel and take out all the metals stored in the earth. We can destroy the lakes, the rivers, and the oceans with pollution, and make the water unfit for use by plants or animals or human beings. We can cause chemical changes in the very atmosphere on which all life depends. These things can happen to our earth. In fact, they are on the way to happening right now.

That is why we must begin to take better care of our earth and its natural resources. But in order to do this, we must understand what the dangers are. We must find out what is happening to our land. And we must learn what we can do to make sure that "Spaceship Earth" will continue to carry its passengers safely now and in the future. These are the big questions to think about as you read and study these topics:

1. The Problem of Pollution
2. Ecology—The Vital Key
3. Energy for Today and Tomorrow
4. Protecting Our Future

CHAPTER

23 Saving the Earth

1 The Problem of Pollution

The world around us, our **environment,** consists of a layer of air, water that covers three fourths of the surface of the globe, and soil upon which we depend for food, clothing, and shelter. Every part of this environment is important to us. When we cause any part of it to become dirty, impure, and contaminated—made unfit for use—it is said to be **polluted.** Pollution can destroy plants and animals, and upset the balance of nature. Among the countless living creatures that pollution harms are the ones that cause it—human beings.

WHY DO WE HAVE POLLUTION?

Pollution may occur when we get rid of something we don't want. Harmful, unburned gases from our automobile engines are added into the air. Unwanted smoke and gases from factories, smelters, power plants, and home furnaces go up millions of smokestacks and chimneys. Ashes, soot, and gases are carried far and wide by the wind and make the air impure. People discard tires, bottles, cans, and even old automobiles along the highways and in streams. Chemical plants and steel mills pour their wastes into rivers, lakes, and oceans.

Why do people pollute their environment? They do it because they started doing it long ago when dumping caused little damage. An early town bought a piece of swampland to serve as its dump. There was plenty of other land, so hardly anyone minded this small-scale damage of the environment. An early factory was built beside a river. It dumped its waste into the river. The river did not belong to anyone in particular, and few people complained. When there were fewer towns and factories scattered throughout our vast land, not many people worried about these methods of getting rid of unwanted refuse.

Since our earlier history, three things have happened that have made these earlier practices unsuitable. First, our population has grown enormously. Every person produces garbage, sewage, and other kinds of waste. The more people we have, the more garbage we produce. As long as our population continues to grow, so will the problem of disposing of our waste.

Second, our economy has developed such enormous capacity that we manufacture and use more and more goods every year. Americans use more than 137 million automobiles, trucks, and buses to move people and goods from place to place. In the United States alone, billions of metal cans and nonreturnable bottles are used every year—and then thrown away.

Third, new inventions have led to products that complicate our trash disposal problem. Plastics do not decay and, if burned, may pollute the air. Detergents may upset the natural balance in streams and lakes.

These are only a few of the new and old products that cause trouble in our environment. Because our economy gives us so much, we have mountains of trash to dispose of and tons upon tons of waste matter polluting the air and water.

AIR POLLUTION

The air we breathe is a unique combination of nitrogen, oxygen, carbon dioxide, and small amounts of other gases. It is a **renewable resource.** That is, it can be replaced. Under good conditions, nature can clean the air of impurities that are breathed into it by people or put into it by furnaces, factories, and automobiles. In recent years, however, nature has been unable to rid the air of the great amount of pollution thrown into it by our modern industrial civilization. As a result, the air over many of our cities is filled with **smog**—a combination of smoke, gases, and fog. Smog burns the eyes, causes coughing, and is dangerous for anyone with a breathing ailment.

Automobiles in America pour more than 100 million tons of pollutants into the air each year. This is nearly half of all our air pollution. Thus, cars we use to get to work, to go shopping, and for pleasure are to blame for much of the bad air we breathe. But automobiles are by no means solely responsible for our bad air. Nearly 50 million tons of pollutants a year are spewed into the atmosphere by the fuel we burn to heat our homes and to power the generators for electricity. Almost 30 million tons each year come from factories. In some parts of the country, factories are the worst polluters of all. In addition, 5 million tons of ashes and gases enter the atmosphere each year from the burning dumps and incinerators near almost all of our cities and towns.

Every year it costs government and business about $30 billion dollars to try to control and reduce air pollution. The pollutants corrode metal, damage crops, and waste our resources. But the damage may be even greater. Changes in the makeup of the air, some scientists say, are changing the earth's climate. Harmful gases and tiny particles of foreign matter are increasing in the upper atmosphere. When the sun's rays strike these particles, the rays are scattered back into space. It will not take long, these scientists say, for this process to cut down the amount of sunlight that reaches the earth. The effect of this will be to reduce plant life and, eventually, to threaten all life on earth.

Pollution from factories, trash burners, and automobiles poisons the air that all of us must breathe.

Already smog has been seen high over the open oceans and even at the North Pole. Airplanes flying at high speeds in the upper atmosphere may increase the danger.

OUR WATER SUPPLY

While there is plenty of air to breathe, even if it is polluted, there is not plenty of fresh water. Ninety-seven percent of all the water in the world is salt water. Of the remaining 3 percent, all but a tiny fraction is frozen in the polar ice caps. Thus, our supply of usable water is strictly limited. But Americans use water as though it were plentiful.

All fresh water comes from the clouds—as rain, snow, or other precipitation. It seeps into the earth, follows underground courses, and forms underground pools. Excess water runs into streams, lakes, and oceans. Eventually, it evaporates and is taken up into the atmosphere to fall again upon the land. This process is called the **water cycle.**

Underground water reserves are one of the keys to life on the land. Underground water nourishes plants. Bubbling out in wells and springs, it helps supply the water needs of humans and of animals. A good supply of underground water is assured when trees, plants, and grasses cover the earth's soil. The roots of trees and other plants help to keep the soil moist. They slow the flow of water. The trees and plants give off moisture into the atmosphere to help keep the water cycle working.

When trees and other plants are removed from great areas of land, the rain tends to rush down slopes instead of sinking slowly into the ground. That has happened in many parts of the United States. Thus, the level of our water under the ground, the **water table,** is slowly sinking. As a result, our supply of usable water is decreasing. Despite this, we are using more water than ever before. Some scientists say that every day we take twice as much from groundwater reserves as flows in. This situation is made worse because we are rapidly polluting much of our surface water—the water of rivers, lakes, and reservoirs.

WHAT ARE THE WATER POLLUTERS?

Anything in the water that makes it less useful or less healthful is a pollutant. Water pollution can be classified into five types: chemical, sewage, thermal, silt, and crud.

Chemical pollutants come mainly from industrial plants. In fact, industry—factories, mills, and mines—accounts for more than half of all water pollution. Agriculture, with its insect sprays and artificial fertilizers, is also responsible for chemical pollution of water.

There are other forms of chemical pollution as well. For instance, the detergents we use contain substances called phosphates. These phosphates make detergents act more quickly. But they also pollute the waters in much the same way fertilizers do.

Sewage comes mainly from cities and other communities that dump their waste, including that of humans, into lakes and streams. Water pollution also comes from sewage treatment plants and septic tanks.

Thermal pollution occurs when industries use cold water from a stream to cool their products, then pump the warmer water back into the streams. Steel plants, nuclear power plants, and others pump warmed water into streams. The temperature of the water, raised in this fashion, may kill fish and other marine life. It also upsets the balance of nature that helps renew the purity of fresh water. Industry uses more water in this way than all the water that Americans drink. For example, it takes about 380,000 liters (100,000 gallons) of water to cool the parts for one automobile. Nuclear energy plants also require huge amounts of water each day to cool their nuclear reactors.

Silt,—soil, sand, or mud washed into streams—comes mainly from sloping land that does not have enough trees or other plants to hold the soil. Silt pollution is often the result of improper mining and agricultural practices, road building, grading, and earth moving.

Crud, usually used as a slang word, can also be used to refer to trash such as old tires, bottles, and other used items. Such things become crud when they are thrown away by careless, thoughtless people into streams and lakes, as well as onto the land.

The cure for water pollution is to rid water of all impurities before it is returned to streams and lakes. Such purification is costly. It requires the building of more and better sewage treatment plants. Urban areas and industries are already spending billions of dollars each year to construct new plants. Americans use about 1,366 billion liters (360 billion gallons) of water a day—for drinking, bathing, industry, and all other purposes. About 70 percent of this water becomes sewage. All of this sewage would have to be treated if we really want our water to be pure.

NOISE POLLUTION

Loud, harsh, irritating sounds have become a part of our modern civilization. The roar of jet planes, the blare of automobile horns, the rumble of trucks, the penetrating sounds of jack hammers and riveting guns—all of these and more cause noise pollution. Long exposure to disturbing noise may lead to heart disease, high blood pressure, stomach ulcers, nervous disorders, and deafness.

To understand the problem of noise pollution we need to know something about the nature of sound. The loudness of sound is measured in **decibels.** We can barely hear the difference of one decibel. We usually speak in tones of about 50 to 60 decibels. When sound reaches about 100 decibels, it becomes uncomfortable. At 140 decibels it is painful. The sound of a jet plane taking off at 150 decibels is harmful to human eardrums. Some workers at airports wear protective devices over their ears. The citizen who endures a daily traffic noise of 80 decibels, or a subway roar of 100 decibels, also suffers.

People have begun to do something about noise pollution. The federal government is spending millions of dollars to lower the noise of jet planes. Federal, state, and local governments have passed laws to control noise levels. There are quieter mufflers for trucks and buses. Quieter machines are being made by industry. Fans of rock music are being urged to lower their music from its loud range of 100 to 160 decibels, which can cause ear troubles. And concerned citizens are working to make the public aware of the many problems of noise pollution.

AN INTERNATIONAL PROBLEM

Pollution does not respect political boundaries. A polluted stream may flow from one state to the next. Polluted air from New Jersey factories drifts over New York City. New York City's polluted water fouls the New Jersey shoreline. Ships dump or spill oil into the oceans of the world. Atomic fallout affects every section of the globe. The children of Japan wear masks to help protect them against smog. Sonic booms from fast flying planes echo over Africa. The problem of pollution calls for international cooperation.

In June 1972, the United Nations held the first global Conference on the Human Environment at Stockholm, Sweden. Delegates from 114 nations attended this conference. Together they made a beginning toward a worldwide fight against pollution. The conference set up 110 stations throughout the world to obtain data on the extent and nature of each area's pollution. The decisions of the conference was referred to the United Nations General Assembly for action. The nations of the world are all affected by what happens to the air and the oceans. The future of the earth as a home for human beings may depend upon how well all of us can work together to control pollution.

CONSIDER AND DISCUSS

Identify. environment / pollution / renewable resource / smog / water cycle / water table / chemical pollutants / sewage / thermal pollution / silt / crud / decibel

Review. 1. What three factors have increased pollution in modern times? 2. How does air pollution affect people? 3. Name five kinds of water pollution. 4. What are the water polluters? 5. What can be done about noise pollution?

Discuss. What are some of the causes of pollution in your locality? What can be done about them?

2 Ecology—the Vital Key

Our environment, the world around us, is changing very quickly. Buildings go up. Highways are built. Jet planes streak through the skies. Of course, these changes can be helpful. But they can also create serious problems.

WHAT IS ECOLOGY?

All living things depend upon each other. All animals, for example, depend on green plants for the oxygen they breathe. Plants take carbon dioxide out of the air. They then break it down into carbon and oxygen. They use the carbon to make their own food. The pure oxygen, which they cannot use, is released back into the atmosphere. Animals breathe in this oxygen, which they need to live. They breathe out carbon dioxide, and the cycle begins again. Without green plants and the oxygen they supply, no animal or human being could live.

There are many other ways in which living things depend upon each other. Bacteria feed on fallen leaves, causing them to decay. This decaying matter enriches the soil, so that more plants and trees can grow. These in turn supply food for many animals, such as rabbits, squirrels, deer, and many kinds of birds. Some birds eat insects that feed on the plants. Tiny marine animals called plankton live in marshes and wetlands and provide food for shrimp, oysters, and minnows. These in turn feed larger fish and make possible the great schools of herring, tuna, salmon, and other seafood so important to humans.

In such ways, all living things, including humans, are like links in a chain. Take away one link of the chain, and all living things depending on that link will suffer. Reduce the amount of forest and field, and the num-

Continued on page 487

ENERGY VS.

WHAT DO YOU THINK?

What would happen if all electric power were suddenly cut off? Try to picture it. Lights would go out. Air conditioners would stop. Elevators would be stuck. Refrigerators would get warm. Electric ovens would stay cold. Television sets would go off. Trains and subways would stop. Factory assembly lines would not run. The entire life of the nation would come to a halt.

Electricity "blackouts" like this really do happen. In 1965, the whole northeastern part of the United States was without electricity for many hours. Since then, blackouts have hit many cities and local areas. In some areas, "brownouts" have become common. These are periods of reduced power, used to save electricity when demands are too high.

Our modern way of life depends very much on electricity. Between 1960 and 1970, our use of electric power doubled. It is expected to double again by the early 1980's. Our population keeps growing. And we use more and more electrical appliances. Where is all the extra electricity going to come from? What price must we pay for more and more power?

Most of our electricity is produced by burning coal, oil, or natural gas. The coal is often mined from open pits, or "strip mines," leaving

POLLUTION

huge scars on the land. Once an area has been mined in this way, not even grass will grow there. To find more oil and gas, companies are drilling offshore wells in the sea bed. Oil spills have become a danger to our shorelines. When burned for power, all of these fuels are dirty. Thus, electric power plants pour pollution into our air and water. They are also using up natural resources that cannot be replaced.

Many people look to nuclear energy as the great power source of the future. A very small amount of radioactive material can produce a great deal of electricity. Nuclear reactors will even be able to produce their own radioactive fuel. Nuclear power plants produced less than 2 percent of our electricity in 1970. By the late 1970's, they produced about 10 percent of all electric power.

A nuclear power plant does not pour smoke into the air, or waste materials into the water. But it can produce a different kind of pollution—heat. The nuclear reactor is usually cooled by taking water out of a nearby river or lake. The water to be poured back is warmer than before. If this water is not cooled, thermal, heat, pollution can kill fish and upset the whole ecology of an area. The water may fill up with algae and begin to smell. Because they must be near water, nuclear plants may ruin scenic landscapes and recreation areas.

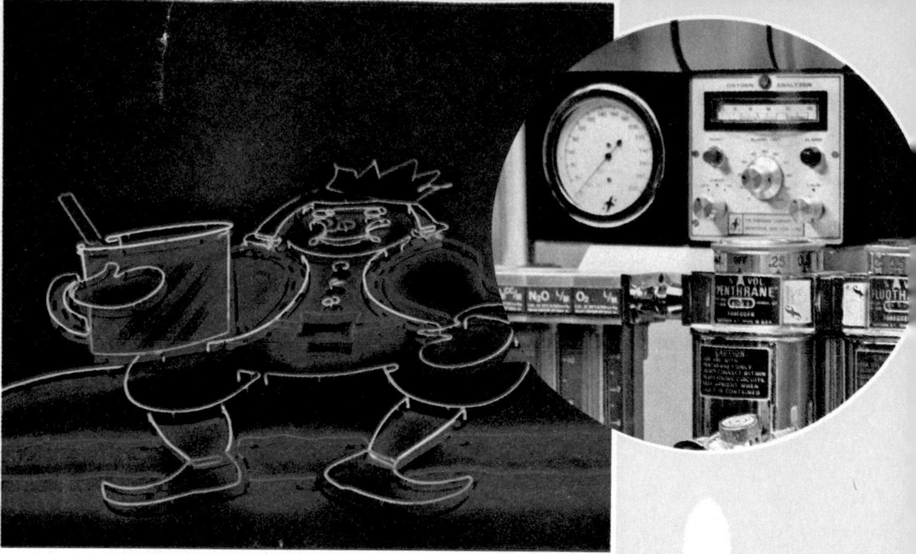

Nuclear power plants also carry all the dangers of radioactivity. Under ordinary conditions, these plants are quite safe. But could an accident happen? Could people be exposed to dangerous radiation? What about radioactive wastes? These will last for thousands of years. How long will our safeguards last? Is there a chance these wastes might some day poison our earth?

How can we balance our rising demand for electricity against the costs to our environment? Strip-mining companies must restore the land by bringing in new topsoil. Will the companies mine less because of the costs? Nuclear plants can build special towers to cool the water they use. But this costs money. All of these added costs mean higher bills. Are we willing to pay this extra money to save our environment? Or will we pay the price in pollution and ugliness instead?

Some people are confident that technology will solve our problems. They have hopes for solar energy, for example. Scientists are trying to find ways for the sun to produce electricity and to heat our homes. But other people warn us that progress has its price. The more dependent we become on electricity, they say, the greater the danger to our environment.

Look around you at all the ways in which we use electricity. Look at the advertisements in magazines. Do we really need all of these gadgets? Do we need more and more of them every year? Look, too, at the ways in which electricity is wasted. Are lights on, or a television set, when nobody is using them? What is the true price of these gadgets and this waste? Are we paying for them with dirty air and polluted rivers?

Do we really want to sacrifice our natural environment for this kind of "progress"? How much of our environment, for how much progress? Many people believe that this is the real choice for the future. It is a choice that you—as a consumer and a citizen—will help to make.

ber of wild birds will be reduced. Without enough birds to eat them, insects will multiply too quickly. Drain or pollute the wetlands, and there will be fewer fish. Reduce the wild areas of the country, and eagles, hawks, coyotes, mountain lions, and other animals will no longer have a home. Without these natural enemies, other animals such as mice and deer will increase too fast. With too many plant-eating animals, not enough plants will decay to enrich the soil and hold moisture. Later there will be fewer plants, and the deer too will suffer.

These are only a few simple examples. Perhaps you can think of some others. The whole subject is very, very complex. It is called **ecology.** Ecology is the study of the **balance of nature** – how all different living things, including humans, relate to one another. It is of great importance because people can do many things to upset the balance of nature. And they may not always see the many harmful side effects of their activities.

AMERICA'S EARLY ENVIRONMENT

Long before any European settlers came here, the North American continent was a land of great natural wealth and beauty. This part of the world had moderate climates, with plenty of sunshine and a good supply of rain in most places. Trees grew thick and tall in the forests. The plains were covered with wild grasses. The river valleys were fertile and green. And many kinds of wild animals lived in balance with each other.

This abundance was the result of natural forces that had been at work over thousands of years. The sun, the wind, and the rain had worn away huge rocks and reduced them to soil. Melting snow had formed streams that carried soil down from the mountains into the valleys. Huge rivers were formed. These rivers dug out great channels and canyons, and left more soil in their paths. Plants grew in this soil and, when they decayed, their leaves and roots enriched the soil. As the soil was built up, trees were able to grow. Some of these grew in rocky places. Their roots helped to break up the rocks and make more soil. Their leaves decayed and built up the soil even more. Then other trees – such as oaks, elms, maples, beeches, pines, and redwoods – took root, and huge forests were born.

These great forests provided protection and food for many kinds of animals. Other animals, such as the great herds of American bison (buffalo), grazed on the open plains. Different species of birds, insects, and animals kept each other in balance. Each plant or animal took what it needed from the environment. In turn, it contributed to the needs of others.

At this time, humans, too, were part of the balance of nature. The Native Americans hunted for food and for animal skins, which they used for clothing and shelter. Hunting with spears or bows and arrows, they rarely killed more than they needed to feed themselves. The Native Americans did not yet have the tools or the technology to make great changes in the environment. Moreover, they had great respect for the earth and for the other creatures with whom they shared it.

UPSETTING AMERICA'S ECOLOGY

The early European settlers were amazed by the natural wealth of the Americas. In Europe, most of the land was divided up and had been farmed for hundreds of years. There were few forests. And those few were the private property of kings and nobles. There was little wild game left. No wonder that the fertile land, the forests, and the wildlife of America seemed unlimited to early European settlers.

America's forests were so thick that in order to grow crops, the settlers first had to clear away the trees. They used part of the wood to build their houses and furniture. They burned what they didn't need. Then they started sending lumber back to Europe. The tallest and straightest trees were used to make the masts of great sailing ships. As the number of settlers increased and the demand for wood grew, more and more forests were cut down. No new trees were planted in their place. If people wanted more wood, there were many more forests to the west.

But forests were not only for people. As the trees disappeared, so did much of the wildlife that depended on them for food and shelter. Many other wild animals were killed, not only for food but also for their furs or for "sport." Beavers were trapped by the millions because beaver hats were popular in Europe. Whole herds of buffalo were shot for hides or for sport, while their meat was left to rot. Other animals and birds of prey—including foxes, bears, mountain lions, owls, hawks, and eagles—were shot as "pests" because they sometimes attacked chickens, cattle, or other livestock. But these creatures fed mostly on other wild creatures, including mice and snakes. This helped to maintain the balance of nature. Many of these species, including the American eagle, have been almost totally destroyed and must now be protected by special laws.

Green plants, trees, deer, and other wildlife all have their place in the balance of nature. How have people upset nature's balance?

FARMING THE LAND

The land that was cleared for farming was at first very fertile. For centuries, decaying matter from plants, plus minerals from rocks, had been building up the soil. This rich soil produced wonderful crops of vegetables, wheat, oats, corn, cotton, and tobacco. But when the farmer planted a crop and harvested it, nothing was left to decay and rebuild the soil. As the land was farmed year after year, the supply of plant food in the soil was used up and nothing was put back. Like the lumber workers in the forests, the farmers thought there would always be more new land.

In the West, cattle raisers and sheep herders took the land for granted, too. Their huge herds ate all the plants on the prairies they roamed. Without plants to hold water, the land dried out. Much good grassland was ruined in this way. There was always more land, most people thought. But was there?

By the early 1900's, our vast continent was filling up with people. There was no longer an endless supply of untouched farmland. Farmers were plowing up more and more of the flat grasslands on the Great Plains. Then, in the 1930's, there was a long dry period in this area. With no grass growing, vast amounts of rich soil blew away. A few years later, all that was left was a barren "dust bowl."

President Franklin D. Roosevelt urged Congress to pass a program to conserve the farmlands of the country. Under this program, called the **"soil bank,"** land owners would stop farming some of their land. The government would pay them to grow trees, grass, or other plant cover on this land instead. In this way, there would be a supply of good land left for the future.

MODERN AGRICULTURE

The population of America was increasing. New farmland was running out. Old farmland was wearing out. And some of it was no longer farmed at all. How were all the new people to be fed?

The answer was found in modern science and technology. With the help of science, farmers can now grow more and more food on less and less land. This miracle was made possible by the use of chemical fertilizers and pesticides. Because of these, farm production has increased enormously in the past few decades.

Fertilizers are special plant foods that make crops grow faster and bigger. The most important are **nitrates,** which contain nitrogen. Nitrates can be mixed with water and pumped into the ground or they can be spread as a powder to soak in with the next rain. When a field is fertilized with nitrates, plants grow so quickly that much more food can be harvested. Nitrates are now used by almost all farmers, and also by home gardeners on their lawns and flower beds.

Pesticides are special chemicals that kill insect pests. Many kinds of insects attack different food plants, and they can ruin a farmer's whole crop. A pesticide called **DDT,** introduced in the 1940's, seemed to be the answer. Farmers mixed DDT with their fertilizer to control the corn borer, the boll weevil, the cabbage moth, and hundreds of other insect pests. People sprayed it on their lawns to get rid of mosquitoes, and on their windows to get rid of flies. Forests were sprayed with DDT by airplane to kill the gypsy moth and other insects that attacked trees. When many beautiful elm trees were attacked by Dutch elm disease, tons of DDT were sprayed on these trees in lawns and parks all over the country.

Science has solved many problems with fertilizers and pesticides. American farmers have been able to produce more and more food. But now we are learning that these chemicals are causing problems that may be worse than the problems they solve. Nitrates and DDT are only two examples of the unexpected and dangerous effects that chemicals have on our environment.

SCIENCE AND ECOLOGY

All different living things, as we now know, are related to each other in complex ways. A change in one link of the chain may cause many other changes.

That is what has happened with nitrates. They are used to make the farmer's crops grow faster. But some of the nitrates also wash away into streams, and then into rivers and lakes. These nitrates speed up the growth of plant life (algae and weeds) in rivers and lakes. Tiny bacteria feed on this plant matter and help to break it down. As the plant life increases, the bacteria multiply faster and faster. But in the process of breaking down plant matter, bacteria use oxygen. Too many bacteria can use up all of the oxygen in the water. Without oxygen, fish die. This has begun to happen in many of our waterways.

DDT has also caused a dangerous "chain reaction." DDT is very good at killing insect pests. But it is a poison that does not break down easily. That is, it is not easily changed into other, less harmful substances. Instead, it remains in the dead insects, on trees, and in the fields. The insects are eaten by small birds and by fish, which are eaten by humans. Many large birds eat the smaller birds. Cattle take in the DDT that has been sprayed in the fields, and the chemicals remain in their meat. DDT has been found in birds, fish, and other animals in every part of the world. This insecticide can prevent them from having young. Therefore, it can cause whole species of animals to disappear.

America's Share of the World's Resources

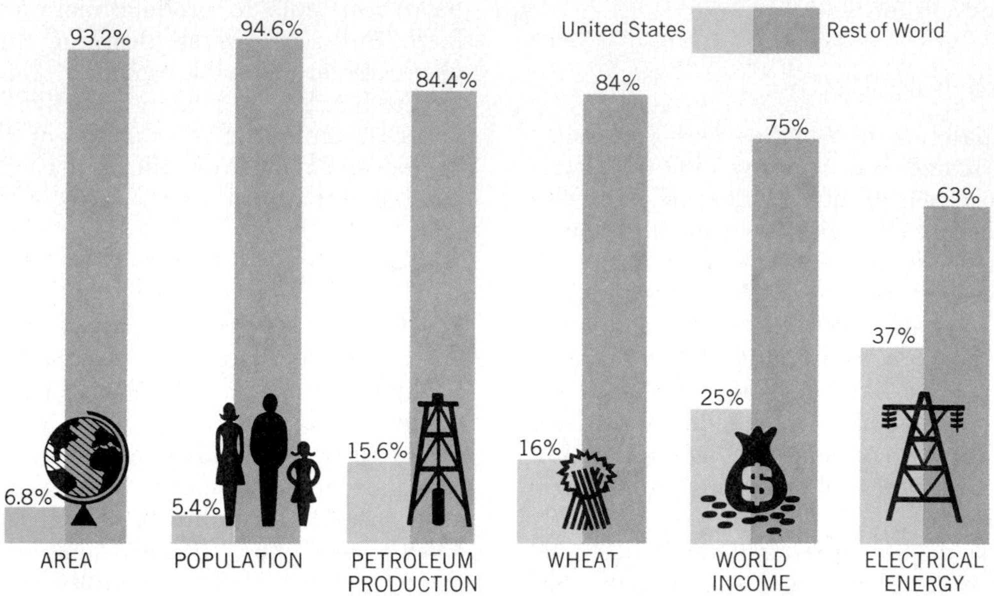

SOURCE: United Nations and United States Department of Commerce, Bureau of the Census. Figures are for 1975.

Nitrates and DDT are two important examples of how modern science and technology can upset the balance of nature. Progress has brought about many benefits. But it has brought many new problems, too. That is why an understanding of ecology is more important today than ever before.

THE FARMER AND THE LAND

No one has a greater stake in the future of the American land than the farmer. Many farmers remember the dark days of the 1930's when dust from the Great Plains blew as far east as Washington, D. C. In other parts of the country, once fine land was ruined by water rushing unchecked down the slopes of farmland. Much land was worn out by planting a single crop, such as cotton or tobacco, year after year. Action has been taken by the federal government to help farmers save and improve one of our most precious resources—the soil.

Farmers have learned how to keep the soil from being worn out. They prevent topsoil from washing or blowing away by many different techniques. Some farmers plow across slopes instead of up and down, a method called **contour plowing.** Many build drainage channels, small dams, and terraces—flat, level spaces on the slopes. They plant **cover crops,** such as clover, soybeans, and hay because they hold the soil better than other crops. They also practice **crop rotation,** planting different crops on the land each year. This helps to restore nitrogen to the soil and increases crop yields.

Soil conservation is only one way in which farmers are safeguarding our land. With the help of scientists and the government, they are constantly trying to find even better ways.

OVERPOPULATION—A THREAT TO OUR RESOURCES

Farmers have proved that they can produce enough food to feed the present population of the United States, with some left over for export. But will they continue to do so in the future as more and more land is covered with cities, dams, highways, and other kinds of development? Consider also the problems of living space, of water supply, and of getting rid of trash and waste as more and more people crowd the earth. How many people can the United States and the rest of the world hold and still provide a decent standard of living for all?

The increase in the world's population has been called a "population explosion." It took more than a million years for the human population to reach 1 billion people by the year 1850. But it took only 80 years to arrive at the second billion, in 1930. Today the world's population is over 4 billion. If it keeps increasing at the same rate, the world's population will reach 6.2 billion by the year 2000. Where will these people live? Where will the resources be found to provide for them all? This rapid growth greatly concerns America. Even now, food must be sent to many nations because they cannot feed all their people. But even with this aid, about one half billion people in the world suffer from starvation each year.

In the United States, the population is increasing at less than 1 percent a year. In the late 1970's there were over 3 million births and almost 2 million deaths a year. Thus, the **natural increase** in our population was a little over a million a year. In addition, about 400,000 immigrants came to the United States each year. Even if we continue at this low rate of growth, we will have over 260 million people by the year 2000. Where will all these people live? Where will we find the resources to provide a high standard of living for so many people? This is a challenge that Americans face for the future.

The problems of population growth have brought many Americans to favor **zero population growth.** That is, the number of births about replaces the number of people who die. In 1970, Congress passed the **Family Planning Services and Population Research Act.** This act made family planning information available to those who wanted it. In 1972 it was recommended that much of the problem of overpopulation could be solved by helping those families who wanted to limit the size of their families. Some people objected to the report because some of its measures were against their religious views. Others claimed that the program was an attempt to limit the growth of population among minority groups. However, most religious leaders, economists, and ecologists agree that the problem of overpopulation must be solved if the world is to be a fit place for people to inhabit in the future.

CONSIDER AND DISCUSS

Identify. ecology / balance of nature / fertilizers / pesticides / nitrates / DDT / contour plowing / cover crops / crop rotation / natural increase / Family Planning Services and Population Research Act / zero population growth

Review. 1. How do plants and animals depend upon each other? 2. What are some of the ways in which humans upset the balance of nature? 3. Give several examples of the way in which resources have been wasted. 4. Why is unrestricted use of DDT dangerous? 5. Name some ways in which farmers can conserve the soil. 6. Why is overpopulation a threat to our resources?

Discuss. What is the place of humans in the balance of nature?

3 Energy for Today and Tomorrow

Until recently many Americans believed that our country's resources would last forever. Ever since the European settlers arrived in America, people have been using up the land and its resources at faster and faster rates.

Americans have covered the land with cement and asphalt, buildings and highways. As the number of people grew, houses spread into the countryside where, often, precious farmland gave way to new buildings. To meet our demand for goods, mountains have been stripped bare for lumber and for coal, copper, silver, gold, and other minerals. America has only about 6 percent of the world's population. But it uses much of the world's petroleum, natural gas, iron ore, and other resources. This places a heavy burden on the earth's limited resources.

OUR ENERGY RESOURCES

Among the resources that we are using up quickly are our **energy resources.** They furnish the power for doing the nation's work. Between 1950 and 1970, we doubled the amount of energy we use to run our machines. Experts think our energy use will double again by 1985. In addition to the United States, there are other industrial nations that use up energy at a fast rate. Moreover, developing nations around the world are demanding a greater share of the world's energy resources.

Unless we take steps now, we will soon be without valuable energy resources—coal, petroleum, and natural gas. These resources are limited. And they are nonrenewable. That is, they can be used only once. Without them, our way of life would be in danger. Our factories would stop running. Our homes would be dark and cold. Our transportation system would come to a halt. And our national defense would be in danger. To understand better why this would happen, let us examine the energy situation.

OIL FOR INDUSTRY

The energy source we depend upon most is **petroleum,** or oil, as it is commonly called. It is a **fossil fuel** that lies deep within the earth in great pools. These pools were formed from microscopic plants and animals that lived millions of years ago. They were covered with mud, rocks, and water. After centuries of decay and pressure from the earth, an energy source of great value was formed. Pumped to the surface and refined, petroleum furnishes the energy to heat our homes, the gasoline to run our cars and trucks, and the lubricating oil to grease the wheels of industry. It also is used to produce a great variety of by-products such as plastics, fertilizers, dyes, and many different chemicals.

There is, however, only so much oil left in the ground. When it is all used up there will be no more. The United States was for many years the leading oil-producing nation in the world. The Trans-Alaska Pipeline began to move oil from the north Alaskan oil fields in 1977. These fields have huge deposits of oil. Despite this, by the late 1970's, we were behind the Soviet Union and Saudi Arabia in oil production. Moreover, we had to import about 50 percent of our oil supplies. Some experts think that the world's oil supply will run out by the year 2000. Of course, the discovery of new oil deposits will give us an additional supply. To aid in the search for more oil, the federal government has leased drilling sites off the Atlantic Coast to oil companies. The companies seek oil beneath the ocean floor.

CONSERVING OIL

Another way to stretch our available oil resources is through **conservation,** or wise use. The lowering of speed limits on highways to 88 kilometers (55 miles) an hour has saved gasoline. It has saved lives as well. The auto industry is cooperating by making smaller cars that use less gasoline. By 1985, new cars are expected to travel about 44 kilometers on every 3.7 liters (or 27.5 miles a gallon).

Homeowners, too, must do their part to conserve heating oil. Lowering home temperatures, insulating attics and walls, and putting in storm windows and doors are some ways to save oil. Certain industries may have to stop using oil and substitute coal and other fuels. In the meantime, we must find new resources to take the place of oil.

A SHORTAGE OF NATURAL GAS

The second most widely used fuel in the United States is **natural gas.** Like petroleum, it is a fossil fuel. Natural gas is usually found with petroleum. At one time, it was burned off as it came out of the oil well. But this clean-burning fuel found favor with homeowners and industry. Therefore, it began to be used in ever larger amounts. Over half of the homes in America are now heated with gas. Industry, too, relies upon gas for almost half of its energy needs.

During the 1960's, energy experts began warning that our natural gas supplies were running low. Production began to fall around 1974. As a result, distributors of natural gas had to cut back on new customers. Then, during the unusually cold winter of 1977, distributors were unable to meet the increased demands for gas. To free enough of the fuel to heat homes, some industries were shut down. Almost a million workers were idled. And a number of schools that used gas heat were closed. Later that year, the Alaskan oil fields, with their large gas deposits, were opened. They were expected to help the nation meet its gas needs.

Some producers blamed the gas shortage on the low price of natural gas. They claimed that producers are unwilling to spend money to find new sources if the price is too low to make a profit. But even if prices rise and new sources of natural gas are found, they will only supply America's needs for a while. We must use what we have now wisely and without waste.

COAL FOR THE FUTURE

The United States is fortunate in having a large supply of coal. We are thought to have enough coal to last for about 300 years. Much of this coal lies deep in the earth where it was formed millions of years ago. Getting this coal out of the ground is hard and dangerous, even with improved methods and machines.

Other deposits of coal lie near the surface and can be reached by stripping off the soil on top. The coal is then scooped up by machine. This **strip mining** has been severely criticized for its effects upon the environment. It often leaves ugly scars on the land. Without trees or plants to hold it together, the soil washes down the hills and into streams. It muddies the water and sometimes clogs waterways. To solve this problem, Congress passed a strip mining act in 1977. It requires mining companies to recover the area with soil, plants, and trees after they have removed the coal.

Coal is looked upon by many as the best energy source for the near future—until other sources have been discovered or developed. To use coal, many industries will have to convert from oil and natural gas. But, as you read earlier, it is difficult to burn coal without polluting the air. Researchers are looking for ways to prevent this from happening. They are trying to change coal into gas and oil so it will burn cleaner and more efficiently. In the meantime, industries will have to install expensive "scrubbing" equipment to prevent polluting materials from reaching our air.

USING NUCLEAR ENERGY

There were over 60 nuclear plants in operation in the United States in the late 1970's. The government hopes to have 300 more by the year 2000. Nuclear reactors run on a small amount of fuel. They produce large amounts of energy efficiently. It was estimated that during the energy crisis of 1977, half a million jobs were saved because of nuclear energy. But nuclear plants may carry the danger of radioactivity and thermal pollution. We must also find ways to store the waste materials from nuclear plants so that they will not be dangerous to the earth in the future. We also need to find ways to make nuclear plants less expensive to build.

ENERGY FROM THE SUN

One of the most promising new sources of energy for the future is energy from the sun—**solar energy.** Research on this type of energy is still in the beginning stages. But it is proving to be a very practical way to heat and cool homes. It may even provide some electricity. To encourage the study and use of solar energy, the federal government is giving grants to people who want to put solar heaters in their homes. This clean and plentiful source of power holds great promise for the future.

OTHER SOURCES OF ENERGY

The continuing energy shortage has convinced many Americans that action is needed to avoid national disaster. Private industry, government agencies, and university research centers are engaged in the search for new and practical sources of energy.

One of the possible sources of energy that is being investigated is **geothermal energy.** Scientists are trying to use the heat from deep within the earth to produce energy. They are also studying ways to expand our use of **hydroelectric power**—energy from water, including the movement of ocean tides and waves. Other possible sources of energy that are being investigated are more efficient windmills and the conversion of manure into methane gas. These and other ideas must be developed if Americans are to have enough energy for the future.

THE DEPARTMENT OF ENERGY

In order to direct our different energy programs, a Department of Energy was added in the executive branch of the federal government in 1977. This department and its Secretary have the responsibility of administering the many energy programs that had been under other departments, as you may recall from Chapter 4. It also has the power to gather data about the energy we have available and its use. The department can order certain steps to conserve energy. In addition, it has control over gas and oil pipelines, nuclear waste management, nuclear plant safety, and federal energy leases off the Atlantic Coast. The Department of Energy also carries out all federal energy laws.

ENERGY AND THE ENVIRONMENT

Americans must be careful about how our new energy resources are developed. Each time we develop an area, we may upset its ecological balance. Development is necessary for the well being of our country. But more and more citizens are determined that in the future our development will not harm the environment, as it did in the past.

Even though we need new sources of energy many Americans do not want new nuclear plants, mines, or dams near areas where they live. Nor do they want oil drilling sites off their coastal shores. Too many oil spills from tankers and barges have ruined our beaches. Over a million tons of oil a year have leaked into the oceans from tankers, barges, oil rigs, and coastal installations.

Because of the harm that has been done to the environment, the federal government and some states and local areas have passed laws to control new development. They require developers of some new plants, mines, and installations to study the effects their development will have on the environment. Before any work can begin, they must prove they will meet the standards that have been set.

DEVELOPMENT VERSUS CONSERVATION

Some Americans are worried about the high costs of keeping our environment clean. They say that the new safeguards and equipment

The Trans-Alaska Pipeline was opened in 1977. It carries oil all the way across Alaska, from Prudhoe Bay in the north to the port of Valdez in the south.

make it too costly to build new plants or to carry out new development. In order to have the energy and raw materials we need, some people think we must continue to use the land and its resources as we have been doing. They feel it may even be necessary to relax some of the standards we have set for a cleaner environment. In the process, we may upset the balance of nature and cause some kinds of wildlife and fish to die out. Would we be any worse off because of that? Would it be better to do without energy and many of the goods we use everyday?

Conservationists say that continuing to pollute the environment or to upset the balance of nature is dangerous. Their study of ecology has convinced them that what affects our land and its wildlife may eventually affect us. In many ways, animals give us timely warnings. Humans developed DDT to destroy insect pests. But it also harmed many birds and animals. People have been warned that they may be next. Much damage can be caused by upsetting our ecological balance.

Conservation is not a miserly saving of resources for some future time. It is "wise use" now. We can make wise use of our resources now in order to make our lives richer, but without endangering our future. And we must be constantly on guard to make sure that there will be a future worth having.

CONSIDER AND DISCUSS

Identify. energy resources / petroleum / fossil fuel / conservation / natural gas / strip mining / solar energy / geothermal energy / hydroelectric power

Review. 1. What are some of the ways in which oil resources may be conserved? 2. What is the chief advantage of using natural gas instead of oil or coal? 3. Why do some groups oppose strip mining? 4. What are the main arguments for and against continuing to develop resources as we have in the past?

Discuss. Should we relax some of the standards that have been set for a cleaner environment? Why or why not?

4 Protecting Our Future

Over 100 years ago, in 1872, the government of the United States set aside a portion of northwestern Wyoming as a national park. Its forests, rivers, waterfalls, geysers, hot springs, and wildlife became the property of all the American people. The land was to remain in its natural state, to be enjoyed as a place of beauty and an area for outdoor recreation. The region was named Yellowstone National Park. Since then, 36 other National Parks, containing over 6 million hectares (15 million acres) of land, have been reserved for recreational use.

EARLY CONSERVATION EFFORTS

The National Park Service of the United States is only one of many agencies that help to preserve the natural resources of our country. Early in the 1900's, President Theodore Roosevelt began this movement by calling a conference of the governors of the states to consider how best to conserve our land and resources. Gifford Pinchot was appointed as the first head of the National Forest Service, which supervises vast areas of our forest land to help conserve the timber in our nation. Later, laws were passed to limit the amount of oil and minerals that could be taken from the ground each year. Laws governing grazing practices helped to stop the destruction of our grasslands. The Department of Agriculture of the federal government, and also the state governments, encouraged and helped farmers to use soil conservation methods.

Under President Franklin D. Roosevelt, as you have read, a program of **soil banks** was established. It set aside land to be improved and renewed. Dams were built to irrigate farm lands and to control floods. The dams also provide electricity for rural areas and furnish recreation areas.

These efforts, however, did not stop waste and pollution. By the 1950's, concerned citizens such as Rachel Carson began to point out that an environmental crisis was at hand. In 1962, in her best-selling book *Silent Spring*, she warned that the entire earth was in danger because of our misuse of resources. Today we know that drastic measures are needed if America is to remain a fit place to live in.

THE FEDERAL GOVERNMENT'S EFFORTS

America has a number of national leaders who are aware of the seriousness of our environmental crisis. They have been responsive to the demands of interested citizens who urge action at once. But have they gone far enough, fast enough? During the 1960's and 1970's, each session of Congress saw new and stricter laws passed for the control of pollution and the restoration of the environment. The following were the most significant of these acts.

THE NATIONAL ENVIRONMENTAL POLICY ACT

Sometimes called the "Environmental Bill of Rights," this act of 1969 set up a **Council on Environmental Quality** to advise the President and to oversee the nation's pollution controls. As a result of advice from this body, stricter laws were passed regulating the use of pesticides, the control of oil spills, and ocean dumping. The council also favored the recycling of paper, more effective noise control, and international cooperation for the improvement of the environment. The National Environmental Policy Act also provides that every federal agency must make and publish an environmental impact statement. This is a study describing the expected effects on the environment of any project to be undertaken with federal aid.

CLEAN AIR ACTS

Originally passed in 1955, an act for cleaning the air was amended and strengthened several times. These **clean air acts** provide funds for research and set standards to be met by all air polluters. They also make it possible for the government to stop certain forms of air pollution. The automobile industry, for example, was given until 1980 to develop engines that would give off minimum amounts of exhaust pollution.

Oil spilled from tankers or offshore wells can wash up on nearby beaches, ruining them for wildlife and for people. These people are trying to clean up after an oil spill.

WATER POLLUTION CONTROL ACTS

As early as 1899, Congress passed a law making it a crime to dump refuse into any navigable waterway. This law was not strictly enforced until recent times. Now it has been strengthened by the Water Quality Act of 1965, which set standards of water quality for the interstate and coastal waters of the United States. Again in 1966 and 1969, clean water acts were passed by Congress. Under these acts, the federal government has helped local communities build sewage treatment plants. In 1972, a law was passed to stop the discharge of wastes into our waters by 1985.

OTHER ACTS OF CONGRESS

Americans in favor of a better environment have also brought pressure on Congress to preserve the beauty of the land and to conserve its wildlife. The **National Wild Rivers Act** and the **Wilderness Act** set aside areas to be kept in their natural state for the pleasure of people. **Endangered Species Acts** have listed wildlife that should be protected. About 1,700 plants and 170 animals in the United States alone are threatened with extinction. Laws have been passed to keep them from dying out and to help them multiply. To save wildlife in other parts of the world, our federal laws forbid the importation of the feathers and skins of many animals for use in clothing and in other unnecessary ways.

THE ENVIRONMENTAL PROTECTION AGENCY (EPA)

Many of the federal bureaus that deal with pollution and other ecological problems have been organized under an independent agency. This government agency reports directly to the President of the United States. Called the **Environmental Protection Agency,** this or-

This rocky coastline is part of a state park. As our land becomes more crowded, it is more important than ever to safeguard our remaining wilderness areas.

ganization includes several offices dealing with water and air pollution. It also oversees the management of solid wastes and radiation. In addition, the agency deals with pesticide problems and carries out studies of ecological systems.

STATE AND LOCAL ACTIVITIES

Every state government and most local governments have laws that help to provide better environments for their citizens. These laws range from provisions for the preservation of the state's natural resources and scenic beauty to local laws governing trash disposal. Some states have taken giant steps forward by studying large areas and launching programs to preserve or restore their ecological balance. The state of Oregon, for example, has placed its entire Pacific shoreline in the public domain. It is also planning to preserve its natural beauty. The state of New York has set up a Department of Environmental Conservation with powers to set standards for purer air and water. It enforces these standards with heavy fines. Some states have passed laws regulating soda bottles. These laws require that soft drinks and some other liquids must be sold in bottles. Customers who return their bottles will receive payments for them.

In our local communities, we can often

see how well or how poorly the environment is being protected. Smoke, for example, is a sign of air pollution. Many communities have laws against open-air burning of leaves, grass, and trash. They also have laws against unnecessary smoke from chimneys and smokestacks. Litter can be seen along roads and in streams. The "litterbug" is often subject to fines. But anti-litter laws are often not enforced as strictly as they should be. Signs of water pollution that may be seen locally are oil slick along our beaches and dead fish in rivers, lakes, and bays, caused by chemical or thermal pollution. Local citizens can also be aware of unpleasant odors in the air, smog, smoldering city dumps, and many other signs of pollution. All of these conditions can be improved if citizens are willing to take action in their own communities.

THE WORK OF CONSERVATION GROUPS

Have you ever heard of the Sierra Club? It is a private organization of citizens whose purpose is to improve our environment. The members of the Sierra Club issue books to inform the public about our environment, and urge needed legislation at state and federal levels. The club members also hire lawyers to bring suits against polluters, and aid research in better ecological procedures.

Other groups work to set aside public park lands and wildlife preserves, and to help restore the balance of nature where it has been interfered with. Among these groups are Friends of the Earth, The National Audubon Society, The National Wildlife Society, and The Isaak Walton League.

CONSERVATION AND THE INDIVIDUAL CITIZEN

Federal, state, and local laws cannot guarantee that our environment will be saved. Even huge amounts of money will not do the job. The future of our nation and of our earth depends upon the cooperation of every inhabitant of this small planet. The task begins with you, the individual citizen. As more and more individuals become actively involved, the hope for the future increases.

Here are some suggestions about steps you and your classmates can take now to help conserve America's resources:

1. *Be careful* of fires when in a forest or wooded area. Put out your campfire with water. Then shovel dirt on it to be sure it is out.
2. *Prevent waste* of all kinds in your home and school. Don't waste food, water, electricity, or anything else.
3. *Take part* with your class in a conservation project, such as tree planting, cleaning up streams, or soil conservation.
4. *Take an interest* in the natural resources that you find all around you in your community. Study ways in which they might be used more wisely. You may wish to join a conservation group such as those you have read about in this chapter.
5. *Participate* in recycling projects. Newspapers, cans, bottles, scrap metal, and other materials can be reused in new products. Find out about companies in your area that accept such materials, and join in collection projects.
6. *Do not destroy* wildlife, or damage forests or other public places. Vandalism is a serious crime against the environment.
7. *Obey laws* against open burning, littering, pollution, and other crimes against the environment.
8. *Keep informed* on ecological problems, and make your opinion felt by writing to your governmental representatives. Attend meetings and back petitions for a better environment.
9. *Be aware* of the sources of noise pollution, and join the fight for a quieter America.
10. *Get the facts* about population growth. Start thinking about what you can do to help keep the world a fit place for people.

CONSIDER AND DISCUSS

Identify. Council on Environmental Quality / clean air acts / water pollution control acts / National Wild Rivers Act / Wilderness Act / Endangered Species Act / Environmental Protection Agency

Review. 1. What have been some of the landmarks in the conservation movement? 2. Why is the National Environmental Policy Act sometimes called the "Environmental Bill of Rights"? 3. Describe the work of the Environmental Protection Agency. 4. How can the average citizen help to conserve our natural resources?

Discuss. What are some of the conservation activities being carried on in your community currently? What things could you do to help?

CHAPTER

Summary

Many of our practices have upset nature's balance. Air and water pollution are among our greatest problems. In recent years, we have also become aware of the dangers of noise pollution. Little has been done so far about pollution, although there has been much publicity about it. Elimination of pollution practices will be costly. But the cost must be met.

To understand the effects of pollution, we must understand ecology—the study of nature's balance and the relation between every part of the environment. Damage to any part of nature may result in damage to all of it, including the welfare of humans themselves.

Unwise development of land and the misuse of natural resources has resulted in the destruction of wildlife, ruin of scenic and recreational areas, and interference with the balance of nature. National problems have been caused by oil spills, land fill, construction of too many dams, highways, and buildings, and the use of DDT and other insecticides. In addition, we are faced with shortages of natural resources, especially of energy resources—oil, natural gas, and coal. Overpopulation is also a threat to the land and its limited resources. The basic environmental question facing the American people is how we can continue to prosper and still conserve our environment.

The conservation movement that began in the early 1900's emphasized the preservation of America's forests and improvement of farming methods. Today's environmental problems have added a new urgency to conservation—now called the "wise use" of natural resources. Federal, state, and local laws are being passed. Conservation groups are active. But the individual citizens must be aware, and do their share and work toward a better environment, now and for the future.

VOCABULARY

List each of the following words in your notebook. Next to each word write a good definition.

renewable resources	environment
ecology	pollution
wildlife	conservation
topsoil	water cycle
erosion	soil bank

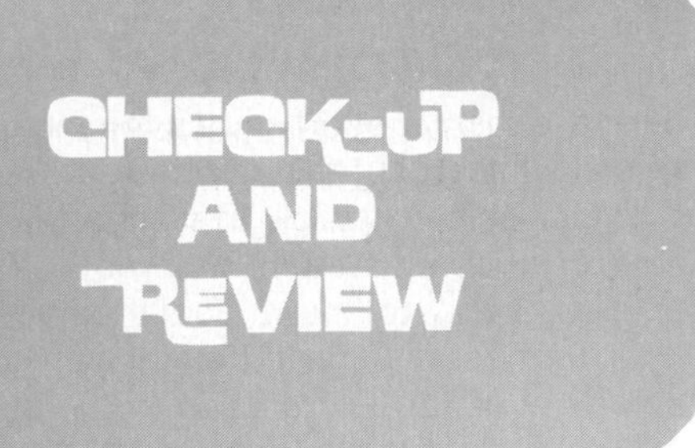

CHECK-UP

Write out brief answers to the following questions, and come to class prepared to discuss each answer.

1. How have humans upset nature's balance in North America?
2. Why has water supply become a problem in the United States?
3. What is ecology and why is it important to each citizen?
4. How have fertilizers and pesticides caused problems for the environment?
5. What are some of the suggested remedies for water, air, and noise pollution?
6. How could air pollution change the earth's climate?
7. Why has the federal government set up national parks and seashores?
8. What are some of the measures taken by farmers to conserve the soil?
9. What are the dangers of overpopulation?
10. How can the individual help to conserve our natural resources?

CITIZENSHIP AND YOU

The following projects are suggested to help you learn more about ecology and conservation.

1. Class Projects

A number of trips may be planned to observe good and bad practices in regard to our habitat. Some might be taken by the entire class and others by committees that report to the class. Places to visit might be a farm where soil conservation is practiced, a forest reserve, local dams, wildlife refuges, and recycling plants.

Invite a forest ranger to visit your class and to describe the work.

Read one of the many excellent books on ecology and discuss its viewpoint.

Participate in an antipollution drive or other local effort to clean up the environment.

2. Group or Committee Projects

Conduct a panel discussion on the topic, "Ecological Problems and Practices in Our State."

An art committee can prepare posters, charts, graphs, and maps for a display on the problems of pollution.

Another idea for a display on ecology in America is to collect pamphlets and booklets from various agencies interested in a better, cleaner America, and to display them in the classroom.

Groups within your class may take part in practical conservation projects close at hand. Some civics groups have improved their school grounds, gathered papers and cans for recycling, and planted trees. They also have distributed literature on antipollution subjects.

3. Individual Projects

Prepare a scrapbook of articles and pictures on problems and practices for improving the environment.

Make a chart showing the water cycle. Explain how humans have interfered with the regular operation of nature's cycle.

Draw a cartoon showing the results of careless camping or of the wasteful use of energy resources.

CIVICS SKILLS

WORKING IN YOUR COMMUNITY

There are many opportunities for you to take part in worthwhile, real-life activities during your study of civics. This textbook has already pointed out some of these possibilities. You could work at part-time jobs to learn about careers and job opportunities. You could help in a political party's campaign in order to learn how our political parties work. Or you can take part in class projects and activities in order to learn to work with others. There are many other useful and interesting things that you can do in your community while you are still a student.

In your study of ecology, for example, you have learned about a number of ways in which you can contribute to a better environment. Drives to collect used papers, cans, bottles, and other materials that can be recycled are practical projects. The school grounds may be beautified by your class or a committee. Information on pollution prevention may be distributed by your group. Local organizations interested in improving your local environment will be glad to get your help.

You can learn more from your studies if you take an active part in learning activities. You can participate in class projects, take part in class discussions, and contribute to such learning activities as bulletin-board displays, art projects, interviews, class surveys, and many others. In this way, you can become an active learner. Taking part in such activities will help you to gain more information. It will also give you valuable practice in skills that will prove useful throughout your life.

PRACTICING YOUR CIVICS SKILLS

Here are some conservation exercises that can be planned and carried out by your class in your local community:

1. Cooperate with groups that are collecting papers, aluminum cans, and other materials for recycling.
2. Find out what groups in your community are active in the movement to protect the environment, and work with them.
3. Prepare posters on conservation topics and display them in schools, store windows, and other suitable places.
4. Prepare the soil, plant a class garden, and harvest a crop.
5. Obtain trees from your state forestry or agricultural department (usually available free) and plant them where they are most needed.
6. Form a group to plan a campaign for cleaning up or beautifying your neighborhood. Try to get parents, store owners, and other adults in the area to participate in the activities.

Take photographs of good and bad conservation practices in your local community. Display the pictures in class. How could your community improve its environmental practices? What does the class think it could do to help?

Glossary of Civics Terms

This glossary is a handy civics dictionary. It contains many of the words you need to understand in your study of civics. After each word there is a brief definition, or explanation, of the meaning of the word or term as it is usually used in civics. Note that the meanings given in this glossary also show the way in which these words and terms are used in your textbook.

The brief definitions in this civics glossary do not always provide you with all the information that you will need about many of these civics words and terms. In most cases, however, your textbook will provide a more complete discussion. Therefore, you will find it useful to turn to the index of this book. The index will tell you the pages of the book on which you can read more about any of the words or terms. Remember, this glossary is included to help you. Develop the habit of making use of it as you continue your study of civics.

Absolute monarch: an all-powerful king or queen.

Addict: a person who is physically dependent, or "hooked," on a habit-forming drug.

Adjourn: to end a session of Congress or of a state legislature.

Alcoholism: addiction to alcohol (liquor).

Alien: a person who lives in or visits a nation but who is not a citizen of that nation.

Alliance: a treaty agreement between nations, usually for purposes of defense.

All-volunteer army: armed forces made up entirely of volunteers, with no draft.

Ambassador: an official who represents his or her government in a foreign country.

Amendment: a change or addition made in the Constitution.

Anthropologist: a social scientist who studies the physical, social, and cultural development of human beings.

Appeal: the right of a convicted person to ask a higher court to review his or her case.

Appellate jurisdiction: the authority given to some courts to review cases that already have been tried in a lower court.

Appropriation bills (or **money bills**): bills that call for the spending of public money.

Articles of Confederation: our nation's first government, in effect from 1781 to 1789.

Assembly: name of the lower house of some state legislatures.

Audit: a careful examination, or study, by an accountant of government or business expenditures.

Auditor: an official who examines the record of the income and expenditures of a government or a business.

Australian ballot: a system that allows the voter to mark a printed ballot in secret.

Bail: a sum of money deposited with a court as a pledge that the accused person will be in court at the time of trial.

Ballot: a list containing the names of candidates for office on which the voter casts his or her vote.

Bank: a business firm that deals in money and credit.

Bicameral legislature: a lawmaking body consisting of two houses.

Bill: a proposed law being considered by a lawmaking body.

Bill of attainder: a law sentencing a person to jail without granting him or her a fair public trial.

Bill of Rights: the first ten amendments to the Constitution, which set forth the basic rights, or freedoms, guaranteed to all Americans.

Blue-collar workers: persons who provide labor for business and industry or who operate special equipment.

Board of directors: the people who direct the affairs of a corporation, and who approve the corporation's business plans and policies.

Board of Education: the governing body of a school district.

Bonds: certificates of debt issued by governments or corporations to persons from whom they have borrowed money.

Budget: a plan of spending; a yearly plan of income and expenses of federal and local governments.

Budget Message: the President's recommendations to Congress on how the federal government is to raise and to spend its money.

Building code: the local laws that regulate the construction and repair of buildings in a community.

Bureaucracy: the individuals who are employed at all levels of federal, state, and local governments.

Cabinet: the people who head the executive departments in the federal government, who also act as advisers to the President.

Calendar: a schedule that lists the order in which bills are to be considered by a lawmaking body.

Candidates: the people who run for election to the offices in governments.

Capital: the property, machines, equipment, and money used to produce goods or provide services.

Capitalism (or **the Capitalistic system**): an economic system based on freedom and private ownership of the means of production.

Caucus: meeting of party leaders to determine the party's policy on proposed laws or to choose the party's candidates for public office.

Censorship: government control over what can be said or written.

Census: an official count of the number of people in the United States taken every ten years.

Certificate of naturalization: a document given to a naturalized American citizen to prove that he or she has been granted citizenship.

Charge account: a form of credit that allows a store's customers to receive goods now and pay for them later.

Charter: a plan of government granted by a state legislature to a local government. *Also* a document permitting a business firm to form a corporation.

Checks: written orders to a bank to have it pay a certain sum of money to the person or to the organization that is named on the check.

Checks and balances: the way in which the powers of government are balanced, or divided, among three branches so that each branch may check, or limit, the other branches.

Chief Executive: the President of the United States.

Chief Justice: the chief judge of the Supreme Court of the United States.

Citizen: a member of a country.

Citizenship: membership in a nation, carrying certain rights, duties, and responsibilities.

City Council: the lawmaking body of a city or town.

City Manager: head of a city government hired by the City Council to enforce city laws and to help govern the city.

Civics: the study of government and good citizenship in your community, school, family, state, and nation.

Civil case: a case between two or more individuals, to settle a dispute.

Civil disobedience: the act of deliberately disobeying a law that one believes to be unjust.

Civil rights: the political rights guaranteed to all American citizens by the Bill of Rights, together with many other social and economic rights.

Civil service: the system used by our federal, state, and local governments to hire workers to fill government jobs.

Closed primary: primary elections in which only voters who are members of the party vote to choose the party's candidates.

Closed shop: a business arrangement in which a worker may not be hired unless he or she is already a member of a union.

Cloture: the limit on debate in the Senate, must be voted by three fifths of the members.

Cold War: the worldwide political struggle that developed between the United States and the Soviet Union after World War II.

Collateral: property used to guarantee that a loan will be paid back.

Collective bargaining: representatives of a labor union and the employer working to reach an agreement about wages or working conditions.

Command economy: a business system in which the government completely controls, or commands, the nation's economy.

Commander-in-Chief: the President as head of the armed forces.

Commercial bank: a bank whose major purpose is to make loans and handle checking accounts.

Commercial treaty: a treaty in which two or more nations agree to trade on favorable terms.

Commissioners: heads of city departments. *Also* the heads of certain federal and state government agencies.

Committee of the Whole: the Senate or House of Representatives acting as one committee to discuss a bill.

Committee on committees: the group within each party, in the Senate and the House of Representatives, that assigns party members to the various standing committees.

Committees: small groups into which Congress is divided in order to consider bills.

Common law: customary law that develops from judges' decisions.

Common stock: corporations' stock on which dividends are paid and which give the owner the right to have a vote in corporate affairs.

Communism: economic theories of Marx and Engels based on the common ownership of property by the people. Basis of the governments of many countries, including the Soviet Union and the People's Republic of China.

Community: a group of people who have common interests, who live in the same area, and who are governed by the same laws.

Community college: a two-year college, often supported by local taxpayers.

Community planning commission: an official group that works to improve conditions in the city by planning programs to end slums, to build parks and roads, and to make other community improvements.

Comptroller: a government official whose job is to make sure that public funds are spent as authorized by law.

Concurrent powers: powers shared by state and federal governments.

Conference committee (See **Joint conference committee.**)

Conglomerate: a large company that controls many different kinds of smaller companies.

Congress: the lawmaking body of the federal government.

Congressional districts: divisions of a state in each of which the voters elect one member of the House of Representatives.

Congressional Record: the official record of all speeches made and votes taken in both houses of Congress.

Conservation: using natural resources wisely in order to insure an adequate supply of these resources in the future.

Constituents: people of a district who are represented by the members of a lawmaking body.

Constitution: a written plan of government describing how a government is organized, listing its purpose, some of the basic laws, and the rights of the people.

Constitution of the United States: the plan of the American government set up in 1789 to be the supreme law of our land.

Constitutional: within the limits and safeguards of the Constitution.

Consul: an American embassy official in a foreign city who works to promote American trade and who aids American citizens who do business there.

Consumer: one who buys or uses products and services.

Containment: American policy of preventing Communism from spreading.

Convention: an official meeting of a political party.

Corporation: a business chartered by a state government and given power to issue stocks, own property, make contracts, and sue and be sued in court.

Council member-at-large: a member of a local council elected by all the voters of the area.

County: subdivision of state government established to carry out state laws, collect taxes, and supervise elections.

County Board: the lawmaking body of a county government.

County Manager (or **County Executive**): an official hired by the County Board to carry on the work of the county government.

County seat: the town or city in which the county government is located.

County-township government: a mixed form of a local government in which county and township governments work side by side to help the people govern their local affairs.

Court of Claims: federal court that hears property claims against the federal government.

Courts of Appeals: federal (or state) courts to which a convicted person may take his or her case for review.

Craft union: a union organized among all members of a craft, or skilled trade.

Credit: a promise to pay money at some future time for goods or services received now.

Credit rating: a record of how well a customer pays his or her bills.

Crime: any act that breaks the law or fails to fulfill some requirement of the law.

Criminal case: a court case in which a person is accused by the state of breaking a law.

Cultural heritage: the knowledge and traditions of a people that are passed from generation to generation.

Currency: the coins and paper bills that are used as money.

Customs Court: federal court that hears cases involving import taxes.

Day care center: place where young children may be left to be cared for while their parents work.

Debt limit: a limit on the amount of money that a government may borrow.

Declaration of Independence: a key document of American freedom, adopted on July 4, 1776, declaring the thirteen American colonies to be free and independent of Great Britain.

Delegated powers: specific powers in the Constitution given to Congress.

Delegates: representatives who attend the convention of a political party.

Democracy: a form of government in which the people rule themselves either directly or through elected representatives.

Depositors: persons who keep checking accounts and savings accounts in a bank.

Depressants: sleeping pills, tranquilizers, and other drugs that depress the nervous system.

Depression: a sharp decline in a nation's business activity, during which workers lose their jobs and in which wages and prices decline.

Dictatorship: a government in which all power is in the hands of one person or a group of persons.

Diplomatic corps: a nation's ambassadors and ministers.

Direct democracy: a form of government in which all the people meet together in one place to make laws and to decide what actions the nation should take.

Discrimination: unfair treatment of someone because he or she belongs to a particular group.

Dissent: to disagree, to hold or express a different opinion.

District Attorney: a government lawyer who presents cases in court for the federal, state, or local government.

District Courts: the federal courts which have original jurisdiction in most cases involving federal laws.

District of Columbia: a federal district in the eastern United States wholly occupied by the city of Washington, the nation's capital.

Dividends: profits paid to the stockholders of a corporation.

Division of labor: a system in which each worker does a portion of a total job.

Domestic Relations Courts: special state courts for cases involving family disputes and the rights of children.

Dropouts: students who leave high school before graduation.

Drug abuse: the taking of drugs in amounts that may cause addiction or be harmful.

Due process: the right of all Americans to the same fair procedures under the law.

Ecology: the relation of all living things to their environment and to each other.

Economic Message: the President's review of the nation's economic condition, presented each year to Congress along with programs to aid the economy.

Economist: a specialist who studies economics.

Economy: a nation's system of producing, distributing, and consuming goods and services.

Education: the process of learning information and skills that are useful and necessary throughout life.

Elastic clause: Article 1, Section 8, of the Constitution, or the "necessary and proper" clause, that allows Congress to extend the powers of the Constitution to cover many other areas.

Election: The method by which citizens vote for officials at the local, state, or federal levels of government.

Electoral College: the men and women who cast the official votes that elect the President and Vice-President.

Environment: our natural surroundings, such as rivers and lakes, trees, earth, the ocean, and air.

Estate tax: a tax on the money, property, and other valuables left when a person dies.

Ex post facto law: a law that is passed making illegal an action that occurred in the past.

Excise tax: a federal tax collected on certain articles produced and sold in the United States.

Executive branch: the branch of our federal, state, or local government that enforces laws.

Executive departments: the twelve major departments in the executive branch of the federal government, the heads of which form the President's Cabinet.

Executive sessions: meetings of Congressional committees that are held in private and are closed to the public.

Exhaustible resources: natural resources that may be used up if they are not conserved.

Expenditures: government and business spending, or expenses.

Exports: goods and services that are sold to other countries.

Extracurricular activities: school activities in addition to classes, such as school clubs, sports teams, band, and social events.

Extradition: returning escaped prisoners or accused persons from one state back to the state where the crime was committed.

Factors of production: the four means of production—land, labor, capital, and management.

Family: a group of persons united by marriage, blood, or adoption.

Farm price-support program: a program of our federal government that pays American farmers part of the price of a crop in order to increase their income.

Farmers' cooperatives (co-ops): groups of farmers who join together to market their crops in order to get the highest prices possible.

Fascism: a dictatorship form of government in Italy and Germany during the 1930's headed by a single strong leader.

Favorite sons: popular men or women in a state party, usually a Governor or Senator, for whom that state's delegates often vote on the first ballot at the National Nominating Convention.

Featherbedding: the practice among some unions of forcing employers to hire or keep workers who are not needed.

Federal government: the national government of our nation.

Federal Reserve System: banking system in the United States that handles banking needs of the federal government and regulates the supply of money.

Federal Union (or **federal system**): the American system of government in which the powers of government are divided between the national government, which governs the whole American nation, and state governments, which govern the people of each state.

Fees: money payments charged by state and local governments for licenses. *Also,* charges for professional services.

Felonies: serious crimes, such as burglary, kidnapping, or murder, usually punishable by more than one year in jail.

Filibustering: a method of delaying or preventing a vote on a bill by making long speeches.

Fines: money paid to local governments as a penalty by citizens who break certain laws.

Floor leaders: party leaders in both houses of Congress who try to pass the bills that their party favors.

Foreign relations (or **foreign policy**): the way a nation conducts its relations with the other nations of the world.

Franchise: a permit granted to a business firm giving it the right to operate a public service.

Free competition: the right of business firms to produce goods and services and to compete with one another for customers.

Free enterprise system: the American economic system, based on the right to own and operate business firms, or enterprises, for the purpose of earning a profit.

Free market: the right to buy and sell any product or service we choose.

Free trade: the exchange of goods between countries without tariffs or any other kinds of trade barriers.

Freedom of assembly: the right to meet with others in public meetings to work together, to discuss problems, and to plan common actions.

Freedom of petition: the right to ask the government to take certain actions.

Freedom of the press: the right to express any idea and opinion in writing.

Freedom of religion: the right to worship or practice any religion or no religion at all.

Freedom of speech: the right to express ideas and opinions as well as to listen to the thoughts and opinions of others.

General elections: elections in which the American voters elect the leaders of their government.

Gift tax: a tax collected on large sums of money given as gifts by individuals.

Government: the authority, or power, that rules on behalf of a group of people.

Governor: the head of the executive branch in our state governments.

Grand jury: the group of persons that hears the evidence in a case and decides whether there is reason enough to bring the accused person to trial.

Great Compromise: the agreement reached by the Constitutional Convention that all the states should have equal representation in the Senate and be represented according to the size of their populations in the House of Representatives.

Gross National Product (GNP): the total value of the goods and services produced in a nation each year.

Habeas corpus: an official paper requiring that a person accused of a crime be brought into court and be given a fair trial without unreasonable delay.

Hallucinogens: drugs that cause hallucinations, for example, LSD, mescaline, and peyote.

Hearings: special meetings called by Congressional committees to consider a bill.

House of Representatives (or **the House**): the lower house of Congress in which states are represented according to their population.

Ideals: basic beliefs or standards

of conduct that people attempt to live up to.

Immigrant: a person who comes to a nation to settle as a permanent resident.

Impeachment: formal charge, or indictment, brought against a government official. In the federal government, the House of Representatives has the power to impeach the President and other high officials.

Implied powers: authority not specifically granted to Congress by the Constitution but which is implied, or suggested, to be necessary in order to carry out the specific powers.

Imports: goods and services that are purchased from other countries.

Inaugural Address: the speech made by the President at the time the oath of office is taken.

Income: a payment of money received for contributing labor, land, capital, or management in the production of goods or services.

Independent agencies: agencies in the executive branch of the federal government established to help the President enforce laws and regulations.

Indicted: formally accused of a crime by a grand jury.

Industrial Revolution: the great expansion of business and industry in the 1800's caused by the introduction of new machines and new forms of power.

Industrial union: a union that includes all workers in an industry.

Inflation: a period of rising prices for goods and services.

Inheritance tax: a tax on money and property received from an estate.

Inner city: term that is used to refer to old, run-down areas of large cities. Often used in the same way as "slum."

Installment buying: a system of buying in which the buyer makes a cash down payment and then pays the balance over a period of time.

Insurance: a planned method of saving by which an individual makes regular payments for protection against emergencies, such as fire, theft, or loss of life.

Interest: payment for the use of money or for a loan.

Internal Revenue Service: the federal agency that collects income taxes.

Interstate Highway System: a network of superhighways connecting all parts of the country, built jointly by the federal and state governments.

Invest: to use money to buy buildings, machinery, or other means of production.

Isolationism: the policy of avoiding all involvement in foreign affairs.

Joint Chiefs of Staff: the group made up of the highest military officer from each service—Army, Navy, Air Force, and Marines—that advises the President on military affairs.

Joint committee: a committee made up of members of both houses of Congress which meets to discuss matters of interest to both houses.

Joint conference committee: a committee made up of members of the two houses of Congress which attempts to resolve the differences in the versions of the same bills passed by the House and the Senate.

Judicial branch: the branch of the federal, state, or local governments that decides if laws have been broken and that punishes lawbreakers.

Judicial review: the power of the Supreme Court to decide whether a law passed by Congress or by state or local governments violates any provision of the Constitution.

Junior college: a college with a two-year program of study.

Jurisdiction: the authority to judge and administer the laws. *Also* the extent or range of that authority.

Jurisdictional strike: a strike to determine which labor union will represent workers.

Jurors: men and women of the trial jury who judge the evidence and determine the verdict in a court case.

Justice Court: a lower state court in rural areas and towns that tries misdemeanors and civil cases involving small sums.

Justice of the Peace: the judge who presides over a state Justice Court.

Justices: title for judges who serve on the Supreme Court.

Juvenile Courts: lower state courts that hear cases involving young persons, usually under 18 years of age.

Juvenile delinquents: young persons, usually under 18 years of age, who commit crimes.

Labor: large groups of workers or the total work force. *Also* any kind of work that helps to produce goods or to provide services.

Labor contract: a written agreement between a labor union and an employer that spells out workers' wages and their working conditions.

Labor unions: organizations of workers established to protect workers' rights and to bargain for higher wages and for improved working conditions.

Land: the soil and all of the natural resources and raw materials used to produce goods.

Law of supply and demand: a general rule which states that the price of an item is determined by the relationship between its availability and its need at any particular time.

Laws: all the rules of conduct of a nation that are enforced by government or by custom.

Legal tender: paper money and coins that all Americans must accept as payment in exchange for goods and services.

Legislative branch: the branch of our federal, state, or local government that makes the laws.

Legislator: a state lawmaker or member of a state legislature.

Legislature: a lawmaking body of the local, state, or federal government.

Literacy test: a test that required voters to prove that they could read and write English before being allowed to vote, now illegal.

Lobbyists: people who are paid to represent a certain group's point of view at Congressional committee hearings and who try to influence the votes of members of Congress.

Local government: term applied to government in a city or town, county-township, or other local area.

Local school board (or **board of education**): a group of individuals who are responsible for managing the public schools in a community or locality.

Magistrate's Court: a type of city court that has an elected judge and that hears minor cases without a jury.

Majority leader: the floor leader of the majority party in Congress and in state legislatures.

Majority party: the political party that has elected the greater number of members of Congress or of a state legislature.

Management: the people who run a business firm and decide how it should operate.

Manslaughter: a legal term that means the unplanned killing of a person. In some states it may be known as second-degree murder.

Marijuana: a drug, usually smoked, with intoxicating effects, whose long-range effects are not fully known.

Marketing: transporting and moving products from the producer to the customer. *Also* refers to the method of selling the goods or services.

Marshal: the official in each federal District Court who makes arrests, issues subpoenas, and carries out the orders of the court.

Martial law: the limitation of people's rights and freedoms, under military authority, during a state of emergency.

Mass marketing: transporting and selling large amounts of goods to millions of customers. Also, the method of selling goods and services to millions of people.

Mass production: producing huge amounts of goods rapidly by machine to supply the needs and wants of many people.

Mass transit: public transportation, including buses, subways, and railroads.

Mayor: the chief executive of a city government.

Medicaid: the federal program to help poor people get hospital and medical services.

Medicare: the federal program of health insurance for people aged 65 and over.

Megalopolis: a continuous urban area that includes many cities and extends over a vast area.

Mental illness: a sickness of the mind caused by damage, stress, drugs, or other factors.

Metropolitan area: a large city and its nearby suburbs and small towns.

Migrant workers: farm workers who move from place to place with the seasons in order to pick crops.

Minority group: a group that is set apart from other people in the same society because of race, nationality, language, customs, or religion and that usually has no political power.

Minority leader: the floor leader of the minority party in Congress and in state legislatures.

Minority party: the political party that has elected less than a majority of the members of Congress or of a state legislature.

Misdemeanors: less serious crimes, such as traffic violations and disorderly conduct.

Mixed economy: a system in which both business and government make decisions that affect the economic situation of the country.

Moderator: the official who presides over a town meeting.

Money: the paper and coins that are a nation's standard means of exchange used to purchase goods and services.

Monopoly: a business firm that produces and markets all or a large part of the total supply of a product or service.

Narcotics: habit-forming, pain-killing drugs such as morphine, codeine, and heroin.

National Committee: the top committee of each American political party.

National debt: the total amount of money owed by the federal government of a country.

National Nominating Convention: a meeting held by the major political parties every four years to draw up the party platform and to choose the party candidates for President and Vice-President.

National Security Council: the group of top advisers to the President of the United States on matters concerning national defense.

Native-born citizens: Americans who are born citizens of the United States.

Natural resources: land, minerals, and other raw materials that nature has provided.

Naturalization: the legal method established by Congress by which aliens become American citizens.

Naturalized citizens: American citizens who were once aliens.

Neutrality: a policy of not favoring one side or the other in a conflict.

Nominate: to name candidates who will run for public office.

Northwest Ordinance: a measure passed by the Congress of the Confederation in 1787 which set up a plan for governing territories and forming them into states.

Oath of office: a declaration made by public officials upon taking office that they will perform their duties well and uphold the Constitution of the United States.

Open primary: a primary election in which the voters may vote for the candidates of any party.

Open shop: a labor arrangement in which workers may be hired by a business firm whether or not they belong to a union.

Ordinances: laws and regulations passed by local lawmaking bodies.

Original jurisdiction: the authority of some courts to hold trials first in certain kinds of cases.

Overpopulation: too many people for the resources of a country, or of the earth, to support.

Pardon: an official act by the President or by a Governor forgiving a person of a crime.

Parliament: the lawmaking body in the British government.

Parochial schools: private schools sponsored by religious groups.

Parole: to release a convicted person from prison (on certain conditions) before completion of the sentence.

Partnership: a business organization in which two or more persons share the ownership, the profits, and the losses of the business firm.

Party (See **Political party.**)

Party caucus (See **Caucus.**)

Party whip: an assistant to the floor leader in each house of Congress who tries to persuade members of the party to vote for all bills the party supports.

Passport: a document issued by the State Department which permits American citizens to travel abroad.

Peace Corps: American volunteer agency founded in 1961. Sends Americans overseas to help people in foreign nations learn needed skills.

Peers: one's equals; people like oneself.

Periodic registration: a system in which a citizen must register each year or every two years in order to vote.

Permanent registration: a system in which a citizen must register only once in order to vote.

Personal income tax: a federal or state tax on the income a person earns.

Personal property: money, stocks, jewelry, clothing, and furniture on which local property taxes may be collected.

Personnel record form: a form on which an employer asks job applicants to supply information about themselves.

Petition: a written request in which citizens ask a government to take certain actions.

Pigeonholing: putting bills aside in committee and not sending them to the whole Congress for further action.

Platform: a written statement that outlines a political party's ideas and describes the program it proposes.

Pocket veto: a means the President has of rejecting a bill passed by Congress. Any bill presented to the President within ten days before the end of the session is "pocket vetoed" if not signed before Congress adjourns.

Police power: the power of the government to regulate certain activities of people in order to insure domestic peace.

Police state: a kind of dictatorship where secret police are all-powerful.

Political party: an organization of citizens who have similar views on public issues and who work for the election of party members to public office in order to put these ideas into effect.

Poll tax: a special tax that had to be paid in order to vote, now illegal.

Polling place: the place where citizens go to vote.

Pollution: the contaminating of our earth, air, or water.

Poverty: having less than the minimum income needed for the necessities of life.

Preamble: the beginning of the Constitution, which describes its purposes. *Also* the beginning of a state constitution.

Precedent: an earlier court decision on which later decisions may be based.

Precincts: the local voting districts in larger cities.

Precinct captain: the political party leader in a local voting district.

Preferred stock: corporation stock on which fixed dividends are paid but which gives the owner no vote in corporate affairs.

Prejudice: an unfair opinion about members of a particular group.

Premiums: the payments made for insurance protection.

President: the Chief Executive, or head, of the executive branch of the federal government.

President pro tempore: the official who presides over the Senate when the Vice-President is absent.

Presidential preference primary: a kind of election held in some states in which voters select the Presidential candidate whom they wish their delegates to support at the party's Nominating Convention.

Presidential succession: the order in which the office of the President is to be filled when the office becomes vacant.

Presidential veto: the President's refusal to sign a bill, which is then sent back to Congress with a message giving the reasons for its rejection.

Price: the money value of a product or service.

Primary election: an election in which the voters of various parties choose their candidates to run for office in the general election.

Priorities: the order of importance of national needs.

Private property: land, equipment, and money owned by individuals and business firms.

Probation: suspension of a sentence of a person convicted of a crime but not yet in prison.

Professional workers: the most highly educated of the labor groups· includes scientists, doctors, teachers, lawyers.

Profit: income that a business has after expenses, paid to the owner of the business or its stockholders.

Propaganda: ideas or beliefs that are widely spread, even if false, in order to influence the way people feel or act.

Property taxes: local and state taxes collected on real property or personal property.

Prosperity: periods in a nation's economy in which business is good and wages are high.

Protective tariffs: high taxes on imported goods intended to protect American industries from foreign competition.

Public sessions: meetings of Congressional committees that are open to the public.

Public utilities: essential services required by people of the community, such as gas, electricity, water, and transportation.

Quorum: the minimum number of members who must be present before a legislative body can do business.

Quota system: a limit on the number of immigrants who may come to America.

Ratification: approval of a Constitutional amendment by the states.

Real property: land and buildings on which local property taxes are usually collected.

Recession: a small decline in a nation's business activity.

Reciprocal trade agreement: agreement by which nations lower tariffs on certain goods imported from each other.

Register: to place one's name in the official record of eligible voters in order to be able to vote.

Regulatory agencies: federal commissions and agencies set up to enforce many laws passed by Congress.

Renewable resources: natural resources that are not expected to run out, such as sunlight, water, and forests.

Rent: the payment for the use of property such as land and buildings.

Representative democracy (also known as a **republic**): a government in which the people elect representatives to do the work of governing.

Representative town meeting: town government in which the voters elect representatives to attend the town meeting and to make decisions for them.

Representatives: members of the House of Representatives.

Reprieve: to postpone carrying out a prison sentence.

Republic: a government in which the people elect representatives to govern for them.

Reserved powers: powers left to the state governments by the Constitution.

Revenue: government income.

Right-to-work laws: state laws that make it illegal to require a person to join a union to get or keep a job; prohibit closed shops and union shops.

Roll call vote: a vote in Congress in which the clerk records how each member votes.

Salary: regular, fixed income paid each week or month.

Sales tax: a state or city tax on any item or service that is sold to the public.

Satellite nations: term used to describe the Communist nations of Eastern Europe under the influence of the Soviet Union.

Saving: keeping money by setting it aside.

Savings bank: a bank whose major purpose is to handle savings accounts and lend and invest money.

School tax: a tax on property collected to support the local public schools.

Search warrant: a legal paper granted by a judge that permits a police officer to enter and search a private residence.

Secretary: the official who heads an executive department in the federal government.

Segregation: separation of people based on race; illegal in the United States in public schools, public accommodations, and in job consideration.

Selectmen: officials who manage a town's affairs during the period between regular town meetings.

Self-employed workers: workers who are in business for themselves.

Senate: the upper house of Congress in which each state has two Senators.

Senators: members of the United States Senate.

Senior Senator: the Senator from each state who was elected first.

Seniority: the status or rank that a member of Congress achieves because of a long period of service.

Separation of powers: the three-way division of power among the branches of the federal government.

Service workers: workers who perform services for the public, for example, repairers, hair cutters, and chauffeurs.

Sheriff: the chief law-enforcemen official in some county governments.

Single proprietorship (or **individual proprietorship**): a business firm owned by one person.

Slum: a rundown city area where apartments and houses need repairs and painting and where families live crowded together.

Social Security program: the system of federal laws that provides aid to unemployed, disabled, and retired workers, paid for by a special tax on workers and their employers.

Solar energy: power that is obtained by using the heat produced by the sun.

Speaker: the presiding officer of the House of Representatives.

Special session: a special meeting of Congress called by the President.

Split ticket: a ballot on which a person has voted for the candidates of more than one political party.

Standard parts: identical parts of a manufactured product that are mass produced and interchangeable.

Standing committee: a permanent Congressional committee that considers bills in a certain field of government.

State Department of Education: a state agency or department that assists the local school districts of the state.

State militia: a voluntary military organization that is called to preserve order during times of emergency; same as the state National Guard.

State of the Union Message: the yearly report of the President to Congress, as required by the Constitution, in which the nation's condition is described and programs are recommended.

State Representatives: members of the lower house of a state lawmaking body.

State Senators: members of the upper house of a state lawmaking body.

State trial courts: state courts that try the more serious civil and criminal cases arising under state laws.

States: the fifty largest units of government in the United States below the federal level.

Steering committee: a party committee in each house of Congress that helps the party floor leader and the party whip to steer, or guide, laws through Congress.

Stimulants: amphetamine, cocaine, diet pills, and other drugs that stimulate the nervous system.

Stock exchange: an organized market for the buying and selling of stocks.

Stocks: shares of ownership of a corporation.

Stockholders: persons who own stock in a corporation.

Straight ticket: a ballot in which a person votes for all the candidates of the same political party.

Strong-Mayor plan: a form of city government in which the Mayor has strong executive powers that are not limited by the City Council.

Subpoenas: official court documents that require persons to appear in court.

Subsidy: a money grant from the government to help support some activity.

Suburb: a residential community located near a large city.

Suffrage: the right to vote.

Summit conference: a term that refers to a meeting between the President of the United States and the leader or leaders of other large nations.

Superintendent of Schools: an official appointed by a local Board of Education to manage its schools.

Supreme Court: the highest court in the United States. *Also* the name given to the highest state courts in many of our states.

Tariff: a tax on imports.

Tax: a payment of money that people are required to make to help pay the costs of government.

Tax assessors: local officials who judge the value of property to determine how much the property tax on it will be.

Tax Court: the court that hears cases involving federal taxes.

Third parties: political organizations in the United States other than the Democratic and Republican parties, usually set up to work for special causes.

Third World: developing nations of Asia, Africa, and Latin America usually not aligned with the Communist or anti-Communist sides.

Totalitarian governments: nations in which the government has total power over the lives of the people.

Town meeting: a form of government in which all citizens of the town meet together to discuss their problems and to decide how to handle these problems.

Townships: local government units in the Middle Atlantic states that maintain local roads and rural schools within the county.

Trades: occupations such as the jobs of carpenters, bricklayers, plumbers, electricians, and others that require special manual training and skills.

Traffic Courts: the state courts for cases involving traffic violations.

Treaty: a written agreement between nations.

Trial jury: the men and women who hear the evidence and decide the verdict in a court case. Between six and twelve people may serve on a jury.

Unconstitutional: going against the Constitution, or beyond the powers granted by the Constitution.

Unemployment insurance: money paid to jobless workers under the Social Security program.

Unicameral legislature: a lawmaking body consisting of one house.

Union shop: a business arrangement in which workers are required to join the union after they are hired; made illegal in some states by right-to-work laws.

Unions (See **Labor unions.**)

Unit price: the price of an item per gram, ounce, pound, or other standard unit.

United Nations: the international organization to which most nations belong, which promotes world peace and progress.

Unwritten Constitution: the traditional ways of doing things in our federal government that are seldom written down or made into laws.

Urban communities: cities and towns with a population of 2,500 or more people.

Verdict: the decision of a jury.

Veto (See **Presidential veto.**)

Voice vote: a vote in which individuals announce aloud how they are voting.

Voting machine: a machine, usually in a large curtained booth, in which voters record their votes by pulling down levers to show the candidates they favor.

Wages: money earned by a worker each hour and paid daily or weekly.

Wards: election districts within cities or counties.

Warrant: an announcement of a town meeting. *Also* a written order for someone's arrest, or an order to pay out government funds.

Weak-Mayor plan: a form of city government in which most of the power is in the hands of the City Council and not in the office of the Mayor.

Welfare programs: the federal, state, and local programs that help support the poor.

White-collar workers: people who generally are self-employed or who do professional, technical, clerical, or sales work.

White House: the official residence of the President of the United States.

Withholding tax: that part of a person's earnings taken out for income tax.

Workers' compensation: benefits paid to a worker who is hurt on the job and cannot work.

Write-in votes: votes cast for a candidate whose name does not appear on the ballot and must be written in by the voter.

Zero population growth: rate of growth that replaces existing population but does not increase it.

Zoning: dividing a city into areas, or zones, each of which is reserved for certain types of building or businesses.

Zoning board: a city board that enforces the local zoning laws.

The Declaration of Independence

In Congress, July 4, 1776

The Unanimous Declaration of the Thirteen United States of America

Why the Declaration Was Written

When, in the course of human events, it becomes necessary for one people to dissolve the political bands which have connected them with another, and to assume, among the powers of the earth, the separate and equal station to which the laws of nature and of nature's God entitle them, a decent respect to the opinions of mankind requires that they should declare the causes which impel them to the separation.

Statement of Basic Human Rights

We hold these truths to be self-evident: That all men are created equal; that they are endowed by their Creator with certain unalienable rights; that among these are life, liberty, and the pursuit of happiness.

Government Must Safeguard Human Rights

That to secure these rights, governments are instituted among men, deriving their just powers from the consent of the governed; that, whenever any form of government becomes destructive of these ends, it is the right of the people to alter or to abolish it, and to institute a new government, laying its foundation on such principles, and organizing its powers in such form, as to them shall seem most likely to effect their safety and happiness. Prudence, indeed, will dictate that governments long established should not be changed for light and transient causes; and accordingly all experience hath shown that mankind are more disposed to suffer while evils are sufferable, than to right themselves by abolishing the forms to which they are accustomed. But when a long train of abuses and usurpations, pursuing invariably the same object, evinces a design to reduce them under absolute despotism, it is their right, it is their duty, to throw off such government, and to provide new guards for their future security.

Abuses of Human Rights by the King

Such has been the patient sufferance of these colonies; and such is now the necessity which constrains them to alter their former systems of government. The history of the present King of Great Britain is a history of repeated injuries and usurpations, all having in direct object the establishment of an absolute tyranny over these states. To prove this, let facts be submitted to a candid world.

He has refused his assent to laws the most wholesome and necessary for the public good.

He has forbidden his governors to pass laws of immediate and pressing importance, unless suspended in their operation till his assent should be obtained; and, when so suspended, he has utterly neglected to attend to them.

He has refused to pass other laws for the accommodation of large districts of people, unless those people would relinquish the right of representation in the legislature, a right inestimable to them, and formidable to tyrants only.

He has called together legislative bodies at places unusual, uncomfortable, and distant from the depository of their public records, for the sole purpose of fatiguing them into compliance with his measures.

He has dissolved representative houses repeatedly, for opposing, with manly firmness, his invasions on the rights of the people.

He has refused, for a long time after such dissolutions, to cause others to be elected, whereby the legislative powers, incapable of annihilation, have returned to the people at large for their exercise; the state remaining, in the mean time, exposed to all the dangers of invasions from without and convulsions within.

He has endeavored to prevent the population of these states; for that purpose obstructing the laws for the naturalization of foreigners, refusing to pass others to encourage their migration hither, and raising the conditions of new appropriations of lands.

He has obstructed the administration of justice, by refusing his assent to laws for establishing judiciary powers.

He has made judges dependent on his will alone for the tenure of their offices, and the amount and payment of their salaries.

He has erected a multitude of new offices, and sent hither swarms of officers to harass our people and eat out their substance.

He has kept among us in times of peace

standing armies, without the consent of our legislatures.

He has affected to render the military independent of, and superior to, the civil power.

He has combined with others to subject us to a jurisdiction foreign to our constitutions and unacknowledged by our laws, giving his assent to their acts of pretended legislation:

For quartering large bodies of armed troops among us;

For protecting them, by a mock trial, from punishment for any murders which they should commit on the inhabitants of these states;

For cutting off our trade with all parts of the world;

For imposing taxes on us without our consent;

For depriving us, in many cases, of the benefits of trial by jury;

For transporting us beyond seas, to be tried for pretended offenses;

For abolishing the free system of English laws in a neighboring province, establishing therein an arbitrary government, and enlarging its boundaries, so as to render it at once an example and fit instrument for introducing the same absolute rule into these colonies;

For taking away our charters, abolishing our most valuable laws, and altering, fundamentally, the forms of our governments;

For suspending our own legislatures, and declaring themselves invested with power to legislate for us in all cases whatsoever.

He has abdicated government here, by declaring us out of his protection and waging war against us.

He has plundered our seas, ravaged our coasts, burned our towns, and destroyed the lives of our people.

He is at this time transporting large armies of foreign mercenaries to complete the works of death, desolation, and tyranny already begun with circumstances of cruelty and perfidy scarcely paralleled in the most barbarous ages, and totally unworthy the head of a civilized nation.

He has constrained our fellow-citizens, taken captive on the high seas, to bear arms against their country, to become the executioners of their friends and brethren, or to fall themselves by their hands.

He has excited domestic insurrection among us, and has endeavored to bring on the inhabitants of our frontiers the merciless Indian savages, whose known rule of warfare is an undistinguished destruction of all ages, sexes, and conditions.

Colonial Efforts to Avoid Separation

In every stage of these oppressions we have petitioned for redress in the most humble terms; our repeated petitions have been answered only by repeated injury.

A prince whose character is thus marked by every act which may define a tyrant is unfit to be the ruler of a free people.

Nor have we been wanting in our attentions to our British brethren. We have warned them, from time to time, of attempts by their legislature to extend an unwarrantable jurisdiction over us. We have reminded them of the circumstances of our emigration and settlement here. We have appealed to their native justice and magnanimity; and we have conjured them, by the ties of our common kindred, to disavow these usurpations, which would inevitably interrupt our connections and correspondence. They, too, have been deaf to the voice of justice and consanguinity. We must, therefore, acquiesce in the necessity which denounces our separation, and hold them, as we hold the rest of mankind, enemies in war, in peace friends.

The Colonies Declare Their Independence

We, therefore, the representatives of the United States of America, in General Congress assembled, appealing to the Supreme Judge of the world for the rectitude of our intentions, do, in the name and by the authority of the good people of these colonies, solemnly publish and declare, That these united colonies are, and of right ought to be, free and independent states; that they are absolved from all allegiance to the British crown, and that all political connections between them and the state of Great Britain is, and ought to be, totally dissolved; and that, as free and independent states, they have full power to levy war, conclude peace, contract alliances, establish commerce, and do all other acts and things which independent states may of right do. And, for the support of this declaration, with a firm reliance on the protection of Divine Providence, we mutually pledge to each other our lives, our fortunes, and our sacred honor.

The Constitution of the United States

The parts of the text crossed out in blue have been changed by the passing of time or by later amendment. Explanations and comments are also in blue.

Preamble

The Preamble lists the reasons for writing the Constitution.

We, the people of the United States, in order to form a more perfect union, establish justice, insure domestic tranquillity, provide for the common defence, promote the general welfare, and secure the blessings of liberty to ourselves and our posterity, do ordain and establish this CONSTITUTION for the United States of America.

ARTICLE 1. Legislative Department

Section 1. Congress

The power to make laws is given to a Congress of two houses.

All legislative powers herein granted shall be vested in a Congress of the United States, which shall consist of a Senate and a House of Representatives.

Section 2. House of Representatives

Members of the House of Representatives are chosen every two years. They are elected directly by the voters who are qualified to vote for members of the state legislature.

1. **Election of Members and Term of Office.** The House of Representatives shall be composed of members chosen every second year by the people of the several States, and the electors in each State shall have the qualifications requisite for electors of the most numerous branch of the State Legislature.

Members of the House of Representatives must be at least 25 years old, and residents of the states that they represent.

2. **Qualifications.** No person shall be a Representative who shall not have attained to the age of twenty-five years, and been seven years a citizen of the United States, and who shall not, when elected, be an inhabitant of that State in which he shall be chosen.

The number of Representatives for each state is based on its population. Direct taxes also must be assessed according to population. [See Amendment 14.]

A federal, or national, census must be taken every ten years.

3. **Division of Representatives and Direct Taxes among the States.** Representatives ~~and direct taxes shall~~ be apportioned among the several States which may be included within this Union, according to their respective numbers, ~~which shall be determined by adding to the whole number of free persons, including those bound to service for a term of years, and excluding Indians not taxed, three fifths of all other persons.~~ The actual enumeration shall be made within three years after the first meeting of the Congress of the United States, and within every subsequent term of ten years, in such manner as they shall by law direct. The number of Representatives shall not exceed 1 for every 30,000, but each State shall have at least one representative; ~~and until such enumeration shall be made, the State of New Hampshire shall be entitled to choose three, Massachusetts eight, Rhode Island and Providence Plantations one, Connecticut five, New York six, New Jersey four, Pennsylvania eight, Delaware one, Maryland six, Virginia ten, North Carolina five, South Carolina five, and Georgia three.~~

Vacancies in the House of Representatives are filled by special elections.

4. **Filling Vacancies.** When vacancies happen in the representation from any State, the Executive authority thereof shall issue writs of election to fill such vacancies.

The House of Representatives has the power of impeachment.

5. **Officers; Impeachment.** The House of Representatives shall choose their Speaker and other officers; and shall have the sole power of impeachment.

Section 3. Senate

1. **Number of Members and Term of Office.** The Senate of the United States shall be composed of two Senators from each State, chosen by the Legislature thereof [see Amendment 17], for six years; and each Senator shall have one vote.

In the Senate, every state is represented equally by two Senators each. [Amendment 17 provides for the direct election of Senators.]

2. **Classification; Filling Vacancies.** ~~Immediately after they shall be assembled in consequence of the first election, they shall be divided as equally as may be into three classes. The seats of the Senators of the first class shall be vacated at the expiration of the second year, of the second class at the expiration of the fourth year, and of the third class at the expiration of the sixth year, so that one third may be chosen every second year; and if vacancies happen by resignation, or otherwise, during the recess of the Legislature of any State, the Executive thereof may make temporary appointments until the next meeting of the Legislature, which shall then fill such vacancies.~~ [See Amendment 17.]

One third of the Senators are elected every two years for a six-year term.

Senate vacancies are filled by new Senators appointed by the Governor of the state. Such Senators serve until the next general election.

3. **Qualifications of Members.** No person shall be a Senator who shall not have attained to the age of thirty years, and been nine years a citizen of the United States, and who shall not, when elected, be an inhabitant of that State for which he shall be chosen.

Senators must be at least 30 years old, United States citizens for at least 9 years, and residents of the state that they represent.

4. **President of the Senate.** The Vice-President of the United States shall be President of the Senate, but shall have no vote, unless they be equally divided.

The Vice-President is the presiding officer of the Senate, but may vote only in case of a tie.

5. **Other Senate Officers.** The Senate shall choose their other officers, and also a President *pro tempore,* in the absence of the Vice-President, or when he shall exercise the office of President of the United States.

The Senate elects a temporary presiding officer from among its members to serve when the Vice-President is absent or when he becomes President.

6. **Trial of Impeachments.** The Senate shall have the sole power to try all impeachments. When sitting for that purpose, they shall be on oath or affirmation. When the President of the United States is tried, the Chief Justice shall preside; and no person shall be convicted without the concurrence of two thirds of the members present.

The Senate has power to try impeachment cases. A two-thirds vote is needed to convict an impeached official.

7. **Penalty for Conviction in Impeachment Cases.** Judgment in cases of impeachment shall not extend further than to removal from office, and disqualification to hold and enjoy any office of honor, trust, or profit under the United States; but the party convicted shall nevertheless be liable and subject to indictment, trial, judgment, and punishment, according to law.

The Senate can remove from office officials convicted on impeachment charges. Such persons also may be tried in courts of law if they have broken any law.

Section 4. Both Houses

1. **Holding Elections.** The times, places, and manner of holding elections for Senators and Representatives shall be prescribed in each State by the Legislature thereof; but the Congress may at any time by law make or alter such regulations, except as to the place of choosing Senators.

Election regulations are set by the states. But Congress may pass laws relating to elections.

2. **Meetings.** The Congress shall assemble at least once in every year, ~~and such meeting shall be on the first Monday in December~~, unless they shall by law appoint a different day.

The meeting time of Congress was changed by Amendment 20. Congress now meets January 3.

Section 5. The Houses Separately

1. **Organization.** Each House shall be the judge of the elections, returns, and qualifications of its own members, and a majority of each shall constitute a quorum to do business; but a smaller number may adjourn from day to day, and may be authorized to compel the attendance of absent members, in such manner, and under such penalties, as each House may provide.

Each house of Congress decides whether its members are qualified and have been elected fairly. A majority of the members, or a quorum, must be present to carry on the work of each house.

Members of either house of Congress may be compelled to attend in order that business may be carried on.

2. **Proceedings.** Each House may determine the rules of its pro-

ceedings, punish its members for disorderly behavior, and, with the concurrence of two thirds, expel a member.

Each house of Congress must keep and publish an official record of its activities.

3. **Journal.** Each House shall keep a journal of its proceedings, and from time to time publish the same, excepting such parts as may in their judgment require secrecy; and the yeas and nays of the members of either House on any question shall, at the desire of one fifth of those present, be entered on the journal.

Neither house of Congress may adjourn for more than three days without the consent of the other house.

4. **Adjournment.** Neither House, during the session of Congress, shall, without the consent of the other, adjourn for more than three days, nor to any other place than that in which the two Houses shall be sitting.

Section 6. Privileges and Restrictions

Members of Congress are paid salaries and receive additional sums of money for certain expenses.

Members of Congress cannot be sued or arrested for anything they say in Congress. But they can be arrested for major crimes while Congress is in session.

Members of Congress cannot hold any other federal office while they serve in Congress.

1. **Pay and Privileges.** The Senators and Representatives shall receive a compensation for their services, to be ascertained by law, and paid out of the treasury of the United States. They shall in all cases, except treason, felony, and breach of the peace, be privileged from arrest during their attendance at the session of their respective Houses, and in going to and returning from the same; and for any speech or debate in either House they shall not be questioned in any other place.

2. **Members Cannot Hold Other Offices.** No Senator or Representative shall, during the time for which he was elected, be appointed to any civil office under the authority of the United States, which shall have been created, or the emoluments whereof shall have been increased, during such time; and no person holding any office under the United States shall be a member of either House during his continuance in office.

Section 7. Method of Passing Laws

Revenue (money) bills must begin in the House of Representatives. But the Senate can suggest changes.

1. **Revenue Bills.** All bills for raising revenue shall originate in the House of Representatives; but the Senate may propose or concur with amendments as on other bills.

A bill passed by Congress must be sent to the President. If the President signs the bill, it becomes a law. If the President vetoes, or refuses to sign the bill, it is returned to the house in which it started.

The President's veto may be overcome by a two-thirds vote of each house of Congress.

The President can let a bill become a law without signing it. But a bill sent to the President during the last ten days of a session of Congress is rejected by a "pocket veto" if the President does not sign it.

2. **How a Bill Becomes a Law.** Every bill which shall have passed the House of Representatives and the Senate shall, before it becomes a law, be presented to the President of the United States; if he approve he shall sign it, but if not he shall return it with his objections to that House in which it shall have originated, who shall enter the objections at large on their journal, and proceed to reconsider it. If after such reconsideration two thirds of that House shall agree to pass the bill, it shall be sent together with the objections, to the other House, by which it shall likewise be reconsidered, and, if approved by two thirds of that House, it shall become a law. But in all such cases the votes of both Houses shall be determined by yeas and nays, and the names of the persons voting for and against the bill shall be entered on the journal of each House respectively. If any bill shall not be returned by the President within ten days (Sundays excepted) after it shall have been presented to him, the same shall be a law, in like manner as if he had signed it, unless the Congress by their adjournment prevent its return, in which case it shall not be a law.

The President must sign or veto every resolution, except those on adjournment, which are passed by both houses.

3. **Presidential Approval or Veto.** Every order, resolution, or vote to which the concurrence of the Senate and House of Representatives may be necessary (except on a question of adjournment) shall be presented to the President of the United States; and, before the same shall take effect, shall be approved by him, or, being disapproved by him, shall be repassed by two thirds of the Senate and House of Representatives, according to the rules and limitations prescribed in the case of a bill.

Section 8. Powers Granted to Congress

The **delegated powers** of Congress are:

The Congress shall have power,

1. To lay and collect taxes, duties, imposts, and excises, to pay the debts and provide for the common defense and general welfare of the United States; but all duties, imposts, and excises shall be uniform throughout the United States;

to levy and collect uniform taxes, pay debts, and provide for the defense and general welfare of the nation.

2. To borrow money on the credit of the United States;

to borrow money

3. To regulate commerce with foreign nations, and among the several States~~, and with the Indian tribes;~~

to regulate commerce, or trade

4. To establish a uniform rule of naturalization, and uniform laws on the subject of bankruptcies throughout the United States;

to set up uniform laws concerning naturalization and bankruptcy

5. To coin money, regulate the value thereof, and of foreign coin, and fix the standard of weights and measures;

to coin money and set standards of weights and measures

6. To provide for the punishment of counterfeiting the securities and current coin of the United States;

to provide for the punishment of counterfeiting

7. To establish post offices and post roads;

to establish post offices and post roads

8. To promote the progress of science and useful arts, by securing for limited times to authors and inventors the exclusive right to their respective writings and discoveries;

to issue patents and copyrights

9. To constitute tribunals inferior to the Supreme Court;

to set up federal courts

10. To define and punish piracies and felonies committed on the high seas, and offences against the law of nations;

to punish piracy

11. To declare war~~, grant letters of marque and reprisal~~, and make rules concerning captures on land and water;

to declare war

12. To raise and support armies, but no appropriation of money to that use shall be for a longer term than two years;

to raise and support armies

13. To provide and maintain a navy;

to maintain a navy

14. To make rules for the government and regulation of the land and naval forces;

to make regulations for the armed forces

15. To provide for calling forth the militia to execute the laws of the Union, suppress insurrections, and repel invasions;

to provide for calling out the militia (National Guard)

16. To provide for organizing, arming, and disciplining the militia, and for governing such part of them as may be employed in the service of the United States, reserving to the States respectively, the appointment of the officers, and the authority of training the militia according to the discipline prescribed by Congress;

to help states maintain the militia

17. To exercise exclusive legislation, in all cases whatsoever, over such district (not exceeding ten miles square) as may, by cession of particular States, and the acceptance of Congress, become the seat of the government of the United States; and to exercise like authority over all places purchased by the consent of the Legislature of the State in which the same shall be, for the erection of forts, magazines, arsenals, dock-yards, and other needful buildings; and

to establish and govern the District of Columbia and govern other federal property

18. To make all laws which shall be necessary and proper for carrying into execution the foregoing powers, and all other powers vested by this Constitution in the government of the United States, or in any department or officer thereof.

to make all "necessary and proper" laws. This clause is the "elastic clause" that allows Congress to take many actions not named in the Constitution.

Section 9. Powers Forbidden to the Federal Government

[Amendments 1 to 10 also directly or indirectly limit the powers of the Federal Government.]

The **powers forbidden** to Congress are:

~~1. The migration or importation of such persons as any of the States now existing shall think proper to admit, shall not be prohibited by the Congress prior to the year one thousand eight hundred and eight, but a tax or duty may be imposed on such importation, not exceeding ten dollars for each person.~~

[to interfere with foreign slave trade]

to suspend the writ of **habeas corpus** except during emergencies
to pass bills of attainder or **ex post facto** laws
to levy direct taxes except in proportion to population [See Amendment 16.]
to tax exports
to pass any laws that would favor the trade of a particular state

2. The privilege of the writ of *habeas corpus* shall not be suspended, unless when in cases of rebellion or invasion the public safety may require it.

3. No bill of attainder or *ex post facto* law shall be passed.

~~4. No capitation or other direct tax shall be laid, unless in proportion to the census or enumeration herein before directed to be taken.~~

5. No tax or duty shall be laid on articles exported from any State.

6. No preference shall be given by any regulation of commerce or revenue to the ports of one State over those of another; nor shall vessels bound to, or from, one State, be obliged to enter, clear, or pay duties in another.

to spend money without appropriating it by law

7. No money shall be drawn from the treasury, but in consequence of appropriations made by law; and a regular statement and account of the receipts and expenditures of all public money shall be published from time to time.

to grant or accept any title of nobility

8. No title of nobility shall be granted by the United States; and no person holding any office of profit or trust under them shall, without the consent of the Congress, accept of any present, emolument, office, or title, of any kind whatever, from any king, prince, or foreign state.

The **powers forbidden** to the states are:

Section 10. Powers Forbidden to the States
[Supplemented by Amendments 14 and 15.]

to make treaties
to coin money
to pass a bill of attainder
to pass an **ex post facto** law
to grant titles of nobility

1. No state shall enter into any treaty, alliance, or confederation; grant letters of marque and reprisal; coin money; emit bills of credit; make anything but gold and silver coin a tender in payment of debts; pass any bill of attainder, *ex post facto* law, or law impairing the obligation of contracts, or grant any title of nobility.

to levy taxes or tariffs on imports or exports without permission of Congress

2. No State shall, without the consent of the Congress, lay any imposts or duties on imports or exports, except what may be absolutely necessary for executing its inspection laws; and the net produce of all duties and imposts, laid by any State on imports or exports, shall be for the use of the treasury of the United States; and all such laws shall be subject to the revision and control of the Congress.

to keep troops or warships in peacetime or deal with another state or a foreign nation without consent of Congress

3. No State shall, without the consent of Congress, lay any duty of tonnage, keep troops or ships of war in time of peace, enter into any agreement or compact with another State, or with a foreign power, or engage in war, unless actually invaded, or in such imminent danger as will not admit of delay.

ARTICLE 2. Executive Department

Section 1. President; Vice-President

Executive power is given to the President, who holds office for a four-year term.

1. **Term of Office.** The executive power shall be vested in a President of the United States of America. He shall hold his office during the term of four years, and, together with the Vice-President, chosen for the same term, be elected as follows:

The President is elected by electors, or delegates, chosen by the voters.

2. **The Electoral System.** Each State shall appoint, in such manner as the Legislature thereof may direct, a number of Electors equal to the whole number of Senators and Representatives to which the State may be entitled in the Congress; but no Senator or Representative, or person holding an office of trust or profit under the United States shall be appointed an Elector.

3. **A Discarded Way of Using the Electoral System.** ~~The electors shall meet in their respective States, and vote by ballot for two persons, of whom one at least shall not be an inhabitant of the same State with themselves. And they shall make a list of all the persons voted for, and of the number of votes for each; which list they shall sign and certify, and transmit sealed to the seat of the government of the United States, directed to the President of the Senate. The President of the Senate shall, in the presence of the Senate and House of Representatives, open all the certificates, and the votes shall then be counted. The person having the greatest number of votes shall be the President, if such number be a majority of the whole number of electors appointed; and if there be more than one who have such majority, and have an equal number of votes, then the House of Representatives shall immediately choose by ballot one of them for President; and if no person have a majority, then from the five highest on the list the said House shall in like manner choose the President. But in choosing the President, the votes shall be taken by States, the representation from each State having one vote; a quorum for this purpose shall consist of a member or members from two thirds of the States, and a majority of all the States shall be necessary to a choice. In every case, after the choice of the President, the person having the greatest number of votes of the electors shall be the Vice-President. But if there should remain two or more who have equal votes, the Senate shall choose from them by ballot the Vice-President.~~

The procedure for electing the President and Vice-President was changed by Amendment 12.

4. **Time of Elections.** Congress may determine the time of choosing the electors, and the day on which they shall give their votes; which day shall be the same throughout the United States.

Today, Presidential elections are held on the first Tuesday after the first Monday in November. Electoral votes are cast on the first Monday after the second Wednesday in December.

5. **Qualifications for the President.** No person except a natural-born citizen, ~~or a citizen of the United States at the time of the adoption of this Constitution,~~ shall be eligible to the office of President; neither shall any person be eligible to that office who shall not have attained to the age of thirty-five years, and been fourteen years a resident within the United States.

The President must be a natural-born citizen of the United States, at least 35 years old, and a resident of the United States for at least 14 years.

6. **Filling Vacancies.** In case of the removal of the President from office, or of his death, resignation, or inability to discharge the powers and duties of the said office, the same shall devolve on the Vice-President, and the Congress may by law provide for the case of removal, death, resignation, or inability, both of the President and Vice-President, declaring what officer shall then act as President, and such officer shall act accordingly, until the disability be removed, or a President shall be elected.

If the President dies, or for any reason cannot carry out the duties of office, the Vice-President will act as President. In the event that both officials are unable to serve, Congress has declared that the order of succession is as follows: (1) Speaker of the House, (2) President **pro tempore** of the Senate, and (3) the cabinet members in the order in which their offices were created. [See Amendment 25 also.]

7. **Salary.** The President shall, at stated times, receive for his services a compensation, which shall neither be increased nor diminished during the period for which he shall have been elected, and he shall not receive within that period any other emolument from the United States, or any of them.

The President receives a salary, the amount of which may not be changed during the term of office.

8. **Oath of Office.** Before he enter on the execution of his office, he shall take the following oath or affirmation:—"I do solemnly swear (or affirm) that I will faithfully execute the office of President of the United States, and will, to the best of my ability, preserve, protect, and defend the Constitution of the United States."

The President takes an oath of office, or is "sworn in," before beginning the duties of office as Chief Executive.

Section 2. Powers of the President

The duties of the President are:

1. **Military Powers.** The President shall be commander-in-chief of the army and navy of the United States, and of the militia of the several States, when called into the actual service of the United States; he may require the opinion, in writing, of the principal officer in each of the

The President is Commander-in-Chief of the armed forces.

The head of each executive department is, in practice, a member of the President's Cabinet.

The President may grant pardons for offenses against the United States, except in cases of impeachment.

executive departments, upon any subject relating to the duties of their respective offices, and he shall have power to grant reprieves and pardons for offences against the United States, except in cases of impeachment.

The President has the power to make treaties and to make appointments, provided that the Senate approves them.

2. **Treaty-making Power; Power of Appointment.** He shall have power, by and with the advice and consent of the Senate, to make treaties, provided two thirds of the Senators present concur; and he shall nominate, and, by and with the advice and consent of the Senate, shall appoint ambassadors, other public ministers, and consuls, judges of the Supreme Court, and all other officers of the United States, whose appointments are not herein otherwise provided for, and which shall be established by law; but the Congress may by law vest the appointment of such inferior officers, as they think proper, in the President alone, in the courts of law, or in the heads of departments.

The President may appoint officials to fill vacancies temporarily without the consent of the Senate when Congress is not in session.

3. **Filling Vacancies.** The President shall have power to fill up all vacancies that may happen during the recess of the Senate, by grant-commissions which shall expire at the end of their next session.

Section 3. Duties of the President

The President is required to send or to read a report on the state of the Union—the condition of the nation—at the opening of each session of Congress. The President also sends special messages to Congress.

The President may call special sessions of Congress.

The President is required to receive ambassadors, to execute the laws of the nation, and to commission all officers of the armed forces.

He shall from time to time give to the Congress information of the state of the Union, and recommend to their consideration such measures as he shall judge necessary and expedient; he may, on extraordinary occasions, convene both Houses, or either of them, and in case of disagreement between them, with respect to the time of adjournment, he may adjourn them to such time as he shall think proper; he shall receive ambassadors and other public ministers; he shall take care that the laws be faithfully executed, and shall commission all the officers of the United States.

Section 4. Impeachment

The President and all civil officers may be removed from office if convicted of treason, bribery, or other high crimes.

The President, Vice-President, and all civil officers of the United States, shall be removed from office on impeachment for, and conviction of, treason, bribery, or other high crimes and misdeameanors.

ARTICLE 3. Judicial Department

Section 1. Federal Courts

Judicial power is given to a Supreme Court and lower federal courts established by Congress.

Federal judges hold office for life. But they may be removed by impeachment.

The Supreme Court and lower federal courts. The judicial power of the United States shall be vested in one Supreme Court, and in such inferior courts as the Congress may from time to time ordain and establish. The judges, both of the Supreme and inferior courts, shall hold their offices during good behavior, and shall, at stated times, receive for their services a compensation, which shall not be diminished during their continuance in office.

Section 2. Jurisdiction of the Federal Courts

Federal courts may try cases involving the Constitution, federal laws, or treaties. They also try cases involving the United States, a state, citizens of different states, and ambassadors and consuls of foreign nations.

1. **General Jurisdiction.** The judicial power shall extend to all cases, in law and equity, arising under this Constitution, the laws of the United States, and treaties made, or which shall be made, under their authority; to all cases affecting ambassadors, other public ministers and consuls; to all cases of admiralty and maritime jurisdiction; to controversies to which the United States shall be a party; to controversies between two or more States, ~~between a State and citizens of another State~~ [see Amendment 11], between citizens of different States, between citizens of the

same State claiming lands under grants of different States, and between a State, or the citizens thereof, and foreign states, citizens, or subjects.

2. **The Supreme Court.** In all cases affecting ambassadors, other public ministers, and consuls, and those in which a State shall be party, the Supreme Court shall have original jurisdiction. In all the other cases before mentioned, the Supreme Court shall have appellate jurisdiction, both as to law and fact, with such exceptions, and under such regulations, as the Congress shall make.

Cases involving ambassadors or officials of foreign nations and cases involving states are tried in the Supreme Court. Other cases begin in lower courts but may be appealed to the Supreme Court.

3. **Conduct of Trials.** The trial of all crimes, except in cases of impeachment, shall be by jury; and such trial shall be held in the State where the said crimes shall have been committed, but when not committed within any State, the trial shall be at such place or places as the Congress may by law have directed. [Expanded by Amendments 5, 6, and 7.]

All federal crimes, except cases of impeachment, are to be tried by jury trials in the states where the crimes were committed.

Section 3. Treason

1. **Definition.** Treason against the United States shall consist only in levying war against them, or in adhering to their enemies, giving them aid and comfort. No person shall be convicted of treason unless on the testimony of two witnesses to the same overt act, or on confession in open court.

Treason is carefully defined as waging war against our nation or helping its enemies.

2. **Punishment.** The Congress shall have power to declare the punishment of treason, but no attainder of treason shall work corruption of blood, or forfeiture, except during the life of the person attainted.

Punishment for treason may not extend to the family of the convicted person.

ARTICLE 4. Relation of the States to Each Other

Section 1. Official Acts

Full faith and credit shall be given in each State to the public acts, records, and judicial proceedings of every other State. And the Congress may by general laws prescribe the manner in which such acts, records, and proceedings shall be proved, and the effect thereof.

All states are required to honor each other's laws, records, and legal decisions.

Section 2. Privileges of Citizens

1. **Privileges.** The citizens of each State shall be entitled to all privileges and immunities of citizens in the several States.

Each state must treat citizens of other states as it treats its own citizens.

2. **Fugitive Criminals.** A person charged in any State with treason, felony, or other crime, who shall flee from justice, and be found in another State, shall, on demand of the executive authority of the State from which he fled, be delivered up, to be removed to the State having jurisdiction of the crime.

An accused person who flees to another state must be returned to the state in which the crime was committed.

3. **Fugitive Slaves.** ~~No person held to service or labor in one State, under the laws thereof, escaping into another, shall in consequence of any law or regulation therein, be discharged from such service or labor, but shall be delivered up on claim of the party to whom such service or labor may be due.~~

This provision for fugitive slaves has not been in effect since Amendment 13 was approved in 1865.

Section 3. New States and Territories

1. **Admission of New States.** New States may be admitted by the Congress into this Union; but no new State shall be formed or erected within the jurisdiction of any other State; nor any State be formed by the junction of two or more States, or parts of States, without the consent of the Legislatures of the States concerned, as well as of the Congress.

New states may not be formed by dividing or joining existing states without the consent of the state legislatures and Congress. New states may be admitted into the Union by Congress.

Congress has power to make laws for the territories and for federal property.

2. **Powers of Congress over Territories and Other Property.** The Congress shall have power to dispose of and make all needful rules and regulations respecting the territory or other property belonging to the United States; and nothing in this Constitution shall be so construed as to prejudice any claims of the United States, or of any particular State.

Each state is guaranteed a republican form of government; that is, government by representatives of the people. The federal government must protect the states against foreign attack or violence within their borders.

Section 4. Guarantees and Protection for the States

The United States shall guarantee to every State in this Union a republican form of government, and shall protect each of them against invasion; and on application of the Legislature, or of the Executive (when the Legislature can not be convened), against domestic violence.

ARTICLE 5. How Amendments Are Made

Amendments may be proposed by a two-thirds vote of each house of Congress or by a national convention at the request of two thirds of the states. Amendments may be ratified, or approved, by the legislatures of three fourths of the states. They may also be ratified by conventions in three fourths of the states.

No amendment may deprive a state of its equal vote in the Senate.

The Congress, whenever two thirds of both houses shall deem it necessary, shall propose amendments to this Constitution, or, on the application of the Legislature of two thirds of the several States, shall call a convention for proposing amendments, which, in either case, shall be valid to all intents and purposes, as part of this Constitution, when ratified by the Legislatures of three fourths of the several States, or by conventions in three fourths thereof, as the one or the other mode of ratification may be proposed by the Congress; provided that ~~no amendment which may be made prior to the year one thousand eight hundred and eight shall in any manner affect the first and fourth clauses in the ninth section of the first article; and that~~ no State, without its consent, shall be deprived of its equal suffrage in the Senate.

ARTICLE 6. General Provisions

The federal government will honor all debts and contracts of the United States made before the adoption of this Constitution.

The Constitution, laws, and treaties of the United States are the supreme law of the nation. No state or local laws may conflict with them.

All federal and state officials must promise to support the Constitution.

Religion may not be a qualification for federal officials.

1. **Public Debt.** All debts contracted and engagements entered into, before the adoption of this Constitution shall be as valid against the United States under this Constitution as under the Confederation.

2. **The Supreme Law.** This Constitution, and the laws of the United States which shall be made in pursuance thereof, and all treaties made, or which shall be made, under the authority of the United States, shall be the supreme law of the land; and the judges in every State shall be bound thereby, anything in the constitution or laws of any State to the contrary notwithstanding.

3. **Oaths of Office.** The Senators and Representatives before mentioned, and the members of the several State Legislatures, and all executive and judicial officers, both of the United States and of the several States, shall be bound by oath or affirmation to support this Constitution; but no religious test shall ever be required as a qualification to any office or public trust under the United States.

ARTICLE 7. Ratification

The Constitution was to become the law of the nation when it was ratified, or approved, by nine states.

The ratification of the conventions of nine States shall be sufficient for the establishment of this Constitution between the States so ratifying the same.

DONE in Convention, by the unanimous consent of the States present, the seventeenth day of September, in the year of our Lord one thousand seven hundred and eighty-seven, and of the Independence of the United States of America the twelfth. *In Witness* whereof we have hereunto subscribed our names.

(Signed by) *G. Washington,*
President and Deputy from Virginia

NEW HAMPSHIRE

John Langdon
Nicholas Gilman

NEW YORK

Alexander Hamilton

NEW JERSEY

William Livingston
David Brearley
William Paterson
Jonathan Dayton

MARYLAND

James McHenry
Daniel of St. Thomas Jenifer
Daniel Carroll

VIRGINIA

John Blair
James Madison

MASSACHUSETTS

Nathaniel Gorham
Rufus King

DELAWARE

George Read
Gunning Bedford
John Dickinson
Richard Bassett
Jacob Broom

SOUTH CAROLINA

John Rutledge
Charles Cotesworth Pinckney
Charles Pinckney
Pierce Butler

CONNECTICUT

William Samuel Johnson
Roger Sherman

PENNSYLVANIA

Benjamin Franklin
Thomas Mifflin
Robert Morris
George Clymer
Thomas FitzSimmons
Jared Ingersoll
James Wilson
Gouverneur Morris

NORTH CAROLINA

William Blount
Richard Dobbs Spaight
Hugh Williamson

GEORGIA

William Few
Abraham Baldwin

Attest: William Jackson,
Secretary

The Bill of Rights: Amendments 1–10

[Adopted in 1791]

Amendment 1. Freedom of Religion, Speech, Press, and Assembly

Congress may not set up an official church. It also may not pass laws that limit freedom of religion, speech, the press, assembly, and the right to petition.

Congress shall make no law respecting an establishment of religion, or prohibiting the free exercise thereof; or abridging the freedom of speech, or of the press, or the right of the people peaceably to assemble, and to petition the government for a redress of grievances.

Amendment 2. Right to Keep Arms

The right of states to have a militia (National Guard) is guaranteed. The right of citizens to keep weapons to resist a tyrannical government is also protected.

A well regulated militia being necessary to the security of a free state, the right of the people to keep and bear arms shall not be infringed.

Amendment 3. Quartering of Soldiers

In peacetime, troops may not take over private houses.

No soldier shall, in time of peace, be quartered in any house, without the consent of the owner, nor in time of war, but in a manner to be prescribed by law.

Amendment 4. Search and Seizure; Warrants

The government is limited in its right to search and take custody of persons and property.

The right of the people to be secure in their persons, houses, papers, and effects, against unreasonable searches and seizures, shall not be violated, and no warrant shall issue but upon probable cause, supported by oath or affirmation, and particularly describing the place to be searched, and the persons or things to be seized.

Amendment 5. Rights of Persons Accused of Crime

A person cannot be tried for an important crime unless indicted (accused) by a grand jury. A person cannot be tried twice for the same crime. A person cannot be forced to testify against himself or herself. No person can be deprived of life, liberty, or property except by lawful means.

No person shall be held to answer for a capital, or otherwise infamous crime, unless on a presentment or indictment of a grand jury, except in cases arising in the land or naval forces, or in the militia, when in actual service in time of war or public danger; nor shall any person be subject for the same offence to be twice put in jeopardy of life or limb; nor shall be compelled in any criminal case to be a witness against himself, nor be deprived of life, liberty, or property, without due process of law; nor shall private property be taken for public use without just compensation.

Amendment 6. Right to Speedy Trial

An accused person is entitled to a speedy, public trial by a jury in the state where the crime was committed. A person is to be told of the charges. A person is entitled to have a lawyer, to question witnesses, and to call defense witnesses.

In all criminal prosecutions, the accused shall enjoy the right to a speedy and public trial, by an impartial jury of the State and district wherein the crime shall have been committed, which district shall have been previously ascertained by law, and to be informed of the nature and cause of the accusation; to be confronted with the witnesses against him; to have compulsory process for obtaining witnesses in his favor, and to have the assistance of counsel for his defence.

Amendment 7. Jury Trial in Civil Cases

A jury trial in civil cases is guaranteed when the matter amounts to more than $20.

In suits at common law, where the value in controversy shall exceed twenty dollars, the right of trial by jury shall be preserved, and no fact tried by a jury shall be otherwise reexamined in any court of the United States, than according to the rules of the common law.

Amendment 8. Excessive Bail or Punishment

Bails, fines, and punishments must not be unreasonable.

Excessive bail shall not be required, nor excessive fines imposed, nor cruel and unusual punishments inflicted.

Amendment 9. Powers Reserved to the People

The enumeration in the Constitution of certain rights shall not be construed to deny or disparage others retained by the people.

The listing of these rights guaranteed in the Constitution does not mean that these are the only basic rights or that other basic rights may be restricted.

Amendment 10. Powers Reserved to the States

The powers not delegated to the United States by the Constitution, nor prohibited by it to the States, are reserved to the States respectively, or to the people.

All powers not given to the federal government are left to the states and to the people.

Amendment 11. Suits Against States (1798)

The judicial power of the United States shall not be construed to extend to any suit in law or equity, commenced or prosecuted against one of the United States by citizens of another State, or by citizens or subjects of any foreign state.

Any suit against a state initiated by a citizen of another state or of a foreign country must be tried in a state court and not in a federal court.

Amendment 12. Election of President and Vice-President (1804)

The Electors shall meet in their respective States, and vote by ballot for President and Vice-President, one of whom, at least, shall not be an inhabitant of the same State with themselves; they shall name in their ballots the person voted for as President, and in distinct ballots the person voted for as Vice-President; and they shall make distinct lists of all persons voted for as President, and of all persons voted for as Vice-President, and of the number of votes for each, which lists they shall sign and certify, and transmit sealed to the seat of the government of the United States, directed to the President of the Senate;—the President of the Senate shall, in the presence of the Senate and House of Representatives, open all the certificates, and the votes shall then be counted;—the person having the greatest number of votes for President shall be the President, if such number be a majority of the whole number of Electors appointed; and if no person have such majority, then from the persons having the highest numbers not exceeding three on the list of those voted for as President, the House of Representatives shall choose immediately, by ballot, the President. But in choosing the President, the votes shall be taken by States, the representation from each State having one vote; a quorum for this purpose shall consist of a member or members from two thirds of the States, and a majority of all the States shall be necessary to a choice. ~~And if the House of Representatives shall not choose a President, whenever the right of choice shall devolve upon them, before the fourth day of March next following, then the Vice-President shall act as President, as in the case of the death or other constitutional disability of the President~~. [See Amendment 20.] The person having the greatest number of votes as Vice-President shall be the Vice-President, if such number be a majority of the whole number of Electors appointed, and if no person have a majority, then from the two highest numbers on the list the Senate shall choose the Vice-President; a quorum for the purpose shall consist of two thirds of the whole number of Senators, and a majority of the whole number shall be necessary to a choice. But no person constitutionally ineligible to the office of President shall be eligible to that of Vice-President of the United States.

Electors (members of the Electoral College) are instructed to vote separately for President and Vice-President. [See Article 2, Section 1.]

Amendment 13. Slavery Abolished (1865)

Section 1. Neither slavery nor involuntary servitude, except as a punishment for crime whereof the party shall have been duly convicted,

Slavery is abolished. Congress is given power to enforce the abolition of slavery.

shall exist within the United States, or any place subject to their jurisdiction.

Section 2. Congress shall have power to enforce this article by appropriate legislation.

Amendment 14. Rights of Citizens (1868)

Citizenship is given to black Americans. The states are forbidden to deny equal privileges and protection by law to any citizen. In effect, the basic protections of the Bill of Rights apply to state governments as well as to the federal government.

Section 1. **Citizenship Defined.** All persons born or naturalized in the United States, and subject to the jurisdiction thereof, are citizens of the United States and of the State wherein they reside. No State shall make or enforce any law which shall abridge the privileges or immunities of citizens of the United States; nor shall any State deprive any person of life, liberty, or property, without due process of law; nor deny to any person within its jurisdiction the equal protection of the laws.

A state's representation in Congress may be reduced if the state denies the right to vote to any eligible adult male citizen.

Section 2. **Apportionment of Representatives.** Representatives shall be apportioned among the several States according to their respective numbers, counting the whole number of persons in each State, excluding Indians not taxed. But when the right to vote at any election for the choice of Electors for President and Vice-President of the United States, Representatives in Congress, the executive and judicial officers of a State, or the members of the Legislature thereof, is denied to any of the male inhabitants of such State, being twenty-one years of age and citizens of the United States, or in any way abridged, except for participation in rebellion or other crime, the basis of representation therein shall be reduced in the proportion which the number of such male citizens shall bear to the whole number of male citizens twenty-one years of age in such State.

Former officials of the Confederate States are barred from holding public office.

Section 3. **Disability for Engaging in Insurrection.** No person shall be a Senator or Representative in Congress, or Elector of President and Vice-President, or hold any office, civil or military, under the United States, or under any State, who, having previously taken an oath, as a member of Congress, or as an officer of the United States, or as a member of any State Legislature, or as an executive or judicial officer of any State, to support the Constitution of the United States, shall have engaged in insurrection or rebellion against the same, or given aid or comfort to the enemies thereof. But Congress may, by a vote of two thirds of each House, remove such disability.

All debts of the federal government connected with the War Between the North and the South are to be paid. All debts of the Confederate States are declared illegal and will not be paid by the federal government.

Section 4. **Public Debt.** The validity of the public debt of the United States, authorized by law, including debts incurred for payment of pensions and bounties for services in suppressing insurrection or rebellion, shall not be questioned. But neither the United States, nor any State shall assume or pay any debt or obligation incurred in aid of insurrection or rebellion against the United States, ~~or any claim for the loss or emancipation of any slave;~~ but all such debts, obligations, and claims shall be held illegal and void.

Section 5. **Enforcement.** The Congress shall have power to enforce, by appropriate legislation, the provisions of this article.

Amendment 15. Right of Suffrage (1870)

Citizens cannot be denied the right to vote because of their race or color, or because they were formerly slaves.

Section 1. The right of citizens of the United States to vote shall not be denied or abridged by the United States, or by any State, on account of race, color, or previous condition of servitude.

Section 2. The Congress shall have power to enforce this article by appropriate legislation.

Amendment 16. Taxes on Income (1913)

The Congress shall have power to lay and collect taxes on incomes, from whatever source derived, without apportionment among the several States, and without regard to any census or enumeration.

Congress is given the power to pass a law taxing personal incomes.

Amendment 17. Election of Senators (1913)

Section 1. The Senate of the United States shall be composed of two Senators from each State, elected by the people thereof, for six years; and each Senator shall have one vote. The electors in each State shall have the qualifications requisite for electors of the most numerous branch of the State legislatures.

Senators are to be elected by the voters of each state.

Section 2. When vacancies happen in the representation of any State in the Senate, the executive authority of such State shall issue writs of election to fill such vacancies. Provided, that the Legislature of any State may empower the executive thereof to make temporary appointment until the people fill the vacancies by election as the Legislature may direct.

A vacancy in the Senate may be filled by a special election. Or the Governor of the state may be given the power by the state legislature to appoint someone to fill the vacancy.

Section 3. ~~This amendment shall not be so construed as to affect the election or term of any Senator chosen before it becomes valid as part of the Constitution~~.

Amendment 18. National Prohibition (1919)

Section 1. ~~After one year from the ratification of this article the manufacture, sale, or transportation of intoxicating liquors within, the importation thereof into, or the exportation thereof from the United States and all territory subject to the jurisdiction thereof, for beverage purposes is hereby prohibited~~.

The making, sale, and transportation of alcoholic beverages in the United States are prohibited. [See Amendment 21.]

Section 2. ~~The Congress and the several States shall have concurrent power to enforce this article by appropriate legislation~~.

Section 3. ~~This article shall be inoperative unless it shall have been ratified as an amendment to the Constitution by the Legislatures of the several States as provided in the Constitution within seven years from the date of the submission hereof to the States by the Congress~~.

Amendment 19. Woman's Suffrage (1920)

Section 1. The right of citizens of the United States to vote shall not be denied or abridged by the United States or by any State on account of sex.

The right of women to vote is guaranteed.

Section 2. Congress shall have power to enforce this article by appropriate legislation.

Amendment 20. Inauguration of President; Sessions of Congress (1933)

Section 1. **Beginning of Terms of Office.** The terms of the President and Vice-President shall end at noon on the 20th day of January, and the terms of Senators and Representatives at noon on the 3d day of January, of the years in which such terms would have ended if this article had not been ratified; and the terms of their successors shall then begin.

The President and Vice-President are to take office on January 20 (instead of March 4). Members of Congress are to take office January 3.

Section 2. **Beginning of Congressional Sessions.** The Congress shall assemble at least once in every year, and such meeting shall begin at noon on the 3d day of January, unless they shall by law appoint a different day.

Congress is to meet once a year.

If the President-elect should die before January 20 or fail to qualify, the office of President is to be filled in the order described.

Section 3. **Presidential Succession.** If, at the time fixed for the beginning of the term of the President, the President-elect shall have died, the Vice-President elect shall become President. If a President shall not have been chosen before the time fixed for the beginning of his term, or if the President-elect shall have failed to qualify, then the Vice-President-elect shall act as President until a President shall have qualified; and the Congress may by law provide for the case wherein neither a President-elect nor a Vice-President elect shall have qualified, declaring who shall then act as President, or the manner in which one who is to act shall be selected, and such person shall act accordingly until a President or Vice-President shall have qualified.

Section 4. **Filling Presidential Vacancy.** The Congress may by law provide for the case of the death of any of the persons from whom the House of Representatives may choose a President whenever the right of choice shall have devolved upon them, and for the case of the death of any of the persons from whom the Senate may choose a Vice-President whenever the right of choice shall have devolved upon them.

Section 5. **Effective Date.** ~~Sections 1 and 2 shall take effect on the 15th day of October following the ratification of this article.~~

Section 6. **Limit on Time for Ratification.** ~~This article shall be inoperative unless it shall have been ratified as an amendment to the Constitution by the legislatures of three fourths of the several States within seven years from the date of its submission.~~

Amendment 21. National Prohibition Repealed (1933)

Amendment 18 is repealed.

Section 1. The eighteenth article of amendment to the Constitution of the United States is hereby repealed.

States may prohibit the sale of alcoholic beverages.

Section 2. The transportation or importation into any State, Territory, or possession of the United States for delivery or use therein of intoxicating liquors, in violation of the laws thereof, is hereby prohibited.

Section 3. ~~This article shall be inoperative unless it shall have been ratified as an amendment to the Constitution by conventions in the several States, as provided in the Constitution, within seven years from the date of the submission hereof to the States by Congress.~~

Amendment 22. Two-Term Limit for Presidents (1951)

A President is limited to two full terms in office. If a Vice-President has already served more than two years as President, this person may be elected President only once.

Section 1. No person shall be elected to the office of the President more than twice, and no person who has held the office of President, or acted as President, for more than two years of a term to which some other person was elected President, shall be elected to the office of the President more than once. ~~But this article shall not apply to any person holding the office of President when this article was proposed by the Congress, and shall not prevent any person who may be holding the office of President, or acting as President, during the term within which this article becomes operative from holding the office of President, or acting as President, during the remainder of such term.~~

Section 2. ~~This article shall be inoperative unless it shall have been ratified as an amendment to the Constitution by the legislatures of three-fourths of the several states within seven years from the date of its submission to the states by the Congress.~~

Amendment 23. Presidential Electors for District of Columbia (1961)

Section 1. The District constituting the seat of Government of the United States shall appoint in such manner as Congress may direct: A number of electors of President and Vice-President equal to the whole number of Senators and Representatives in Congress to which the District would be entitled if it were a State, but in no event more than the least populous State; they shall be in addition to those appointed by the States, but they shall be considered, for the purposes of the election of President and Vice-President, to be electors appointed by a State; and they shall meet in the District and perform such duties as provided by the twelfth article of amendment.

Residents of the District of Columbia are given the right to vote for President and Vice-President. The District of Columbia is given three electoral votes.

Section 2. The Congress shall have power to enforce this article by appropriate legislation.

Amendment 24. Prohibition of Poll Tax Requirement for National Elections (1964)

Section 1. The right of citizens of the United States to vote in any primary or other election for President or Vice-President, for electors for President or Vice-President, or for Senator or Representative in Congress, shall not be denied or abridged by the United States or any state by reason of failure to pay any poll tax or other tax.

A poll tax may not be a requirement for voting for federal officials.

Section 2. The Congress shall have power to enforce this article by appropriate legislation.

Amendment 25. Filling the Empty Offices of President and Vice-President (1967)

Section 1. **Filling the Empty Office of President.** In case of the removal of the President from office by his death or resignation, the Vice-President shall become President.

If a President dies or resigns from office, the Vice-President becomes President.

Section 2. **Filling the Empty Office of Vice-President.** Whenever there is a vacancy in the office of the Vice-President, the President shall nominate a Vice-President who shall take the office upon confirmation by a majority vote of both Houses of Congress.

If the office of Vice-President becomes empty, the President may appoint someone to fill this office, with the agreement of Congress.

Section 3. **When the Vice-President Acts as President.** Whenever the President transmits to the President pro tempore of the Senate and the Speaker of the House of Representatives his written declaration that he is unable to discharge the powers and duties of his office, and until he transmits them a written declaration to the contrary, such powers and duties shall be discharged by the Vice-President as Acting President.

If the President feels unable to carry out the duties of office, the President shall tell Congress so in a written message. The Vice-President shall act as President until the President is again able to carry out the duties of office.

Section 4. **When Congress Decides Who Shall Be President.** Whenever the Vice-President and a majority of either the principal officers of the executive departments, or of such other body as Congress may by law provide, transmit to the President pro tempore of the Senate and the Speaker of the House of Representatives their written declaration that the President is unable to discharge the powers and duties of his office, the Vice-President shall immediately assume the powers and duties of the office as Acting President.

Thereafter, when the President transmits to the President pro tempore of the Senate and the Speaker of the House of Representatives his written declaration that no inability exists, he shall resume the powers and duties of his office unless the Vice-President and a majority of either the principal officers of the executive department, or of such

If the Vice-President and a majority of the Cabinet members feel the President is unable to carry out the duties of office, they shall tell Congress so in a written message. The Vice-President then acts as President. When the President feels ready to carry out the duties again, the President shall declare so to Congress. But if the Vice-President and a majority of the Cabinet members do not agree, then Congress must decide by a two-thirds vote within 21 days who is President.

other body as Congress may by law provide, transmit within four days to the President pro tempore of the Senate and the Speaker of the House of Representatives their written declaration that the President is unable to discharge the powers and duties of his office. Thereupon Congress shall decide the issue, assembling within 48 hours for that purpose if not in session. If the Congress, within 21 days after receipt of the latter written declaration, or, if Congress is not in session, within 21 days after Congress is required to assemble, determines by two-thirds vote of both houses that the President is unable to discharge the powers and duties of his office, the Vice-President shall continue to discharge the same as Acting President; otherwise, the President shall assume the powers and duties of his office.

Amendment 26. Voting Age Lowered to 18 (1971)

The minimum voting age is lowered to 18 in all federal, state, and local elections.

Section 1. The right of citizens of the United States, who are 18 years of age or older, to vote shall not be denied or abridged by the United States or any state on account of age.

Section 2. The Congress shall have the power to enforce this article by appropriate legislation.

Proposed Amendment 27

The proposed 27th Amendment to abolish discrimination on account of sex was approved by the Congress and sent to the states for ratification in March of 1972.

Equality of right under the law shall not be denied or abridged by the United States or by any State on account of sex.

Index

Italicized page numbers preceded by *c*, *m*, or *p* refer to a chart (*c*), map (*m*), or picture (*p*) on the page.
Boldface page numbers refer to definitions of important terms.
For list of Charts, see pp. x and xi. For list of Special Features, see p. xii.

Acknowledgments

KEY: *(t)* top; *(c)* center; *(b)* bottom; *(l)* left; *(r)* right.

COVER: HBJ Photo.

TITLE PAGE PHOTOGRAPHS: page ii, *(t)* Sybil Shackman–Monkmeyer, *(cr)* Peter Vadnai–Editorial Photocolor Archives, *(cl)* Tommy Noonan–UNIPHOTO, *(middle)* Bob Wick–Tom Stack, *(br)* Frieda Leinwand–Monkmeyer, *(bl)* Owen Franken–Stock, Boston; iii, William Hamilton–Shostal Associates.

UNIT ONE: page 1, Dennis Stock–Magnum; 3, William Hamilton–Shostal Associates; 4, painting by George Catlin, American Museum of Natural History; 5, Fred Olson–Shostal Associates; 7, Culver; 8, *(t)* HBJ, *(c)* Hugh Rogers–Monkmeyer, *(b)* HBJ; 9, *(t)* Frederic Lewis, *(c)* Mimi Forsyth–Monkmeyer, *(b)* Michael Collier–Stock, Boston; 12, Fred Ward–Black Star; 14, HBJ; 16, Eric Carle–Shostal Associates; 23, Ernest S. Bernard–Shostal Associates; 25, Lizabeth Corlett Forsyth–DPI; 35, The Historical Paintings Collection–Continental Insurance Co.; 37, Ginger Chih; 38, *(l)* Charles Rotmil, *(r)* Alon Reininger–De Wys; 39, *(l)* Tom Brakefield–Taurus, *(r)* Alon Reininger–De Wys.

UNIT TWO: page 45, Dennis Brack–Black Star; 47, Pictorial Parade; 50, PHOTRI; 53, U.S. Capitol Historical Society; 58, Bruce Wolfe–UNIPHOTO; 59, Ellis Herwig–Stock, Boston; 60, *(both)* Tommy Noonan–UNIPHOTO; 63, U.S. Capitol Historical Society; 64, White House Photo; 73, Ron Sherman–Nancy Palmer; 76, UPI; 78, White House Photo; 82, Tom McHugh–Photo Researchers; 85, Susan McElhinney–Woodfin Camp; 86, *(both)* Dennis Brack–Black Star; 93, Susan McCartney–Photo Researchers; 95, HBJ; 100, UPI; 102, *(t)* Chris Casewell–Photo Researchers, *(b)* Rona Beame–DPI; 103, *(l)* Lawrence Fried–Magnum, *(r)* Michael Philip Manheim–Photo Researchers; 104, *(l)* Bob Smith–Rapho/Photo Researchers, *(r)* HBJ; 106, Burt Glinn–Magnum; 108, Hugh Rogers–Monkmeyer; 113, Grant Heilman; 114, NASA; 118, USDA; 120, *clockwise (tl)* Larry Fried–Magnum, J. P. Laffont–Sygma, Marion Bernstein, Hy Simon–Photo Trends, NASA; 122, *(t wedge)* Tom Ehenhoh–Black Star, *(rectangle)* USDA, *(bl wedge)* Cary Wolinsky–Stock, Boston, *(rectangle)* Charles Gatewood, *(br wedge)* Owen Franken–Stock, Boston, *(rectangle)* Monkmeyer; 124, UPI; 126, Grant Heilman; 128, USDA; 133, *(l)* FPG, *(r)* HBJ.

UNIT THREE: page 137, Jim Vines–Tom Stack Associates; 139, Michal Heron–Monkmeyer; 142, USDA; 147, Mimi Forsyth–Monkmeyer; 150, Alex Webb–Magnum; 152, Shostal Associates; 159, J. Paul Kirouac–Monkmeyer; 162, Karen Collidge–Taurus; 164, Hanson Carroll–Peter Arnold; 166, Jon Seeman–DPI; 169, 174, DPI.

UNIT FOUR: page 179, Peter Arnold; 181, UPI; 183, *(both)* White House Historical Society; 188, John Running; 191, Joel Gordon; 194, Culver; 195, Ken Touchton–Globe Photos; 196, NBC-TV; 203, P. Wright–Shostal; 208, NASA; 209, Mimi Forsyth–Monkmeyer; 211, HBJ; 212, John Running–Stock, Boston; 215, HBJ.

UNIT FIVE: page 221, George E. Jones III–Photo Researchers; 223, HBJ; 224, Nebraska State Historical Society; 226, HBJ; 227, Rocky Weldon–De Wys; 230, HBJ; 235, Owen Franken–Stock, Boston; 236, "New England Country School" by Winslow Homer, St. Louis Art Museum; 241, HBJ; 242, Peter Vadnai–Editorial Photocolor Archives; 244, 247, HBJ; 253, Eric Carle–Shostal Associates; 254, Ellis Herwig–Stock, Boston; 255, Doug Wilson–Black Star; 256, PHOTRI; 258, Ross Lewis; 259, Tom Stack Associates; 260, *(tl)* PHOTRI, *(tc)* DPI, *(tr)* Peter Robilotta, *(b)* HBJ; 261, *all* Owen Franken–Stock, Boston *except*, *(tr)* Lawrence Frank–Rapho/Photo Researchers, *(cl)* Jan Lukas–Photo Researchers; 262, *(tl)*, *(b)* James Smith–Photo Trends, *(tr)*, *(c)* HBJ, *(tcr)* Hinton–Monkmeyer; 265, Pittsburgh Convention and Visitors Bureau.

UNIT SIX: page 269, Lizabeth Corlett Forsyth–DPI; 271, Lawrence Lowrey–Rapho/Photo Researchers; 273, HBJ, courtesy "Furniture-In-The-Raw"; 276, HBJ; 278, Bruce Roberts–Rapho/Photo Researchers; 283, HBJ; 289, John Zoiner; 292, J. A. Brown–Shostal Associates; 294, Shostal Associates; 296, HBJ; 299, John Nicolais–Woodfin Camp; 300–301, HBJ; 302, *(c)* Ted Russell, *(b)* Richard Balagur–Nancy Palmer; 309, Shostal Associates; 310–311, Bureau of The Mint; 317, Bob Combs–Rapho/Photo Researchers 321, Bill Powers–Nancy Palmer; 329, AFL–CIO News; 335, HBJ; 337, Jeffrey Foxx–Photo Trends; 340, *(tl)* PHOTRI, *(cr)* Tony Spina; 341, *(t)* Inger McCabe–Rapho/Photo Researchers, *(c)* Milt and Joan Mann, *(b)* Harry Wilks; 342, *(t)* George Gardner, *(c)* Shostal Associates, *(b)* George Gardner; 344, HBJ; 348, Bob Wick–Tom Stack Associates; 352, Dorothea Lange–Library of Congress; 354, drawing by Hoaglund, © 1978, Time, Inc.; 359, Frieda Leinwand–Monkmeyer; 361, Sybil Shackman–Monkmeyer; 363, Irene Bayer–Monkmeyer; 364, John Zoiner; 368, Jeff Smith; 369, Joshua Tree–Editorial Photocolor Archives; 370, *(tl)*, *(bl)*, *(br)* HBJ, *(tr)* Owen Franken–Stock, Boston; 371, *(t)* William McCracken–Nancy Palmer, *(tc)* Joel Gordon, *(bc)* Chester Higgins–Rapho/Photo Researchers, *(b)* HBJ; 372, *(t)* Mimi Forsyth–Monkmeyer, *(tc)*, *(bc)* HBJ, *(b)* Kenneth Karp; 374, HBJ; 377, Charles Gatewood; 379, HBJ.

UNIT SEVEN: page 383, HBJ; 385, White House Photo; 387, Dennis Brack–Black Star; 391, Brown Brothers; 392, The National Archives; 394, B. Glander–Shostal Associates; 397, United Nations; 403, Wally MacNamee–Woodfin Camp; 404, TASS–Sovfoto; 405, John Launois–Black Star; 407, Sovfoto; 408, Stan Wayman–Photo Researchers; 410, UPI; 413, James Pickerell–Black Star; 415, Wally MacNamee–Woodfin Camp; 416, Imperial War Museum; 417, PHOTRI; 421, HBJ.

UNIT EIGHT: page 425, John Zoiner; 427, HBJ; 430, Allan Tannenbaum; 433, Ernest Baxter–Black Star; 434, Charles Gatewood; 436, Joel Gordon; 437, Marc and Evelyne Bernheim–Woodfin Camp; 439, T. Linck–Shostal Associates; 440, *(l)*, Kenneth Murray–Nancy Palmer, *(tr)* Owen Franken–Stock, Boston, *(br)* and 441 *(l)*, Hugh Rogers–Monkmeyer; 441, *(tc)* Michal Heron–Monkmeyer, *(bc)* Hanson Carroll–Peter Arnold, *(r)* John Running–Stock, Boston; 442, *(tl)* PHOTRI, *(bl)* Erik Anderson–Stock, Boston, *(r)* Hella Hamid–Rapho/Photo Researchers; 447, Bill Powers–Nancy Palmer; 453, Olivier Rebbot–Woodfin Camp; 455, Raimondo Borea–Photo Researchers; 459, Charles Gatewood; 461, UPI; 462, John Gray–Nancy Palmer; 465, Maxwell Coplan–DPI; 470, George Gardner; 471, *(background)* Peter Menzel–Stock, Boston, *(insert)* Inger McCabe–Rapho/Photo Researchers, *(tr)* PHOTRI, *(br)* Lynn Karlin; 472, *(t)* George Gardner, *(c)* Leonard Freed–Magnum, *(b)* Chester Higgins–Rapho/Photo Researchers; 474, Syd Greenberg–DPI; 479, NASA; 481, Charles Gatewood; 484, *(tl)* Charles Belinsky–Photo Researchers, *(bl)* Sandbach, *(tr)* Inger McCabe–Rapho/Photo Researchers, *(br)* Orville Schell; 485, *(tl)* Hugh Rogers–Monkmeyer, *(bl)* Luis Villota–Monkmeyer, *(tr)* HBJ, *(cr)* George Gardner, *(br)* Christopher Harris–Photo Trends; 486, *(tl)* Shostal Associates, *(bl)* Fred Lyon–Rapho/Photo Researchers, *(c)* Philip Jon Bailey–Stock, Boston, *(r)* Marion Bernstein; 488, Tom Andrews–Photo Trends; 495, Carlson–Rockey & Associates; 497, Sam Falk–Monkmeyer; 498, Shostal Associates.

F 3
G 4
H 5
I 6
J 7